The Psychobiology
of Emotions

EMOTIONS, PERSONALITY, AND PSYCHOTHERAPY

Series Editors
Carroll E. Izard, *University of Delaware, Newark, Delaware*
and
Jerome L. Singer, *Yale University, New Haven, Connecticut*

THE EMOTIONAL BRAIN: Physiology, Neuroanatomy, Psychology, and Emotion
P. V. Simonov

EMOTIONS IN PERSONALITY AND PSYCHOPATHOLOGY
Carroll E. Izard, ed.

FREUD AND MODERN PSYCHOLOGY, Volume 1: The Emotional Basis of Mental Illness
Helen Block Lewis

FREUD AND MODERN PSYCHOLOGY, Volume 2: The Emotional Basis of Human Behavior
Helen Block Lewis

GUIDED AFFECTIVE IMAGERY WITH CHILDREN AND ADOLESCENTS
Hanscarl Leuner, Günther Horn, and Edda Klessmann

HUMAN EMOTIONS
Carroll E. Izard

LANGUAGE IN PSYCHOTHERAPY: Strategies of Discovery
Robert L. Russell

THE PERSONAL EXPERIENCE OF TIME
Bernard S. Gorman and Alden E. Wessman, eds.

THE POWER OF HUMAN IMAGINATION: New Methods in Psychotherapy
Jerome L. Singer and Kenneth S. Pope, eds.

THE PSYCHOBIOLOGY OF EMOTIONS
Jack George Thompson

SHYNESS: Perspectives on Research and Treatment
Warren H. Jones, Jonathan M. Cheek, and Stephen R. Briggs, eds.

THE STREAM OF CONSCIOUSNESS: Scientific Investigations into the Flow of Human Experience
Kenneth S. Pope and Jerome L. Singer, eds.

A Continuation Order Plan is available for this series. A continuation order will bring delivery of each new volume immediately upon publication. Volumes are billed only upon actual shipment. For further information please contact the publisher.

The Psychobiology of Emotions

Jack George Thompson

Centre College
Danville, Kentucky

Plenum Press • New York and London

Library of Congress Cataloging in Publication Data

Thompson, Jack George.
    The psychobiology of emotions.

    (Emotions, personality, and psychotherapy)
    Bibliography: p.
    Includes indexes.
    1. Emotions—Physiological aspects. 2. Psychobiology. I. Title. II. Series. [DNLM: 1.
Emotions—physiology. 2. Psychophysiology. WL 103 T473p]
QP401.T46   1988   152.4   88-5937
    ISBN 0-306-42843-1

© 1988 Plenum Press, New York
A Division of Plenum Publishing Corporation
233 Spring Street, New York, N.Y. 10013

Printed in the United States of America

Preface

Regardless of culture, most adult humans report experiencing similar feelings such as anger, fear, humor, and joy. Such subjective emotional states, however, are *not* universal. Members of some cultures deny experiencing specific emotions such as fear or grief. Moreover, within any culture, individuals differ widely in their self-reports of both the variety and intensity of their emotions. Some people report a vivid tapestry of positive and negative emotional experiences. Other people report that a single emotion such as depression or fear totally dominates their existences. Still others report flat and barren emotional lives.

Over the past 100 years, scientists have proposed numerous rival explanations of *why* such large individual differences in emotions occur. Various authors have offered anthropological, biochemical, ethological, neurological, psychological, and sociological models of human emotions. Indeed, the sheer number of competing theories precludes a comprehensive review in a single volume. Accordingly, only a representative sample of models are discussed in this book, and many equally important theories have been omitted. These omissions were not intended to prejudice the reader in favor of any particular conceptual framework. Rather, this selective coverage was intended to focus attention upon the empirical findings that contemporary theories attempt to explain.

Two deceptively simple issues have dominated emotion research. First, what *causes* us to experience a given emotion? Are emotions caused by biological events such as changes in the biochemistry of the brain? Are emotions caused by psychological events such as specific memories or thoughts? Are some emotions triggered primarily by biological events, and other emotions elicited primarily by psychological events? Are biological and psychological causes of emotions inseparable? Throughout this book, we will examine the relative merit of each of these positions.

Second, what are the biological and psychological *consequences* of expressing our feelings? Some theorists argue that "acting out" our emotions produces

v

catharsis (emotional release) that promotes mental and physical health. Other theorists, however, argue that overtly expressing our emotions may lead to mental and physical illnesses. We will examine the empirical evidence on this issue throughout this book. For example, does essential hypertension (high blood pressure) occur more commonly in individuals who express or inhibit their feelings?

Discussion of the causes and consequences of emotions often presumes that the reader has a basic understanding of human anatomy and physiology. Obviously, it is impossible to grasp the potential role of prolactin in human emotions unless one is aware of what prolactin is (a hormone) and what it does (effects the tissues of both the breast and brain). For the benefit of readers with a limited background in biology, Chapters 2 through 10 each contain a brief review of the anatomy and physiology of the specific organ system being discussed.

Although the book was intended for use as a text in either undergraduate or graduate courses in emotion, the depth and breadth of the coverage may appeal to a wider audience. For example, nursing and medical students may find the discussions of somatopsychic (body–mind) and psychosomatic (mind–body) disorders extremely beneficial. Because a general understanding of human emotions is important in a wide variety of occupations and professions, a concerted effort was made to clearly define technical terms such as *somatopsychic* throughout the text.

The study of human emotions can be a frustrating experience. Some human emotions such as anxiety have been intensively examined, and thus we are often faced with sorting through a conflicting mass of empirical findings. Conversely, research on other emotions such as embarrassment has been extremely sparse. Hence, we are often confronted with large gaps in our current knowledge about human emotions. Some readers may legitimately feel overwhelmed by the sheer complexity of "what we know," whereas other readers may be legitimately disappointed by "what we don't know." It is my personal hope that the reader will persevere and rediscover the excitement of intellectual discovery that we all experienced as children.

I would like to express my gratitude to all students in my undergraduate course on human emotion. Your constructive criticisms and comments were invaluable in revising the early drafts of this work. Special thanks are due to Lisa Blouin, Jenny Boyle, Debbie Finkel, Kim Helton, and Margi Lacy for proofreading various drafts of the manuscript. Special recognition is also due to Tammy Day for translating my often vague ideas into clear and informative illustrations.

I am greatly indebted to my editor, Carroll Izard, for his insightful comments and his assistance in shortening my original manuscript by approximately 150 pages. Special thanks to Robert Simons and Brent White for reading and commenting on portions of the manuscript. I am also grateful to my editor, Eliot Werner, and the production staff at Plenum Press for transforming my manuscript into book form.

Background research for this book was partially supported through a series of summer grants from the Centre College faculty development fund and through a sabbatical leave. I would like to express my personal thanks to the Centre College library staff for their assistance in locating reference materials. Thanks are also due to Pat Martin and Glenys Haine for their help in preparing the final draft of the manuscript.

Jack Thompson

Danville, Kentucky

Contents

II. PHYSIOLOGICAL SYSTEMS

4. The Cardiovascular System 67

5. The Thermoregulatory System 93

6. The Respiratory System 121

I

The Mind–Body Puzzle

As we will discuss in Chapter 1, all definitions of emotions reflect their authors' beliefs about the nature of reality (metaphysics). Scientists disagree over whether emotions should be viewed as biological (physical) events, as psychological (mental) events, or as products of the complex interaction of mind and body. One of the central issues in this mind–body debate is the temporal sequence of biological and psychological events. Specifically, do bodily changes occur before, during, or after our feelings? Are biological events causes, components, or the consequences of our emotions?

Given the importance of the mind–body debate in the study of emotion, we will begin with a discussion of the two biological systems that control the physiological activity of the other organs in the body. We will focus on the role of the nervous system in emotional states in Chapter 2 and concentrate on the role of the neurohormonal system in emotional states in Chapter 3.

Mind and Body

All cats are grey in the dark.

—Thomas Lodge (1597)

Emotions are integral components of human existence. Most people report that their everyday subjective experiences consist of a kaleidoscope of positive and negative feelings. Indeed, we often intentionally behave in specific ways in order to elicit specific emotions. We may consciously choose to read depressing news reports, pick fights, or cheer ourselves up. Intuitively, we realize that emotions are literally the subjective spices of life. Without tears of joy or sorrow, the laughter of amusement or sadism, the pounding heart of love or hate, life would be a barren experience.

Despite the importance of emotions in everyday life, the question "what are emotions?" is extremely difficult to answer. Most people report that they experience their emotions as distinct mind–body (psychobiological) states. Thus, a particular emotion such as anger is usually perceived as a unique feeling (subjective mental state) coupled with a distinct pattern of physiological responses such as increased heart rate (physical state). However, subjective feelings of emotions and physiological responses may be disconnected (dissociated) in at least some individuals. For example, researchers have identified two different types of personality traits, repression and alexithymia, which are associated with physiological reactions to emotional stimuli *without* the subjective awareness of emotional states.

Repressors tend to selectively deny negative emotions such as fear and to be highly defensive (for example, "I don't have any problems"). Because researchers cannot read the subjects' minds, it is impossible to determine whether repressors are consciously lying or actually unaware of their negative emotional states. Repressors score extremely high on self-report measures of social desirability, extremely low on self-report measures of anxiety, and show high levels of physiological reactivity to stressors (Weinberger, Schwartz, & Davidson, 1979; Asendorpf & Scherer, 1983). For example, Cook (1985) found that female repressors reported less subjective distress but showed greater physiological responses to stressors than other subjects. Thus the repressors' self-reports of low anxiety did not match their physiological reactions.

Alexithymia is characterized by inability to express either positive or negative emotion in words and by an extremely barren fantasy life (lack of daydreaming, night-dream recall). Alexithymics often use actions to unconsciously express their emotions, such as slamming a door without being consciously aware of anger. Although they may be consciously aware of physiological arousal during emotions, they often misattribute their arousal to a physical cause (for example, "I must be getting the flu"). Thus, for alexithymics, emotions appear to be biological rather than psychobiological events (Neill & Sandifer, 1982; Ford, 1983).

As we will discuss later in this chapter, a third personality profile, psychopathy, is characterized by the lack of *both* subjective and physiological emotional reactions. To further complicate matters, individuals with *multiple personality disorders* consciously experience specific emotions as *different* people. In this rare disorder, the same individual alternates between two or more distinct personalities. Each personality has its own unique emotional reactions, habits, and memories. Contrary to popular belief, multiple personality is *not* a form of schizophrenia but, rather, is a *dissociative disorder* like amnesia. Individuals with multiple personalities display a bizarre but effective method of coping with emotional situations. When the conscious personality cannot cope effectively with specific emotions, he or she simply "becomes" someone else who can.

Sybil was a classic example of a multiple personality. As a child, she was repeatedly mentally and physically tortured and sexually abused by her own mother. As an adult, Sybil was incapable of experiencing anger. In anger-inducing situations, Sybil "disappeared" and was replaced by one of her other 15 personalities (Schreiber, 1974). Similarly, Winer (1978) reported the case of Nancy who had been sexually molested by her great-grandfather when she was 6 years old and then raped twice by one of her mother's boyfriends when she was 13. These repetitive sexual traumata left Nancy incapable of consciously experiencing either anger or sexual arousal. Accordingly, her two alter egos, Kitty and Lillian, expressed Nancy's anger and sexuality for her.

The existence of alexithymics, multiple personalities, psychopaths, and repressors makes it difficult to generate a universal definition of human emotions. Not surprisingly, there is still no generally accepted definition of emotion. Various researchers define an emotion as (a) a biochemical response such as an increase in hormone levels in the bloodstream; (b) a physiological response of internal organs such as an increase in heart rate; (c) a physiological response of skeletal muscles such as smiling; (d) an observable psychological response such as cursing; (e) an unobservable psychological response such as a specific stream of thoughts or images; (f) any combination of (a) through (e); or (g) the subjective awareness of any or all of the preceding behaviors. However, selecting any one of these definitions may accidently result in two different types of logical errors.

First, when we adopt a specific definition of emotions, we risk arbitrarily defining events as either emotional or nonemotional. That is, when we define what an emotion *is*, we are also simultaneously defining what we think an emotion is *not*. Thus we may accidently "solve the problem by definition" (Zajonc, 1984a). Suppose we select a purely biochemical definition of emotion. By defining the biochemical event *as* the emotion, we have ruled out the possibility that an observable biochemical event may act as either the *cause* of an emotion or may occur as a *consequence* of an emotion. Moreover, we are also excluding the possibility that an emotion may occur *without* a distinct biochemical event occurring. Thus, rather than basing our judgment upon empirical evidence, we have defined the relationship between biochemical events and emotions *a priori*.

Second, we risk tautological (circular) reasoning with any definition of emotion we select. Suppose we define emotions as observable physiological responses such as crying. Would observing an individual crying allow us to conclude that he or she is experiencing an emotion? Of course not. They may be crying in response to a speck of dirt in their eyes, or they may be an actress or actor voluntarily producing tears on cue.

Based upon the preceding discussion, it should be clear that most definitions of emotions imply that emotions consist of both mental "stuff" and physical "stuff." Yet, if emotions consist of a "mental" event and a "physical" event, why do both occur? How can an ethereal mind effect a physical body? Conversely, how can a physical body alter mental processes? Obviously, it is impossible to discuss human emotions without becoming immediately mired in the philosophical issue of the "nature" of mind and body. The reader should be warned that philosophical discussions often tend to be reminiscent of the children's story of Brer Rabbit and Tarbaby (Harris, 1914). Once you become involved, it becomes increasingly difficult to extract yourself.

1.1. PHILOSOPHICAL TARBABIES

Metaphysics is the philosophical study of the nature of existence (ontology) and of the universe (cosmology). In brief, metaphysics attempts to answer the question, "what is reality?" Western philosophers and theologians have hotly debated the relationship between mind and body from the days of Socrates. Over the centuries, philosophers have offered four different views of reality: materialism, mentalism (or idealism), parallel dualism, and interactionism.

The materialist position is that only physical events exist and that mental events are merely illusions (epiphenomena). How could purely physical events produce mental-like phenomena? Materialists cite the example of modern digital computers. Both computers and computer programs are purely physical entities. Yet, when a computer executes a program, it performs a variety of "mental" operations (forms images, performs mathematical computations, strings together words, etc.). According to the materialists, similar somatopsychic (body–mind) processes account for human mental activity. For example, psychoactive drugs can produce a variety of different psychological states, including emotions. The materialist view of emotion will be discussed in Chapters 12 and 13.

The strict mentalistic position is that only mental phenomena exist and that physical events are purely illusions. Mentalists argue that because our subjective mental experiences are our only proof of physical events, we have no way of objectively proving that physical events exist independent of an observer. A less radical "as-if" variation of the mentalist position is that physical events do exist but that our perception of the physical world is determined by psychological factors. For example, cross-cultural studies have found that individuals from many cultures do not "see" depth in drawings or photographs (Deregowski, 1972). Mentalists postulate that emotions are not caused by physical events but rather by how the individual subjectively perceives the event. Receiving a "B" grade on a paper may elicit despair in one student and elation in another. Mentalistic models of emotion will be discussed in Chapter 14.

The parallel dualism position is that both mental and physical phenomena exist but that mental and physical events are independent of each other. For example, it is possible to be physically exhausted but mentally alert. However, if mental and physical events are actually independent, why do they often appear to co-vary, as during emotional states? Leibniz and other philosophers argued that mental and physical processes exist in *parallel* states such as two clocks set at exactly the same time. Because a supernatural entity (God) is usually invoked to account for why such parallel states exist, parallel dualism has been relatively unpopular among scientists.

The interactionist position is that mental and physical phenomena interact in a reciprocal fashion. Thus, physical events can produce mental events (somatopsychic determinism), and mental events can produce specific physical changes in the body (psychosomatic determinism). For example, if I poured a hot cup of coffee on your lap, you would probably experience anger. Conversely, if you close your eyes and vividly imagine having hot coffee dumped in your lap, you may notice physical changes (increased pulse, clenched fists, etc.). From an interactionist viewpoint, somatopsychic (body–mind) and psychosomatic (mind–body) processes are inseparable. As John Dewey once dryly noted, "Only in wonderland can the grin be divorced from the cat" (Tillman, Berofsky, & O'Conner, 1967, p. 3). Interactional models of emotion will be discussed in Chapters 15 and 16.

1.1.1. Metaphysics of Illness

Metaphysical questions also dominate any discussion of the role of emotions in health and illness. Traditionally, Western cultures have espoused a dualistic distinction between "mental"-health illness and "physical"-health illness. Although this mental-physical distinction was originally made on philosophical grounds, it does have some degree of empirical validity. In the majority of cases of mental illness, no physical cause can be found for the individuals' abnormal behaviors. Conversely, in the majority of cases of physical illness, a specific physical cause for the disorder can be identified. The minority cases, however, deserve careful attention. Some mental patients' emotional states appear to trigger or to directly aggravate physical illnesses. Conversely, some physical illnesses appear to trigger or aggravate mental illness. To further complicate matters, physically ill individuals often report psychological symptoms, and mentally ill individuals often report physical symptoms.

Defining the distinctions between "mental" and "physical" illnesses is an extremely difficult task. The American Psychiatric Association has repeatedly attempted to differentiate between mental disorders, physical disorders, psychosomatic disorders, and somatopsychic disorders. Although numerous objections have been raised concerning the APA's use of "mixed metaphysics," their diagnostic guidelines are widely used in clinical practice. Accordingly, diagnostic categories employed in the *Diagnostic and Statistical Manual (DSM) of Mental Disorders* (3rd ed.), or DSM-III (1980), of the American Psychiatric Association will be used in the following discussion of the role of emotions in mental and physical illnesses.

DSM-III criteria differentiate between health and illness and between types of disorders on the basis of the presence or absence of specific symptoms such as reporting hallucinations. The occurrence of specific symptoms, however, does not automatically imply that a given individual is mentally ill. For example, wandering around campus naked may represent either a severe loss of contact with reality or participation in a college prank.

Healthy individuals may consciously attempt to fake either mental or physical disorders as a form of psychological self-protection (*primary gain*). For example, approximately 20% of undergraduate students report high levels of test anxiety, but only approximately half of these students are underachievers, that is, receive grades much lower than those predicted on the basis of their academic ability. Smith, Snyder, and Handelsman (1982) observed that many college students may use test anxiety as an excuse for failure or an "academic wooden leg." If they perform well, they can claim that they overcame their handicap, that is, "I was a nervous wreck, and I still pulled out an A." If they fail, they can blame their failure on anxiety. When such high test-anxious students are placed in a testing situation where test anxiety is not a viable excuse for failure, many students adopt an alternative excuse of reduced effort ("I didn't try").

Healthy individuals may also attempt to fake mental or physical illness for a variety of external rewards or *secondary gain* (attention, disability payments, exemption from responsibilities, etc.). If the individual's apparent goal in faking illness is secondary gain, the behavior is labeled *malingering*. Although chronic malingering may be considered socially deviant, it is not classified as a mental disorder.

Faking illness when secondary gain is absent, however, is considered a form of mental illness and is diagnosed as a *factitious disorder*. A classic example of a factitious disorder is called the *Munchausen syndrome*. Munchausen patients make elaborate attempts to gain admission into medical hospitals. They may deliberately cut or burn themselves or ingest drugs to produce physical symptoms such as blood in their urine or high blood pressure. To avoid detection, they migrate from hospital to hospital. They often demand and unfortunately receive unnecessary surgery. Pankratz (1981) cited the case of one Munchausen patient who boasted that he had undergone 48 surgeries.

In both factitious disorders and malingering, the individual is consciously aware that he or she is "faking." *Somatoform disorders* (hypochondriasis and conversion disorder) are characterized by the lack of conscious awareness that illness is being faked. For example, hypochondriacs are preoccupied with body functions and disease. They make no attempt to fake physical symptoms and appear to quite honestly believe that every minor ache or physical irregularity represents a symptom of disease. Hypochondriacs often migrate from physician to physician, hoping to find medical confirmation that they are physically ill. Because hypochondriacs are physically healthy, their disorder is labeled a *mental illness*.

Conversion disorders have characteristics of both mental and psychosomatic disorders. The individual has physical symptoms (i.e., blindness, deafness, paralysis, sexual dysfunctions) that have no physical basis and that do not correspond to the symptoms of known physical diseases. For example, a conversion patient may display paralysis of only the hand or foot. Neurologically, such glove-and-socklike paralysis is simply impossible because the limbs are controlled by a number of different nerve bundles (see Figure 1-1). Thus, it is physically possible to have *only* "more" or "less" paralysis than shown by conversion patients.

Conversion disorders also have a number of other characteristics that distinguish them from physical illnesses. First, the symptoms of conversion patients often appear suddenly and disappear just as suddenly through "miraculous cures." Second, the physical symptoms of conversion disorders often

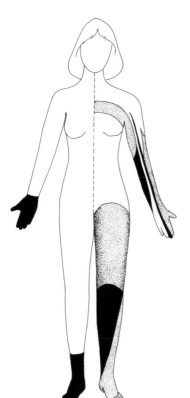

Figure 1-1. Shaded areas on the left side of the figure represent areas commonly affected by "glove" or "sock" conversion paralysis. Shaded areas on the right side of the figure represent patterns of paralysis observed in neurological disorders.

disappear during sleep. Thus, an individual whose hand is paralyzed when awake may move his or her hand while asleep. Third, patients with physical illnesses often report strong emotional reactions to their symptoms (e.g., anger, anxiety, depression, fear). Conversion patients, however, show little emotional reaction (la belle indifference) to sudden blindness, deafness, or paralysis. Fourth, the specific symptoms such as blindness shown by a given conversion patient often appear to be obvious "solutions" to personal emotional conflicts. The following case nicely illustrates a "textbook" conversion disorder:

A 29-year-old woman discovered that her husband had had a series of affairs. Two weeks later she and her husband were arguing in their car when they were involved in a minor traffic accident. Three days after the accident, she complained of radiating pains in her arms, legs, and spine. Neither orthopedic nor neurological examinations identified any physical cause for her pain. The patient reported that because of her pain she is no longer capable of engaging in sexual acts (Spitzer, Skodol, Gibbon, & Williams, 1981).

Although the symptoms of somatoform disorders are physical, the individual's disorder is mental. Conversely, a number of physical disorders can produce mental symptoms. For example, *organic brain disorders* are characterized by observable physical damage to the brain produced by a physical agent (injury, ingestion of toxins) or by genetic defects. These physical disorders may produce a variety of somatopsychic changes in mental functioning (memory, problem solving, etc.), including emotional responses. Organic brain patients often display sudden emotional outbursts (crying, laughing, screaming) or an apparent lack of emotions. It should be stressed that somatopsychic changes in emotional reactions have also been observed with a variety of physical illnesses that involve organs other than the brain (Jefferson & Marshall, 1981). Such somatopsychic emotional reactions are often indistinguishable from the emotional reactions of psychiatric patients who have no known physiopathology.

To further complicate matters, "mental" illness may cause or aggravate physical illnesses. For example, a stomach ulcer is a physical disorder that may be initiated by psychological stress. Ulcers are not "in the patient's head" but rather are pathological physical conditions where stomach acid has eaten through the protective coating of the gastrointestinal system and is damaging the walls of the stomach. Yet ulcers can easily be produced in animals by repeatedly presenting psychological stressors.

DSM-III uses the rather awkward title *psychological factors affecting physical condition* for psychosomatic disorders. This label is used to denote *any* physiological disorder (excluding sexual dysfunctions) that is caused *or* aggravated by psychological reactions. The older DSM-II labeled psychosomatic illnesses as *psychophysiologic disorders* and listed only a small number of physical disorders as psychosomatic (asthma, colitis, headaches, high blood pressure, etc.). Based on the empirical observation that emotional states may affect a wide variety of physical illnesses, DSM-III dropped the distinction between purely psychosomatic and purely physical disorders. Thus any physical illness can be viewed as psychosomatic. For the purpose of brevity, the older term, *psychophysiologic disorder*, will be employed in this book.

Differentiating between physical illness and psychophysiological disorders is an extremely difficult task. Many disorders such as headaches may be traced to either organic causes, psychological stress, or a combination of organic and psychological causes. Moreover, psychophysiological disorders appear to be quite common in the general population. For example, Schwab and his associates conducted a survey of a large random sample of adults living in a county in northern Florida. More than 50% of their respondants reported experiencing at least one psychophysiological symptom on a regular basis, and 17% of their sample reported regularly experiencing two or more psychophysiological symptoms. Paradoxically, 25% of the subjects who reported two or more symptoms also rated their own physical or mental health as good to excellent (Schwab, Fennell, & Warheit, 1974).

The purpose of the preceding discussion was to illustrate the "mixed metaphysics" employed in psychiatric diagnoses. Some psychiatric disorders are labeled *physical,* some are labeled *mental,* and some are labled *psychobiological.*

One of the major criticisms of DSM-III is that the "need" for psychiatric diagnosis is based on the dualistic assumption that both "mental" and "physical" disorders exist. Materialists object to DSM-III on the grounds that all forms of mental illnesses are merely misdiagnosed forms of organic brain disorders. For example, the materialists note that long-term follow-up studies have found that about 60% of conversion disorders are later diagnosed as organic brain disorders (Slater & Glithero, 1965; Whitlock, 1967). They argue that "mental" illnesses may merely be the early symptoms of brain pathologies that are not detectable with current technology. Similarly, strict mentalists argue that because only the mind exists, all physical illnesses are actually forms of mental illnesses.

The interactionists' objections focus on the specification of cause, or etiology, in DSM-III. Although DSM-III claims to list only a "known" etiology, interactionists argue that designation of disorder A as a "physical illness" or disorder B as a "mental illness" violates the fundamental unity of mind and body. For example, heavy cigarette smoking greatly increases the risk of lung cancer. Concluding that lung cancer is purely a physical disorder produced by a physical cause (i.e., cigarette tar) ignores the obvious fact that cigarette smoking is a behavior, not a virus. Although DSM-III does attempt to identify maladaptive behaviors such as cigarette smoking that contribute to physiopathology, it does not endorse the interactionist view that all disorders are psychobiological.

The intended purpose of DSM-III was not to issue a metaphysical statement on illnesses but rather to increase the reliability and validity of psychiatric diagnosis. Whether DSM-III does improve the accuracy of psychiatric diagnosis can be debated on purely empirical grounds. DSM-III has been criticized for implicitly defining "health" as the absence of specific clusters of mental or physical symptoms. Although only about 10% of the population meets DSM-III criteria for psychiatric disorders, a relatively large percentage of the rest of the population reports many of the same symptoms as psychiatric patients. For example, Srole and his associates interviewed a large random sample of the population of New York City. Less than 25% of their respondents were judged "well adjusted" (Srole, Langner, Michael, Opler, & Rennie, 1962).

The current debate over the validity of DSM-III nicely illustrates how our own metaphysical beliefs distort our perception of collectively observable events. Rather than asking the reader to accept a specific metaphysical position, it is sufficient for the purposes of our discussion for the reader to merely agree that collectively observable events exist. The metaphysical issue of whether reality is a collection of physical events, a collective illusion, a parallel existence, or an inseparable unity of mental and physical phenomena may never be resolved. However, the phenomena we label *emotions* are collectively observable. Specific emotions have been consistently reported by humans from all cultures studied. Emotional behaviors and the physiological manifestations of emotion can be objectively recorded by physical instrumentation (cameras, physiological recorders, etc.). Moreover, a temporal association between emotions and mental and physical illnesses has been repeatedly demonstrated. These empirical observations will be examined in detail throughout the remainder of this book.

1.1.2. Abnormal and Normal Emotional Reactions

From a psychiatric viewpoint, emotions are considered "healthy" *unless* they represent very extreme and/or inappropriate reactions. For example, reacting with extreme depression to the death of a loved one is considered a perfectly normal response in our culture. Experiencing severe depression on the thirtieth anniversary of the death of one's pet goldfish, however, would qualify one for a psychiatric interview.

DSM-III list two major classes of psychiatric disorders that are characterized by the presence of inappropriate emotional states. Delineating the boundary between abnormal and normal emotional reactions, however, is a difficult task. The "appropriateness" of any given behavior often varies from culture to culture. Crying at a wedding is considered normal in some cultures and abnormal in others. Moreover, within any given culture, the appropriateness of the same behavior may vary from situation to situation. Screaming in private may be considered abnormal, whereas screaming in public may be considered normal.

Anxiety disorders are a set of different disorders (generalized anxiety, obsession-compulsion, panic, and phobic) that were traditionally labeled *neurotic behaviors*. In generalized anxiety, panic, and phobic disorders, the individuals display extreme emotional reactions to stimuli that other observers from our culture label *nonthreatening*, for example, extreme anxiety reactions to taking a shower. Obsessive individuals report involuntary repetition of images or thoughts that are often anxiety- or guilt-producing. For example, a student may become obsessed with the thought of standing up and screaming obscenities in the middle of a lecture. Compulsions are repetitive actions that often appear to be overt attempts at anxiety reduction such as checking and rechecking that a door is locked.

DSM-III also lists post-traumatic stress disorders (PTSD) under the general category of anxiety disorders. This designation has been repeatedly questioned. Unlike other anxiety disorders, individuals with PTSD have experienced external stressors that objective observers label as highly anxiety-producing (combat, fire, floods, rape, etc.). Moreover, PTSD patients often report guilt (why did I survive?) or blunted (reduced) emotional reactions rather than anxiety. A number of studies, however, suggest that PTSD may legitimately represent a "delayed" reaction to anxiety-provoking stimuli (see Stretch, Vail, & Maloney, 1985).

Affective disorders consist of a set of related psychiatric disorders that are all characterized by intense feelings of depression or elation that are "inappropriate" in the context of the individual's current life. *Manic episodes* are characterized by experience of elation over at least a 1-week period accompanied by increased activity and talking and self-reports of racing thoughts, inflated self-esteem, and decreased need for sleep. *Dysthymic disorders* are characterized as chronic or intermittent experiences of mild depression over at least a 2-year period. Affective disturbances are much more severe in *major depressive episodes* and are accompanied by a variety of symptoms such as disturbances of appetite, sleep, sex drive, and motor behavior. The occurrence of one or more major depressive episodes (without a history of mania) is labeled *major*, or *unipolar depression*. Individuals who alternate between major depressive episodes and manic episodes are diagnosed as displaying a *bipolar disorder* (manic-depression). The mild form of bipolar disorder is labeled a *cyclothymic disorder*.

DSM-III also lists a number of psychiatric disorders that are characterized by the *absence* of appropriate emotional reactions. For example, *psychopaths*, or sociopaths, are individuals who are apparently incapable of experiencing normal emotional states such as anxiety, fear, or guilt. Free from emotional inhibitions, psychopaths often behave in an aggressive, exploitative, and impulsive manner. They often appear to be charming individuals because they cynically attempt to manipulate other people. Not surprisingly, psychopaths often commit criminal acts. However, unlike "normal" criminals, psychopaths are incapable of long-range planning and do not appear to learn from punishment. For example, a normal criminal may steal a car with the rational intent of selling the vehicle. A psychopath may steal a car "because" the keys were in the ignition. Moreover, when punished, a normal criminal is likely to learn from his or her experience. Some criminals learn to abstain from criminal behaviors, whereas others use their prison experiences to improve the methods they use in the commission of crimes. Psychopaths, however, are often punished for repeating the same anti-social behaviors.

Psychopaths are not mentally retarded and often have above average intelligence. Rather, their learning disability appears to be directly related to their inability to experience emotions. In both normal criminals and noncriminals, anxiety and fear signal the individual that he or she is being threatened. Action may then be taken to either avoid or master the threatening situation. Similarly, guilt and shame discourage the individual from repeating punished acts. Lacking these emotional cues, psychopaths often commit impulsive and purposeless crimes. For example, a psychopath interviewed by one of my colleagues had amassed a small fortune smuggling drugs. Yet, he was arrested for writing a bad check for a hotel bill that he could have easily paid.

Males comprise the vast majority of cases of psychopathy. However, female psychopaths are extremely similar to their male counterparts. Schachter and Latene (1964), for example, cited the interesting case of a 20-year-old female psychopath who was referred to psychotherapy by her father. She had a history of chronic lying, petty thefts, and sexual promiscuity, but she reported deriving little pleasure from her antisocial acts. Her descriptions of her emotional reactions were vague and flat. Although she purportedly was fond of animals, she showed only a superficial reaction when her dog was killed by an automobile.

To distinguish between "normal" and psychopathic criminals, DSM-III uses the diagnostic label *adult antisocial behavior* for nonpsychopathic criminals and the label *antisocial personality disorder* for psychopaths. Again, for the purpose of brevity, the older term, *psychopath*, will be used in this book.

Shallow or nonexistent emotional responses are also observed in a variety of other psychiatric disorders. For example, schizophrenics often show blunted or inappropriate affective responses. *Schizophrenia* is a class of disorders characterized by bizarre behaviors, social withdrawal, and severe distortions in emotions, perception, and thought. Unlike multiple personalities, schizophrenics do not show alternating personalities but rather display a fragmentation of personality into loosely associated components. For example, schizophrenics often report hearing voices. Such auditory hallucinations appear to be due to the schizophrenics confusing their own thoughts with the perception of external voices (Gould, 1949). Moreover, multiple personalities are quite capable of functioning in social roles (e.g., student), whereas schizophrenics show marked impairment in everyday living.

The preceding discussion was intended only to introduce the reader to psychiatric diagnostic categories that are commonly cited in emotion research, and it should not be misinterpreted as a summary of DSM-III. There are a large number of psychiatric disorders that are unrelated to emotional disorders that have been omitted from our discussion. Moreover, DSM-III criteria include descriptions of the essential features (symptoms) of psychiatric disorders, associated features, diagnostic criteria, differential diagnosis (symptoms that differentiate related disorders), and five sets of diagnostic dimensions to assist in the evaluation of personality, psychosocial, psychiatric, and medical aspects of an individual's adjustment problems. Readers interested in a more detailed discussion of psychiatric criteria are referred to DSM-III (1980) and to Spitzer *et al.* (1981).

Psychiatric disorders provide a number of interesting insights into normal emotions. First, psychiatric disorders serve as useful conceptual anchors. Some psychiatric patients experience emotional states of abnormal duration and intensity, whereas other patients may not experience emotions at all. Second, psychiatric patients' symptoms provide numerous clues to the relationships between normal emotional states and mental and physical illnesses. Third, the effectiveness or ineffectiveness of the various medical and psychological treatments of psychiatric disorders helps illuminate the relative importance of mind and body during emotional states.

1.2. AN OVERVIEW

The organization of this book is designed to introduce the reader to the complex topic of the psychobiology of emotions. Chapters 2 and 3 deal with the complicated neural and neurohormonal control systems that regulate physiological activity during emotional states. Chapters 4 through 11 focus on the role of individual physiological systems during emotions. Each of these chapters begins with a brief discussion of the anatomy and physiology of the organ system. Studies of the psychobiological activity of the organ system during specific emotions are then reviewed. Chapters 12 through 16 cover some of the major materialistic, mentalistic, and interactionistic models of emotions. Chapter 17 is intended to provide the reader with an integrated view of the relationships between mind and body during emotions.

Given the important role that metaphysical beliefs play in the study of emotion, the reader may be legitimately puzzled over why the chapters on theories of emotion were placed at the end of this book. This organization was selected to encourage the reader to carefully examine the available literature on the biology, psychobiology, and psychology of emotions before drawing his or her own conclusions about the validity of specific theories of emotions.

In science, theories serve the useful function of providing conceptual frameworks for organizing empirical observations and for generating testable hypotheses. Unfortunately, theories also encourage dogmatism. Although faith may be a virtue in theology, it is an anathema in science. Scientific theories are not absolute truths but merely testable models of reality. One of the major advantages of an empirical approach to the study of emotion is that it forces us to make our theories fit collective observations rather than permitting us to distort the facts to fit our theory. However, readers who are unfamiliar with research methodology should be cognizant of the three major risks inherent in blind empiricism.

First, research on inductive reasoning has consistently found that humans tend to fall into the *confirmation trap*, that is, we sift through empirical findings to find evidence that supports our own existing beliefs or hypotheses. A classic example of the confirmation trap is the persistence of social stereotypes. If you hold to the belief that "fat people are jolly," you tend to look only for cases of happy fat people and dismiss cases of unhappy fat people as "exceptions." Moreover, you are also likely to ignore the subjective happiness of thin or average-weight individuals. Unless you are willing to examine *all* of the available evidence, you can never discover whether your existing beliefs are empirically true or false.

Second, in science, truth is often partial rather than absolute. That is, a given principle may be valid in one situation and invalid in another. For example, the folk saying, "what goes up, must come down," is only partially true. If an object achieves sufficient velocity to escape the earth's gravitional field, it will never "come down." In science, the validity of a given theory rests on the *degree* to which it can describe, explain, and predict empirical findings. If a given theory can accurately predict the emotional responses of only 21% of subjects tested and a second theory can accurately predict 75% of the cases, we do not label the first theory *false* and the second *true*. Obviously, both theories are only partially valid. Rather, we assume that the second theory is a better model of emotion because it accounts for a higher proportion of observed cases. The limited predictive validity of both theories may stimulate other researchers to either obtain additional evidence or to generate new models in an attempt to predict more that 75% of the subjects' responses.

Third, to paraphrase George Orwell's *Animal Farm*, "all facts are equal, but some facts are more equal than others." Some so-called empirical facts are artifacts, that is, errors produced by shoddy research designs or procedures. Although artifacts do serve the useful function of helping us improve our research methodologies, they also tend to obscure valid research findings. For example, research suggests that in our culture males are trained to inhibit facial expressions of emotion (e.g., the poker face). A researcher who tested only male subjects might erroneously conclude that facial reactions play no role in human emotional reactions. Conversely, a researcher who tested only female subjects would erroneously draw the opposite conclusion. Obviously, sex difference in facial reactivity can be observed only when subjects of both sexes are tested. Unfortunately, such biased samples are relatively common in emotion research. One survey of published psychophysiology studies found that approximately 55% of the studies tested only male subjects and 7% tested only female subjects (Bell, Christie, & Venables, 1975).

Artifacts occur even when sample bias and other obvious sources of error are controlled. Four different research strategies are commonly used in emotion research: self-report, observation, correlation, and experimentation. None of these research methods should be considered "better" than the others because each method produces its own characteristic artifacts. Moreover, different experimental designs (how subjects are assigned to experimental treatments) also produce their own characteristic artifacts. Because the discussion of these issues is beyond the scope of this book, interested readers are referred to texts on experimental design and research methodology.

The purpose of the preceding discussion was to encourage readers to actively criticize the research and theories discussed in the following chapters and to recognize their own metaphysical biases. Excluding Chapter 17, the author has consciously attempted to suppress his own prejudices and to objectively present an accurate representation of both the available scientific literature and theoretical explanations of human emotions. It is the author's personal hope that the reader will also "suspend judgment." In the dark, all cats may appear gray. As long as we are unwilling to turn on a light, we can cling to the comfort of our metaphysical beliefs that "all cats" are really black or white. Perhaps, some cats are actually gray or butterscotch.

SUGGESTED READINGS

The following books are excellent introductions to the complex criteria employed in psychiatric diagnoses:

Al-Issa, I. *The psychopathology of women.* Englewood Cliffs, N.J.: Prentice-Hall, 1980.

Leon, G. R. *Case histories of deviant behavior* (3rd ed.) Boston: Allyn & Bacon, 1984.

Spitzer, R. L., Skodol, A. E., Gibbon, M., & Williams, J. B. *DSM-III Casebook.* Washington, D.C.: American Psychiatric Association, 1981.

Neural Control Systems

Like other multicelled animals, the cells of the human body are organized into highly specialized organs and organ systems that perform specific biological functions (digestion, physical movement, respiration, etc.). The primary function of the nervous system is to coordinate the physiological activity of the different organ systems in response to the demands of the external environment.

2.1. MICROANATOMY AND PHYSIOLOGY

The human nervous system is primarily composed of neurons and neurologia (or glial) cells. Neurons are living cells that transmit information throughout the body. Nobel laureate David Hubel (1979) estimated that the human brain alone contains between 10 billion and 1 trillion individual neurons. Glial cells are approximately 10 times more numerous than neurons and form a dense network within the nervous system.

Traditionally, anatomists assumed that glial or so-called "glue" cells merely physically supported and protected the more delicate neurons. Over the past 50 years, however, researchers have discovered that glial cells perform a number of important functions. First, neurons are not in direct contact with the circulatory system. Glial cells pass oxygen and nutrients from the blood to the neurons and collect cellular waste products from the neurons. Second, the glial cells and the tissues of the blood vessels act as a selective filter to prevent many chemicals in the blood from reaching the neurons. This "blood–brain" barrier helps protect the neurons from toxic chemicals and microrganisms carried in the blood. Third, glial cells play an important role in the growth of the brain. During prenatal development, glial cells develop before the neurons and thus provide "directional" cues to help the growing neurons form the appropriate connections (Cowan, 1979). Fourth, glial cells digest dead neurons and thus allow new neural connections to form between healthy neurons.

Figure 2-1 represents a typical neuron. The three major structural components of the neuron are dendrites (input), soma (cell body), and axon (output). Although there is tremendous variation in the size and shape of neurons, the majority of neurons consist of these anatomical structures. The notable exceptions are sensory neurons. The photoreceptive cells in the eye, for example, have no dendrites and extremely small axons that function quite differently from typical axons.

A neuron's ability to conduct electrical impulses is due to its ability to create an electrical potential across the cell membrane. In brief, each segment of the cell membrane acts like a simple flashlight battery. Positively charged sodium (Na) ions are concentrated on the outside of the cell membrane, whereas negatively charged chloride (Cl) ions are concentrated inside the cell. This *polarization* of ions produces a small voltage potential (70 to 90 millivolts) between the inside and outside of the cell membrane. Transmission of an electrical signal along the cell membrane is produced by temporarily allowing sodium to move through the cell membrane. This ionic shift causes a shift in electrical potential (depolarization) that moves along the surface of the neuron. Because depolarization eliminates the voltage potential at a given location, there is a brief period of time (absolute refractory period) when no additional impulses can be transmitted until the cell membrane is repolarized. The average axon can depolarize at a rate of about 1,000 times per second (for a more detailed discussion of the neural transmission, see Stevens, 1979).

Communication between neurons (synapse) is also chemical. As shown in Figure 2-1, each axon terminates in a small knob that contains small vesicles that store chemicals (neurotransmitters). Each neuron is physically separated from the next neuron by a microscopic gap called the synaptic cleft. When a neural impulse reaches the end of the first (presynaptic) neuron's axon, neurotransmitters are released and diffuse across the synaptic cleft to the second (postsynaptic) neuron. There are currently approximately 30 known or suspected neurotransmitters in the human nervous system. The use of multiple neurotransmitters is actually highly efficient. Neurons are extremely densely packed together in the nervous system. By using different neurotransmitters, adjacent neurons can minimize chemical "cross-talk" between circuits. Moreover, different neurotransmitters serve different functions. Some of these neurotransmitters are excitatory and cause depolarization to occur in the postsynaptic neuron. Other neurotransmitters are inhibitory and hyperpolarize (prevent depolarization) in the postsynaptic neuron.

After the chemical message has been sent, the neurotransmitters must be removed from the synaptic cleft in order to permit additional synaptic transmission to occur. Some neurotransmitters are reabsorbed by the presynaptic neuron, whereas others are biochemically degraded by special enzymes. Research suggests that drug or hormonally induced emotional states may be traced to changes in the levels of specific neurotransmitters in the nervous system. We will discuss this issue in detail in Chapters 3 and 12.

Compared with other forms of electronic communications, neurons appear to be slow and highly inefficient. For example, in man-made electronic circuits, the speed of conduction of electrical energy is almost instantaneous. Neurons, however, are not simply "wires" in a telephone system, but, rather, each neuron actually functions as an independent computer. A single postsynaptic neuron may receive signals from up to 10,000 other neurons. Some of these synapses are excitatory, whereas others are inhibitory. This anatomical arrangement

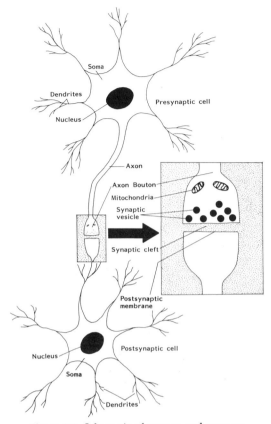

Figure 2-1. Schematic of neuron and synapse.

allows the neuron to average incoming excitatory and inhibitory signals and transmit this information along the axon in a simple binary (on/off) code. This coding may not appear terribly sophisticated unless the reader is aware that the man-made computers operate with the same type of binary code. Given that the brain alone contains an estimated 100 trillion synapses, the information-processing capacity of the nervous system is extremely difficult to comprehend.

2.2. MACROANATOMY AND PHYSIOLOGY

The nervous system is divided into two major anatomical units. The central nervous system, or CNS, is composed of all neurons whose somas are contained within the spine and skull. The peripheral nervous system consists of neurons in the remainder of the body. Although this distinction was originally purely anatomical, physiologists have noted fundamental differences between central and peripheral nervous system neurons. For example, neurons in the peripheral nervous system have the capacity for axonal regeneration. If the axon is cut, the two parts will grow back together, if they have not been pulled too far out of spatial alignment by the injury. Cajal (1968) observed that CNS neurons in mammals show only the initial stages of regeneration and then the neurons die. It should be noted that Cajal's observation was based on *natural* healing. Later researchers have claimed that CNS regeneration can be artifically induced.

Another fundamental difference between central and peripheral nervous system neurons is the type of neurotransmitters used in synaptic transmission. Of the 30 known or suspected neurotransmitters in the human body, only three of these chemicals (acetylcholine, epinephrine and norepinephrine) are commonly found in the peripheral nervous system.

The structure of the nervous system is extremely complex and thus it is easy to become confused over the location and functions of specific subcomponents. Fortunately, anatomists use different terms to identify similar structures in the central and in the peripheral nervous systems. For example, in the peripheral nervous system clusters of axons traveling together are called *nerves* while in the central nervous system the same structures are labeled *tracts*. Similarly, clusters of somas are labeled *ganglion* in the peripheral nervous system but called *nuclei* in the CNS. As shown in Table 2-1, anatomists also use a number of specific prefixes to define the spatial location of specific structures. For example, the ventral medial nuclei identify a cluster of somas in the CNS that are located on the belly side (ventral) on the midline of the body (medial). Although many readers may find such terminological distinctions confusing, a general understanding of anatomical terms is extremely useful in forming a clear cognitive map of the nervous system.

Table 2-1. Commonly Used Anatomical Terms[a]

Spatial coordinate	Anatomical label
Front	Anterior
Back	Posterior
Above	Superior
Below	Inferior
Midline	Medial
To the side (left–right)	Lateral
Bellyside	Ventral
Backside	Dorsal
Nose	Rostral
Tail	Caudal
Near	Proximal
Far	Distal

[a]These anatomical terms were originally intended to describe the spatial references of quadrupeds such as a cat. In humans and other bipeds, these anatomical coordinates refer to different spatial relationships. For example, the terms ventral and anterior both refer to the front of a human's body but not a cat's.

2.2.1. The Peripheral Nervous System and Spinal Cord

The human body contains 12 pairs of cranial nerves that originate or terminate in the brain itself and 31 pairs of spinal nerves that originate or terminate in the spinal cord. Eleven of the cranial nerves carry information to the brain from the sensory organs (eyes, ears, vestibular apparatus, skin of the head, and tongue), and/or control the motor movements of the muscles of the head. Although the vagus nerve (cranial nerve X) originates in the brain, it does not travel within the spine but rather parallels the spinal cord and terminates in the internal organs (viscera) located in the trunk.

The spinal nerves carry sensory information to the spinal cord and motor commands from the spinal cord. The somas of sensory neurons are located posterior to the spinal cord in clusters called *dorsal root ganglia*. Each ganglion receives input from touch receptors located in a specific region of the skin's surface called a *dermatome*. Thus, the CNS receives a precise sensory "map" of the exterior of the body. The axons of these fibers enter the spinal cord. Some axons continue upward toward the brain, whereas others synapse with specialized cells in the spinal cord called *interneurons* that, in turn, synapse with motor neurons on both sides of the spinal cord. This anatomical arrangement allows sensory information to be forwarded to the brain while at the same time permitting the spinal cord to perform a primitive form of thought called the spinal reflex. Specifically, the sequence receptor>interneuron>motor neuron allows the spinal cord to make a meaningful "local" response to stimuli. For example, if you step on a piece of broken glass in your bare feet, you will reflexively jerk the cut foot off the glass before the pain message reaches your brain.

The peripheral nervous system is divided into two functionally different subsystems, the somatic and autonomic nervous systems. The somatic nervous system consists of the sensory and motor neurons that are connected to the skin and skeletal muscles. The autonomic nervous system consists of the sensory and motor neurons of the viscera.

As shown in Figure 2-2, the autonomic nervous system is subdivided into two antagonistic systems—the parasympathetic and sympathetic nervous systems. The parasympathetic system, or PNS, controls physiological activity of the viscera when one's body is "resting." For example, if one has eaten a large meal and sits down to watch TV, his or her parasympathetic system slows down the heart and speeds up the digestive system. Conversely, the sympathetic system or SNS assumes control of the viscera during "emergencies." For example, if one is watching a horror movie, one may notice a number of SNS responses such as an increase in heart rate.

2.2.2. Emotions and the Peripheral Nervous System

As we will discuss in detail in later chapters, many theories of emotion are based on the assumption that physiological activity of the autonomic and/or somatic nervous systems plays an integral role in human emotional reactions. For example, William James postulated that different emotional states are char-

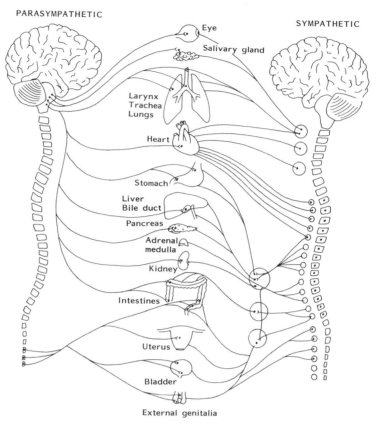

Figure 2-2. Parasympathetic and sympathetic divisions of the autonomic nervous system.

acterized by different patterns of physiological activities and that the sensory feedback about these patterns allows the individual to differentiate between emotions.

Researchers have adopted two different strategies for investigating the role of the peripheral nervous system in emotional states. The most common approach is to record physiological activity (blood pressure, stomach contractions, etc.) during emotions. These psychophysiological studies will be discussed in detail in Chapters 4 through 11.

An alternative method for studying the role of the peripheral nervous system is to examine the emotional reactions of individuals who have damaged spinal cords. This approach is based on the logic that if the peripheral nervous system plays an important role in emotional reactions, then individuals who are deprived of sensory information from the peripheral nerves should show reduced emotional reactions. Because sensory information is lost below the point of nerve damage, researchers have focused on the emotional experiences of paraplegic and quadriplegic individuals.

Hohmann (1966) interviewed 25 adult males with various spinal injuries. Self-reports of feelings of anger and fear varied inversely with the loss of sensory and motor control. Specifically, individuals with damage to the lower spine (and who thus experienced minimal loss of sensory feedback) reported normal emotional reactions. Individuals with damage to the upper spine (and greater loss in sensorimotor feedback), however, reported decreases in emotional states of anger and fear. Interestingly, some of these quadriplegic patients reported displaying emotional behaviors *without* experiencing emotional states. For example, one patient reported cursing at others when he thought anger was appropriate but claimed that he did not "feel" anger.

Other researchers, however, have failed to find changes in emotions of individuals with spinal injuries. Nestoros, Demers-Desrosiers, and Dalicandro (1982) asked paraplegic and quadriplegic individuals to complete the Zung self-rating scales of anxiety and depression and found no difference between the two groups.

These apparently contradictory findings nicely illustrate the methodological problems inherent in studying emotional states. Because both Hohmann's and Nestoros's studies employed self-report methods, it is quite plausible that the results of either study may be artifacts. For example, Hohmann (who himself is a paraplegic) noted that other paraplegics often confessed that they were reluctant to talk honestly with "normal" interviewers. Conversely, a paraplegic interviewer may have biased the responses of spinal patients.

An alternative explanation for these findings is that only *some* emotional states may depend on feedback from the peripheral nervous system. Specifically, Hohmann found that feelings of anger and fear varied with the level of spinal injury, whereas Nestoros found that feelings of anxiety and depression did not. It is quite reasonable that the subjective experience of anger and fear may be more dependent on autonomic and somatic arousal (i.e., heart rate increases, skeletal muscle tension) than on emotions such as anxiety or depression.

One method for empirically testing this hypothesis would be to mimic spinal damage by injecting healthy individuals with a paralyzing drug such as curare (d-turbocurarine) or scoline (succinylcholine chloride dihydrate) and then systematically assess the subjects' emotional reactions. Presumably, any emotion that depends upon feedback from skeletal muscles should be eliminated by this procedure. Surprisingly, despite a number of studies on the effects of paralyzing drugs on humans, relatively little is known about emotional reactions during temporary paralysis. For example, Campbell, Sanderson, and Laverty (1964) produced brief (90–130 second) respiratory failure by injecting six alcoholics and an unspecified number of presumably nonalcoholic physicians with scoline. All but one subject reported experiencing terror during the drug-induced involuntary cessation of breathing. However, because the drug dose used in this experiment did not produce complete muscle paralysis, it is impossible to determine whether the subjects' experience of terror was due to sudden loss of muscular control over respiration or a sudden drop in oxygen in the blood stream. These two potential sources of feedback can be separated by artificially resuscitating the subjects. Thus, rather complete striate muscle paralysis can be induced while blood oxygen levels remain constant.

Smith, Brown, Toman, and Goodman (1947) induced complete curare paralysis in a single subject while his breathing was artificially controlled. Examination of the subject's original log reveals that, although he later reported being completely conscious the entire time, he did *not* report experienced anxiety reactions during paralysis (for a general review and methodological critique of the curare–scoline studies, see McGuigan, 1978).

2.2.3. Emotions and the Central Nervous System

The human brain is composed of a complex network of nuclei and tracts. Although our general understanding of global brain functions is still extremely primitive, over the past 50 years information on both neuroanatomy and neurophysiology has increased at an exponential rate. We now have a general outline of which brain structures are involved in emotional states and emotional behaviors.

Traditionally, anatomists have divided the brain into three large structural units: the hindbrain, midbrain, and forebrain. However, physiologists have noted that physiological activity does not follow these anatomical divisions. For example, raising your hand involves the activation of structures in the hind-, mid-, and forebrain. To provide the reader with a clear cognitive map of regions of the brain involved in emotions, both anatomical and functional organizations will be presented in our discussion.

As shown in Figure 2-3, the hindbrain is composed of the spinal cord and

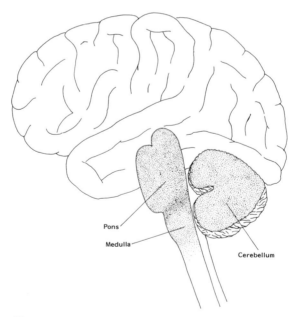

Figure 2-3. Major anatomical structures of the hindbrain.

three major brain structures (the cerebellum, medulla, and pons) located at the base of the brain. The cerebellum helps control the coordination of motor activity. The medulla contains nuclei that control digestion, heart rate, blood pressure, and respiration. The pons contains nuclei that function as a biological "clock" and help mediate the sleep–wake cycle. As you have probably guessed from their functions, all three hindbrain structures are involved in emotional reactions. It should be stressed that the term *control* should not be taken literally. The brain contains numerous interacting "control" centers for specific functions. For example, you can consciously decide to stay awake for 150 to 200 hours without drugs and stay awake. Thus, within limits, higher brain structures may override lower brain centers.

The midbrain contains a number of nuclei and tracts, including the reticular activating system (RAS) and the pain and pleasure tracts that are all involved in emotional reactions. Although these three midbrain tracts normally function in a coordinated manner, for purposes of clarity, we will discuss each tract separately.

The RAS consists of a diffuse network that stretches between the hindbrain and the forebrain (see Figure 2-4). Although the RAS receives input from all of the senses except smell (olfaction), the RAS does not function as a sensory processing tract. Rather, the RAS uses the ongoing level of sensory information to adjust the level of arousal of the CNS. If the external level of stimulation is low, the RAS reduces the overall level of arousal. Conversely, if external stim-

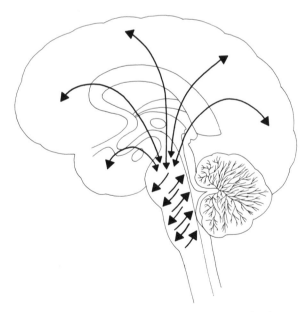

Figure 2-4. The reticular activating system (RAS) that connects the sleep–wake centers in the hindbrain with the entire brain. Arrows indicate ascending and descending neural tracts.

ulation is high, the RAS stimulates the activation of relatively large regions of the CNS, including the motor neurons of the spinal cord (Moruzzi & Magoun, 1949; Jouvet, 1967). It should be noted that the forebrain also influences RAS activity. You can consciously decide to take a nap in a highly stimulating environment or stay wide awake and attentive during the most boring lecture. Thus the RAS should be conceptualized as a component of the CNS arousal system rather than as the "control" center for arousal.

Numerous theorists have postulated that RAS activity may account for why emotional states may either facilitate or interfere with performance on specific tasks. These theories are based on the assumption that, for any given task, there is an "optimal level of arousal." That is, peak performance occurs only at a specific level of CNS activity. If arousal is either too low or too high for a given task, performance suffers. For example, students who experience either very low or very high levels of academic anxiety often perform poorly on tests. Moreover, researchers have generally found an inverse relationship between the complexity of the task and the point of optimal arousal. That is, the more complex the task, the lower the level of physiological arousal needed to achieve optimal performance. Thus, peak performance in a simple motor task (sprinting) occurs at a higher level of physiological arousal than a more complex task (playing football). Not surprisingly, athletes often "choke" when levels of arousal are extremely high. Although the relationship between arousal and performance is commonly labeled the Yerkes–Dodson (1908) *law*, it should be noted that empirical support for this law has been mixed. Wilkinson, El-Beheri, and Gieseking (1972), for example, reported that an inverted U-shaped relationship between arousal and performance may occur only when other variables that influence performance (information load, practice, etc.) are held constant.

Other theorists have postulated that RAS activity may account for why emotional states may either facilitate or interfere with sleep patterns. For example, anxiety is associated with complex patterns of often contradictory changes in sleep patterns. Specifically, both anxiety states and trait anxiety (an individual's predisposition to experience anxiety states) are associated with an increase in the frequency of nightmares (Cellucci & Lawrence, 1978; Starker & Hasenfeld, 1976). However, state anxiety is associated with insomnia or loss of sleep (Haynes, Follingstad, & McGowan, 1974), whereas trait anxiety is paradoxically associated with increased sleep time (Hartmann, 1973).

Insomnia nicely illustrates the role of the RAS in emotionally induced sleep disorders. Insomnia is characterized by a 30- to 60-minute delay in sleep onset and an increase in the number of waking periods during sleep. Estimates of the incidence of insomnia range from 5% of pediatric patients to 32% of psychiatric patients (Bixler, Kales, & Soldatos, 1979). Insomniacs tend to report two different types of symptoms: elevated physiological arousal (somatic insomnia) and racing or repetitive thoughts (cognitive insomnia). Although researchers currently disagree on the relative incidence rates of somatic and cognitive insomnias, both disorders appear to directly involve overactivation of the RAS. For example, Haynes, Adams, and Franzen (1981) found that, when awake, insomniacs show larger heart rate responses to stressors than noninsomniacs. Such physiological overreactivity may directly produce the "tossing-and-turning"

symptoms of somatic insomnia. Similarly, Lichstein and Rosenthal (1980) note
that the majority of severe insomniacs blame disturbing thoughts for their disorder. Such cognitive activation presumably produces RAS activation that in turn
delays sleep onset.

Hartmann (1973) noted that human subjects tend to report an increased
need for sleep after emotional stress and a decreased need for sleep during
nonstress periods. He postulated that both emotional states and the need for
sleep were determined by the balance of neurotransmitters in the CNS. Specifically, emotional states such as anxiety and depression may be produced by the
depletion of specific neurotransmitters, whereas sleep may help restore neurotransmitter levels. We will discuss the validity of Hartmann's model in Chapter
12.

The pain tract is another major midbrain structure that is directly involved
in emotional states (see Figure 2-5a). The pain tract is called the *periventricular
system* (PS), and it connects the nucleus gigantocelluaris in the medulla with
structures in the forebrain. The pain tract runs parallel to the RAS, and the two
tracts share numerous interconnections. This intimate anatomical relationship
accounts for both the attention-getting and arousing characteristics of pain.

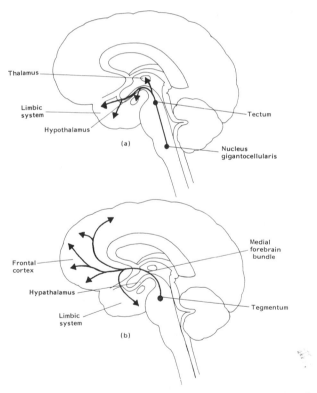

Figure 2-5. The "pain" (periventricular) and "pleasure" (medial forebrain bundle) tracts in
the human brain.

The pleasure tract is called the *medial forebrain bundle* (MFB) and also runs parallel to the PS (see Figure 2-5b). The two tracts are interconnected at many points that may account for why pleasure is normally conditional. In moderate quantities, biological rewards (food, sex, water, etc.) are usually experienced as pleasurable. However, in large quantities, the same "rewards" may become aversive. For example, consuming a single candy bar may be perceived as pleasurable, whereas eating 100 candy bars at one sitting would become painful. Valenstein and Valenstein (1964) observed that when rats were given the opportunity to control the duration of (presumably) pleasurable electrical stimulation, they did not choose continuous stimulation but rather turned the signal on and off. Moreover, the length of time the rats turned the current on varied inversely with the intensity of the current. Thus, it would appear that continuous stimulation of the pleasure tract may trigger associated structures in the pain tract.

The pain–pleasure tracts were discovered by accident by Olds and Milner (1954) during an experiment that was intended to study the effects of electrical stimulation on the RAS. During the surgical implantation of the stimulating electrodes, one of the electrodes bent and was accidently implanted in the MFB. When this particular rat was stimulated, he kept returning to the spatial locations where stimulation occurred as if he was waiting for the event to be repeated. After observing this odd behavior, Olds and Milner then intentionally implanted electrodes in the MFB of other rats and allowed the animals to electrically stimulate themselves by pushing a lever. They found that the rats would self-stimulate themselves at very high rates up to the point of exhaustion. Olds (1958a,b) then conducted a series of experiments that examined the properties of electrical stimulation of the MFB and PS. He repeatedly found that stimulation of the MFB acted as a potent reward and stimulation of the PS acted as a potent punishment.

Since Olds and Milner's discovery of the MFB and PS tracts, numerous researchers have documented the existence of "pleasure" and "pain" tracts in a wide variety of species (chickens, dogs, cats, monkeys, etc.). Unfortunately, nonhuman research tells us only that the animal is willing to work to obtain or avoid electrical brain stimulation and does not prove that the animal is experiencing pleasure or pain. The obvious advantage of experimentation with human subjects is that they can report their subjective experience. Given the ethical issues raised by direct electrical stimulation of the MFB and PS, research with human subjects has been restricted to "volunteers" from samples of criminals, epileptics, mental patients, and chronic pain patients. Obviously, the ethics of using such subjects for brain research is also highly questionable.

Humans receiving electrical stimulation to the MFB behave very similarly to nonhuman subjects. Specifically, both human and nonhuman subjects will self-stimulate at rates of over 1,000 times per hour (Heath, 1964) and ignore biological rewards such as food (Bishop, Elder, & Heath, 1963). Conversely, the self-reports of human subjects, however, fail to support the view that stimulation of the MFB produces "pure" pleasure. The subjective experiences produced by electrical stimulation appear to be mediated by the specific location in the MFB stimulated. Subjects reported intense orgasmiclike pleasure only when a few specific points in the MFB were stimulated. At the majority of sites tested, however, subjects reported much lower levels of pleasurable sensations that ranged from mild tingling to sexual stimulation without achieving orgasm. MFB stimulation also produced self-reports of "positive" emotions such as happiness, humor, and general euphoria. When other sites in the MFB are stimulated, subjects denied either pleasure or positive emotional states but rather reported an overwhelming compulsion to repeat the behavior that produced the stimulation (Bishop *et al.*, 1963; Heath, 1964; Delgado, 1971).

Human research on stimulation of the PS tract has also failed to support the position that stimulation of the PS produces "pure" pain. Although both humans and nonhumans will work to avoid stimulation of the PS tract, human subjects report intense pain only when a relatively small region of the PS is stimulated (Valenstein, 1973). Stimulation of other areas produces self-reports of negative emotions such as anxiety, depression, or fear (Delgado, 1971).

Based on research with human subjects, it would appear that the MFB may contain specific control centers for pleasurable affective states and the PS may contain specific control centers for negative affective states. Such simplistic conclusions, however, are highly questionable. Neurons, like other electrical circuits, conduct currents for great distances from the point of origin. Thus, stimulating the brain at point A may inadvertently produce activation of other neural structures at point Z. It is just as plausible to attribute the emotional experience produced by electrical stimulation to activation of structure Z as to activation of structure A or to *any* structure between point A and Z. As you will see in our following discussion of the forebrain, the concept of "emotional control center" appears to have limited value when discussing the human brain.

Anatomists divide the forebrain into an inner and an outer layer. Because the inner layer contained the major nuclei for the sense of smell, it was traditionally called the *smell brain* (rhinencephalon), whereas the outer layer or "peel" was labeled the *cortex*. Papez (1937) proposed that emotional behaviors were controlled by structures collectively labeled the limbic system contained in the rhinencephalon, whereas emotional experiences were localized in the cortex. Although subsequent research suggests that many of the specific details of Papez's model are incorrect, research has consistently supported his general model.

The major structures of the limbic system are shown in Figure 2-6. Research suggests that each of these structures may perform multiple functions. First, a given structure may contain nuclei that elicit highly organized patterns of emotional and/or motivational behaviors. For example, the amygdalas are two small structures located on both sides of the limbic system. Electrical stimulation of nuclei in the amygdala elicits rage behaviors where the organism launches a savage attack on external targets. Thus, the amygdalas appear to contain "local control centers" for rage. Such behavior patterns are highly species-specific. Rage reactions of cats are characterized by hissing and unsheathing claws, whereas human rage reactions are characterized by bared teeth and clenched fists. Such rage behaviors are also normally directed at appropriate targets (i.e., provokers) in the external environment.

Second, a given limbic structure may help control a specific behavior by exciting or inhibiting other parts of the brain. For example, Kluver and Bucy

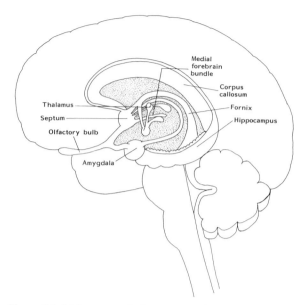

Figure 2-6. Major anatomical structures of the limbic system.

(1937) discovered that surgical removal of the amygdalas and overlying cortex can eliminate rage behaviors in monkeys. However, the surgery also produces a pattern of abnormal motivational behavior patterns now labeled the *Kluver–Bucy syndrome*. These animals display bizarre eating behaviors and often attempt to eat nonfood items (bolts, shoes, etc.). Moreover, the animals display hypersexuality and attempt to copulate with members of the same and opposite sex, members of other species, and even inanimate objects.

Bard's (1928, 1934) research on the effects of surgical removal of sections of cats' brains on rage behaviors provides another example of the functional unity of the CNS. Bard found that when the entire cortex was removed, the animals failed to show rage reactions when attacked. If the majority of the cortex and the limbic system above the hypothalamus were removed, the animals showed a bizarre pattern of behaviors called *sham rage*. These cats displayed normal rage reactions (i.e., hissing), but the behaviors were no longer aimed at appropriate targets in the environment and terminated as soon as the provocation stopped. If the entire cortex and limbic system were removed, the animals showed only fragments of rage behavior, that is, unsheathed their claws and simultaneously purred.

Both the Kluver–Bucy syndrome and sham rage research suggest that the amygdalas may "control" normal rage reactions. However, other studies have found that destruction of both amygdalas may lead to an *increase* in ragelike behaviors (Bard & Mountcastle, 1948). Surprisingly, both findings have been repeatedly replicated. Some researchers have found that destruction of the amygdalas produces placid animals, whereas other researchers have reported that the operation produces savage, uncontrollable animals. How can the same surgical operation produce opposite behavioral effects? The key word to understanding these paradoxical research findings is the word *same*. Traditionally, neuroscientists have attempted to identify the functions of neural structures by surgically destroying the structure or by electrically or chemically stimulating the structure and then observing changes in behavior. Due to the amygdalas' location in the brain, however, it is physically impossible to surgically destroy both amygdalas without damaging other structures in the limbic system and in the cortex. Although two researchers may perform the "same operation," a difference of a few millimeters in a surgical incision will produce two radically different patterns of brain damage. For example, the hypersexuality observed in the Kluver–Bucy syndrome appears to be due to damage to the cortex adjacent to the amygdalas rather than to damage of the amygdalas *per se* (Kluver & Bucy, 1939). Thus it is quite plausible that the apparently contradictory findings on the effects of destroying the amygdalas may be due to differences in the degree of damage to adjacent neural structures.

The research on the functions of the amygdalas nicely illustrates the danger in taking the concept of "control center" too literally. Research findings consistently suggest that the brain does not contain specific "control" centers" but rather is organized into a series of interlocking and redundant control circuits. Damage to one component of the nervous system may produce changes in other "unrelated" behaviors. Moreover, damage to a specific area of the brain may produce either permanent changes or only temporary disruptions in a given behavior. Although CNS tissue does not regenerate, other areas of the brain may assume control of components of the lost behavior (e.g., recovery of function). Thus, the individual may recover behaviorally, if not neurologically. Although we will treat specific limbic and cortical structures "as if" they control specific emotional or motivational behaviors, the reader should keep in mind that these structures are components of larger neural organizations and are not isolated control centers.

The hypothalamus is a small structure located at the base of the forebrain. Research has revealed that the hypothalamus is quite complex and contains a number of different nuclei, each controlling different emotional and/or motivational behaviors. The hypothalamus illustrates three basic principles of the functional organization of the CNS.

First, the CNS contains distinct excitatory and inhibitory control centers. For example, stimulating the anterior hypothalamus excites the PNS and simultaneously inhibits the posterior hypothalamus from triggering SNS (sympathetic nervous system) activation. Conversely, stimulation of the posterior hypothalamus stimulates the SNS and inhibits the anterior hypothalamus from exciting the PNS. Such antagonistic "ON-OFF" control circuits are common throughout the CNS. Numerous researchers have reported that surgical damage to specific hypothalamic nuclei produces changes in behaviors that are the exact opposite of the behaviors elicited by chemical or electrical stimulation. Specifically, stimulation of the lateral nucleus elicits eating behaviors, and the animal will overeat until it becomes extremely obese or hyperphagic (Anand & Dua, 1955). Surgical damage to the lateral nucleus produces hypophagic animals that refuse to eat and may starve to death even though they are surrounded by food (Anand & Brobeck, 1951). Similarly, stimulation of the ventromedial nucleus will produce hypophagia (Miller, 1960), whereas surgical destruction of the ventromedial nucleus causes hyperphagia (Brobeck, 1946). Thus, the physiological effect of destruction of an excitatory (ON) nucleus is equivalent to stimulation of an inhibitory (OFF) nucleus and vice versa. It should be noted that although these hypothalamic nuclei appear to be the primary "control centers" for eating, some recovery of function can occur if these nuclei are destroyed (Teitelbaum & Stellar, 1954).

Second, the same small area of the brain may control a number of different behaviors. For example, the lateral hypothalamic nucleus controls (at least) three separate behavior patterns—eating, drinking, and directed aggression. How does an extremely small region of neural tissue manage to control different behaviors without mixing up neural signals? One possible explanation is that the microcircuits involved in different behaviors may use different neurotransmitters to avoid "cross-talk" between circuits. Grossman (1960, 1964), for example, found that injections of norepinephrine into the lateral nucleus elicits eating, whereas injections of acetylcholine at the same site elicits drinking. Thus, it would appear that the behaviors elicited by stimulating a given site in the limbic system may be determined by a number of different neurotransmitters.

Third, the neural circuits that control "emotional" and "motivational" behaviors are intimately connected. For example, Flynn (1967; Flynn, Vanegas, Foote, & Edwards, 1970) reported that the behaviors elicited by electrical stimulation of hypothalamic nuclei vary with the intensity of the electrical current. Low stimulation to the anterior nuclei elicits eating behaviors in cats, whereas high levels of stimulation cause the cat to stop eating and quietly attack and kill a rat (directed aggression). Similarly, low levels of stimulation to the ventromedial nuclei will stop a cat from eating, whereas high levels of stimulation produce sham rage (affective aggression). Although researchers have often arbitrarily distinguished between emotions and motivations, this distinction has little neurological basis. Emotions and motives share many of the same neurological tracts and may be elicited simultaneously. Moreover, in everyday life, humans often engage in motivational behaviors (eating, sex, etc.) to fulfill emotional needs. Conversely, the gratification of motives may elicit positive emotions such as joy, whereas the frustration of motives often elicits negative emotions such as rage.

Based on the preceding discussion, it might appear that only two components of the limbic system—the amygdala and hypothalamus—are involved in the excitation and inhibition of rage behaviors. However, at least three other limbic structures, the cingulate gyrus, the septal area, and the hippocampus, also control rage reactions. Stimulation of the cingulate gyrus (Siegel & Chabora, 1971) or the septal area (Siegel & Skog, 1970) blocks the aggressive behaviors normally elicited by hypothalamic stimulation. Conversely, stimulation of the hippocampus may elicit rage reactions (Naquet, 1954). Thus it would appear that the limbic system contains a complex "rage" circuit with multiple control centers. Similarly, research suggests that the limbic system contains a complex "fear" circuit. Fearlike behaviors can be elicited by electrically stimulating the amygdala, cingulate gyrus, and posterior hypothalamus (Roberts, 1958; Miller, 1961; Goddard, 1964).

Given the complex interconnections between limbic system structures, many researchers have questioned whether the effects of electrical stimulation are due to the activation/inhibition of specific emotional centers in the CNS or to the disruption of ongoing mental activities. Kelley and Stinus (1984), for example, argued that emotional behaviors elicited by hippocampal stimulation may be due to disruptions in spatial memory and other cognitive functions.

Case reports of humans with tumors located in specific limbic structures tend to closely parallel the research findings on nonhuman subjects. For example, violent behaviors can be triggered by abnormal activity of the amygdalas and hippocampus (Mark & Ervin, 1970). However, Valenstein (1973) has cautioned against generalizing from animal limbic system studies to humans and cited a number of differences between humans and nonhumans. First, in nonhuman subjects, stimulation of hypothalamic nuclei elicits specific emotional or motivational behaviors. Human subjects, however, often do not report either emotional or motivational states when the same areas of the limbic sytem are stimulated. Second, there are wide individual differences in emotional experiences reported when specific limbic structures are stimulated. For example, different subjects have reported anxiety, orgasm, terror, or "no effect" when the ventrolateral area of the thalamus is stimulated. Third, if the same site in the brain is stimulated at different times, a given individual may report different emotional states. For example, stimulation of the amygdala may elicit reports of rage or fear at different times from the same patient. Thus it would appear that in humans the emotional states elicited by limbic stimulation may vary with the activity of other brain structures.

The cerebral cortex is the complex mass of forebrain tissue that covers the majority of the rest of the brain. As shown in Figure 2-7, the plural term, *cortices*, is actually more appropriate than cortex because the cerebrum is structurally divided into two distinct halves or hemispheres. These two hemispheres are connected by a large bandlike tract called the *corpus callosum* and a number of smaller tracts called *commissures*. Each hemisphere is anatomically divided into four regions or lobes by fissures in the surface of the cortex.

Although the two cortices contain the most sophisticated information-processing areas in the CNS, more information is currently available about the functions of specific cortical lobes than about the entire rest of the brain. This rather odd state of affairs is due to the cortices' anatomical position as the outermost layers of the brain. Because the cortices are located adjacent to the skull, they are most likely to be damaged by blows to the head. Over the past 150 years, numerous case studies have been published on the behavioral changes that occur when humans have specific regions of the cortices damaged. Moreover, their spatial location makes recording, stimulation, or surgical destruction of the cortices much simpler than for other areas of the brain. Not surprisingly, researchers have been able to construct a rather detailed map of the functions of specific cortical lobes. Because a general understanding of cortical structure–function relationships is needed to understand the role of the cortices in emotions, we will begin our discussion with a brief review of these relationships.

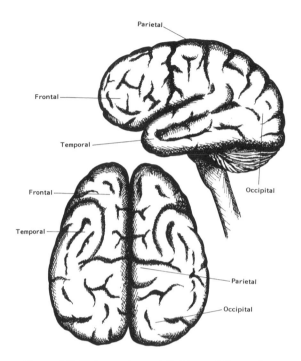

Figure 2-7. Major anatomical divisions of the cortices.

The primary function of the occipital lobes is processing visual information. The visual tract is organized such that information from the extreme right visual field is represented only in the left hemisphere and information from the extreme left visual field is represented only in the right hemispheres. Objects in the center of the visual field are represented in both hemispheres. Normally, this odd mapping goes unnoticed because the two hemispheres communicate via the corpus callosum.

The temporal lobes contain a number of interesting anatomical structures. First, the temporal lobes contain six different sensory-processing centers for hearing. Second, temporal lobes contain a small region called *Wernicke's area* that controls language comprehension. If Wernicke's area is destroyed, the individual can speak normally, but the content of his or her speech consists of meaningless word strings such as "cows float red shoes." Moreover, such individuals have also lost their ability to comprehend the speech of others.

In the majority of individuals, Wernicke's area is found only in one of the two temporal lobes. One method for confirming which hemisphere contains Wernicke's area is to temporarily anesthetize one half of the brain by injecting the drug sodium amytal into either the left or right carotid artery. If the subject stops understanding speech, then the anesthetized hemisphere contains Wernicke's area. About 95% of right-handers and 70% of left-handers have language localized in the left hemisphere. About 5% of right-handers and 15% of left-handers have language localized in the right hemisphere. Surprisingly, the remaining 15% of left-handers have bilateral (both hemisphere) language centers (Springer & Deutsch, 1981). Sex differences in the pattern of verbal and nonverbal intelligence test performances after temporal lobe damage suggests that right-handed females may also be more likely to have bilateral language (McGlone, 1978).

Each parietal lobe contains two sensory-processing areas for touch. Somatosensory area 1 is a detailed representation of touch information from receptors located along the exterior surfaces of the opposite side of the body. If we electrically stimulate a point in this region, you will experience a touch sensation (pressure, cold-hot, pain) at some point on the opposite side of your body. It should be noted that the cortical representation of the body's surface is *not* an isomorphic (one-to-one) map. The amount of cortical area representing a given region of the body reflects the relative sensory sensitivity of the skin surface (somatotonic map). That is, areas of your body that contain a large number of sensory receptors, such as your face, are represented by a relatively large area of the cortex.

Somatosensory area 2 of each parietal lobe receives touch information from both your skin and your viscera. Surprisingly, this area is almost randomly mapped such that sensory information from your arm may be adjacent to sensory input from your heart. This unusual neurological organization accounts for the phenomenon of *referred pain*. Pain signals from internal organs are normally misperceived as originating from regions of the skin that are displaced from the organ. For example, the pain associated with a heart attack is often misperceived as originating from the armpit or arm.

The strip of each frontal lobe adjacent to the parietal lobe controls motor movement on the opposite side of the body. These cortical representations of the muscles are also not isomorphic. The area of the cortex that represents a specific muscle group is proportional to the degree of fine motor movement needed. Areas of your body such as your hand or face that contain a relatively large number of small muscles are represented by a larger area of cortex than areas of your body that contain large muscles such as your arms.

The frontal lobe also contains a small area that controls speech production, called *Broca's area*. Destruction of Broca's area leaves the individual capable of comprehending speech but incapable of speaking normally. These individuals have extreme difficulty speaking words and often become extremely frustrated because they know what they want to say but cannot say it. Surprisingly, they can still hum and may actually be able to sing familiar songs if someone else starts the song. Moreover, such patients can also curse. Like Wernicke's area, Broca's area is usually found only in the left hemisphere. The localization of language centers in only one hemisphere led researchers to postulate that the language hemisphere was "dominant" and controlled the other hemisphere like a slave computer. We will examine the validity of this hypothesis later in this chapter.

Most of the frontal lobes are not involved in either motor movements or speech but appear to control "higher" intellectual functions such as decision making, memory for complex behaviors, and planning. Accordingly, many researchers consider the frontal lobes as the neurological equivalent of a computer's CPU (central processing unit). Other researchers, however, have noted that the frontal lobe has numerous connections with the limbic structures and could be legitimately classified as a component of the limbic system. Clues about the role of the cortices in human emotions comes from four different sources: case reports, electrical stimulation studies, surgical studies, and electroencephalographic (EEG) recording.

The case reports technique is based on the systematic correlation of patterns of "naturally occurring" brain damage with changes in behaviors or psychological abilities. For example, systematic evaluation of case reports led to the discovery of both Broca's and Wernicke's areas. Based on case reports, there is little evidence that damage to the occipital, parietal, or temporal lobes *per se* produces changes in human emotional reactions. Any emotional changes observed after damage to these regions of the cortex appear due to either damage to underlying limbic structures or psychological reactions to loss of other functions (e.g., the patient became depressed about being blinded). Damage to the frontal lobes, however, appears to directly alter emotional reactions (Curt, Jacobsen, & Marcus, 1972). Specifically, the individual may experience either a marked decrease or increase in anxiety, depression, euphoria, and other emotional states. Davidson (1983a, 1984) noted that these clinical findings suggest that different emotional states may be localized in either the left or right frontal lobes. Both positive and negative emotions appear to be localized in the left frontal lobe, whereas only negative emotions are localized in the right frontal lobes. Such findings support the view that the frontal lobes should be classified as a component of the limbic system.

The case report literature provided strong but *indirect* evidence that highly localized areas of the cortices perform specific functions. Direct evidence for localization of cortical function has been obtained during neurosurgery by a technique called *electrical mapping*. A weak electrical current is run between two points on the cortex in the areas adjacent to diseased or damaged tissues. If this tissue is also diseased, it will react with an abnormal pattern of high-amplitude and high-frequency electrical spikes characteristic of epileptic seizures. Thus, the neurosurgeon can systematically map the extent of tissue damage and avoid accidently destroying healthy brain tissue during surgery. It should be noted that this technique causes no discomfort to the patient. Although the tissues adjacent to skull and blood vessels of the head contain pain receptors, the brain does not. Only local anesthesia (for removal of sections of skull) is needed during neurosurgery, and the patient is conscious and capable of communicating with the surgeon.

Penfield and his associates employed the electrical mapping technique to explore localization of cortical functions (Penfield, 1954, 1958, 1975; Penfield & Rasmussen, 1950; Penfield & Jasper, 1954). Specific points of the cortex were stimulated (or unknown to the patient *not* stimulated), and the surgeons simply asked, "What do you feel now?" Stimulation of the motor cortex produced robotlike (automation) motor movements on the opposite side of the body. Stimulation of the primary visual or somatosensory areas produced simple hallucinations (i.e., colored dots or pressure on a point on the skin). Surprisingly, stimulation of the temporal lobes did not produce simple auditory hallucinations but rather led to self-reports of complex and vivid movielike hallucinations that incorporated multiple sensory experiences (sights, sounds, smells, tastes, etc.) and complex memories. For example, the patient may report, "I'm sitting in the opera and someone nearby is giving off a foul body odor." Penfield discovered that he could repeatedly elicit the same hallucination in a given patient by stimulating the same site on his or her cortex.

One important characteristic of the hallucinations induced by temporal lobe stimulation is that they are emotionally "flat." For example, one patient matter-of-factly reported "seeing a small boy in danger." Penfield also repeatedly failed to elicit emotional reactions by stimulating other regions of the cortex, including the frontal lobes (Penfield & Jasper, 1954). These findings led Penfield to con-clude that the cortices function in a computerlike fashion and that both emo-tional behaviors and experiences were mediated subcortically.

The apparently contradictory findings of the case report and electrical stim-ulation studies raise the issue of what role (if any) the cortex plays in emotions. One possibility is that structures in the frontal and temporal lobes actively inhib-it limbic system activation. Although the notion of "higher" cortical centers suppressing "animalistic" emotional impulses has a certain Victorian appeal, it cannot account for the available data. If the cortex functions as an "off" center for emotions, then electrical stimulation would (and apparently does) fail to elicit emotional reactions. However, as discussed previously, destruction of inhibito-ry areas is equivalent to stimulation of excitatory centers. If the cortices act as inhibitory centers, then destruction of these cortical areas should consistently produce increases in emotional reactions (which it does not).

Studies of the surgical removal (ablation) of cortical tissue suggest the cortex may play a complex role in human emotions. For example, neurosurgeons have experimented with the removal of sections of the frontal lobes (prefrontal lob-otomy) in an attempt to alleviate the suffering of cancer patients. The rationale for this procedure was the attempt to eliminate pain by cutting the connections between the pain tracts in the limbic system and in the cortex. These operations failed to alter the sensory components of pain but curiously eliminated the emotional components of pain. Thus, the patients reported that they still experi-enced pain but no longer "cared" about it (Delgado, 1971; Valenstein, 1973). These findings suggest that the frontal lobes may play an important role in the *conscious* experience of emotions.

Prior to the discovery of psychoactive drugs in the 1950s, prefrontal lob-otomies were also rather routinely performed to "cure" mental patients. Moniz (1936) reported that prefrontal lobotomies produced decreases in abnormal emo-tional reactions of mental patients, and his procedure soon became popular as a form of "surgical tranquilizer." Between 1945 and 1955, an estimated 40,000 lobotomies were performed in the United States alone (Valenstein, 1973). One reason for the popularity of the prefrontal lobotomy was that in 75% to 85% of the cases, the operation eliminated abnormal emotional experiences without grossly altering intelligence, memory, or other cognitive functions.

Careful evaluation of lobotomized patients, however, revealed that lob-otomies produce a curious pattern of side effects. Although the surgery reduced emotional experiences (conscious awareness of anxiety, depression, etc.), it led to a dramatic increase in emotional behaviors (i.e., crying, laughing). Patients often impulsively acted out their emotions or motives without regard to the social consequences. The observed increase in emotional behaviors after lobotomy does not appear to be due to the loss of cortical inhibition but rather due to the loss of specific cognitive abilities. Lobotomized patients show marked deficits in judgment, planning, and problem solving on a variety of tasks. The inability to "think about the consequences" coupled with the loss of inhibitory emotional experiences (i.e., anxiety) appears to produce the increase in emotional behaviors.

Studies of lobotomized patients suggest that the frontal lobes coordinate "cold" computerlike decision making with conscious emotional experiences to selectively inhibit (or not inhibit) emotional behaviors. The issue of "consciousness," however, reintroduces the mind–body debate into our materialistic discussion of the neurological basis of emotion. To avoid recapitulation, I would simply like to remind the reader that even strict materialists concede that consciousness (as an epiphenomenon) exists.

Unfortunately, even when we strip away the metaphysical disagreements, there is still little agreement among researchers as to the meaning of the term *consciousness*. Some researchers use the term to denote a primitive awareness of external and internal stimuli. According to this definition, both computers and the spinal cord can be defined as conscious. Other researchers reserve the term *consciousness* for the subjective "awareness of awareness" (I know that I know). Still other researchers argue that consciousness involves a more abstract form of meta-awareness (I know that I know that I know). Such definitions inevitably lead to such questions as "what is awareness?" and "what is knowledge?" To avoid such philosophical regression, we will use the traditional Freudian definitions of conscious, preconscious, and unconscious processes in the remainder of our discussion.

According to the Freudian view, consciousness is a momentary state of "awareness of awareness." Thus, any external or internal stimuli that "I am aware that I am attending to" are defined as conscious. Preconsciousness is defined as all stimuli that I potentially could attend to, if I shifted my attention. For example, I am currently unaware of the time of day. By shifting attention, I have made "time" conscious rather than preconscious. Thus, preconsciousness can be viewed as all material that is accessible to attention. Unconsciousness is defined by Freudian theorists as a primitive form of awareness that cannot be attended to, rather than a comalike lack of awareness. For example, healthy adults "know" how to rise smoothly out of a chair to a standing position without falling over. Obviously, some portion of one's CNS is "aware" of body position in space, gravity, and one's state of muscle contraction. Yet, it is extremely difficult to become conscious of (let alone describe) the complex temporal pattern of muscular contraction and relaxation needed to perform such a "simple" motor act.

The literature on surgical treatment of epilepsy provides some important information on the role of the cortices in conscious emotional experiences. Epilepsy is not a disease *per se* but rather a set of different disorders characterized by the periodic occurrence of abnormal patterns of neural activity or seizures in the CNS. Subtypes of epilepsy are classified by both the size of the area of the cortices effected by a seizure (partial or local, generalized or global) and the severity of the seizure (petit, mal, grand mal). The two major known causes of epilepsy are brain tumors and scar tissue from earlier injuries to the brain. In either case, epilepsy should be viewed as a symptom rather than as a disease.

The majority of epileptic patients respond well to anticonvulsive drug therapies, and neurosurgery is now recommended only when a tumor is suspected or when the patient does not respond to medication. However, prior to the discovery of anticonvulsive drugs, neurosurgeons employed a variety of surgical techniques in an attempt to cure epilepsy. One surgical procedure of particular interest is commonly called the *split-brain* operation. In order to prevent the spread of epiletic seizures between hemispheres, the two hemispheres are surgically "split" by cutting the corpus callosum and the commissures. This operation is remarkably effective in reducing both the severity and frequency of epiletic seizures. Moreover, the operation appeared to produce little change in intelligence, personality, or everyday behaviors.

Gazzaniga (1967, 1977) and Sperry (1968) doubted that the destruction of an estimated 200 million neurons in the split-brain operation had "no effect" and designed a clever procedure for testing split-brain patients. As discussed previously, information presented in the right visual field is processed in the left hemisphere, whereas information presented in the left visual field is processed in the right hemisphere. Normally, information is shared between hemispheres via the corpus callosum. However, after the split-brain procedure, this information-sharing capacity is lost. Thus, flashing words in gther the left or right visual field of a split-brain patient allowed the researchers to communicate separately to the subject's left and right hemispheres.

Flashing words to the right visual field (left hemisphere) produced conscious recognition ("I see the word *spoon*"), and the subjects were able to reach under a cloth and locate the target object with their right hands. When words were flashed to the left visual field (right hemisphere), subjects would respond that they had "seen nothing," yet correctly identified the object with their left hands. If asked to guess what object their left hands were holding, the patients replied "nothing." If they were allowed to look at their left hands, they were surprised that they were holding an object and denied conscious control over the hand's activity ("I didn't do that!"). Subsequent testing revealed that the patients' right hemispheres were quite capable of rather sophisticated decision making and would occasionally "correct" their left hemispheres. For example, when a patient's left hemisphere made a mistake, his or her head might suddenly start shaking from side to side, and the patient would remark "Oh, maybe I was wrong."

The overall pattern of results of testing split-brain subjects does not support the traditional view that the right hemisphere is a passive "slave" computer. The right hemisphere in humans appears capable of highly intelligent decision making and of generating complex behavior. Moreover, right hemisphere performance is better on global-holistic tasks (music, spatial relationships, etc.) than that of the "dominant" left hemisphere. However, the right hemisphere apparently has limited language skills and performs poorly on serial-analytical tasks (language, mathematics, etc.).

The split-brain studies suggest that the operation produces "two minds" in the same body. Researchers, however, disagree over whether both hemispheres are conscious. Gazzaniga (1967, 1977) argued that each hemisphere is clearly "aware that it is aware" and that the split-brain operation simply reveals the two hemispheres have different cognitive abilities.

Other researchers, however, argued that the nonverbal and nonlinear thought processes characteristic of the right hemisphere are virtually identical to the "primary-process" form of thought that Freud attributed to the unconscious. Similarly, the verbal-serial thought processes of the left hemisphere are virtually identical to the "secondary-process thinking" Freud attributed to consciousness (Galin, 1974; Ornstein, 1977).

Given that the right hemisphere has extremely limited means of communications (i.e., pointing, drawing), it is difficult to determine whether the right hemisphere functions at a conscious or unconscious level. Gazzaniga and LeDoux (1978) tested one split-brain patient with some degree of bilateral language and found clear evidence of "awareness of awareness" in both hemispheres. However, this case does not provide any information on whether verbal abilities are needed for "consciousness" in the right hemisphere.

Laboratory tests of split-brain patients suggest that both hemispheres are capable of processing emotional stimuli and of generating "appropriate" emotional behaviors. In one study, the subjects were presented with a series of photographs of ordinary objects to identify followed by the photograph of a nude woman. The subjects found the unexpected presentation of the nude funny, *regardless* of which hemisphere was stimulated. For example, when one female subject had the nude presented to her left hemisphere, she laughed and then correctly identified the photograph. When the same subject had the nude presented to her right hemisphere, she denied seeing anything but blushed and began giggling.

Anecdotal reports of split-brain patients also suggest that both hemispheres are capable of generating emotional behaviors. One dramatic example of "mixed emotions" was the case of a patient who was consciously angry with his wife. His left hand suddenly reached out to grab her while his right hand tried to stop the left (Gazzaniga, 1970).

Galin (1974) noted that the split-brain patients displayed more intense emotional reactions when the right hemisphere was stimulated. For example, the female patient discussed previously laughed when she had the nude presented to the left hemisphere but blushed and giggled when the nude was presented to the right hemisphere. Similarly, the male patient's *left* hand attempted to grab his wife. Galin hypothesized that if the right hemisphere plays a more important role in emotional reactions than the left, then somatic expressions, psychosomatic disorders, and conversion disorders should occur more frequently on the left side of the body. Consistent with these predictions, Stern (1977) found that conversion disorder symptoms occurred most frequently on the left side of the body in both right- and left-handed individuals.

Studies of nonclinical populations provide only mixed empirical support for

Galin's hypothesis. For example, Sackeim, Gur, and Saucy (1978) reported that subjects judged the emotional expressions on the left side of the face (controlled by the right hemisphere) as more intense than on the right side. Similarly, subjects' moods affect the memory of faces when the faces are presented to the right but not the left hemisphere (Gage & Safer, 1985). Electroencephalography (EEG) studies of brain activity, however, suggest that *both* hemispheres may play an important role in emotions.

In EEG recordings, electrodes are pasted to the surface of the scalp, and powerful amplifiers are used to detect the weak electrical signals produced by the physiological activity of the brain. These "brain waves" represent the collective electrical activity of the hundreds of thousands of neurons directly below each electrode. Because different parts of the brain may be activated or deactivated at any given point in time, different electrode locations on the scalp can produce entirely different patterns of brain waves. For example, imagining your living room tends to produce activation in the right hemisphere and deactivation in the left. Conversely, performing mathematical computations tends to produce the opposite pattern of brain activity.

EEG studies have found an inconsistent pattern of brain activity during emotional states. As predicted by Galin's model, some experimenters have found greater right than left hemisphere activation during either positive or negative emotional states. However, other studies have found the exact opposite pattern of hemispheric activation. After reviewing the EEG literature, Davidson (1983a,b, 1984) concluded that hemispheric asymmetries may reflect approach/avoidance motives rather than specific emotions *per se.* He argued that emotions that involve approach motives (anger, happiness, humor, etc.) appear to involve greater activation of the left hemisphere, whereas emotions that involve avoidance motives (anxiety, depression, etc.) appear to involve greater right hemisphere activation.

Based on the preceding discussion, it should be clear that a crude map of the emotional circuits in the CNS is currently available. These circuits are connected in a hierarchical fashion so that each level of the brain contributes to a more organized level of emotional behaviors and emotional states. The hindbrain elicits somatic and visceral activity during emotional reactions and forwards sensory information to higher brain centers. The midbrain contributes to emotional reactions by stimulating cortical arousal (via the RAS) and providing the pleasure–pain aspect (hedonic tone) of emotions (via the MFB and PS). The limbic system contains a number of separate excitatory and inhibitory centers for specific emotional experiences and emotional behaviors. The frontal lobes of the cortex integrate ongoing sensory information from both the external environment and body with images, plans, and memories and then decide whether to excite or inhibit specific emotional behaviors. Moreover, the cortices appear to be the locus of conscious emotional experiences, whereas the limbic system (and perhaps the right hemisphere) are the locus of unconscious emotional experiences.

It should be stressed that our map of the CNS is still extremely crude. Humans experience a wide variety of emotional states (anger, amazement, contempt, disgust, fear, joy, etc.). Yet, researchers have only identified the neural substrate of a small number of emotions (anger, anxiety, and fear). Whether each emotion has its own unique "circuit" or is represented by the pattern of activation in a small number of primary circuits is unknown.

SUGGESTED READINGS

Scientific American, 1979, 241(No. 3)

A special edition devoted to original articles on the anatomy and physiology of the nervous system. Although some of the information discussed is already dated, these articles are easy to read and quite thought-provoking.

Valenstein, E. S. *Brain control: A critical examination of brain stimulation and psychosurgery.* New York: Wiley, 1973.

Provides a general review of the history of psychosurgery in human and nonhuman species.

Neurohormonal Control Systems

As discussed in Chapter 2, the central nervous system directly controls physiological activity throughout the body. Hormones secreted by the endocrine gland system also exert a direct influence on physiological activity of specific organs. The CNS and endocrine gland system interact in reciprocal fashion. CNS stimulation can stimulate or inhibit the release of hormones by the endocrine glands, and endocrine hormones can stimulate or inhibit specific areas of the CNS. The CNS and endocrine gland system normally act in unison to produce integrated physiological activity. Accordingly, this "secondary" control system is called *neurohormonal*.

3.1. ANATOMY AND PHYSIOLOGY

The neurohormonal system consists of the hypothalamus and the endocrine glands (see Figure 3-1). Although the hypothalamus is a neural structure, it also functions as an endocrine gland and plays a central role in integrating neural and hormonal activities. The hypothalamus is connected with the posterior pituitary by neural fibers and with the anterior pituitary by a portal system of blood vessels. Researchers have identified a number of hypothalamic "releasing hormones" (RH) that cause the pituitary gland to secrete specific hormones into the bloodstream (Schally, 1978). Thus, the hypothalamus can stimulate or inhibit the pituitary gland through either neural activity or chemically with hormones. The hypothalamus also contains chemical receptors that are stimulated by endocrine gland hormones circulating in the bloodstream.

3.1.1. Pituitary Gland

The pituitary gland is often labeled the *master* gland of the endocrine system because it releases hormones that stimulate other endocrine glands. The anterior

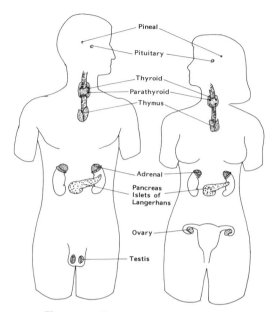

Figure 3-1. The major endocrine glands.

pituitary secretes three hormones (growth hormone, melanocyte-stimulating hormone, and prolactin) that directly influence physiological activity of specific body tissues. The anterior pituitary also secretes the following four tropic hormones that stimulate other endocrine glands to release hormones; adrenocorticotropic hormone (ACTH), thyroid-stimulating hormone (TSH), follicle-stimulating hormone (FSH), and luteinizing hormone (LH). The posterior pituitary releases oxytocin that stimulates contractions of the uterus and milk ejection and vasopressin, an antidiuretic hormone that stimulates reabsorption of water by the kidneys.

As you will see throughout this chapter, excessively high or low levels of hormones are associated with a variety of emotional states. In this section, we will focus on two pituitary hormones, prolactin and growth hormone, that act directly on the body's tissues rather than on another endocrine gland. Because other pituitary hormones control the activity of the endocrine glands, abnormal activity of the pituitary may produce a wide variety of endocrinological disorders. For the purpose of clarity, these disorders will be discussed in the context of abnormal activity of the target glands.

Prolactin is produced by the pituitary in both sexes, but it is considered a "female" hormone because it is normally produced in much larger quantities in females than in males. Prolactin is normally released into the bloodstream during the menstrual cycle and helps prepare the ducts of the breasts for milk production (lactation) if pregnancy should occur.

Excessively high levels of prolactin (hyperprolactinemia) may produce abnormal emotional reactions in both sexes. For example, hyperprolactinemic females report significantly higher levels of anxiety, depression, and hostility than other female patients (Fava, Fava, Kellner, Serafini, & Mastrogiacomo, 1981). Similarly, O'Moore and his associates found elevated levels of both anxiety and prolactin in women seeking treatment for idiopathic infertility. Autogenic relaxation training produced parallel decreases in both self-reports of anxiety and blood levels of prolactin (O'Moore, O'Moore, Harrison, Murphy, & Carruthurs, 1983). Hyperprolactinemic males report higher levels of anxiety but do not differ from other males in self-reports of depression or hostility (Fava, Fava, Kellner, Serafini, & Mastrogiacomo, 1982).

Growth hormone (GH), or somatotrophin, is another pituitary hormone that acts directly on the tissues of the body. GH is released throughout the entire life span, and in adults it plays an important role in stimulating the body to repair damage of skin and bone. During childhood and adolescence, GH helps stimulate physical development. Endocrinological researchers have noted that the release of GH may be related to emotional adjustment.

Gardner (1972) reported that even with adequate nutrition, emotionally deprived children often "fail to grow" physically and show low levels of growth hormone. Gardner labeled this syndrome *deprivation dwarfism* and cited numerous cases where parental hostility led to slow physical growth in offspring. For example, one mother was abandoned by her husband 4 months after giving birth to male and female twins. She evidently directed the hostility she felt about her husband toward her son. Her daughter's growth rate remained normal while her son's growth rate dramatically slowed. When the son was removed from the mother and hospitalized his growth rate quickly improved. Reconciliation between the parents was also followed by accelerated growth in their son.

3.1.2. Pineal Gland

The pineal gland is located deep in the brain under the corpus callosum. Until the 1960s, the function of the pineal was unknown, and many biology textbooks did not list the pineal as a "gland." Environmental lighting directly controls pineal activity. In fish, amphibians, and reptiles, the pineal contains light-sensitive tissue like the retina. In mammals, the pineal does not directly receive light but rather receives neural input from the visual system. The pineal secretes the hormone melatonin in dark environments. During seasons with short periods of daylight (fall and winter), large amounts of melatonin are released. Conversely, during seasons with long periods of daylight (spring and summer), melatonin secretion declines. Because melantonin inhibits the activity of the ovaries and testes, the pineal produces seasonal breeding patterns in many species. Removal of the pineal in sheep, for example, produces year-round mating. Whether the pineal exerts a similar effect on human reproduction has been debated. Ehrenkranz (1983) reported that both melatonin levels and births vary seasonally among the Eskimos.

3.1.3. Thyroid and Parathyroid Glands

The thyroid and parathyroid glands are located in the neck. The thyroid gland releases the hormones thyroxin and triiodothyronine that help regulate the energy-producing biochemical activities (metabolism) of individual body cells. TSH from the pituitary stimulates the release of both hormones that, in turn, inhibit pituitary release of TSH. The thyroid also secretes thyrocalcitonin that increases the calcification of bone and decreases calcium excretion by the kidneys. Thus, thyrocalcitonin decreases blood levels of calcium. The four parathyroid glands secrete parathorome that increases the amount of calcium in the blood.

Either over- or underactivity of the thyroid gland can mimic a variety of psychiatric disorders (Hall, 1983). Patients with overactive thyroid glands (hyperthyroidism) often display symptoms associated with severe anxiety reactions such as elevated heart rates (tachycardia), irregular heart beats (palpitations), and excessive sweating (hyperhidrosis). Patients often report high levels of anxiety and display a high degree of emotional lability (i.e., spontaneous crying or anger for no apparent reason). Severe hyperthyroidism may mimic manic-depressive psychosis. Conversely, the symptoms of severe hypothyroidism often resemble those of a variety of psychiatric disorders such as depression, paranoia, and schizophrenia.

Either over- or underactivity of the parathyroid glands can also mimic psychiatric disorders. Patients with severe hyperparathyroidism tend to show psychoticlike symptoms (hallucinations, paranoia, etc.), whereas depression is commonly observed in less severe cases (Peterson, 1968). Hypoparathyroidism is characterized by muscle spasms, intellectual impairment, and tactile hallucinations (i.e., insects crawling on the skin). Although a variety of psychiatric disorders (anxiety, depression, agitated psychosis) have been observed in hypoparathyroid patients, symptoms associated with low calcium levels tend to be idiosyncratic (Jefferson & Marshall, 1981).

3.1.4. Thymus Gland

The thymus gland is located in the upper chest at the base of the trachea. Although specific thymic hormones have not been clearly identified, thymic hormones appear to perform two important functions. Thymosin stimulates the body's immune system, and one or more thymic hormones appear to inhibit pituitary production of growth hormone. Hans Selye's (1956) research on the physiological effects of stress suggests that the thymus gland may play a central role in adaptation to stress. We will discuss Selye's research in detail later in this chapter.

3.1.5. Adrenal Glands

The two adrenal glands are located on top of each kidney. The outer glands (adrenal cortex) secrete three classes of hormones: mineralocorticoids, glucocorticoids, and sex hormones. Mineralocorticoids such as aldosterone are steroids that help maintain the body's balance of fluids and minerals. Glucocorticoids such as cortisol are steroids that help control the metabolism of proteins and sugars. The adrenal cortices of both sexes produce "male" hormones (androgens) and "female" hormones (estrogens). Adrenal sex hormones promote the development of secondary sexual characteristics (breasts, body hair, etc.) during puberty. The inner adrenal glands (medulla) are innervated by the sympathetic nervous system. Excitation of these sympathetic fibers causes the adrenal medulla to release two hormones, epinephrine and norepinephrine, which stimulate the cardiovascular system.

Jefferson and Marshall (1981) noted that because the adrenal cortices produce three different classes of hormones (aldosterone, androgen, and cortisol), abnormal functioning of the adrenals may produce three distinct classes of disorders. Although individuals with either aldosterone or androgen disorders may experience psychosocial adjustment problems, neither class of disorders is associated with abnormal emotional states. Cortisol disorders, however, may produce marked psychological changes that mimic psychiatric disorders.

Excess production of cortisol (hyperadrenalism, or Cushing's syndrome) is associated with severe depression, and about 10% of hyperadrenalism patients attempt suicide. Psychotic reactions (paranoia, hallucinations, etc.) are also occasionally reported. Paradoxically, depression is also the most commonly observed psychiatric syndrome associated with a shortage of cortisol in the bloodstream (hypoadrenalism). However, depression in hypoadrenal patients often is episodic, and hypoadrenal patients may fluctuate between depression, symptom-free periods, and anxiety and paranoid states.

3.1.6. Pancreas

The pancreas is located below the stomach and secretes two hormones, glucagon and insulin. Glucagon stimulates the liver to convert stored sugars into blood sugars. Insulin stimulates metabolism of blood sugar by the body's cells. Thus, insulin acts to decrease levels of blood sugar. Diabetes and other disorders of the pancreas lead to abnormal blood sugar levels. Maniclike states are commonly associated with excessive blood sugar levels (hyperglycemia), whereas shortages of blood sugar (hypoglycemia) are associated with anxiety states, outbursts of anger, and fuguelike states.

3.1.7. Reproductive Glands

The gonads or reproductive glands of both sexes are identical up to the fourth to sixth week after conception. If high levels of androgens are present in the bloodstream, the gonads form into "male" testes glands that secrete an androgen (testosterone) that stimulates the development of a male urinogenital system (penis, scrotum, etc.) and development of a "male" reproductive system occurs in either genetic sex. There are a number of rare disorders (e.g., the androgenital syndrome) that are characterized by genetic females having a partial or almost completely formed male phenotype. Conversely, low levels of androgens prenatally produce the development of a female urinogenital system (uterus, vagina, etc.) in either genetic sex. Again, there are a number of rare disorders (e.g., androgen insensitivity syndrome) where genetic males are born with female reproductive organs (Money & Tucker, 1975).

In normal adults, physiological activity of males' testes and females' ovaries are controlled through a complex interaction with the pituitary gland. Due to prenatal effects of androgen on the development of the hypothalamus, the release of sex hormones in males is relatively constant or tonic, whereas in females, sex hormones are secreted cyclically (Pfeiffer, 1936; Goy, Phoenix, & Young, 1962). We will discuss the male and female reproductive cycles later in this chapter.

3.1.8. Neurohormonal Controls

The neurohormonal control system is continually modulating physiological activity in the body. Some endocrine gland activity is directly influenced by levels of chemicals in the blood. For example, parathyroid activity is controlled by a simple negative feedback loop. Decreases in blood calcium levels stimulate parathyroid secretion, whereas increases in blood calcium inhibit parathyroid secretion. Conversely, a simple positive feedback loop controls secretion of insulin by the pancreas. Increases in the levels of blood glucose produce increases in insulin secretion.

Control of hormonal secretion of other endocrine glands is much more complex. Although the hypothalamus and pituitary "control" other endocrine glands, hormones from the target glands also alter the activity of the hypothalamus and pituitary. For example, at least three neurotransmitters (dopamine, histamine, peptides) inhibit pituitary release of prolactin, whereas at least six hormones and neurotransmitters stimulate prolactin release. These complex interactions between the components of the neurohormonal system are best illustrated by examining specific hormonal cycles. Two endocrine cycles involved in human emotions, the stress cycle and the reproductive cycle, will be examined in detail later in this chapter.

3.1.9. Methodological Issues in Neurohormonal Research

The physiological characteristics of hormones present numerous problems for researchers. First, human hormones are often secreted into the blood in minute quantities, and concentrations of hormones may fall as low as a few picograms (trillionth of a gram) per milliliter (Ryan, 1975). To further complicate matters, hormones often quickly "disappear" from the bloodstream. Some hormones are quickly absorbed by target organs, whereas others are chemically unstable. For example, epinephrine and norepinephrine have half-lives of less than a minute. Low blood levels of a given hormone may mean that very little hormone was secreted or that the hormone has already been absorbed by the target organ or broken down into chemical by-products (metabolites). Oken (1967) noted that delayed blood samples are worthless if we are interested in acute hormonal reactions.

Second, hormones are highly related biochemically. For example, all adrenal steroids are derived from cholesterol (Ryan, 1975). Through biosynthesis, cholesterol is converted into either progesterone or androstenedione. Progesterone can be converted into either aldosterone or cortisol. Androstenedione is synthesized into testosterone that is a precurser of estrogens. Similarly, the body converts dopa into norepinephrine that is the precurser of epinephrine. Moreover, changes in the level of one hormone may facilitate or inhibit the production of other hormones. For example, cortisol speeds the biochemical transformation of norepinephrine into epinephrine. Increases in cortisol levels are accompanied by increases in epinephrine but decreases in norepinephrine. Conversely, decreases in cortisol are accompanied by decreases in epinephrine but increases in norephinephrine. Obviously, the release of multiple hormones during stress reactions may produce complex *patterns* of hormonal changes.

Third, the same chemical, norepinephrine, serves the dual function of a hormone and a neurotransmitter. Thus norepinephrine metabolites found in urine may be either hormonal or neural in origin. Mass, Fawcett, and Dekirmenjiam (1972) estimated that between 25% and 60% of urinary norepinephrine metabolites may originate from the CNS. Obviously, given a potential error rate of 35%, measures of the levels of the "hormone" norepinephrine are always suspect.

Fourth, hormonal activity varies as a function of circadian rhythms. For example, blood concentrations of ACTH (Ney, Shimizu, Nicholson, Island, & Liddle, 1963), GH (Taskahashi, Takahashi, Takahashi, & Honda, 1974), prolactin and testosterone (Sassin, 1977) are highest during sleep and progressively decline during waking hours. Thus blood or urine samples taken early in the morning will differ from those taken from the same individual in the afternoon or evening. Ryan (1975) argued that 24-hour samples are needed to accurately estimate hormonal levels in a given individual. Although 24-hour sampling techniques are employed in hospitals, they are less common in laboratory research because they "average out" acute hormonal reactions. Consequently, the hormone levels reported by different researchers may reflect the time of day that the samples were taken.

Despite the low concentrations and chemical instability of hormones in body fluids, modern chemical assay techniques, such as gas chromatography, can accurately detect hormones in blood samples and their metabolites in urine. These chemical assays are relatively complex but can be performed in most modern biochemistry laboratories. Obtaining samples of blood or urine to assay, however, creates one of the major methodological problems in studying human hormonal activity. Many people will not volunteer for experiments that involve either extracting blood or giving urine samples. Obviously, the subjects who do participate in hormonal research may not be representative of the general population. Moreover, marked individual differences in emotional reactions to giving blood or urine samples are often observed among volunteer subjects. For many subjects, having a needle stuck in a vein or being handed a cup and asked to urinate are highly emotionally arousing experiences. Thus, the collection of a hormone sample may itself alter hormonal activity.

Another major methodological issue is the time intervals between assessment of emotional states and hormonal levels. If hormonal levels are conceptualized as indices or *biological markers* of emotional reactions, then subjects' emotional reactions of different time intervals *prior* to the collection of blood or urine are of specific interest. Conservely, if hormones are conceptualized as a component of emotional reactions, then subjects' emotional reactions at different time intervals *after* sample collection are critical. Although neither hormonal levels nor emotional states remain constant over time, few studies have examined the temporal relationships between emotions and levels of specific hormones. For example, Ward and her associates observed that epinephrine levels recovered quickly after stress, whereas norepinephrine levels often remained elevated. Marked individual differences in recovery rates for epinephrine and norepinephrine were also observed (Ward *et al.*, 1983).

The appropriate time interval between emotional states and the collection of urine samples is also a difficult methodological issue. In order for hormone metabolites to be detected in urine, the kidneys must first extract the metabolites from the blood. Thus, urine samples collected during a stressor may reflect prestress rather than stress hormonal levels. Although collecting a series of urine samples from the same individuals might appear to be the ideal solution, frequent urination may also alter hormonal measurements. Levi (1972) argued that in order to make accurate estimates of blood levels of epinephrine and norepinephrine a 2-hour delay is needed between urine samples. Forsman (1981), however, found that accurate estimates of epinephrine and norepinephrine could be made with only a 75-minute delay between samples.

3.2. EMOTION AND THE NEUROHORMONAL SYSTEM

Research on the role of hormones in emotional states has focused on three general topics: neurohormonal stress reactions, reproductive hormones, and the relationships between specific hormones and specific emotional states.

3.2.1. Neurohormonal Stress Studies

As discussed in Chapter 2, the sympathetic nervous system is activated by a wide variety of physical stressors and emotional states. During SNS arousal, the neurohormonal system reacts in a global fashion (Oken, 1967). Excitation by the SNS stimulates the adrenal medulla to secrete epinephrine and norepinephrine that raise heart rate and blood pressure. Excitation of the amygdalas and other areas of the limbic system stimulate the hypothalamus to signal the pituitary to release tropic hormones. The pituitary signals the adrenal cortex to release aldosterone, cortisol, and sex hormones into the bloodstream and the thyroid gland to secrete thyroxin to speed metabolism. Thus, the endocrine glands help mobilize the body for "fight or flight."

Endocrine hormones also play an important role in terminating physiological stress reactions. Adrenal corticoids stimulate the hypothalamus to inhibit the pituitary. Excitation of the hippocampus and other areas of the limbic system also produces inhibition of the pituitary. Thus, stress hormones act as a negative feedback signal to the brain to terminate stress reactions. Other researchers, however, postulate that stress hormones may exert more complex effects on emotions. For example, Jacobs and Nadel (1985) hypothesized that cortisol may facilitate learning and recovery of phobias by blocking neural activity in the hippocampus.

Researchers have repeatedly demonstrated that the hormonal stress response may be elicited by a variety of physical and psychological stressors. For example, Ward *et al.* (1983) measured hormone levels by continuous blood withdrawal while male subjects were exposed to (a) passive painful stressors (venipuncture, immersing a hand in ice water), (b) active physical stressors (isometric handgrip, knee bends), (c) a psychological stressor (mental arithmetic), and (d) a standard physical examination procedure (blood pressure cuff readings). Blood levels of epinephrine increased significantly from baseline to all stressors and showed a marginal increase during blood pressure readings. Epinephrine showed the largest increases during the psychological stress period. Norepinephrine levels also increased from baseline in response to all stressors, but the largest norepinephrine increases occurred during the passive stressor periods. Marked individual differences were observed in both hormonal stress reactions and in recovery from stress (return to baseline).

In a review of endocrinological studies, Frankenhaeuser (1978) noted that even after mathematically correcting hormone data for body weight, males show more pronounced increases in epinephrine and cortisol in stressful situations than females. However, this sex difference appears to be age-dependent. Aslan, Nelson, Carruthers, and Lader (1981) tested endocrine reactions of 22- to 35-year-old and 50- to 67-year-old females and males. Only the younger female subjects failed to show marked epinephrine and norephinephrine responses to stressors.

Numerous authors have noted that the observed sex differences in adrenal responses parallel the sex differences in incidence rates of heart disease and high blood pressure. Prior to menopause, women have lower incidence rates of cardiovascular diseases than males. The observed sex differences in adrenal secretion and cardiovascular disease led researchers to postulate that high estrogen levels may inhibit the adrenals and thus, "protect" younger women from cardiovascular disorders.

Empirical evidence to support the "estrogen-protection" hypothesis, however, is equivocal. Numerous studies have found higher adrenal and cardiovascular reactions in male than female subjects during stress. For example, Forsman and Lindblad (1983) found that male medical students showed much higher blood pressure and epinephrine responses to mental stress than female medical students. Frankenhauser (1978), however, reported that women in "nontraditional" roles (e.g., engineering school) tend to show neurohormonal stress reactions similar to males their age. Moreover, epinephrine responses do not fluctuate with the menstrual cycle (Patkai, Johannson, & Post, 1974).

Although the majority of research studies have focused on epinephrine and norepinephrine, sex differences in other hormonal responses to stressors have been reported. Studies of Finnish high-school students have found both sexes showed elevation in urine levels of epinephrine, norepinephrine, cortisol, and a norepinephrine metabolite, MHPG (3-methyoxy-4-hydroxy-phenylethylene glycol) during a 6-hour matriculation examination. Males, however, showed significantly greater increases in both epinephrine and MHPG during the examination (Frankenhauser 1978; Rauste-von Wright & von Wright, 1981).

Vaernes, Ursin, Darragh, and Lambe (1982) attempted to assess the patterns of relationships between emotional reactions during stress and endocrine gland activity. The subjects were all nonswimmers who were required to jump from a 5-foot high platform into the deep end of a swimming pool as part of military training. Subjects completed mood questionnaires and gave blood samples before and after the jump. A urine sample was also collected after the stress experience, and subjects completed a questionnaire on psychological defense mechanisms. Multiple hormonal assays were performed on the samples. Prior to the jump, the nonswimmers showed elevations in all hormone levels. Cortisol and prolactin showed moderate increases, pre- to postjump. No change was observed in either growth hormone or testosterone. Only postjump measures were taken of epinephrine-norepinephrine so no change scores were reported.

Vaernes *et al.* (1982) found no relationship between hormone levels and subjects' self-reports of fear or anxiety. However, they observed a number of interesting relationships between self-reports of emotion, strategies for coping with emotion, and hormonal levels. Specifically, hormone levels during stress were related to three ego defense mechanisms: ignoring emotional significance of a stimulus (isolation), childish reactions (regression), and statement of the opposite motive (reaction formation). Subjects who scored high in isolation had lower postjump epinephrine–norepinephrine levels. Subjects who scored high in regression had lower testosterone levels. Subjects who scored high in reaction formation had elevated cortisol levels. Significant interactions were also observed between emotional states, degree of defensiveness, and hormonal levels. Subjects who reported both high degree of fear or anxiety *and* defensiveness showed elevations in prolactin.

Vaernes's findings suggest that patterns of hormone activation during stress may be related to both subjects' affective reactions and their attempts to psychologically cope with both the stressor and their affective states. Consistent with this hypothesis, Bandura and his associates found that epinephrine and norepinephrine levels were low when subjects perceive themselves as either completely capable or totally incapable of coping with a stressor. The highest levels of epinephrine and norepinephrine were found when subjects perceived themselves as moderately capable of coping with the stressor (Bandura, Taylor, Williams, Mefford, & Barchas, 1985).

The hormonal studies we have discussed up to this point all have employed brief exposures to physical or physiological stressors. Selye (1956), however, postulated that *repeated* SNS activation eventually produces psychophysiological symptoms such as ulcers. He found that animals showed systematic changes in their endocrine reactions when presented with repetitive stressors. Because these hormonal changes could be elicited by a variety of noxious stimuli (heat, cold, toxins, etc.), Selye labeled this process the *general adaptation syndrome* (see Figure 3-2). During the initial arousal or alarm stage of the general adaptation syndrome, the adrenals and other endocrine glands secrete large quantities of hormones. If the stressor continues for a prolonged period or is presented repeatedly, the animal enters a resistance stage characterized by tonic (baseline) elevation of hormone secretion. Selye postulated that the high levels of ACTH are released during the alarm and resistance stages to maintain high levels of blood glucose that increases energy and the repair of damaged tissues. Unfortu-

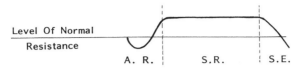

Level Of Normal
Resistance

A. R.   S.R.   S.E.

Figure 3-2. The general adaptation syndrome. From *The Stress of Life* by H. Selye, 1956, New York: McGraw-Hill. Copyright 1956 by McGraw-Hill. Reprinted with permission.

nately, high levels of ACTH also suppress the immune system and thus make the animal more vulnerable to infection. If the stressor is intense or prolonged, the animal enters the exhaustion stage where hormonal secretions cease. The animals often died during the exhaustion stage, and autopsies revealed enlargement of the adrenal glands, atrophy of the thymus gland, and massive stomach ulceration. Selye observed that stress appeared to weaken the animals' resistance to later stressors. Animals adapted to a given stressor (i.e., cold) showed a lower tolerance for novel stressors (i.e., heat) and entered the exhaustion stage more rapidly.

Selye noted that an epidemic of "air-raid ulcers" occurred in Britain during World War II and argued that the general adaptation syndrome might account for the development of psychophysiological disorders in humans. Normally, the gastrointestinal system is protected from its own digestive enzymes by an inflammatory barrier. Excessive quantities of adrenal hormones suppress this protective coating and thus may produce ulcers. Selye postulated that other psychophysiological disorders such as high blood pressure may also be produced by the general adaptation syndrome and that a given individual may be genetically predisposed to develop a specific stress-related disorder.

Research on nonhuman species' stress responses have consistently supported Selye's model. For example, a number of studies have found that chronic stress may produce rather permanent changes in an organism's adrenal glands' ability to synthesize and release the two catecholamine hormones, epinephrine and norepinephrine. In a series of studies of rats, Kopin (1980) demonstrated that chronic stress causes a marked increase in the release of adrenal catecholamines that does not return to prestress baseline. Consistent with Selye's model, Kopin found that rats that had been previously stressed showed exaggerated levels of catecholamine release when later presented with a new stressor. These findings suggest that chronic stress may sensitize the adrenals to overrespond to stressors. Kopin also noted that different strains of rats showed marked differences in both the magnitude of the catecholamine response and in tissue reactions to the catecholamines. Spontaneous hypertensive rats (SHR strain) showed the greatest elevation of catecholamine during stress and the greatest increase in blood pressure to a fixed dose of catecholamines. Thus this particular strain of rats appears to be genetically predisposed to show exaggerated catecholamine responses and tissue hypersensitivity.

Empirical support for Selye's model of human physiological disorders, however, has been equivocal. The results of some human studies clearly parallel Selye's findings with nonhumans. Poteliakhoff (1981), for example, observed that medical patients who reported chronic fatigue had significantly lower blood cortisol levels and were also more likely to report a history of severe and recurring stress than other patients. Similarly, Rauste-von Wright and von Wright (1981) reported that adolescent females' and males' self-reports of their histories of psychosomatic symptoms were negatively related to their neuroendocrinological reactions during stress. That is, subjects who reported the fewest psychosomatic complaints tended to show the strongest endocrine reactions. Both the patients' and adolescents' lower hormonal responses after a history of stress are obviously similar to Selye's animals during the exhaustion stage.

The results of other hormone studies, however, clearly do not support Selye's model. For example, Bloom, Von Euler, and Frankenhaeuser (1963) found no difference in either epinephrine or norepinephrine responses of veteran and novice parachutists during jump periods. Thus, despite repeated exposure to the stressor, the experienced parachutists showed no evidence of either habituation or sensitization to the stressor. Frankenhaeuser and Rissler (1970) observed that humans' epinephrine reaction to electric shock varied inversely with the degree of control subjects were given over the shocks. The more control the subject had over the situation, the lower his or her epinephrine response. Similarly, Bourne (1970) reported that American soldiers in Vietnam showed lower hormonal stress reactions during combat than had been observed in other wars and noted that the lower hormonal response was correlated with higher levels of ego defense mechanisms (denial, projection, etc.).

Studies of psychiatric patients also only partially support Selye's model. For example, consistent with Selye's model, anxiety patients (Miyabo, Asato, & Mizushima, 1979) and reactive depression and acute schizophrenic patients (Sachar, 1980) show elevated corticosteroid responses to stressors. Moreover, many depressed patients also display a *chronic* elevation in cortisol levels that is independent of either stressors or the sleep–wake cycle. Contrary to Selye's model, such chronic elevation in blood cortisol has rarely been observed in either anxiety patients (Rosenbaum et al., 1983) or schizophrenic patients (Carroll, Curtis, & Mendels, 1976).

Carroll and his associates found that the abnormal cortisol secretion observed in depressed patients could be traced to abnormal functioning of the steroid-sensitive cells in the hypothalamus (Carroll et al., 1976; Carroll et al., 1981; Carroll, Martin, & Davies, 1983). In healthy individuals, cortisol is normally secreted episodically during a 24-hour period, and peak secretion tends to occur between 4 and 8 A.M. (Weitzman, 1980). High blood levels of cortisol and other corticosteroids stimulate hypothalamic neurons to inhibit the pituitary's release of ACTH. Injections of the synthetic steroid, dexamethasone, mimic the effects of high blood levels of corticosteroids and inhibits ACTH secretion. Surprisingly, dexamethasone may have no effect on the abnormally high ACTH secretion in many depressed patients. Specifically, dexamethasone inhibits ACTH in about 90% of control subjects but in only about 51% of depressed subjects (Carroll et al., 1981). Thus, it would appear that in a large number of depressed patients, either the steroid-sensitive hypothamalic cells are malfunctioning or that this feedback mechanism is being overridden by abnormal neural signals from other regions in the limbic system.

In summary, research on nonhuman species suggests that both physical and psychological stressors may produce permanent changes in endocrine gland activity that, in turn, may lead to the development of psychophysiological disorders (high blood pressure, ulcers, etc.) and to increased vulnerability to physical illnesses due to suppression of the immune system. In humans, however, stressors often produce less dramatic effects on the neurohormonal system. This species difference does not appear to be biological. Some psychiatric patients do display hormonal changes similar to those observed in nonhumans. However, in most healthy individuals and psychiatric patients, coping strategies appear to play a major role in mediating their hormonal stress responses.

3.2.2. Reproductive Hormone Studies

The term *sex hormone* is misleading because the adrenal glands of both sexes produce both "male" hormones (androgens) and "female" hormones (estrogens). Adult males normally have much higher blood levels of androgens than females due to the additional androgen (testosterone) produced by the testes. Conversely, adult females normally have much higher blood levels of estrogen than males due to additional estrogen produced by the ovaries.

3.2.2.1. Androgens and Emotion

The male reproductive hormone cycle is a classic example of a positive feedback system. Starting at puberty, the pituitary releases relatively constant amounts of FSH and interstitial cell-stimulating hormone (ICSH, the male equivalent of LH) into the bloodstream. These gonadotropic hormones cause the testes to produce both sperm and testosterone. Testosterone stimulates the hypothalamus to stimulate the pituitary to release more FSH and LH into the bloodstream. Thus, the male hormonal cycle is relatively constant or tonic. However, the blood level of testosterone does follow a circadian rhythm. The average male shows peak levels of testosterone after waking from sleep (Sassin, 1977). Other researchers have argued that males' reproductive cycles may show longer fluctuations or rhythms. Doering, Brodie, Kraemer, Becker, and Hamburg (1978) found that males tend to show 3- to 30-day cycles in testosterone levels and that their self-reports of anxiety, depression, and hostility were related to their testosterone levels.

Research with nonhuman species suggests that blood levels of testosterone and other androgens may mediate specific motivational behaviors. Elevated androgen levels are associated with high levels of aggression and increased frequency in sexual behaviors. For example, removal of the testes (castration) produces a gradual decline in both aggression and sexual responsiveness of nonhuman males. Injecting castrated male animals with androgen can restore aggressive and sexual behaviors to precastration levels (Bermant & Davidson, 1974).

Research on human males, however, has produced conflicting results. Kreuz and Rose (1972) found that male prisoners with elevated levels of testosterone had a history of more violent crime than other criminals. However, testosterone levels did not predict which prisoners behaved violently while in prison. Rada, Laws, and Kellner (1976) reported that testosterone levels were higher in extremely violent rapists than in *other* rapists. Similar patterns of contradictory findings have been reported with research on human males' sexual behaviors. After puberty, castration does not eliminate either aggressive or sexual behaviors. Money and Erhardt (1972) noted that in some males, the decline in sexual responsiveness may not occur until years after castration.

Adrenal androgens may play an important role in the sexual behavior of human females. Removal of the ovaries (ovariectomy) has little or no effect on women's sexual behaviors. However, removal of the adrenals (adrenalectomy) produces a sharp decline in a woman's sexual behaviors. Conversely, injections of androgens can produce increased sexual drive in women, but the effect appears to be most pronounced with sexually experienced women (Kennedy, 1973; Norris & Lloyd, 1971).

Research on the role of naturally occuring androgen in females' sexual behavior is both sparse and equivocal. Perksy (1978), for example, found no relationship between sex drive and blood androgen levels in a sample of college women. Bancroft, Sanders, Davidson, and Warner (1983) reported that females' androgen levels correlated with masturbation frequency but were unrelated to the frequency of sexual behaviors with a partner. Schreiner-Engle, Schiavi, Smith, and White (1981) found insignificant correlations between androgen levels and sexual arousal. However, women with high levels of androgen did report higher sexual drive than women with low levels of androgen.

The available literature suggests that in both men and women numerous psychological and social factors may mediate the role of androgens in human aggression and sex (O'Leary, 1977; Dolye, 1983). For example, male heterosexuals, homosexuals, and transsexuals do not differ in androgen levels (Rose & Sachan, 1981).

As we will discuss later in Chapter 9, one of the major methodological problems in sex hormone research is that researchers have often failed to differentiate between behaviors, emotional states (feelings), and motives (desire to engage in specific behaviors). Aggression may be physical or verbal, direct or indirect, an attempt to reach a specific goal (instrumental), or a display of anger (an emotional state).

3.2.2.2. Estrogens and Emotions

The release of female reproductive hormones is a more complex process than the release of male hormones. In males, sex hormones are secreted relatively constantly. In females, blood levels of both pituitary and ovarian hormones vary over time in a distinct reproductive or menstrual "cycle." Although the "textbook" menstrual cycles last 28 days, the length of actual cycles is highly variable. The same woman may experience marked variation in length of her cycles, and there are also large individual differences in cycle length between women. "Normal" menstrual cycles range from 8 to 40 days in length. By convention, the first day of menstrual bleeding is labeled *Day 1* of the cycle.

On the first day of the cycle, the pituitary secretes small amounts of FSH that stimulate the growth of one or more follicles in the ovary. As the follicle matures, it releases estrogen into the bloodstream. Estrogen stimulates the growth of the lining of the uterus and signals the hypothalamus to stimulate the pituitary to release more FSH. This positive feedback loop continues, and estrogen rises to a sufficient level to stimulate pituitary to begin releasing LH. On about the fourteenth day, the pituitary releases a relatively large quantity of LH into the bloodstream. This LH "surge" causes the follicle to rupture, releasing the egg (ovulation), and causes the remaining cells of the follicle to form a special structure called the *corpus luteum*. The corpus luteum acts as a temporary endocrine gland and releases the hormones estrogen and progesterone. Progesterone helps maintain the uterine lining and signals the hypothalamus to inhibit FSH and LH secretion.

If pregnancy does not occur, the corpus luteum dies. The resulting drop in estrogen and progesterone levels causes the breakdown and expulsion of the uterine lining (menstrual bleeding) and allows the pituitary to resume FSH secretion. However, if pregnancy does occur, the fertilized egg secretes a hormone (chorionic gonadotropin) that prevents the corpus luteum from degenerating. Soon after the egg is implanted in the uterine wall, the placenta develops. The placenta also acts as a temporary endocrine gland and secretes estrogen and progesterone. The continued high levels of progesterone prevent the pituitary from releasing FSH and maintain the uterine lining during pregnancy.

Researchers have focused on two fascinating topics: the effects of estrogen on emotions and the effects of emotions on the menstrual cycle.

3.2.2.3. Menstrual Mood Shifts

Numerous studies have found that between 50% to 75% of menstruating women report periodic shifts in mood during the menstrual cycle. Reports of positive moods (happiness, elation, etc.) tend to occur around ovulation when estrogen levels peak. Conversely, reports of negative affect (anxiety, depression, and hostility) tend to cluster during either premenstrual or menstrual phases, when estrogen and progesterone are both at low levels (Gottschalk, Kaplan, Gleser and Winget, 1962; Ivey & Bardwick, 1968; Moos et al., 1969). However, it should be noted that across studies, at least 25% of the women tested do *not* report experiencing menstrual mood shifts (Hyde & Rosenberg, 1976).

If mood shifts are hormonally induced, why do some normally menstruating women not experience them? One plausible explanation is that individual differences in mood shifts may reflect individual differences in expectations. Menstruation is the subject of numerous cultural stereotypes, folk myths, and taboos (Weideger, 1976; Paige, 1977). For example, Clarke and Ruble (1978) reported that 12-year-old girls who had not started menstruating expected negative moods and pain to accompany menstruation. Koeske and Koeske (1975) observed that both female and male subjects attributed a menstruating females' emotional reactions to menstruation rather than situational factors. Obviously, such culturally acquired stereotypes may directly influence how an individual woman may react to premenstruation and menstruation. Parlee (1973) observed that many women often "adopt" stereotypical symptoms to appear "normal" to others.

For sexually active women, premenstruation may also trigger a multitude of pregnancy fears and fantasies. Specifically, for women who want to become pregnant, premenstrual symptoms signal "failure" and thus may trigger depression. Conversely, premenstruation may be a highly anxious "waiting" period for women who are terrified of becoming pregnant. For example, Birtchnell and Floyd (1975) reported that many cases of "premenstrual suicide" attempts are unmarried women who believe they are pregnant because of delayed menstrual bleeding.

Consistent with this "expectation" hypothesis, a number of researchers have found *positive moods* premenstrually or during menstruation. For example, May (1976) asked 30 women not taking birth control pills to rate their positive and negative moods at different phases of the menstrual cycle. Increased depression premenstrually was reported by 50% of the sample. However, another 40% of the subjects reported their most positive moods premenstrually and reported increased depression during the menstrual phase. Subjects' reports of mood changes were unrelated to either physical symptoms or the degree of distress reported during premenstrual or menstrual phases. Similarly, Moos and Leiderman (1978) observed that 13% of their sample reported only one premenstrual or menstrual symptom—an increase in *positive* moods.

An alternative explanation for individual differences in mood shifts is that they may reflect individual differences in the magnitude of hormonal changes. Schildkraut (1965) noted that drugs that increased levels of norepinephrine in the CNS (tricyclics, etc.) acted as antidepressants, whereas drugs that decreased CNS norepinephrine (e.g., reserpine) produced depression. Thus, high levels of norepinephrine are associated with elation, whereas low levels are associated with depression. Grant and Pryse-Davies (1968) hypothesized that estrogen and progesterone may alter CNS levels of norepinephrine and emotions by acting upon monoamine oxidase (MAO) levels in the CNS. MAO is an enzyme that is found in many parts of the body, including inside neurons. MAO breaks down epinephrine and norepinephrine. Drugs that inhibit MAO increase norepinephrine and thus act as antidepressants. Grant and Pryse-Davis argued that estrogen acts as a MAO inhibitor, whereas progesterone stimulates MAO activity. Thus positive moods at ovulation may be due to increased levels of norepineprhine, and negative premenstrual moods may be produced by norepinephrine decreases.

A third explanation for individual difference in mood shifts is that they reflect individual differences in premenstrual and menstrual symptoms. The premenstrual drop in estrogen and progesterone may produce a variety of physical symptoms (backaches, breast tenderness, headaches, swelling, etc.) that in turn may elicit negative moods (Paige, 1971). A minority of women report severe physical symptoms either premenstrually or menstrually (dysmenorrhea). Although most women do not experience dysmenorrhea, the majority of women report some degree of physical discomfort premenstrually or menstrually (Rouse, 1978).

Birth control pills provided the ideal test of these three rival hypotheses. First, because birth control pills help women avoid unwanted pregnancies, birth control pills act as an "antianxiety" medication for sexually active women. Second, birth control pills differ in their hormonal composition. Combination birth control pills contain high levels of estrogen and progesterone and thus mimic pregnancy. Sequential pills mimic the normal menstrual cycle. The pills for days 4 through 14 contain only estrogen, whereas the pills for days 20 to 24 contain both estrogen and progesterone. Third, birth control pills help eliminate menstrual irregularities or discomfort. If mood shifts are due to either psychological expectations or physical symptoms, then both combination and sequential pill users should show reduced mood swings. Conversely, if mood shifts are related to shifts in estrogen levels, then the combination pill users should report more stable moods than either normally menstruating women or sequential pill users.

Comparisons of birth control pill users and normally menstruating women have produced a mass of conflicting reports concerning the relationships between birth control pills, physical symptoms, and emotions (Paige, 1971; Worsely & Chang, 1978; Banks & Beresford, 1979; Ruble & Brooks-Gunn, 1979; Slade, 1984). Across studies, some women report either expectation-induced, symptom-induced, or hormone-induced mood shifts, whereas others do not.

Given this conflicting pattern of results, researchers have shifted their attention to a minority of women who report both hormone- and symptom-related mood shifts. The term *premenstrual syndrome* (PMS) is commonly used to describe any regularly occurring set of *severe* premenstrual symptoms (congestive dysmenorrhea, sudden mood shifts, asthma, headaches, etc.), and most researchers argue that the incidence rate of PMS is between 2% to 8% of adult women (Rose & Sachan, 1981; Clarke, 1985). Dalton (1979) argued that PMS accounts for the higher incidence rates of abnormal behaviors (child abuse, psychiatric admissions, suicide, violent crime, etc.) premenstrually than during other phases of the menstrual cycle. Dalton postulated that PMS symptoms are produced by excessive progesterone deficits and has claimed that she has successfully treated 20,000 PMS cases with progesterone suppositories.

Studies of PMS patients have failed to support Dalton's "progesterone" hypothesis. Zola and his associates reported that psychotic women were more likely to report PMS symptomatology (Zola, Myerson, Reznikoff, Thornton, & Concool, 1979). However, they found no difference between psychotic women admitted to a mental hospital premenstrually and other psychotic women admitted during other phases of their menstrual cycles. Sanders and her associates noted that women who were receiving treatment for PMS, women with a history of PMS, and women without PMS report similar mood shifts and physical symptomatology during premenstruation (Sanders, Warner, Backstrom, & Bancroft, 1983). Comparison of women who report high or low degrees of mood shifts revealed no differences in levels of androstenedione, estrogen, progesterone, or testosterone (Backstrom et al., 1983). Andersch and Hahn (1985) found no difference in PMS symptom relief produced by progesterone and a placebo.

Carroll and Steiner (1978) proposed that individual differences in prolactin levels may account for both menstrual mood shifts and PMS. They postulated that prolactin interacts with estrogen and progesterone to produce specific emotions. High levels of prolactin, estrogen, and progesterone presumably produce elation. High levels of prolactin combined with low levels of estrogen presumably produce depression, and high levels of prolactin combined with low levels of progesterone presumably produce anxiety and hostility. Thus, both menstrual mood shifts and PMS would be experienced only by women with excessively high levels of prolactin.

The Fava *et al.* (1981, 1982) studies of hyperprolactinemic patients would appear to provide rather strong empirical support for Carroll and Steiner's model. However, reports on the effectiveness of the prolactin-suppressing drug, bromocriptine, on premenstrual symptoms have been mixed. Early studies reported that bromocriptine was effective in relieving both physiological (breast and abdominal discomfort) and psychological (depression) premenstrual symptoms (Benedek-Jaszmann, & Hearn-Sturtevant, 1976; Horrobin *et al.*, 1976). Later research, however, failed to demonstrate that bromocriptine is more effective than a placebo (Ghose & Coppen, 1977; Tolis, 1980; Steiner, 1983).

3.2.2.4. The Effect of Emotions on the Menstrual Cycle

Primary amenorrhea or failure of a female to menstruate by 18 years of age may be traced to a variety of organic causes. Interruption of the menstrual cycle once it has begun is called *secondary amenorrhea*. The most common organic cause of secondary amenorrhea is pregnancy. Other organic causes of amenorrhea include hyperprolactinemia and a low percentage of fat in the body produced by self-starvation (Frisch & McAuthur, 1974) or by strenuous physical activities such as professional or Olympic-class athletics (Webb, Millian, & Stoplz, 1979).

Various psychological factors may also produce secondary amenorrhea. For example, numerous studies have found that the emotional stress associated with a novel or an institutional environment may produce amenorrhea. Specifically, the following incidence rates of amenorrhea have been reported: 25% of young women visiting a foreign country (Shanan, Brezezinski, Sulman, & Sharon, 1965), 73% of women entering the U.S. Military Academy (Anderson, 1979), 25% of female army recruits (Drillien, 1946), 16% of women entering a religious order (Drew & Stifel, 1968), and 6% of student nurses (McCormick, 1975). Obviously, it is difficult to separate the psychological effects of novel environments from changes in diet and physical conditioning.

Emotional trauma has also been reported to produce amenorrhea (Russell, 1972), and spontaneous recovery from emotional trauma-induced amenorrhea often occurs within 6 to 18 weeks (Jones & Jones, 1981). However, trauma-induced amenorrhea may be quite prolonged. Fishkin and King (1982) cited a case of a 22-year-old who had amenorrhea for a year and a half after a violent argument with her mother-in-law and husband. Coldsmith (1979) described an interesting case history of prolonged trauma-induced amenorrhea. The patient was menstruating normally up until her first marriage. On their wedding night, her husband savagely beat and abused her. During their 6 years of marriage and 2 years following their divorce, she had amenorrhea. After she became engaged to her second husband, she immediately resumed a normal menstrual cycle.

Pseudocyesis, or false pregnancy, is a unique type of amenorrhea accompanied by enlargement of the abdomen and breasts. Pseudocyesis patients may show other symptoms of pregnancy (e.g., morning sickness) and report fetal movement or "labor" pains. Murray (1979) noted the following characteristics of cases of false pregnancy: about 75% are married; about 75% are of reproductive age (15 to 39 years old); almost 50% have had a previous pregnancy that terminated in a miscarriage or stillbirth, and, in about 50% of the patients, pseudocyesis lasts 9 months. Conflicts between fear and desire for pregnancy, high levels of sex guilt, and depression are commonly reported with women reporting false pregnancies.

Due to the complexity of the neurohormonal control system, identifying the psychobiological mechanism that produces either amenorrhea and/or pseudocyesis has proven to be extremely difficult (see Brown & Barglow, 1971; Starkman, Marshall, LaFerla, & Kelch, 1985). Specifically, altering the levels of any CNS neurotransmitters (acetylcholine, dopamine, enkephalin, GABA, norepinephrine, or serotonin) produces a unique pattern of stimulation and suppression of pituitary hormones (Frohman, 1980). For example, GABA stimulates the release of growth hormone and prolactin without effecting other pituitary hormones. Conversely, sex hormones (androgen, estrogen, progesterone, and prolactin) and stress hormones (cortisol, thyroxine) are each absorbed at different sites in the limbic system and presumably influence different neurotransmitters (McEwen, 1980).

3.2.3. Hormones and Emotional States

A number of studies have reported elevations in epinephrine in anxiety states and elevation in norepinephrine during anger (Elmadjian, Hope & Lamson, 1957, 1958; Elamadjian, 1959; Silverman, Cohen, & Zuidema, 1957; Silverman, Cohen, Shmavonian, & Kirschner, 1961). Other researchers, however, have reported that elevations in both epinephrine and norepinephrine occur in a variety of emotional states (Levi, 1965; Patkai, 1971; Mathew, Ho, & Taylor, 1981). Low levels of epinephrine, norepinephrine, and cortisol are associated with self-reports of boredom (Thackray, 1981). Increased blood levels of cortisol have also been observed during anxiety, anger, and depression (Persky *et al.*, 1958). Thus, hormonal responses would appear to be relatively nonspecific markers of the intensity of emotional states.

Rather than collecting hormone samples during emotional states, a number of researchers have attempted to artificially produce emotional states by injecting subjects with hormones. Maranon (1924) noted that about one-third of subjects injected with epinephrine reported feeling "as-if" emotions, for example, "I feel *as if* I'm anxious or *as if* I'm angry." If these subjects were asked to talk about personally emotional events (i.e., a recent death in the family), they reported "real" rather than as-if emotional states. Maranon's findings have been basically replicated using epinephrine (Hawkins, Monroe, Sandifer, & Vernon, 1960), norepinephrine (Frankenhauser, Jarpe, & Matell, 1961), and combinations of epinephrine and norepinephrine (Frankenhauser & Jarpe, 1962). One plausible explanation for these findings is that the physiological changes produced by epinephrine or nonepinephrine may remind subjects of emotion-induced arousal.

An alternative explanation for hormonally induced as-if emotions is that hormones may not cause specific emotional experiences but rather produce global physiological arousal that subjects may or may not interpret as emotional. Thus, as-if emotions observed with injections of epinephrine and norepinephrine may not be produced by the effects of the hormones *per se* but rather are due to the subjects' perception of the testing situation as "emotional."

Schachter and Singer (1962) examined the role of perception in hormonally induced emotion by manipulating both the subjects' physiological arousal and their perception of the testing situation. Three groups of subjects were injected with epinephrine to induce cardiac acceleration and systolic BP increases. One group of subjects was correctly informed of the side effects of epinephrine (i.e., heart palpitation, muscle tremor, skin flush). A second group of subjects was misinformed about the side effects (i.e., told to expect numbness in feet, itching, headache), and the third group was given no information. To assess the effects of epinephrine, a fourth group of subjects received a placebo injection (saline). After receiving the injection, each subject was then placed in a room with a confederate. Half of the subjects in each treatment group were assigned to different induction conditions. In one condition, the confederate acted euphoric and attempted to engage the subject in playful activities (i.e., flying paper airplanes). In a second condition, the confederate displayed anger when asked to complete a long questionnaire that contained a number of embarrassing questions (e.g., Do you bathe frequently?). The effects of the confederate's behavior on the subjects' moods and behavior varied with the treatment conditions. Placebo and informed subjects were relatively unaffected by the social induction. Subjects in the misinformed and no-information groups reported emotions similar to those of the confederate. That is, subjects exposed to the euphoric confederate felt euphoric and those exposed to an angry conferate felt angry.

Schachter and Singer argued that the failure of the social induction procedure *per se* to elicit emotions in placebo subjects indicates that physiological arousal is needed to produce emotion states. However, the subjects' cognitive appraisal of physiological arousal rather than the arousal *per se* appears to produce specific emotional states. Subjects in the informed group showed cardiovascular arousal but not emotional arousal. Only subjects that lacked an appropriate explanation for cardiovascular arousal (misinformed and no-information groups) used the situational cues to label their autonomic arousal as specific emotions. Schachter and Singer postulated that autonomic arousal does not directly elicit specific emotional states but rather elicits an evaluative need. If the subject has a plausible explanation for arousal (e.g., my heart is pounding because I've been running), no emotion is presumably experienced. However, when arousal is unexplained, subjects may interpret their own cognitions (e.g., my heart is pounding because I was thinking about my final exam) or situational cues (e.g., my heart is pounding because I am watching a basketball game) as the "cause" of arousal. *If* the thoughts or situations are emotional, the individual will then label arousal accordingly (I'm anxious, I'm happy).

Publication of the Schachter and Singer study acted as a catalyst for a series of interesting studies on the role of cognition and autonomic perception in emotional states that we discuss later in Chapter 4. It should be noted, however, that a number of authors have raised serious methodological questions about their original report (Plutchik & Ax, 1962). Moreover, two attempts to replicate

Schachter and Singer's findings with epinephrine injections have found that epinephrine induces negative emotional reactions regardless of the situational cues (Marshall & Zimbardo, 1979; Maslach, 1979). Schachter and Singer (1979), in turn, have offered serious methodological criticisms of the latter two experiments.

One of the major issues in the controversy surrounding the original Schachter and Singer study is the physiological effects of the injection of different dosages of epinephrine (Plutchik & Ax, 1962; Schacter & Singer, 1979). In very low doses, epinephrine may produce decreases in BP, whereas in high doses, epinephrine elicits BP increases. Moreover, epinephrine is only one component of a complex neural-neurohormonal control system, and physiological changes induced by epinephrine injections trigger other cardiovascular controls (Oken, 1967).

The overall pattern of research on normal subjects suggests that cognitive activity (coping, strategies, self-appraisal, etc.) may alter both hormonal responses and emotional states. In contrast, studies of patients with endocrinological disorders suggest that excesses or shortages of specific hormones may induce specific emotional states (anxiety, depression, etc.).

One possible explanation for these apparently contradictory findings is that hormones may exert different physiological effects when they are chronically present than when they are episodically released. The neurohormonal control systems of healthy subjects normally prevents their bodies from accumulating excess levels of any single hormone. In endocrinological disorders, the abnormal release of high levels of a single hormone may sufficiently alter the biochemistry of the CNS to deactivate normal neurohoromonal controls and simultaneously stimulate neural tracks associated with specific emotional states.

An alternative explanation for the apparent different effects of hormones on the emotions of healthy individuals and endocrinological patients is that the effects of hormones on the CNS are inverted U-shaped functions. Specifically, in moderate levels, specific hormones may exert relatively little influence on neural functioning. However, extremely high or low levels of hormones may directly alter specific tracts in the CNS and thus mimic naturally occurring emotional states.

Obviously, both interpretations of endocrine disorders are highly complementary. We will return to the fascinating issue of the role of CNS biochemistry in emotional states in Chapter 12.

SUGGESTED READINGS

Krieger, D. T., & Hughes, J. C. (Eds.). *Neuroendocrinology.* Sunderland: Sinaur, 1980.

An interesting collection of original articles on the anatomy and physiology of the neurohoromonal system and on the behavior effects of hormones.

Jefferson, J. W., & Marshall, J. R. *Neuropsychiatric features of medical disorders.* New York: Plenum Press, 1981.

A useful discussion of specific somatic disorders that mimic psychiatric disorders.

Schachter, S., & Singer, J. E. Cognitive, social and physiological determinants of emotional states. *Psychological Review*, 1962, *69*, 379–399.

Pioneering study of the importance of cognitions in eliciting emotional states.

Selye, H. *The stress of life*. New York: McGraw-Hill, 1956.

Classic study of the physiological effects of physical and psychological stressors.

Physiological Systems

Anatomically, the billions of living cells in the human body are organized in structures called *organs*. Each individual organ performs a unique set of physiological functions. Organs that perform similar functions are collectively labeled a *system*. For example, the heart and blood vessels function as the primary system for transporting chemicals throughout the body.

In Chapters 4 through 11, we will examine the role of each of the major physiological systems in human emotions. Each of these chapters begins with a brief review of the anatomy and physiology of the system and a brief discussion of some of the methodological problems involved in studying its activity. We will then focus on the central issue of whether the biological activity of the system should be viewed as a cause, component, or consequence of specific emotional states.

The Cardiovascular System

In order to maintain normal metabolic activity, the cells of the human body must ingest oxygen and nutrients and excrete toxic chemical waste products. The cardiovascular system serves the vital function of circulating oxygen and nutrients throughout the body and removing waste products. As we will discuss later in Chapter 5, the cardiovascular system also plays a major role in maintaining internal body temperatures.

4.1. ANATOMY AND PHYSIOLOGY

As its name implies, the two major components of the cardiovascular system are the heart and blood vessels. These two subsystems are composed of different types of muscle tissues. The heart is composed of specialized muscle tissue that is not found in any other organ of the body. The anatomical structure of cardiac muscle resembles that of the skeletal muscles. However, the physiological properties of cardiac muscle are similar to those of the smooth muscle tissue of the blood vessels and other internal organs. Both cardiac and smooth muscles share the property of elasticity (i.e., the ability to stretch and contract without tissue injury). Both cardiac and smooth muscles also contract rhythmically without stimulation from the CNS. The heart muscle contains a built-in pacemaker (sinoatrial node) that stimulates the heart to spontaneously contract about 72 times per minute. The rhythmical contractions of smooth muscles are at a much slower rate of about 5 times per minute. Cardiac and smooth muscles also differ in the strength of contraction. Cardiac muscle displays rather strong but brief contraction, whereas smooth muscles generally exhibit weak but prolonged contractions.

As shown in Figure 4-1, the human heart contains four chambers. The atria, or upper two chambers, receive blood from the body and then force the blood into the ventricles, or lower chambers. Oxygen-depleted blood enters the right atrium and is pumped into the right ventricle. Contraction of the right ventricle forces blood to the lungs to be reoxygenated. Oxygen-enriched blood returns to the heart through the left atrium and then is pumped into the left ventricle. The

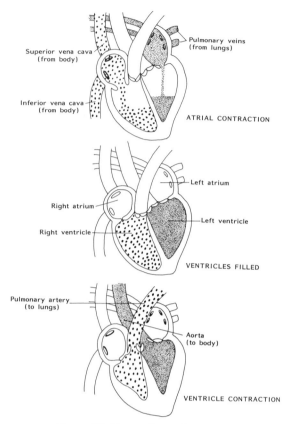

Figure 4-1. The cardiac cycle.

contraction of the left ventricle forces the blood to flow throughout the entire body. Four internal valves inside the heart normally insure that blood flows only in the proper direction. The two atrial-ventricle valves (tricuspid and mitral) are closed during ventricular contraction (systole) and open during ventricular relaxation (diastole). Conversely, the two ventricle valves (pulmonary and aortic) are open during ventricular systole and closed during ventricular diastole.

The oxygen-enriched blood that leaves the heart from the left ventricle circulates throughout the body through a complex network of blood vessels that are divided into three anatomically distinct subsystems: arteries, capillaries, and veins.

The arteries are a series of strong tubes that carry blood away from the heart. Each artery is composed of three layers. The inner layer consists of an elastic membrane. The middle layer of the artery consists of thick bands of smooth muscle fibers arranged in a circular fashion. The outer layer of the artery is composed of relatively inelastic connective tissue. This anatomical arrangement allows the arterial muscles to exert fine control over the diameter of the internal vessel (lumen). When the muscles contract, the lumen is constricted. When the muscles relax, the lumen is dilated, but the inelastic outer layer limits dilation of the artery itself. As shown in Figure 4-2, the major arteries all sequentially branch from the aorta. Each time an artery divides, the diameters of the branches are smaller than that of the parent artery. Eventually, the branches become extremely small and are called *arterioles*.

Arterial branching produces gradients in both blood pressure and blood velocity that promote the flow of blood from the heart to the capillary system. In

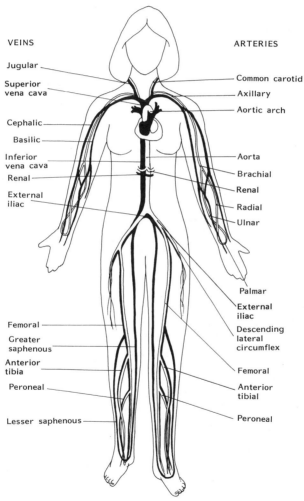

Figure 4-2. The vascular system. Darkened areas represent major veins and the light areas represent major arteries.

the aorta, the average blood pressure is equivalent to 100 to 120 millimeters of mercury (mm Hg), and average blood velocity is about 400 mm per second. At the arteriole–capillary junctions, average blood pressure drops to about 35 mm Hg, and blood velocity decreases to about 1 mm per second. The differences in aorta and arteriole blood pressure and velocity effectively prevent blood from flowing backward in the arterial systems.

The capillary system consists of an extremely dense network of microscopic passages between the body tissues. The slow movement of blood, coupled with extremely thin capillary walls, maximizes the exchange of oxygen, nutrients, and metabolic waste products between the blood and individual cells. If blood flow to a region of the capillaries is inadequate for the metabolic demands of the tissues (ischemia), cellular metabolism shifts from aerobic (oxygen-present) to anaerobic (oxygenless). Cellular wastes (lactic acid and carbon dioxide) accumulate in the tissues, causing mild to severe pain. The muscle pains caused by vigorous exercise or by cutting off blood flow with a tourniquet are examples of ischemic pain.

Oxygen-depleted blood is collected from the capillaries by small tubes called *venules*. Venules are the tributaries of small veins that, in turn, feed into progressively larger veins. Eventually, all the veins from the lower body empty into the inferior vena cava vein, and all the veins in the upper body converge into the superior vena cava vein. Blood enters the right atrium from the vena cava and repeats its journey throughout the body.

Although anatomically veins resemble arteries, veins contain much less smooth muscle tissue than arteries. Thus, venous contraction alone is insufficient to return blood to the heart from the extremities. Two anatomical features of the human body prevent blood from pooling in the veins and inhibiting circulation. The larger veins of the limbs contain a series of one-way valves that prevent blood from flowing backward. Moreover, many veins are sandwiched between skeletal muscles. Body movement effectively squeezes the veins and forces blood toward the heart. For example, if you sit motionless for any length of time, your hands, feet, or buttocks may "fall asleep." Stretching the muscles helps restore normal circulation.

The heart–artery–capillary–vein route is the primary pathway of blood flow. There are also two secondary pathways that play important roles in distributing or shunting blood to areas of high metabolic demand and in maintaining blood pressure. Anastomoses are small arteries that branch from an artery, travel a short distance, and then rejoin the main artery. Anastomoses are commonly found in parts of the body (abdominal organs, brain, etc.) that show large periodic shifts in metabolic demand. The anastomoses permit rather large quantities of blood to be distributed to a localized region without producing a sharp increase in the blood pressure of the main arteries. Another secondary pathway for blood flow is the system of arteriovenous anastomoses, or shunts. These vessels directly connect arterioles and venules and thus bypass the capillary system. Arteriovenous shunts are commonly found near the skin and are quite numerous in the ears, fingers, lips, nose, and toes. These vessels allow blood to be diverted to and from the skin and play an important role in thermoregulation.

Given the importance of supplying cells with a continuous blood flow, it is not surprising that the body contains a complex system of both neural and neurohormonal controls over the cardiovascular system. The vasomotor area in the medulla is the primary neural control center for both cardiac and vascular activity. The normal cardiac cycle (contraction of both artria followed by contraction of both ventricles) is controlled by a special conduction system embedded inside of the heart. The medulla can override the heart's own pacemaker through excitation of either parasympathetic fibers of the vagus nerve or sympathetic fibers of the chain ganglia. Parasympathetic excitation leads to a decrease in heart rate, whereas sympathetic excitation produces cardiac acceleration. The medulla receives sensory information from stretch receptors located within the walls of the heart, aortic and carotid arteries, and vena cava veins. If blood pressure rises too high, these receptors signal the medulla to stimulate cardiac deceleration and thus reduce blood pressure. If blood pressure drops too low, these receptors signal the medulla to speed up cardiac activity.

The medulla also controls blood pressure by altering the amount of contraction of blood vessels through the sympathetic nervous system. Stimulation of the muscle layers of arteries and veins constricts the vessels and causes an increase in blood pressure. The medulla produces vasodilation by *not* stimulating the vascular muscles. Vascular constriction-dilation plays an important role in maintaining blood pressure and in thermoregulation. It also allows the medulla to divert or shunt blood to local areas of high metabolic demand. For example, after eating a large meal, a large proportion of blood (25%–30%) is diverted to the gastrointestinal tract. During vigorous exercise, the medulla responds to the muscles' increased demand for oxygen by increasing both heart rate and blood pressure and by shunting about 80%–85% of blood flow directly to the muscles (Astrand & Rodahl, 1970).

As discussed in Chapter 2, the term *neural control center* should not be taken literally. A complex network of neural tracts connects the medulla with the limbic system and cortex. For example, the hypothalamus signals the medulla to make the cardiovascular adjustments needed for the complex muscular activity involved in emotional-motivational (digestive, sexual, and thermoregulatory) behaviors. The hypothalamus, in turn, receives inputs from other areas of the limbic system and from the cortex.

The neurohormonal system also exerts a direct influence on cardiovascular activity. Sympathetic nervous system arousal causes the adrenal glands to release epinephrine and norepinephrine into the bloodstream. Epinephrine acts directly on the neural and muscle tissues of the heart to increase heart rate. Epinephrine also produces constriction of the small blood vessels in the skin and dilation of arterioles to the muscles. Norepinephrine causes vasoconstriction in almost all arterioles. The adrenal glands also help control blood pressure with the hormone aldosterone. Aldosterone causes the kidneys to retain water in the body and to release the hormone renin. Renin causes the blood to form the chemical angiotensin that acts as a powerful vasoconstrictor. Thus the general effect of stimulation of the neurohormonal system is increased blood pressure.

The interaction of the neural and neurohormonal systems gives the body great flexibility in shunting blood between organ systems while maintaining relatively constant pressure in the vessels. Blood pressure in the arteries is normally determined by three factors: heart rate, stroke volume (the amount of blood pumped), and the degree of constriction of the arteries. Increasing any one of these factors while the other two remain constant results in increased blood pressure. For example, injections of norepinephrine do not directly alter cardiac output but raise blood pressure through vasoconstriction. Paradoxically, the body reacts to norepinephrine-induced BP increases by reflexively reducing heart rate. Thus heart rate and blood pressure co-vary in a complex fashion.

4.1.1. Methodological Issues in Cardiovascular Research

Researchers employ a variety of different recording techniques and measures of cardiovascular activity. For example, tonic (baseline) and phasic (change) heart rate in beats per minute (bpm) are both commonly used indices of cardiovascular activity. Heart rate can be detected mechanically (manual pulse or stethoscope), by electrical amplification of the electrical changes in the heart (electrocardiogram, or EKG), by sound waves (Doppler Electrograph), and by using light sensors to detect changes in blood density in the skin as blood pulses through the vascular beds (photoplethysmography). Similarly, human blood pressure (BP in mm Hg) can be measured directly in an artery (arterial cannulization) or indirectly by using a pressure cuff (sphygmomanometer) or photoplethysmography. Measures of vascular dilation-constriction (skin temperature and infrared photography) will be discussed in Chapter 5.

Each recording technique produces its own characteristic errors or artifacts. For example, in the pressure cuff method of BP measurement, an arm band is placed above the elbow and inflated until arterial blood flow is cut off. The cuff is then slowly deflated while the observer listens through a stethoscope to the brachial artery for the sound of blood returning to the artery (Korotkoff sounds). The first sound is recorded as maximum, or systolic blood pressure. As the cuff continues to deflate, the sounds gradually fade. The last audible sound is recorded as minimum, or diastolic blood pressure. Given that the observer must make a perceptual judgment of the points at which Korotkoff sounds begin and end, even highly trained observers normally differ by 2 to 5 mm Hg in their estimates of the BP of the same subject.

"Objective" electrical recording techniques such as EKG also produce artifacts. The powerful amplifiers used in physiological recording inadvertently pick up extraneous electrical noise (e.g., radio signals, elevator motors, false electrical signals produced by subject movement). Although modern physiological recorders use sophisticated electronic filters to minimize artifacts, no instrument is "error-free." For a more complete discussion of the technical limitations of various physiological recording techniques, see Martin and Venables (1980).

The intrusive nature of physiological recording techniques creates one of the major methodological problems in the study of emotion, namely that the subject may react emotionally to the testing situation itself. For example, Pickering (1982) examined daily shifts in the blood pressure of individuals with normal BP (normotensive), mildly elevated BP (borderline hypertensive), and high BP (hypertensive) using a 24-hour monitoring device. Subjects also had their blood pressure recorded in a physician's office to provide a comparison with more traditional medical BP recording techniques. For normotensive subjects, blood pressure recorded at home was equivalent to blood pressure recorded in the physician's office. The blood pressure readings of both hypertensive groups, however, were much higher in the physician's office than at home. Thus the same testing situation (physician's office) appears to have been a neutral stimulus for the normotensive individuals and an emotional stimulus for the hypertensive subjects.

Another problem in identifying cardiovascular correlates of emotion is that tonic levels of cardiovascular activity partially determine both the direction and magnitude of phasic activity. This phenomena is called the *law of initial values* (Benjamin, 1963). If initial values or tonic levels are extremely high, then the cardiovascular control system tends to resist any further increases in heart rate or blood pressure. When a stressor is presented to individuals with high initial values, they may display paradoxical decreases (rather than increases) in cardiovascular activity. For example, both females and males have very high heart rates (180 bpm) during sexual intercourse. However, if you have a live tarantula dropped on your face during lovemaking, it is highly doubtful that you will show phasic heart acceleration. Rather, you are likely to show a sudden cardiac deceleration. Conversely, if tonic levels of cardiovascular activity are extremely low, the neurohormonal control system resists decreasing heart rate and blood pressure any further and may produce paradoxical increases in cardiovascular activity.

Given the complex relationship between tonic and phasic responses, it should be noted that tonic cardiovascular activity varies with the subject's age, sex, and race. Tonic heart rate tends to decrease with age, whereas tonic blood pressure tends to increase with age. Prenatal heart rates average about 140 bpm. Average heart rate is about 90 in children and about 72 in adults. At any given age, females tend to have higher heart rates. The average systolic/diastolic ratio (in mm Hg) for males is 128/75 for 20-year-olds, 132/81 for 40-year-olds, and 156/91 for 60-year-olds. For 20-, 40-, and 60-year-old females, average BP is 121/72, 132/80, and 158/90, respectively. Marked racial differences in BP have also been reported. For example, black Americans tend to have higher BP than white Americans (Voors, Bererson, Dalfere, Webber, & Schuler, 1979). An individual's physique and state of physical conditioning also influence tonic cardiovascular activity. For example, normal resting heart rate is about 60 bpm for the average adult, but it is often as low as 30 bpm in athletes (Sprague, 1981). Tonic cardiovascular activity also fluctuates with postural changes (Victor, Weipert, & Shapiro, 1984), diurnal rhythms (Luce, 1971), and the menstrual cycle (Little & Zahn, 1974; Hastrup & Light, 1984).

In a series of experiments, Lacey and his associates found that even when individual differences in tonic activity are eliminated, individuals show sharp differences in phasic responses to physical stressors (Lacey, 1950; Lacey, Bateman, & VanLehn, 1953; Lacey & VanLehn, 1952; Lacey & Lacey, 1958). Regardless of the type of stimulation, some subjects consistently show large cardiovascular changes. Other subjects display small cardiovascular reactions but large changes in other physiological systems. This phenomenon is called *individual response specificity*, or *stereotypy*. Lacy argued that such idiosyncratic patterns of physiological activity are due to genetic variability in the reactivity (lability) of specific physiological systems.

To further complicate matters, intense levels of stimuli may produce a distinct physiological pattern in all individuals (response specificity or stereotypy). For example, submerging a limb in ice water (cold pressor test) produces increases in heart rate and blood pressure. Conversely, immersing the face in ice water produces a sharp decrease in heart rate (diving reflex). Obviously, such response stereotypy may mask individual differences produced by either the law of initial values or by individual stereotypy.

4.2. EMOTION AND THE CARDIOVASCULAR SYSTEM

As we will disuss later in Chapters 12 through 16, almost all twentieth-century theories of emotion postulate some type of linkage between human emotional experiences and physiological activity. Materialists argue that specific *patterns* of physical arousal cause the individual to experience specific emotional states. On the opposite extreme, mentalists argue that specific thought processes trigger specific emotional states and thus may be accompanied by a variety of physiological changes. Interactionists argue that emotional states, physiological activity, and thought processes are related in a dynamic fashion. As you will see in the following discussion of research, cardiovascular activity during emotions partially supports all three views of emotions.

4.2.1. Laboratory Studies

In the typical laboratory study, the experimenters attempt to artifically elicit specific emotions. For example, Ax (1953) examined the physiological patterns associated with socially induced anger and fear. A total of 43 adult females and males agreed to serve in a purported study of high blood pressure. Subjects were attached to the polygraph and told to relax to music. The fear-induction procedure consisted of a series of staged "accidents" intended to convince the subjects that they were in danger of being electrocuted by the recording equipment. In the anger-induction procedure, the polygraph operator verbally abused the subjects. Subjects' self-reports confirmed that both manipulations were effective in eliciting the appropriate emotions.

The major finding of Ax's study was that different patterns of physiological activities occurred during fear and anger. Increases in systolic and diastolic BP and decreases in heart rate were observed with both emotions. However, phasic diastolic BP increases and heart rate decreases were significantly greater in the anger than in the fear condition, and phasic increases in systolic BP were slightly higher in the fear condition. Ax noted that the cardiovascular correlates of anger were similar to combined epinephrine–norepinephrine reactions, whereas the fear pattern appeared more similar to an epinephrine response.

Ax's findings appear to provide strong support for the materialist view that specific patterns of physiological activity are yoked with specific emotions. To help clarify this complex issue, we will briefly examine the cardiovascular correlates of three sets of emotional states: anger, anxiety-fear, and happiness-sadness.

4.2.1.1. Anger

Anger is a complex negative emotional-motivational state characterized by intense and unpleasant physiological arousal coupled with the desire to obliterate the real or imaginary stimulus of arousal. Accordingly, anger can be legitimately viewed as either an emotion or a motive.

Are there specific cardiovascular correlates of anger? Researchers have consistently replicated Ax's finding of anger-associated increases in BP (Schwartz, Weinberger, & Singer, 1981)). However, empirical support for anger-induced cardiac deceleration has been equivocal. Some studies have found heart rate increases during anger, whereas other studies have found heart rate decreases. For example, Weerts and Roberts (1976) instructed subjects to "vividly imagine" anger or fear stimuli. Consistent with Ax's findings, their subjects showed increases in systolic BP to both scenes and greater increases in diastolic BP to anger than to fear images. However, contrary to Ax's report, their subjects showed increased heart rate to both anger and fear imagery.

Marked individual differences in the magnitude of anger-associated BP increases have been consistently reported. Hokanson (1961) compared the cardiovascular reactions of male college students who scored either extremely high or low on self-reports of hostility. Both groups of subjects showed an increase in systolic BP after being insulted by the experimenter, but the high-hostility group showed BP increases that were almost twice as large as those of the low-hostility group. Gentry (1970) compared cardiovascular reactions of female and male college students to being insulted by the experimenter and to frustration (task failure). Both sexes showed elevated systolic and diastolic BP to both manipulations. Male subjects, however, showed larger systolic increases.

In a series of studies, Hokanson and his associates examined whether aggression has a cathartic (emotion-releasing) effect upon the cardiovascular system. The basic design employed in these studies was social induction of anger followed by either an aggressive or nonaggressive task. The induction procedure consisted of having subjects complete either a low- or high-frustration task. The low-frustration task was counting backward from 100 by 3, and the high frustration task was being frequently interrupted by the experimenter while counting backward. This manipulation is apparently quite effective. High-frustration subjects showed marked increases in both systolic BP and in heart rate, whereas low-frustration subjects did not. Subjects were then given outlets for emotional arousal. For example, Hokanson and Burgess (1962a) allowed subjects to either (a) physically retaliate (give electric shocks to the experimenter), (b) verbally retaliate (fill out an evaluation of the experimenter), (c) retaliate through fantasy (write a story), or (d) they were not given any opportunity to retaliate. Subjects in the physical and verbal aggression condition showed a rapid decrease in BP to prefrustration levels, whereas BP remained elevated in the fantasy and no-aggression subjects. Thus it would appear that overt (physical or verbal) aggression produces decreases in cardiovascular arousal, whereas covert (fantasy or cognitive) aggression does not.

Other researchers have found that viewing aggressive films may increase rather than decrease BP. Geen and Stonner (1974) examined the effects of physical stress on later emotional reactions to an aggressive film. Half the subjects received an electric shock prior to viewing the film. The subjects who had received the shock prior showed higher BP after the film than subjects who had not been shocked. Thus it would appear that the physical arousal elicited by the shock had an "anticarthartic" effect of producing stronger physiological reactions to viewing aggression. In a second experiment, subjects who had been shocked prior to viewing a film of "real" violence showed greater BP increases than subjects who had received shocks but were presented with a film of "fictional" violence (Geen, 1975).

The overall pattern of frustration–aggression studies suggests that the cathartic effects of aggression are mediated by a complex combination of variables. Subjects who retaliate against a low-status (student) antagonist show a decrease in BP, whereas subjects who retaliate against a high-status (professor) antagonist do not (Hokanson & Shetler, 1961; Hokanson & Burgess 1962b). Aggression directed against a substitute (innocent) human target does not produce a marked decrease in BP (Hokanson, Burgess, & Cohen, 1963). Moreover, the cathartic effect of aggression appears to depend at least partially on the subjects' characteristics. As a group, low-guilt subjects show postaggression BP decreases, whereas high-guilt subjects do not (Gambaro & Rabin, 1969). Similarly, males are more likely to show a postaggression BP decrease, whereas females are more likely to show a catharticlike BP decrease if allowed to make a friendly counterresponse to aggression (Hokanson & Edelman, 1966; Hokanson, Willers, & Koropsak, 1968).

The observed sex differences led Hokanson to postulate that postresponse BP reductions may be conditioned responses to successful avoidance, rather than "catharsis" in the traditional Freudian sense of the term. To test this hypothesis, Hokanson (1970) rewarded subjects for making "unconventional" avoidance responses. For example, in one study, female subjects could avoid electric shocks by making aggressive responses to a confederate. After relatively brief training, the women showed both an increase in aggressive responses and postaggression decreases in BP. In another study, female and male subjects were reinforced for "masochistic" (self-shock) behavior. Again, subjects showed both an increase in targeted behavior and postmasochistic BP decreases.

4.2.1.2. Anxiety-Fear

Anxiety, distress, and fear are closely related negative emotional states associated with physical or psychological harm. These three emotions can be differentiated by the temporal relationship between the feeling and the potential threat. Anxiety is characterized as the anticipation of harm in the future, whereas fear is characterized as the anticipation of being harmed in the present. Distress is characterized by the awareness of being harmed at this specific moment. Obviously, these three emotions may merge into a single diffuse state. For example, if you are having a tooth extracted, you may simultaneously experience distress to the unpleasant physical sensations, fear that your discomfort may suddenly increase, and anxiety over the anticipated bill.

In order to differentiate anxiety and fear from distress, researchers may threaten but then not administer a painful stimulus such as electric shocks. If the temporal delay before the anticipated shock is longer than 5 minutes, subjects tend to show a highly irregular pattern of heart rate acclerations-decelerations. If "time of the shock" is less than 5 minutes away, subjects show a marked heart rate acceleration (Folkins, 1970; Lundberg, Ekman, & Frankenhaeuser, 1971). These findings suggest that heart rate acceleration may be characteristic of fear but not anxiety.

Marked individual differences have been reported in fear-related heart rate increases. Hodges and Spielberger (1966) recorded the heart rates of subjects who reported high or low trait anxiety. After completion of a verbal learning task, half of the subjects were told that they would receive several strong electric shocks during the next block of trials, and bogus "shock electrodes" were attached to their ankles. Both high- and low-anxiety groups showed a marked increase in heart rate in the threat condition. Cardiac acceleration, however, was directly related to subjects' reports of fear of electric shock. Subjects in both the high- and low-anxiety groups who had previously indicated moderate to extreme fear of electric shock showed the greatest cardiac acceleration.

Numerous studies have found that the direction of phasic cardiac reactions may differentiate individuals who experience high- and low-fear reactions to a specific stimulus. For example, Hare (1973; Hare and Blevings, 1975) compared the cardiac responses of a group of subjects who reported high-fear reactions to spiders and a group that reported low spider fear. When presented with slides of spiders, the high-fear subjects showed phasic cardiac acceleration, whereas the low-fear subjects showed phasic deceleration in heart rate. Similar patterns of cardiac acceleration-deceleration with high- or low-fear subjects have been found with slides of homicide victims (Hare 1972), mutilated accident victims (Klorman, Wiesenfeld, & Austin, 1975), and snakes (Klorman, 1974).

4.2.1.3. Happiness-Sadness

Happiness is commonly defined as a positive emotional state associated with a real or imaginary gain, whereas sadness is defined as a negative emotional state associated with a real or imaginary loss. Although these two emotions would appear to be polar opposites, both emotions are accompanied by increases in heart rate and blood pressure (Rusalova, Izard, & Simonov, 1975; Schwartz et al., 1981; Ekman, Levenson, & Friesen, 1983). Happiness appears to elicit smaller heart rate changes but larger diastolic BP increases than sadness. Conversely, sadness elicits larger systolic BP increases and greater drops in skin temperature than hapiness.

In summary, distinct patterns of cardiac and vascular responses appear to be characteristic of specific emotional states. Anger appears associated with the largest increases in blood pressure. Distinct, but smaller, increases in BP are characteristic of fear, happiness, and sadness. Irregular patterns of cardiac acceleration-deceleration have been observed with both anger and anxiety. Fear appears associated with marked heart rate acceleration.

4.2.1.4. The Role of Cognitions in Cardiovascular Responses

Depending upon your metaphysical biases, the observed patterns of cardiovascular responses during anger, anxiety-fear, and happiness-sadness can be interpreted either as the cause of the emotions or as the emotions themselves or as the consequences of the specific emotional states. Various researchers have argued that at least four different types of cognitive processes may alter an individual's cardiovascular responses.

Lacey (1967) postulated that heart rate acceleration occurs when the individual attends to his or her own thoughts and ignores external stimuli (environmental rejection), and heart rate deceleration occurs when the individual attends to external events (environmental intake). Thus the direction of phasic cardiac activity may merely reflect shifts in attention. For example, the presentation of a "fear" stimulus appears to elicit environmental rejection (heart rate increases) in high-fear subjects but environmental intake (heart rate decreases) in low-fear subjects (Hare, Wood, Britain, & Shadman, 1971).

Obrist (1976) argued that different coping strategies would produce either heart rate increases or decreases. Attempting to actively cope with a threatening situation would lead to increases in muscle tension that would increase the body's metabolic demands. These metabolic changes, coupled with sympathetic nervous system arousal, would produce marked heart rate acceleration (Wood & Hokanson, 1965). Conversely, passively coping with an unavoidable aversive event would lead to a decrease in physical mobility and in heart rate. Moreover, if the event is perceived as nonaversive by the individual, then no "coping" is required. Such indifference may also produce a decrease in physical mobility and a subsequent decrease in heart rate. Thus the differential phasic responses in high- and low-fear subjects may be at least partially an artifact of the degree of somatic activation (Obrist, Webb, Sutterer, & Howard, 1970).

Both Lacey's and Obrist's models accurately predict the observed differences in phasic cardiac activity of high- and low-fear subjects. Numerous studies can be cited to support either the environmental intake–rejection or active–passive coping hypothesis. Neither model alone, however, appears adequate to account for the available empirical findings. For example, Rusalova *et al.* (1975) instructed actors and nonactors to imagine and act out anger, fear, joy, and sadness (environmental rejection with active coping), to imagine but not act out these emotions (environmental rejection with passive coping), and to act out but not imagine the emotions (environmental intake with active coping). The highest heart rates were observed during environmental rejection–active coping and the lowest heart rates were observed during environmental intake–active coping. These findings suggest that attentional and coping strategies may interact in a complex fashion. For example, environmental rejection and active coping may occur concurrently when high-fear subjects are presented with threatening stimuli. Conversely, presenting low-fear subjects with morbidly fascinating stimuli may elicit both environmental intake and passive coping.

The Lacey–Orbist controversy has tended to obscure the major finding that humans' emotional reactions are often determined by the subjective meaning of the stimulus to the observer and not the stimulus *per se.* For example, Gottschalk (1974) reported an interesting self-case study. He imagined a variety of stimuli (anxiety-dream content, fishing, numbers, sleeping, etc.) during physiological recording. Increases in heart rate were observed only when he imagined or remembered personally stressful events or images.

Bennett and Holmes (1975) examined whether specific thought sequences can reduce cardiovascular arousal and emotional reactions to affective situations. They informed one group of female undergraduates that they had failed an important test (high threat) and a second group that they had passed (low threat). Subjects from both groups were randomly assigned to one of four treatment conditions. Subjects in the first treatment condition (prestress) were instructed to mentally "redefine" the test as unimportant before they received their grades. In the second treatment condition (poststress), subjects were instructed to mentally "redefine" the meaning of the test after they had received their grades. Subjects in the third treatment were instructed, after they received their grade, to think about their friends' performance on the test (projection), and subjects in the fourth treatment received no cognitive instructions. Subjects in the high threat, poststress, projection, and no-information treatments had higher heart rates and subjective reports of anxiety than other subjects. Subjects in the high-threat prestress condition, however, were indistinguishable from low-threat subjects. Thus altering the subjective meaning of the stressor by adopting a specific mental coping strategy (denial) before its onset appears to reduce both cardiovascular and emotional reactions to the stressor.

As we discussed previously in Chapter 3, Schachter and Singer (1962) demonstrated that the individual's subjective interpretation of epinephrine-induced cardiovascular responses may determine whether or not he or she experiences a specific emotion. Similar findings have been reported using exercise-induced cardiovascular arousal (Zillman, Kaycher, & Milavsky, 1972; Zillman, Johnson, & Day, 1974; Cantor, Zillman, & Bryant, 1975; Clark, Milberg, & Erber, 1984).

Zillman (1972) postulated that recovery from the presentation of physical stressors occurs in three distinct phases: initial decay in excitation, residual excitation, and recovery. During the initial decay period, the subject correctly attributes physiological arousal to the stressor and any emotional reactions (fear, anger, etc.) are associated with the stressor. During the residual excitation period, physiological arousal has not yet returned to baseline, and the subject may misattribute arousal to other situational cues and thus experience a different emotional state. Zillmann et al. (1972, 1974) tested this hypothesis by inducing physiological arousal through exercise and then angering the subjects. Subjects given the opportunity to immediately retaliate against the experimenter responded much less aggressively than subjects who retaliated after a delay.

Other researchers have also reported exercise-induced emotional states. Cantor et al. (1975) induced physiological arousal in male subjects through exercise and then presented them with an erotic film in either the initial arousal, residual excitation, or complete recovery periods. Subjects who viewed the film during the residual excitation period reported the highest sexual arousal and most positive evaluations of the film. Clark et al. (1984) examined whether residual arousal produced by exercise could alter subjects' judgments of the emotional reactions of others. In both laboratory and naturalistic studies, they found that after exercise-induced arousal, subjects perceived others' positive emotional states as more positive but did not perceive negative stimuli more negatively.

Researchers have also attempted to manipulate subjects' emotional states by employing Valins's (1966) "false feedback" technique to give subjects the illusion of cardiac arousal. In this procedure, subjects have EKG electrodes attached. They are informed that they will be given auditory or visual biofeedback to their own heart rates but actually receive bogus EKG signals prerecorded by the experimenter. Subjects are then simultaneously presented with affective stimuli (nudes, snakes, etc.) and with bogus information about whether their heart rate accelerates, decelerates, or shows no change. The results of the majority of studies employing false feedback suggest that subjects react more emotionally to stimuli paired with false feedback of phasic cardiac activity (acceleration-deceleration) than stimuli paired with false tonic cardiac activity. Valins (1970) interpreted these findings as indicating that the perception of autonomic arousal rather than actual autonomic arousal may determine whether emotions are experienced.

Critics of the false feedback procedure have argued that either the affective stimuli or the false feedback may induce phasic cardiac responses (Harris & Katkin, 1975). Goldstein, Fink, and Mettee (1972) found that when male subjects were presented with mildly emotional stimuli (*Playboy* female nudes), subjects' emotional reactions were positively correlated with false feedback. However, when the male subjects were exposed to highly arousing stimuli (male nudes), they disregarded the bogus feedback and showed marked cardiac and emotional reactions to the stimuli. Similarly, Truax (1980) found that the intensity of physiological arousal and situational cues may determine whether perceived or actual autonomic arousal determines the type of emotion experienced. In instances where physiological arousal is mild, situational cues such as false feedback or the behavior of others may determine whether or not an emotion is experienced. When physiological arousal becomes intense, actual autonomic arousal appears to determine the type of emotion experienced.

In summary, cardiovascular and emotional arousal appear to be altered by four different types of cognitive processes: attention, coping strategies, subjective appraisal of the stimulus, and subjective appraisal of physiological arousal. Conversely, cardiovascular and emotional arousal may override cognitive processes. For example, you may experience heart palpitations and terror during a "horror" movie even though you are consciously aware that "it's only a movie."

4.2.2. Naturalistic Studies

One general criticism of laboratory studies of emotion is that the artificial nature of the testing situation may produce only pseudoemotions. In everyday life, the majority of adults rarely receive (or give strangers) electric shocks or stare at photographs of dead babies. Are the cardiovascular correlates of emotion observed in the laboratory similar to cardiovascular changes during naturally occurring emotional states? Studies of the physiology of emotion in natural settings provide some rather interesting answers to this question.

Fenz and Epstein (1967) compared the physiological reactions and self-ratings of fear of novice and experienced sport parachutists to an actual parachute jump. A portable physiological recorder was used to monitor the subjects' heart rate and other psychological measures from the moment they arrived at the airport. The data were analyzed for subjects' reactions to different phases of the jump sequence (e.g., waiting to board the aircraft, at the jump altitude, and after landing). Both novice and experienced subjects showed heart rate increases from the point they arrived at the airport, checked their equipment, and boarded the airplane. Once aboard the aircraft, however, the two groups showed markedly different patterns of cardiovascular responses. The heart rates of the novice parachutists continued to increase up to the actual jump and showed a sharp decrease after landing. The heart rates of the experienced group showed only mild acceleration during the taxiing–jump sequence and mild acceleration after landing.

The authors noted that because the experienced group jumped at altitudes 2,000 to 13,000 feet higher than the novices, the heart rate increases observed in the experienced jumpers might be due to altitude-induced shortages of oxygen in the bloodstream (hypoxia). When the data were corrected for hypoxia effects, the novice group still showed a sharp cardiac acceleration during the taxiing–jump sequence. Experienced jumpers, however, show cardiac deceleration from the takeoff to the jump altitude.

The cardiovascular data appeared to suggest that the experienced parachutists had extinguished their fear reactions. Analysis of the subjects' self-reports of fear, however, revealed that both novice and experienced jumpers reported the same inverted-U pattern of fear. That is, over time, subjective fear rose to a peak and then declined. The novice subjects' fear reports paralleled their cardiovascular reactions, that is, peaked at the point of the jump. The experienced jumpers reported the highest levels of fear in the morning of the day of the jump and then reported progressively less fear as the time for the actual jump approached. Thus, during the preboarding period, the experienced group's self-reports of fear are negatively correlated with their cardiovascular activity.

Fenz and Epstein argued that the observed differences between novice and experienced subjects were due to differences in coping strategies. Presumably, the experienced parachutists inhibited their fear during the actual taxiing–jump sequence by learning to detect and inhibit fear-induced autonomic arousal at progressively lower levels. Thus, the experienced jumpers used their own anticipatory physiological reactions as cues to induce psychological coping mechanisms that then inhibited later physiological arousal. The novice subjects presumably do not detect their autonomic arousal until it reaches much higher levels and lack coping strategies (e.g., controlled breathing or thought patterns) to reduce arousal. The failure to cope with arousal produces progressive increases in both fear and arousal.

Solomon and Corbit (1974; Solomon, 1980) offered a radically different interpretation of the parachutist data based on their opponent-process model of emotion and motivation. As shown in Figure 4-3, they postulate that specific events that initially produce a large physiological response such as a sharp increase in heart rate are followed by a physiological overshoot in the opposite direction (e.g., decrease in heart rate past baseline) when the event is terminated. The emotion experienced during the rebound phase tends to be the exact opposite of the emotion epxerienced during arousal. For example, the novice parachutists showed sharp increases in both heart rate and fear up to the point

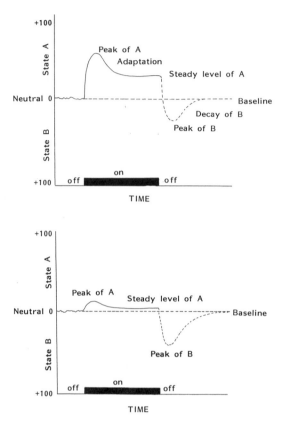

Figure 4-3. Temporal relationship of physiological reactions to stimuli with (a) relatively novel stimuli and (b) repeated presentation of the same stimulus. From "An Opponent Process Theory of Motivation: I. Temporal Dynamics of Affects" by R. L. Solomon and J. D. Corbit, 1974, *Psychological Review, 81*, pp. 119–145. Copyright 1974 by American Psychological Association and Richard Solomon. Reprinted with permission.

of the jump. After landing, they showed heart rate deceleration and presumably relief. Solomon and Corbit argue that, after repeated exposure to the event, the initial arousal is lowered through habituation, but the magnitude of the rebound response and its accompanying emotional state increases.

A third plausible interpretation of Fenz and Epstein's findings is that self-selection may account for the observed differences between novice and experienced parachutists. Specifically, individuals who experience terror at the thought of a parachute jump are highly unlikely to sign up for parachute training. Thus the novice group probably was composed of individuals who either showed lower fear reactions or failed to anticipate their own fear response. Individuals who show only mild reactions to their first parachute jump are more likely to continue jumping and thus become experienced parachutists. Individuals who respond with strong fear reactions, however, may terminate training.

Fenz and Epstein's study nicely represents the relative strengths and weaknesses of naturalistic studies. Because naturalistic studies lack the careful controls (internal validity) of laboratory research, their results are much more difficult to interpret. Conversely, emotional reactions observed in naturalistic research are probably more representative of the individual's reactions in real-life settings (external validity). Other naturalistic studies have found cardiac acceleration in response to a variety of real-life stressors. For example, elevation in heart rate has been observed in undergraduates during debates (Murray, 1963), naval pilots on practice missions (Roman, Older, & Jones, 1967), physicians during stressful work periods (Ira, Whalen, & Bogdonoff, 1963), scuba divers underwater (Gooden, Feinstein, & Skutt, 1975), ship pilots maneuvering ships in hazardous situations (Cook & Cashman, 1982), test pilots during landings (Roscoe, 1980), and 12-year-old girls during immunization injections (Shapiro, 1975).

Roth, Tinklenberg, Doyle, Horvath, and Kopell (1976) examined the cardiovascular and emotional reactions of healthy adult females and males (age range 20–37 years) to ordinary daily activities. A portable EKG was used to record heart rate for a continuous 24-hour period. Subjects were instructed to keep a log of ongoing activities and to rate their anxiety-tension level during each activity. At the end of the 24-hour monitoring period, subjects completed the Profile of Mood States (POMS) questionnaire. Individual subjects showed marked fluctuations in heart rate during a day. For example, the difference in one male subject's sleeping and running heart rates was 72 bpm. Analysis of the data also revealed marked sex differences. Although the men and women reported similar levels of activities, heart rates for the female subjects were significantly higher during both sleeping and waking hours. During sleep, the average female's heart rate was 68.6 bpm, whereas the male average was 56.1 bpm. The relationships between cardiovascular activity and moods also differed between the sexes. During sitting activities, male subjects' heart rates were unrelated to self-ratings of anxiety during a given activity. Male average heart rates, however, were positively correlated with the amount of tension they experienced during the day. Female subjects' heart rates during sitting activities were positively correlated with self-ratings of anxiety. Average female cardiovascular activity was unrelated to the amount of anxiety experienced during the day but correlated with reports of depression and social discomfort.

Roth's findings are highly suggestive and illustrate the need for monitoring both physiological and emotional reactions to everyday events on a prolonged basis. Unfortunately, there have been very few attempts to examine these relationships. One notable exception was a study reported by Epstein (1979). Forty-five male and female undergraduates kept daily records of their pulse rates, social behaviors, physical symptoms (i.e., headaches), and emotional states for 14 consecutive days. Self-reports of anxiety were positively correlated with daily ratings of tension and negatively correlated with soundness of sleep and physical symptoms. Mean heart rate showed a high degree of stability across the 2-week period ($r = +.94$) but was unrelated to self-reports of either positive or negative emotions. Heart rate range, however, correlated positively with self-reports of both undercontrolled hostility and subjective distress over hostile feelings. Thus, subjects who showed the greatest lability in heart rate tended to report higher levels of anger and guilt.

Naturalistic studies not only allow us to observe spontaneously occurring emotions, they also permit us to test whether laboratory results can be replicated in the "real world." Dutton and Aron (1974) attempted to replicate Schacter and Singers' situational effects on emotion by examining male subjects' reactions to conflicting fear and sexual situational cues. A high suspension bridge served as a "fear" stimulus. This bridge was constructed of wooden planks mounted on steel cables suspended 230 feet over a river canyon. The bridge had very low handrails and a tendency to sway in the wind. A second bridge served as a "neutral" stimulus. This bridge was a solidly constructed wooden bridge about 10 feet above a small river. Male passersby were interviewed by physically attractive female and male experimenters. Subjects tested on the neutral bridge responded similarly to male and female experimenters. Subjects tested on the high bridge by a female experimenter made more sexual responses on the TAT projective test and made more sexual advances to the female experimenter. Evidently, given two rival situational cues for arousal, these male subjects chose the macho (sexual) interpretation over the more realistic (fear) interpretation. An alternative explanation is that sympathetic arousal elicited by the fear stimulus may have facilitated sexual arousal. As we will discuss later in Chapter 9, sexual arousal may be associated with a variety of emotions, including terror.

4.2.3. Clinical Studies

The subjects in the laboratory and naturalistic studies discussed in the preceding sections were presumably "healthy" adults (i.e., did not meet medical or psychiatric criteria for abnormality). For example, an individual may report high fear of a given object or event but his or her behaviors may not match DSM-III (1980) criteria of phobic reaction. In the following section, we will examine the cardiovascular activity of clinical populations, for example, samples of medical and psychiatric patients.

4.2.3.1. Psychiatric Populations

One popular research strategy has been to test a sample of patients with the same diagnostic label (anxiety reaction, unipolar depression, etc.) and compare their physiological and emotional reactions to a group of "normal" individuals. However, numerous methodological problems are inherent in such research. For example, psychiatric patients often are receiving medications that alter both physiological and emotional responses. Lader (1975) argued that when extraneous variables like drug use are controlled, the reactions of anxious and depressed psychiatric patients differ quantitatively but not qualitatively from those of normal subjects. For example, both normal subjects and anxiety patients show the similar cardiovascular reactions to fear stimuli. However, when instructed to relax, the anxiety patients had significantly higher tonic heart rates than the normal subjects.

Grings and Dawson (1978) point out that individuals from different psychiatric diagnostic groups are often indistinguishable on any single physiological measure but differ in their overall patterns of physiological reactions. Specifically, patients with anxiety reactions, depression, and schizophrenia all show elevations in heart rate when compared with normal subjects. Anxiety patients also show elevation in tonic BP, whereas schizophrenics' BPs are either higher or lower than normal.

A number of theorists have argued that psychiatric diagnostic criteria ignore important individual differences in symptomatology. For example, DSM-III criteria for generalized anxiety disorder require that the individual display symptoms from three of the following categories: (a) motor tension, (b) autonomic hyperactivity, (c) apprehensive expectations, or (d) vigilance and scanning. Excluding diagnostic errors, the cluster of symptoms reported by anxiety patients should be fairly homogeneous. Empirical evidence, however, suggests that the converse may be true. Cameron (1944), for example, found that anxiety patients reported either striate muscle (motor) symptoms or smooth muscle (autonomic) symptoms or mixed striate-smooth muscle symptoms. However, patients within each of these three categories could be divided into subgroups of patients with similar symptoms. For example, patients in the smooth muscle category tended to report either cardiovascular symptoms or gastrointestinal symptoms. Thus patients within a single psychiatric category may report a heterogeneous pattern of symptoms.

Other researchers have noted that anxious individuals' reports of cognitive anxiety (worry) are independent of their reports of somatic anxiety (Liebert & Morris, 1967; Davidson & Schwartz, 1976; Davidson, 1978). Specifically, some individuals report high levels of cognitive anxiety in the apparent absence of somatic arousal. Conversely, other individuals report high levels of somatic arousal (emotionality) in the absence of cognitive anxiety. A third group of anxious individuals reports a mixture of cognitive and somatic symptoms.

Obviously, the observed patterns of anxiety symptoms may merely reflect errors in the diagnostic process rather than flaws in the diagnostic criteria. However, it is also quite plausible that DSM-III criteria may inadvertently combine heterogeneous subsets of patients into homogeneous categories. For example, Hare (1975) noted that the MMPI profiles of diagnosed psychopaths clustered into three distinct subgroups. Type I individuals fit the textbook description of psychopathology. Type II individuals reported both neurotic and psychopathic symptoms, and Type III individuals reported a mixture of paranoid, psychopathic, and schizophrenic symptoms. Hare reported that these three subtypes of psychopaths can be discriminated on the basis of their cardiovascular response patterns. For example, when presented with an 80-db tone, all three types of psychopaths show cardiac deceleration. When a 110-db tone was presented, Type III pyschopaths showed cardiac acceleration. When the intensity was increased to 120 db, Type II psychopaths also showed cardiac acceleration, but Type I psychopaths still reacted with deceleration. Type III individuals also showed marked vasoconstriction with higher intensity tones, whereas Types I and II psychopaths did not.

4.2.3.2. Psychophysiologic Populations

Cardiovascular diseases are the primary cause of death in the United States. Almost 1 million Americans die each year from either heart attacks (myocardial infarction) or strokes (destruction of brain tissue produced by the rupture of cranial blood vessels).

Emotional reactions have been implicated as either precipitating or aggravating factors in a variety of cardiovascular disorders. In this chapter, we will focus on the role of emotions in high blood pressure and in heart disease. Disorders that involve highly localized vascular activity (migraine headaches, Raynaud's disease, sexual dysfunctions, etc.) will be discussed in Chapters 5 and 9.

a. Essential Hypertension. Abnormally high blood pressure (hypertension) is defined as tonic pressure in the brachial artery of the arm in excess of 140/90 mm Hg. Estimates of the incidence rate of hypertension range from 10% to 30% of the adult population (Stamler, Stamler, Reidlinger, Algers, & Roberts, 1976). The uncertainty over the prevalence of hypertension is partially due to the nature of the disorder. Because the symptoms of hypertension are difficult to perceive, many hypertensive adults do not seek medical treatment.

Chronic hypertension can be produced by either elevations in tonic heart rate or by chronic vasoconstriction (Taylor & Fortmann, 1983). In 10% to 15% of all cases of hypertension, elevations in BP can be traced to specific physical causes (arteriosclerosis, adrenal disease, kidney disease, etc.). For example, in arteriosclerosis (hardening of the arteries), a layer of fat deposits narrows the arterial lumen and reduces the elasticity of the arterial walls. The increased resistance to blood flow produces abnormally high systolic pressure and abnormally low diastolic pressure. In the remaining 85% to 90% of cases of hypertension, however, no physical cause can be discovered. These latter cases are diagnosed as essential (idiopathic) hypertension.

The failure to identify physical causes for essential hypertension has led many authors to discuss the disorder as if it were purely psychogenic. However, it should be stressed that physiological factors may also play an indirect role in the development of hypertension. A number of life-style characteristics (high salt and fat diets, heavy cigarette smoking, obesity, and sedentary leisure activity) may contribute to the development of hypertension.

A number of researchers have postulated that hypertension may be a genetic disorder and that individual response stereotypy may account for why only some individuals develop hypertension in high stress situations (Biron, Mongeau, & Bertrand, 1975; Manuck, Giordani, McQuaid, & Garrity, 1981). Presumably, individuals with highly labile cardiovascular systems would repeatedly react to physical and psychological stress with increased BP that eventually reduces the elasticity of the arteries and produces chronic hypertension. Support for this model of hypertension, however, has been equivocal. Svensson and

Theorell (1982), for example, found that hypertensive 18-year-old military draftees showed much larger increases in systolic BP during an interview than normotensives. Other researchers, however, have noted that normo- and hypertensives often show extremely similar cardiovascular reactions to various stressors and that hypertensives may show exaggerated lability only to specific stimuli (Groen et al., 1982; Drummond, 1983).

Alexander (1950; Alexander, French, & Pollock, 1968) sparked the ongoing debate over the role of emotional states in hypertension. He postulated that hypertensives were characterized by overcontrolled hostility and nonassertiveness and that conflicts over expressing anger led to chronic elevation in BP. According to this view, suppressed anger plays both a causal and maintenance role in essential hypertension.

The results of a number of the laboratory and naturalistic studies discussed in the preceding section are consistent with Alexander's position that anger is associated with elevations in BP and that the expression of anger is associated with "cathartic" reductions in BP. Holroyd and Gorkin (1983) examined the relationship between suppressed anger and parental history of hypertension. Suppressed anger and a parental history of hypertension were unrelated in their sample, but both variables independently predicted which subjects showed the strongest cardiovascular reactions to a social stress situation.

Alexander's prediction that suppressed anger eventually causes hypertension, however, has received equivocal support from longitudinal studies of the same individuals over a period of years. Thomas and Greenstreet (1973) found that the level of anger, anxiety, or depression reported by college students did not predict which individuals developed hypertension 16 years later. Conversely, McCelland (1979) reported that college students' scores on suppressed anger did predict the development of hypertension 10 to 12 years later.

Equivocal support has also been found for Alexander's view that anger plays a critical role in the maintenance of chronic hypertension. Lynch, Long, Thomas, Malinow, and Katcher (1981) reported that when asked to speak about "your work," both normotensive and hypertensive subjects show a marked elevation in systolic and diastolic BP while talking. However, hypertensive subjects showed much larger increases in BP. Whitehead, Blackwell, DeSilva, and Robinson (1977) instructed a group of female and male hypertensives to rate their emotions and take their own blood pressure four times per day for a period of 7 weeks. Correlations between self-reports of anxiety and systolic and diastolic BP were consistently higher than the correlations between self-reports of anger and either systolic or diastolic BP. Other researchers have noted that, although difficulty expressing anger may be fairly common in hypertensive samples, it is also frequently found in normotensives (Ford, 1983; Taylor & Fortmann, 1983).

Since the early 1970s, there have been literally hundreds of attempts to teach hypertensive patients how to lower their own blood pressure without medication. Although different treatment programs have employed a wide variety of therapeutic techniques, the common emphasis of these programs has been on teaching patients to reduce autonomic arousal through self-relaxation (Stoyva, 1976; Luthe & Blumberger, 1977; Jacobson, 1938; Weiss, 1980).

Reviews of hypertension treatment literature have consistently reported that the various treatment programs are highly beneficial to some patients but not others (Schwartz & Shapiro, 1973; Patel, 1977; Silver & Blanchard, 1978; Seer, 1979; Hart & Weiss, 1982). The reviewers note that patients who are willing to continue practicing self-relaxation at home appear to derive the benefit from treatment. One interpretation of this finding is that the various treatment programs may only be successful for patients willing to use relaxation as a coping technique (see Goldfried, 1971; Goldfried & Trier, 1974). Such patients may also be more willing to alter their life-styles or have higher expectations of success (Wadden, 1984).

Green, Green and Norris's (1980) report on the high success rate (75%–80%) of the Menninger Foundation's treatment program is consistent with the view that treatment protocols that emphasize coping skills may be most beneficial for hypertensives. Each patient is given training in a complex combination of self-relaxation techniques (autogenics, BP and thermal biofeedback, controlled breathing and visualization) and psychotherapy. The patients are also actively encouraged to practice self-relaxation at home. After completing the training program, the majority of patients have become normotensive without medication.

b. Heart Disease. Diseases of the heart are divided into two general categories: congestive and coronary. Abnormalities of the heart itself are labeled *congestive*, and abnormalities of the arteries leading to the heart muscle are classified as *coronary*. Congestive and coronary heart diseases are highly related, and both are characterized by progressive damage to the cardiac muscle fibers.

In congestive heart diseases, the heart may beat normally, but structural defects in the heart cause the congestion or pooling of blood in the veins. For example, heart murmurs indicate that one or more of the heart valves is not closing properly and allowing blood to leak back toward the veins. Congestive heart failure occurs when the heart is weakened to the point where normal circulation is impaired and a shortage of oxygen in the blood stream (anoxia) occurs. Severe anoxia, in turn, produces additional damage to the cardiac muscle.

In coronary heart diseases, the arteries supplying oxygen to the heart muscle are narrowed or blocked. For example, arteriosclerosis produces both hypertension and a reduction in blood flow to the heart. Arteriosclerosis also promotes the formation of blood clots inside the coronary vessels (thrombosis) that further restrict blood flow. During everyday activities, the reduction in blood flow may be sufficient for the metabolic needs of the heart. However, if cardiac activity increases suddenly, the narrowed arteries are incapable of supplying sufficient oxygen, and severe chest pain called *angina pectoris* is experienced.

A heart attack (myocardial infarction) occurs when a portion of the muscle suffers a severe shortage of oxygen and dies. Because the area of dead tissue cannot contract, cardiac output drops suddenly, and congestive heart failure may occur. If a large area of the heart muscle is destroyed, death may occur almost instantly. If only a small area of the heart has been damaged, the neural and neurohormonal control systems attempt to compensate for the sudden drop in cardiac output with sympathetic arousal. Both heart rate and contractile force of the undamaged tissues increase, and vasoconstriction occurs. These compensatory changes in cardiovascular activity may be sufficient to restore circulation. However, the heart has been weakened and hence is highly susceptible to additional damage. If the individual ignores the symptoms of a heart attack (angina, cold skin, fainting, nausea, and sweating) and continues placing stress on the heart, a minor heart attack may escalate into massive heart damage and death.

About 50% of all new cases of coronary disease can be traced to a sedentary life-style accompanied by overeating, heavy smoking, and excessive use of alcohol (Jenkins, 1971; Russek & Russek, 1976). Freidman and Rosenman (1974) proposed that an individual's style of coping with stress may also increase the risk of heart attack. They noted that individuals whose behaviors are characterized by high achievement orientation, competitiveness, hostility, and a sense of time urgency (Type A) have a much higher incidence rate of heart disease than individuals who lack this pattern of behaviors (Type B). One plausible interpretation of the higher rate of heart disease in Type A individuals is that the Type A coping style is associated with poor health habits. Numerous studies, however, have found that when physical risk factors are controlled statistically, Type A individuals still have twice the incidence rate of Type B individuals (Bakal, 1979).

A number of studies have examined Type A and Type B individuals' cardiovascular reactions to stress. For example, Blumenthal et al. (1983) measured Type A and B subjects' reactions to tasks with either no incentive or a monetary reward for high performance. In the monetary reward condition, both Type A and B subjects showed increased heart rate and systolic BP. In the no-incentive condition, the Type A individuals also showed sympathetic arousal, whereas Type B subjects responded with slight cardiac deceleration. Thus it would appear that Type A individuals may have highly labile cardiovascular systems. Similar findings were reported by Siegel, Mattews, and Leitch, 1983. The blood pressure of female and male adolescents was measured in two presumably "nonstress" physical exams 8 months apart. Both the raw data and data adjusted for age, sex, and weight indicated that the Type A teenagers had significantly higher systolic peaks and greater variability in systolic BP.

Other researchers have found that the Type A individuals' cardiovascular lability may be situationally determined. Van Egeren, Abelson, and Sniderman (1983) found no difference in heart rate or the EKG waveform components of Type A and B male and female undergraduates when they played a competitive computer game. Holmes and his associates reported that Type A female and male undergraduates had higher heart rates and systolic BP than Type B students only on cognitively challenging tasks (Holmes, Solomon, & Rump, 1982; Holmes, McGilley, & Houston, 1984). When tested with intellectually unstimulating stressors, no differences in cardiac activity were observed between Type A and Type B subjects. Ortega and Pipal (1984) found that not only do Type A male undergraduates show higher heart rates to challenging tasks, they choose more difficult tasks than Type B individuals.

The challenge-seeking hypothesis provides a plausible explanation for the development of heart disease in managerial personnel. Indeed, the Type A stereotype is the hard-driving executive, working 16 hours a day, 7 days a week. However, other researchers have found that many blue-collar occupations (assembly line workers, bus drivers, etc.) also have a high incidence rate of heart disease (Karasek, Baker, Marxer, Ahlbom, & Theorell, 1981) and that the lack of intellectual challenge at work was also associated with a higher incidence of coronary disease. Thus it would appear that too much or too little opportunity for selecting task difficulty may increase the risks of heart disease.

An alternative explanation for the development of heart disease in Type A individuals is that the Type A's only experience stress when they discover that a given situation is uncontrollable. Glass (1977; Burnam, Pennebaker & Glass, 1975) argued that Type A behavior represents the individual's need to maintain a sense of control over events. When confronted with uncontrollable events (e.g., death of a spouse), Type A's experience higher levels of stress and initially exert greater efforts to master the situation than Type B's. Paradoxically, Type A's are more likely than Type B's to stop coping and show learned helplessness when it becomes apparent that the situation is uncontrollable. Glass (1977) hypothesized that the neurohormonal reactions associated with high levels of stress and with learned helplessness may trigger coronary disease.

Neither the challenge nor learned helplessness hypotheses appears capable of explaining the marked sex difference in the incidence of heart disease. Traditionally, women have had less challenging occupations than men but much higher incidence of learned helplessness (i.e., depression). Yet, males are twice as likely as females to have heart disease. One plausible explanation for this sex difference is that both male and female Type A's have a high risk of heart disease, but, because of sex role stereotyping, there are fewer Type A women than men. The available data, however, only partially support a sex role stereotype model. Waldron (1976) noted that Type A women do have a higher incidence rate of heart disease than either female or male Type B's. However, Type A women also had a lower incidence rate of heart disease than Type A males.

A commonly cited explanation for the lower rate of heart disease in women is that female sex hormones protect women from heart disease until menopause. Support for this position, however, is equivocal (Al-Issa, 1980). An alternative explanation for lower heart disease in women is that women may cope with events differently than men. For example, Witkin-Lanoil (1984) noted that although women suffer the same or more severe levels of job- and home-related stress as men, women also derive more social support from their co-workers and families.

There have been a number of experimental treatment programs that have attempted to reduce the Type A individuals' risk of heart attacks by teaching them to cope more effectively with anger and stress. Although these treatments appear promising in reducing Type A behaviors, their effectiveness in reducing the incidence rate of later heart attacks is currently unknown (Hart & Weiss, 1982; Rosenman & Chesney, 1982; Appel, Saab, & Holroyd, 1985).

In summary, the clinical literature on both high blood pressure and heart disease is consistent with laboratory findings that anger and cardiovascular lability are closely yoked. However, as we will discuss in later chapters, both expressed and suppressed anger may play important roles in the development of disorders of other physiological systems.

SUGGESTED READINGS

Ax. A. F. The physiological differentiation between fear and anger in humans. *Psychosomatic Medicine*, 1953, *15*, 433–442.

> Classic study of the physiological correlates of anger and fear. However, it should be noted that the methodology employed in this experiment would now be considered unethical according to U.S. Department of Health and Human Services guidelines for the treatment of human subjects.

Fenz, W. D., & Epstein, S. Gradients of physiological arousal in parachutists as a function of an approaching jump. *Psychosomatic Medicine*, 1967, *29*, 33–51.

> An intriguing study of the emotional reactions of novice and experienced sport parachutists to an actual parachute jump.

Friedman, M., & Rosenman, R. *Type A behavior and your heart.* New York: Knopf, 1974.

> Theoretical discussion of the relationships between personality and heart disease.

Hokanson, J. E. Psychophysiological evaluation of the catharsis hypothesis. In E. I. Megargee & J. E. Hokanson (Eds.), *The dynamics of aggression.* New York: Harper & Row, 1970.

> A general review of the early literature on the cathartic and anticathartic effects of aggression on blood pressure.

Solomon, R. L., & Corbit, J. D. An opponent-process theory of motivation: Temporal dynamics of affect. *Psychological Review*, 1974, *81*, 119–145.

> An interesting theoretical explanation of the relationships between emotions and motives. For example, why do people pay to view horror movies?

The Thermoregulatory System

The living cells of the body produce (metabolize) energy from the chemicals absorbed from food during digestion and oxygen absorbed by the lungs in a complex series of relatively inefficient chemical reactions. Only about 20% of the energy produced is used to perform work, and the remaining 80% is converted to heat. Accordingly, metabolism is measured in units of heat called *Calories* or *kilogram calories* (1 Calorie = 1,000 calories). A Calorie is the amount of heat needed to raise the temperature of 1 kilogram of water 1°C.

A daily diet of 2,400 Calories produces about 1,900 Calories in excess heat or enough heat to boil approximately 24 liters of water. In humans, the respiratory, gastrointestinal, and urinogenital systems dissipate about 300 Calories daily in excess body heat. These sources of heat loss, however, leave the body with a net heat gain of about 1,600 Calories. Without additional heat loss, the cells of the human body would quickly be destroyed by the heat produced by their own metabolic processes (hyperthermia).

Paradoxically, an extreme drop in cellular temperature (hypothermia) is also potentially lethal. As cellular temperatures decrease, metabolic processes slow down and eventually stop. Moreover, at extremely low temperatures, ice crystals will form within the cellular fluids and destroy the cell.

Obviously, all living organisms face the difficult task of balancing heat gained through metabolic processes with heat gained from or lost to the external environment. The survival of "cold-blooded" animals (poikilotherms) depends on their physiological ability to tolerate wide fluctuations in internal (core) temperature. Conversely, the survival of humans and other "warm-blooded" animals (homeotherms) depends on their ability to maintain relatively constant core temperatures despite fluctuations in environmental temperature.

5.1. ANATOMY AND PHYSIOLOGY

The human thermoregulatory system has four major components: the skin, cardiovascular system, sweat glands, and striate muscles. Each of these subsystems plays an important role in helping to maintain constant body temperatures.

The skin is a passive conductor of heat that absorbs and emits thermal energy in the infrared range. The average adult has a large skin surface area and thus, the skin functions as an effective radiator. Approximately 60% of the nude body's heat loss or gain to the external environment is in the form of infrared radiation. The skin also passively gains and loses heat through conduction with objects (clothing, furniture, etc.) in the external environment. Normally, conduction to objects accounts for only about 3% of all body heat loss.

In the cardiovascular system, blood absorbs excess heat from the cells of the brain and other internal organs. When the blood passes near the skin's surface, heat is conducted through the skin and emitted into the environment. As shown in Figure 5-1, the arteriovenous anastomoses regulate the amount of blood that passes through the vascular beds under the skin's surface. To maximize heat loss, the arteriovenous shunts are closed, and blood flows freely to the surface blood vessels. Vasodilation of the skin produces a series of temperature gradients across the skin surface. Due to proximity to the internal organs, skin temperatures of the head and trunk may approach core temperature. Skin temperature progressively declines in the extremities so that hands and feet temperatures are normally 5°F to 10°F cooler than core temperature.

If heat loss is too rapid, the arteriovenous anastomoses open and divert blood away from the skin's surface (see Figure 5-2). Vasoconstriction of the surface vessels produces a drop in skin temperatures and thus, reduces infrared radiation. In a cold environment, blood flow is diverted to the internal organs in the head and trunk, and skin temperatures in the extremities drop dramatically.

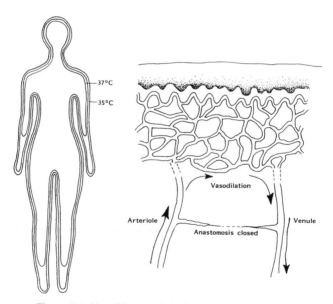

Figure 5-1. Vasodilation of the blood vessels of the skin.

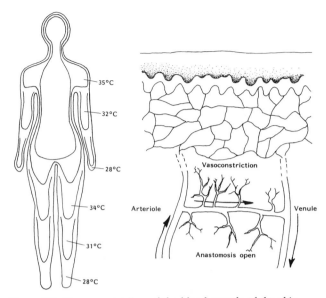

Figure 5-2. Vasonconstriction of the blood vessels of the skin.

At environmental temperatures between 66°F and 87°F, the naked body can successfully regulate internal body temperature through vasodilation and constriction alone. If environmental temperatures rise above 87°F or internal temperatures increase due to sudden increases in metabolic activity, the sweat glands of the body are activated. The body contains two different types of sweat

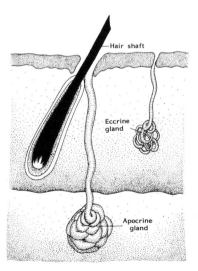

Figure 5-3. Sweat glands.

glands, eccrine and apocrine (see Figure 5-3). Two to 3 million eccrine glands are distributed irregularly over the skin surface and are highly concentrated in the armpits, forehead, palms of the hands, and soles of the feet. The ducts of eccrine glands terminate directly at pores on the skin surface. Eccrine sweat is "odorless" and composed of 99% water and 1% organic salts. Apocrine glands' ducts terminate at the ducts of body hairs and are concentrated in the armpits and pubic areas. Apocrine secretions produce body odors.

At temperatures between 66°F and 87°F, the sweat glands daily produce about 1 pint of perspiration that evaporates too quickly to be visible. When environmental temperatues rise above 87°F, "visible" sweating occurs. In extremely dry air, sweat very quickly evaporates from exposed skin, and sweating can produce up to 25% of the body's heat loss. As the relative humidity in the air increases, the rate of evaporation and of heat loss decreases. Similarly, clothing traps sweat against the skin and thus reduces the amount of heat removed by evaporation.

When environmental temperatures drop below 66°F, muscle activity helps prevent a drop in core temperature by raising the level of metabolic heat produced by the body. Even in moderately warm environments, reflexive contraction and relaxation of muscles (shivering) may occur. If environmental temperatures drop, the rate of shivering increases dramatically until the entire body shakes and the teeth chatter. Extreme cold also elicits reflexive contraction of the small muscles attached to body hairs (goose bumps) and voluntary motor movements such as hand rubbing. The net effect of involuntary and voluntary motor activities is an increase in core temperature that allows a naked human to successfully balance heat loss with heat production in environments as cold as 50°F. At colder temperatures, the naked human body has extreme difficulty preventing a drop in core temperature, and death may occur if core temperature falls below 77°F.

The hypothalamus contains the primary neural control centers for global thermoregulation. Neural impulses from temperature receptors located in the skin and internal organs are transmitted to the anterior hypothalamus that also contains temperature receptors that monitor the temperature of blood in the brain. Sharp increases in skin or core temperature stimulate the hypothalamus to increase the body's heat loss. The anterior hypothalamus directly increases sweat gland activity through sympathetic stimulation and also indirectly produces global vasodilation by inhibiting the posterior hypothalamus from eliciting sympathetic vasocontriction.

The anterior hypothalamus also mediates the body's reaction to a sharp drop in skin or core temperatures by chemically stimulating the pituitary gland to release thyroid-stimulating hormone (TSH). The thyroid gland responds to TSH by releasing the hormone thyroxin that increases the level of cell metabolism and, thus, core temperature. The anterior hypothalamus also stimulates the posterior hypothalamus to increase sympathetic vasoconstriction and to trigger the shivering reflex.

Many biology texts discuss the human thermoregulatory system as if it is a simple heating–air-conditioning system with the hypothalamus serving as a "thermostat." Such simplistic descriptions ignore the fascinating complexity of the thermoregulatory system (Hensel, 1981). For example, presentation of a hot or cold stimulus against the skin can elicit thermoregulatory responses in highly localized areas of the human body. If you simultaneously place your left hand in hot water and your right hand in cold water, you will produce vasodilation in the left hand and vasoconstriction in the right. Zimny and Miller (1966) reported that vasoconstriction can be elicited in a single finger by local application of a cold stimulus. Such local thermal reactions are at least partially independent of the hypothalamus. Paraplegics sweat on the lower halves of their bodies in response to hot stimuli (McCook, Randall, Hassler, Mihaldzic, & Wurster, 1970) but fail to react to cold stimuli until core temperature falls (Downey, Miller, & Darling, 1969).

In humans without spinal injuries, local presentation of hot or cold stimuli elicit both local physiological reactions and global thermoregulatory adjustments. Vasodilation-constriction occurs in three distinct regions: the extremities (ears, feet, hands, lips, and nose), the trunk and upper limbs, and the head. Blood flow in the extremities is under CNS control. Vasodilation in the hands or feet is produced by decreases in sympathetic stimulation. In contrast, the other two regions show both passive vasodilation in response to decreased sympathetic stimulation and active vasodilation induced by the sweat glands releasing the chemical bradykinin. Within the upper limbs, trunk, and head areas, there is also considerable variation in localized reactions to hot or cold stimuli. Rate of sweating increases dramatically when the forehead is warmed and decreases dramatically as the forehead is cooled. Presenting the same stimuli to the thighs produces much smaller sweat gland reactions. Thus stimulation of local thermal receptors may induce either global thermoregulatory responses mediated by the CNS or highly localized physiological responses.

5.1.1. Methodological Issues in Thermoregulatory Research

Techniques for recording the body's thermoregulatory responses fall into two general classes: cardiovascular measures and measures of sweat gland (electrodermal) activity. Cardiovascular techniques provide information about vasodilation and constriction and internal metabolic activity, whereas electrodermal recordings measure electrical (ionic) changes in sweat gland activity.

5.1.1.1. Cardiovascular Measures

Temperature measurement is one of the most common techniques for measuring cardiovascular activity. Small temperature-sensitive probes can be taped to various locations on the skin and provide a record of local vasodilation or constriction. There are two major methodological problems with skin temperature recording. First, recordings are highly localized and thus provide a poor index of global skin vasodilation and constriction. Plutchik (1956) observed that skin temperatures in the extremities are differentially effected by increases and decreases in environmental temperature. When environmental temperatures increase, skin temperature rises in the fingers before it increases in the toes. Conversely, when environmental temperatures decrease, larger decreases in skin temperature are observed in the toes than in the fingers. Second, the thermoregulatory system responds differently to changes in environmental temperature and changes in metabolic activity. Thermal regulatory responses to a drop in external temperature tend to be highly global. Blood flow is restricted to both the skin and muscles in the limbs. However, during exercise, blood flow is diverted from the skin to the muscles. Thus skin temperature provides only a crude measure of global vascular activity. A drop in skin temperature may indicate either global vasoconstriction or the shunting of blood to underlying muscles.

One alternative method for measuring skin vasodilation and constriction is photoplethysmography. This technique involves shining a small light against the skin and using a light sensor to measure the amount of light reflected from the tissues. Because the density of the skin varies with the amount of blood passing underneath, photoplethysmography provides a beat-by-beat record of vasodilation (see Figure 5-4). The number of peaks per minute represents pulse rate, and the height of each wave represents blood volume (BV). Increases in BV represent local vasodilation, and decreases in BV indicate local vasoconstriction. Unlike skin temperature recording, photoplethysmography can differentiate between blood flow in the skin and blood flow in the underlying muscles. When the sensor is attached to nonmuscular parts of the body (ear lobe or finger tips), the photoplethysmograph detects primarily changes in cutaneous blood flow. When the sensor is attached to skin over muscular parts of the limbs (forearm or calf) blood flow to the muscles is primarily detected. Although photoplethysmography has obvious advantages over skin temperature recording, both techniques provide only highly localized measures of cardiovascular activity.

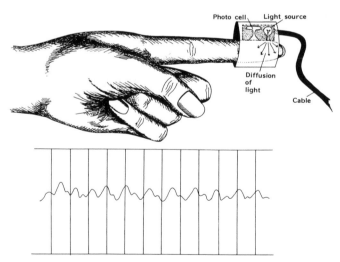

Figure 5-4. Photoplethysmographic recording of blood volume. Each large peak represents the pulse of blood through the skin tissue.

Internal temperature recordings (eardrum, mouth, nose, rectum, or vagina) are used to produce measures of core metabolic activity. Each recording site tends to produce slightly different estimates of core temperature. For example, rectal temperature is usually about 1°F higher than oral temperature. Even at the same recording site, temperature readings fluctuate between 1°F to 3°F during a 24-hour period. Moreover, shifts in body temperature also accompany the menstraul cycle in adult women. Average body temperature is about 1°F cooler in the preovulation phase of the cycle than in the postovulatory phase. Thus a core temperature of 98.6°F (37°C) should be viewed as purely a statistical average rather than "normal."

One of the potential artifacts of thermal recordings is that the majority of recording techniques require that thermal probes be attached to or inserted within the subjects' bodies. Although medical personnel may accept such physical contact with strangers as "normal," other subjects may react emotionally to the recording techniques *per se*. Infrared photography is the only technique for studying vasodilation and constriction that does not require direct physical contact with the subjects. Because the skin absorbs and emits heat in the form of infrared radiation, photographic equipment sensitive to infrared bandwidths can detect thermoregulatory responses. Two different types of infrared photographic techniques are commonly used. The simplest type of infrared photography uses a conventional 35-mm camera and special infrared-sensitive film. As shown in Figure 5-5, this technique produces clear photographs of otherwise "invisible" surface veins (Eastman Kodak, 1973). An alternative technique is called thermography. A thermographic camera has infrared sensors that allow a "heat" picture to be constructed (see Figure 5-6). Although both infrared recording techniques can provide excellent records of global patterns of vascular activity, it should be noted that infrared radiation is partially or completely blocked by clothing. Obviously, asking subjects to partially or completely disrobe will provide better infrared recordings but may elicit emotional responses.

The major disadvantage of all vascular thermoregulatory measures is that compared with cardiac responses, vascular reactions are relatively slow and diffuse. Heart rate shows sharp phasic responses to emotional stimuli. Vascular reactions, however, occur more slowly over time. For example, skin vasodilation is followed by a gradual rise in skin temperatures. Similarly, changes in core temperature occur gradually. Thus vascular measures primarily represent changes in tonic thermoregulatory activity during emotional states.

5.1.1.2. Electrodermal Measures

Changes in the electrical potentials of the skin due to local sweat gland activity are called *electodermal*. As sweat gland activity increases, the electrical resistance of the skin decreases, and the skin becomes a better conductor of electiricty. As shown in Table 5-1, there are two common methods for measuring electrodermal activity (EDA). In the Fere or "galvanic skin reflex" (GSR) method, a weak electrical current is run between two electrodes attached to the skin surface, and skin resistance is directly measured. Accordingly, this technique is called *skin resistance* (SR) or *skin conductance* (SC). (Note that although conduc-

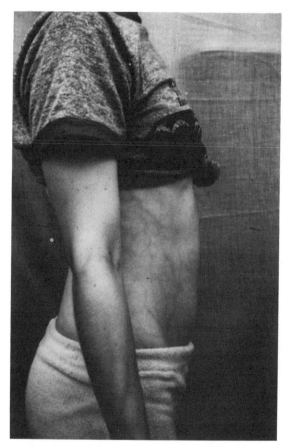

Figure 5-5. Vasodilation recorded with a 35-mm camera and Kodak infrared film. The varicose pattern of the veins on the skin surface was invisible to the naked eye. Photographed by the author.

tance is the mathematical reciprocal of resistance, the two units are not equivalent. For a more detailed discussion of this issue see Hassett, 1978.) In the Tarchanoff method, fluctuations in the skin's electrical activity or skin potential (SP) are measured directly, and no external current is employed. Researchers now use SR or SP to indicate which method of measuring EDA was employed, and no longer use the older term *GSR*. Researchers also differentiate between tonic or "level" of EDA, phasic or "response" EDA, and changes that occur in the absence of external stimulation (spontaneous EDA).

Readers who are unfamiliar with electrodermal research may find the use of six different measures of EDA at best confusing. However, researchers have found that the EDA produced by the "simple" sweat gland is surprisingly complex. During emotional states, electrodermal levels, responses and spontaneous activity often vary independently. Moreover, skin conductance and skin

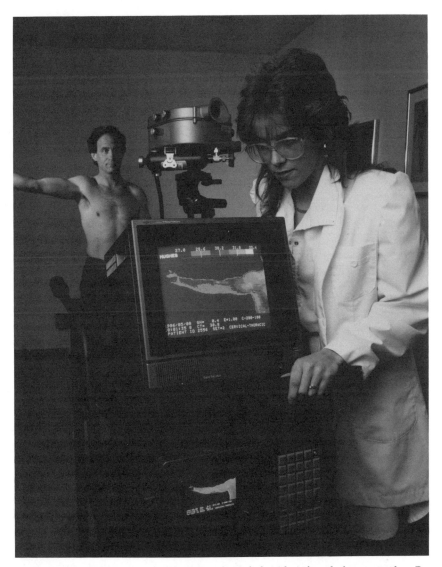

Figure 5-6. Vasodilation and constriction recorded with infrared thermography. Reproduced by permission of Hughes Aircraft Company, Carlsbad, California.

potential recording techniques give different estimates of EDA. Although it would greatly simplify our discussion to use a single generic term such as *EDA*, the distinctions between tonic, phasic, and spontaneous EDAs are too important for scientists to ignore. Nevertheless, readers who are overwhelmed by the sheer complexity of electrodermal activity should feel free to substitute the generic label *EDA* for *any* of the specific measures of sweat gland activity.

Table 5-1. Commonly Used Measures of Electrodermal Activity (EDA)

Physiological activity	Measure
Tonic	Skin resistance level (SRL) or skin conductance level (SCL)
	Skin potential level (SPL)
Phasic response to external stimulus	Skin resistance response (SRR) or skin conductance response (SCR)
	Skin potential response (SPR)
Phasic response, no external stimulus	Spontaneous skin resistance response (SSRR) or spontaneous skin conductance response (SSCR)
	Spontaneous skin potential response (SSPR)

As with cardiovascular measures, large individual differences in both tonic and phasic EDAs have been consistently reported. However, the physiological basis of individual differences in sweat gland activity is very poorly understood. For example, marked racial differences in EDA have been observed (Bernstein, 1965; Lazarus, 1967), but whether these differences are due to genetic differences in the distribution of sweat glands, genetic differences in EDA, or cultural differences is unknown. Similarly, conflicting sex differences in EDA have been reported. Some researchers have found much higher EDA in females (Aronfreed, Messick, & Diggory, 1953), whereas others report higher EDA in males (Buck, Savin, Miller, & Caul, 1972). Again, whether these contradictory findings are due to sample biases such as fluctuations in EDA with the menstrual cycle (Little & Zahn, 1974), sex differences in physical conditioning (Henane, 1981), artifacts of the testing situation (e.g., temperature of the testing room), or sex differences in emotional reactions is unknown.

5.2. EMOTION AND THE THERMOREGULATORY SYSTEM

Thermoregulatory responses are commonly observed during various emotional states. For example, anger, embarrassment, and sexual arousal are often accompanied by skin vasodilation, that is, blushing or skin flush. Conversely, skin vasoconstriction is often observed during anxiety or fear reactions. Specifically, cold hands and feet are commonly reported during anxiety reactions, and terror is often characterized as "white from fear."

Cannon (1934) argued that "emotional" thermoregulatory responses were indicative of the "flight-or-fight" reflex. According to his model, all emotional states trigger global sympathetic arousal that aids the organism to escape (flight) or defend itself (fight) from stressors. For example, suppose you are suddenly confronted by a large snarling dog. Vasoconstriction of the skin serves two different adaptive functions. First, it reduces blood loss if you are bitten. Second, it facilitates the divergence of blood into the muscles and, thus, increases muscular efficiency to help you flee or fight.

Edelberg (1973) argued that sweat gland activity during emotions may also serve a variety of adaptive functions. Vasoconstriction of the skin coupled with increased metabolic activity of the muscles during emotions traps a large quantity of heat inside of the body. "Cold sweat" allows the body to dissipate some of this excess heat through evaporation. Moreover, the wetness (hydration) of the skin determines the amount of friction between the skin and external surfaces. If the skin is extremely dry or extremely wet, there is relatively little friction between the skin and other surfaces. Moderate hydration on the soles of the feet and palms of the hands may facilitate flight-or-fight reactions by providing the optimal friction to run or grasp. High levels of skin hydration make the human body a "slippery" target. Hydration also protects the skin from abrasion. Dry skin is easily torn, whereas wet skin resists ripping.

Although most researchers concede the merit of Cannon's view of the adaptive advantages of emotional responses, numerous authors have questioned whether global sympathetic arousal can account for emotional thermoregulatory responses. Specifically, emotional "thermoregulatory" responses clearly differ from physiological reactions to hot or cold stimuli. For example, both emotional and cold-induced shivering begin in the muscles of the lower arm and leg. However, the locus of emotional shivering remains in the extremities, whereas, after a brief period, cold-elicited shivering spreads to the thigh and upper arm muscles (Golenhofen, 1981). Similarly, thermal-induced vasodilation is observed primarily in the limbs, whereas during emotional blushing, vasodilation tends to be restricted to the skin of the face, neck, and chest. Marked differences are also observed between emotional- and thermal-induced electrodermal activities. Emotional sweating occurs primarily in the palms of the hands and soles of the feet (Herrmann, Prose, & Sulzberger, 1951), whereas heat-induced sweating occurs rather diffusely across the surface of the body.

Given these different patterns of responses, it would appear that "emotional" thermoregulatory responses do not simply represent global sympathetic arousal. However, the "meanings" of emotional cardiovascular and electrodermal responses are still hotly debated. Proponents of a revised version of Cannon's model argue that although emotional- and thermal-induced responses may be mediated by different neural circuits, both sets of responses represent global sympathetic arousal. According to this position, thermoregulatory responses may provide a valid index of the *intensity* of emotional states but provide relatively little information about *which* specific emotion an individual is experiencing.

Critics of this global arousal position argue that the thermoregulatory system is capable of producing a number of complex patterns of localized responses and that different patterns of thermoregulatory activity may indicate different emotional states. For example, sexual excitement is associated with vasodilation of the genitals *and* chest while during embarrassment vasodilation is restricted primarily to the face.

As you will see in the following discussion, laboratory, naturalistic, and clinical research all suggest that both views of emotional thermoregulatory responses may be correct. That is, the magnitude of thermoregulatory responses generally reflects the intensity of emotional states while localized patterns of responses may occur during specific emotional states.

5.2.1. Laboratory Studies

Using a variety of recording techniques, psychophysiological studies of physically healthy adults have generally found that global vasoconstriction occurs during a variety of emotional states. For example, decreases in peripheral blood flow have been observed during discussions of anxiety-provoking topics (Mittelmann & Wolff, 1943; Crawford, Friesen, & Tomlinson-Keasey, 1977; Smith, Houston, & Zurawski, 1984), during socially induced anger (Ax, 1953), and during distress or fear induced by the threat of electric shocks (Ax, 1953; Boudewyns, 1976; Bloom & Trautt, 1977). Conversely, global vasodilation has been commonly reported during relaxation (Boudewyns, 1976). Such findings would appear to provide strong support for the flight-or-fight interpretation of cardiovascular responses during emotional states. Specifically, emotional states would appear to mimic the body's reaction to cold (vasoconstriction), whereas relaxation appears to mimic the body's response to heat (vasodilation). However, it should also be noted that laboratory studies have documented vasodilation during at least one emotion—sexual excitement.

Masters and Johnson (1966) found that in both sexes vasodilation of the genitals during sexual arousal was often accompanied by vasodilation of the chest. Specifically, nipple erection and vasodilation of the skin of the chest and upper abdomen (sex flush) commonly occurred in both men and women during the early stages of sexual arousal.

Later researchers have repeatedly replicated Masters and Johnson's findings. For example, Abramson and Pearsall (1983) used thermography to record blood flow in the chests of three men and three women during masturbation. Both sexes showed clear vasodilation of the chest, and vasodilation was much higher in the right side of the chest than on the left in both sexes. This latter finding would appear to contradict Galin's hypothesis (discussed in Chapter 2) that physiological arousal is higher on the left side of the body during emotional-motivational behaviors.

The observation of sex flush during sexual excitement raises the interesting question of whether patterns of localized vasodilation or constriction are characteristic of any other emotional states. Unfortunately, laboratory research on this issue is extremely sparse. For example, despite clear naturalistic and clinical evidence that facial vasodilation (blushing) commonly occurs during embarrassment, laboratory documentation of blushing is nonexistent. Similarly, research on cardiovascular changes during *positive* emotional states such as humor or joy is also extremely sparse. Schwartz and Logue (1977) used infrared thermography to study facial blood flow during positive and negative affective thoughts. They found highly localized patterns of blood flow changes were characteristic of different types of emotional thoughts. The area around the subjects' mouths was warmer during "happy thoughts" and colder during "sad thoughts."

Based on the available laboratory data, it would be fair to conclude that global vasoconstriction appears to be the norm for at least four emotions (anger, anxiety, distress, and fear) and that distinct patterns of localized vasodilation are characteristic of at least one emotion (sexual excitement). Thus the global arousal and pattern models may each account for cardiovascular changes during different sets of emotions.

Paradoxically, laboratory research on EDA during emotional states has produced a conflicting mass of empirical findings that do not fit neatly into either a global aroual or a pattern interpretation of thermoregulatory responses. For example, consistent with the global arousal model, changes in EDA can be elicited by a wide variety of "emotional" stimuli including giving a brief speech (Baker, Sandman, & Pepinsky, 1975), imagining fear-producing situations (Waters & McDonald, 1973), the physical approach of an experimenter (McBride, King, & James, 1965), subliminal presentation of taboo words (Dixon, 1958), reading ego-threatening sentences (Russell & Brandsma, 1974), or threats of electric shocks (Katkin, 1966). Although these findings would appear to suggest that EDA may be a valid index of "emotional arousal," numerous researchers have also failed to produce changes in EDA using identical stimuli. For example, Aronfreed, Messick, and Diggory (1953) failed to find any difference in EDA to taboo and neutral words presented subliminally. Rimm and Litvak (1969) failed to find any difference in EDA when subjects read ego-threatening sentences. Grossberg and Wilson (1968) observed no difference in EDA when subjects imagined fear and neutral scenes. And so on.

Three explanations are commonly cited to account for the contradictory EDA literature. The most obvious explanation is that EDA is an unreliable index of "emotionality." According to this position, "emotional" EDA can be traced to the physiological linkage between EDA, respiration, and heart rate. For example, taking a deep breath elicits a large SR or SP response. Thus, EDA may provide only an indirect and therefore a less reliable index of emotions than either cardiac or respiratory responses.

One major theoretical weakness of the "EDA unreliability" hypothesis is that it fails to account for why EDA, respiration, and cardiac responses do not all co-vary with emotional states. Specifically, if cardiac and respiratory activities are reliable indices of emotionality and EDA is yoked to these physiological systems, why would EDA reflect emotional reactions in only "some people, some of the time"? Lang and his associates postulated that Lacey's environmental intake–rejection hypothesis (see Chapter 4) may account for apparent unreliability of EDA as an index of emotion (Lang, Kozak, Miller, Levin, & McLean, 1980; Lang, Levin, Miller, & Kozak, 1983). They argue that EDA is lower during environmental rejection and higher during environmental intake. Task-related environmental rejection (emotional thoughts, imagery, etc.) would minimize EDA and make cardiac responses appear more salient. Conversely, both EDA and cardiac responses would provide reliable indexes of emotional arousal during environmental intake.

Another commonly cited explanation for the contradictory EDA literature is that only some measures of EDA may co-vary with emotional arousal. Kilpatrick (1972), for example, reported that spontaneous electrodermal responses co-varied with emotional or "hot" cognitions, whereas baseline or tonic EDA co-varied with intellectual or "cold" cognitive activity. In Kilpatrick's study, male undergraduates' SCs were measured during conditions of high and low ego threat. Subjects in the low-threat condition were informed that the purpose of the experiment was to examine the relationship between task preferences and physiological responses. In the high-threat condition, subjects were informed that they would be asked to complete a test of "brain damage" that was also a reliable index of intelligence. Tonic SC increased while performing the cognitive task, but these changes in tonic SC were unrelated to the stress manipulation. Conversely, the number of spontaneous SC responses increased in the high-threat condition and were unrelated to performing the cognitive task. Thus, tonic sweat gland activity appears to be yoked to "cognitive activity," whereas phasic sweat gland responses appear to reflect subjects' "emotional reactions."

Inspection of the EDA literature would appear to provide at least moderate support for Kilpatrick's hypothesis. Phasic electrodermal responses (SRRs, SSRRs, SPRs, and SSPRs) are more frequently reported to vary with the intensity of emotional reactions than are measures of tonic EDA (SRL and SPL). However, it should be noted that tonic and phasic physiological activities are not independent but interact in a complex nonlinear fashion (Boucsein, Baltissen, & Euler, 1984). That is, changes in tonic EDA directly effect the magnitude of phasic responses.

A third commonly cited explanation for the contradictory EDA literature is that EDA may be yoked to the individual's cognitive strategies for coping with emotional arousal. Presumably, effective coping strategies should minimize both subjective emotional arousal and EDA. Conversely, ineffective coping strategies should lead to increased subjective emotional arousal and EDA.

Consistent with these predictions, Lazarus and his associates have found that subjects' cognitive appraisal of "emotional" stimuli rather than the stimuli *per se* mediated their emotional reactions (Lazarus, 1982). For example, in one study, middle-level airline executives and undergraduates viewed a film entitled *Subincision* (Spiesman, Lazarus, Mordkoff, & Davison, 1964). This film depicts an Australian aborigine puberty rite during which adolescent males' penes are repeatedly slashed with a stone knife. The film was presented with either (a) no sound track, (b) a trauma sound track (which emphasized the pain and cruelty of the ritual), (c) an intellectualization sound track (which emphasized a detached scientific attitude) or (d) a denial reaction formation sound track (which denied the negative aspects of the film and emphasized how the adolescents were looking forward to the benefits of adulthood). Across treatment conditions, subjects reported marked distress and showed sharp increases in skin conductance during each of the operation scenes. During nonoperation scenes, both ratings of subjective distress and measures of skin conductance dropped. Subjects in the trauma condition showed much higher levels of skin conductance than subjects in the other three conditions during the film. Both intellectualization and the denial reaction formation narratives produced decreased levels of skin conductance. The executives showed the lowest EDA with the denial narrative, whereas undergraduates showed the lowest EDA with the intellectualization narrative.

Lazarus and Alfert (1964) examined whether presenting a denial reaction formation set prior to the film *Subincision* would lead to reduced EDA during the film. Male undergraduates were assigned to three condigions: (a) silent film, (b) denial set and narrative, or (c) denial orientation (set and no narrative). Although subjects in both denial conditions showed lower EDA during the film, the denial orientation group showed the lowest level of EDA. Paradoxically, in the silent condition, subjects who scored high on personality measures of denial (repressors) reported less subjective distress but showed higher levels of EDA than subjects who scored low on denial (sensitizers). The authors argue that repressors may be more receptive to external denial messages and thus show reductions in EDA when such cues are available.

An alternative explanation for the higher EDA of repressors is that denial may be an effective short-term coping mechanism but fails to reduce autonomic arousal if it is habitually employed. Mullen and Suls (1982) reviewed 26 studies that had reported physiological correlates of attending to or rejecting (denial) of a stressor. Studies that examined the immediate physiological reaction to stressors found that rejection produces lower physiological arousal than attention. However, studies that measured long-term adaptation to stressors (3-week to 3-year periods) found that attention produced a lower physiological arousal.

Another explanation for repressors' elevated EDA is that the physiological effects of denial may be mediated by whether denial is conscious or unconscious. Conscious denial may produce decreases in physiological arousal, whereas unconscious denial may produce increases. Consistent with this position, numerous studies have found that repressors tend to show elevated physiological reactions to a variety of stressors. For example, Learmonth, Ackerly, and Kaplan (1959) examined the spontaneous SP responses of female student nurses to a sentence completion test, a stressful interview, and to a series of physical stressors (firing a gun behind the subject's head, an electric shock, and placing the subject's foot in ice water). Regardless of the type of stressor, the number of SP responses correlated positively with subjects' scores on personality measures of repression. That is, subjects who should report the greatest tendency to deny negative affective states showed the highest EDA.

It should be noted that all three explanations of repressors' elevated physiological responses are highly complementary. Repressors may so habitually use denial as a conscious coping strategy that they are no longer consciously aware of their own denials. Moreover, their cognitive set of "nothing is wrong" may predispose repressors to search for confirming evidence.

The EDA literature nicely illustrates the complexity of human emotions. Changes in both tonic and phasic EDA can be reliably observed across a variety of emotional states. However, EDA appears to be directly yoked to the complex interaction of "hot" (emotional) and "cold" (attention, coping strategies) cognitive processes. Although the average person usually displays a clear positive relationship between the intensity of EDA and of emotions, repressors show the exact opposite pattern. Such findings highlight the importance of individual variability in emotions. Any given individual may display an idiosyncratic pattern of physiological reactions during emotions that may vary significantly from the "average" response. As you will see in the following discussion of naturalistic and clinical studies, such individual response stereotypy appears to be the rule rather than the exception in thermoregulatory research.

5.2.2. Naturalistic Studies

Naturalistic studies of cadiovascular activity during emotions have focused on an easily observable response during embarrassment—blushing. Blushing is produced by the sudden vasodilation of the capillaries of the skin. In Caucasians, blushing usually causes the skin to appear flushed or bright red. In a minority of individuals, blushing takes the form of rasklike red spots (erythema fugax). Similar patterns of blushing also occur in members of other races but the blushing response may be partially masked by skin pigmentation. Blushing usually occurs in the skin of the face; however, some individuals also show blushing on the upper abdomen, chest, and neck. Darwin (1872) noted that even blind individuals blushed and postulated that because blind individuals could not have learned the response through social modeling, then blushing must be genetically determined.

Buss, Iscoe, and Buss (1979) examined the development of embarrassment in 3- to 12-year-old children by asking their parents to complete a questionnaire about their offsprings' behavior over the previous 6 months. Although embarrassment was reported for 59% of the 5-year-olds and 73% of the 6-year-olds, embarrassment was reported for only 26% of the 3- and 4-year-olds. In both sexes, blushing was reported in 57% of the children during embarrassment. The authors postulated that the development of blushing and embarrassment may indicate the child's development of the perception of a "social self."

Abe and Masui (1981) investigated the incidence of anxiety and phobic symptoms in 11- to 23-year-old females and males. Although there were no observed sex differences in the incidence rate of blushing, females were more likely to report fear of blushing (erythrophobia). For both sexes, the incidence of erythrophobia reached a peak during adolescence. For females, the peak incidence rate of erythrophobia (30%) occurred at age 15, whereas, for males, the highest incidence of erythrophobia (20%) was found among 17-year-olds.

Due to our cultural norms of modesty, adults often report blushing and feeling "naked" (vulnerable) and embarrassed when asked to disrobe for a medical examination. Yet studies have documented a notable lack of blushing and embarrassment by individuals at nudist camps. This apparent "lack of shame" is often interpreted as evidence that nudists are exhibitionists. However, studies of the personality profiles of nudists suggest that, except for their attitudes about public nudity, social nudists may be indistinguishable from the general population (Hartman, Fithian, & Johnson, 1970; Casler, 1971).

Weinberg (1965, 1968) argued that embarrassment associated with nudity is situationally determined. For example, the situational norms of nudist camps may help eliminate embarrassment associated with public nudity by encouraging the beliefs that nudity is (a) unrelated to sexuality, (b) not inherently shameful, (c) associated with mental and physical health, and (d) an expression of personal freedom. Weinberg noted that many social nudists report that they would feel very embarrassed if other people saw them in the nude at home. Thus, depending upon situational cues, even nudists may feel naked. Conversely, many nonnudists may feel comfortable disrobing in front of strangers when the situational cues (locker room, medical examining room, etc.) define public nudity as "appropriate."

Naturalistic studies have also documented changes in EDA during a variety of emotional states. For example, Valone, Goldstein, and Norton (1984) examined the EDA of parents and adolescent females and males during discussions of family problems. The parents were scored on the degree of negative emotions (criticism, hostility, and overinvolvement) that they expressed toward their offspring. Prior to the discussion, increases in tonic SC occurred in adolscents who were to talk with a parent who expressed high levels of negative affect. No such "anticipation" effect was observed in the parents' EDA. During the discussion, both highly negative parents and their offspring showed marked elevations in SCL that increased as their discussion or, more accurately, confrontation progressed.

Grings and Dawson (1978) argued that the results of naturalistic studies like Valones's should be interpreted with caution. In such complex social situations, changes in EDA and other physiological processes may reflect emotional states or mental activity or muscle tension or a combination of these factors.

5.2.3. Clinical Studies

Based on the assumption that psychiatric disorders represent exaggerated versions of normal emotional reactions, numerous authors have postulated that psychiatric patients' thermoregulatory responses should differ from those of subjects drawn from the general population. However, researchers disagree over exactly how psychiatric patients' responses differ. Proponents of the global "flight-or-fight" view of emotional arousal argue that psychiatric patients' thermoregulatory responses should be higher than "normals" but should not differentiate between psychiatric groups. Conversely, Lader (1975) and other proponents of the pattern model of emotional arousal argue that some psychiatric disorders may be characterized by elevated thermoregulatory responses, whereas other psychiatric disorders may be characterized by lower than normal thermoregulatory responses. As we will see in the following section, research with psychiatric patients appears to clearly support the pattern model.

5.2.3.1. Psychiatric Populations

Although panic attacks (spontaneous episodes of intense fear) are commonly reported in both the general and psychiatric populations, relatively little is known about the physiological correlates of these naturally occurring emotional states. Lader and Mathews (1970) observed three panic attacks while conducting psychophysiological studies of anxious and phobic psychiatric patients. In all three cases, the cause of the panic attack was idiopathic (no external fear stimulus was present). Each of the panic attacks lasted 2 to 5 minutes, and sharp physiological changes occurred at the onset of the attack. Heart rate increased about 50 bpm. Vasoconstriction in the extremities was coupled with an approximately 10-fold increase in blood flow in the forearm muscles. The level of skin conductance increased dramatically, and numerous spontaneous fluctuations in skin conduction were observed. No change in striate muscle activity was observed in two patients, and the third patient showed a delayed increase in forearm muscle tension. Thus the physiological markers of the onset of panic attacks appear to be the autonomic components of the thermoregulatory system. We will discuss panic attacks later in greater detail in Chapter 12.

Kelly (1966, 1971) reported that anxiety patients had higher resting forearm blood flow but showed smaller increases in forearm blood flow during stress than control subjects. For example, Kelly, Brown, and Shaffer (1970) found that resting forearm blood flow correlated positively with both self-ratings ($r = +.43$) and observer ratings ($r = +.71$) of anxiety but was unrelated to ratings of depression. Similarly, Kelly and Walter (1969) found that resting forearm blood flow correlates with self-reports of anxiety but not depression in severely depressed patients. Lader and Wing (1964) found that anxious patients showed higher tonic SC and more frequent spontaneous SCRs than normals. When presented with a series of 100-db tones, all normal subjects, but only 6 of 20 anxious patients, showed habituation.

In general, the overall pattern of findings with psychiatric patients is consistent with Lader's (1975) hypothesis that highly anxious individuals have higher tonic levels of sympathetic arousal but smaller phasic responses to stress than control subjects. Lader argues that the law of initial values may account for the "failure" of physiological measures to differentiate high- and low-anxious individuals in stress situations.

Studies of phobic patients suggest that their fear reactions may be highly specific. Geer (1966) reported that phobic patients showed increased EDA when shown photographs of their specific fear stimuli. Lang et al. (1983) compared the physiological reactions of snake phobics and speech phobics during a math test, during exposure to a live snake, and while giving a speech to an audience. Both groups of phobics showed higher heart rates preceding and during exposure to their respective fear stimuli. EDA also increased in each group of phobics during anticipation and exposure to their respective fear stimuli, but the observed differences in EDA did not reach statistical significance. EDA paralleled subjects' self-reports of fear during anticipation periods, whereas heart rate did not. Conversely, during exposure periods, snake phobics showed accelerated heart rates to both snake and speech tasks, whereas speech phobics showed heart rate increases only during the speech. The subjects' EDA did not match these heart rate patterns.

A number of studies have reported that depressed patients may have lower EDA than normal subjects. For example, Iacono and his associates reported that depressed subjects "in remission" have significantly lower SCL and smaller SCRs than normal subjects to a wide variety of stimuli (Iacono et al., 1983; Iacono et al., 1984). Specifically, depressed subjects showed lower EDA to breath-holding exercises, blowing up a balloon until it burst, to a series of loud tones and loud familiar sounds such as a dog barking. Depressed and control subjects, however, did not differ in the frequency of spontaneous SCRs. The reduced EDA observed in Iacono's studies does not appear to be due to medication. Drug-free samples of chronically depressed subjects show similar patterns of reduced EDA (Donat & McCullough, 1983). Moreover, Lenhart (1985) found that college students identified as at high risk for bipolar disorders showed lower EDA to tones than control subjects.

Research with schizophrenic patients has produced a mixed pattern of EDA. Some studies have reported elevated EDA in schizophrenics (Zahn, Rosenthal, & Lawlor, 1968), whereas other studies have found reduced EDA (Bernstein, 1970). One explanation for these apparently contradictory findings is that schizophrenic samples may contain two distinct subpopulations—hyperreactive patients and hyporeactive patients (Gruzelier & Venables, 1972; Rubens & Lapidus, 1978). Other researchers have argued that the reduced EDA may be the dominant characteristic of schizophrenic populations (Ohman, 1981; Bernstein *et al.*, 1982). Although the EDA of schizophrenics clearly differs from the EDA of the general population, the available evidence suggests that observed differences in EDA may not be physiological in origin but rather are due to differences in attention. For example, about 40% of both active schizophrenics (Ohman, 1981) and schizophrenics in remission (Iacono, 1982) are electrodermal "nonresponders" to auditory tones. However, many schizophrenic "nonresponders" show normal EDA activity when meaningful stimuli are substituted for tones (Gruzelier & Venables, 1973; Bernstein, Schneider, Juni, Pope, & Starkey, 1980).

Psychopathy is characterized by emotional "flatness," an inability to learn to avoid punishments in avoidance tasks and, paradoxically, normal learning on positively rewarded tasks. Numerous authors have proposed that psychopaths' lack of emotion may be due to abnormal physiological responses to stress. For example, Schachter and Latane (1964) proposed that a psychopath's lack of affect may be due to highly labile cardiovascular systems that

> react sympathetically to events that are labeled frightening by others, but he also reacts to events labeled as relatively harmless by others. Such generalized, relatively indiscriminate reactivity is, we would suggest, almost equivalent to no reactivity at all. If almost every event provokes strong autonomic discharge, then, in terms of internal autonomic cues, the subject feels no differently during times of danger than during relatively tranquil times. Bodily conditions that for others are associated with emotionality are, for the sociopath, his "normal" state. (pp. 266–267)

Research on criminal populations has consistently failed to support Schachter and Latane's hyperreactivity model of psychopathy. Hare and Quinn (1971), for example, compared the physiological responses of psychopathic and nonpsychopathic male criminals to positive (female nude) and negative (strong electric shock) conditioned stimuli in a classical conditioning experiment. No differences were observed between the groups in either cardiac or digit vascular responses. The only vascular difference observed was that nonpsychopaths responded to shock with cranial vasoconstriction, whereas psychopaths showed cranial vasodilation. The psychopaths showed lower EDA to both positive and negative stimuli. In a series of experiments, Hare and his associates found that psychopathic criminals showed lower EDA and equal or slightly higher cardiovascular responses than nonpsychopathic criminals to stressful stimuli (Hare & Craigen, 1974; Hare, 1975; Hare, Frazelle, & Cox, 1978). However, the cause of psychopaths' reduced EDA is unknown. Hare (1972) injected psychopathic and nonpsychopathic criminals with epinephrine and with saline. Both groups showed similar cardiovascular, respiratory, and striate reactions to epinephrine. However, the two groups differed in their electrodermal reactions to the injections. Nonpsychopaths showed sharp increases in SC following both injections, whereas psychopaths showed much smaller SC increases. Both nonpsychopaths and psychopaths showed much slower recovery in SC after epinephrine than after saline injection, and no group differences in recovery rates were observed. Thus the observed differences in EDA do not appear to be due to differential sensitivity to epinephrine but rather to different psychological reactions to the injection.

Hare (1975) noted that one of the major weaknesses in the literature on psychopathy is the lack of information about psychopaths who avoid being arrested. Research on the EDA of antisocial adolescents has produced conflicting findings. Some studies have found psychopathic delinquents to have reduced EDA, whereas others reported no differences between psychopathic and nonpsychopathic delinquents. Raine and Venables (1984) examined the EDA of 15-year-old males who were rated by their teachers on antisocial behaviors (destructiveness, fighting, etc.). No difference in initial EDA to novel stimuli was observed between subjects who scored high or low on measures of antisocial tendencies. Approximately 78% of the subjects who scored high on antisocial tendencies were electrodermally responsive, but 80% of nonresponders were from the high antisocial subgroup. Subsequent analysis revealed that antisocial nonresponders scored high on measures of schizoid tendencies. Thus the adolescents who were electrodermally nonresponsive appear to be a high risk group for later schizophrenia rather than psychopathy.

In general, the results of studies of psychiatric populations (Lader & Wing, 1964; Grings & Dawson, 1978) suggest that specific patterns of thermoregulatory responses may differentiate between psychiatric patients and controls and between anxiety patients and other psychiatric disorders. Tonic levels of skin conduction and the frequency of spontaneous skin conduction responses are higher than normal in anxious patients and lower than normal in depressives, psychopaths, and nonresponsive schizophrenics. Tonic peripheral vasoconstriction and forearm blood flow are higher in anxious patients than in other psychiatric patients.

5.2.3.2. Psychophysiologic Populations

The global arousal (flight-or-fight) model of emotional thermoregulatory responses predicts that emotional stress may initiate or aggravate global physiological dysfunctions. Conversely, the pattern model of emotion argues that emotions may produce or aggravate highly localized dysfunctions in the thermoregulatory system. As you will see in the following discussion, all of the psychophysiological thermoregulatory disorders involve highly localized dysfunctions of either the sweat glands (chronic perspiration) or the vascular system (chronic blushing, chronic headaches, Raynaud's disease).

a. Chronic Perspiration. Chronic perspiration or hyperhidrosis may be a symptom of a wide variety of endorcrinological, metabolic, or neurological organic disorders. For example, episodic hyperhidrosis is often a symptom of CNS disorders of the corpus callosum (Lewitt *et al.*, 1983). Holzle (1983) argued that the pattern of eccrine gland hyperactivity is often indicative of specific disorders. Endrocrinological and metabolic disorders commonly produce global or generalized hyperhidrosis, whereas irregular patterns of sweating on the head and trunk are characteristic of neurological disorders. Sweating localized in the palms of the hands (palmar hyperhidrosis), soles of the feet (plantar hyperhidrosis), or armpits (axillary hyperhydrosis) is often idiopathic and presumably psychogenic in origin.

Idiopathic or essential hyperhidrosis is characterized by chronic emotional sweating (Engels, 1982). The onset of hyperhidrosis usually occurs before the age of 20 and rarely after the age of 25. Patients often report concurrent autonomic symptoms such as diarrhea, tachycardia and tremors, and a family history of chronic sweating (Lerer, 1977). Oda (1983) reported that concordance rate of hyperhidrosis is significantly higher in identical than in fraternal twins. Thus it appears reasonable to assume that essential hyperhidrosis patients may have a genetic predisposition to profuse emotional sweating.

Although emotions are commonly cited as producing or aggravating hyperhidrosis (Eller, 1974; Engels, 1982; Holzle, 1983; Lerer, 1977), there have been relatively few studies of the emotional reactions of hyperhidrosis patients. Dosuzkov (1975) cited a case report of a 29-year-old male hyperhidrosis patient who reported idrosophobia (fear of social encounters), preoccupation with his appearance, and delusions of physical offensiveness (i.e., body odor). Obviously, idrosophobia and hyperhidrosis may interact in a reciprocal manner. The more an individual worries about his or her appearance, the higher the rate of emotional sweating. Conversely, the higher the rate of sweating, the more reason the individual has to worry about physical offensiveness. Bar and Kuypers (1973) also reported that hyperhydrosis patients display sudophobia (fear of sweating) and an inability to express their emotions. Lerer, Jacobowitz, and Wahba (1980) reported that hyperhidrosis patients' and control subjects' scores on standardized personality tests differed significantly. As a group, hyperhidrosis patients tend to score lower in overall coping ability and anxiety but higher on avoidance and impulsivity. The authors observed that 25% of the hyperhidrosis patients had abnormally *low* anxiety scores. It should be noted that the pattern of low self-reports of anxiety and high autonomic arousal is characteristic of repressors. Other researchers have postulated that hyperhidrosis patients' poor psychosocial adjustment may manifest itself in other psychophysiological disorders. For example, Wabrek (1984) observed that 80% of a sample of males being treated for premature ejaculation also had palmar hyperhidrosis.

If hyperhidrosis is psychogenic in origin, then teaching patients to reduce their emotional arousal should produce symptom relief. Bolzinger and Ebtinger (1971) reported that a combination of psychotherapy and hypnosis was successful in eliminating the excessive sweating of an 11-year-old girl with palmar hyperhidrosis. A 1-year follow-up confirmed prolonged symptom relief. Duller and Gentry (1980) treated 14 hyperhidrosis patients with visual biofeedback from a water vapor analyzer. Six weeks after the termination of training, 8 patients showed clinically significant reductions in sweating, and 3 additional patients reported some degree of symptom relief. The patients who did reduce sweating reported they did so through self-relaxation.

b. *Chronic Blushing.* Blushing is normally a brief reaction to embarrassment. However, some individuals experience prolonged and exaggerated blushing in presumably nonthreatening situations. Although there has been relatively little research on chronic blushing, the available evidence suggests that chronic blushing is psychogenic in origin.

Zimbardo, Pilkonis, and Norwood (1974) observed that 53% of high school and college students who reported themselves as "shy" also reported chronic blushing. Other autonomic responses (butterflies in the stomach, heart palpitations, increased pulse, and perspiration) were also more commonly reported by shy respondants. Zimbardo (1977) cited numerous case histories of chronic blushing associated with shyness. Blushing was usually triggered by the subjects' feelings of social anxiety or embarrassment in social situations. However, some individuals reported blushing in private when they recalled past embarrassments or anticipated socially stressful situations. It should be noted that the specific types of social situations that elicited chronic blushing were idiosyncratic. Some shy individuals blushed only when interacting with strangers, whereas other shy individuals blushed only when interacting with people they knew. Zimbardo cited an interesting example of a 21-year-old female undergraduate who could not speak in class without blushing. After classes she worked as a nude model and purportedly never blushed while posing nude for strange males.

Unfortunately, there is little information available on the relationships between normal blushing, chronic blushing, and erythrophobia. Tomkins (1963) speculated that occurrence of blushing may increase the individual's embarrassment and thus lead to additional blushing and embarrassment. Thus habitual embarrassment may produce both chronic blushing and erythrophobia. Other researchers argue that intense emotional experiences may be needed to produce chronic blushing. Van Pelt (1975) argued that superconcentration during intense emotional states may trigger a self-hypnotic production of symptoms such as chronic blushing. Consistent with Van Pelt's position, a number of authors have reported that chronic blushing can be cured through hypnosis (Welsh, 1978). Schneck (1967) postulated that both repressed hostility and repressed sexuality may produce chronic blushing. Zimbardo *et al.* (1974) provide some empirical support for Schneck's model. Specifically, repressed hostility, repressed sexuality, chronic blushing, and erythrophobia were all commonly observed in shy subjects.

Given the consistent finding that chronic blushing is a psychophysiological disorder, it is rather surprising that there are few reports on psychological treatment of chronic blushing and erythrophobia. Salter (1950) reported successfully treating one case of chronic blushing with assertiveness training. Case studies have also reported that the technique of "paradoxical intention" may be successful in controlling blushing (Lamontagne, 1978; Boeringa, 1983). With this technique, the patients are encouraged to force themselves to blush ("I am going to look like a beet!"). Gotestam, Melin, and Olsson (1976) reported successful treatment of blushing and erthrophobia of two patients with temperature biofeedback in conjunction with counterconditioning.

   c. Chronic Headache. An estimated 10% to 15% of the population suffer from chronic headaches (Bakal, 1979). Medical textbooks traditionally divided headache sufferers into three general categories: organic, migraine (vascular), and tension (muscle contraction). Organic headaches are symptoms of specific physical disorders such as brain tumors or hypertension and account for only 5% to 10% of all headache cases. In the remaining 90% to 95% of the cases, the headache is the primary disorder. Because no physical causes for either migraine or tension headaches were known, it was traditionally assumed that both types of headaches were psychogenic in origin.

   Our discussion will focus on *migraine headaches,* which account for approximately 40% to 50% of all chronic headaches. Migraines are characterized by debilitating head pain that lasts for between 2 and 24 hours. Two subtypes of migraines are commonly reported. *Classic* migraines are characterized by the occurrence of a variety of neurological symptoms (numbness, speech difficulties, sensitivity to everyday sounds, vertigo, visual disorders, etc.) prior to the onset of the headache. During the headache, pain is unilateral (localized in the temporal area on one side of the head) and is usually accompanied by nausea and vomiting. *Common* migraines occur without warning. During the headache, pain may be experienced either unilaterally or bilaterally, and nausea and vomiting may not occur. Often the same individual will report experiencing both types of migraines at different times.

   Although migraines may be triggered by a wide variety of stimuli (anxiety, food allergies, glare, hunger, lack of sleep, menstruation, temperature changes, etc.), most authors agree that all migraines are produced by a common physiological mechanism—localized spasms of the extracranial arteries of the head (see Graham & Wolff, 1938). Migraine attacks presumably develop in three stages. In the preheadache stage, the superficial temporal artery and other extracranial arteries show intense vasoconstriction. In the onset stage, the extracranial arteries suddenly stretch and become excessively dilated. The pulsation of blood through the distended arteries stimulates pain receptors in the arterial walls and produces a "throbbing" pain sensation. The congestion of blood in the head causes fluids from the blood to be forced into the arterial walls and the arteries become swollen and rigid. This arterial edema helps maintain the headache. During the edema stage, pain is often experienced as constant rather than throbbing.

   Why a given individual is susceptible to chronic headaches is currently unknown. Nonchronic headaches are extremely common in the general population. In one survey, 87% of females and 74% of the males reported having had at least one headache during the previous 6 months (Phillips, 1977). Moreover, the headaches reported by the general population are often as severe and as debilitating as those reported by chronic headache patients (Ziegler *et al.*, 1977). The two groups differ primarily in the *frequency* of headaches. Members of the general population may report experiencing one migraine attack per year or per decade or per lifetime, whereas chronic headache patients are experiencing headaches once a month or once a day.

Traditionally, researchers assumed that specific personality characteristics predisposed the individual to chronic headaches. Migraine sufferers were stereotyped as "obsessional perfectionists," and tension headache patients as "coping ineffectively with stress." Empirical support for these stereotypes, however, is both sparse and contradictory (Martin, 1983).

Many authors have postulated that the development of specific types of chronic headaches may be due to a genetic predisposition to headaches coupled with repetitive stress. Presumably, individuals with highly labile vascular systems are susceptible to migraines and other vascular headaches, whereas individuals with highly labile striate musculature are suspectible to tension headaches. Empirical support for this view, however, is mixed. Studies that compared the physiological responses of headache patients and control subjects generally support the lability hypothesis. For example, compared with healthy controls, migraine patients tend to have higher tonic levels of peripheral vasoconstricfion (Appenseller, 1969; Price & Tursky, 1976; Werbach & Sandweiss, 1978; Price and Clark, 1979), show different patterns of extracranial vascular responses to psychological stress (Drummond, 1982), and show different patterns of peripheral, extracranial, and intracranial vascular responses to heat (Sovak, Kunzel, Sternbach, & Dalessio, 1978). Similarly, tension headache patients tend to have higher tonic levels of muscle tension in facial and neck muscles than controls (Martin & Mathews, 1978). Marked lability has also been observed when headache patients are tested during headache-free periods and during headaches. Migraine patients tend to show a sharp increase in pulse amplitude in the superficial temporal artery during headaches (Allen & Mills, 1982), whereas tension headache patients show increases in neck muscle tension and cephalic vasodilation (Haynes *et al.*, 1983). Studies that have compared different diagnostic groups of headache patients, however, have often failed to find different patterns of lability. For example, Anderson and Franks (1981) reported marked personality differences between migraine and tension headache patients but could not discriminate between the two groups on the basis of either cardiovascular or muscular activity.

Numerous theorists have postulated that specific emotions (anxiety, depression, and hostility) may trigger headache attacks. The results of studies of samples of the general population suggest that emotions may play an important role in the etiology of headaches. Ziegler, Rhodes, and Hassanein (1978), for example, asked 711 unselected adults to complete a battery of psychological tests and a medical history as part of a "medical project." Regardless of age or sex, subjects who reported a history of disabling or severe headaches scored significantly higher on measures of anxiety and depression than subjects who reported mild or no headaches.

Studies of psychiatric patients also suggest that headaches may be related to anxiety and depression. Headaches are relatively commonly reported by both anxious and depressed patients, and antidepressant medications often provide symptom relief (Lance, 1978; Raskin, 1982).

Paradoxically, studies of chronic headache patients have frequently failed to find any relationship between emotional states and headache attacks. Arena, Blanchard, and Andrasik (1984) asked migraine, tension, and mixed headache patients to self-monitor their moods and headaches for 28 to 35 consecutive days. No relationship was found between headache attacks and emotional states on either the 2 days before or the 2 days after a headache attack. On the day of the headache, only 23% of the patients reported increases in either anxiety, anger, or depression. Thus the patients' conscious emotional states appear to be unrelated to headache onset.

Numerous explanations have been offered for the failure of researchers to demonstrate a simple cause-and-effect relationship between emotions and chronic headache attacks. Some researchers argue that all headaches are organic in origin and that emotional states may play little or no role in triggering headache attacks. Psychoanalytic researchers argue that suppressed emotions rather than conscious emotional states may trigger headaches. Consistent with the psychoanalytic position, headache researchers have consistently noted that a significant minority of chronic headache patients are repressors who tend to deny emotional stress (Martin, 1966; Featherstone & Beitman, 1984).

Literally hundreds of reports have been published on treatment programs designed to teach chronic headache patients how to reduce the frequency and severity of headaches without medication. The majority of these studies have employed some form of biofeedback either alone or in conjunction with self-relaxation techniques. The most popular treatments for vascular headache patients have been finger (digit) temperature biofeedback, cranial artery photoplethysmography biofeedback, or a combination of these two techniques. Although proponents of biofeedback have often reported impressive (75%) cure rates with chronic headache patients, reviews of the headache treatment literature have consistently questioned the effectiveness of biofeedback training (Alexander & Smith, 1979; Surwitt, Williams, & Shaprio, 1982; Holmes & Burish, 1983). For example, Knapp (1982) found that 1 year after training, both cognitive stress-coping training and photoplethysmographic biofeedback led to equal reductions in headaches of chronic migraine patients.

d. Raynaud's Disease. Raynaud's disease is characterized by spasmodic vasoconstriction in the digits of the hands and feet that has no known organic cause (see Krupp & Chatton, 1975; Surwitt, Williams, & Shapiro, 1982). At the onset of an attack, the digits suddenly blanch as blood is diverted from the extremities. The digits then turn blue (cyanosis) due to the oxygen shortages in the tissues, and the patients report mild to severe pain. The vasospasm normally ends spontaneously but often can be terminated by placing the affected extremities in hot water. During the recovery phase, the digits turn red as blood rushes back into the fingers or toes (reactive hypermia). The recovery phase may last several hours during which the patient often experiences burning sensations until normal circulation is restored.

The age of onset of Raynaud's disease ranges from 15 to 45 years and Raynaud's patients often report a family history of vasospastic disorders (Krupp & Chatton, 1975). Approximately 20% of adolescents and young adults suffer mild to severe forms of Raynaud's disease (Lewis, 1949). The incidence rate of Raynaud's disease is about five times higher in females than in males. The average patient reports one to two attacks of varying severity per day. Global exposure to cold and emotional stress are the two most commonly reported triggers of vasopasms in Raynaud's patients.

Mittelmann and Wolff (1939) examined the relative importance of cold temperatures and emotions in triggering vasospasms in Raynaud's patients. Exposure to cold alone was not sufficient to trigger vasospasms, and attacks occurred most frequently when cold temperatures and emotional stress were present. For example, one subject consistently showed decreases in skin temperature of 9.5°C when discussing emotional issues. In a latter study, Mittelmann and Wolff (1943) demonstrated that vasoconstriction in the skin could be elicited by a variety of emotional states and that the degree of vasoconstriction appeared to vary with the intensity of the emotion.

Other researchers have replicated Mittelmann's findings. Graham (1955) noted that peripheral vasoconstriction occurred in both normal controls and in Raynaud's patients during interviews that elicited either anxiety or hostility. Graham, Stern, and Winokur (1958) observed that digit vasoconstriction could be induced in normal subjects through hypnotic suggestions of anxiety or hostility. Freedman and Ianni (1985) found that both normal controls and Raynaud's patients displayed finger vasoconstriction to general stress images, but only Raynaud's patients responded to images of cold stressors with a drop in finger temperature. The results of these studies strongly suggest that Raynaud's disease may represent an exaggerated version of the peripheral vasoconstriction normally observed in anxiety states or in reaction to cold.

A number of researchers have attempted to teach Raynaud's patients to control vasospasms through the use of digit temperature biofeedback and self-relaxation techniques. Blanchard (1979) reviewed 19 case histories of biofeedback treatments of Raynaud's patients and noted that there was at least anecdotal evidence of improvement in 89% of the patients. More recent reviews of the biofeedback literature noted that, after treatment, the average patient learned to reduce the frequency of vasopasms about 50% to 93% (Freedman, Ianni, & Wenig, 1985).

5.2.3.3. Emotions and Thermoregulatory Disorders

The available literature on psychophysiological thermoregulatory disorders nicely illustrates (a) our relative ignorance of the physiology of thermoregulation; (b) the difficulty inherent in separating psychological and organic causes of disorders and (c) the complex relationships between emotional states and thermoregulatory responses. Given the sheer complexity of this literature, it is easy to overlook three extremely important empirical findings. First, most physiological disorders tend to be mutually exclusive. Patients who chronically blush, for example, rarely report chronic headaches and vice versa. Second, a single emotion may be associated with attacks of different psychophysiological disorders in different individuals. Thus, anger may trigger a migraine headache in one patient, but it may trigger a Raynaud attack in another. Third, the symptoms of psychophysiological disorders are only partially yoked to conscious experiences of emotional states. As you will see throughout the remainder of the book, these three features appear to be characteristic of a variety of psychophysiological disorders.

SUGGESTED READINGS

Bakal, D. A. *Psychology and medicine: Psychobiological dimensions of health and illness.* New York: Springer, 1979.

   A good general introduction to the scientific literature on headaches and other psychophysiological disorders.

Hensel, H. *Thermoreception and thermal regulation.* New York: Academic Press, 1981.

   A comprehensive discussion of the anatomy and physiology of human thermoregulation.

Lazarus, R. S. Thoughts on the relations between emotion and cognition. *American Psychologist,* 1982, *37(9),* 1019–1024.

   A theoretical discussion of the relationships between cognitive coping strategies (e.g., denial), emotional states, and physiological activity.

The Respiratory System

The term *respiration* refers to the exchange of gases. Biologists label the interchange of gases within a cell as *true respiration*. During aerobic metabolism, oxygen combines with carbon and hydrogen to produce carbon dioxide and water. The exchange of oxygen and carbon dioxide between the blood cells and body cells is called *internal* respiration. The exchange of gases between the bloodstream and the external environment is labeled *external* respiration. Thus, technically, the respiratory system consists of every living cell in the body. The term *respiratory system*, however, is more commonly used to denote the lungs and other organs involved in external respiration.

6.1. ANATOMY AND PHYSIOLOGY

The respiratory system consists of a series of tubes that form the air passages, the lungs, the skeletal bones of the chest (ribs and spine), and two major groups of skeletal muscles (diaphragm and intercostal).

Four interconnected tubes form a passageway that connects the lungs and the external environment (see Figure 6-1). Inhaled or inspired air passes from the nasal cavities into the pharynx. The pharynx is a wide tube that connects the nasal cavities, the oral cavity (mouth), the larynx (voice box), and the esophagus. This anatomical arrangement allows the mouth to serve the dual functions of digestion and respiration. Food entering the mouth passes to the esophagus, whereas air entering the mouth passes to the larynx. The entrance to the larynx is shielded by a leaf shaped cartilage structure called the *epiglottis* that blocks food or fluids from entering the larynx during swallowing.

The trachea or wind pipe is a cartilage-lined tube that connects the larynx with the large passageways, or bronchi, in the lungs. The lungs are two spongelike organs contained in the upper two-thirds of the chest cavity. Air enters the lungs through the bronchi, which progressively divide into small tubes called *bronchioles*. Unlike the larynx, trachea, and bronchi, bronchioles are not composed of cartilage but rather of rings of smooth muscle that can contract or dilate. Parasympathetic stimulation causes the bronchioles to constrict,

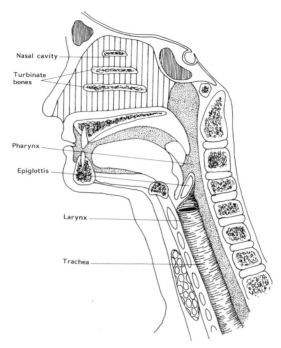

Nasal cavity

Turbinate
bones

Pharynx

Epiglottis

Larynx

Trachea

Figure 6-1. Major anatomical structures of the upper respiratory system.

whereas sympathetic stimulation causes the bronchioles to dilate. The bronchioles branch into finer tubes (alveolar ducts) that in turn terminate in 750 million sacs called *alveoli* (Best & Taylor, 1966). The walls of the alveoli are only one cellular layer thick and are surrounded by beds of capillaries. Because the blood is separated from the air only by the walls of the alveoli and capillaries, oxygen can move rather freely from the lungs to the blood, whereas carbon dioxide can move freely from the blood to the lungs.

The lungs are like balloons and cannot inflate or deflate themselves. The rib cage (ribs, spine, and sternum) and muscles of the chest mechanically inflate the lungs at sea level air pressure. Attached to the base of the rib cage is a strong band of skeletal muscle called the *diaphragm* that acts like a piston. Contraction of the diaphragm pulls the lungs downward and thus mechanically expands them. Air pressure inside the lungs drops below atmospheric pressure and outside air rushes into the lungs (inhalation). Exhalation is normally a much more passive process. Both the diaphragm and the lungs are elastic and tend to "snap back" to their original shape. Thus relaxation causes the diaphragm to move upward and allows the lungs to collapse inward. This mechanical compression causes air pressure inside the lungs to become higher than atmospheric pressure, and air rushes out of the lungs. Under resting conditions, diaphragm movement (more commonly called abdominal breathing) moves about one-half a liter of air (tidal volume) in and out of the lungs during each inhalation–exhalation cycle.

Although the tidal volume is adequate for metabolic needs at rest, it is insufficient for the sudden increase in oxygen needed during strenuous physical activity. The physical movement of the diaphragm is limited by the viscera in the abdominal cavity. One method for increasing the volume of air exchanged during respiration cycles is to increase the distance traveled by the diaphragm by voluntarily forcing the abdominal muscles outward. This abdominal movement pulls the viscera downward and outward and allows the diaphragm to contract fully. Conversely, contraction of the abdominal muscles forces the viscera inward and upward and thus helps compress the lungs. Such forced abdominal breathing increases respiration volume to about 2 liters.

A second way to increase respiration volume is to increase the size of the rib cage. Two pairs of muscles, the external and internal intercostals, are located between each rib. Contraction of the external intercostal muscles causes the ribcage to move upward and outward and thus facilitates inhalation. Conversely, contraction of the internal intercostal muscles compresses the rib cage and lungs, forcing exhalation. The external muscles of the chest (pectoralis major and minor) and back (latissimus dorsi) can also assist the intercostals in expanding and contracting the rib cage. Due to mechanical limits of the rib cage, intercostal breathing can increase respiratory volume by only about 1 liter of air.

Both in terms of the increase in respiration volume and in the amount of physical effort required, abdominal breathing is more "cost-effective" than intercostal breathing. Yet researchers have consistently found that a large percentage of adults in our culture habitually suppress abdominal breathing and show intercostal breathing. A number of theorists have speculated on the psychological significance of such ineffective respiration patterns, and these theoretical positions will be discussed later in this chapter.

The skeletal muscles involved in respiration are commonly labeled as *voluntary* muscles and, to a degree, respiration is under voluntary control. Yet, paradoxically, these same muscles also act as *involuntary* muscles and relax and contract rhythmically without conscious effort. Researchers have discovered that the CNS contains multiple interlocking control centers that stimulate the respiratory muscles in a periodic fashion and thus produce an involuntary pattern of rhythmical breathing.

The medulla contains both an inspiration and expiration center that function in an antagonistic fashion. Stimulation of the inspiration center stimulates the respiratory muscles and temporarily inhibits the expiratory center. Conversely, stimulation of the expiration center simultaneously causes contraction of the expiration muscles and the temporary relaxation of the inspiration muscles by inhibiting the inspiration center. This oscillatory inhibition produces a crude pattern of rhythmical breathing. However, if the brain stem is cut above the medulla (leaving the inspiration–expiration centers intact), breathing becomes an abnormal pattern of gasps.

The second set of respiratory control centers is found in the pons. The pons inhalation (apneustic) and exhalation (pneumotaxic) centers act as "timers" to produce smooth rhythmical patterns of respiration.

The hypothalamus provides the third level of respiratory control. The hypothalamic nuclei can trigger either sympathetic arousal that produces deeper and faster breathing or parasympathetic arousal that produces shallower and slower breathing. Given that a number of limbic structures stimulate the hypothalamus, it should be stressed that the term *hypothalamic control center* should not be taken literally.

Broca's area and the motor areas of the cortex are the fourth level of respiratory control. Speech production involves a complex pattern of expiration, vocal cord contraction, and tongue movements. Activation of Broca's area temporarily overrides the rhythmical respiration cycle produced by subcortical control centers. Similarly, behaviors such as holding your breath or playing a wind musical instrument demonstrate that the motor cortex can also temporarily supercede subcortical control centers. It should be noted that such cortical control is quite transient and is inhibited by either an excess or a shortage of carbon dioxide in the bloodstream.

The respiratory centers in the CNS are stimulated by a wide variety of sensory receptors. Specifically, CNS respiratory centers receive input from pressure and chemical receptors in the carotid artery and the aorta; from stretch receptors in the lungs, the skeletal joints, and the anal sphincter; from blood temperature receptors in the hypothalamus; and from pain and cold receptors located in the skin. These various sources of sensory feedback allow the respiration control centers to produce reflexive adjustments in respiration rate and depth. For example, despite the importance of oxygen to true respiration, the CNS control centers are surprisingly hyposensitive to blood oxygen levels but are hypersensitive to blood levels of carbon dioxide. Even large changes in blood oxygen levels have rather delayed effects on respiration, but sudden small shifts in blood carbon dioxide levels induce reflexive changes in respiration. Increasing carbon dioxide levels elicits increased respiration, whereas decreasing carbon dioxide levels inhibits respiration.

The sensitivity of the brain to carbon dioxide levels is extremely easy to demonstrate. If you lie down and force yourself to breath very deeply (hyperventilate) for about 2 minutes, you will expel an excessive amount of carbon dioxide and produce a shortage of carbon dioxide in the blood called *acapnia*. As carbon dioxide levels drop, you will become dizzy and experience sensory hallucinations such as tingling in the limbs. Your breathing will involuntarily stop temporarily (apnea), which allows your blood levels of carbon dioxide to return to normal. If you repeat the demonstration while breathing into a paper bag, however, the symptoms do not occur because you are reinhaling carbon dioxide that you expelled during hyperventilation.

Hyperventilation is normally inhibited by acapnia-induced apnea. However, some individuals may react emotionally to the symptoms of hyperventilation and thus inadvertently prolong hyperventilation. We will discuss panic (anxiety)- and asthma-related hyperventilation attacks later in this chapter.

6.1.1. Methodological Issues in Respiration Research

Respiration volume can be measured directly by having subjects breathe through a gas mask and by recording the amount of air inhaled and exhaled. Although this spirometer technique is still employed in medical research, subjects often report that breathing through a mask for any prolonged period of time is extremely uncomfortable. Thus spirometer recording may, itself, act as a stressor. To minimize stress to the subjects, psychophysiologists commonly employ indirect recording techniques such as thermal recording and pneumography.

In thermal respiration recording, a sensitive electronic thermometer is taped or held in place in a mask next to the nostrils. Inhalation draws environmental air past the thermometer producing a temperature decrease, whereas exhalation releases air that has been warmed in the lungs and thus produces a temperature increase. These temperature changes can be plotted by a chart recorder to produce an accurate record of respiration rate but not depth.

Pneumography is another commonly used indirect technique for recording respiration. In this technique, air-filled rubber bellows are strapped around the chest and/or abdomen. A small tube connects the bellows with a pressure transducer. As the chest or abdomen expands suring inspiration, air pressure decreases in the bellows. Conversely, as the chest or abdomen contracts during expiration, air pressure increases inside the bellows. The plot of these pressure changes appears similar to that produced by thermal recording. However, with the pneumographic method, the height of each wave does reflect respiration depth *if* both chest and abdominal recordings are made simultaneously (Hassett, 1978). The need for simultaneous recording at both the chest and abdomen reflects individual differences in breathing "style." Subjects who habitually breathe abdominally may show marked increases in respiration depth with little change in chest diameter. Conversely, subjects who breathe intercostally may show marked increases in respiration depth with little change in abdominal diameter.

Kovats, Kiss, Naszlady, and Nemeskeri (1981) have experimented with the use of different photographic techniques (projection of rectangular grids, virtual prisms, mirrors, and stroboscopic lighting) to measure respiration rate and depth in freely moving human subjects. Although photographic techniques may eventually provide a nonintrusive method for quantifying respiration, such methods are not currently employed by most respiration researchers.

Due to the relative simplicity of recording techniques, respiration research is less prone to equipment artifacts than other physiological research (Stern, Ray, & Davis, 1980). The most common artifacts in respiration research are reactive effects and sample bias.

Reactive effects are due to the intrusive nature of the recording techniques and are of particular concern because subjects have a higher degree of voluntary control over respiration than most other physiological responses. Moreover, subjects may react emotionally to discomfort produced by the recording equipment (e.g., "I can't breathe normally with this damn mask on") or to the sexual connotations of the chest bellows in pneumographic recording.

Sample biases are another major source of artifacts in respiration research. Like cardiovascular activity, respiration activity varies with a number of subject variables (age, body size, physical conditioning, sex, etc.). For example, the average respiration rate (inspiration–expiration cycles per minute) is 44 for infants, 26 for children, 17 for young adults, and 20 for elderly adults. The higher respiration rates of infants and children are partially due to their higher metabolic rates. Another contributing factor to higher respiration rates during infancy and childhood is that the total volume of air that can be inspired varies with body (and therefore lung) size.

Sex is another potential source of sample bias. Although no sex differences in respiration are observed prior to puberty, after puberty women consistently show lower oxygen consumption but higher pulse rates during exercise than men (Astrand & Astrand, 1978). When respiratory data are adjusted for body weight, women still average about 80% of the oxygen consumption of men. This sex difference appears to be due to a number of physiological factors (Falls, Baylor, & Dishman, 1980). First, given that the average adult male is physically larger than the average adult female, it is not surprising that lung capacity of the average male is 1.4 liters greater than the average female. Second, adult women have a higher percentage of body fat and a smaller percentage of active muscle mass than adult men. Because muscle absorbs more oxygen than fat, the observed sex difference in respiration may be due to sex differences in body composition. Third, an adult woman's blood has lower oxygen-carrying capacity (hemoglobin concentration) than a man's blood. Fourth, women's respiration and heart rates vary with the menstrual cycle and are slower during preovulation than postovulation (Little & Zahn, 1974). It should be noted that the observed sex differences in respiration do not imply that males have a biological advantage. Indeed, Hannon (1978) found that females adapted faster than males to the respiratory stress of high altitudes.

Sex differences in clothing may also partially account for the observed sex differences in respiration. Although "sticking your chest out and pulling your stomach in" is stereotyped in our culture as "good posture" for both sexes, the use of girdles and other restrictive clothing to achieve this posture has traditionally been stereotyped as feminine. Not surprisingly, the higher incidence of intercostal breathing patterns has been reported in women rather than in men (Clausen, 1951). Simply removing the subjects' clothing may not eliminate the sex differences in clothing-related respiration patterns. Women who habitually wear girdles adapt their breathing to restricted abdominal movement. Although removing the girdle theoretically allows the individual to breathe abdominally, she may continue breathing intercostally due to habit.

6.2. EMOTIONS AND RESPIRATION

During the early 1900s, a number of researchers reported that specific emotional states such as anger could be distinguished on the basis of respiration patterns alone. Contradictory findings, however, soon led researchers to conclude that respiration was an unreliable index of emotional states (Woodworth & Schlosberg, 1952; Hassett, 1978). Accordingly, prior to the early 1970s, laboratory research on the relationship between respiration and emotion was extremely sparse. For example, Ax (1953) reported that respiration rate increased during fear and decreased during anger. Such reports, however, were generally ignored as researchers focused upon "more" reliable physiological indices of emotional arousal such as EDA and cardiovascular activity.

Over the past two decades, research on the issue of "voluntary versus involuntary responses" has led to a mild resurgence in interest in the relationship between respiration and emotional states. Scientists have debated whether humans are capable of learning to consciously control "involuntary" autonomic responses either directly (e.g., mentally lower your heart rate) or indirectly by consciously manipulating other physiological responses such as decreasing heart rate by decreasing skeletal muscle tension. Given that respiration is paradoxically both an involuntary and voluntary response, it is not surprising that respiration has played a central role in the "self-control" debate.

6.2.1. Respiration as an "Involuntary" Response

Critics of the "self-control" position argue that humans, like other animals, are genetically programed to display specific involuntary responses during emotional states. For example, crying consists of an inspiration followed by a series of short convulsive expirations accompanied by vocal cord vibrations. Laughter involves an almost identical pattern of respiration as crying, and often the two responses merge into an indistinguishable pattern (e.g., "I laughed so hard that I cried"). Sobbing involves a series of convulsive inspirations followed by a single long expiration. Screaming involves a long forced expiration accompanied by high-pitch vocalizations. Such emotional respiratory behaviors are found cross-culturally and, thus, are presumably genetically determined.

Although such emotional respiratory behaviors can be both voluntarily suppressed and "faked," such attempts at self-control may themselves produce distinct involuntary changes in respiration. To examine this issue, we will focus on two fascinating research areas—lie detection and humor.

6.2.1.1. Lie Detection Research

The lie detector, or field polygraph, exam is based on the assumption that humans have little conscious control over the physiological correlates of emotional states. Presumably, both guilt associated with lying and fear of detection elicit distinct patterns of autonomic arousal that can be detected by simultaneously recording EDA, pulse rate, BP, and chest and abdominal pneumography (Smith, 1967). The actual polygraph exam consists of a structured interview in which the subject is instructed to answer "yes" or "no" to a series of carefully constructed questions.

The most commonly used form of lie detection interview is called the control question technique. Some of the questions are "neutral," items, such as "Is your name John [Jane] Doe?" Mixed in with neutral questions are "critical" (crime-related) questions, such as "Did you steal X dollars from your employer?" Presumably, higher physical arousal to the critical rather than neutral questions is indicative of lying. One potential problem with this technique is that an innocent individual may also respond emotionally to critical questions.

A less commonly used polygraph interview technique is called the *guilty knowledge test*. The subject is asked a series of highly related questions, such as "did you stab her with a knife? Scissors? An icepick?" Presumably, only the guilty party has specific information about the *details* of the crime and thus should show higher physiological arousal to the actual murder weapon. An emotionally aroused but innocent subject should respond equally to all three weapons.

The use of field polygraph exams in criminal investigation dates back to the 1890s with the pioneering work of the Cecsare Lombroso (Hassett, 1978). Although the average person associates lie detection with criminal investigations, American courts rarely accept polygraph exams as evidence. Polygraph exams are more commonly used to screen employees in both government and industry. Lykken (1974) estimated that several million polygraph exams are given every year in the United States alone.

Laboratory researchers have long suspected that the field polygraphers' claims of "95% to 99% accuracy" were highly inflated (Munsterberg, 1908). Empirically testing the accuracy of polygraph exams, however, is extremely difficult. In order to determine whether the results of the polygraph were correct or in error, one must know the individual's absolute guilt or innocence.

One approach used to estimate the validity of polygraph exams is *post hoc* analysis. Court cases are selected in which the defendants were administered polygraph exams *prior* to trial. Individuals who later confessed or were convicted are classified as guilty, and individuals who were later acquitted are classified as innocent. The court outcome can then be compared to polygraphers' judgment of guilt or innocence. Across studies, the accuracy rate of polygraph exams (defined by later convictions or acquittals) ranges from 88% to 94% (Grings & Dawson, 1978). Lykken (1979) noted that when the field polygraph operators score the charts blindly (i.e., without interviews), their accuracy rates drop to 64% to 71%. Similarly, Kleinmuntz and Sczuko (1984) found that when six professional polygraph operators were asked to score the physiological records blindly, they misclassified 39% of the innocent individuals as guilty. One "professional" operator misclassified 62% of the innocent subjects.

The major flaw with the *post hoc* analysis approach is that the individual's guilt or innocence is never absolutely known. Innocent people confess (for whatever reason) to crimes they did not commit. Moreover, juries convict some unknown percentage of innocent people and free some unknown percentage of guilty people. Indeed, if human judgments were infallible, there would be no need for polygraph exams.

In order to control subjects' guilt or innocence, researchers attempted to reproduce the testing situation of field polygraph exams in the laboratory by employing a social induction technique called the *mock* crime (Lykken, 1959). Each subject is given a "role" (spy, police officer, hardened criminal, etc.), and an elaborate script of a "crime" to act out. For example, the subject may be instructed to "steal" an object from a faculty member's office. Commission of the mock crime and, thus, each subject's "guilt" or "innocence" can be objectively documented.

One methodological problem laboratory researchers face is how to score physiological data for "lying." Field polygraph operators use a variety of scoring systems and many rely on a global, or Gestalt, pattern of sympathetic arousal (Smith, 1967). In order to establish a more standardized scoring system, researchers have attempted to identify the types of physiological changes that field operators intuitively use. For example, field operators commonly interpret sudden stoppage (respiration blocks) or slowing of respiration rate as indicative of lying (Reid & Inbau, 1977). Although respiration blocks are unambiguous, "slowing" is not. How much does respiration rate have to decrease to indicate lying? To avoid intuitive judgments, laboratory researchers employ statistical criteria such as scoring respiration rate as "slowed" when it drops below the mean respiration rate for neutral items or for the 30-second period preceding presentation of a critical item.

Perhaps the most interesting finding to emerge from the mock crime literature was that respiration changes may be reliable indices of lying. A number of studies have found that either respiration depth, respiration rate, or both provide a valid clue to guilt or innocence (Ellson, Davis, Saltzman, & Burke, 1952; Barland & Raskins, 1972, 1975a,b; Cutrow, Parks, Lucas, & Thomas, 1972). For example, Ellson et al. (1952) obtained an accuracy rate of 77% when decreases in respiration depth were used as the sole criterion of guilt in a mock crime situation. Similarly, Szucko and Kleinmuntz (1981) found that both chest and abdominal respiration measurements were significantly related to guilt and innocence. These findings raise a puzzling question, namely if lie detection is based on discovering subjects' involuntary physiological responses to lying, why does respiration (which is partially voluntary) often provide a more valid clue to deception than other autonomic responses?

One plausible explanation for the importance of respiration data in lie detection is that respiration changes may themselves be valid indices of deception. Smith (1967) noted that subjects' attempts to "fake" answers are often accompanied by distinct changes in respiration. Given that other respiratory behaviors (crying, laughing, screaming, etc.) accompany emotional states, it is highly plausible that the "breath-holding" type of behavior observed during polygraph exams may represent an involuntary response elicited by the guilt and/or fear that may accompany conscious deception.

An alternative explanation is that respiration changes per se may not indicate deception. However, guilt-related respiration changes may trigger changes in BP, EDA, and HR that, in turn, are easily detected in the polygraph record. For example, Stern and Anschel (1968) reported that changes in respiration depth and rate elicit reflexive adjustment in finger pulse volume, heart rate, and skin resistance. Thus respiration changes may allow the operator to distinguish between respiration- and nonrespiration-induced autonomic changes. Consistent with this view, a number of researchers have noted that combinations of physiological measures are more accurate at determining deception than any single response measure (Cutrow et al., 1972; Szucko & Kleinmuntz, 1981).

The results of post hoc analysis and laboratory studies of lie detection are remarkably similar. In both cases, the polygraph exams accurately identified an average of about 90% of the guilty subjects and about 82% of the innocent (Grings & Dawson, 1978). Although these statistics appear impressive, it should be noted that most researchers have ignored the base rates of guilt and innocence. For example, suppose 10 out of 1,000 employees are dishonest. If we use a polygraph to decide who to dismiss, we might successfully identify 9 of the 10 thieves. However, we would also inadvertently fire at least 190 innocent employees. In such situations, the use of a polygraph to detect dishonest employees is analogous to using a howitzer to kill flies. Both approaches are "effective" but raise serious ethical questions about their social implications.

6.2.1.2. Humor Research

Emotion researchers have the reputation of being preoccupied with negative emotions (anger, anxiety, depression, embarrassment, guilt, etc.). However, most researchers also have a sense of humor and occasionally we even study it. As early as 1916, researchers observed that laughter was associated with unique patterns of respiration (Feleky, 1916). For example, "belly laughs" are associated with spasmodic contractions of the abdominal muscles.

Numerous studies have documented respiration changes during humor. Averill (1969), for example, randomly assigned 54 male subjects to either a comedy film, a sad film, or a control film and recorded their chest respiration during the film. Subjects' self-reports confirmed that the respective films elicited mirth, sadness, and no emotion. Subjects who viewed the comedy showed significantly more respiration irregularities and higher respiration rates. Comparison of the subjects' respiration records with tape recordings of the noises they made during the film revealed that respiration irregularities correlated significantly with laughter (+.86), whereas respiration rate did not (+.11).

Sveback (1975) compared the chest and abdominal responses of 12 men and 13 women to a "candid camera"-type comedy film. Increases in abdominal respiration depth were associated with laughter in the female subjects but not in the male subjects. Sveback speculated that the observed sex differences may be due to sex differences in habitual breathing patterns. However, it is also equally plausible that the females found the film "funnier" than the males.

Sveback's study nicely illustrates many of the methodological problems inherent in studying humor. "What's funny?" varies with cognitive development (McGee, 1979), personality (Eysenck, 1942), and a variety of other factors. For example, depending upon the social context, at least seven distinct types of laughter (apologetic, anxious, derisive, humorous, ignorant, social, and tickle-induced) can be discriminated (Giles & Oxford, 1970). An individual who would respond with humorous laughter to a "dirty joke" in private may display anxious or social laughter if the same joke were told in public.

6.2.2. Respiration as a "Voluntary" Response

Proponents of self-control argue that both the lie detection and humor literatures suggest that at least a significant minority of individuals can successfully "fake" emotional behaviors and inhibit displays of emotional states. Researchers, however, disagree over how such physiological self-regulation could be achieved. As we will discuss in greater detail in Chapter 10, actors commonly use two techniques for reproducing emotional behaviors. In "nonmethod" acting, the actor attempts to consciously produce the desired response such as crying. In "method" acting, the actor concentrates on a memory or mental image associated with the appropriate emotional state and thus attempts to consciously trigger an "involuntary" response. Researchers examined whether either of these acting techniques may be effective in controlling "involuntary" autonomic responses.

Researchers who adopt the "nonmethod" approach simply instruct subjects to consciously produce a specific physiological response. For example, Engel and Chisms (1967) instructed subjects to either increase or decrease their respiration rate by 20% for a 10-minute period. In both conditions, heart rate remained constant and finger pulse volume decreased. However, respiration rate produced differential changes in the beat-by-beat variability in heart rate. Slow breathing increased heart rate variability, whereas fast breathing decreased it. Similarly, Sroufe (1971) found that changes in respiration rate produced changes in the beat-by-beat variability in heart rate, whereas changes in respiration depth produced changes in both heart rate level and variability. Deep breathing produced an increase in heart rate and variability. Conversely, shallow breathing produced decreases in heart rate and variability. Thus the common advice of "take a deep breath and relax" may produce (not reduce) cardiac arousal.

The observed yoking of respiration and other autonomic responses led researchers to explore whether teaching subjects to breathe at specific rates (paced respiration) would be effective in reducing autonomic arousal to stressors. Harris, Katkin, Lick, and Habberfield (1976) randomly assigned male subjects to either a paced respiration condition (8 inspirations per minute) or one of two control groups. Subjects in the paced respiration group were presented with a light that blinked on and off and were instructed to inhale when the light was turned on. After the experimental subjects were given 10 minutes of training synchronizing their breathing with the light, all subjects were informed that they would be presented with two tones that might be accompanied by an electric shock. Three minutes later, the tone was presented and followed by a painful electric shock. After another 90 seconds, the second tone was presented but was not followed by an electric shock. Subjects in the paced respiration group showed lower EDA to the electric shock than control subjects. However, no reduction in cardiac responses to shock was observed in the paced respiration group.

Holmes, McCaul, and Solomon (1978) examined whether teaching subjects to maintain a normal resting breathing rate and depth would reduce their reaction to stressors. Experimental subjects were given a record of their own resting respiratory patterns and instructed to attempt to duplicate the model with the movement of the polygraph pen by controlling their breathing. This biofeedback procedure allowed subjects to duplicate both respiration rate and depth. However, the respiration biofeedback training had no effect on either subjects' emotional or cardiac arousal to the threat of electric shocks. In a second experiment, subjects were assigned to either slow respiration (8 inspirations per minute), normal respiration (16 inspirations per minute), or control conditions (McCaul, Solomon, & Holmes, 1979). Slow respiration produced reductions in EDA and pulse volume responses to the threat of electric shock but had no effect on heart rate. Subjects in the slow respiration group also reported lower anxiety than subjects in the other two conditions. In a third experiment, male and female subjects were taught to inhale quickly but to exhale slowly in order to slow respiration to about 6 inspirations per minute (Cappo & Holmes, 1984). Again, slow respiration produced reductions in both EDA and subjective arousal to the threat of electric shocks.

One of the major criticisms of the paced respiration studies is that subjects are given minimal training at controlling respiration prior to the presentation of the stressors. Clinical stress-reduction programs that incorporate breathing exercises (autogenics, progressive relaxation, etc.) generally encourage clients to practice their exercises on a daily basis for weeks *before* attempting to use their exercises to cope with stressful situations. In sharp contrast, laboratory studies have often given subjects 10 minutes of practice at paced respiration. Obviously, the degree of mastery of respiration that subjects acquire after such brief training is highly questionable. For example, in one paced respiration study conducted in my laboratory, we noted that a large percentage of subjects who received brief training "forgot" to breathe regularly when presented with stressors (Beck, Thompson, & Adams, 1981). Such observations suggest that paced respiration may be ineffective as a "brief" form of stress-reduction training. Whether prolonged training would improve subjects' abilities to pace their respiration in stressful situations is currently an open question.

Fenz and Epstein's (1967) naturalistic study of experienced and novice parachutists strongly suggest that paced respiration may be an effective self-control technique. Novice parachutists showed a marked increase in respiration rate from the time they arrived at the airport until the time they jumped from the plane. In contrast, experienced parachutists showed only a modest increase in respiration rate during takeoff and then reductions in respiration rate (despite increasing altitude) until the point of the jump. These respiration changes occurred *prior* to changes in EDA and HR in the experienced jumpers. The authors speculated that

> if the assumption is made that an inhibitory process is responsible for the decline in response of experienced parachutists, then respiration is inhibited first and skin conductance last, with heart rate more similar to skin conductance. It is noteworthy that the order corresponds to the degree to which conscious control of, and feedback from, the different system is possible. (p. 41)

The overall pattern of results of the paced respiration studies suggests that in stressful situations respiration appears to be yoked with EDA but only partially yoked with cardiac activity. These findings are puzzling only if we conceive of sympathetic arousal as a unitary phenomenon. Numerous researchers have argued that the complex system of interlocking CNS controls causes physiological systems to function in a quasi-independent fashion (Lacey, 1959; Obrist, Howard, Lawler, Galosy, Meyers, & Gaeblein, 1974). As discussed previously in Chapter 4, the coupling-decoupling of cardiac activity and other physiological responses appears to be dependent on both attention (environmental intake rejection) and on the active-passive coping behaviors used to deal with the threat.

Given that both attention and active-passive coping behaviors reflect subjects' cognitive coping strategies, it would appear that cognitive activity and physiological arousal may be intimately related. Not surprisingly, numerous authors have argued that techniques such as "method" acting that focus on consciously manipulating cognitions may be effective means of physiological "self-control." For example, studies have consistently found that respiratory changes may accompany emotional images. Lang, Melemed, and Hart (1970) reported that subjects showed higher respiration rates visualizing fear than neutral scenes. Similarly, Craig (1968) noted that respiration rate decreased during a cold pressor test but increased when subjects imagined or witnessed another subject taking a cold pressor.

Clearly, "hot" (emotional) cognitions can elicit distinct changes in respiration. However, researchers disagree over what constitutes a "hot" cognition. Specifically, are "hot" cognitions vivid representations of external events, or are they codes for emotional physiological responses, or both?

Carroll, Marzillier, and Merian (1982) examined whether imagery instructions that focus on stimulus characteristics (mental pictures) or that emphasize response characteristics (somatic sensations such as vomiting) were more effective at eliciting emotional arousal. A total of 24 female and male subjects were divided into stimulus imagery or response imagery conditions. Each subject was instructed to vividly imagine three relaxing scenes and three arousing (anxiety or excitement) scenes. In the response condition, the mean respiration rate increased 5 cycles per minute (cpm) with arousal images and decreased 2 cpm with relaxation images. In the stimulus condition, arousal images produced only a 2-cpm increase, and relaxation images produced only a 1-cpm decrease. Thus response imagery instructions appeared to have had a much greater effect on respiration than did stimulus imagery instructions.

Other researchers, however, have failed to demonstrate the importance of response components of "hot" cognition. Kantner and Ascough (1974), for example, examined the physiological effects of two cognitive techniques (focusing and induced affect) for eliciting emotional states in psychotherapy. In the focusing technique, the subject is instructed to concentrate on a specific emotion (i.e., anxiety) or ongoing emotions and then try to mentally deepen the emotional experience. In the induced affect technique, the subject is first instructed to concentrate on a specific emotion and then is reinforced for any appropriate emotional behavioral display or self-report of the emotional state. Forty female subjects were assigned to focusing instruction, induced affect instructions, and no-treatment conditions. Subjects in the two treatment groups received three 8-minute periods of relaxation, anxiety, and relaxation instructions. During the anxiety period, subjects in the focusing condition reported the highest anxiety and had the highest respiration rates. Thus the focusing procedure appeared to be more effective than the induced affect technique at eliciting emotional arousal.

Current literature on respiration suggests that respiration changes during emotions may be paradoxically either "involuntary" or "voluntary" responses. For example, the same individual who is incapable of inhibiting screaming on a rollercoaster may easily inhibit screaming during a horror movie by focusing his or her attention on the artificial aspects of the special effects.

6.2.3. Respiration in Psychiatric Populations

If you ask any group of psychotherapists to name a single common characteristic that their patients share, a surprisingly large proportion will respond that "they breathe funny." Scattered throughout the clinical literature are literally hundreds of anecdotal comments about patients with a variety of diagnoses who showed rapid shallow respiration, excessive sighing, or hyperventilation.

Psychophysiological studies of psychiatric patients tend to support the validity of clinical observations. As a group, psychiatric patients tend to have shallower respiration depth but higher respiration rates than normal subjects. Roessler, Bruch, Thum, and Collins (1975), for example, recorded a variety of physiological responses from a 23-year-old female patient during four psychotherapy sessions. Ratings of the intensity of her expressed emotions were positively correlated with respiration rate (mean $r = +.40$) and negatively correlated with respiration depth (mean $r = -.33$).

Consistent with case reports, abnormal respiration patterns have also been documented in large samples of psychiatric patients. Balshan-Goldstein (1965) tested three groups of psychiatric patients (psychotics, anxiety reactions, and personality disorders) and a control group of "normal" subjects. All four groups were matched on sex and race and were drug-free at the time of testing. A number of physiological responses (including respiration rate but not depth) were recorded while subjects rested and while they were presented with loud "white" noise, that is, a combination of sound waves from all frequency bands that is commonly described as meaningless hissing. All three groups of psychiatric patients showed a slight elevation in tonic resting respiration rate (about 1.5 cpm faster than normals). When the white noise was presented, psychotic and anxiety reaction patients showed the largest increase in respiration rate (about 3 cpm), whereas normal subjects showed the smallest increase (1 cpm). Personality disorder patients showed an intermediate (1.5 cpm) increase in respiration rate.

Clinical researchers have also found that psychiatric patients are more likely to experience difficulty breathing (dyspnea). For example, Dudley, Martin, and Holmes (1968) found that anger- and anxiety-induced dyspnea were related to hyperventilation, whereas depression-induced dyspnea was associated with hypoventilation.

Burns (1971) compared a sample of depressed patients who complained of dyspnea with patients with obstructive airway disease (OAD) and noted numerous differences in the symptoms reported by these two groups of patients. For example, OAD patients complained primarily of difficulty exhaling, whereas the depressed patients complained of difficulty inhaling. Approximately 91% of OAD patients' respiratory distress was positively correlated with their level of physical exertion. In contrast, only 9% of the depressed patients reported exercise-related dyspnea, and 88% reported rest-related dyspnea attacks. About 63% of the depressed patients reported experiencing a "weight" on their chest at rest that fluctuated with their depressed mood. About 82% of the depressed patients also reported panic attacks accompanied by hyperventilation and a fear of death.

Steinhardt (1970) argued that separating psychogenic and organic respiratory dysfunctions is often extremely difficult. Patients with organic lung disease such as emphysema frequently report emotion-related respiratory distress. Conversely, patients with conversion or psychophysiological respiratory disorders may consciously deny any connection between respiratory distress and their emotional states.

One commonly cited explanation for the abnormal respiration patterns of psychiatric patients is that, because respiration depth is highly dependent on posture, psychiatric patients may simply be more likely than normal individuals to adopt postures that restrict respiration. Mechanically, the respiratory systems of animals function optimally in an quadruped posture (i.e., on all fours). In this position, gravity pulls the viscera outward and thus allows the diaphragm to move freely. Upright postures place a greater mechanical strain on the respiratory system. When you stand in an upright posture, gravity pulls downward on both the viscera and the diaphragm. Thus gravity impedes deep breathing by compression of the diaphragm against the viscera during inhalation and by opposing the elastic return of the diaphragm during exhalation. In order to breathe deeply, you must force your abdomen forward to increase the amount of diaphragm movement. Standing in either a military "chest-out" posture or in a "gorilla" posture with your shoulders hunched forward further increases the mechanical effort needed to breathe deeply. Abdominal movements are similarly restricted in sitting postures.

Alexander and his followers argued that, due to learned postural irregularities, abnormal respiratory patterns are common in both psychiatric patients and in the general population (Metheny, 1952; Alexander, 1969; Barlow, 1973; Jones, 1976). Alexander systematically examined individual differences in the body movements involved in performing everyday activities. He noted that the average person habitually performed simple motor acts, such as rising from a chair, in an awkward and mechanically inefficient manner. That is, due to postural irregularities, the average person expended much more energy than was needed to perform the task. Alexander and his followers observed that simple physical exercises designed to teach clients how to correct postural irregularities also produced symptom relief from a variety of somatic and psychological disorders (Tinbergen, 1974).

Observational studies of psychiatric patients have consistently supported Alexander's hypothesis of posture-induced respiration irregularities. As a group, psychiatric patients are more likely than normal individuals to habitually adopt postures that impede respiration. For example, exaggerated gorilla postures are commonly observed in depressed patients, where contorted postures are often displayed by psychotic patients. (We will discuss these observational studies in Chapter 11.)

Reich and his student, Lowen, proposed an alternative theoretical explanation for both respiratory and postural abnormalities in psychiatric patients (Reich, 1961; Lowen, 1967, 1973, 1974, 1976). They argued that somatic symptoms are physical manifestations of unconscious psychological conflicts. For example, an individual who feels a strong but socially unacceptable impulse to scream obscenities as his or her boss may consciously deny the impulse (ego defense) while simultaneously inhibiting the emotional behavior by tensing the neck muscles to choke off the scream (body armor). Reich (1961) observed that when individuals were induced to relax abnormally tense skeletal muscles, they frequently experienced a cathartic release of specific emotional or motivational impulses. That is, the individual may spontaneously cry, laugh, scream, become sexually aroused, and so forth. Conversely, Reich observed that patients' psychological improvement was often paralleled by decreases in muscle tension. (We will discuss these findings in more detail in Chapter 11).

Both Alexanderian and Reichian therapies are fascinating attempts to expand respiration research beyond the simplistic concept of "sympathetic arousal." Unfortunately, both approaches share a common methodological flaw, namely the overreliance on clinical observation. If improvement in posture or psychological functioning does produce improvements in the depth of respiration, then such changes could be easily documented by recording respiration patterns before and after therapy. Yet after 100 years of Alexanderian therapy and about 50 years of Reichian therapy, no such documentation of the efficacy of therapy has been reported.

6.2.4. Psychophysiological Respiratory Disorders

Prior to DSM-III, only one respiratory disorder (bronchial asthma) was considered psychosomatic. Recently, researchers have identified a second psychophysiological respiratory disorder, the hyperventilation syndrome or HVS.

6.2.4.1. Bronchial Asthma

The incidence rates of asthma during childhood range from 0.7% (Sweden) to 4.9% (USA), and in adults they range from 0.6% (United Kingdom) to 5.7% (United States). The incidence of asthma also varies with age and sex (Weiner, 1977). During childhood, male asthmatics outnumber females two or three to one, whereas during adolescence, the sex ratio approaches 1:1. In females, the incidence rate of asthma increases with age, and women over the age of 45 have two to three times the incidence of asthma than do younger women. In males, asthma is most common in boys under the age of 5 and men over the age of 45.

Bronchial asthma attacks are characterized by the narrowing of the air passages inside the lungs. A number of different physiological mechanisms are involved in asthma attacks. The smooth muscles in the walls of the bronchioles and bronchi constrict spasmodically. The walls of the bronchioles swell with fluid (edema) and increase the amount of mucous secreted into the air passages. These three physiological mechanisms interfere primarily with exhalation rather than inhalation. Air flows rather freely into the lungs as they expand but then becomes trapped in the alveoli as the lungs contract. Exhalation of air through the narrowed air passages produces the wheezing and coughing characteristic of asthma attacks. In severe asthma attacks, inhalation may also be impeded by the distension of the lungs by air trapped in the alveoli and by the partial collapse of the walls of the bronchi and trachea.

Hypersensitivity to environmental antigens (allergy-triggering agents such as pollen) accounts for between 30% and 50% of all asthma cases (Holman & Muschenheim, 1972). However, researchers have also found that, in any given patient, asthma attacks can be induced by a wide variety of other physical stressors (cold, exercise, hyperventilation, infections, odors, smoke, etc.) and by psychological stressors, including emotional states. Although a given asthmatic patient may be more likely to react to antigens or infections or psychological stress, about 70% of all asthma attacks are triggered by a combination of stimuli.

The documentation of "psychophysiological" asthma attacks has unfortunately led to the development of the dangerous folk myth that asthma is "in the patient's head" (Purchell & Weiss, 1970). Regardless of whether the triggering stimuli are physical or psychological, asthma is a potentially life-threatening disease, and it accounts for about 0.6% of all deaths (Rees, 1956). In the most severe form of asthma (*status asthmaticus*), the patient suffers a continuous attack that is extremely resistent to medical treatment, and he or she may die from either heart or respiratory failure.

Mathis (1964) cited an interesting case of lethal "psychophysiological" asthma. A 59-year-old man decided to sell his business against the wishes of his domineering mother. His distraught mother repeatedly warned him that "something dire will happen to you" for being a disobedient son. Although he had no history of respiratory disease, he suffered a mild asthma attack 2 days later. Over the following 8 months, he suffered a series of violent asthma attacks after arguments with his mother. Despite repeated medical and psychiatric treatments, he died from his "imaginary" symptoms.

The most obvious approach to identifying which specific emotions trigger asthma attacks is to interview asthmatics. Surprisingly, the asthmatics' responses sound like a list of human emotional states. Common responses include anger, anxiety, depression, disgust, embarrassment, excitement, fear, guilt, humor, jealousy, joy, sadness, shame, and sexual arousal. Based on asthmatics' self-reports, it would appear that emotional arousal *per se* rather than specific emotional states triggers asthma.

Consistent with the emotional arousal hypothesis, researchers have confirmed that a variety of emotional states may trigger impaired respiration in asthmatics. For example, Clarke (1970) found that hypnotic suggestions of asthma and anger or asthma and fear elicited greater decreases in forced expiration volume than suggestions of asthma alone. Similarly, Tal and Miklich (1976) reported that instructing asthmatic children to imagine either anger or fear stimuli produced decreases in expiration flow rates. Levenson (1979) found that asthmatics displayed an empathic increase in respiratory resistance in response to a film about hospitalized asthmatic children. Stevenson and Ripley (1952) observed that adult asthmatic patients showed prolonged expiration to a variety of emotional themes, including anger, anxiety, depression, and guilt. Six of their 15 asthmatic subjects apparently experienced attacks at the beginning of, or during, the interview. Thus it would appear that *any* emotional state may trigger asthma attacks in susceptible individuals.

Purchell and Weiss (1970), however, voiced four objections to the emotional-arousal hypothesis. First, asthma attacks may be triggered by specific emotional behaviors (crying, laughing, screaming, etc.) rather than by specific emotional states. A patient who reports that depression and joy trigger his or her attacks may be ignoring a common emotional behavior (crying). Second, asthmatics may have been repeatedly told by physicians that their attacks are triggered by emotions and, thus, may mistakenly associate any concurrent emotional state with their asthma attacks. Third, asthmatics may confuse their emotional states during or after attacks with emotional triggers. Between attacks, asthmatics often react to their disease with anxiety, disgust, and embarrassment. During attacks, asthmatics often report (rather realistically) anxiety and fear. Fourth, asthmatics, like other humans, may deliberately misreport their emotional states. Moreover, a number of studies suggest that a significant minority of asthmatics are alexithymics or repressors (Dahlem & Kinsman, 1978; Kleiger & Dirks, 1980).

Purchell and Weiss (1970; Purchell, 1963) do not dispute that emotions can trigger asthma attacks. Indeed, based on clinical observations, they argued that only three negative emotional states (anger, anxiety, and depression) appear to be distinct triggers of asthma attacks. Although the results of a number of other clinical studies would appear to support this hypothesis, additional research is clearly needed to identify *which* emotions may elicit asthma attacks.

Researchers have experimented with biofeedback, muscle relaxation, and other self-control techniques to teach asthmatics to voluntarily inhibit their asthma attacks. Various reviews of these treatment programs have concluded either that they are highly promising (Knapp, 1977; Fritz, 1983) or useless (Richter & Dahme, 1982). Given the heterogenity of asthma populations, both conclusions may be valid. It is highly plausible that self-control treatment may be highly effective with asthmatics whose attacks are primarily triggered by emotions and ineffective with asthmatics whose attacks are primarily triggered by antigens or infections.

6.2.4.2. Hyperventilation Syndrome

As discussed earlier in this chapter, voluntary depletion of blood carbon dioxide levels by forced deep breathing (hyperventilation) produces a variety of symptoms that mimic the symptoms of a number of physical and psychological disorders. Specifically, hyperventilation produces cardiovascular symptoms (chest pain, rapid and irregular heartbeat), CNS symptoms (dizziness, fainting, visual problems), gastrointestinal symptoms (belching, flatulence), motor symptoms (numbness, pain, tremor, or stiffness) and respiratory symptoms (excessive sighing, shortness of breath). Hyperventilation may also produce psychological symptoms such as intense anxiety or fear or fuguelike states (Lum, 1975; Grossman & DeSwart, 1984). The physiological mechanism believed to produce both physical and psychological symptoms is reflexive vasocontriction of the peripheral and cerebral arteries in response to the low levels of blood carbon dioxide (Sim, 1963) and the resulting increase in blood pH (alkalinity).

Involuntary hyperventilation produces symptoms identical to those of voluntary hyperventilation and can be triggered by a variety of physical diseases, psychological stressors, emotions, or respiratory habits (Pfeffer, 1978). This disorder is called the *hyperventilation syndrome*, or HVS.

Currently, little is known about HVS. The incidence rate of HVS in medical patients is estimated to be in the range of 6% to 11%. However, the similarities between HVS and other disorders make misdiagnoses common (Lum, 1975; Grossman & DeSwart, 1984). The frequency of HVS in the general population or in psychiatric populations is unknown. Numerous researchers have reported high incidence rates of psychiatric disorders in HVS patients, including agoraphobia and other assorted phobias, anxiety reactions, character disorders, conversion disorders, depression, malingering, and schizophrenia (Pfeffer, 1978; Brodtborg, Sulg, & Gimse, 1984; Singh, 1984).

Given that respiration abnormalities are common among psychiatric patients, why are only a subset of patients prone to hyperventilation? Singh (1984) tested the hypothesis that hyperventilators may be hypersensitive to carbon dioxide. Three groups of psychiatric patients (anxiety, depression, and anxiety hyperventilators), a group of transcendental mediators, and a normal group were tested for CO_2 sensitivity using a rebreathing test. (The subjects reinhale their own breath so the concentration of CO_2 increases). Unexpectedly, all three groups of psychiatric patients were found to be hyposensitive to CO_2. However, inspection of the respiration record revealed that all three groups of psychiatric patients were hyperventilating *prior* to the CO_2 test. Singh speculated that psychiatric patients perceived the testing situation itself as a stressor.

Grossman, DeSwart, and Defares (1985) examined the effectiveness of pace respiration training with two groups of HVS patients. Control subjects were instructed to breathe abdominally at their normal resting rates, and experimental subjects were paced at a slower, more regular rate. At the end of 10 weeks of training, both groups showed some reduction in HVS symptoms but a much higher percentage of the experimental subjects showed "marked improvement" in respiratory function and in reduction of HVS symptomology. Although these findings appear promising, it should be noted that these HVS patients were not tested in a psychologically stressful situation.

The clinical literature nicely illustrates the paradoxical involuntary-voluntary nature of respiration. Both asthmatics and HVS patients' respiratory symptoms may be involuntary reactions to emotional states. Yet both asthmatic and HVS patients may learn to consciously control their respiration to abort their symptoms.

SUGGESTED READINGS

Barlow, W. *The Alexander technique.* New York: Knopf, 1973.

> Clear introduction to the principles of Alexander therapy. It includes a number of interesting case reports on the role of posture in respiratory and pain disorders.

Lykken, D. T. The detection of deception. *Psychological Bulletin,* 1979, *86,* 47–53.

> A critical review of the uses and abuses of "lie detectors". Lykken is one of the leading opponents of the use of polygraph exams in government and industry.

Weiner, H. *Psychobiology and human disease*. New York: Elsevier, 1977.

A detailed introduction to the massive literature on asthma. It also contains comprehensive reviews of research on other psychophysiological disorders.

Woodworth, R. S., & Scholsberg, H. *Experimental psychology* (2nd ed.). New York: Holt, Rinehart & Winston, 1952.

This work contains a concise historical review of the early literature on the respiratory correlates of emotions.

7

The Gastrointestinal System

Both aerobic (with oxygen) and anaerobic (without oxygen) cellular metabolisms require simple hydrocarbons. Although the tissues of both plants and animals are composed of hydrocarbons, these organic compounds are too complex chemically for use in cellular metabolism. The two basic functions of the gastrointestinal (GI) system are to chemically break down the complex hydrocarbons contained in food into simple hydrocarbons and to expel chemical wastes such as fiber that cannot be digested.

7.1. ANATOMY AND PHYSIOLOGY

The gastrointestinal system is a complex series of specialized organs and glands (see Figure 7-1). The alimentary canal, or GI tract, is a coiled hollow tube that stretches an average of 7.6 to 9.1 m from your mouth to your anus. The walls of the GI tract are composed of smooth muscles that rhythmically and sequentially contract (peristalsis) to propel food toward the anus. The GI tract is also segmented by valves or sphincters that help prevent food from moving backward.

The mouth, pharynx, and esophagus form the first segment of the GI tract. The mouth contains six salivary glands that secrete saliva to lubricate the food. Chewing aids the digestive process by helping crush solid foods into a semiliquid mass called a bolus. Swallowing involves a complex mixture of voluntary and reflexive motor acts. The tongue lifts the bolus backward toward the pharynx and against the roof of the mouth (soft palate). The soft palate moves upward to block off the nasal cavities, and the bolus passes through the pharynx into the esophagus.

The esophagus is a 25- to 30-cm-long tube that connects the pharynx with a valve called the cardiac sphincter that separates the esophagus and stomach. The muscle walls of the esophagus produce relatively weak contractions that help propel the bolus toward the cardiac sphincter. The pressure of the bolus against the esophagus walls causes the cardiac sphincter to relax and the bolus enters the stomach. This process is reversed during the vomiting reflex.

141

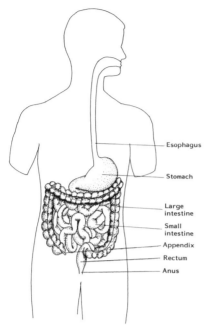

Esophagus

Stomach

Large
intestine

Small
intestine

Appendix

Rectum

Anus

Figure 7-1. Major anatomical structures of the gastrointestinal system.

The stomach is the second segment of the GI tract. Its primary function is to chemically and mechanically convert food into a liquid form (chyme). The stomach is composed of three layers of smooth muscle. Contractions of the stomach walls produce both peristalsis and mixing movements. Peristalic movements force the stomach contents to gradually move from the cardiac sphincter to the pyloric sphincter at the base of the stomach. Mixing movements circulate and expose food to the digestive juices. A mucus coating normally protects the inner lining of the stomach from damage by its own secretions of hydrochloric acid and pepsin (an enzyme that breaks down proteins). Ulcers occur when gastric juices penetrate the mucus coating and begin digesting the walls of the stomach itself.

The small intestine forms the third segment of the GI tract. The name *small* intestine is based on its diameter (about 2.5 to 5 cm) rather than its length (about 6.7 to 7.6 m). The primary function of the small intestine is to absorb minerals and nutrients from the chyme produced by the stomach. Two anatomical features help protect the inner walls of the small intestine from damage by stomach acid. First, three glands (the liver, gallbladder, and pancreas) secrete alkaline substances into the upper small intestine (duodenum) that help neutralize stomach acid. Second, irritation of the small intestine reflexively inhibits stomach contractions. Unfortunately, neither anatomical mechanism may be sufficient to prevent ulceration of the duodenum.

The large intestine or colon is the fourth segment of the GI tract and is separated from the small intestine by the ileocecal sphincter. The large intestine follows a rather curious anatomical route from the ileocecal sphincter to the rectum. The large intestine first ascends, then traverses across the abdomen and then descends. Although this 1.7-m journey may appear rather illogical, it serves the important physiological function of delaying expulsion of waste products while the large intestine reabsorbs water. The contents of the large intestine are gradually converted from fluid into a semisolid mush and then into a solid mass of waste products called *feces*. Slow movement of the contents through the large intestine causes constipation, whereas rapid movement produces diarrhea.

The rectum is a 15-cm-long tube that forms the final segment of the GI tract. The rectum is separated from the large intestine by the internal sphincter and from the environment by the external sphincter, or anus. Although the anus is commonly referred to as the only "voluntary" sphincter of the GI tract, it should be stressed that defecation is normally an involuntary reflex. In most animals (including human infants), pressure from feces against the walls of the rectum causes the opening of the anus and contraction of the rectal muscle. Humans are among the few species that can be trained to inhibit defecation.

Like cardiac muscle, the smooth muscles of the GI tract can function independently of the CNS. If the GI tract is surgically separated from the nervous system, the walls of the GI tract will continue to rhythmically contract and relax. However, normally the two branches of the autonomic nervous system control GI tract activity in an antagonistic fashion. Parasympathetic stimulation increases the rate of secretion of digestive juices (saliva, pepsin, etc.) and the rate of peristalic muscle contractions. Conversely, sympathetic stimulation inhibits the digestive processes. The two primary GI-tract control centers are located subcortically (medulla and hypothalamus). However, the cortices play an important role in exciting and inhibiting digestion. For example, simply fantasizing about your favorite food may produce both salivation and audible stomach contractions.

7.1.1. Methodological Problems in GI-Tract Research

Both the anatomical and physiological characteristics of the GI tract create numerous technical difficulties in recording its physiological activity. Recording devices attached to tubes can be inserted down the pharynx into the stomach or through the rectum into the descending large intestine. However, the convoluted shape of the GI tract effectively limits the insertion of recording devices beyond these points.

The physiological characteristics of the GI tract also make skin surface recording difficult. Compared with electrical signals produced by other internal organs, the voltages produced by GI-tract activity are extremely weak. Thus the electrical activity of the heart and skeletal muscles tends to mask the biopotentials produced by the GI tract. Moreover, the frequency of GI-tract contractions is extremely low compared with skeletal or cardiac muscle. Unfortunately, the slow waveforms produced by the GI tract are often difficult to discriminate from equipment artifacts (electronic drift, etc.).

GI-tract researchers have invented a number of ingenious recording techniques to circumvent the anatomical and physiological barriers to studying GI-tract activity. Because internal and external recording techniques each create their own unique methodological problems, we will discuss these two classes of techniques separately.

The oldest internal recording devices were balloons that were inserted into the stomach or rectum and then inflated. Mechanical contraction of the stomach or rectum increases the air pressure in the balloon that then can be detected by an external pressure transducer. For example, Whitehead, Engels, and Schuster (1980) used a series of three balloons to simultaneously record activity of the large intestine, internal sphincter, and external sphincter. The major methodological criticism of the balloon technique is that the balloon itself may stimulate abnormal contractions of the walls of the stomach or rectum.

To avoid internally stimulating the walls of the GI tract, smaller internal recording devices have been invented. For example, muscle tension sensors can be mounted inside a small plastic tamponlike probe and inserted into the rectum. Orr (1983) described a rather clever device for simultaneously recording pressure at different points of the esophagus. Three pressure transducers are mounted at different intervals inside a narrow plastic tube. The tube is inserted down the subject's nose until the transducers enter the stomach. The tube is then slowly withdrawn producing a series of simultaneous recordings of pressure gradients along the esophagus.

The major methodological problem produced by insertion recording devices is that the recording techniques are "intrusive" and therefore may cause the subject to experience both physical and psychological discomfort. For example, many subjects report feeling apprehensive about "choking to death" when recording devices are mechanically inserted into the esophagus. Similarly, due to our cultural taboo about anal intercourse, both men and women commonly report feeling "sexually violated" when recording devices are inserted into their rectums. Such emotional reactions to the recording procedures clearly constitute a major artifact in studies of the role of emotion in GI-tract activity.

An alternative technique for internally recording GI-tract activity is to have the subject swallow a target (radioactive dye, magnet, radiotransmitter, etc.) that can be tracked by external sensors. For example, Jacobson (1938) used radioactive dye to demonstrate the role of skeletal muscles in psychophysiological disorders of the GI tract. Like other soft tissues, the muscles of the GI tract are translucent in X-ray records. Ingestion of radioactive dye, however, makes the GI tract clearly visible on X-rays. Jacobson documented that teaching patients to relax skeletal muscles also produced relaxation of the underlying GI muscles. Although the ingestion technique is less intrusive than insertion techniques, it should be stressed that, due to individual differences in GI-tract motility, the researcher has limited control over the location of the target. Averill (1969), for example, intended to study stomach movements during sad and comic films by having subjects swallow a small plastic-covered magnet. Magnetometer readings, however, indicated that the magnet passed too quickly through the stomach to provide a valid record of stomach activity during a film.

A less intrusive technique for recording GI activity is commonly called the electrogastrogram (EGG) because it is most often used to record stomach motility. However, the same technique is employed to measure small and large intestine activities. Surface electrodes are pasted to the skin surface over specific organs to detect the electrical signals produced by GI-muscle contractions.

The main technical problem with EGG recording is locating electrodes directly over the target organ. The location of the stomach and other components of the GI tract shifts radically, depending on whether the organ is empty or full and whether the subject is standing, sitting, or reclining. A number of researchers have reported that the use of multiple recording sites minimizes the problem of organ displacement and that EGG records show a relatively good correspondence to muscle contractions recorded by internal probes (Abell, Tucker, & Malagelada, 1983; Holzle, 1983; Koch & Stern, 1983).

One of the major problems in GI-tract research is that the recording techniques themselves may produce subject self-selection and thus biased samples. Ethically, participants in experiments are supposed to give their "informed consent." However, once informed that internal recording techniques will be used, many potential subjects may refuse to consent.

Another major methodological problem in GI-tract research is that subjects' expectations may alter GI-tract activity. Sternbach (1964) recruited six undergraduate subjects for a "drug" experiment. The subjects were informed that they each would be given three different drugs at different times. One drug was a stimulant that would increase stomach contractions; the second drug was a relaxant that would reduce stomach contractions, and the third drug was a placebo. All three drugs were plastic-coated magnets used to record stomach movements. Four of the six subjects showed the "expected" pattern of stomach motility. That is, they showed increased stomach contractions to the "stimulant" and decreased stomach contractions to the "relaxant."

7.2. EMOTIONS AND GI-TRACT ACTIVITY

Although many of our subjective descriptions of emotional states (lumps in the throat, knots in the stomach, etc.) clearly refer to sensations of changes in GI-tract activity, laboratory research on GI activity of healthy humans during emotional states is extremely sparse. Indeed, many psychophysiology books simply omit the GI tract completely. As you will see in our following discussion, the available literature clearly indicates that specific emotional states may either excite or inhibit the activity of specific components of the GI system.

7.2.1. Mouth and Esophageal Activity

Although salivation is relatively easy to measure, relatively few researchers have attempted to use salivation as an index of emotion. In a series of recent studies, Morse and his associates reported that both the volume and chemical characteristics of saliva differ during anxiety and relaxation (Morse, Schacterle, Furst, & Bose, 1981; Morse, Schacterle, Esposito, Furst, & Bose, 1981; Morse, Schacterle, Furst, Brokenshire, Butterworth, & Cacchio, 1981; Morse, Schacterle, Furst, Goldberg, Greenspan, Swiecinski, & Susek, 1982). Specifically, salivary volume and pH decreased during stressful situations (dental surgery, classroom exams), whereas salivary proteins increased. Conversely, salivary volume and pH increased and salivary proteins decreased during relaxation (anesthesia, meditation, hypnosis). Borgeat, Chagon, and Legault (1984), however, failed to replicate Morse's findings using stressful intellectual tasks to induce anxiety. They found that salivary characteristics did not vary before and after stress or relaxation manipulations but rather differed between stress and relaxation testing sessions. They argued that salivary characteristics reflect "general apprehension" rather than state anxiety.

Spasmodic nonpropulsive contractions of the esophagus have been frequently observed in medical patients during periods of emotional stress. Stacher, Schmierer, and Landgraft (1979) found that esophageal contractions could be elicited by loud tones. Stacher, Steinringer, Blau, and Landgraft (1979) repeated this experiment but included measures of heart rate, respiration, and skeletal muscle tension. Because the tone-induced esophageal contractions roughly paralleled heart rate increases, the authors concluded that esophageal contractions were a component of the defense reflex.

7.2.2. Stomach Activity

The earliest documentation of stomach (gastric) changes during emotional states was reported by Beaumont (1833). One of his patients had suffered a gunshot wound in the stomach that healed incompletely creating a fistula (artificial hole). Beaumont observed that the patient showed increased gastric activity (blood flow and contractions) when angry. Over a century later, Wolf and Wolff (1947) confirmed Beaumont's findings and noted that specific emotions such as depression and fear produced decreases in gastric activity (acid secretion, blood flow, motility), whereas anger and resentment produced increases.

Despite the clear evidence that different patterns of gastric activities may reflect different emotions, the bulk of the available literature has focused on the relationships between the perception of gastric activity, emotions, and eating behaviors. In a series of experiments, Stunkard and his associates attempted to isolate the relationship between the perception of stomach contractions and obesity (Stunkard, 1959; Stunkard & Koch, 1964; Griggs & Stunkard, 1964). In these experiments, stomach contractions were recorded by an intragastric balloon while the experimenters periodically asked subjects if they felt "hungry" or "not hungry." Normal-weight individuals' self-reports of hunger were positively correlated with stomach activity. That is, hunger was generally reported during periods of stomach contractions. Obese individuals' self-reports of hunger, however, were almost randomly related to stomach contractions.

Based on Stunkard's findings, Schachter hypothesized that obese individuals were hypersensitive to external hunger cues (food smells, food taste, time of day, etc.) but hyposensitive to internal hunger cues such as stomach motility (Schachter, 1967, 1968, 1971). Schachter and other researchers have conducted a series of experiments that generally support the hypothesis that obese individuals' eating patterns may be controlled by external stimuli. For example, Schachter, Goldman, and Gordon (1968) manipulated the stomach load (empty or full) and emotional state (fear, no fear) of normal-weight and obese subjects. The threat of a painful electric shock was used as a fear stimulus. All subjects were given a "cracker-tasting" task and informed that they should eat as many crackers as they needed to make the perceptual judgment. Normal-weight subjects in either the full stomach or fear condition ate significantly fewer crackers. The obese subjects ate approximately the same amount of crackers regardless of whether their stomachs were empty or full or whether they were anxious or nonaxious. However, the obese subjects ate about 15% more in the fear condition, which suggests that they misperceived the physiological arousal associated with fear as "hunger."

Rodin, Elman, and Schachter (1974) found that obese subjects may be hyperresponsive to external cues to emotion as well as to food. After listening to audiotapes with either neutral content (rain) or emotional content (i.e., atomic bombing of Hiroshima), obese subjects reported that they were much more upset by the emotional stories than normal-weight subjects. In a second study, the maze learning of normal-weight and obese subjects was tested under low threat (mild electric shock) and high threat (strong electric shock) conditions. Performance of the obese subjects was most disrupted by the threat of strong shock.

Other researchers have basically replicated Schachter et al.'s (1968) finding that obese subjects may misperceive the physiological arousal associated with a variety of affects as "hunger" (McKenna, 1972; White, 1973; Slochower, 1976). However, clinical studies do not support the view that obese individuals are more likely than normal-weight individuals to confuse hunger and emotional states. Leon and Chamberlain (1973), for example, conducted a 1-year follow-up of a group of 49 females and 7 males who had successfully completed a diet program. About two-thirds of these subjects had regained more than 20% of the weight that they had originally lost. The authors compared the self-report responses of these "regainers" with the remaining subjects (maintainers) and a control group of normal-weight nondieters. Approximately 29% of the regainers, 23% of the maintainers, and 8% of the control subjects reported that eating was elicited by a variety of positive and negative emotional states. In addition, approximately 26% of the regainers, 36% of the maintainers, and 28% of the control group reported that eating was primarily triggered by "boredom and loneliness." Clearly, a sizable minority of all three groups recognized that their eating patterns were yoked to "labeled" emotional states.

Pine (1985) found that stress-related eating occurred in both obese and nonobese Native Americans. He argued that the observed differences in stress-related eating patterns between Caucasian and Native American samples may reflect cultural rather than genetic differences toward food consumption.

One of the most puzzling findings in the clinical literature on dieting is that regardless of weight, some individuals eat more when they are emotionally upset, whereas other individuals eat less. Herman and Polivy (1975) proposed that individual differences in emotionally induced appetite may be mediated by an individual's biological "set point." According to the set-point model of hunger, the number of fat cells in the body mediate daily caloric demand. If actual caloric intake falls below the fat-determined set point, the individual presumably feels hungry. Herman and Polivy hypothesized that regardless of body weight, individuals who report "unrestrained" eating patterns are at or above their biological set points. Such individuals should behave like Schachter's normal-weight subjects and lose their appetite when emotionally upset. Conversely, individuals who report high levels of self-control of eating (restrained style) are presumably below their biological set points and therefore should behave like Schachter's obese subjects and eat more when emotionally upset.

Consistent with these predictions, Polivy and Herman (1976) found that both anxiety and depression produced weight losses in unrestrained subjects and weight gains in restrained subjects. Similarly, Ruderman (1985; Ruderman, Belzer, & Halperin, 1985) reported that both mood and anticipated food intake differentially influenced the eating behaviors of restrained and unrestrained eaters.

The overall pattern of findings of obesity research suggests that the "simple" motive of hunger is a complex product of hypothalmic activation, gastric motility, perception of gastric motility, emotional arousal, the salience of external cues to eating and to emotions, and a host of other factors. Perception of gastric motility appears to play a key role in mediating eating behaviors but only for unrestrained normal-weight individuals. For these individuals, negative emotional states appear to influence eating patterns indirectly by reducing gastric motility. For restrained obese individuals, gastric motility appears to play a minor role in eating behaviors, and emotions may play a more direct role in triggering eating. These individuals are more likely to both confuse emotional arousal with hunger and paradoxically to attribute their eating behaviors to specific emotional states.

7.2.3. Intestinal Activity

Studies of intestinal activity during emotional states are relatively sparse. Almy, Hinkle, Berle, and Kern (1949) observed colon motility with a proctoscope during discussions of emotionally stressful topics. (A number of authors have noted that the observational technique *alone* may have been highly stressful to subjects.) They reported that the discussion of topics that elicited anger or fear produced increases in colon motility. In a more recent study, Latimer and his associates recorded colon motility with a pressure transducer and observed marked individual differences in colon activity during emotional states (Latimer, Sarna, Campbell, Latimer, & Daniel, 1981). Some subjects showed a marked increase in colon motility, whereas other subjects showed a sharp decrease. Such individual stereotypy may account for why some individuals experience diarrhea when stressed (high motility), whereas other individuals experience constipation (low motility).

7.3. CLINICAL STUDIES

7.3.1. Psychiatric Populations

Given the sparse literature on GI-tract correlates of emotion in healthy subjects, it is hardly surprising that little information is available on GI-tract activity in psychiatric patients. However, the readers should be reminded that psychophysiological recording with psychiatric patients is also at best difficult. First, psychiatric patients' self-reports are of dubious value. For example, patients who report abdominal cramps may be reporting legitimate physical symptoms. Unfortunately, they may also be reporting delusions (e.g., they believe snakes live in their intestines), illusions (misperceptions of normal GI-tract activity), or hallucinations (e.g., "devils keep poking my abdomen with pitchforks"). Second, psychiatric patients tend to be highly reactive to physiological recording. Patients often express fears that the recording apparatus will "electrocute them" or "read their minds." The intrusive nature of most GI-tract recording techniques simply aggravates such reactive effects. Third, disruption in GI-tract activity is one of the most frequent side-effects of psychoactive medications. For example, a psychiatric patient's dry mouth may be medication-induced and be totally unrelated to his or her emotional state.

7.3.1.1. Mouth and Esophageal Activity

Although salivation is a relatively unintrusive measure, relatively few studies have reported salivation data on psychiatric patients. Toone and Lader (1979) measured salivation volume in anxious, depressed, and schizophrenic patients and found no relationship between salivation and psychiatric diagnoses. Salivation, however, was positively related to subjective appetite ratings. Thus it would appear that salivation provides an index of global GI-tract activity rather than the patient's emotional state.

Two spasmodic esophageal disorders, globus dysphagia (difficulty swallowing) and cardiospasm (blockage to the esophageal-stomach valve), were traditionally regarded as forms of conversion disorders. However, later researchers have documented organic causes for both disorders (Jacobs & Kilpatrick, 1964; Smith, 1970).

Diffuse esophageal spasm (involuntary constriction of the esophagus) is most commonly observed in anxiety patients. However, the experimental evidence suggests that this disorder is not psychogenic but rather psychophysiological. Kronecker and Metzer (1883) observed that spasmodic (nonpropulsive) contractions of the esophagus occurred during emotional arousal. Later researchers have repeatedly documented that esophageal spasms can be elicited by discussions of emotional topics (Jacobson, 1938; Falkner, 1940; Wolf & Almy, 1949; Rubin, Nagler, Sprio, & Pilot, 1962).

7.3.1.2. Stomach Activity

Research on gastric activity in psychiatric patients has focused primarily on two related research topics, eating disorders (anorexia nervosa, bulimia) and psychogenic vomiting. Although some eating-disorder patients do vomit chronically, these patients consciously induce vomiting to avoid gaining weight. Thus vomiting by eating-disorder patients should be viewed as irrational but "purposeful." In contrast, psychogenic vomiters either lack conscious control over the behavior, induce vomiting to "prove" they are physically ill, or intentionally regurgitate so they can rechew and reswallow the same food (rumination).

a. Eating Disorders. Anorexia nervosa is a severe psychiatric disorder characterized by delusions and illusions of obesity, bizarre eating behaviors intended to lose (imaginary) excess weight, the refusal to eat, and low sexual drive. Until the 1960s, the incidence rate of anorexia was extremely low, and anorexia was considered an "exotic" psychiatric disorder. However, during the 1960s and 1970s, the incidence rate of anorexia increased dramatically (Duddle, 1973), and by the early 1980s had reached epidemic proportions. In a survey of nine British schools, Crisp, Plamer, and Kalucy (1976) found incidence rates of anorexia averaged 1 per 100 female students over the age of 15. Anorexia is most common in Caucasian adolescent and young adult females. For example, in one study of the demographics of 30 anorexic patients being treated at an outpatient clinic, 30 were Caucasian, 29 were female, and the patients' ages ranged from 14 to 32 years (Herzog, 1982).

Anorexia is an extremely life-threatening disorder. The patients suffer a variety of malnutrition-induced disorders, including heart failure. An average of about 9% of anorexics die from their disorder or commit suicide. Because of both the physiopathologies and high suicide risk associated with anorexia, neither medical nor psychiatric treatment alone is adequate. Unfortunately, the long-term prognosis for anorexics after medical treatment coupled with psychotherapy is also extremely poor. Approximately 40% show long-term recovery, and an additional 30% show "improvement" (Garfinkel & Gardner, 1982).

Bulimia is characterized by secretive eating binges of large quantities of food that are terminated by abdominal pain, sleep, self-induced vomiting, or consumption of massive dosages of laxatives. Unlike anorexics, bulimics report average levels of sexual drive and behaviors. Bulimics are consciously aware that their eating patterns are abnormal and frequently go to great lengths to hide their binges. They often binge in private or migrate from restaurant to restaurant eating only a "normal" amount of each location. During binges, bulimics often report experiencing guilt, shame, and the fear that they have lost control and cannot voluntarily stop eating. After the binge is terminated, bulimics frequently report depression.

The incidence rate of bulimia, like anorexia, is currently at epidemic levels. For example, Halmi, Falk, and Schwartz (1981) reported that 13% of the college sample they tested were bulimic. Other studies have found incidence rates of bulimia ranging from 5% to 20% in samples of 13- to 23-year-old American females. Like anorexics, the majority of bulimics are Caucasian females. Most researchers attribute the sudden epidemics of anorexia and bulimia to the development of the cultural ideal that slenderness is attractive and healthy (Bruch, 1973, 1978; Palazzoli, 1978).

Unlike anorexics, bulimics often "maintain" normal or obese body weights. However, weight fluctuations greater than 10 pounds are relatively common due to alternating fasts and binges. Common medical complications of bulimia include cardiac abnormalities and failure, hernias, loss of tooth enamel (from regurgitating stomach acid), and ulcers. Estimates of the mortality rate of bulimia range from 1% to 10%. Thus, like anorexia, bulimia is a life-threatening disorder.

Researchers currently disagree about whether anorexia and bulimia are two separate disorders or simply different behavioral manifestations of the same disorder. A significant minority of anorexics display bulimiclike behaviors (habitual vomiting), and an estimated 65%–75% of anorexics later develop bulimia. Moreover, both anorexics and bulimics frequently report the symptoms of depression. For example, Ben-Tovin, Marilov, and Crisp (1979) compared 12 anorexic "food abstainers" and 9 anorexic "habitual vomiters." They found no personality or symptom differences between the two samples and noted that depression and obsessions were common in both groups of patients. Herzog (1982) reported that 75% of his sample of bulimics met at least three DSM-III criteria for depression.

One plausible explanation for the observed overlap in symptoms between anorexics, bulimics, and clinically depressed patients is that eating disorders may cause later depression. Anorexics often report becoming increasingly dissatisfied with their (imaginary) "inability" to lose weight and their (imaginary) overweight bodies. Thus, the onset of anorexia may precede self-reports of symptoms of depression. Similarly, bulimics commonly report feeling depressed after eating binges and not before them. Williamson and his associates compared personality self-report data of groups of bulimic, normal-weight, and obese women. The bulimics reported higher levels of anxiety, depression, and distortions in body image. Interestingly, both the bulimics and the obese subjects reported elevated levels of guilt (Williamson, Kelley, Davis, Ruggiero, & Blouin, 1985).

An alternative explanation for the concordance between anorexia, bulimia, and depression is that depression may cause both eating disorders. Consistent with this view, researchers have found that psychoactive drugs commonly used to treat depression may be beneficial in the treatment of eating disorders (Herzog, 1982; Halmi, 1983). However, if anorexia and bulimia are both variants of depression, why do anorexics, bulimics, and clinically depressed patients show different behavioral patterns? One possible explanation is that the three groups differ in their awareness of gastric activity. Specifically, anorexic-prone individuals may be hyposenstive to internal hunger cues, whereas bulimic-prone individuals may be hyposensitive to internal satiation cues.

Consistent with the self-perception hypothesis, Striegel (1981) found that both obese and anorexic subjects had lower correlations between self-ratings of hunger and stomach contractions than normal-weight subjects. When the subjects were given a stomach load (liquid diet formula), self-ratings of satiation were positively correlated with internal sensation for anorexic and normal-weight subjects but negatively correlated for obese subjects. Striegel's findings suggest that anorexia may be characterized by hyposensitivity to internal hunger cues coupled with slightly heightened sensitivity to internal satiation cues.

b. Psychogenic Vomiting. Psychogenic vomiters lack both the food phobias of anorexics and the food compulsions of bulimics and do not use vomiting as a "weight control" technique. However, like anorexia and bulimia, psychogenic vomiting is an extremely life-threatening disorder. Psychogenic vomiters suffer the same malnutrition disorders as anorexics and the same medical complications of regurgitation as bulimics. Not surprisingly, the mortality rate of psychogenic vomiting is estimated at between 15% to 20%. In their review of the psychogenic vomiting literature, Pazulinec and Sajwaj (1983) noted that research on psychogenic vomiting is extremely sparse and has generally consisted of individual case histories. Incidence rate, sex ratios, and/or demographic information about psychogenic vomiting are simply unavailable.

The term *psychogenic vomiting* is commonly used to denote three distinct syndromes of childhood disorders: rumination, chronic vomiting, and cyclical vomiting.

Rumination is most commonly observed in infants and is characterized by habitual regurgitation of small quantities of food that is rechewed and re-swallowed. The infants display no discomfort and apparently enjoy the act. Ruminating infants also often display a variety of other self-stimulationg behaviors such as genital manipulation, head banging, and rocking (Richmond, Eddy, & Green, 1958).

Two explanations are commonly cited for rumination. Psychoanalytic theorists argue that rumination is a symptom of anxiety and depression produced by pathological mother–child relationships. They note that the mothers of ruminating infants often have a history of psychiatric disorders and tend to be highly immature and emotionally unresponsive. Moreover, although infants cannot report their emotional states, older ruminators can. Ruminating children do tend to report anxiety, depression, and poor social relationships. Behavioral theorists argue that rumination is a learned habit that can be extinguished. Consistent with the behaviorist position, researchers have found infants can be quickly taught not to ruminate by punishing the behavior with electric shocks to the leg (Lang & Melamed, 1969) or injecting lemon juice into the mouth (Sajwaj, Libet, & Agras, 1974) or by rewarding nonrumination behaviors by training the mothers to cuddle the children (Richmond *et al.*, 1958).

Chronic vomiting is characterized by vomiting episodes that may occur as frequently as 10 times per day. Chronic vomiting usually begins in childhood and adolescence and may continue for a period of years. Kanner (1972) observed that chronic vomiting is often self-induced by hypochondriacs who use vomiting as "proof" that they are physically ill. A number of cases of self-induced chronic vomiting have also been reported with mentally retarded and psychotic adolescents and adults (Pazulinec & Sajwaj, 1983). In such cases, vomiting is clearly voluntary.

Chronic vomiting may also be an involuntary response to emotional stress (Morgan, 1985). For example, Lang (1965) reported the case of an anxious 23-year-old nurse who lost her appetite and vomited only when she was placed in new situations or received social disapproval. Similarly, Burgess (1969) reported a case of an 18-year-old woman who vomited only on the "morning after" heterosexual dates. Her vomiting initially appeared as a symbolic reaction to being sexually propositioned but thereafter occurred after all of her heterosexual dates.

Cyclical vomiting is characterized by 2- to 6-day vomiting episodes that recur at intervals of weeks or months. During the vomiting episode, the individual exhibits marked personality changes (depression, hostility, etc.) and often displays regressive behaviors (Davenport, Xrull, Kuhn, & Harrison, 1972). The episodes may occur without warning but are often precipitated by anger, disappointment, or other strong emotional states. Unlike chronic vomiting, cyclical vomiting tends to terminate during adolescence (Feldman & Fordtran, 1978).

Psychoanalytic and behavioral theorists disagree about the causes of chronic and cyclical vomiting. Psychoanalytic theorists note that psychogenic vomiters often show anxiety, depression, and poor social adjustment and hypothesize that the vomiting is a symptom of pathological family relationships. Behavioral theorists argue that self-induced vomiting is often socially reinforced. For example, if a child vomits, then his or her parents are likely to let the child stay home from school. Behavioral theorists argue that involuntary vomiting may also represent a classically conditioned response to emotional stressors. It should be noted that both the psychoanalytic and behavioral explanations of psychogenic vomiting are highly compatible. Pathological family relationships may increase the probability that the child will learn maladaptive behaviors such as vomiting.

7.3.1.3. Intestinal Activity

Cameron (1944) observed that intestinal complaints (constipation, diarrhea, excess gas) were commonly reported by anxiety patients. Later researchers refer to these symptoms as the *irritable bowel syndrome* (IBS) that we will discuss later in this chapter.

Coprophilia is a rare psychiatric disorder characterized by experiencing sexual excitement during the act of defecation or sexual arousal associated with feces. We will discuss coprophila with related disorders in Chapter 8.

7.4. PSYCHOPHYSIOLOGICAL POPULATIONS

Psychophysiological research has focused on two major disorders of the GI system: ulcers and the irritable bowel syndrome.

7.4.1. Ulcers

The term *ulcer* denotes a localized wound in the surface of the skin or a mucus membrane. If the wound is deep enough to produce bleeding, it is labeled a *perforated ulcer*. Ulcers can develop at any point of the GI tract. However, the two most common sites for ulceration are the interior walls of the stomach (gastric ulcer) and proximal segment of the small intestine (duodenal ulcer). The term *peptic ulcer* is commonly used to refer to either disorder. Although ulcers are commonly believed to be a "stomach" disorder, duodenal ulcers are actually four times more common than gastric ulcers.

The most commonly cited estimate of the incidence rate of ulcers in the United States is that 1 out every 10 Americans will suffer an ulcer during his or her lifetime. Every year, about 4 million Americans have ulcers, and between 6,000 to 10,000 die from the disorder (Weiner, 1977). Although the peptic ulcer mortality rate is relatively low in comparison to eating disorders, it should be noted that perforation can produce potentially lethal internal bleeding.

In his review of the cross-cultural incidence rates of peptic ulcers, Pflanz (1978) observed that both incidence rates and sex ratios of ulcers have fluctuated wildly within any given country over the past 150 years. He noted that statistical artifacts such as rates of hospital admission, autopsies, or changes in diagnostic procedures could not account for these changes. Similar patterns of changes in ulcer incidence and sex ratios were found in European countries, Canada, and the United States. Specifically, between 1850 and 1900, perforated ulcers were twice as common in women than in men, and women under the age of 25 accounted for approximately 50% of all cases. Between 1900 and 1940, the incidence rate stabilized for women but increased dramatically for men. During World War II, there was an increase in the incidence of ulcers in males but not females. After World War II, however, incidence rates gradually stabilized for males but increased dramatically for women. For example, the female/male sex ratio of ulcer mortality was 1:4.3 in 1951 but only 1:1.9 in 1972. Pflanz noted that radically different incidence rates and sex ratios of ulcers have been observed in non-Western countries during the same time periods. For example, in 1978, young African black males were nine times more likely to develop ulcers than their female peers. Pflanz argued that both intracultural and cross-cultural shifts in incidence and sex ratios of ulcers reflect cultural changes in sex role stereotypes and employment-related stress.

Pflanz's hypothesis that psychosocial stressors (e.g., employment) account for sex differences in ulcers is based on the assumption that psychological stressors can precipitate or aggravate peptic ulcers. Before we discuss the empirical validity of this assumption, it is important that the reader be aware of the current terminological confusion in the stress literature. Early researchers such as Hans Selye carefully distinguished between external noxious stimuli (stressors) and the organism's response (stress). Unfortunately, many later researchers have used the terms *stress* and *stressor* interchangeably. The terminological distinction between stressors and stress, however, is nontrivial. In the case of phobias, both humans and nonhuman species show stress reactions to presumably harmless stimuli. Conversely, in the case of masochism, both humans and nonhumans show nonstress reactions to harmful stimuli. Thus the presence of a stressor does not automatically imply that the organism is experiencing stress, nor does the absence of a stressor insure the absence of a stress response. For the purpose of clarity, we will use the term *stressor* to denote external noxious stimuli and the term *stress* to denote the organism's behavioral, physiological, and psychological responses.

As discussed previously in Chapter 3, Selye (1956) demonstrated that repetitive presentation of various physical stressors produces a hormonal stress response that eventually leads to the destruction of the animal's immune system and to massive gastric ulcers. Weiner (1977) noted that similar "stress ulcers" often occur in humans after severe physical injuries or ingestion of large quantities of aspirin or other medications. Thus both laboratory and clinical evidence indicate that physical stressors can produce gastric ulcers.

Animal research indicates that psychological stress may also play an important role in ulceration. Porter, Brady, Conrad, Mason, Galambos, and Rioch (1958) conducted an experiment on avoidance learning in monkeys. Each monkey was strapped in a restraining chair and received a brief electric shock to its feet every 20 seconds, unless it pushed a lever to postpone the shock for another 20 seconds. Surprisingly, a number of the monkeys died of ulceration during training.

In a subsequent experiment, Brady, Porter, Conrad, and Mason (1958) attempted to isolate the effects of physiological and psychological stresses on ulceration. Four pairs of monkeys were strapped into adjacent chairs and received electric shocks every 20 seconds. One member of each pair (the "worker") was given a disconnected lever and thus could not prevent the occurrence of the shock. The other monkey (the "executive") was given a working lever that postponed the shocks that *both* monkeys received. If the executive failed to push the lever, both monkeys received equal electric shocks. This experimental yoking procedure was cleverly designed to insure that both monkeys experienced equal physiological stress (identical shocks) while experiencing different psychological stresses. Presumably, the executive monkeys experienced the psychological stress of decision making, whereas the workers experienced the psychological stress of helplessness. Within 25 days from the beginning of training, three of the four executives died. All four executive monkeys showed extensive GI ulceration, whereas no GI abnormalities were found in the worker monkeys. The original report did not indicate the location of the ulcers, but, in a later paper, Brady (1958) commented that at least one of the executives had died from a perforated duodenal ulcer.

Serious questions were raised about the validity of Brady's study when other researchers failed to replicate his findings (Foltz & Miller, 1964; Natelson, 1977). Weiss (1968) hypothesized that Brady's results may have been an artifact of subject bias. He noted that Brady's executive monkeys had not been randomly selected but rather picked because they had made a high number of avoidance responses on a pretest. Thus the "executives" may have been more emotional than the "workers." Weiss tested his hypothesis by randomly assigning 14 trios of rats to avoidance (executive), helpless (yoked worker), and no-shock conditions. Surprisingly, the avoidance rats had significantly fewer gastric ulcers than the helpless rats, and the most severe ulceration was observed in the helpless group.

Weiss (1971a) postulated that the conflicting results of active coping on ulceration might be due to the animals' certainty or uncertainty about receiving the shock. He repeated his experiment but gave the trios of animals either a warning beeping tone, a progressive (ascending) warning tone, or no warning. In all three conditions, the avoidance groups developed less ulceration than the helpless animals. The presence of the warning signals, however, reduced ulceration in both avoidance and helpless animals. Weiss theorized that stress ulceration varied as a function of both the number of coping responses the animal made and the amount of relevant feedback it received. Situations (such as Brady's study) where the avoidance animals make a high number of coping responses but receive only negative feedback (shocks for mistakes) should produce high degrees of ulceration. Conversely, situations where the animal makes few responses but receives a large amount of positive feedback (safety signals) should produce little ulceration. In a series of experiments, Weiss (1970, 1971b,c) demonstrated that both coping behaviors and feedback mediated ulceration. For example, in one study, the animals received negative feedback (a shock) every time the avoidance animal made the correct response. In this conflict situation (high response rate-negative feedback), the avoidance animals suffered more severe gastric ulceration than the helpless animals (Weiss, 1971b).

Weiss's findings suggest that both attempts to cope and feedback on the success or failure of coping efforts may play an important role in the development of gastric stress ulcers. Whitehead and Schuster (1982) have questioned the relevance of such animal studies in understanding human ulcers. Their major objection is that 80% of human ulcers are duodenal, whereas the majority of ulcers found in animal studies were gastric. Although this objection is valid, it misses the key finding in animal research, namely that the combination of physical and psychological stressors may play a key role in the development of gastric ulcers and that even "physiological stress" ulcers may be mediated by psychological factors. For example, research with human subjects suggests that smoking and ingestion of specific drugs (alcohol, coffee, pain killers) greatly increase the risk of peptic ulcers. However, research also suggests that neither smoking or drinking alone may cause ulceration.

First, as in animal research, not all humans exposed to specific physical stressors develop ulcers. For example, nicotine acts as a stimulant to the GI tract. Although smoking may increase the risk of ulceration, not all smokers develop ulcers. Conversely, some individuals not exposed to specific stressors (i.e., non-smokers) do develop ulcers.

Second, nicotine and other drugs are not simply "stressors." Drug consumption is a learned behavior that may increase in frequency with psychological stress. For example, Castelnuovo-Tedesco (1962) noted that 12 of the 20 perforated gastric and duodenal patients he studied were alcoholics. Because alcohol stimulates stomach acid secretion, the author surmised that alcohol may have triggered the onset or recurrence of their perforations. Consistent with this prediction, he found that increased alcohol consumption had preceded perforation. However, emotional stress had also preceded increased alcohol consumption.

The overall pattern of findings of both laboratory and clinical studies strongly suggests that emotional states may play a central role in the onset and recurrence of peptic ulcers. Yet identifying how emotions may produce ulceration has proved to be an extremely difficult task. Emotions may directly produce ulceration by triggering abnormal gastric activity. Most researchers currently believe that such psychophysiological processes may be important in the development of duodenal ulcers but not gastric ulcers (Weiner, 1977). Emotions may also indirectly trigger ulceration by eliciting exaggerated coping attempts or maladaptive behaviors (e.g., alcohol consumption). Thus emotions may merely increase the individual's vulnerability and/or exposure to physical stressors rather than directly produce ulceration. Based on the available evidence, it would appear that such indirect psychophysiological processes may contribute to the development of gastric ulcers. To further complicate matters, ulceration may produce specific emotional states. For example, a survey of residents of Cincinnati, Ohio (Whitehead, Winget, Fedoraavicious, Wooley, & Blackwell, 1981), found that individuals with a history of peptic ulcers were almost twice as likely than other respondents to report either anxiety (40% vs. 20%) or depression (44% vs. 28%). The higher incidence of anxiety and depression in peptic ulcer patients may reflect either their emotional reactions to the disorder or the cause of their original ulceration.

After interviewing upper- and upper-middle-class peptic ulcer patients, Alexander (1934, 1950) noted that these patients shared a common personality profile characterized by strong conscious needs for independence coupled with strong unconscious needs for dependence. He postulated that such pseudoindependent individuals were psychologically vulnerable to specific types of life events (business reversals, family quarrels, etc.) that simultaneously threatened their conscious sense of independence and triggered their unconscious dependency needs. The occurrence of such life events may trigger strong emotional reactions that further threaten the individual's self-image and lead to maladaptive coping responses, stomach hyperactivity, and eventually to ulceration. Thus the individual's failure to adequately cope with emotions rather than emotions *per se* may produce ulceration. For example, being "dumped" by a boyfriend or girlfriend is a fairly common emotional trauma. Most people react to this situation with a combination of anger ("how could they do this to me?"), depression ("I'll miss them") and guilt ("maybe if I tried harder, the relationship would have worked"). Alexander argued that the people with an "ulcer-prone" personality experience quite a different emotional reaction because being "dumped" activates their unconscious dependence needs and threatens their conscious self-image. Presumably, they experience intense guilt over their own dependency needs and not over the breakup of the relationship. Accordingly, guilt does not lead to longing for their "lost love" (bereavement) but rather triggers intense anxiety. The individual attempts to cope with anxiety in an exaggerated fashion (overcompensation, reaction formation, repression), and these exaggerated coping efforts produce gastric hyperactivity and eventual ulceration.

Alexander's model has been the focus of considerable research interest. A few studies have strongly supported the model. For example, Weiner and his associates were able to predict 7 of the 10 cases of ulcers in a sample of 120 army recruits *with* elevated blood levels of pepsinogen (a precursor of pepsin) on the basis of projective assessment of independence–dependence conflicts (Weiner, Thaler, Reiser, & Mirsky, 1957). Other studies, however, have found only partial support for Alexander's model. For example, Cohen, Silverman, and Magnussen (1956) reported that the personality characteristics of 200 female duodenal ulcer patients clustered in three distinct groups. One group was composed of "feminine" women who were psychologically well adjusted and were proud of their feminine roles (housewife, mother). Ulceration in this group was commonly preceded by life events (gynecological surgery, menopause, birth of a grandchild, pregnancy of younger female relatives) that were a threat to their femininity. A second group of patients were characterized as "immature", that is, overtly maladjusted and highly dependent. Although their personality profile does not match Alexander's ulcer-prone personality, the most common antecedent of ulceration in this group was the loss of someone upon whom they depended. The third group was described as "masculine and aggressive" and corresponds roughly to Alexander's ulcer-prone personality. In this group, the loss of someone they depended upon was also the most common antecedent of ulceration.

After reviewing the literature on the personalities of ulcer patients, Weiner (1977) concluded that the bulk of the evidence suggests that ulcer patients are not a homogeneous group but rather a heterogeneous population containing a number of clusters of distinct personality types. Weiner noted that the strongest evidence that supports Alexander's model is based primarily on studies of upper- and upper-middle-class males and speculated that Alexander's model may be a valid "micromodel" that explains ulceration in this subgroup of patients. However, given that the majority of ulcer patients are blue-collar or poor (Kahn, 1969; Whitehead *et al.*, 1981) and that a sizable minority are women, the utility of Alexander's original model is highly questionable.

Although the empirical evidence does not support Alexander's concept of an "ulcer-prone" personality, it should be noted that empirical findings do generally support Alexander's prediction that specific types of psychosocial stressors (life events) may precipitate both emotional states and ulceration in humans. For example, all three groups of women in Cohen's study reported experiencing a major psychological "loss" (femininity, loved one) prior to the onset of ulcer symptoms. Similarly, Davis and Wilson (1937) reported that 84% of 205 peptic ulcer patients reported that they first experienced symptoms shortly after a major stressful life event.

As discussed previously in this section, the presence of stressors does not automatically produce ulceration in either humans or nonhuman species. The critical issue is whether a specific type of psychosocial stressor is associated with ulceration or whether a variety of stressors may trigger a common factor (coping style, emotional state, etc.) that produces ulceration.

Craig and Brown (1984) examined whether different types of antecedent life events differentiate patients with organic GI diseases (i.e., peptic ulcers, colitis) from patients with nonorganic (functional) GI-tract disorders (i.e., irritable bowel syndrome) and healthy control subjects matched on age, sex, marital status, social class, and other variables. All the patients were undiagnosed at the time of the assessment and had reported symptoms of abdominal pain. All subjects were given a structured interview that included questions about ongoing personal problems and stressful life events that had occurred during the previous 38 months. The subjects' later medical diagnoses were used to assign patients to the organic or functional disorder groups. Marked differences were observed in the types of life events reported by the three groups. The majority (57%) of functional disorder patients reported that a severe and personally threatening life event had occurred during the pre-illness period. Surprisingly, the majority of specific events reported by these patients involved losses and disappointments similar to those reported by psychiatric groups of depressed patients. In contrast, goal frustration (blockage of personal plans by an event) was much more commonly reported by organic disease patients. Although not statistically significant, differences were observed between the diagnostic subgroups of organic illnesses. For example, a higher proportion of upper-GI-tract-disease (esophageal, gastric, and duodenal ulcers) patients reported goal frustration than did lower-GI-tract-disease patients (67% vs. 41%). Both severe life events and goal frustration were much less frequently reported by control subjects than by either group of patients. The authors observed that organic disease patients tend to report tenacious coping efforts in the face of negative feedback prior to the disease onset. For example, one businessman was sued for not paying what he considered an unfair bill. Against the advice of his legal council, he repeatedly refused to pay and countersued twice. The net result was that he lost both cases and a fairly large sum of money in legal fees. The authors speculate that anger associated with such goal frustrations may play a central role in the development of organic GI-tract diseases.

7.4.2. Irritable Bowel Syndrome

Irritable bowel syndrome, or IBS, is characterized by abdominal pain and either diarrhea or constipation in the absence of organic disease. In many cases, diarrhea alternates with constipation. Other gastrointestinal complaints (excessive gas, heartburn, lump in the throat, nausea, and vomiting) are commonly reported by IBS patients. Historically, researchers failed to agree on a diagnostic label for IBS. Latimer (1983a) observed that 30 different diagnostic labels, ranging from adaptive colitis to vegetative neurosis, have been used. To avoid confusion with organic disorders, such as Crohn's disease and ulcerative colitis, the diagnostic label *IBS* is now commonly used.

The incidence rate of IBS is extremely high, and a diagnosis of IBS is made in between 13% to 52% of the patients examined in gastrointestinal clinics. A total of 218,000 cases of IBS were reported in American hospitals in 1976 alone. Onset generally occurs during adolescence. The sex ratio (female/male) is 2:1 in the general population (Latimer, 1983a). Among the elderly, the sex ratio is 4:1 (Sheehy, 1983). The mortality rate of IBS is zero. Schuster (1983) commented that a "few" IBS patients were suicidal but did not report incidence rates of either attempted or successful suicides by IBS patients.

IBS patients have extremely high incidence rates of psychiatric disorders (anxiety, depression, somatoform disorders). Young and his associates found a psychiatric incidence rate of 18% in control subjects and of 72% in IBS patients (Young, Alpers, Norland, & Woodruff, 1976). Other researchers have reported that psychiatric symptoms occur in 80% to 90% of IBS patients (Chaudhary & Truelove, 1962; Fielding, 1977). Moreover, these psychiatric symptoms are not reactive to the disorder. Young (1979) found that 65% of IBS patients had psychiatric symptoms prior to the onset of the disorder. In 85% of IBS patients, psychiatric symptoms occurred prior to or simultaneously with IBS symptoms. Moreover, Craig and Brown (1984) noted that IBS patients report the same types of precipitating stressful life events as psychiatric groups of depressed patients.

Given the large overlap between IBS and psychiatric populations, why do

IBS patients experience GI-tract distress, whereas other individuals with similar psychological problems do not? Latimer (1983b) noted that the following five hypotheses are commonly cited to account for IBS: (a) IBS patients have chronic abnormal (hyper- or hypo-) GI-tract motility; (b) IBS patients have episodic stress-related abnormal GI-tract motility; (c) IBS patients are hypersensitive to normal GI-tract motility; (d) IBS reports of symptoms may be unrelated to GI-tract activity; and (e) hypotheses a through d may be true for different IBS patients or the same patient at different times. Latimer argued that the clinical evidence supports the latter hypothesis that IBS patients represent a heterogeneous population. Latimer (1983a) noted that not only do IBS patients report a variety of concurrent GI-tract and psychiatric symptoms, they also concurrently report a wide variety of somatic complaints. For example, concordance rates of 26% for painful urination, 33% for painful sexual intercourse, 50% for headaches, 63% for frequent urination, and 90% for dysmenorrhea have been reported with IBS patients.

A number of studies have attempted to teach patients to reduce the frequency and severity of both organic and functional GI-tract disorders using psychoanalytic therapy, behavior therapy, various relaxation training procedures, and biofeedback. Reviews of the treatment literature concluded that, with the notable exception of traditional psychoanalytic therapy, psychotherapeutic treatments have been highly successful in producing symptom relief from a variety of GI-tract disorders (Whitehead, 1978; Whitehead & Schuster, 1982). Paradoxically, success rates have frequently been higher with patients with organic disorders. One possible explanation for this finding is that there is little secondary gain in organic disorders such as ulcers. Hence organic-disease patients may be highly motivated to learn specific coping skolls and/or to modify their lifestyles.

The GI system represents one of the major frontiers in emotion research. The few available studies suggest that folk expressions such as "you make me sick" may be at least partially valid. Moreover, the observed linkage between self-perception, GI-tract activity, emotions, and eating behaviors raises numerous interesting questions about the relationships between emotions and motives.

SUGGESTED READINGS

Burch, H. *The golden cage: The enigma of anorexia nervousa.* Cambridge: Harvard University Press, 1977.
    A good introduction to the clinical literature on eating disorders.

Holzl, R., & Whitehead, W. E. (Eds.). *Psychophysiology of the gastrointestinal tract.* New York: Plenum Press, 1983.
    An excellent collection of original articles on GI-tract correlates of emotions.

Jacobson, E. *Progressive relaxation* (2nd ed.) Chicago: University of Chicago Press, 1938.
    A classic study of the effects of skeletal muscle tension on psychophysiological disorders.

The Urinary System

The major by-products of cellular metabolism are heat, carbon dioxide, water, inorganic salts, and nitrogen compounds. In excess quantities, any of these by-products are toxic, and unless they are excreted from the body, the cells would eventually be destroyed by their own metabolic processes. The skin (Chapter 5) plays a major role in excreting excess heat, and the respiratory system (Chapter 6) plays a major role in excreting carbon dioxide. Except in extremely hot environments, the skin and lungs combined do not excrete sufficient water or salts to balance the quantities produced by cellular metabolism. Moreover, neither system excretes nitrogen compounds such as urea in any quantity. The urinary system performs the complex task of maintaining the chemical balance in the body. Without a functioning urinary system, excess nitrogen compounds accumulate in the blood (uremia), the blood becomes acidic (acidosis), and excess water accumulates in the tissues (edema). Within a few days, the individual lapses into a coma, and death occurs within 2 weeks.

8.1. ANATOMY AND PHYSIOLOGY

Three of the major components of the urinary system (kidneys, ureters, and bladder) are identical in both sexes (see Figure 8-1). The only major anatomical difference in the urinary systems of females and males is in the tube (urethra) that connects the bladder with the external environment. In females, the urethra is anatomically adjacent to but separated from the reproductive system. In males, the urethra is a component of both the urinary and reproductive systems.

The kidneys are a pair of organs that are located at the base of the rib cage. Each kidney is surrounded by a capsule (tubica fibrosa) and is embedded in a mass of fat and connective tissue that helps protect the organ from injury. The interior of each kidney contains a massive network of arterioles from the renal branch of the abdominal aorta artery and venules that are tributaries of the inferior vena cava vein. Approximately 1 million small tubular structures called *nephrons* separate the arterioles and venules in each kidney.

Each nephron functions as a two-stage filter. The entering (afferent) ar-

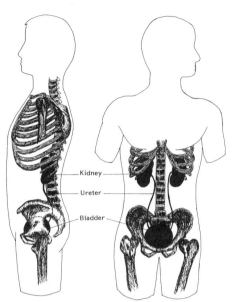

Figure 8-1. Major anatomical structures of the urinary system.

teriole branches into a looping mass of about 50 capillaries called the *glomerulus*. Blood pressure normally forces the fluid (plasma) and small molecules in the blood through the capillary walls, whereas the blood cells, plasma proteins, and other large molecules pass through the glomerulus to an exiting (efferent) arteriole. Kidney failure often occurs when blood pressure drops below 70 mm Hg systolic and becomes too low to operate this first stage of the filtering process. About 110 liters of filtrate (filtered plasma) are formed by the nephrons of both kidneys during a 24-hour period. The filtrate passes through a series of looping tubules that are surrounded by a network of capillaries that join the efferent arterioles and the venules. These capillaries reabsorb large quantities of water, glucose, sodium, chloride, amino acid, and other useful substances into the bloodstream and reduce the volume of filtrate from 110 liters to 1 to 1.5 liters of concentrated solution that is now called *urine*. Urine is composed of about 85% water, and the remaining 15% is composed of inorganic compounds (calcium, chloride, magnesium, iron, phosphorus, potassium, sodium, and sulfur) and nitrogen compounds (ammonia, creatinine, urea, and uric acid). Urine flows from the collecting tubules of each nephron into the ureters.

Each ureter is a 27-cm-long tube that connects one kidney with the base of the bladder. The walls of the ureters are composed of smooth muscle, and slow peristaltic contractions (1 to 5 per minute) force the urine toward the bladder. The ureters enter the bladder through two small slits in the wall of the bladder. As the bladder fills, internal pressure forces the ureteral orifices to be closed unless peristaltic contractions of the ureters forces more urine against the orifices.

The bladder is a balloonlike smooth muscle that can easily expand to accommodate 0.5 liters of urine without distension. If kidneys produce an abnormally high volume of urine (polyuria), the bladder can distend to accommodate more than 1 liter. The base of the bladder is located behind the symphysis pubis bone of the pelvis and is supported from below by a broad band of skeletal muscles collectively called the *urinogenital diaphragm*. The urethra connects the bladder with the external environment and contains two sphincters (see Figures 8-2 and 8-3). The internal sphincter is located at the beaklike junction of the bladder and urethra and is composed of smooth muscle. The external sphincter is located at the junction of the urethra and the pubococcygeus, or PC, muscles of the urinogenital diaphragm and is composed of skeletal muscle. Normally, both spincters are contracted (closed). This prevents urine from leaking from the bladder while the bladder is filling.

Urination (micturation) is a spinal reflex elicited by the internal pressure produced by between 0.2 and 0.3 liters of urine in the bladder. The urination reflex begins with weak rhythmical contractions of the detrusor muscle of the bladder. These contractions gradually become stronger and force the bladder downward toward the urinogenital diaphragm. These strong preurination contractions are normally perceived as the "need" to urinate. During urination, the detrusor contracts tonically while the internal sphincter simulateously relaxes

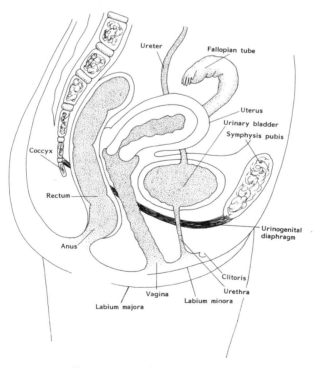

Figure 8-2. The female urinary tract.

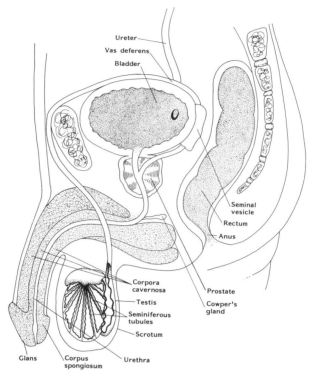

Figure 8-3. The male urinary tract.

(opens). Urine flows against the closed external sphincter that in turn reflexively relaxes (opens) and thus allows urine to flow down the urethra.

In adult females, the urethra is only about 4 cm long, and its length varies with body position. In upright positions, the female urethra averages about 4.3 cm in length, whereas, when lying down in a supine position, the urethra is compressed to about 3.8 cm (Lapides, Ajemian, Stewart, Brekey, & Lichtwardt, 1960). The external urethral orifice is located between the clitoris and vagina and enclosed by the minor and major labia (see Figure 8-2). Thus, in females the urethra is adjacent to but anatomically separate from the reproductive system.

In males, the urethra is about 20 cm long and is a component of both the reproductive and urinary systems. As shown in Figure 8-3, the male urethra passes through the prostate gland, and the ejaculation ducts join the urethra between the internal and external sphincters. During the urination reflex, the ejaculation ducts are closed while the urethral sphincters are opened. During sexual arousal, the penis becomes engorged with blood (erect) while the internal and external sphincters show increased muscle contraction. During orgasm, the ejaculation ducts open, the external sphincter relaxes, and semen is propelled down the urethra.

In most species, urination is purely a reflex act. The bladder fills until the urination reflex is stimulated, and animals urinate wherever they happen to be. Such reflexive urination occurs both in human infants and in human adults with spinal damage. Species such as cats and dogs that use urine odors (pheromones) to mark their territories display voluntary control over the urination reflex. These animals inhibit urination until they can locate a suitable object (tree, your living-room drapes, etc.) to mark with urine. Electrical stimulation studies have revealed that both the limbic systems and cortices of such species contain multiple control centers that inhibit the urination reflex (Ruch, 1966).

Research suggests that humans may also be a "marker" species and that the ability of humans to voluntarily control urination may be due to CNS centers that originally evolved to control marking behaviors. A musklike compound extremely similar molecularly to exaltolide (a synthetic compound used in perfumes) is secreted in the urine of both male and female humans. Although the concentration of this compound is approximately two times higher in male than female urine, males are extremely insensitive to its odor. Studies of exaltolide (instead of the urine) have found marked variation in females' sensitivity to the compound. Like males, prepubescent and postmenopausal women are also insensitive to the scent of exaltolide. Menstruating women, however, easily detect the odor and describe it as "pleasant or sweet" (Schiffman, 1982). Moreover, menstruating women's sensitivity to exaltolide varies with the menstrual cycle and peaks around ovulation (Vierling & Rock, 1967). Assuming that the exaltolide and the exaltolidelike compound found in human urine produce similar effects, it would appear that the sexually attracting properties of perfume may derive from genetically inherited sensitivity to urinary pheromones. We will discuss the role of pheromones in human sexual behaviors in Chapter 9.

The term *voluntary urination* implies that the organism can both inhibit and excite the urination reflex. Most biology textbooks state that voluntary inhibition of urination in humans involves the CNS inhibition of the spinal reflex centers and voluntary contraction of the external sphincter. Conversely, voluntary excitation of urination presumably involves disinhibition of the spinal reflex and increased intraabdominal pressure produced by the contraction of the abdominal muscles and the respiratory diaphragm. (Various texts disagree about whether the external sphincter can be voluntarily relaxed or whether it relaxes only when it is not voluntarily contracted.) Research, however, suggests that this "standard" explanation of voluntary urination is much too simplistic.

Kegel (1949) observed that about 80% of female patients who suffered the loss of control of urination during physical activities (stress incontinence) had extremely weak PC muscles. He reasoned that because the PC muscles directly controlled the muscle tone of the external urethral sphincter, vagina, and rectum, exercising the PC muscle by isometrically contracting the vaginal and rectal muscles should restore voluntary control of urination. Consistent with his prediction, he found that teaching women simple vaginal exercises cured incontinence in a number of female patients but also produced an unexpected increase in the women's sexual responsiveness (Kegel, 1952; Ladas, Whipple, & Perry, 1982). In the context of the present discussion, the important aspect of Kegal's findings is that both the urinogenital diaphragm and related skeletal muscles may play an important role in mediating voluntary urination.

Lapides, Sweet, and Lewis (1957) examined whether voluntary urination could occur in the absence of skeletal muscle contractions. To eliminate skeletal muscle activity, they injected one female and six male subjects with the drug curare and filled their bladders with 0.3 liters of saline through a catheter. As discussed in Chapter 2, curare paralyzes skeletal muscles but does not effect either consciousness or the majority of smooth muscles. Theoretically, the curare injection should have eliminated voluntary control over urination by relaxing the external sphincter. However, all seven subjects demonstrated that they could consciously start urination within 5 seconds after a signal and stop urination within 15 seconds after a signal without the use of their skeletal muscles.

Both Kegel's and Lapides's findings suggest that the voluntary control of urination in humans involves a complex mixture of "voluntary" skeletal muscle and "involuntary" smooth muscle responses. This sophisticated control system may account for the difficulty many children have in learning to inhibit urination and for the wide range of individual differences in the ages at which children are completely "toilet trained." Some children have mastered the control of urination by as early as a year and a half, whereas other equally intelligent children still have difficulty inhibiting urination when they are 5 or 6 years old. Learning to inhibit urination during sleep appears to be a much more difficult skill to acquire. As we will discuss later in this chapter, a fairly large proportion of children who can voluntarily control urination when awake routinely urinate involuntarily when asleep.

The CNS also plays an important role in coordinating the chemical composition and volume of urine produced daily by the kidneys. The hypothalamus serves as the major control center for balancing fluid intake (drinking behaviors) and the volume of fluid lost through sweat, urine, and feces. The osmotic pressure of the blood serves as the primary stimulus for hypothalamic activity. When large volumes of fluid are excreted from the body, the blood becomes more concentrated (higher percentage of solids), and osmotic pressure increases. Osmoreceptors, clustered in the lateral preoptic area and scattered throughout the hypothalamus, detect the increase in osmotic pressure and stimulate the posterior pituitary gland to release the antidiuretic hormone (ADH). ADH stimulates the nephrons in the kidneys to increase the amount of water reabsorbed that in turn, lowers osmotic pressure in the blood. Conversely, if a large quantity of fluid is ingested, the blood becomes more diluted. This drop in osmotic pressure inhibits ADH secretion, and, in the absence of ADH, the nephrons decrease water reabsorption and increase the volume of urine formed.

The sympathetic nervous system (SNS) also alters kidney function via the hormone epinephrine and the neurons that stimulate contraction of the arterioles within the kidneys. Small doses of epinephrine and weak neural signals produce a local increase in blood pressure (BP) in the glomerulus by causing the efferent arterioles to constrict more than the afferent arterioles. The increase in BP increases the volume of urine formed. Conversely, large dosages of epinephrine and strong neural signals cause the afferent arterioles to constrict more than the efferent arterioles. The drop in glomerulus BP leads to a decrease in urine volume (Grollman, 1964). Given that SNS arousal accompanies emotional states, it is not surprising that emotional states may produce marked increases or decreases in urine formation. Clinical observations suggest that mild but persistent emotional states (e.g., anxiety) are associated with an increase in daily urine volume, whereas strong but transient emotional states (e.g., terror) are associated with a decrease in daily urine volume.

8.1.1. Methodological Issues in Urinary Research

Like gastrointestinal recording, urinary recording techniques are highly intrusive. For example, medical researchers commonly use a technique called *retrograde cystometry* to measure bladder pressure. A catheter is inserted up the urethra into the bladder. The tube is filled with fluid and attached to an external pressure gauge. Because the urethra is much shorter, straighter, and slightly wider in females than in males, females report less physical discomfort during this procedure than males. However, because the technique requires that the patients expose their genitals, both sexes may experience much psychological stress during the procedure. An alternative technique for directly recording bladder pressure without catheterizing the urethra is called *direct cystometry*. A needle catheter is inserted directly through the walls of the abdomen into the bladder. Again, the technique is highly intrusive.

Radiological cystography is another commonly used medical technique for studying the physiology of urination. Like other soft body tissues, the bladder normally appears as a shadowy mass on X-ray film. In order to make clearer X-ray pictures, chemicals that partially block X-rays are injected into the bladder and cause the bladder to appear as an opaque outline on X-ray film. During urination, the passage of these chemicals also outlines the flow of urine down the urethra.

Electromyography (EMG) is a third commonly used technique for studying urinary physiology. Like EKG discussed in Chapter 4, an EMG instrument is a powerful amplifier that detects and records the electrical signals (biopotentials) produced by muscle contraction. Bladder and sphincter contractions can be detected by surface electrodes placed on the skin of the abdomen and of the perianal (between genitals and anus) region. Unfortunately, surface electrodes also simultaneously detect the contractions of adjacent muscle groups (abdominals, urinogenital diaphragm, etc.). Although the activity of adjacent muscles is of interest, their biopotentials often obscure signals from the urinary tract. In order to produce accurate recordings of urinary tract activity, medical researchers frequently combine surface and internal recording of EMG. One common method of internal EMG recording is to insert needle electrodes into the walls of the detrusor, internal, and external sphincters. Although needle EMG records are highly accurate, this procedure does produce some degree of physical discomfort for the subject.

An alternative instrument for recording internal muscle tension is a small plastic probe containing EMG electrodes called a *perineometer* (see Ladas *et al.*, 1982). In female subjects, contraction and relaxation of the PC muscles can be accurately detected when a perineometer probe is inserted in either the urethra, vagina, or rectum. In males, the probe is inserted in the rectum. Subjects report that the insertion of the perineometer probe is no more uncomfortable than the insertion of a tampon or suppository.

Given the highly intrusive nature of urinary tract recording techniques, sample bias is one of the major methodological problems in studies of the role of emotion in urinary activity. Subjects in psychophysiological studies of urination are almost exclusively drawn from populations of medical, psychiatric, and psychophysiologic patients. Obviously, whether results obtained with such clinical samples can be generalized to the general population is debatable.

Another major confound in urination research is that individuals in our culture acquire rather strong emotional reactions to the discussion of elimination processes. Knapp (1967), for example, noted that humans generally react to eliminative processes with a mixture of disgust and satisfaction. Some individuals report that their feelings of disgust are mixed with a constellation of negative emotional states (guilt, shame, etc.), whereas other individuals report their feelings of satisfaction are mixed with pleasurable erotic feelings.

Consistent with Knapp's observations, there are numerous anecdotal reports of individuals who display strong negative or positive reactions toward urination. For example, many individuals of both sexes report feeling embarrassed and self-conscious when using public restrooms. Conversely, many (presumably) mentally healthy adults confess that they derive much satisfaction from engaging in "socially unacceptable" forms of urination. As a group, males are more likely to report enjoying "aggressive" acts of urination such as urinating upon another person's car. Conversely, many females report that they secretly enjoy "urinating like a man" in a standing position, whereas few males report enjoying "urinating like a woman." Both sexes frequently report enjoying urinating in socially unacceptable situations (during bathing, swimming, etc.). Such anecdotal reports raise serious questions about the validity of self-report studies of urination. Like defecation and sexual behaviors, the topic of urination elicits a complex mixture of emotional reactions that subjects may consciously attempt to conceal from researchers.

8.2. EMOTIONS AND THE URINARY SYSTEM

Research on the effects of emotional states on urination has focused on four basic issues—the frequency and volume of urination, emotional inhibition of urination (psychogenic continence), the relationship between urination and psychosexual disorders, and psychophysiological disorders of the urinary tract.

8.2.1. Volume and Frequency of Urination

Numerous self-report studies have found that state anxiety is associated with more frequent urination and with increased daily urine volume. For example, one study of 11- to 23-year-old females and males found that across age groups about 15% of the females and 20% of the males reported more frequent urination when anxious (Abe & Masui, 1981). Similarly, Wenderlein (1980) reported that emotionally unstable postmenopausal women were three times more likely than their emotionally stable peers to report increased frequency of urination during periods of psychological stress and two times more likely to report increases in volume of urine.

The consistency of self-report data suggests that at least one emotional state (anxiety) may produce an increase in the frequency and volume of urination. However, there are four plausible explanations for why such a relationship may occur. First, during emotional states, the individual may simply become more consciously aware of his or her body sensations, including bladder distension. Thus the individual may feel a "need" to urinate more frequently without an actual increase in bladder distension or may misperceive normal urinary output as increased output. For example, Klimo, Durindova, Simko, and Durinda (1975) cited two cases of depression patients who reported a sharp increase in consumption of fluids (polydipsia) and in urine volume (polyuria). In both cases, fluid intake and urine volume were normal, and the patients were simply hyperaware of their drinking behaviors and urination patterns.

Second, emotional states may actually trigger polydipsia that, in turn, leads to polyuria. Coe (1980) noted that polydipsia-induced polyuria is frequently observed in psychiatric patients. Such patients ingest large quantities of fluids and may void over 3 liters of urine in a 24-hour period.

Third, emotional states may lead to increased consumption of diuretics (alcohol, coffee, tea, etc.). In such instances, increased frequency and volume of urination are attributable to emotionally induced drug use and not to the emotional state *per se*. For example, Boulenger, Uhde, Wolff, and Post (1984) reported that caffeine consumption was positively related to the intensity of state anxiety in panic-anxiety patients but not in depressed patients. Mikkelsen (1978) reported the case of a female schizophrenic whose mounting sense of anxiety prior to a psychotic episode led to a marked increase in coffee consumption.

Fourth, sympathetic arousal during emotional states may increase the production of urine and/or bladder contractions. Thus polyuria may occur in the absence of polydipsia or diuretic use. Smith (1959) reported the case of a student who showed abnormally low urinary output (oliguria) on the days prior to an examination and polyuria after the examination.

The available evidence suggests that all four explanations of the association between increased frequency and volume of urination and emotional states may be valid for different individuals or valid for the same individual at different times. However, numerous authors have noted that subjects often have extreme difficult discriminating between polyuria (increase in urine volume) and increased frequency of urination in the absence of polyuria, for example, frequent voiding of small quantities of urine. Self-report data suggest that emotional states may elicit increased frequency of urination with or without polyuria. The latter cases suggest that emotional states may directly alter bladder activity.

8.2.2. Psychogenic Continence

The psychological "need" to inhibit the urinary reflex varies inversely with the frequency and strength of bladder contractions. Physiological recording of bladder activity confirmed that a variety of emotional states may directly alter the rate of bladder contractions. Masso and Pellacani (1882) demonstrated that bladder contractions increased during fear. Straub, Ripley, and Wolf (1949, 1950) reported that different emotional states during psychiatric interviews produced increases in bladder contractions. Topics that elicited aggression, anxiety, or sexual arousal were accompanied by increases in the rate of bladder contractions. Conversely, cognitive coping strategies (repression or withdrawal) were associated with marked decreases in bladder contractions.

To assess whether these changes were artifacts of skeletal abdominal muscle contractions, Straub, Ripley, and Wolf (1950) had patients perform a variety of motor movements (cough, sit up, tense their abdominal muscles, etc.) intended to increase intraabdominal pressure. Such movements produced only minor increases in bladder contractions. Stressful topics during psychiatric interviews, however, produced extremely strong bladder contractions in the same patients.

The observed increase in bladder activity during emotional states conflicts with the simplistic notion that emotional states involve global sympathetic arousal. Stimulation of sympathetic fibers causes the detrusor muscle to relax (not contract) and causes the internal sphincter to contract (not relax). Conversely, stimulation of parasympathetic fibers produces bladder contractions and relaxation of the internal sphincter. Thus, although other physiological systems tend to show global sympathetic arousal during emotional states (e.g., increase in BP), the urinary system displays a clear pattern of parasympathetic activation.

There are three plausible explanations for observed increase in bladder activity during emotional states. One explanation is that strong SNS activation may reflexively elicit PNS activity. According to this PNS rebound model, increased bladder contraction during emotional states is due to initial SNS activation. Specifically, SNS relaxation of the bladder elicits PNS contractions that may alternate in a cyclical fashion.

An alternative explanation is that PNS contractions of the bladder may be directly elicited by a variety of different emotional states. According to this response-fractionation model, PNS excitation of the bladder occurs concurrently with SNS activation of other physiological systems. Thus different organ systems may receive PNS or SNS excitation during emotional arousal.

A third explanation is that bladder relaxation or contractions may occur during specific emotional states. This biospecificity model argues that PNS-induced bladder contractions may occur during some emotions, whereas SNS-induced bladder relaxation may occur during other emotional states.

Research on emotional inhibition of urination (psychogenic continence) tends to support a parasympathetic rebound explanation of bladder activity during embarrassment. Urologists have frequently reported that embarrassed patients display a "spurting" pattern of urination. It was traditionally assumed that this stop-and-start pattern was produced by spasmotic closure of the external sphincter that intermittently blocked the flow of urine through the urethra. Although healthy humans can mimic spurting urination with voluntary contractions of the external sphincter, this response appears to be involuntary during embarrassment. For example, Jeffcoate (1961) observed spurting urination during a radiological examination of an embarrassed female patient. During periods of urine flow, normal contractions of the bladder and relaxation of the internal sphincter were observed. During the periods of urine stoppage, the bladder relaxed and the internal sphincter contracted. Thus it would appear that the spurting pattern was produced by alternating cycles of PNS and SNS activities.

Consistent with this finding, Hutch and Elliot (1968) found that, although females have weaker external sphincters than males, spurting urination during embarrassment was more common in female than male patients.

Middlemist, Knowles, and Matter (1976) performed a field study on the role of psychosocial stressors on urination in males. An observer hid in a toilet stall in a college men's room and used a periscope to record delay and length of urination. Psychosocial stress was manipulated by having no one else present (control condition), a confederate stand at a urinal adjacent to the subject (high threat), or with one-urinal separation (moderate threat). Compared with the control group, urination in the high-threat group was delayed by 3.5 seconds, and the duration of urination was shortened by 7.4 seconds. These findings are consistent with Jeffcoate's observation of alternating contraction and relaxation of the bladder during embarrassment. It should be noted that numerous authors have questioned the ethics of Middlemist's study.

Although the alternating PNS–SNS control of bladder activity during embarrassment appears to be well documented, there is little evidence to support the view that the increase in bladder contractions during other emotions represents PNS rebound. For example, in Straub's studies discussed previously in this section, PNS-induced muscle contractions were observed in the data from the beginning of each emotional episode, and there was no evidence of SNS-induced bladder relaxation occurring at the onset of emotional states. Similarly, recordings of bladder activity during emotional states have rather consistently failed to find the emotion-induced bladder relaxation predicted by the biospecificity model. However, it should be noted that relatively few emotions (aggression, anxiety, embarrassment, fear, and sexual arousal) have been observed during urinary tract recording. It is quite possible that bladder relaxations may occur during other emotional states (e.g., joy). Clearly, more research is needed before we can assess the validity of the biospecificity model.

8.2.3. Psychosexual Disorders

The discovery of PNS-induced bladder contractions during emotional states has helped clarify the frequently observed linkage between urination and psychosexual disorders. As we will discuss in greater detail in Chapter 9, urination and sexual arousal are extremely similar neurologically. Specifically, both responses are spinal reflexes that are excited or inhibited by higher CNS centers. Both responses are elicited by PNS excitation and inhibited by SNS excitation. Bors and Comarr (1971) argued that the anatomical and neurological overlap between the gastrointestinal, reproductive, and urinary systems make the overlap between various disorders not only comprehensible but perhaps inevitable. The reader may recall from Chapter 7 that IBS patients have extremely high incidence rates of both urinary tract and reproductive tract disorders.

Other researchers contend that the observed overlap between bowel, bladder, and reproductive disorders may be attributed to cultural taboos about both elimination and reproductive functions. According to this social learning model, children in our culture are still exposed to the Victorian belief that excretatory functions (defecation, sweating, vomiting, urination) and reproductive functions (menstruation, sexual behaviors) are at best "socially unacceptable" topics and are at worst "disgusting." Given the negative social connotations of excretion and reproduction, it is not surprising that the average American may still receive little factual information on either excretatory or reproductive functions during childhood and adolescence. The lack of information, however, may lead to confusion of excretatory and sexual sensations and the development of specific psychosexual disorders. As you will see in the following sections, the available empirical evidence tends to support both neurological and social learning views of the linkage between urination and psychosexual disorders.

Contemporary sex researchers distinguish between sexual arousal produced by mechanical stimulation of the urethra (sexual urethralism) and sexual arousal associated with the act of urination and/or urine (urophilia). Meeks and Heit (1982), however, argued that these two psychosexual disorders are closely related. The nineteenth-century pioneer of sex research, Havelock Ellis (1900), observed that sexual urethralism and urophilia were also closely related to other psychosexual disorders such as coprophilia, exhibitionism, fetishism, sadomasochism, and voyeurism.

For the purpose of clarity, we will discuss each psychosexual disorder separately. However, in clinical practice, it is not uncommon for the same patient to report various combinations of these disorders. For example, Ellis cited the case of "Florrie," a 37-year-old upper-class Victorian lady who had never engaged in sexual intercourse in 7 years of marriage and who very rarely masturbated. Her primary sources of sexual gratification were beating herself with a riding crop (fetishism-masochism), urinating while she beat herself (urophilia-fetishism-masochism), watching other people urinate (urophilia-voyeurism), and urinating in public, in the bathtub, on furniture, and in her hands (urophilia). She also reported producing sexual arousal by constructing elaborate sadomasochistic fantasies of having a male beat and/or urinate upon her. Although Florrie admitted to engaging in these unusual behaviors since early childhood, she had managed to keep her sexual practices a secret and was described by "her husband and all her friends [as] a stable normal person" (1900, p. 191).

Sexual urethralism is defined as obtaining sexual gratification from stimulation of the urethra. Differentiating urethralism from "normal" sexuality, however, is extremely difficult. Many normal males and females report deriving erotic gratification from stimulation of the urethral orifice (meatus) during masturbation or during manual or oral stimulation from a partner. Moreover, a large proportion of females report that mild stimulation of the urethral meatus during sexual intercourse is highly erotic (Clark, 1970). Such cases are not classified as urethralism because the pleasure derived from urethral stimulation is secondary to another sexual act. In true cases of urethralism, stimulation of the urethra itself is the primary goal, and the individual may masturbate to orgasm by massaging the urethral meatus alone. This behavior is almost exclusively auto-erotic (self-stimulation) and rarely involves a hetero- or homosexual partner.

Stoller (1977) argues that urethralists frequently become bored with stimulation of the urethral meatus and often experiment with inserting thin rodlike objects into the urethra.

Occasionally, a person will gradually work at enlarging the urethral meatus so that it can accept penetration of a penis or a penis-sized object. In the most bizzare cases, one finds reports of remarkable foreign bodies emplaced in the rectum or bladder: electric light bulbs, door knobs, ping-pong balls and the like in the rectum, and nails, needles and even snakes in the bladder. (p. 213)

Both the incidence rate and sex ratio of sexual urethralism are unknown. Hospital records indicate a higher percentage of female than male patients, but such sex differences may be purely an artifact of sex differences in anatomy. Meeks and Heit (1982) noted that because the urethra is much shorter in females than males, female urethralists have a much higher risk of lodging an object inside the bladder (and therefore having their behavior detected) than their male counterparts. Because urethralism is a solitary behavior, urethralists are rarely detected *unless* they injure themselves. Urethralists evidently derive much sexual and emotional gratification from their behavior and rarely seek psychiatric help voluntarily.

Researchers disagree over whether sexual urethralism is a distinct psychosexual disorder or should be classified as a form of fetishism (sexual arousal to objects) or a form of masochism (sexual arousal to pain). Weiss (1982) interviewed seven urethralists whose ages ranged from 14 to 55 years and concluded that urethralism was neither a fetish nor a sadomasochistic disorder but incorporated features of both disorders. He speculated that urethralism may represent a "midpoint" disorder that shares features with other psychosexual disorders.

Urophilia, or sexual arousal from urination and/or urine, may occur alone or in conjunction with other psychosexual disorders. Like urethralism, urophilia is also difficult to differentiate from "normal" behaviors. Many adults will freely admit to having engaged in some form of unorthodox act of urination at some point in their lives. These acts vary from innocent acts of public urination (i.e., urinating in a swimming pool) or malicious pranks (urinating upon a friend's front door). Nevertheless, most individuals do not report deriving the intense sexual and emotional gratification reported by urophiles. Moreover, the average person may describe emptying a full bladder as pleasurable, but he or she is unlikely to label the experience *sexual*. Many urophiles report an obsessive-compulsive need to experiment with socially unacceptable forms of urination and may devote much time to experimenting with new positions to urinate in and new techniques to urinate in public without detection. Urophiles frequently report that they find the scent or feel of urine highly erotic and that they may deliberately urinate on their own legs or hands. For some urophiles, urine becomes a fetish, and they cannot become sexually aroused unless their own or their partner's clothing smells of urine.

Explaining *why* urophiles associate urine and sexual arousal is a difficult task. The most commonly cited explanation is that the close proximity of the urinary and reproductive organs leads urophiles to confuse sensory signals from the different systems. For example, some urophiles also report copropilia (sexual arousal associated with defecation) and/or kilsmaphilia (sexual arousal associated with enemas). However, Ellis (1900) noted that despite the physiological association between urination and defecation, urophilia and coprophilia are rarely found in the same patient. Thus, misperceptions of the sensory signals from the GI, reproductive, and/or urinary systems does not appear to be sufficient for the development of urophilia.

Other biological factors may also predispose a given individual to become a urophile. For example, during a class discussion of urophilia, one of my students raised the interesting question of whether urophiles might not simply be hypersensitive to the exaltolidelike compounds found in human urine. Although I am not aware of any empirical data on this issue, researchers have found large individual differences in sensitivity to odors, including pheromones. Hypersensitivity to exaltolide would clearly account for the fetishlike attachment to urine odors displayed by many urophiles.

Another potential biological cause of urophilia is the distribution of touch receptors. Researchers have repeatedly documented wide individual differences in both touch sensitivity and the actual distribution of touch receptors. Such genetic variation may produce a minority of individuals whose urethras are hypersensitive to pressure and, thus, they may actually experience erotic sensations when their urethras are stimulated.

Although biological variability may contribute to the development of urophilia, it cannot account for why urophilia is often found in conjunction with one or more other psychosexual disorders. Indeed, as you will see in the following discussion, it is often impossible to classify a given urophile in any single diagnostic category.

Voyeurism is defined as deriving sexual excitement from watching other people engage in "private" acts. The most common types of voyeurs are individuals who are sexually aroused by observing others undress or engage in sexual acts. Such voyeurs generally "peep" through bedroom windows or into dressing rooms. A minority of voyeurs, however, are clearly urophiles because they report experiencing sexual arousal while watching other people urinate. Such urophilic voyeurs usually "peep" through bathroom windows or holes in restroom stalls. Although 90% of voyeurs who are arrested are male, it is impossible to determine whether this 9:1 sex ratio is also true for urophilic voyeurs.

Urophilia may also occur in conjunction with exhibitionism (sexual arousal obtained from exposing one's genitals to other people). Unlike other exhibitionists or other urophiles, urophilic exhibitionists enjoy having other people watch while they urinate and derive sexual gratification from their audience's emotional reactions (disgust, sexual arousal, shock, etc.). Although the vast majority of exhibitionists who are arrested are male, arrest records may underestimate the incidence of exhibitionism in females. Until quite recently, occupations that allowed exhibitionists to expose themselves for a profit (nude dancer, pornography model, etc.) were almost exclusively female.

Urophilia is often commonly reported in conjunction with sadomasochism. In its pure form, sadism involves deriving sexual pleasure from inflicting physical or psychological pain on a sex partner. Urophilic sadists enjoy urinating on a partner, and female prostitutes report this act is fairly commonly performed by male patrons. Stoller (1977) dryly noted that, although males may urinate on women who are not prostitutes, "one cannot always find a mate so well matched that she cooperates without charge" (p. 200). Conversely, in its true form, masochism involves experiencing sexual pleasure by having a partner inflict physical or psychological pain. In contrast, urophilic masochists enjoy being urinated upon. Hunt (1974) estimated that about 4.5% of the adult population has engaged in sadomasochistic acts. The proportion of urophiles contained in the sadomasochistic population, however, is unknown.

Although the literature on sexual urethralism and urophilia is extremely sparse, the high concordance rates between these disorders and other psychosexual disorders suggests a common psychological etiology. As a group, psychosexual patients have lower than average social skills. Because they lack "how-to-act" skills, these individuals encounter much frustration when they attempt to form normal hetero- or homosexual relationships. Hence, they develop fewer than average social contacts. The lack of social contacts, however, produces lower than average social skills. Thus psychosexual patients receive less exposure to socially acceptable models of normal behaviors, including sexual behaviors. Such individuals may then copy abnormal models depicted in pornography or discover socially unacceptable sexual behaviors through experimentation. In some cases, childhood and adolescent experiences may provide abnormal adult or peer models. For example, during Florrie's childhood, her father often beat her sadistically with a riding crop until she wet her pants, and her nurse used to force her to urinate in the woods to "avoid" toilet accidents in other people's houses. Obviously, many of Florrie's later abnormal behaviors were clearly derived from these early exposures to abnormal models. Why Florrie and other urophiles, however, substitute such behaviors for more conventional sexual stimulation is the key issue in understanding urophilia.

8.3. PSYCHOPHYSIOLOGICAL POPULATIONS

Psychophysiological research has focused on three distinct disorders: loss of voluntary control over urination while asleep (enuresis); loss of voluntary control over urination while awake (incontinence); and pain associated with urination (chronic pelvic pain).

8.3.1. Enuresis

Enuresis (bed-wetting) is the loss of bladder control during sleep, and it may be produced by a variety of urological and neurological disorders. For example, Anders (1976) noted that bed-wetting is often frequently associated with sleepwalking (somnabulism), another sleep disorder. Traditionally, it was believed that sleep disorders represented "emotional problems" reactiviated during dream (REM) sleep. However, researchers have found that sleep disorders tend to occur during nondream (NREM) periods during the sleep cycle (Broughton, 1968). Accordingly, researchers currently believe that the majority of cases of sleep disorders can be traced to neurological deficits in the RAS. In the majority of adults, the sensations of a full bladder are usually sufficient to wake the individual and elicit a nocturnal visit to the bathroom. In bed-wetters, however, these physiological signals do not appear to wake the individual.

Researchers speculated that the high incidence rate of bed-wetting during childhood is due to immaturity of the CNS and that as the individual's CNS matures, he or she may "outgrow" bed-wetting and other sleep disorders.

Although the types of neurological deficits postulated by sleep researchers are impossible to detect with current medical technology, both the age incidence and sex ratio data on enuresis are consistent with the view that the majority of cases of enuresis may be due to delayed physical maturation. Specifically, the incidence rates of enuresis average 15% to 20% in children under the age of 12. During adolescence, the incidence rates decline to 3% to 6% and by adulthood averages around 1%. Across age groups, the sex ratio (female/male) averages 1:2 to 1:3 (Doleys, Weiler, & Pegram, 1982). Given that males as a group physically mature at a slower rate than females, the higher incidence of enuresis in males is clearly consistent with the CNS immaturity hypothesis.

The diagnostic label of *functional nocturnal enuresis* is used to designate individuals older than 3 years who bed-wet on a weekly basis in the absence of physiopathology. Although the "absence" of a physiological disorder is extremely difficult to prove or disprove, the belief that functional enuresis is psychogenic is highly questionable. Researchers have consistently found that the incidence of psychiatric disorders is no higher in enuretics than in nonenuretics (Schaffer, 1973). Moreover, although some psychiatric patients will habitually ingest large quantities of fluid and thus produce large volumes of urine (polyuria), the majority of these individuals are noneuretic and display nocturia, that is, frequent nocturnal visits to the bathroom (Coe, 1980). A small minority of children and adults may deliberately fake bed-wetting either for primary gain (attention) or secondary gain (avoid going away to camp, medical discharge from the military, etc.). Although such cases of bed-wetting may be psychogenic, they are clearly not psychophysiologic.

The label *psychophysiologic enuresis* may be appropriate only for the subset of enuretics who develop enuresis *after* at least a 6-month period of noctural continence, have no detectable physiopathology, *and* whose enuretic episodes are preceded by emotional stress. A variety of diagnostic labels (acquired enuresis, discontinuous enuresis, secondary enuresis) have been used to designate this type of enuresis.

Psychophysiological enuresis patients share a number of interesting characteristics. First, the patients often display loss of bladder control during both waking and sleeping hours. Second, they often have a history of painful urination due to urethral or bladder infections. Third, they often have a history of harsh toilet training and/or strong sexual inhibitions. Do these characteristics account for why these normally continent individuals develop enuresis after emotional stress? Perhaps. One plausible explanation is that these individuals have learned to associate groin sensations with pain or negative emotional states (guilt and shame). Unlike hypochondriacs who have learned to overattend to weak internal body sensations, these individuals have apparently learned *not* to attend to relatively strong internal sensations. They often do not detect the need to urinate until their bladders are extremely full and frequently have to race to find a toilet. Not surprisingly, they may occasionally accidently wet themselves (urge incontinence). This lack of "body awareness" may predispose such individuals to enuresis during strong emotional states when both urine output and bladder contractions may increase suddenly.

It should be noted that the incidence rates of both psychogenic and psychophysiological enuresis are quite low. Bors and Commar (1971) estimate that the combined incidence of both disorders may account for only about 5% of all cases of enuresis.

8.3.2. Incontinence

Urinary incontinence refers to a class of disorders characterized by the loss of voluntary control over urination while awake. Stress incontinence is used to denote involuntary urination during physical activities (coughing, climbing stairs, sexual intercourse, etc.). Stress incontinence occurs most commonly in postmenopausal women and is frequently associated with urethral atrophy and weak pelvic muscles. In older males, stress incontinence is associated with prostate disorders. Urgency or urge incontinence is characterized by poor awareness of the need to urinate and is associated with a variety of organic disorders (urethral and bladder infections, spinal damage, etc.). Overflow incontinence is produced by partial urethral blockages. Mechanical incontinence is produced by either genetic defects or surgical injury. Although these different types of incontinence all have clearly identifiable organic causes, it should not be concluded that psychological factors play no role in incontinence episodes. Wenderlein (1980), for example, found that 48% of postmenopausal women who scored high in anxiety reported stress incontinence compared with only 12% of the nonanxious women. Thus it would appear that emotional states may aggravate organic forms of incontinence.

The term *psychogenic incontinence* is used to denote cases of incontinence where no anatomical or physiological abnormality can be found to account for the loss of bladder control. Although urologists agree that psychogenic incontinence does exist, they disagree over the incidence rate of the disorder. Bors and Comarr (1971), for example, estimated that psychogenic incontinence accounts for approximately 10% of female incontinence cases and a lower (unspecified) percentage of male cases. These authors cited numerous cases of psychogenic incontinence. For example, one middle-aged woman became incontinent after being involved in an auto accident. Although her urinary tract was undamaged by the accident, she lost bladder control every time she approached a car. In this case, the incontinence-inducing stressor was clearly psychological (the sight of cars) and not physical (i.e., walking). Other urologists argue that the incidence of psychogenic incontinence is much lower than 10% (Gill & Coe, 1980). When psychogenic incontinence is confirmed, many patients may refuse psychiatric help. For example, in one treatment study of psychogenic incontinence, one-third of the patients either refused or dropped out of psychotherapy prematurely (Hafner, Stranron, & Guy, 1977).

8.3.3. Chronic Pelvic Pain

Cystitis is a bacterial infection of the bladder and is characterized by a burning or painful sensation in the urethra during urination, an increase in the frequency of waking urination and nocturia, and pain localized in the lower abdomen and genitals. The pain sensations (with the exception of urethral burning) are usually more salient when the individual is *not* urinating. Because the urethra is shorter in females than males, cystitis is more common in females (Gill & Coe, 1980).

Chronic pelvic pain (CPP) is a somatoform disorder that mimics cystitis. Older diagnostic labels for CPP include chronic glandular urethrotrigonitis, functional bladder syndrome, and psychosomatic cystitis (Gill & Coe, 1980). Like cystitis, CPP is more common in females than males, and CPP patients report many of the same symptoms reported by cystitis patients (i.e., burning urination, abdominal pain) with two notable exceptions. First, CPP patients do not report the nocturia that is characteristic of cystitis. Second, CPP patients report that pain is aggravated by urination (Malinak, 1980). Despite CPP patients' reports of cystitislike symptoms, extensive gynecological, neurological, and urological tests reveal no organic pathology. CPP patients usually reject the diagnosis that their pain is psychogenic and refuse psychiatric treatment (Nadelson, Norman, & Ellis, 1983).

Like IBS patients, CPP patients often report a variety of concurrent psychophysiological symptoms including dysmenorrhea, headaches, hyperventilation, and painful sexual intercourse (dyspareunia). CPP patients frequently have a history of sexual trauma such as incest or rape (Gross, Doerr, & Caldirola, 1980), conflicts over sexuality (Nadelson *et al.*, 1983), and/or severe psychosocial stress (Leon, 1984). Two emotional states, anxiety and depression, are commonly cited as precipitating factors in CPP. For example, Castelnuovo-Tedesco and Krout (1970) reported that anxiety states and panic attacks are common in CPP patients. Wenderlein (1980), however, noted that depression appears to play a more important role in the development of CPP in older women. In his sample of menopausal women, 44% of depressed subjects reported burning or pain during urination, whereas only 13% of the nondepressed subjects reported this symptom.

Given the high degree of overlap between organic, psychogenic, and psychophysiological symptoms, it is extremely difficult to isolate the role of emotions in urinary tract disorders. The presence of physiopathology (e.g., stress incontinence) does not preclude emotional states from aggravating the disorder. Thus individuals with weak sphincters or PC muscles may experience incontinence only when physical activity is coupled with emotional stress. Conversely, the presence of emotional stress in the apparent absence of physiopathology does not imply that a given patient's symptoms are psychogenic. For example, Andrew and Nathan (1965) cited the case of an apparently healthy 48-year-old woman who reported symptoms of enuresis, waking incontinence, urge incontinence, and nymphomania. Although any or all of these disorders could have been psychogenic, all of her symptoms were caused by a limbic system tumor, and her disorders disappeared once the tumor was removed.

There have been numerous attempts to teach organic, psychogenic, and psychophysiological patients to regain voluntary bladder control through psychotherapy and biofeedback. In general, various treatment programs have had some degree of success with organic disorder patients. For example, the success rate of behavioral conditioning treatment programs for enuresis have averaged 75% to 100% (Doleys *et al.*, 1982). Similarly, biofeedback treatment programs for stress incontinence also have been moderately successful. Burglo, Whitehead, and Engel (1983) observed that 100% of their patients reported at least 55% decreases in the frequency of incontinence episodes after biofeedback treatment. Similarly, Stanton (1981) reported that 59% of his patients were objectively cured of incontinence after biofeedback and relaxation training. Paradoxically, the success rate of psychological and biofeedback treatment programs with psychogenic patients has been extremely low (Hafner *et al.*, 1977; Nadelson *et al.*, 1983). Evidently, psychogenic patients derive sufficient primary and secondary gain from their disorders that they resist treatment programs that might eliminate their symptoms.

In summary, the sparse literature on urinary tract activity provides some tantalizing clues about the complex relationships between physiological activity and emotional states. For example, embarrassment appears associated with a unique pattern of urinary tract activity. Conversely, research on urophilia suggests that humans may acquire diverse sets of emotional associations to urination.

SUGGESTED READINGS

Lapides, J., Sweet, R. B., & Lewis, L. W. Role of striate muscle in urination. *Journal of Urology*, 1957, 77, 247–250.

A fascinating study of the role of "voluntary" and "involuntary" muscles in urination.

Middlemist, R. D., Knowles, E. S., & Matter, C. F. Personal space invasions in the lavatory: Suggestive evidence for arousal. *Journal of Personality and Social Psychology*, 1976, 33, 541–546.

An interesting example of how the Faustian obsession with knowledge can lead to unethical research. This study has been repeatedly questioned as an invasion of privacy.

Stoller, R. J. Sexual deviations. In F. A. Beach (Ed.), *Human sexuality in four perspectives*. Baltimore: Johns Hopkins University Press, 1977.

A concise introduction to psychosexual disorders.

Straub, L. R., Ripley, H. S., & Wolf, S. Disturbance of bladder function associated with emotional states. *Journal of American Medical Association*, 1949, 141, 1139–1143.

Pioneering study of the psychological correlates of bladder activity.

The Female and Male Reproductive Systems

Like all living organisms, humans have finite life spans. Without sexual reproduction, the human species would become extinct.

9.1. ANATOMY AND PHYSIOLOGY

The major external anatomical structures of the female reproductive system are the labia minora, labia majora, and the clitoris (Figure 9-1). The labia minora are two thin folds of skin that enclose the external meatus of the urethra and the entrance to the vagina. The labia majora are two larger folds of skin that surround the labia minora. The clitoris is a small shaftlike structure at the apex of the labia minora and is almost completely covered by a hoodlike fold of skin. All three structures contain a large number of blood vessels and neural receptors. During sexual arousal, these structures become engorged with blood and become highly sensitive to mechanical stimuli.

The major internal female reproductive organs are the ovaries, fallopian tubes, uterus, and vagina. As discussed previously in Chapter 3, the ovaries function as endocrine glands. A complex hormonal feedback system between the hypothalamus-pituitary and the ovaries controls both the cyclical production of ovum by the ovaries and the cyclical growth and degeneration of the uterine lining.

The external male reproductive organs consist of two major structures, the penis and scrotum (Figure 9-2). Three spongy cylindrical masses of tissue form the shaft and the caplike tip (glans) of the penis. These structures are richly supplied with blood vessels and become engorged with blood during sexual arousal. The male urethra transverses through the base of the penis and terminates at the external meatus in the glans.

The internal male reproductive system is composed of four major glands and a series of interconnecting tubes. Like the ovaries, the testes function as

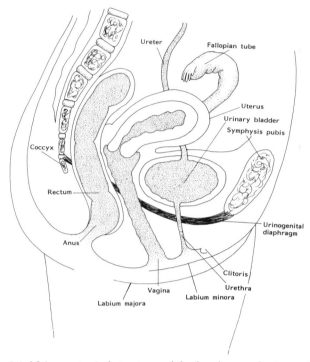

Figure 9-1. Major anatomical structures of the female reproductive system.

endocrine glands and insure the tonic production of sperm through a hormonal feedback loop with the hypothalamus and pituitary. The testes also act as exocrine (external secretion) glands by producing sperm—the male reproductive cells. Mature sperm migrate from the testes through the vas deferens to the seminal vesicles. The seminal vesicles act as a storage area for mature sperm and as an exocrine gland. The vesicles produce an alkaline fluid that helps neutralize the acidity of the vagina. During ejaculation, a mixture of sperm and seminal fluid is expelled into the urethra through the ejaculation ducts. The prostate gland secretes a large quantity of alkaline fluid that mixes with the ejaculate to form semen. After semen passes through the external sphincter, it passes two small glands that are joined to the urethra. These bulbourethral or Cowper's glands secrete an alkaline lubricant that helps neutralize the acidity of the male urethra and facilitates the movement of semen through the urethra.

Prior to the 1960s, little was known about the physiology of the human reproductive systems. Masters and Johnson (1966) published their landmark study, *Human Sexual Response,* which summarized the physiological responses of 382 women and 312 men during masturbation and sexual intercourse. Masters and Johnson observed that the sexual response cycle occurred in four distinct physiological stages in both sexes: excitement, plateau, orgasm, and resolution.

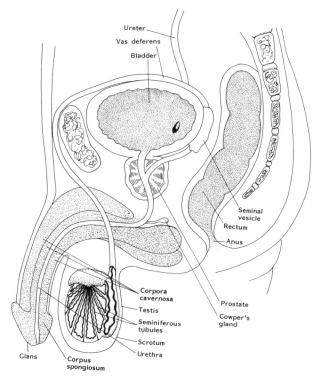

Figure 9-2. Major anatomical structures of the male reproductive system.

The global physiological changes and local genital responses associated with each of these stages are virtually identical in both sexes.

The excitement phase is characterized by parasympathetic dilation of the blood vessels of the genitals of both sexes. In females, the labia majora, clitoris, and walls of the vagina become engorged with blood. This local increase in blood flow forces cellular fluid from the walls of the vagina that lubricates the inner lining of the vagina. Some females also display sex flush (vasodilation of the chest). In males, the penis becomes engorged with blood, and the scrotum muscles partially contract.

In both sexes, the plateau phase is characterized by an increase in global sympathetic arousal (rapid heart rate, respiration rate, etc.) and by chest and genital vasodilation. In females, the outer one-third of the vagina becomes increasingly engorged with blood. The entrance of the vagina decreases by about 30% in diameter, whereas the inner two-thirds of the vagina expand slightly. The clitoris contracts toward the pubic bone as the labia minora become engorged with blood. In males, the glans becomes engorged with blood, and Cowper's gland secretions may begin to leak from the urethral meatus. The scrotum contracts fully and presses the testes against the floor of the pelvis. In both sexes, there is a sharp increase in skeletal muscle tension during the plateau stage, particularly in the buttocks and thighs.

The orgasm stage is characterized by global sympathetic arousal accompanied by intense muscular contractions. In females, the anal sphincter, PC (pubococcygeus) muscles, vagina, and uterus rhythmically contract. In males, orgasm occurs in two distinct substages. The first substage is called *ejaculation inevitability* and is characterized by rhythmic contractions of the prostate and seminal vesicles. During the second substage, rhythmic contractions of the PC muscles, penis, prostate, and urethra expel semen out of the urethral meatus. In both sexes, the number and intensity of muscle contractions varies from individual to individual.

The resolution stage is characterized by hyperventilation and perspiration. Global sympathetic arousal gradually declines, and the body slowly relaxes. Muscular contractions divert blood flow from genital tissues, and pelvic blood flow returns to baseline.

Although Masters and Johnson found little evidence for unique "female" or "male" sexual responses, they did observe that the sexual response cycle was highly stereotyped in males but highly variable in females. Specifically, males all showed the same basic response cycle and differed only in the length of time each stage lasted. In females, however, three distinct patterns of sexual responses were observed. Some women showed a clear pattern of multiple orgasms (Pattern 1). Other women displayed a prolonged plateau stage without orgasm (Pattern 2), and still other women showed an irregular pattern of physiological arousal during the plateau stage followed by an extremely rapid orgasm and resolution stages (Pattern 3).

Critics of Masters and Johnson's research have raised serious questions about whether their sample of subjects was representative of the general population. Although the incidence rate of sexual dysfunctions averages about 30% in 20-year-old women, individuals with sexual dysfunctions were eliminated from Master and Johnson's sample. Whether similar physiological reactions occur in individuals with sexual dysfunctions will be discussed later in this chapter.

Ladas, Whipple, and Perry (1982) argued that elimination of individuals with "sexual dysfunctions" from Masters and Johnson's sample also eliminated an interesting subgroup of women—female urethral ejaculators. Cases of females who ejaculated fluid from the urethra at orgasm have been reported for centuries, but researchers have traditionally dismissed such cases as stress incontinence, that is, stress-related loss of bladder control.

Perry and Whipple (1981) documented numerous cases of female ejaculators and argued that the female and male reproductive systems may be even more similar than Masters and Johnson believed. They found that pressure against the anterior wall of the vagina near the mouth of the bladder initially produced an urge to urinate that was followed by an intense orgasmic experience. In a number of women, a small amount of fluid spurted from the urethra. Chemical analyses revealed that the fluid was not urine but rather similar to semen without sperm. The authors speculated that the fluid was produced by the female equivalent of the prostate gland (Grafenberg or G-spot) located at the base of the bladder. Although the percentage of women who ejaculate is unknown, Ladas *et al.* (1982) estimate that between 10% and 40% of adult females may be capable of ejaculation but that many women may inhibit their ejaculation response out of the fear of "losing bladder control."

The sexual response cycle is controlled by a complex mixture of spinal reflexes and CNS centers. For example, research with male paraplegics has confirmed that genital responses are controlled by spinal reflexes. Stimulation of the genitals produces a normal erection and orgasm, although the patients cannot "feel" their own physiological responses. Researchers speculate that the same spinal reflexes control females' genital responses, but data on female paraplegics is currently unavailable (Hyde, 1982). Like urination, higher centers in the CNS excite or inhibit the sexual spinal reflex centers. Electrical stimulation studies with monkeys suggest that the primary CNS centers for exciting-inhibiting sexual responses are clustered in the septal area and thalamus and scattered throughout the rest of the limbic system.

In humans, the cortices clearly play an important role in mediating sexual arousal. The majority of humans report that they can produce or inhibit sexual arousal through cognitive activity alone. For example, if you vividly imagine a scene that you personally find erotic, you may notice that sexual arousal occurs rather rapidly. Conversely, sexual arousal may quickly disappear if you imagine your parents bringing guests into your room while you are having sexual intercourse.

9.1.1. Methodological Issues in Reproductive Physiology Research

Physiological changes during the human sexual response cycle can be divided into four general classes: global autonomic responses, CNS activity, skeletal muscle activity, and genital autonomic responses (Davidson, 1980). Different forms of instrumentations are needed to record each of these classes of responses.

Since the publication of Masters and Johnson's original study, measures of cardiovascular activity (BP, heart rate, skin temperature) and respiration have become commonly used indices of sexual arousal. However, as discussed in earlier chapters, each of these measures produces its own unique artifacts.

CNS activity can be recorded using surface electrodes attached to the scalp and powerful amplifiers to detect the weak electrical signals produced by the brain. The results of sleep studies suggest that subjects may become quickly habituated to this electroencephalogram (EEG) recording procedure. Given the relatively nonintrusive nature of EEG recording, there has been surprisingly little research on brain-wave activity during sexual behaviors.

Cohen, Rosen, and Goldstein (1976) recorded left and right hemisphere EEGs of three female and four male subjects during masturbation and found that sudden shifts in brain-wave patterns occurred in the right (but not the left) hemisphere at orgasm. In a later study, Cohen, Rosen, and Goldstein (1985) compared EEG patterns of normal and sexually dysfunctional males to auditory and visual presentation of erotic stimuli. The normal males showed greatest right-hemisphere activation and sexual arousal during the visual presentation. The sexual dysfunctional males, however, showed greatest right-hemisphere activation but lowest degree of sexual arousal during auditory presentation.

The overall pattern of Cohen's findings are consistent with Galin's hypothesis that the right hemisphere may play a more important role in emotional-motivational behaviors than the left hemisphere (see Chapter 2). However, Cohen's findings may also merely represent shifts in attention. For example, it is quite plausible that at the point of orgasm, subjects shifted their attention from erotic imagery (presumably a right-hemisphere activity) to their own internal body sensations. Such a sudden shift in attention would also produce a sudden shift in brain-wave patterns.

Over the past two decades, internal EMG probes, discussed previously in Chapter 8, have become increasingly popular in sex research. Graber and Kline-Graber (1979), for example, used a vaginal perineometer to record PC muscle contractions of sexually dysfunctional women, women who achieve orgasm through clitoral (but not vaginal) stimulation, and women who achieved orgasm through vaginal (but only indirect clitoral) stimulation. These three groups of women differed in the strength of their PC muscles. The sexually dysfunctional women had the weakest PC muscles, whereas the women who experienced vaginal orgasm had the strongest PC muscles. These findings would appear to support Kegal's hypothesis that PC muscle tone may directly affect bladder, bowel, and reproductive physiology. However, studies of the effectiveness of teaching sexually dysfunctional women to strengthen their PC muscles have been equivocal (Chambless & DeMarco, 1985; Jayne, 1985).

The development of instruments to measure autonomic changes in the female genitals during the sexual response cycle has proven to be a difficult task. For example, researchers have experimented with taping electronic thermometers to the clitoris or labia and inserting thermometers into the vagina in order to detect vasocongestion (Zuckerman, 1971). Such thermal probes, however, not only tend to interfere with sexual behaviors, but depending upon placement, they also tend to fall off or out during sexual activity.

Sintchak and Geer (1975) developed a device called the *vaginal photoplethysmograph* to provide a more accurate record of vaginal blood flow. As discussed in Chapter 5, photoplethysmography detects vasodilation and constriction by recording the amount of light reflected from the skin surface. To record blood flow within the walls of the vagina, Sintchak and Geer mounted a small light bulb and light sensor in a tamponlike plastic probe. Although some authors have questioned the accuracy of vaginal photoplethysmography (Beck, Sakheim, & Barlow, 1983), this technique is now commonly used in sexual research.

Autonomic changes in the male genitals can be easily recorded using a simple device called a penile ring. The penile ring consists of a mercury filled tube that conducts a weak electrical current. When the ring is stretched, the electrical resistance in the circuit changes. The penile ring fits on the base of the penis like the rubber ring of a condom. As the penis expands in diameter during the excitement and plateau stages of the sexual cycle, the penile ring is also stretched. Bancroft and Bell (1985) challenged the validity of penile ring recording. They simultaneously recorded penile diameter with a penile ring and penile pulse volume with a photoplethysmograph during viewing a sexually explicit film and during sexual fantasy. Across subjects, five different patterns of relationships were observed between penile diameter and pulse amplitude. Thus, it would appear that penile diameter *per se* may be a relatively unreliable index of male sexual arousal.

The intrusive nature of the physiological recording techniques used in sex research creates three potential artifacts. First, the recording procedures themselves may interfere with normal behavioral or physiological responses. Although both researchers and equipment manufacturers argue that subjects quickly habituate to the recording equipment, the validity of their claims is highly questionable. Both males and females may (at least initially) show rather strong emotional reactions to the recording procedures.

Second, sexual recording requires that the subjects be sexually aroused. Experimenters commonly instruct the subjects to engage in a specific sexual behavior (most commonly masturbation) or present subjects with stimuli that the experimenter has judged "erotic." Either procedure may produce rather strong emotional reaction by the subjects. In our culture, many adults report embarrassment, guilt, or shame when asked to even discuss masturbation (Abramson & Mosher, 1975). Obviously, instructing subjects to masturbate may elicit even stronger emotional reactions. Similarly, the experimenter's and subjects' conceptions of erotica may not match, for example, subjects may find the experimenter's "erotic" stimuli either obscene or boring.

Third, volunteer bias is a major concern in sex research. For example, Hatfield, Specher, and Traupmann (1978) observed that when they showed explicit films on masturbation in a human sexuality class, students who were the same sex as the model began sneaking out of the classroom. The authors hypothesized that students may have experienced negative reactions to same-sex models rather than to the act of masturbation *per se.* To test this hypothesis, they had female and male undergraduates rate their reactions to films that depicted actors or actresses engaged in masturbation, heterosexual, or homosexual sex acts. Both female and male subjects reported greater sexual arousal to films that depicted models of the *opposite* sex engaging in either masturbation or homosexual behaviors. Thus the female subjects rated the films of male masturbation and homosexuality more erotic than the female versions of the films, whereas the males rated the female models more arousing.

Kenrick and his associates examined whether subjects who volunteer for sex research experiments differed systematically from individuals who decline to participate (Kendrick, Stringfield, Wagenhals, Dahl, & Ransdell, 1980). In one study, they gave female and male undergraduates a choice of viewing a "hard-core" or "soft-core" erotic film. A disproportionate number of females chose to view the soft-core film. In a second study, subjects were given a choice between viewing a hard-core film or a soft-core film or participating in a study of spatial perception (neutral task). A disproportionate number of female subjects volunteered for the neutral task. About a month after subjects had been contacted to participate in the second experiment, they were asked to complete the Bem Sex Role Inventory. A clear sex difference in volunteering-declining participation rates were found in sex-typed subjects. Masculine males were most likely to volunteer to view hard-core films (91%) whereas feminine females were least likely to volunteer (31%). No sex differences, however, were observed among androgynous (mixed masculine-feminine trait) subjects. Approximately 60% of the androgynous males and 67% of the androgynous females volunteered for the erotic experiment. Thus it would appear that sex role stereotyping may mediate which individuals volunteer to participate in sexual research experiments.

Another major source of artifacts in sexual research is the subjects' perceptions of the experimenter's attitudes. For example, Martin (1964) found that subtle differences in the experimenter's behavior produced marked effects on male undergraduates' reactions to erotic stimuli. In two different experiments, subjects were randomly assigned to either "permissive" or "inhibitory" experimenter conditions. In the permissive condition, the experimenter acted in a warm and friendly manner and suggested that the subjects would probably enjoy participating. In the inhibitory condition, the experimenter acted in a cold and clinical fashion. All subjects were then given photographs of female nudes and landscapes and instructed to pick out the three photographs that they found most appealing. In both experiments, subjects in the inhibitory condition spent much less time viewing the nude photographs and showed higher EDA than subjects in the permissive condition.

9.2. EMOTIONS AND THE REPRODUCTIVE SYSTEMS

The literature on human sexuality suggests that a given individual's sexual attitudes, behaviors, emotions, motives, and physiological arousal may be totally unrelated. That is, what individuals say they believe about specific sexual acts, what sexual acts they engage in, what they experience emotionally during a sexual act, why they engage in specific sexual behaviors, and how their bodies respond may only partially match. For example, female prostitutes often report that, although they regularly engage in heterosexual acts, their motives are purely financial and they experience no physical arousal during their business transactions. Moreover, they also frequently report that they experience a mixture of contempt and disgust toward their clients and a realistic fear that their clients may injure or kill them.

Unfortunately, many researchers have often failed to distinguish between sexual attitudes, behaviors, emotions, motives, and physiological arousal. The term *sexual arousal* has been loosely used to refer to positive attitudes toward sexuality, to approach behaviors to sexual stimuli, to emotional excitement elicited by sexual stimuli, to the motive to engage in sexual acts, and to physiological arousal. For the purpose of clarity, the term *sexual arousal* will be used only to denote physiological arousal in the following discussion. To denote the positive emotional state associated with sexual arousal, the term *sexual excitement* will be used.

The majority of laboratory studies of sexual excitement have focused on emotional traits (the individual's disposition to experience specific emotions) and on emotional states during sexual arousal.

9.2.1. Emotional Trait Studies

The emotional trait approach is based on the assumption that a given individual's habitual emotional reactions may predispose him or her to adopt specific beliefs, display specific behaviors, experience emotional reactions, and display physiological reactions. The Mosher Sex Guilt Scale is currently the most popular self-report trait measure in sex research (Mosher, 1961, 1965, 1966, 1979). This inventory consists of a series of statements related to sex guilt, such as "If I commit adultery, I hope I enjoy it," which are presented in either a true-false or forced-choice format.

In a series of experiments, Mosher and his associates have found that the amount of sex guilt reported by an individual appears to be directly related to his or her sexual attitudes, behaviors, motives, and sexual arousal. For example, early studies of sex guilt focused on subjects' ability to detect sexual words in a perceptual defense task. In this procedure, words are flashed at speeds too fast to be consciously read, and subjects are instructed to guess what they think each word is. The length of time that each word is presented is gradually increased until the subject can correctly identify all the words. Presumably, longer exposure times needed to identify taboo words (e.g., "whore") than neutral words (e.g., "ocean") indicate a high degree of defensiveness. Both male (Mosher 1961, 1965) and female (Ridley, 1976) high sex guilt undergraduates showed delayed recognition of taboo words, whereas low sex guilt subjects did not. High sex guilt subjects' apparent defensiveness about sexual words has also been observed in word association tasks (e.g., What is the first word you think of when I say "salt?"). Galbraith and Mosher (1968) found that high sex guilt male undergraduates were more likely than other subjects to inhibit sexual associations to double entendre words such as "screw."

High sex guilt appears to partially inhibit sexual behaviors. Both female and male undergraduates who score high on sex guilt report fewer experiences with specific sexual behaviors and are more likely to report inhibiting sexual behaviors on moral grounds (Mosher & Cross, 1971; Abramson & Mosher, 1975). However, high sex guilt is associated with different sexual motives in males and females. High sex guilt males tend to disapprove of attempting to sexually exploit dates and report that they rarely attempt to convince their dates to engage in sexual acts (Mosher, 1971). Thus, to avoid experiencing guilt, high sex guilt males tend to renounce the conservative attitude of "male sexual domination." Paradoxically, high sex guilt females appear to desire a sexually dominant partner to reduce their own feelings of guilt. Moreault and Follingstad (1978) asked female undergraduates to fill out a questionnaire about their sexual fantasies and to write an erotic story based on one of their own personal fantasies. High sex guilt subjects reported fewer and less explicit fantasies than other subjects but were more likely to display *greater* physiological sexual arousal during an erotic videotape. The author noted that her sample was biased because women who reported extremely high levels of sex guilt chose not to participate in the study.

Although high sex guilt women report fewer than average sexual experiences, they are a high-risk group for unwanted pregnancies. For example, Lindemann (1974) concluded on the basis of clinical interviews that high sex guilt may deter contraceptive use but not sexual intercourse. Gerrard (1977) found that female undergraduates seeking abortions had much higher levels of sex guilt than other sexually active women who had avoided becoming pregnant. In a later study, Gerrard (1982) found that high sex guilt female undergraduates were more likely to report using ineffective or no contraception than other women. These results clearly parallel Moreault and Follingstad's finding that high sex guilt women's fantasies emphasize the lack of female responsibility over engaging in sexual behaviors.

Byrne and his associates argued that sex guilt may be only one component of a complex cluster of personality traits that mediate sexual behaviors. They postulated that, during socialization, a given individual is exposed to a variety of rewards and punishments associated with sexuality and may acquire both strong positive and negative emotional reactions. Rather than accept these emotional reactions as personal experiences, the individual projects his or her feelings to the external stimulus. Thus an individual's positive and negative emotional reactions to sexuality may quickly evolve into a complex belief system that, in turn, may determine the individual's later attitudes, behaviors, emotional reactions, motives, and physiological responses. Specifically, some individuals (erotophiles) report extremely positive attitudes and emotional reactions to erotic stimuli. Other individuals (erotophobes) report extremely negative attitudes and emotional reactions to the same stimuli (Byrne, Fisher, Lamberth, & Mitchell, 1974; Byrne, Jazwinski, Deninno, & Fisher, 1977).

Consistent with Byrne's model, other researchers have found that personality characteristics other than sex guilt may mediate sexuality. For example, Hollender, Luborsky, and Harvey (1970) found that females who reported a strong need for body contact (being held, caressed, touched, etc.) also reported extremely positive attitudes about sexuality.

Personality traits, other than sex guilt, also mediate contraceptive use. In a study of undergraduate women seeking abortions, Rader, Bekker, Brown, and Richardt (1978) found that pregnant undergraduates scored higher on measures of denial and masochism but not higher on sex guilt than nonpregnant peers. Leary and Dobbins (1983) found that female and male undergraduates who reported high levels of heterosexual anxiety also reported fewer sexual experiences and a higher preference for condoms than nonanxious subjects. The authors speculated that the clear preference for condoms expressed by highly anxious women may be due to their limited experience with intercourse.

One alternative explanation of Leary and Dobbins's findings is that highly anxious women, like high sex guilt women, may refuse to accept responsibility for engaging in sexual acts. Specifically, the highly anxious women preferred *male* contraceptives (condoms) rather than female contraceptives (i.e., diaphragms). Another alternative interpretation of these findings is that highly anxious females may find "planning to have sex" anxiety producing and prefer to risk pregnancy during "spontaneous" sexual encounters.

Although researchers currently disagree over whether global traits such as erotophilia-erotophobia or specific traits such as sex guilt or anxiety are better predictors of human sexuality, the available literature clearly indicates that emotional traits do exert a strong influence on human sexuality.

9.2.2. Emotional State Studies

The overall pattern of results of trait studies clearly suggests that "erotic stimuli" may elicit a wide variety of positive and negative emotional states from different individuals. Research on the relationships between sexual arousal and emotional states has focused on the fascinating issue of what mechanism produces such diverse emotional reactions during sexual arousal. In most non-human mammals, sexual behavior (and presumably sexual excitement) is controlled by four interdependent biological mechanisms: hormonal levels, pheromones, the perception of a suitable partner (sign stimuli), and sensory feedback from the genitals (Davidson, 1980). Researchers have examined whether any of the biological mechanisms observed in nonhuman species also influence human sexual behaviors.

In nonhuman species, androgen and estrogen play an important role in triggering sexual behaviors. As discussed previously in Chapter 3, androgens also play an important role in the sexual behaviors of both male and female humans. Surgical removal of the testes and adrenals in males or removal of the adrenals in females eventually leads to elimination of sexual drive. However, reducing estrogen levels by removal of the ovaries has no effect on sex drive in humans.

Consistent with these findings, researchers have repeatedly failed to demonstrate estrogen-related shifts in sexual behaviors in normally menstruating women. For example, Udry and Morris found that frequency of both intercourse and orgasm peaked around ovulation and was lowest around menstruation in normally menstruating women and in birth control pill users (Udry & Morris, 1968, 1970). Schreiner-Engel, Schiavi, Smith, and White (1981) asked 30 normally menstruating women to keep daily records of sexual excitement and behaviors. A vaginal photoplethysmograph was used to record their physiological reactions to fantasy and erotic tape recordings during the postmenstrual, ovulation, and premenstrual phases of their menstrual cycles. Subjective reports of sexual arousal did not vary systematically during the three phases of the cycle. Sexual arousal, however, was highest during the post- and premenstrual phases. Bancroft, Sanders, Davidson, and Wraner (1983) found that, excluding women with marked menstrual mood shifts, normally menstruating women tended to report higher subjective sexual arousal during the post- and premenstrual phases and to report the highest incidence of sexual behavior during the postmenstrual phase.

Although these findings may appear totally contradictory, it should be noted that researchers agree that the lowest frequency of sexual behaviors occurs during menstruation. Why would women who do not experience congestive dysmenorrhea abstain from sexual behaviors during menstruation? Paige (1977) hypothesized that the apparent reluctance of many American women to engage in sexual behaviors during menstruation was due to cultural menstrual taboos found in 73% of the world's cultures. Although American women have presumably developed more positive attitudes toward menstruation, Paige noted that a large proportion of samples of undergraduate women still report that intercourse during menstruation would be distasteful, embarrassing, or unsanitary.

In nonhuman species, pheromones often play a central role in sexual behaviors. As discussed in Chapter 8, both female and male humans do excrete a musklike pheromone in their urine. Other human pheromones have been identified in human apocrine sweat (Kirk-Smith, Booth, Carroll, and Davies, 1978) and in human vaginal secretions (Michael, Bonsall, and Warner, 1974). However, despite the popularity of scented soaps, oils, perfumes, and deodorants, there is absolutely no scientific evidence to support the claim of sociobiologists that humans' sexual behaviors are influenced by pheromones (Rogel, 1978). Cross-cultural studies have found marked cultural differences in reactions to specific odors. In some cultures, the scent of human sweat is considered erotic, whereas in other cultures the odor of sweat is considered repulsive. Moreover, there are marked individual differences within a given culture that appear due to individual sexual experiences.

In nonhuman species, sexual behavior is often triggered by specific "sign stimuli" such as a display of colored plumage. Compared with other primates, adult human females have extremely large breasts and adult human males have extremely large penes. Sociobiologists have argued that these anatomical characteristics may function as human "sign stimuli" (Diamond & Karlen, 1980). However, cross-cultural studies have found that neither female breasts nor male penes are considered sexual stimuli in all cultures (Ford & Beach, 1951).

Sensory feedback from the genitals plays an important role in the sexual behaviors of nonhuman species. Davidson (1980) noted that although male animals with anesthetized penes will begin to copulate, they quickly lose interest without genital feedback. Heiman (1977) examined the importance of genital feedback in human sexual excitement. She compared males' and females' subjective reports of sexual arousal with their actual sexual arousal during a series of erotic and nonerotic tapes and during fantasy. Correlations between subjective arousal and sexual arousal were virtually identical for both sexes and ranged from +.4 to +.68. However, analysis of the data by the degree of sexual arousal revealed a curious sex difference. At high levels of sexual arousal, 100% of the male subjects reported subjective sexual arousal, whereas 42% of the females denied sexual arousal. Further analysis revealed that female subjects were most likely to deny sexual arousal in the absence of erotic cues (neutral tapes). Thus their reports do not appear to be an artifact of social desirability but rather appear to represent an inability to perceive sexual arousal in the absence of external cues.

Heiman interpreted her findings on the basis of Schachter and Singer's model of emotion (see Chapter 3). She argued that females' apparent dependence on external cues was due to anatomical differences in sexual arousal. In males, penile erection provides an unambiguous cue to sexual arousal and, thus, males may accurately label sexual arousal in either the presence or absence of appropriate external cues. Sexual arousal in females, however, is a relatively vague event (tingling sensation in the clitoris, vaginal lubrication, etc.). In the absence of external cues, women may have difficulty in identifying and labeling these physiological changes as sexual arousal. Even in the presence of sexual cues, some subjects may still mislabel sexual arousal. For example, both high sex guilt (Morokoff, 1985) and sexually dysfunctional (Rook & Hammen, 1977) females may show physiological arousal to erotica, yet deny experiencing sexual excitement. For a more complete discussion of the cognitive labeling hypothesis of female sexual arousal, see Gagnon and Simon (1973).

An alternative interpretation of Heimen's findings is that males and females may focus their attention differently during sexual arousal. In our culture, males are encouraged to attend to their own genital responses during sexual acts, whereas females are encouraged to attend to external cues such as romantic relationships (Korff & Geer, 1983). According to this attentional hypothesis, the observed sex difference in awareness of sexual arousal may be an artifact of sex differences in attention.

Korff and Greer (1983) tested the validity of the attentional hypothesis by randomly dividing 36 women into three attention instruction groups. One group received explicit instructions to attend to their own genital responses. A second group was instructed to focus their attention on nongenital responses (i.e., heart rate), and a control group received no attention instructions. All the women were then presented with erotic slides and asked to rate their subjective sexual arousal while their actual sexual arousal was recorded, using a vaginal photoplethysmograph. Correlations between subjective and objective arousal ranged from $+.48$ to $+.69$ for control subjects. Subjects in the nongenital attention group showed a much higher degree of accuracy (mean r-values $= +.72$ to $+.86$), and subjects in the genital attention condition showed the highest degree of accuracy (mean r-values $= +.82$ to $+.9$). Thus, consistent with the predictions of the attentional hypothesis, it would appear that women *can* identify sexual arousal as accurately as males *if* they shift their attention to their own physiological responses.

The overall pattern of these findings suggests that genital feedback is a psychobiological control mechanism in humans rather than a purely biological control mechanism. Clearly, the relative importance of genital feedback is mediated by psychological factors (cognitive sets, attention). Research on the biological and psychological effects of alcohol on sexual arousal have yielded some interesting insights into this psychobiological mechanism.

Researchers have long been puzzled by the effects of ethyl alcohol on human sexuality. Biologically, alcohol inhibits sexual arousal. The greater quantity of alcohol consumed, the less capable the individual becomes of sexual arousal. Yet, paradoxically, subjective sexual arousal increases with alcohol intoxication in both sexes (Briddell & Wilson, 1976; Wilson & Lawson, 1976b). Thus, actual and subjective arousal (which are normally positively correlated) become negatively correlated after alcohol consumption.

The most commonly cited explanation for the paradoxical effects of alcohol on sexuality is called the *disinhibition hypothesis.* Presumably, alcohol directly inhibits sexual arousal by stimulating sympathetic vasoconstriction of the genitals (via the hypothalamus) while simultaneously inhibiting areas of the frontal lobes that normally inhibit sexual arousal. Thus, the pseudoaphrodisiac qualities of alcohol may be due to the disinhibition of the limbic system from cortical inhibition (Block, 1965).

Wilson (1977) argued that the disinhibition effects of alcohol may be more psychological than biological. He noted that a relatively high percentage of adults report the (erroneous) belief that alcohol increases sexual arousal. For example, in one survey, 68% of the female respondents and 45% of the male respondents reported that alcohol enhanced sexual pleasure (Athanasiou,

Shaver, & Yavris, 1970). Wilson hypothesized that such expectations that alcohol acts as an aphrodisiac may play a more important role than cortical disinhibition in alcohol-related increases in subjective sexual arousal.

In a clever series of experiments, Wilson and his associates separated the effects of psychological expectations from the biological effects of alcohol by giving subjects either alcohol (vodka) or a nonalcoholic beverage that tastes like vodka and then comparing subjects' sexual arousal and subjective sexual arousal to erotic stimuli.

Wilson and Lawson (1976a) divided 40 male undergraduates into two expectation treatment conditions. One group of subjects was told that they would be asked to drink vodka and tonic, whereas the other group was informed they would be drinking only tonic. A bogus breath analyser was used to reinforce these expectations. Half of the subjects in each group actually drank vodka. All the subjects then viewed an explicit erotic heterosexual film and a male homosexual film while sexual arousal was recorded with a penile ring. Regardless of the actual alcohol content of their drinks, subjects who *believed* they had consumed alcohol showed higher sexual arousal and reported greater subjective sexual arousal to both films.

Wilson and Lawson (1976b, 1978) repeated their experiment, using female subjects and vaginal photoplethysmographic recording. They found no effect of expectation instructions. The women who had consumed alcohol showed lower sexual arousal but reported higher subjective arousal to an explicit heterosexual film and a female homosexual film.

The observed sex difference in response to alcohol may be an artifact of a number of biological and psychological sex differences. First, in our culture, males tend to consume alcohol more frequently and in greater quantities than women. Thus, males may develop a higher tolerance for low dosages of alcohol than females. At higher blood levels of alcohol, males also show a paradoxical decrease in sexual arousal and an increase in subjective sexual arousal (Briddell & Wilson, 1976).

Second, the observed sex differences may be an artifact of sex differences in attention to genital responses. At low dosages of alcohol, males may simply be more accurate at detecting sexual arousal. At higher dosages, both sexes may base their judgments of sexual arousal on other physiological cues. For example, alcohol is a cardiac stimulant. With increased intoxication, both men and women may misattribute alcohol-induced increases in heart rate to sexual arousal.

Third, in our culture, males tend to report lower levels of sex guilt than females. This sex difference in sex guilt may produce different motives for alcohol consumption prior to sexual activity. Males may be more likely to use alcohol as a tool for sexual exploitation. (Candy is dandy but liquor is quicker.) Conversely, women may be more likely to use alcohol to avoid experiencing sex guilt, for example, "I was drunk at the time." Research with male subjects suggests that the "disinhibition" effects of alcohol-related expectancies are most pronounced in high sex guilt subjects (Lang, Searles, Lauerman, & Adesso, 1980; Lansky & Wilson, 1981). Moreover, males show greater sexual arousal and report greater subjective arousal to deviant stimuli (rape, sadism) when they *believe* they have consumed alcohol (Bridell *et al.*, 1978). Abrams and Wilson

(1983) found that the effects of alcohol-related expectancies on delay of gratification were unrelated to sex guilt *per se* but were related to erotophobia. Unfortunately, the equivalent studies have not been performed with female subjects. Thus, the role of sex guilt and of erotophobia in females' alcohol-related expectancies is currently unknown.

Weaver, Masland, Kharazmi, and Zillmann (1985) have provided some interesting additional support for Wilson's psychological disinhibition hypothesis. Male undergraduates were given either no, a low, or a high dose of alcohol and asked to view either subtle or slapstick humorous videotapes. With increased alcohol intoxication, subjects rated the slapstick tape funnier. Thus, whereas alcohol intoxication may impair subjects' ability to comprehend subtle humor, it may give the individual a socially acceptable excuse to react to more primitive forms of humor.

Overall, the pattern of findings of emotional state studies suggests that a complex interaction of cognitive factors (cognitive sets, attention), situational cues, and personality traits may mediate the role of genital feedback in humans' subjective experience of sexual arousal. However, it should be stressed that the majority of researchers have used the term *subjective sexual arousal* extremely loosely and have not differentiated between the awareness of genital sensations (self-perception), the emotional experience of sexual excitement, and the motive to engage in sexual acts.

Another major limitation of this research area is that the majority of studies have used only male subjects. Given the observed sex differences in both sexual arousal and subjective sexual arousal, generalizing from male samples to female populations is clearly unwarranted. Although we will discuss some additional studies of female sexual responses in the following section on clinical populations, additional research on nonclinical samples of females is clearly needed to clarify why women misperceive their own genital responses at even low dosages of alcohol. Carpenter and Armenti (1971) commented that the then-available literature on the effects of alcohol on sexual behavior made it appear "as if" only males consumed alcohol or engaged in sexual acts. Unfortunately, their comment is still valid.

9.3. CLINICAL POPULATIONS

Sex researchers have identified a large number of distinct clinical populations. For example, DSM-III lists the following eight major psychosexual disorders or paraphilias (amiss loves) as psychiatric disorders: exhibitionism, fetishism, masochism, pedophilia, sadism, transvestism, voyeurism, and zoophilia. The diagnostic category of "atypical psychosexual disorder" is used for less common paraphilias such as urophilia. Sex researchers have also studied criminal populations (incestual parents, pedophiles, rapists, etc.) and their victims. Because reviewing the entire clinical literature on human sexuality is beyond the scope of this book, we will focus our discussion on two specific clinical populations: rape victims and sexual dysfunctions.

9.3.1. Rape Victims

The actual incidence of rape is extremely difficult to estimate. Most researchers argue that only about 1 out of every 10 rapes is ever reported to any authority (police, hospitals, etc.). In 1979, there were over 76,000 rapes reported, and an estimated 600,000 individuals were raped in the United States during that year alone (Crooks & Baur, 1983). In the majority of rape cases, the assailant is male and the victim is female.

In a minority of rape cases, the assailant and victim are the same sex (homosexual rape). Such homosexual rapes are most common in prisons. For example, Davis (1980) documented 156 cases of homosexual rapes in the Philadelphia prison system during a 26-month period. Based on victims' unwillingness to cooperate with authorities due to feelings of shame and fear of retaliation, Davis estimated that the actual incidence of homosexual assaults was about 1,900 cases or roughly 1 out of every 30 inmates.

In a small minority of rape cases, the assailant is female and the victim is male. Although many people in our culture have difficulty believing that women can rape men, a number of such assaults have been documented. Female rapists tend to employ deadly weapons (guns, knifes, etc.) rather than physical force in their assaults and to target "defenseless" (intoxicated) adult males or smaller adolescent males or boys. Contrary to their depictions in pornography, female–male rapes are usually as violent as male–female rapes. In many cases, the female assailant denigrates the victim's masculinity and threatens to castrate the victim (Sarrel & Masters, 1982).

Studies of female victims of heterosexual rapes suggest that rape may elicit a complex set of emotions. During the assault, most victims report experiencing a variety of *negative* emotional reactions (anger, embarrassment, humiliation, terror, etc.). Victims who do become sexually aroused during the assault usually report experiencing disgust at their own physiological reactions. After the assault, the victims generally experience negative emotional reactions for a prolonged period of time. Burgess and Holstrom (1974) noted that rape victims tend to report similar adjustment problems (rape trauma syndrome) and hypothesized that postrape adjustment may occur in two distinct phases. During the first few weeks after the assault (acute phase), the victims report a variety of emotional reactions (anger, disbelief, fear, etc.). About half of the women show "expressive" reactions (crying, restlessness, etc.), whereas the remaining women show "controlled" reactions and appear abnormally calm. During the following year (long-term reorganization phase), the individual may experience depression, rape-related fears, social adjustment problems, and sexual dysfunctions (McCahill, Meyer, & Fischman, 1979; Nadelson, Notman, Zackson, & Gornick, 1982).

Other researchers have argued that women's postrape adjustment may be a more prolonged and complex process than Burgess and Holstrom's findings would indicate. For example, Calhoun, Atkeson, and Resnick (1982) tested 115 rape victims 2 weeks and 1, 2, 4, 8, and 12 months postrape. Compared with other women, rape victims reported higher levels of fear during the first month after the assault. Although the rape victim's levels of fear had declined somewhat by the 2-month testing session, it was still higher than other women's and remained elevated 10 months after the assault. Other researchers have found that rape-related emotional changes may last years. Ellis, Atkeson, and Calhoun (1981) found a higher incidence of depression in rape victims 1 to 16 years after the assault. Moreover, the assault also had long-term effects on the victims' sexual behaviors. Of the 27 women in their sample, 5 had abstained from sexual activity, 5 developed sexual dysfunctions, 5 became promiscuous, and 2 became lesbians after the assault.

Norris and Feldman-Summers (1981) examined the factors related to postrape adjustment. Their sample consisted of 119 rape victims who had been assaulted an average of 3.4 years earlier. The victims reported that, after the assault, they experienced an increase in a variety of psychophysiological symptoms and in the fear of being out alone. They also reported a decrease in sexual frequency and sexual satisfaction. The severity of the assault (i.e., victims' injuries) was positively correlated with the development of psychophysiological symptoms. The presence of understanding men and women (social support network) was negatively correlated with fears of going out alone. Vulnerability to claims of responsibility (e.g., the victims' behaviors that may have precipitated the assault) were positively related to going to bars alone. None of the four predictor variables was related to the decrease in sexual satisfaction.

The same individual may, unfortunately, be raped on more than one occasion. Ellis, Atkeson, and Calhoun (1982) compared the prerape adjustment of 25 women who had been raped once and 25 multiple-incident victims. All the women were tested about 2 weeks after the most recent rape. Multiple-incident victims had a higher incidence of psychiatric problems prior to the most recent rape. For example, 52% of the multiple-incident and only 16% of the single-incident victims had previously attempted suicide. The multiple-incident victims also reported fewer friends and lower sexual satisfaction than the single-incident victims.

Ellis raised the interesting question of whether the multiple-incident victims' poorer psychological adjustment made them more vulnerable to repeated rapes. One possibility is that these women are targeted because rapists assumed that these women would be less credible witnesses because "everyone knows she's crazy." Alternatively, these women's poor adjustment and higher unemployment rates may have forced them to live in high-crime neighborhoods where all women have a higher risk of rape. However, it should be noted that vulnerability in no way implies "responsibility." Women who are mentally ill or poor do not "deserve" to be raped. Moreover, in the case of multiple-incident victims, there is a strong possibility that their previous assault contributed to both their psychiatric problems and poverty (see Myers, Templer, & Brown, 1985; Wieder, 1985).

Clinical studies of male victims of homosexual rapes (Groth & Burgess, 1980; Kaufman, Divasto, Jackson, Voorhees, & Christy, 1980) and heterosexual rapes (Sarrel & Masters, 1982) suggest that male victims' reactions to sexual assault are quite similar to females' reactions. Regardless of the sex of the assailant, male victims report experiencing negative emotional reactions during the assault similar to those reported by females. There is some evidence that male victims may suffer more severe postrape adjustment problems than females. Male victims of homosexual and of heterosexual rapes report feeling "stigmatized" by the assault and are extremely reluctant to tell anyone about the incident. Moreover, postrape psychosocial adjustment problems, psychiatric disorders, and sexual dysfunctions appear to be more common and more severe in male than in female victims. However, Kaufman *et al.* (1980) noted that male rapes generally include characteristics that are also associated with poorer postrape adjustment in female victims. For example, compared to female victims, male victims are more likely to be attacked by multiple assailants (gang raped), to be forced to engage in multiple sexual acts, and to be severely injured during the assault. Such factors are negatively related to postrape adjustment in both sexes.

9.3.2. Sexual Dysfunctions

From the preceding discussion, it should be obvious that there is considerable overlap between clinical populations of rape victims and sexual dysfunction patients. The degree of overlap, however, is almost impossibe to estimate. Sarrel and Masters (1982) noted that many male rape victims who seek treatment for sexual dysfunctions at least initially deny that they were ever sexually assaulted. Such "silent rape" victims of both sexes frequently volunteer information about their current symptoms and attempt to conceal their histories of sexual assault. Conversely, many rape victims with sexual dysfunctions do not seek treatment.

The term *sexual dysfunction* is used to denote a class of physiological disorders of the sexual response cycle. For example, vaginismus is characterized by severe involuntary contractions of the entrance to the vagina. This disorder is classified as a sexual dysfunction because it makes intercourse painful or even physically impossible. Masters, Johnson, and Kolodny (1982) noted that not all sexual problems are classified as sexual dysfunctions. For example, individuals with a history of sexual assault (incest, rape, etc.) frequently experience irrational fears of sexual activity and tend to avoid engaging in sexual activity (sexual aversion or phobia). Usually, such individuals show perfectly normal sexual response cycles *if* they can overcome their fears. Thus sexual aversions are behavioral disorders rather than sexual dysfunctions.

Researchers currently believe that the majority of sexual dysfunctions are true psychophysiological disorders. However, sexual dysfunctions may also be produced by a variety of organic disorders, psychiatric disorders, and drugs (Degen, 1982; DeLeo & Magni, 1983; Wise, 1983). To further complicate matters, organic and psychological factors may interact in a complex fashion to produce sexual dysfunctions. For example, a male who experiences difficulty maintaining an erection while intoxicated may become anxious and depressed about becoming impotent. On later sexual encounters, his emotional stress may also interfere with his sexual arousal. If he consumes alcohol to reduce his sexual anxieties, the alcohol will further aggravate both his inability to maintain an erection and his sexual anxieties. In such cases, the symptoms are caused by the interaction of the drug and psychological distress.

Obviously, isolating the specific cause or causes of a patient's sexual dysfunction can be quite difficult. Kolodny, Masters, and Johnson (1979) estimated that organic factors (illnesses, drugs) are the primary cause of 10% to 20% of all cases of sexual dysfunctions and that organic factors may contribute to an additional 15% of the cases.

Karacan (1982) devised a clever diagnostic test to differentiate organic and psychogenic causes of sexual dysfunctions. Numerous researchers have reported that sexual arousal normally occurs during REM (dream) sleep periods in both males (Fisher, Gross, & Zuch, 1965) and females (Abel, Murphy, Becker, & Bitar, 1979) and that both sexes may experience nocturnal orgasms (Kinsey, Pomeroy, Martin, & Gebhard, 1953). Karacan reasoned that if psychogenic sexual dysfunctions were similar to conversion symptoms, then sexual dysfunctions should disappear when the patients were asleep. Consistent with this prediction, Karacan found that many males who were impotent while awake showed normal patterns of nocturnal erections. Moreover, this nocturnal response is absent in male patients whose sexual dysfunctions can be traced to specific organic causes. Although this test is also potentially useful in diagnosis of sexual dysfunctions in female patients, to date there has been relatively little research with female patients.

DSM-III criteria are based on the assumption that most psychiatric disorders are mutually exclusive. For example, the same individual would generally not display the symptoms of schizophrenia and a major depressive episode simultaneously. However, because sexual dysfunctions may be concurrent with other psychiatric disorders, DSM-III does permit a dual diagnosis. Specifically, a diagnosis of sexual dysfunction is appropriate with organic or psychiatric patients, if the patient's sexual dysfunction cannot be accounted for entirely by either (a) his or her other disorder or (b) the medications used to treat her or his other disorder. Thus, a given individual may be diagnosed as both an alcoholic and impotent or as both depressed and impotent. DSM-III groups sexual dysfunctions by the phase of the sexual response cycle where the symptoms occur: prearousal, excitement-plateau phase, or orgasm phase.

DSM-III lists only one disorder of the prearousal phase—hypoactive sexual desire. Such individuals are hyposensitive to sexual stimuli and report few sexual fantasies or interest in sexual behaviors. DSM-III states that hypoactive sexual desire is more prevalent in females than males but does not give either the incidence rate or the sex ratio of female to male patients. Hypoactive sexual desire should not be confused with celibacy. Celibate individuals usually have normal sexual desires but consciously choose to abstain from sexual activity for religious or philosophical reasons. In the majority of cases of hypoactive sexual desire, the individual has a history of other psychiatric disorders (alcoholism, depression, or sexual dysfunctions) or of sexual trauma (incest, rape, etc.). In a minority of cases, organic causes of this disorder (endocrine disorders, kidney disease, etc.) can be identified. For example, Schwartz and Bauman (1981) estimated that hyperprolactinemia may account for 10% to 20% of the cases of male hypoactive sexual desire.

Curiously, DSM-III does not list hyperactive sexual desire as a sexual dysfunction. Hypersexual males (satyrs) and females (nymphomaniacs) report a compulsion to engage in frequent sexual activities and that they experience little gratification from sexual activity despite frequent orgasms with numerous partners. Such individuals often seek psychotherapy only when their sexual behaviors interfere with their everyday activities and social relationships.

Disorders of the excitement-plateau phase of sexual arousal are subdivided by the patient's sex. Two common female disorders are vaginismus and general sexual dysfunction. The latter disorder is characterized by inadequate vasodilation and lubrication of the vagina. The male equivalent of this disorder is labeled erectile dysfunction or impotence. In both sexes, the individual experiences difficulty in maintaining adequate physiological arousal *on a regular basis*. Transient episodes of general sexual dysfunction and impotence are fairly common and may be due to fatigue, psychological stress, or a variety of other causes. Such acute episodes are not considered sexual dysfunctions. For example, Hoon, Wincze, and Hoon (1977) found that anxiety may either facilitate or inhibit sexual arousal in healthy female subjects. Similarly, the Dutton and Aron "bridge" study (discussed in Chapter 4) suggests that under some circumstances anxiety may facilitate sexual arousal in males. Clinical studies, however, indicate that chronic anxiety may play a major role in both general sexual dysfunction and impotency (Cooper, 1969a,b).

Sexual dysfunctions of the orgasm phase are also designated by the patient's sex. In males, two common disorders are premature ejaculation and retarded ejaculation. Premature ejaculation is characterized by a brief plateau phase followed by an orgasm elicited by minimal stimulation. Although the terms *brief* and *minimal* are difficult to objectively define, in the typical case of premature ejaculation, the male achieves orgasm before insertion of the penis into the vagina or after a few pelvic thrusts. Retarded ejaculation is characterized by prolonged plateau phase and delayed orgasm despite vigorous stimulation. Again, the terms *prolonged* and *vigorous* are difficult to define objectively.

Heiman and Rowland (1983) compared the sexual arousal of sexual dysfunctional and of normal males to erotic audiotapes and to self-generated sexual fantasies. Each subject was tested once with "high performance demands" instructions (concentrate on how erotic the material is) and once under low performance demands (relaxation). The healthy male subjects showed higher sexual arousal to the high performance demand instructions, whereas the dysfunctional males showed higher arousal during the relaxation instructions. Across testing conditions, the sexually dysfunctional males showed lower sexual arousal than healthy males and reported more negative emotional reactions (anxiety and depression).

Female sexual dysfunctions of the orgasmic phase are collectively labeled *anorgasmia*. Primary anorgasmia is used to denote cases where the woman has never experienced an orgasm through any form of stimulation. Cases where the individual has previously experienced orgasms but is no longer achieving orgasm are labeled *secondary anorgasmia*. A subset of women report that they can achieve orgasm only through clitoral stimulation (coital anorgasmia) or can achieve orgasm with only some partners (situational anorgasmia) or only irregularly (random anorgasmia). Given that many anorgasmia patients do experience orgasms in some situations, the older diagnostic term, *frigidity*, has little meaning.

Wincze, Hoon, and Hoon (1976) compared the sexual arousal of healthy and sexually dysfunctional women to an erotic film of a couple engaging in foreplay. The healthy women showed higher vaginal engorgement during the film than the dysfunctional women, yet both groups of women rated their subjective sexual arousal equivalently. Thus self-reports of subjective sexual arousal correlated with sexual arousal for healthy women but not for the sexually dysfunctional women.

Researchers have consistently reported that a variety of therapeutic approaches may be highly effective in the treatment of sexual dysfunctions. For example, Masters and Johnson (1970) employed behavioral therapy to treat female and male sexual dysfunctions. For female patients, the success rates of their treatment program average 78% and range from 71% with situation anorgasmia patients to 99% with vaginismus patients. Similarly, their success rates of sexual therapy for male patients averaged 85% and ranged from 67% with primary impotence patients to 96% with premature ejaculation patients (Masters, Johnson, & Kolodny, 1982).

Although the success rates of Masters and Johnson's treatment program are quite impressive, other researchers have argued that alternative treatment programs may produce even higher success rates (Lobitz & LoPiccolo, 1972; LiPiccolo, Heiman, Hogan, & Roberts, 1985). However, the issue is not whether psychotherapy can be effective with sexual dysfunctions but rather *which* type of therapy is most effective with *what* type of client.

Research on human sexuality has had numerous implications for theories of emotion. First, individuals may learn to associate sexual excitement with a wide variety of socially acceptable and unacceptable stimuli. Second, depending on an individual's personality traits, sexual arousal may be associated with a wide variety of positive or negative emotions. Third, emotions may interfere with or facilitate sexual arousal. Fourth, sexual arousal and sexual excitement may become dissociated. For example, during alcohol intoxication, sexual excitement may occur in the absence of sexual arousal. Similarly, individuals with sexual dysfunctions may be unaware of their own sexual arousal. Fifth, sexual traumata such as rape may have long-term emotional consequences. As we will discuss later in Chapters 12 through 16, many contemporary theories of emotion have difficulty accounting for this diverse pattern of findings.

SUGGESTED READINGS

Davidson, J. M. The psychobiology of sexual experience. In J. M. Davidson & R. J. Davidson (Eds.), *The psychobiology of consciousness.* New York: Plenum Press, 1980.

A comparative discussion of neural and neurohormonal control of mammalian sexual behaviors.

Kendrick, D. T., Springfield, D. O., Wagnals, W. L., Dahl, R. H., & Ransdell, H. J. Sex differences, androgyny and approach response to erotica: A new variation on the old volunteer problem. *Journal of Personality and Social Psychology*, 1980, *38*, 517–524.

A clever study of sample biases in sexual research.

Ladas, A. K., Whipple, B., & Perry, J. D. *The G spot: And other recent discoveries about human sexuality*. New York: Holt, Rinehart & Winston, 1982.

A controversial discussion of female "ejaculation."

Masters, W. H., & Johnson, V. E. *Human sexual response*. Boston: Little, Brown and Company, 1966.

Landmark study of the physiology of female and male sexual responses.

Mosher, D. L. The meaning and measurement of guilt. In C. E. Izard (Ed.), *Emotions in personality and psychopathology*. New York: Plenum Press, 1979.

A useful review of the literature on guilt and human sexuality.

The Skeletal Muscle System I
Nonclinical Populations

Like other overlearned behaviors, adults tend to take their own perceptual-motor skills for granted and are often mystified by the obvious difficulty infants and young children display when they attempt to perform "simple" motor movements. Yet, even "simple" physical movements are actually extremely complex acts. Fitts (1964), for example, noted that the motor movements needed to hit a baseball are so complex that the computer program needed to command a robot arm to perform the same act would be as sophisticated as a computer program designed to play chess.

10.1. ANATOMY AND PHYSIOLOGY

The skeletal muscle system is composed of five major anatomical units: bones, joints, ligaments, tendons, and striate (striped) muscles. Because each of these anatomical units plays a important role in motor movement, we will briefly discuss each anatomical component separately.

The 206 bones in the adult human's skeleton perform four basic mechanical functions. First, the skeleton provides some protection from mechanical injury for the internal organs. Second, the skeleton provides a framework of mechanical support for the viscera. Third, the bones serve as a mechanical leverage system for exerting force against the internal organs. For example, the bones of the rib cage help inflate and deflate the lungs. Fourth, the bones serve as a mechanical leverage system for exerting force against the physical environment. The human skeleton represents a compromise between the conflicting mechanical needs for rigidity and for flexibility. To provide the rigidity needed to protect and support internal organs, some of the bones of the skull, hip, and spine are fused together. The remainder of the bones of the skeleton are jointed to provide a flexible framework for exerting leverage on either the external or internal environment.

The joints are the second major anatomical unit of the skeletal muscle system. Technically, the term *joint* merely defines the space between two bones and thus refers to the juncture of either fused or movable bones. For the purpose of clarity, the term *joint* will be used in our present discussion only to refer to movable joints. A joint consists of a coating of articular cartilage on the end of each bone and either a disc of fibrous cartilage or a fluid-filled sac (bursa). Both the cartilage and bursa act as shock absorbers. The fluid in the bursa also acts to reduce friction between the bones. Some joints such as the knee are enclosed by a lubricating membrane called a *synovia*. Joints are classified according to the type of movement that they produce. Saddle joints (found only in the thumbs) produce a variety of movements. Ball-and-socket joints such as the hip and shoulder produce rotary movement in a variety of directions. Pivot joints allow two bones to rotate and are found between vertebra. Hinge joints such as the knee only flex (bend) or extend (straighten).

Ligaments are broad bands of connective tissue that hold two bones together at a joint. The ligaments are quite elastic and allow the joint to move rather freely while preventing the two bones from being pulled out of alignment. Thus ligaments play only a passive role in joint movement.

Tendons are bands of strong elastic tissue that connect a bone to a muscle. By extending across joints, tendons allow the contractions of a muscle attached to one bone to pull against a second bone.

Over 400 individual striate muscles in the human body are the fifth major component of the skeletal muscle system. Unlike either cardiac or smooth muscle, striate muscles do not contract spontaneously and thus require neural stimulation to contract. Each muscle is composed of long thin fibers that are functionally organized into groups called motor units. As shown in Figure 10-1, each motor unit is innervated by a single motor neuron that synapses with all the fibers. The cell membrane of each muscle fiber acts as a postsynaptic neuron and depolarizes when stimulated by acetylcholine. Depolarization causes the muscle fiber to temporarily contract or shorten. The cell membrane then repolarizes, and the muscle fiber relaxes. Because all of the fibers of a single motor unit are innervated by the same neuron, they all contract and relax simultaneously.

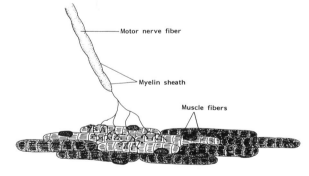

Motor nerve fiber

Myelin sheath

Muscle fibers

Figure 10-1. The motor unit.

Two different physiological mechanisms control the degree of muscle contraction. First, each action potential produces a single contraction. Increasing the frequency of neural stimulation increases the average amount of contraction of a single motor unit. The second physiological mechanism for increasing muscle contraction is to stimulate an additional number of motor units. At rest, only a small number of motor units within a given muscle are stimulated at any one time. This produces a steady state of partial muscle contraction called *muscle tone*. If these weak contractions are blocked by a muscle relaxant drug such as curare, you would collapse into a limp jellylike mass. When a greater degree of contraction is needed for movement or to provide force against external objects, progressively more motor units are activated.

Anatomically, the majority of skeletal muscles are arranged in antagonistic pairs. For example, when you straighten your leg, your anterior thigh muscles (quadricep femoris) contract while your posterior thigh muscles relax (see Figure 10-2). Conversely, when you bend your knee, your anterior thigh muscles relax while your posterior thigh muscles contract. Complex body movements involve the coordinated activity of multiple pairs of antagonistic muscles that contract and relax in a synergistic (cooperative) fashion. For example, the leg movements involved in walking are produced by the sequential contraction-relaxation of 24 major muscles in each leg (Wells, 1971). Given that walking also normally involves holding your back and head erect while you swing your arms in opposition to your legs, it should be obvious that a large proportion of your skeletal musculature is actively involved in the "simple" act of walking.

Skeletal muscles are commonly classified by their location in reference to the skin's surface (Basmajiam & Blumenstein, 1980). Muscles that are adjacent to skin are labeled *superficial*. The major superficial muscles of the human body are shown in Figure 10-3. Many major skeletal muscles, however, are covered by the

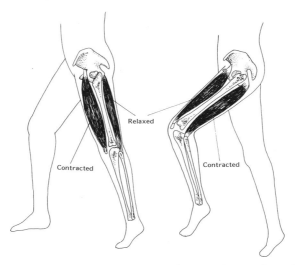

Figure 10-2. Antagonistic contraction–relaxation of pairs of muscles.

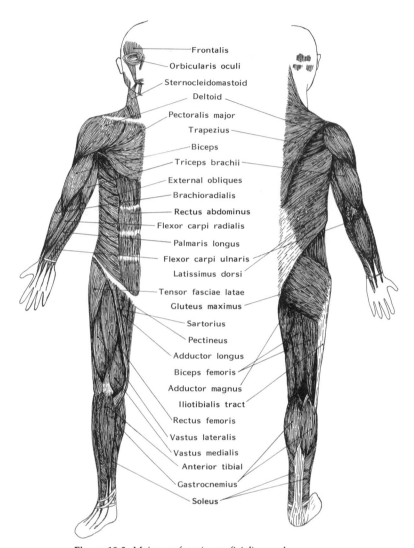

Figure 10-3. Major surface (superficial) muscle groups.

superficial muscles. Such "deep" muscles may run obliquely, parallel, or perpendicular to overlying superficial muscles. Moreover, deep muscles may contract in an antagonistic, synergistic, or unrelated fashion to the superficial muscles. Thus, attempting to describe global (bodywide) skeletal muscle activity during even a "simple" movement is somewhat like trying to describe the simultaneous state of 400 or so independently occurring events. Readers who are interested in a more detailed discussion of kinesiology are referred to Wells (1971) and Broer (1966).

Given the complexity of coordinating body movement, it should not be surprising that a relatively large proportion of the human central nervous system from the cortex to the spinal cord is involved in coordinating skeletal muscle activity. In order to successfully perform a purposeful movement, we first need to perceive the following information: (a) The physical characteristics of the environment. Are the surfaces soft or hard, smooth or rough, flat or tilted? (b) Our orientation in the environment. Are we lying, sitting, or standing? Are we floating or falling? and (c) the current state of our skeleton and muscles. Where are our legs? Four major sensory systems are involved in providing the sensory information needed to initiate and successfully complete motor movements: the visual system, the vestibular (balance) system, the haptic (touch) system, and the kinesthetic (joint position) system. The anatomy and physiology of these four sensory systems is beyond the scope of this book. For a detailed discussion of these sensory systems, see Schiffman (1982) and Ludel (1978).

Research on humans' ability to adapt to distorted (prism) vision illustrates the importance of sensory input to the skeletal muscle system. Kohler (1962, 1964) asked human subjects to wear prisms that produced a mirror reversal (left-right) of the retinal image. Initially, the conflicting information from the visual and other sensory systems produced a marked disruption in motor behaviors. After a few days, the subjects adjusted their motor behaviors to match their "new" retinal images. After wearing the prisms for about 2 months, some subjects had become so accustomed to their distorted retinal image that they were now performing complex motor acts like skiing.

Held (1965) argued that the remarkable adaption of humans to prism distortions reported by Kohler and other researchers may have occurred only because the subjects were given the opportunity to actively explore their environment. Held postulated that if subjects were given only passive experience to visual distortions, they would fail to adapt. In a clever series of experiments, Held provided subjects with either active or passive experience with distorting prisms. For example, in one study, subjects wearing prisms either walked around a room (active movement) or were pushed around the same room in a wheelchair (passive movement). Held found that subjects who were allowed to actively perform motor tasks while wearing prisms eventually adapted to the distorted image, whereas subjects who were given only passive experience did not. Thus it would appear that prism adaption depends upon subjects' exposure to both their own motor commands and sensory feedback that the task has been performed erroneously.

The results of prism adaptation studies suggest that information from the visual system tends to dominate over feedback from the other three sensory systems. Specifically, the motor errors produced when wearing prisms are due to the subjects' disregarding accurate feedback from their haptic and kinesthetic systems and using the erroneous visual information to guide their movements (Rock & Harris, 1967). However, other researchers counter that both blindfolded and blind humans can make extremely accurate body movements. Thus, feedback from the vestibular, haptic, and kinesthetic systems are sufficient to control motor movement in the total absence of visual information (see Schiffman, 1982). Although the debate over the relative importance of these sensory systems to motor movements is theoretically important, it obscures the basic fact that we normally receive *redundant* information from all four sensory systems. For example, if you tilt your head to one side while looking in a mirror, your CNS simultaneously receives input from your visual, vestibular, haptic, and kinesthetic systems that your head is tilted. For the purpose of controlling body movement, the information "head tilt 106 degrees" is more critical than which sensory system supplied the information.

The CNS contains at least four distinct "motor command systems" for controlling skeletal muscle activity. The reflex system is the simplest form of motor command system in the sense that only a small number of synapses are involved in initiating and completing the motor movement. As discussed previously in Chapter 2, the spinal cord directly controls a number of motor reflexes. The majority of spinal reflexes are elicited by stimulation of skin receptors. However, the stretch reflex is elicited by receptors located in the muscle spindles. If a muscle is mechanically stretched, the spinal cord signals the muscle to contract to compensate for the load. Merton (1972) hypothesized that the stretch reflex plays an important role in regulating voluntary body movements by acting like powersteering in a car. For example, when you lift a heavy suitcase with your right hand, the additional weight stretches the muscles on the left side of your body and elicits the stretch reflex. The contractions of the muscles on the left side of the body cause you to bend to the left to compensate for the weight imbalance produced by the suitcase.

Most textbook discussions of reflexes focus primarily on spinal reflexes that are elicited by either haptic or kinesthetic stimuli. However, it should be noted that reflexive motor behaviors are also elicited by other sensory stimuli via subcortical structures. For example, loud sudden auditory stimuli elicit orienting and startle reflexes via the inferior colliculus. If I fire a gun 5 feet away from your head, you will reflexively jump and turn your head toward the sound source. Similarly, moving visual stimuli elicit orienting and defensive reflexes via the superior colliculus (Gordon, 1972). If an object moves in the periphery of your visual field, you reflexively turn your head and eyes toward the movement. If the moving object happens to be a brick being thrown at your head, you will reflexively duck. Although the cortex cannot initiate motor reflexes, it clearly can inhibit or facilitate reflexive motor movements. For example, your reflexive reaction to a gun's being fired is mediated both by your knowledge (or lack of knowledge) that the event will occur and your cognitive appraisal of the direction in which the gun is pointed. If you know when the event will happen and that the gun is pointed away from you, you may completely inhibit your startle reaction. Conversely, if you are unaware when the event will occur but are aware that the gun is pointed at your face, you may display a highly exaggerated motor response.

The remaining three motor control systems all involve three major brain structures: the frontal lobes of the cortex, the basal ganglia located in the limbic system, and the cerebellum in the hindbrain. Given the high degree of overlap in neural "control centers," it might appear more logical to conclude that the brain contains a single gigantic motor control circuit. However, research suggests that the cortex, basal ganglia, and cerebellum may each control a different type of motor movement. For the purpose of discussion, we will adopt Evarts's (1973, 1979) model of the cortex, basal ganglia, and cerebellum as functionally separate but interdependent motor control systems.

The cortical-pyramidal tract system was traditionally believed to be the primary CNS motor control system. Broca and other nineteenth-century neuroanatomists recognized that damage to areas in the frontal lobes caused paralysis in muscles on the opposite side of the body. With the advent of electrical mapping techniques, researchers repeatedly explored the surface of the cortex and consistently found that discrete motor movements could only be elicited when specific areas of the frontal lobes were stimulated. As shown in Figure 10-4, five major motor areas in the frontal lobes have been identified. Area 4 is commonly referred to as the motor cortex because electrical stimulation of this region produces an involuntary robotlike motor movement such as raising an arm on the side of the body opposite to the lobe stimulated. Each lobe is topologically organized so that each lobe contains a "map" of the muscles of the opposite side of the body. The size of muscle representation in Area 4 is determined not by the actual size of the muscle mass but rather by the degree of fine motor behavior it produces. Thus muscles that make extremely fine movements (face, hands, and tongue) have relatively large representations in the motor cortex, whereas muscles that make rather crude movements such as the legs have rather small cortical representations. Area 6 is commonly referred to as the premotor cortex because electrical activity in Area 6 precedes neural activation of Area 4. Areas 8, 44, and 45 are called *supplementary motor areas* because they represent muscles that are also represented in Area 4.

According to the traditional view of motor control, the premotor area functions as the link between the "higher" cognitive functions of the frontal lobes (planning, anticipating consequences, etc.) and overt motor acts. According to this view, the premotor area selects the appropriate motor behavior, and the motor cortex translates the behavioral "plan" into specific motor commands.

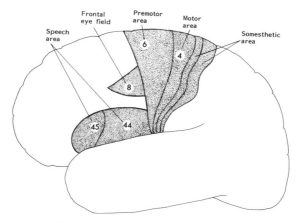

Figure 10-4. Motor areas of the cortex.

Consistent with this view of motor control, electrical recordings of monkeys' cortices during delayed movement have found that not only is the premotor cortex activated *prior* to the motor cortex, but different clusters of premotor neurons are activated depending upon both the muscles needed for the movement and the direction of the movement (Niki, 1974; Niki & Watanabe, 1976).

The pyramidal tract is usually described as an "express route" for motor commands. The axons of motor cortex neurons descend through the forebrain and midbrain along a section of the pyramidal tract called the *internal capsule*. At the level of the midbrain, fibers descending from the left and right hemispheres form parallel tracts. Some pyramidal fibers branch off from the primary tract and synapse with neurons located in a number of subcortical structures. At the medulla, about 80% of the fibers cross over to the opposite side of the body. Some fibers pass through the medulla and descend down the spinal cord before synapsing with spinal cord neurons. The remaining pyramidal fibers terminate at motor neurons located in the medulla. The axons of these postsynaptic fibers branch. Some medulla fibers form the cranial nerves that innervate the muscles of the head, whereas others descend down the spinal cord and eventually synapse with motor neurons of the spinal nerves.

Two subcortical structures, the basal ganglia and the cerebellum, are connected by a looping series of tracts that are collectively labeled the *extrapyramidal* or *supplementary motor tract*. Anatomists traditionally assumed that the extrapyramidal tract did not initiate motor movements but rather coordinated posture and balance during movement. For example, complete destruction of the cerebellum does not cause paralysis but rather produces jerky uncoordinated movements. However, Evarts (1973, 1979) and other researchers have argued that the results of both clinical and laboratory studies suggest that the extrapyramidal system contains two additional motor control systems—the cerebellum and the basal ganglia—that may independently initiate as well as coordinate movement.

The cerebellum-extrapyramidal control system consists of a multisynaptic looplike circuit that connects the motor cortex and the cerebellum. Pyramidal tract fibers synapse with three subcortical structures (nuclei pontis, lateral reticular nucleus, and inferior olive) that then relay the signals to the interposed nucleus and other areas of the cerebellum on the opposite side of the brain. Thus motor cortex commands to the muscles are simultaneously forwarded to the cerebellum on the *same* side of the body as the intended movement. Axons from the dentate nucleus of the cerebellum cross back over to the opposite side of the brain and synapse with cells in the thalamus. Axons from the thalamus then project back to the area of the motor cortex that initiated the movement (see Eccles, 1973).

The basal ganglia-extrapyradmidal system is composed of a series of interlocking subcortical structures (caudate nucleus, globus pallidus, putamen, and substania nigra) that are collectively labeled the *basal ganglia*. The extrapyramidal tract of the basal ganglia is composed of a complex series of multisynaptic tracts that loop between the cortex and spinal cord. Descending tracts lead from the basal ganglia to the spinal cord, whereas ascending tracts via the thalamus terminate in both the premotor and motor cortexes. The basal ganglia receives neural input from both the RAS and a large area of the cortex. Destruction of the basal ganglia, like the cerebellum, does not produce paralysis but rather produces abnormal patterns of movement. Based on this clinical observation, researchers traditionally assumed that the basal ganglia also does not initiate movement but rather functions as a "higher-level cerebellum" to help coordinate posture and balance during motor movements.

A number of researchers have attempted to clarify the sequence of CNS control of movement by recording the electrical signals from multiple sites in the brain while monkeys performed specific sequences of movements. Based on the traditional model of motor control, it was assumed that activation of the motor cortex would always precede activation of subcortical structures. Surprisingly, researchers have discovered that electrical activity often occurs in the basal ganglia (DeLong, 1974), dentate nucleus (Thach, 1970a,b, 1978) and the thalamus (Evarts, 1971) *prior* to electrical activity in the motor cortex.

Clearly, activation of the subcortical "feedback" system *prior* to the "feed" from the motor cortex contradicts traditional explanations of neural control of motor movements. Evarts (1973, 1979) proposed that both the cerebellum and basal ganglia do initiate movement but that each structure initiates a different *type* of motor behavior. He noted that opposite patterns of movement abnormalities are produced by destruction of either the cerebellum or basal ganglia.

Damage to the cerebellum produces a set of motor disorders that are all characterized by disruption of fast ballisticlike movements that require a sequence of coordinated motor movements, for example, running. Movements are jerky and the patient often may under- or overshoot a desired limb position. Muscle tremors are most severe in patients with cerebellum damage when they attempt to perform a fine motor act such as playing a musical instrument and may disappear when the patient is resting or performing slow motor acts.

An opposite pattern of motor abnormalities is observed in patients with damage to the basal ganglia. For example, Parkinson's disease is a neurological disorder that primarily affects the globus pallidus and substantia nigra. Symptoms of Parkinson's disease include difficulty in initiating movements, loss of spontaneous emotional facial expressions, muscle tremor, postural rigidity, and difficulty performing slow motor movements. Parkinson's-disease patients, however, may perform rapid motor movements almost normally. Evarts argued that these clinical findings suggest that the cerebellum and basal ganglia act as complementary motor control centers with the cerebellum controlling fast movements and the basal ganglia controlling slow movements. Note that, according to Evarts's model, destruction of either the cerebellum or basal ganglia would be expected to produce highly specific motor abnormalities but *not* paralysis.

Evarts's subcortical model is a promising attempt to explain how the CNS performs the complex process of integrating sensory information and motor commands to produce fluid patterns of body movements. Evarts's model also may help account for why patients with a variety of neurological disorders may show a marked disassociation between voluntary and involuntary emotional displays. For example, Gilles de la Tourette syndrome patients curse involuntarily, whereas pseudobulbar palsy patients may suddenly laugh or cry involuntarily. In such cases of *emotional lability*, the patients often struggle unsuccessfully to inhibit their own involuntary emotional displays. Thus the subcortical motor control centers appear capable of initiating emotional displays independent of the motor cortex.

Rinn (1984) argued that the overall pattern of clinical findings suggests that the pyramidal system controls voluntary or "social" emotional displays, whereas the extrapyramidal system controls involuntary or genuine emotional displays. In healthy adults, the pyramidal system usually inhibits or masks extrapyramidal motor commands. In infants and emotional lability patients, however, the extrapyramidal system may dominate.

10.1.1. Methodological Issues in Skeletal Muscle Research

As discussed throughout the preceding chapters, researchers frequently emphasize the importance of distinguishing between emotional behaviors and emotional states. Emotional behaviors are defined as overt or covert displays of emotions. Examples of *overt* emotional displays include vocalizations (e.g., screaming), autonomic responses that are visible to external observers (blushing and sweating), and a variety of motor responses such as posture, involuntary movements (e.g., facial expressions), and voluntary motor acts (e.g., hitting). *Covert* emotional displays are physiological responses, such as heart rate, that are normally "invisible" to the external observer but that are (at least theoretically) observable with the appropriate recording equipment. Emotional states represent the individual's conscious activity (thoughts, perceptions, images, etc.) at a given point in time. Because external observers cannot verify the content of an individual's conscious activity, researchers *infer* emotional states on the basis of their observations of the individual's overt and covert emotional behaviors.

Obviously, the accuracy of an external observer's inference about your current emotional state is mediated by both the accuracy of the observer's observations and your ability to consciously control your overt emotional behaviors. For example, the major methodological weakness in the self-report studies is that regardless of how carefully the experimenter constructs a questionnaire or structures an interview, the subject can consciously choose to lie. Because the subject has 100% control over self-report behaviors (oral or written responses), he or she may easily deceive the experimenter. Thus the validity of self-report data is always questionable. Researchers have attempted to "objectively" verify subjects' self-reports by simultaneously recording the subjects' overt and/or covert emotional behaviors.

Anatomists traditionally assumed that the autonomic nervous system responses were "involuntary" (0% conscious control), whereas somatic nervous system responses were "voluntary" (100% conscious control). However, skeletal muscle responses are not always voluntary. During emotional states, individuals may spontaneously display a variety of reflexive and learned motor responses. Even if they are conscious of their own overt emotional behaviors, they may or may not be able to inhibit their responses.

As we will discuss in detail later in this chapter, researchers have employed a variety of techniques to circumvent human subjects' ability to consciously fake overt emotional displays. For example, a common research strategy is to employ concealed observation. Hidden observers or cameras are used to record subjects' spontaneous reactions to emotional tasks such as anticipating electric shocks. Another common research strategy is to inform subjects that they are being observed but to deceive them about the purpose of the observation. In such experiments, subjects might be informed that they will be photographed during an interview because the experimenter is interested in "eye movements," when in reality the experimenter is interested in postural movements. If the subjects believe the experimenter's deception, they may make such a conscious effort to fake their eye movements that they neglect to conceal postural reactions. A third research strategy is to induce subjects to become coexperimenters by challenging them to consciously deceive a group of observers. Assuming that subjects comply with the experimenter's request, this technique allows the researcher to compare the subjects' spontaneous overt behaviors with their consciously deceitful emotional displays. The specific methodogical limitations of each approach will be discussed later in the context of specific experiments.

One major potential confound in all three observational approaches is clothing. In his study of cross-cultural postural behaviors, Hewes (1957) noted that differences in clothing may account for a number of cultural and sex differences in postures and movements. For example, females in our culture are trained to sit differently when wearing slacks than when wearing skirts.

Clothing also effectively conceals many skeletal responses. If the subject is wearing a short-sleeve blouse or shirt, tensing the forearm is an overt behavior. However, when the subject is wearing a long-sleeve blouse or shirt, the same response is effectively a covert behavior. As discussed previously in Chapter 6, both Alexanderian and Reichian therapists have systematically observed the skeletal muscle reactions of clients who were either wearing tight-fitting leotards or who were nude. These clinical studies have found that the effects of emotional states on posture and movement are often mediated by skeletal muscles groups (abdominal, back, chest, etc.) that are normally concealed by everyday attire (see Lowen, 1968; Barlow, 1973).

A second major potential confound in all observational studies is that skeletal muscle responses may be either overt behaviors or covert behaviors. Individuals may consciously choose either to "act out" their emotional states (overt responses) or may decide to attempt to inhibit their overt motor behaviors by consciously tensing antagonistic muscle groups. Thus muscle responses that may not be detected by an external observer can be detected by an electromyographic (EMG) recording of the electrical activity of the specific muscle groups.

EMG recording, like other forms of electrophysiological recordings, creates its own unique set of artifacts. For example, the electrical signals of both deep and superficial muscles may be detected by surface electrodes attached to the skin. Determining the source of the electrical signal, however, is often difficult. A given EMG signal may originate from either the underlying superficial or deep muscles. In medical research, experimenters often employ needle recording electrodes to separate the electrical activity of superficial and deep muscles. In laboratory settings, researchers rely on a less precise surface electrode technique that is commonly called *muscle belly* recording. Two small surface electrodes are located close together on the skin directly parallel with the main mass or belly of a specific muscle. (For a more detailed discussion of EMG recording artifacts and electrode placement, see Basmajiam & Blumenstein, 1980; Martin & Venables, 1980.)

Like other types of electrophysiological recording techniques, EMG recording is a "reactive" procedure. That is, the subjects are consciously aware of "being studied" and of which muscles are being recorded by the location of electrodes attached to their skin. Thus the results of many EMG studies may reflect reactive effects to the testing situation rather than subjects' spontaneous skeletal muscle reactions to emotional stimuli.

10.2. EMOTIONS AND THE SKELETAL MUSCLE SYSTEM

Although Charles Darwin is commonly associated with the theory of evolution, Darwin was also one of the early pioneers of observational study of overt emotional behaviors. Darwin (1872) proposed a rather comprehensive theory of overt emotional behaviors. Based on cross-cultural observations of humans and cross-species observations, Darwin postulated that emotional displays of both human and other species fell into three general categories: (a) learned habits, (b) antithesis movements (involuntary responses that are mirror images of learned habits), and (c) reflex actions (genetically determined or "species-specific" behaviors). Because Darwin's theory is often erroneously referred to as a *genetic* or *sociobiological* model of emotion, the reader should be aware that Darwin placed a strong emphasis on the importance of learning in emotional expressions. He argued that unless a specific behavior was displayed by *all* members of a given species, the behavior should not be considered "reflexive." For example, Darwin ruled out kissing as a human reflex because, in many cultures, individuals do not kiss. He argued that both individual and cultural differences in emotional displays were due to learning.

After a careful review of the cross-cultural literature on emotional expression, Darwin concluded that only a small number of human emotional expressions should be classified as "reflexes." Specifically, Darwin noted that only a few autonomic responses (blushing, crying, sweating), a few vocalizations (gasping, laughing, screaming, and weeping) and a few nonfacial muscle patterns ("dancing" with joy and shrugging one's shoulders in helplessness) were observed in humans across cultures. However, a number of human emotional facial expressions (e.g., frowning) appeared to be universal across cultures. Later researchers have found strong empirical support for at least three major tenets of Darwin's model.

First, Darwin predicted that very *few* nonfacial emotional displays (gestures, postures, etc.) would be found universally across cultures. Consistent with this prediction, later cross-cultural research has found large cultural differences in nonfacial emotional expressions (Morris, 1977).

Second, Darwin predicted that some emotional facial patterns should be observed across cultures. Again, cross-cultural studies have found that at least six facial patterns (e.g., smiling) are almost universally recognized as expressing specific emotional states such as happiness (Ekman, Sorenson, & Friesen, 1969). Thus it would appear that specific facial patterns may represent species-specific emotional displays.

Third, Darwin predicted that cultures may attempt to train children to inhibit specific emotional displays. For example, Darwin commented that (at least properly educated Victorian) English children did not shrug their shoulders and noted that English parents punished their children for emotional displays that they considered "French." Cross-cultural studies also indicate that cultures differ radically in whether such nonverbal emotional displays are exaggerated or inhibited (Eibl-Eibsefeldt, 1972). In cultures where emotional displays are socially accepted, adults of both sexes characteristically make theatrical displays of emotional behaviors. Conversely, in cultures where displays of emotions are considered socially unacceptable, adults of both sexes may appear unemotional to observers. Moreover, in cultures that stereotype emotional displays by sex, marked sex differences in emotional expression are observed. For example, in our culture, emotional displays have traditionally been stereotyped as "feminine," and males are taught that only a limited number set of emotional behaviors (anger, joy, and sexual excitement) are "masculine." Not surprisingly, American males tend to display fewer emotions but more physical and sexual aggression than American females.

Given that Darwin based his model on observations of a relatively small number of species and on observations of a relatively small number of human cultures, the validity of his model is absolutely astounding. However, it should be stressed that some aspects of Darwin's theory have received only equivocal support. For example, Darwin postulated that emotional displays have an "anticathartic" effect on emotions. That is, "acting out" your emotions should increase the intensity of emotional arousal and suppressing your emotional displays should reduce arousal. However, as we discussed previously in Chapter 4, cardiovascular research suggests that the relationships between emotional displays, emotional states, and physiological arousal are highly complex. Depending upon both the situation and the individual's personality, "acting out" your emotions may produce either cathartic reductions in emotional and physiological arousal or anticathartic increases in the intensity of arousal.

Laboratory studies of the role of skeletal muscles in emotional states have focused on two fascinating research issues raised by Darwin's theory: nonverbal communication and anticatharsis.

10.2.1. Nonverbal Communication

Darwin (1872) argued that the evolutionary function of emotional displays was to communicate a given individual's intentions to members of the same species. For example, monkeys can learn to avoid electric shocks by observing only the "fear" facial displays of other monkeys (Miller, 1967). However, Darwin did concede that humans may learn to voluntarily mimic displays of emotions that they are *not* experiencing and to voluntarily suppress displays of emotions that they are experiencing.

Given that humans may intentionally "fake" nonverbal displays of emotions, how accurate are humans at guessing another individual's true emotional state? In the typical nonverbal communication experiment, photographs of human emotional displays are used as stimuli, and subjects are asked to guess what the person in the photograph is feeling. For example, Zuckerman, Hall, DeFrank, and Rosenthal (1976), secretly videotaped female and male undergraduates while they viewed two pleasant and two unpleasant films and while they discussed their emotional reactions to the films. The subjects were then asked to pose in an appropriate facial response to express their reaction to each film. The same subjects were later asked to judge the emotional states of the facial expressions of other subjects during the films, talking about the films and posing. They found that (a) judgments of spontaneous and posed facial expressions were similar, (b) females were more accurate judges of facial expressions than males, (c) a subject's ability to serve as a stimulus was positively but weakly related to his or her ability to judge the emotional expressions of other people, and (d) the intensity of subjects' emotional reactions was positively correlated with the accuracy of observers' judgments.

Zuckerman et al.'s study was selected as an example of nonverbal communication research for two important reasons. First, this experiment illustrates the methodology typically employed in nonverbal communication studies. Second, although their findings appear rather clear-cut in isolation, they must be interpreted in the context of the available literature. Other researchers have reported results that contradict all four of the major findings in the Zuckerman et al. study. Such contradictory findings do not necessarily imply that the results of any given experiment are "false" but rather illustrate the complexity of the process of communication. For example, verbal communication is a dynamic (active) and dyadic (speaker–listener or author–reader) relationship. Obviously, the speaker's (or author's) ability to express (encode) his or her thoughts into verbal messages influences the accuracy of communication. However, the listener's (or reader's) ability to decode verbal messages also influences the accuracy of communication. Thus the accuracy of communication depends on the degree of agreement between the speaker's encoding and listener's decoding. Similarly, the accuracy of nonverbal communication is also influenced by the clarity of the sender's nonverbal display and by the observer's ability to decode nonverbal messages.

Both the encoding and decoding processes may be influenced by any number of variables. For example, Clark, Milberg, and Erber (1984) found that physical arousal (playing a game of tennis) increased observers' judgments of the intensity of positive facial expressions (i.e., joy), but did not alter observers' judgments of negative facial expressions such as anger. Similarly, Gaelick, Bodenhausen, and Wyer (1985) found that members of married and cohabiting couples were relatively accurate in judging their partner's *negative* emotional displays but were surprisingly inaccurate at identifying their partner's positive emotional displays. As a group, females tended to misperceive the *lack* of expressed hostility as an expression of their partner's love. Conversely, males tended to misperceive the *lack* of positive emotional displays as hostility.

Researchers have attempted to isolate specific variables that influence the accuracy of nonverbal communication. For example, one potentially important variable is the presence or absence of verbal cues during emotional displays. Wallbott and Scherer (1986) videotaped three professional actresses and three professional actors who were each instructed to portray anger, joy, sadness, and surprise. A total of 43 German graduate students were then asked to judge either audiovisual or audio only or visual only or distorted audio samples of the emotional displays. Although the results of this study are highly complicated, data analyses revealed three interesting findings. First, the actresses and actors differed markedly on their encoding abilities. Some encoders were judged more accurately than others on specific emotions or specific scenes or on the basis of audio or visual cues. Although this finding may appear to be purely "common sense," it should be stressed that these were professional actors portraying stereotypical emotional displays. Second, auditory cues did not improve the accuracy of decoders' judgments. Based on auditory cues alone, decoders could differentiate the emotional displays at better than chance levels (37% accuracy); however, visual presentation alone had higher levels of decoding accuracy (63%). Adding sound to the videotape did not improve the accuracy of observers' judgments. Third, the decoders' accuracy varied with the emotion portrayed. Anger and sadness were easier to recognize than either joy or surprise.

Verbal messages contain both semantic (content) and nonverbal (quality) cues to the encoder's emotional state. They also contain cues about other characteristics of the encoder (i.e., age, ethnic origin, sex, socioeconomic class). Gallois and Callan (1986) examined whether the encoder's accent alters decoders' judgments of nonverbal emotional displays. Female and male Anglo-Austrilian judges were presented audiovisual, audio-only, or visual-only samples of emotional displays of female and male Australian, British, or Italian encoders. Overall, female observers were more accurate than male observers only when audiovisual samples were presented. Although observers were equally accurate at judging visual-only presentations of the three ethnic groups' behaviors, the Italian encoders were judged less accurately in the sound-only condition. Adding sound to the videotape reduced the accuracy of observers' judgments of Italian males' but not females' neutral and negative nonverbal displays. Thus it would appear that, although verbal cues such as accent may bias the observer, they do not automatically distract the observer's attention from the encoder's nonverbal behaviors.

Another major variable that affects nonverbal communication is whether observers base their judgments of other people's emotional states on facial and/or postural cues. Dittman, Parloff, and Boomer (1965) presented groups of psychotherapists and professional dancers with a film of an actress during a bogus interview and asked the observers to rate the pleasantness-unpleasantness of her emotional states during 15 segments of the film. In 5 of the film segments, the actress portrayed positive facial and postural expressions (e.g., smiled and had a relaxed posture), and in another 5 segments, the actress portrayed negative facial and postural expressions (e.g., frowned and fidgeted). In the remaining 5 segments, the actress portrayed a mismatch between facial and postural cues (smiled and fidgeted). Because the psychotherapists judged her emotional state as pleasant in the 10 film segments with positive facial expressions, they apparently based their judgments on the actress's facial cues alone. The professional dancers, however, noticed the 5 instances where facial and postural cues mismatched and rated these segments as less pleasant than segments with both positive facial and postural cues. The authors then showed their film to a dance therapist who rated the mismatched segments as highly unpleasant. These findings suggest that the perception of an individual's emotional states may vary with whether the observer attends to the sender's face, body, or both.

Ekman and Friesen (1969b) hypothesized that observers' attentional patterns may influence their accuracy at detecting nonverbal cues of deception. They argued that, in Western cultures, individuals learn to censor their facial cues more than their postural cues during lying. Thus postural behaviors may also provide valid cues to deception. Consistent with this prediction, McClintock and Hunt (1975) found that self-manipulations (touching oneself) and postural shifts (gross movements of the trunk) both commonly occurred during discussions of unpleasant topics and when the respondents attempted to deceive the interviewer. Facial expressions, however, appeared to differentiate unpleasant topics and deception. During unpleasant topics, smiling increased, whereas, during deception, smiling decreased. Although both the senders' facial and nonfacial responses appear to be valid cues to deception, a number of studies have found that observers tend to ignore nonfacial cues. Ekman and Friesen (1974), for example, found that both undergraduate females and males tended to base their judgments of deception on facial cues alone. Instructing subjects to attend to body cues did not increase their accuracy of detecting deception *unless* they were first shown an example of the senders' postural behaviors when they were responding honestly. (For a more detailed discussion of nonverbal cues to deception, see Ekman, 1985.)

Clearly, both the encoder and the decoder influence the accuracy of nonverbal communication. Lanzetta and Kleck (1970) examined whether an individual's ability to encode nonverbal cues was related to his ability to decode nonverbal cues. They secretly videotaped undergraduate males while they were receiving electric shocks. Each subject was later shown the videotape of himself and videotapes of five other subjects and asked to guess whether the person received a shock or no shock on each trial. They found no relationship between a subject's ability to judge his own emotional displays and his ability to judge the emotional displays of other subjects. Contary to Darwin's "anticatharsis" hypothesis, subjects' EDA during shock anticipation was negatively related to how accurately other subjects judged their facial displays. Thus subjects who showed the strongest autonomic reactions were the poorest "stimuli."

DePaulo and Rosenthal (1979) examined the interesting question of whether individuals who are skilled at detecting nonverbal cues to deception are also more accurate at judging the senders' actual emotional states. They videotaped female and male undergraduates while they discussed people that they strongly disliked, liked, both liked and disliked, and were indifferent about. On half the trials, subjects were instructed to intentionally lie. Later, the subjects were asked to judge the honesty-dishonesty and true emotional states of their peers during the interview. No relationship between skills at detecting deception and the ability to guess others' emotional states was found. They also found no sex differences in either the ability to judge deception or the senders' true emotional states. Rather, they observed that subjects of both sexes who adopted a theatrical "hamming" style of deception tended to successfully mislead both female and male judges.

A number of other researchers have examined the role of the encoder's and decoder's sex in nonverbal communication. For example, Buck, Savin, Miller, and Caul (1972) compared females' and males' judgments of facial displays. Their subjects were randomly assigned to same-sex pairs. One member of each pair served as a "sender" and viewed slides of facial injuries, landscapes, mothers and children, nudes, and unusual photographic effects (i.e., double exposures). The senders' facial responses during the slide presentations were secretly recorded on closed-circuit TV. The second member of each pair (observer) sat in a separate room and watched their partner's face on TV. Their task was to guess the specific emotion the senders were experiencing and the intensity of their emotional reaction. Observers of both sexes were able to guess their partners' emotional states at better than chance levels. However, the female observers were more accurate than male observers. Moreover, consistent with Lanzetta and Kleck's findings, the senders' EDAs were negatively related to the accuracy of the observers' judgments. Buck, Miller, and Caul (1974) repeated their experiment but randomly assigned subjects to either same- or opposite-sex pairs. They found that judgments of the emotional states of female "senders" were more accurate than judgments of male "senders" but that there were no sex differences in the accuracy of the observers. Thus the higher accuracy rates of female pairs observed in their first study appear to be an artifact of the sex of the senders. Again, EDA was negatively related to the accuracy of nonverbal communication.

10.2.2. Anticatharsis–Catharsis Studies

The results of the nonverbal communication studies discussed in the preceding section appear to refute Darwin's prediction of the "anticathartic" effects of behavior displays. Thus it would appear that "acting out" your emotions may be cathartic. However, as we will discuss in the following section, a number of studies have found that emotional displays can also be "anticathartic."

In a series of three experiments, Lanzetta, Cartwright-Smith, and Kleck (1976) examined whether instructing subjects to conceal or exaggerate facial reactions to electric shock would alter their physiological and psychological reactions to the shock. Female and male subjects were informed that they would receive a series of electric shocks and that on each trial they would be signaled as to the intensity (no, low, medium, high) of the shock. The subjects were then informed that their facial responses would be videotaped and later rated by judges. The subjects were then instructed to either conceal or exaggerate their facial responses to the shocks. In all three experiments, voluntarily altering facial responses led to consistent changes in autonomic activity. When subjects were instructed to conceal their reactions, they showed lower EDA and reported less pain than when they received no instructions. Conversely, subjects who were instructed to exaggerate their responses showed higher EDA and reported higher levels of pain than when they received no instructions. These findings were replicated in a later study using a live observer (Kleck *et al.*, 1976).

One plausible explanation of Lanzetta *et al.*'s findings is that they were artifacts of the subjects' coping strategies. Specifically, instructing subjects to "exaggerate" their responses may elicit active coping strategies, whereas instructing subjects to "conceal" their responses may elicit passive coping. As discussed previously in Chapter 4, active coping strategies produce increases in autonomic arousal, whereas passive coping strategies produce decreases.

Given that Lanzetta's subjects were aware that they were "acting," it is impossible to determine whether the observed anticatharic effects were due to the emotional displays or to subjects' coping strategies. Laird (1974) devised a clever technique to separate the effects of acting and emotional displays. He posed subjects' faces in specific emotional expressions *without* their awareness that they were making emotional facial patterns. To produce this deception, Laird employed an elaborate set and script. Subjects were recruited for a study of the role of facial muscles in "perception." When the subjects arrived in the laboratory, they were shown an impressive-looking polygraph machine and had a number of electrodes attached to their facial muscles. No EMG recordings were actually made. Subjects were then informed that because emotional facial reactions were a major "artifact" in this experiment, the subjects would be asked to hold a fixed pose and report their emotional states to "control" for this artifact. In two experiments, Laird had undergraduate male subjects "smile" or "frown" by instructing them to tense specific facial muscles. Approximately 16% of the subjects correctly guessed that they were asked to pose in an emotional expression, and their data were discarded. In both studies, subjects who smiled reported higher levels of happiness than control subjects, and subjects who were frowning reported higher levels of anger. These findings suggest that emotional displays may increase the intensity of emotional states and predispose subjects to experience specific emotions.

Laird's "posing" procedure has become a popular method for eliciting emotional displays (presumably) without the subjects' knowledge. For example, McArthur, Solomon, and Jaffe (1980) used Laird's methodology to compare the emotional responses of overweight and normal-weight subjects. They found that "smiling" and "frowning" altered the self-reports of emotional states of the normal-weight but not the overweight subjects.

Ekman, Levinson, and Friesen (1983) asked 12 professional actors and 4 scientists to pose their facial muscles in the patterns of six different emotions (anger, disgust, fear, happiness, sadness, and surprise). The subjects were instructed to contract specific muscles (i.e., wrinkle your forehead) and presumably did not guess that they were being asked to reproduce specific emotional expressions. The subjects were then asked to "relive" a past experience associated with each of the six emotions. For both the actors and scientists, specific facial patterns elicited distinct patterns of autonomic arousal. With angry facial expressions, both heart rate and skin temperature increased. With both fear and sad facial patterns, heart rate increased, but skin temperature decreased. Heart rate decreased with disgusted, happy, and surprised facial patterns.

Although the Ekman *et al.* findings suggest that facial patterns alone may trigger autonomic responses, it should be noted that there are two serious methodological flaws in this study. First, the study lacks any of the elaborate deceptions employed in Laird's original experiment. Second, Ekman *et al.*'s subject samples (actors and scientists) represent two populations that are most likely to guess the meaning of the facial poses. For example, Synder (1974) found that professional actors were highly sensitive to their own emotional expressions. Similarly, the scientists who served as subjects in the Ekman *et al.* study were all experts on facial communication. Given the sample bias in this study, it would be premature to conclude that facial patterns *alone* may elicit emotional reactions.

The available literature on emotional facial displays suggests that both the anticatharsis and catharsis hypothesis may be partially valid. In some circumstances, emotional displays appear to increase autonomic arousal (anticatharsis), whereas, in other instances, emotional displays appear to decrease autonomic arousal (catharsis). Theorists who have attempted to reconcile these contradictory findings commonly cite Jones's (1950) theory of internalizers-externalizers as an explanatory device. Jones postulated that when children are punished for emotional displays, they are simultaneously learning to inhibit emotional behaviors and to substitute autonomic arousal for overt responses. (Learning theorists would label Jones's "substitution" a conditioned emotional response, or CER.) Children who are repeatedly punished for emotional displays will eventually learn to "internalize" their emotional responses as autonomic arousal, whereas children who are not punished should continue to "externalize" their emotional displays. Given that boys are more likely to be punished for expressing emotions in our culture than girls, adult males should be more likely to be "internalizers," whereas adult females should be more likely to be "externalizers." Consistent with this prediction, Buck *et al.* (1972, 1974) found that a disproportionate number of males were internalizers, that is, poor nonverbal "senders" and displayers of high EDA.

Jones's theory nicely accounts for cathartic effects of emotional displays. Paradoxically, Jones's model may also at least partially account for the anticathartic effects of emotional displays. Assuming that internalizers have a history of punishment for facial displays, posing an internalizer's face in an emotional expression or asking the subject to "exaggerate" his or her facial display would act as a conditioned stimulus that would elicit a strong CER. Conversely, instructing internalizers to "conceal" their facial reactions would be consistent with their usual avoidance of facial displays and thus might help minimize the intensity of the CERs by removing the precipitating stimuli (facial expressions). Thus, Jones's model may also account for internalizers' higher EDA when they express their emotions than when they conceal them. Jones's original model, however, has difficulty accounting for anticathartic effects of emotional displays by externalizers.

Asendorpf and Scherer (1983) hypothesized that Jones's model may also account for externalizers' behavior if the personality dimension of repression-sensitization is also considered. They argued that "externalizers" may be composed of two distinct subgroups: nonanxious individuals and repressors. In anxiety-provoking situations, the nonanxious subjects would show low autonomic arousal whereas the repressors would show elevated autonomic arousal.

Experimental manipulations that emphasize the emotional nature of the testing situation may have little effect on low-anxiety subjects (e.g., "Why worry? It is only an experiment"). However, such manipulations directly conflict with repressors' normal coping style (denial) and should therefore increase repressors' psychological stress. Thus, when asked to exaggerate facial displays, repressors may show elevated autonomic reactions and emotional displays but continue to deny feeling anxious. Consistent with these predictions, Buck *et al.* (1972) found that internalizers tended to score high on sensitization but, as a *group*, externalizers did not score high on repression.

Although Jones's hypothesis provides an excellent *post hoc* explanation for contradictory facial display literature, additional research is clearly needed to confirm or refute his predictions. Moreover, it should be stressed that not all experiments have found either anticatharsis or catharsis.

As discussed previously in Chapter 6, clinical observations have found that stooped (gorillalike) postures are fairly common in depressed patients. In a series of three experiments, Riskind (1984) tested the role of posture feedback in emotions by posing subjects in either stooped or upright postures while subjects either succeeded or failed at specific tasks. He found that when an upright posture was appropriate (i.e., the subject had succeeded), stooping decreased both motivation and sense of control over the situation. However, when stooping was appropriate (i.e., the subject had failed), stooping produced lower self-reports of depression and higher motivation than an upright posture. Riskind noted that these findings do not fit either a simple anticatharsis or catharsis explanation of posture and speculated that posture may play an active role in subjects' information processing. Based on Lacey's environmental intake-rejection model discussed previously in Chapter 4, Raskin hypothesized that posture may influence whether individuals direct their attention toward the external environment (i.e., environmental intake) or toward internal sensation and thoughts (i.e., environmental rejection). Specifically, stooping appears to elicit environmental rejection that is adaptive in failure situations but maladaptive in success situations. Conversely, upright postures appear to elicit environmental intake that is adaptive in success situations but maladaptive in failure situations.

10.2.3. The Role of Cognitions in Emotional Displays

As discussed in the preceding section, specific types of cognitive processes (attention, coping strategies, defense mechanisms, etc.) may account for the contradictory literature on the cathartic effects of emotional displays. Other researchers have attempted to clarify this issue by examining the effects of cognitions on emotional displays and emotional arousal.

Professional actors usually employ one of two techniques to produce convincing emotional displays on stage. One commonly employed acting technique is to reproduce the facial expressions, postures, and vocal patterns that are stereotyped as a specific emotional display in a given culture. Thus, if an actor bares his teeth, clenches his fists, and screams, an audience (at least in our culture) will attribute anger to the character that the actor is portraying. This acting technique is generally referred to as "nonmethod" acting. An alternative acting technique for portraying emotional states is to spontaneously recreate emotional displays by mentally concentrating on a personal memory or image associated with a given emotion. This technique is referred to as "method" acting, or the Stanislavsky technique. Stern and Lewis (1968) examined whether these two acting techniques produced differential autonomic arousal. They recruited 10 method and 11 nonmethod actors and actresses and tested their ability to voluntarily produce EDA. Although three professional directors could not differentiate between method and nonmethod actors/actresses on the basis of their emotional displays, the method actors/actresses showed much greater control over EDA and could voluntarily produce larger EDA than nonmethod actors/actresses.

One of the major criticisms of Stern and Lewis's study is that they compared self-selected (static) groups of subjects. That is, each actor/actress habitually employed method or nonmethod acting techniques *prior* to the experiment. Why a given individual selected method or nonmethod acting is unknown. For example, it is quite plausible that externalizers might be attracted to nonmethod acting's focus on emotional displays, whereas internalizers are attracted to method acting's emphasis of internal mental activity. Thus the observed differences in EDA may reflect personality differences of the actors/actresses rather than their acting techniques *per se*.

As discussed previously in Chapter 4, Rusalova *et al.* (1975) examined the relationship between mental imagery and facial displays when the same individual employed either method or nonmethod acting techniques. Their subjects were 23 professional actors and drama students and 12 laboratory assistants. The subjects' first task was to vividly imagine situations that elicit feelings of anger, fear, joy, and sadness. The second task was to reproduce the same emotional images while maintaining a blank (poker) face. The third task was to reproduce the facial expression for each emotion while not producing an emotional image. For both groups of subjects, the highest heart rates occurred during the first task (spontaneous imagery), and the lowest heart rates occurred during facial expressions alone. In the actors, different patterns of facial muscle tension accompanied each of the four emotional images. In the nonactors, such differential facial muscle activity was observed only with joy and sadness images.

Both Stern's and Rusalova's findings suggest that autonomic arousal may be more closely linked to emotional mental activity than to overt emotional displays. In a series of experiments, Schwartz and his associates have systematically examined the relationship between patterns of facial muscle activity and emotional thoughts and images (Schwartz, Fair, Greenberg, Friedman, & Klerman, 1974; Schwartz, Fair, Greenberg, Mandel, & Klerman, 1974; Schwartz, Fair, Salt, Mandel, & Klerman, 1976a,b; Schwartz, Brown, & Ahern, 1980; Friedlund, Schwartz, & Fowler, 1984). In these experiments, subjects were instructed to "think about" and to vividly imagine situations associated with specific emotional states while EMG was recorded from a number of facial muscles and the subject's face was videotaped. Schwartz consistently found that thoughts or images about a specific emotion such as happiness elicit a pattern of covert muscle activity that is virtually identical to the subjects' overt emotional displays. That is, even when the subjects' faces appear to be expressionless, their facial muscles are contracting "as if" they were making a facial expression appropriate for that specific emotion. (Prior to the 1950s, researchers commonly referred to such covert muscle activity as *anticipatory motor responses.*) In one study, Friedlund *et al.* (1984) demonstrated that these covert facial responses to emotional images were distinct enough to be recognized by a computer. Thus the computer was able to correctly "guess" the subjects' mental image by analyzing subjects' facial muscle activity. It should be noted that consistent with the view that males in our culture are trained to inhibit overt emotional displays, Schwartz *et al.* (1980) observed marked sex differences in covert facial patterns during imagery. Specifically, distinct facial patterns to specific emotional images are much more common in female than in male subjects.

As we will discuss later in Chapters 13 and 15, various theorists have noted that facial responses may represent *either* causes *or* effects of human emotions. Although Schwartz's findings would appear to provide rather strong evidence that facial responses play a central causal role in emotions, the reader should avoid the logical fallacy of "reversibility." If "A occurs with B," this does not in any way imply that "B must occur with A". For example, covert or overt "smiling" appears to reliably occur during "happy thoughts." However, smiling may also occur during a variety of negative emotional states (Hagar & Ekman, 1983; Sullivan & Brender, 1986). Thus, whereas happy thoughts may produce smiling, smiling *per se* may not indicate "happy thoughts." Whether the overall pattern of facial activity could be used to differentiate "happy smiles" from brave, embarrassed, or nervous smiles is currently an open question.

SUGGESTED READINGS

Darwin, C. R. *The expression of emotion in man and animals.* New York: Appleton and Company, 1896. Originally published in London by Murray in 1872.

   Classic comparative study of emotional behaviors. This work represents the first "modern" theory of emotion.

Ekman, P. *Telling lies.* New York: Norton, 1985.

   An excellent review of literature on deception in nonverbal communication.

Evarts, E. V. Brain mechanisms of movement. *Scientific American,* 1979, *241(3),* 164–179.

   A clear discussion of the anatomy and physiology of voluntary movement.

Rinn, W. E. The neuropsychology of facial expression: A review of the neurological and psychological mechanisms for producing facial expressions. *Psychological Bulletin,* 1984, *95(1)* , 181–187.

   A somewhat technical discussion of the anatomy and physiology of facial expressions. However, it contains an excellent discussion of the clinical literature on emotional lability.

The Skeletal Muscle System II
Clinical Populations

Studies of skeletal muscle activity in clinical populations have focused on two overlapping issues. First, what are the relationships between skeletal muscle tension and abnormal emotional states (clinical anxiety, depression, etc.)? Second, what relationships exist between skeletal muscle tension and psychophysiological disorders?

11.1. PSYCHIATRIC POPULATIONS

As discussed in previous chapters, high levels of autonomic arousal are characteristic of anxiety disorders. However, postural movements (fidgeting, pacing, finger tapping, etc.) are also commonly observed in anxiety patients. The joint occurrence of both autonomic arousal and emotional displays in anxiety patients would appear to violate Jones's theory of internalizers-externalizers.

Numerous explanations have been offered for the elevated autonomic and skeletal muscle activity in anxiety patients. First, it is possible that anxiety patients are actually internalizers and that their elevated skeletal muscle activity represents nonverbal cues that they are attempting to conceal their emotional states. Consistent with this hypothesis, Wishner (1953) found that the physiological pattern displayed by anxiety patients during stress is typical of internalizers. He compared the facial (frontalis and masseter) muscle activity and heart rates of 11 anxiety patients and 10 control subjects during a variety of physical stressors (cold pressor test, hyperventilation, loud horn blast) and psychological stressors (oral math test, Rorschach inkblot test). The cold pressor test elicited the greatest physiological differences between the anxiety patients and the controls. At the end of the cold pressor test, the anxiety patients showed much higher heart rates but much lower facial muscle tension than control subjects.

Studies of depressed patients have also found that unusual patterns of facial muscle activity may be characteristics of psychiatric patients. In a series of experiments, Schwartz and his associates have observed that depressed and control females react differently to only very specific emotional images (Schwartz, Fair, Greenberg, Friedman, & Klerman, 1974; Schwartz, Fair, Greenberg, Mandel, & Klerman, 1974; Schwartz, Fair, Salt, Mandel, & Klerman, 1976a,b). Specifically, when asked to generate images of angry or sad scenes, depressed patients and control subjects display very similar patterns of facial muscle activity. However, when asked to generate happy images or images of a "typical day," marked group differences in facial activity occurred. The control subjects displayed a covert "smiling" facial pattern, whereas the depressed women displayed a mixed angry-sad facial pattern. These findings are consistent with the self-reports of depressed patients who often complain that they "can't imagine" being happy.

Another plausible explanation for the joint occurrence of autonomic and skeletal muscle activity in samples of anxiety patients is that elevated autonomic arousal may be characteristic of some patients, whereas elevated skeletal activity may be characteristic of other patients. Consistent with this individual response stereotypy hypothesis, Cameron (1944) found that, although the majority of anxiety patients reported skeletal muscle symptoms, a significant minority of patients reported only cardiovascular or gastrointestinal symptoms. Cameron also observed that when the patients' level of anxiety increased, most patients experienced global physiological arousal. Thus patients who normally reported only cardiovascular symptoms also reported gastrointestinal and/or skeletal muscle symptoms during acute anxiety attacks. It would appear, therefore, that anxiety-induced response stereotypy may mask individual stereotypy.

A similar pattern of individual response stereotypy has also been observed in samples of depressed psychiatric patients. Balshan-Goldstein and her associates found that some depressed patients showed primarily elevated autonomic responses to stress, whereas other depressed patients showed increases in skeletal muscle tension (Balshan-Goldstein, Grinker, Heath, Oken, & Shipman, 1964; Shipman, Oken, Balshan-Goldstein, Grinker, & Heath, 1964).

A third plausible explanation for the joint occurrence of autonomic arousal and skeletal muscle tension in anxiety patients is that autonomic arousal may indicate the patients' emotional state, whereas elevated skeletal muscle activity may represent the patients' attempts to inhibit their emotional displays. As discussed previously in Chapter 6, Reichian therapy is based on the assumption that individuals learn to inhibit specific emotional displays by tensing specific skeletal muscles. Although such muscular contractions are initially voluntary, these responses become involuntary and unconscious through repetition. Thus, any given individual may form idiosyncratic patterns of involuntary skeletal muscle contractions (body or muscular armor) to specific emotional stimuli (Wright, 1982).

Consistent with the Reichian model, there have been numerous case reports of idiosyncratic patterns of muscle tension in anxiety patients (Plutchik, 1954; Barlow, 1959). Moreover, Malmo and his associates have demonstrated that psychiatric patients may show elevated tension in specific muscles that are related to their personal emotional conflicts (Malmo, 1949; Malmo, Shagass, &

Davis, 1950; Shagass & Malmo, 1954). For example, patients who have difficulty expressing anger tend to show increased tension in their arm muscles, whereas patients who have difficulty expressing their sexuality tend to show elevated tension in their leg or lower back muscles.

A fourth plausible explanation for the joint occurrence of autonomic arousal and skeletal muscle tension in anxiety patients is that autonomic arousal may be yoked to skeletal muscle activity. As discussed in Chapter 4, Obrist (1976) postulated that an individual's strategy for coping with stress may mediate both skeletal muscle and autonomic activities. Active coping should produce increases in both skeletal muscle and autonomic activities. Conversely, passive coping should produce decreases in both skeletal muscle and autonomic arousal.

Consistent with Obrist's predictions, Balshan-Goldstein (1965) found that, regardless of psychiatric diagnosis, anxious patients showed elevated autonomic and skeletal muscle reactions to stress. The subjects in this study were drug-free female and male psychiatric patients who had recently been admitted into a mental hospital and who had not yet begun psychotherapy. These patients had been diagnosed as either anxiety reactions, depression, personality disorders, psychoses, or somatoform disorders. Hospital personnel served as a (presumably) normal control group. Measures of autonomic activity included EDA, heart rate, and respiration rate. Skeletal muscle tension was recorded from seven major facial and nonfacial muscles. After recording electrodes were attached, the subjects were asked to rest for 1 hour and 15 minutes to habituate to the recording equipment. The subject was then presented with 1 minute of loud white noise. The physiological responses of the personality disorder patients and somatoform patients were similar to those of the control subjects. Anxiety, depression, and psychotic patients, however, all showed heightened autonomic and skeletal muscle reactions to the stressor. The depressed patients showed the greatest autonomic reactions, whereas the psychotic patients showed the largest increases in skeletal muscle tension. The author noted that the one common characteristic in these three groups of patients was high self-reports of state anxiety.

A fifth commonly cited explanation for the joint occurrence of autonomic arousal and skeletal muscle activity in anxiety patients is that autonomic arousal may be yoked to muscle tension in a few "key" skeletal muscles. Alexander and Smith (1979) speculated that two different physiological mechanisms could produce covariance between autonomic arousal and EMG-levels in a specific subset of skeletal muscles.

One potential biological mechanism is that emotional stress may simultaneously elicit both autonomic arousal and anticipatory responses in a small subset of skeletal muscles. For example, if the individual is anticipating "flight," tension would increase primarily in the leg muscles. If the individual is anticipating "fight," EMG levels would increase primarily in the arm muscles. Such anticipatory responses would *not* represent body armor because the individuals are preparing to *express* their emotional display rather than *suppress* it (Balshan-Goldstein, 1964).

An alternative biological mechanism is that skeletal muscle activity may directly alter the physiological activity of underlying internal organs. For example, contraction of the lower abdominal muscles directly increases intraabdominal pressure on the bladder, rectum, and vagina. Contraction of the upper abdominal muscles increases the pressure on the stomach and diaphragm. Thus increases in EMG levels of specific skeletal muscles may alter autonomic activity not by increasing metabolic demands on the body but rather by directly affecting specific organs. For example, using radioactive dye to identify esophageal and intestinal spasms, Jacobson (1938) documented that these GI-tract disorders may co-vary with superficial muscle tension and that relaxation of the superficial muscles can produce symptom relief. Similar findings have been reported with a variety of psychophysiological disorders (muscle tension headaches, urinary incontinence, chronic pelvic pain, anorgasmia, etc.). However, it is also important to recall that the phrase "in some cases of . . ." should be used to describe these relationships. Researchers have consistently noted marked individual differences in the EMG activity of psychophysiological disorder patients. Some psychophysiological patients show clear elevations in EMG activity in symptom-related muscles, whereas other patients do not.

Based on the preceding discussion, it might appear that the available literature on the skeletal muscle activity of psychiatric patients is composed of a hopelessly tangled mass of conflicting empirical findings and rival hypotheses. This conclusion is basically correct. This confused state of the clinical literature nicely illustrates the importance of differentiating between emotional states (what emotion the individual is currently experiencing) and emotional traits (the individual's predisposition to experience specific states).

Psychiatric labels denote traits, *not* states. Specifically, a psychiatric diagnosis of an anxiety disorder implies *only* that the individual has an abnormally high predisposition to experience state anxiety and tells us nothing about his or her current emotional state. Similarly, the psychiatric diagnosis of depression implies *only* that the individual is predisposed to state depression and tells us nothing about his or her current emotional state. Indeed, both clinical and laboratory studies suggest that anxiety patients may also be prone to state depression and that depressed patients may also be prone to state anxiety. For example, Clancy, Noyes, Hoenk, and Slymen (1978) reported that the incidence rate of state depression was 42% in anxiety patients but only 7% in surgical patients. Cameron (1945) found a high incidence of state anxiety in a sample of depressed patients. Moreover, positive correlations between trait anxiety and trait depression have also been found with nonpsychiatric samples of Army recruits (Naditch, Gargan, & Michael, 1975) and college students (Johnson & Sarason, 1978).

Given the positive relationship between trait anxiety and trait depression, isolating the effects of state anxiety, trait anxiety, state depression, and trait depression on skeletal muscle tension is extremely difficult. In their study of depressed patients, Balshan-Goldstein *et al.* (1964; Shipman *et al.*, 1964) found that, across four testing sessions, state depression and trait anxiety were both negatively correlated with bicep muscle tension. Thus both the patients who were feeling the most depressed and patients who were most prone to experience anxiety had the lowest bicep EMG readings. Patients who scored highest in state anxiety and in trait anxiety had the lowest EMG levels in the frontalis and quadricep muscles. Given that all of the subjects were diagnosed as meeting psychiatric criteria for depression (high trait depression), it is impossible to determine whether the observed relationships are simple interactions (e.g., high trait depression and state depression) or complex interactions (e.g., high trait anxiety, high trait depression, and state depression).

To further complicate matters, clinical observations suggest that neither anxiety nor depression is a unitary state but rather may represent sets of related substates. For example, anxiety patients frequently report that their feelings fluctuate between global free-floating anxiety and panic attacks. Although both states are labeled *anxiety reactions*, these states are clearly different both psychologically and psychophysiologically.

As discussed in the preceding chapters, numerous researchers have argued that the term *anxiety* is commonly used to denote two unrelated syndromes: cognitive anxiety (worry) and somatic anxiety (emotionality). Cognitive anxiety is characterized by relatively uncontrollable negative thoughts and images about a personal problem that has potentially negative outcomes. Because the symptoms of cognitive anxiety are quite similar to those of obsessive disorders, it should be noted that the mental content of the individual's repetitive thoughts clearly differentiates the two disorders. During cognitive anxiety states, the individual's repetitive thoughts are *meaningful* to the patient and represent conscious (if ineffective) attempts at problem solving (Borkovec, Robinson, Pruzinsky, & DePree, 1983). In contrast, the repetitive thoughts of obsessive individuals are often lyrics from advertising or other strings of phrases that are *meaningless* to the patients.

Somatic anxiety is characterized by a variety of physical and psychosomatic complaints that the individual consciously recognizes as linked to stress. It should be noted that the individual's conscious awareness of a relationship between symptoms and stress differentiates somatic anxiety from somatoform disorders (conversion disorders and hypochondriasis). Specifically, somatoform patients consciously deny any connection between their symptoms and emotional states. According to the cognitive-somatic anxiety model, a given individual may be prone to experience either cognitive anxiety symptoms or somatic anxiety symptoms or mixed cognitive-somatic symptoms. Obviously, the existence of three distinct subgroups of "anxiety" patients may account for many of the contradictory findings in the clinical literature on anxiety.

Clinical observations of depressed patients also suggest that depression is not a "unitary" disorder and that patients may display either "agitated" depression (hyperarousal) or "retarded" depression (hypoarousal). For example, Balshan-Goldstein *et al.* (1964) commented that both agitated and retarded reactions were common in their sample of depressed patients. Some patients responded to stressors with elevated autonomic and skeletal activity, whereas other patients went "limp." Given that the same patient may alternate between agitated and retarded depression, researchers currently disagree over whether agitated depression is a mixture of state anxiety and state depression or is a unique form of state depression.

The overall pattern of results of psychiatric studies clearly suggests that marked individual differences in skeletal muscle activity occur within groups of psychiatric patients with the same diagnosis. Such intragroup differences, however, do not imply that skeletal muscle activity is unrelated to psychiatric patients' emotional states. Rather, it would appear that such individual differences indicate that there are at least five distinct subgroups of psychiatric patients that can be identified on the basis of their psychophysiological responses during emotional states. The first subgroup of patients are literally "uptight" and display global (bodywide) increases in skeletal muscle tension during stress. Although such patients were traditionally labeled *neurotic*, this subgroup would appear to include at least a minority of agitated depressed or psychotic patients. A second subgroup of patients display highly localized increases in skeletal muscle tension during stress and often report highly localized psychophysiological symptoms such as headaches. This subgroup also appears to be composed primarily of anxiety, agitated depressed, and agitated psychotic patients. A third subgroup of patients show marked decreases in global skeletal muscle activity during stress. This subgroup appears to be composed primarily of retarded depressed patients. A fourth group of patients display little or no change in skeletal muscle activity during stress but show marked autonomic reactions. Such patients often report more global psychophysiological symptoms such as IBS or CPP. Anxiety and depressed patients appear to constitute the majority of this subgroup. A fifth subgroup of patients display skeletal muscle and autonomic responses to stress that are indistinguishable from those of normal subjects but report a variety of physiological symptoms. This latter subgroup is composed primarily of somatoform patients. The observed individual differences in psychophysiological reactions to stress within specific psychiatric groups has two interesting implications for psychotherapists.

First, skeletal muscle activity may provide a valid index of emotional stress but *only* in specific subgroups of patients. For example, Fisch, Frey, and Hirsbrunner (1983) found that recovery from retarded depression was accompanied by (a) a general increase in body movement, (b) an increase in the complexity of body movements and (c) more rapid initiation of motor responses. The authors noted, however, that there were marked individual differences both in the degree of psychomotor retardation during depression and the amount of movement after recovery. They speculated that the complexity of body movements rather than the amount of body movement *per se* may be indicative of recovery from depression.

Second, therapeutic techniques that focus on the patients' skeletal muscle activity such as Reichian therapy, relaxation training, and EMG biofeedback should be highly beneficial for some patients but not others. Review of the clinical literature clearly supports the empirical validity of this prediction. For example, progressive relaxation training (Jacobson, 1938; Bernstein & Borkovec, 1973) consists of a series of yogalike exercises designed to teach the individual how to consciously recognize abnormal levels of skeletal muscle tension and then to voluntarily relax his or her muscles. Progressive relaxation training is commonly used in conjunction with other therapeutic techniques to help clients cope more effectively with anxiety (Suinn & Richardson, 1971) and with specific phobias (Wolpe, 1958). However, the results of studies of the effectiveness of these treatment programs are equivocal. A number of studies have found that decreases in skeletal muscle activity were directly related to reductions in anxiety or phobic behaviors (Lomont & Edwards, 1967; Paul, 1969; Sherman & Plummer, 1973; Thompson, Griebstein, & Kuhlenschmidt, 1980). Other studies have found only a weak relationship (Rachman, 1965, 1968; Waters, McDonald, & Koresko, 1972) or no relationship between skeletal muscle activity and the success of treatment (Cooke, 1968; Agra et al., 1971; Connor, 1974).

Reviews of the EMG biofeedback literature have also found an equivocal pattern of findings (Alexander & Smith, 1979; Tarler-Benlolo, 1978; Gatchel, 1979). Some biofeedback studies find a strong relationship between reductions in muscle tension and reduction in anxiety or fear, whereas other studies find no relationship between muscle tension and emotional states. Even the sparse literature on the therapeutic effects of back massage reveals marked individual differences in treatment outcomes (Madison, 1973; McKechnie, Wilson, Watson, & Scott, 1983).

Davidson (1978) argued that these contradictory patterns of findings may merely reflect the heterogeneity of samples of anxious patients. He postulated that muscle relaxation or EMG biofeedback training may be effective only for patients with high levels of somatic anxiety and that clients with high levels of cognitive anxiety may derive little or no benefit from treatment. Although Davidson's hypothesis provides an excellent *post hoc* explanation for the conflicting clinical findings, additional research is needed to determine whether the mixed success of skeletal muscle therapies is attributable to cognitive anxiety.

11.2. PSYCHOPHYSIOLOGICAL POPULATIONS

As discussed in the preceding chapters, a number of psychophysiological disorders of the viscera appear to be directly related to abnormal levels of tension in superficial muscles. Researchers have also focused on four stress-related disorders of the skeletal muscle system itself: arthritis, muscle pain, muscle spasms, and muscle tics.

11.2.1. Arthritis

Arthritis is a generic diagnostic label that is used to represent about 100 different disorders characterized by pain or inflammation of a joint. An estimated 20 million Americans have moderate to severe arthritis and the estimated female/male sex ratio of the disorder is approximately 3 : 1. Almost all types of arthritis, including the most prevalent form (osteoarthritis), are organic disorders of the joints. One notable exception is rheumatoid arthritis. Based on the idiosyncratic nature of rheumatoid arthritis symptoms and the pattern of abrupt onsets and remissions of symptoms, researchers have long suspected that emotional stress may play a major role in the onset and maintenance of this disorder.

Rheumatoid arthritis is characterized by inflammation of the synovial membrane and accumulation of fluid within the joint. The highest incidence of rheumatoid arthritis occurs between the ages of 25 and 50. Unlike other forms of arthritis, the symptoms of rheumatoid arthritis are highly idiosyncratic. Some patients have only one or two joints affected, whereas other patients have a large number of joints affected. Some patients report a gradual onset of symptoms, whereas other patients report an abrupt onset of symptoms. Some patients show progressive deterioration of the joint and are gradually crippled as the synovial membrane loses its ability to produce lubricating fluid and the cartilage gradually deteriorates. Other patients experience sudden remissions in symptoms that may last for decades. Moreover, there is little or no relationship between the patients' subjective reports of pain and loss of joint mobility and the actual physiopathology of the affected joints. Some patients with marked degeneration of the joints show normal mobility and report little discomfort. Other patients with relatively minor physiopathologies report intense pain and complete loss of joint mobility.

Clinicians have reported numerous cases where the appearance and disappearance of rheumatoid arthritis symptoms clearly paralleled emotional stresses in the patients' everyday life. For example, Ludwig (1967) noted that one female patient's arthritis symptoms reoccurred on the anniversaries of the deaths of loved ones and also *after* expressing anger toward her (living) husband and mother. Consistent with such case reports, systematic surveys of rheumatoid arthritis patients also revealed that onset or aggravation of symptoms was frequently *preceded* by psychologically stressful events (Ludwig, 1954, 1967; Cobb, Schull, Harburg, & Kasl, 1969; Shochet et al., 1969; Heisel, 1972).

The observed relationship between the occurrence of rheumatoid arthritis symptoms and emotional stress strongly suggests that this specific form of arthritis may be a psychophysiological rather than an organic disorder. Identifying the specific psychophysiological mechanism that produces rheumatoid arthritis, however, has been a long and difficult task. Inflammation (the major symptom of rheumatoid arthritis) normally signifies that the body's immune system is responding to a local infection or injury. Yet, prior to the pioneering research of Hans Selye (1956), few researchers believed that the immune system was activated during stress reactions. As discussed previously in Chapter 3, the Selye research strongly suggested that immunological reactions were an integral component of the body's hormonal response to stressors. Selye also demonstrated that arthritislike symptoms could be produced in rats by injecting noxious chemicals (croton oil, formalin) into the rats' paws.

Like most scientific research, Selye's findings raised more questions than they answered. First, if rheumatoid arthritis is a by-product of the body's hormonal stress response, why are arthritis symptoms localized in only specific joints? Second, why do rheumatoid arthritis symptoms often mysteriously appear and disappear? Third, when exposed to emotional stressors, why do only some people develop rheumatoid arthritis? Researchers now suspect that the answers to all three questions may be highly interrelated.

Most contemporary theories of rheumatoid arthritis assume that the individual is infected by a dormant pathogen (bacteria or virus) that takes up residence in a specific joint or set of joints. The pathogen may remain dormant for years until accidently activated by the body's hormonal stress response to a physical or psychological stressor. The immune system then responds to the now active infection and produces localized inflammation and pain. The body responds to this new stressor by releasing more hormones into the bloodstream, thus inadvertently activating more pathogens. According to this pathogen model, rheumatoid arthritis can be conceptualized as either a chronic low-grade infection or as a chronic malfunction in the hormonal control system. Similarly, sudden remission of symptoms may indicate either that the immune system has finally managed to eradicate the active pathogens or that the neurohormonal control system has finally managed to terminate the activation of the immune system. Most theories also assume that susceptibility to rheumatoid arthritis is genetically determined (Amkraut & Solomon, 1974). Thus the development of rheumatoid arthritis may be mediated by (a) exposure to a pathogen, (b) exposure to stressors, and (c) a genetic predisposition.

11.2.2. Muscle Pain Syndromes

Before we review the literature on muscle pain syndromes, it important that we first define *abnormal* muscle reactions. For example, should a brief involuntary muscle contraction be labeled a *spasm, tic,* or *twitch?* Unfortunately, researchers have failed to agree on a common set of diagnostic labels and, thus, the clinical literature is laced with apparently overlapping or synonymous diagnostic jargons. Commonly used diagnostic terms for muscle activity include chorea, convulsion, cramp, flaccid paralysis, freezing, immobility, muscular hypertension, muscular hypotension, myoclonic jerk, rocking, spasm, tic, tremor, twitch, and rigid paralysis. To further confuse matters, only a few researchers have operationally defined their diagnostic labels. For example, Yates (1970) described a clear set of diagnostic criteria (rate of muscle contraction, change in reflexes, etc.) that he employed to differentiate between chorea, spasms, tics, and tremors. Regardless of the validity of Yates's diagnostic criteria, it should be noted that the majority of other researchers have completely failed to define "what they mean" when they employ a given diagnostic label such as "tic."

Anyone who has ever experienced a muscle cramp can testify that prolonged contraction of a muscle can be extremely painful. As discussed in previous chapters, a variety of painful psychophysiological disorders (muscle tension headaches, chronic pelvic pain, vaginismus, etc.) may be produced by abnormal contraction of striate muscles. Researchers suspect that at least three additional pain syndromes (facial, neck/upper back and lower back) may also be psychophysiological disorders. For example, Leavitt, Garron, and Bieliauski (1979) reported that, after a series of exhaustive medical tests of 148 lower-back-pain patients, "definite" organic disease was confirmed in only 57 patients. A panel of nine surgeons agreed that an additional 51 patients should be diagnosed as "probable" organic disease and that the remaining 40 patients had a "nonorganic" disorder.

Findings similar to Leavitt's are commonly reported throughout the facial pain, neck/upper-back-pain and lower-back-pain literature. In a significant minority of patients, no known organic disorder can be identified that accounts for the degree of pain reported. The absence of demonstrable organic disease, however, does not necessarily mean that a given patient's pain is psychophysiological in origin. In their discussion of the chronic pelvic pain syndrome, Pearce and Beard (1984) noted that there are three different plausible explanations for "non-organic" pain cases: (a) the patient's pain is a symptom of the early stages of organic pathology or of an organic pathology that is difficult to detect with existing technology; (b) the patient's pain may be psychophysiological in origin, or (c) the patient's pain may be a symptom of a somatoform disorder. Conversely, Ross (1977) argued that the presence of an "organic pathology" does not automatically rule out the possibility that stress may aggravate the patient's disorder. Accordingly, studies like Leavitt's that select groups of organic and nonorganic patients on the basis of medical diagnosis alone should be interpreted with some caution.

The majority of theories of psychophysiological muscle pain postulate that the various pain syndromes are all produced by the same psychobiological mechanism. Presumably, muscle pain patients react to emotional stress with abnormal tonic or phasic elevations in very specific muscle groups. The specific muscles most affected would determine the specific pain syndrome the patient experiences. The increase in muscle tension initially leads to increased blood flow to these regions to supply the muscles with oxygen and to remove metabolites. However, if the muscle contractions are abnormally long (tonic) or intense (phasic), lactic acid and other metabolites accumulate in the muscle tissue and these metabolites, in turn, excite local pain receptors (Holmes & Wolff, 1952; Dorpat & Holmes, 1955; Barlow, 1959). As discussed previously in this chapter, emotion-related increases in muscle tension may represent either the expression or the inhibition of emotional displays. For example, muscle-contraction headache patients showed larger stress-related increases in facial muscle tension but displayed less facial/postural emotional behaviors than control subjects (Traue, Gottwald, Henderson, & Bakal, 1985).

11.2.2.1. Facial Pain

Although there are a variety of "psychogenic" facial pain syndromes, only one, temporomandibular joint (TMJ) syndrome, is considered a psychophysiological disorder. TMJ is characterized by restricted jaw movement and by dull to intense aching pain that is perceived as originating from the joint between the jawbone and skull and from the muscles (e.g., the masseter) that are involved in chewing. TMJ pain is often unilateral, and EMG recordings reveal muscular hypertension on the side of the face where pain is localized (Gessel & Alderman, 1971). Estimated incidence rates of TMJ in the general population are as high as 20%. Reports of the female/male sex ratio of TMJ range from approximately 3:1 to 4:1. The incidence of TMJ syndrome is also age-related, and the disorder is most commonly reported in young and middle-age women.

TMJ patients often show clear physical evidence of tooth damage from habitually clenching and grinding their teeth (bruxism). Based on the close linkage between TMJ and bruxism, dentists traditionally assumed that abnormalities in the patients' bite (malocclusion) produce both bruxism and TMJ. Presumably, bruxism-related muscular hypertension of the masseter muscle eventually leads to spasmodic contractions of the muscle that, in turn, produce pain and other TMJ symptoms.

Although researchers still suspect that bruxism-related increases in muscle tension may be the primary cause of TMJ, most researchers now doubt that malocclusion *per se* is the primary cause of either bruxism or TMJ. A number of studies have reported that the incidence of malocclusion in TMJ patients is no higher than in the general population and that dental treatments to correct TMJ patients' bite are relatively ineffective (Laskin, 1969; Kopp, 1979). Moreover, "cures" of TMJ symptoms produced by corrective dental work may be due to placebo effects. Goodman, Greene, and Laskin (1976) informed 25 TMJ patients that because their malocclusions were the major cause of their symptoms, their symptoms should abate after their bites were corrected by selectively grinding. The subjects then received a placebo treatment (grinding nonoccluding surfaces). Following treatment, 16 of the 25 patients reported almost complete symptom remission.

One notable difference between bruxism and TMJ patients is the incidence of psychiatric disorders. Bruxism patients are no more likely to be diagnosed as mentally ill than other members of the general population. However, researchers have consistently reported high incidence rates of psychiatric disorders in samples of TMJ patients. For example, Feinmann (1983) reported that in a sample of 50 TMJ patients, approximately 57% met British psychiatric criteria for either neurosis or depressive neurosis. Moulton (1955) reported that, although the typical TMJ patient was neurotic (obsessional and perfectionistic), a significant number of other TMJ patients were repressors. Thus it would appear that TMJ patients represent a more emotionally disturbed subset of the bruxism population.

A growing body of literature suggests that bruxism and TMJ may both be caused by psychological stress-related hypertension in the masseter muscles. First, psychological stress-related increases in masseter tension have been demonstrated in both bruxism patients (Yemm, 1969a,b) and in TMJ patients (Thomas, Tiber, & Schireson, 1973; Scott & Gregg, 1980; Moss, Garrett, & Chiodo, 1982). Second, progressive muscle relaxation, EMG biofeedback, and other forms of muscle relaxation therapy have been reported to be as or more effective than traditional dental therapies in the treatment of both bruxism and TMJ (Brooke & Stenn, 1983; Casas, Beemsterboer, & Clark, 1982; Gessel, 1975; Rugh and Johnson, 1981; Rugh and Solberg, 1974; Rugh, Perlis, & Disraeli, 1977). Third, a high percentage of both bruxism (Brown, 1977) and TMJ (Feinmann, 1983) patients report that stressful life events preceded or were concurrent with the occurrence of their symptoms.

11.2.2.2. Neck/Upper Back Pain

The trapezius muscle group extends from the neck to the middle of the back. Accordingly, injury to the trapezius muscles may produce pain in the neck and/or upper back. However, neck/upper back (interscapular) pain is frequently referred to as *psychogenic* in medical textbooks (Ross, 1977; Makin & Adams,

1980; Thompson, 1980). Presumably, upper-back-pain patients are characterized by (a) a high incidence of cases with no identifiable physiopathology *except* muscular hypertension and spasms, (b) a high female/male sex ratio, (c) self-reports of anxiety- or stress-related attacks, or (d) postural abnormalities.

Given the frequency with which upper back pain is labeled *psychogenic* in the medical community, one is prepared to wade into a conflicting mass of empirical literature. Surprisingly, literature on upper back pain is virtually non-existent. The "characteristics" of upper-back-pain patients cited by Ross and others appear to be derived from the case reports of Alexanderian therapists. Although these case reports do suggest a direct linkage between anxiety, posture, and pain, it should be emphasized that Alexanderian therapists observed this triadic relationship in patients of both sexes and that both anxiety and abnormal postures were linked with headache pain, neck pain, upper back pain, lower back pain. and buttock pain.

Aside from the case reports of Alexanderian therapists, searches of both the medical and psychiatric data bases reveal very few published reports on experimental studies that are even remotely related to psychogenic upper back pain. For example, Jacobs and Felton (1969) compared effects of EMG biofeedback on relaxation in 14 women with injuries to the trapezius muscle and 14 healthy female control subjects. Consistent with the view that women are prone to muscular hypertension in upper back muscles, neither group was able to produce significant trapezius relaxation prior to feedback. With biofeedback, the injured group had more difficulty learning to relax than the healthy group, but both groups eventually learned to voluntarily relax their trapezius muscles after feedback. Although these findings can be interpreted as consistent with earlier case studies, it should be noted that no male subjects were included in the study. Whether males also experience difficulty in voluntarily relaxing upper back muscles is currently unknown.

Cram and Steger (1983) compared EMG levels of 6 upper-back/neck pain, 9 lower back pain, 14 headache pain, and 21 mixed-pain patients. A total of 11 (left-right) pairs of muscles were measured while each patient was in a sitting and in a standing position. Consistent with Barlow's (1959, 1973) clinical observations, postural abnormalities were associated with muscular hypertension in both upper- and lower-back-pain patients. However, additional research is clearly needed to examine the validity of the often cited "characteristics" of upper-back-pain patients such as a high incidence of anxiety disorders.

11.2.2.3. Lower Back Pain

Lower back pain is a generic diagnostic label that is used to represent a number of organic disorders. Chronic or acute pain localized in the lower back and/or buttocks may be produced by a variety of structural and physiological abnormalities of the spine and nervous system and injury to the back muscles through physical strain. Lower back pain may also be a "referred" pain produced by a variety of organic diseases, physiopathologies, or injuries to internal organs. For example, menstrual backaches are referred pains. Because of the number of potential organic causes that can produce backaches, identifying the cause of a given patient's lower back pain often requires a rather extensive diagnostic procedure (Makin & Adams, 1980). However, even after exhaustive medical and neurological testing, there remains a number of low back pain patients whose only organic signs are either muscular hypotension or muscular hypertension and spasms. In the Leavitt et al. (1979) study, this "nonorganic" group represented almost one-third of their lower-back-pain population. Given that such cases are often extremely difficult to treat medically, these patients are usually labeled as *somatoform disorders* or *malingering*. However, it should be emphasized that a medical opinion is *not* a psychiatric diagnosis.

Eliminating an organic basis for a given patient's back pain actually tells us very little about the origin of his or her pain. Specifically, muscle-related chronic lower back pains may be either conversion symptoms, hypochondriacal delusions, psychophysiological disorders, or outright malingering. Ross (1977) noted that three studies that had used the Minnesota Multiphasic Personality Inventory (MMPI) to screen low back patients had all found marked elevations on the Hypochondriasis, Depression, and Hysteria scales. Ross argued that these patients' MMPI scores suggest that they are suffering from specific psychiatric disorders rather than malingering. Consistent with Ross's position, other researchers have found high incidence rates of psychiatric disorders in samples of nonorganic back pain patients (Leavitt, 1985a,b; McCreary, 1985). For example, approximately 66% of the female patients' and 79% of the male patients' MMPI profiles in McCreary's study would be classified as conversion reactions, depression, hypochondriacs, or other psychiatric disorders. Thus the nonorganic pain population appears to include a heterogeneous sample of psychiatric patients.

A number of researchers have postulated that the backaches of psychiatric patients may be psychophysiological in origin. For example, psychotherapists have consistently reported that muscular hypotension and a "slumped" posture are characteristic of retarded depression. This emotion-related postural abnormality places additional mechanical stress on the muscles of the lower back and, thus, may produce back pain. Conversely, muscular hypertension and abnormal postures have been frequently observed in samples of anxious, agitated depressed, and agitated psychotic patients. This combination of elevated muscle tension and imbalanced postures may eventually produce painful spasms in the lower back. Thus, if we exclude somatoform patients, psychiatric patients' reports of back pain may be legitimate, although their reports of the intensity of pain might still be highly questionable.

Consistent with this psychophysiological interpretation, Leavitt et al. (1979) found that nonorganic lower-back-pain patients' self-reports of stressful life events over the preceding year were positively correlated with their reports of severe emotional discomfort, state anxiety, and pain sensations of throbbing pressure. None of these relationships were observed in either their group of "definitely" organic patients or their group of "probably" organic patients.

Flor, Turk, and Birbaumer (1985) reported some rather convincing evidence that the pain experienced by "nonorganic" lower-back-pain patients may be psychophysiological in origin. They compared back EMG levels of chronic back pain patients, general pain patients, and healthy controls to personally relevant and irrelevant stressors. Only the chronic back pain patients displayed abnormal elevations and delayed recovery in back muscle tension in response to personally relevant stressors (pain and personal stress). Interestingly, the back pain patients did not show localized increases in back muscle EMG to *nonrelevant* stressors.

The EMG biofeedback studies provide some additional support for a psychophysiological interpretation of nonorganic lower back pain. For example, Belar and Cohen (1979) found that EMG biofeedback from back muscles was moderately successful in teaching a female lower-back-pain patient how to voluntarily reduce the frequency of her backaches. Similarly, Gottlieb and his associates reported that a comprehensive rehabilitation program that incorporated EMG and GSR biofeedback was moderately effective in treating a group of lower-back-pain patients (Gottlieb *et al.*, 1977).

11.2.3. Muscle Spasm Syndromes

Although muscle spasms may play an important role in a variety of muscle pain syndromes, these disorders are considered "pain disorders" rather than spasmodic disorders because pain is the patients' primary symptom. The term *spasmodic* denotes a disorder characterized by alternating periods of spasm and relaxation in a given muscle. Unfortunately, the term spasmodic has also been loosely used in the clinical literature to denote milder muscle contractions such as twitches or tremors that rapidly alternate with relaxation. To further confuse matters, the term *tic*, which implies a conversion reaction, has been often used interchangeably with both *twitch* and *spasm*. Obviously, the use of ill-defined terms often makes it difficult to guess what type of muscle reaction the researcher observed and whether or not the researcher believed the muscle reaction was a symptom of a conversion disorder. As you will see in the following discussion, it is often extremely difficult to distinguish between organic, psychogenic, and psychophysiological spasmodic disorders.

11.2.3.1. Occupational Cramps

Occupational cramps are muscles spasms that disrupt a learned motor behavior involved in a given vocation. Although "writer's" cramp is the most commonly cited example, the clinical literature suggests that occupational cramps may occur in any profession. The vocations of occupational cramp patients range from waiters to dentists. Occupational cramps were traditionally classified as conversion symptoms because the patients' motor disorders often occur *only* when performing specific job-related motor acts. For example, a concert pianist may experience severe cramps while playing a piano, yet have no difficulty writing or threading a needle.

Moldofsky (1971) and other researchers have repeatedly challenged the view that all occupational cramps are conversion disorders. Moldofsky argued that some cases of occupational cramps are organic in origin and can be traced to job-related nerve damage. For example, models who sit with their knees crossed for any extended period of time may damage the peroneal nerve. If such patients are given a neurological exam, clear evidence of nerve damage is observable.

Moldofsky also argued that some cases of occupational cramps may be psycho-physiological rather than somatoform disorders. This subset of patients reacted to job-related frustrations with muscular hypertension. Because this increased muscle tone interfered slightly with fine motor skills, it became an additional source of job-related stress as patients tried to force themselves to "do the job right." This vicious cycle continued, and eventually the patients began experiencing occupational cramps. Moldofsky reported that such cases can be cured through muscle relaxation to reduce muscular hypertension and muscular re-education training to unlearn maladaptive motor movements.

11.2.3.2. Spasmodic Torticollis

Spasmodic torticollis is a rare disorder characterized by spasms of the muscles on one side of the neck that pull the head to one side in an involuntary and often awkward movement. Although spasmodic torticollis can occur at any age, the average age of onset for the disorder is about 35 years. Because torticollis patients' reports of spasm-related pain range from very mild discomfort to intense pain, this disorder is classified as a spasmodic rather than as a pain syndrome.

Although many contemporary medical texts list spasmodic torticollis as a neurological disorder, as early as the 1860s, researchers recognized that the symptoms of spasmodic torticollis can be produced by *either* infection-induced neurological damage to the extrapyramidal tracts *or* by psychiatric disorders. The organic form of torticollis may be caused by a variety of infections (encephalitis, malaria, rheumatic fever, syphilis, etc.) and is considered intractable (untreatable) because the patient's neurological damage is irreversible. Psychogenic spasmodic torticollis patients, however, may recover with or without psychotherapy. Although early researchers suspected that psychogenic spasmodic torticollis was a conversion symptom, there has been little agreement among researchers on the specific characteristics that distinguish organic cases from psychogenic cases. Neither the patient's history of infections *per se* nor evidence of neurological damage *per se* has proven to be a reliable index of the organic form of the disorder (Meares, 1971).

Meares (1971) designed a clever experiment to identify which patient characteristics differentiated organic and psychogenic cases of spasmodic torticollis. He reasoned that if the only known discriminator of the psychogenic torticollis was recovery, he should compare patients who later recovered with the remaining nonrecovered cases. A total of 32 patients were interviewed and given a battery of psychological tests and a neurological exam. Fifteen patients showed no sign of neurological damage. However, 2 of the 8 cases who had recovered by the time of the follow-up had originally been diagnosed as "unequivocally organic" cases. Although the nonrecovered group was treated "as if" it consisted of a heterogeneous group of organic patients for statistical comparison, it should be noted that this group of 24 patients contained 9 cases with no known neuropathology. Obviously, some percentage of these "organic" patients may have recovered at a later date.

Meares observed four different types of spasmodic attacks in his sample of

32 patients: slow head turning, jerking of the head, "aching" onset (patient reported neck and back pain prior to the attack), and idiosyncratic head movements (e.g., head bobs). All 8 of the recovered group and only 8 of the 24 patients in the nonrecovered group showed either the jerking or aching pattern at the time of their neurological exam. No other neurological signs differentiated between the recovered and nonrecovered groups. The psychological test scores also showed marked differences between the two groups. The patients who later recovered had significantly higher scores on neuroticism and anxiety measures. The recovered group also reported poorer sexual and/or marital adjustment than the nonrecovered group, although the observed group differences were not statistically significant.

The overall pattern of Meares's findings would appear to contradict the traditional view that "psychogenic" spasmodic torticollis is a conversion disorder. Unlike conversion symptoms, torticollis did not always disappear when the patient was asleep. Moreover, the psychogenic patients in his sample did not deny anxiety but rather reported high levels of anxiety. Together, these two findings suggest that these patients' disorder was psychophysiological rather than psychogenic. Consistent with this hypothesis, Meares and Lader (1971) found that patients' neuroticism scores were positively correlated with increases in neck (sternomastoid) EMG during stress.

Meares's findings suggest that at least a minority of spasmodic torticollis cases are psychophysiological in origin and thus may be successfully treated through psychotherapy or EMG biofeedback. Consistent with this prediction, later studies have found that a relatively high percentage of torticollis patients are indeed treatable. For example, Brudny and his associates reported that 19 of 48 torticollis patients showed significant long-term improvement after EMG-biofeedback therapy (Brudny *et al.*, 1976). Similarly, Cleeland (1973) reported that 6 of 10 torticollis patients showed significant long-term improvement after treatment with a combination of EMG-biofeedback and aversion therapy.

It should be noted that some clear cases of "psychogenic" spasmodic torticollis have also been reported in the clinical literature. For example, Brierley (1967) cited two torticollis cases whose symptoms closely resembled occupational cramps. The first patient was a 32-year-old male draftsman whose symptoms were triggered by taking a management course in college. Initially, his symptoms only occurred while studying or sitting in class. Gradually his symptoms worsened to the point that he could no longer work or drive a car. The second patient was a 32-year-old nurse who belonged to a religious order of nursing nuns. Her symptoms were triggered by reassignment to a ward for epileptic children. Both patients had extremely low neuroticism scores on the Eysenck Personality Inventory, and both reported low levels of anxiety. After treatment with aversion therapy, both patients showed marked remission in their torticollis symptoms. A follow-up revealed that the male patient had been completely free of symptoms for a year and the female patient was symptom-free except for two brief reoccurences of torticollis during the following 18 months.

Occupational cramps and torticollis represent two spasmodic disorders where researchers have documented that a given patient's symptoms may be either organic or psychophysiological or psychogenic (somatoform). However, the distinction between these three classes of disorders is often extremely difficult to make. For example, Brierley (1967) commented that both reoccurrences of torticollis in his female patient after therapy were triggered by severe psychological stressors. Thus, although the patient's characteristics at onset of her disorder clearly met the diagnostic criteria for a conversion reaction, her two relapses after therapy could be interpreted as either a defense against anxiety (conversion reaction) or a stress-related (psychophysiological) disorder.

At this point, the reader may be feeling overwhelmed by the sheer complexity of the skeletal muscle literature. As discussed in Chapter 10, emotional displays are clearly a complex mixture of innate reflexes and culturally acquired movements and inhibitions. As you have seen in this chapter, individual response stereotypy is also characteristic of both psychiatric and psychophysiological patients. Such findings suggest that striate muscle activity may be yoked with emotional states *but* that the skeletal muscle responses of any given individual may be highly idiosyncratic.

SUGGESTED READINGS

Cram, J. R., & Steger, J. C. EMG scanning in the diagnosis of chronic pain. *Biofeedback and Self Regulation*, 1983, *8*, 229–241.

This study nicely illustrates the methodological problems in isolating the role of muscular hypertension in pain disorders.

Moldofsky, H. Occupational cramp. *Journal of Psychosomatic Research*, 1971, *15*, 439–444.

An excellent discussion of the difficulties in discriminating between organic, somatoform, and psychophysiological disorders.

Yates, A. J. Tics. In C. G. Costello (Ed.), *Symptoms of psychopathology*. New York: Wiley, 1970.

An interesting theoretical discussion of the criteria used to diagnose abnormal muscle activity.

III

Theories of Emotion

Unlike modern digital computers, humans have extreme difficulty manipulating large quantities of information. For example, a computer can easily store and retrieve the huge mass of information needed to construct an automobile. A human cannot. Our memories are too fallible to recall the thousands of individual components needed. Even if we are given an external memory aid such as a parts list, our span of consciousness is too limited to grasp how all of these components fit together to form an automobile.

One potentially useful strategy for dealing with large masses of information on a specific object or event is to construct a simplified representation or model of the phenomenon. For example, even a crude plastic model of an automobile helps us identify major functional units such as doors and wheels. Obviously, a more detailed model would provide additional insights into how automobiles are assembled. The utility of our model, however, is determined by how well it corresponds to the actual phenomenon. If we want to assemble a Mercedes-Benz convertible, a highly accurate model of a Yugo may be of little value.

The purpose of the preceding discussion is to remind the reader of the functions and limitations of scientific theories. Theories are conceptual models that help us describe, explain, and predict empirical events. Like other models, their utility depends upon how accurately they correspond to the actual phenomenon.

We will briefly review a small sample of the major models of emotion in the following chapters. Each theory was selected to represent a specific metaphysical position. Materialistic models of emotion are discussed in Chapters 12 and 13, mentalistic models are presented in Chapter 14, and interactionistic models are covered in Chapters 15 and 16.

A general summary of the empirical findings on human emotions is presented in Chapter 17. The reader may find it useful to skim Chapter 17, prior to reading Chapters 12 through 16.

Biochemical Models

As we discussed briefly in Chapter 1, the strict materialist position of meta-physics is that only the physical universe exists and that all "mental" processes are purely by-products (epiphenomena) of physical events. Materialist theories of emotion can be divided into two general classes: biochemical models and physiological models. Both classes of materialist models share the same basic assumption that specific emotional states are produced by physical changes in the body. We will discuss physiological models of emotion later in Chapter 13.

Many researchers view biochemical models of emotion as either extremely "simplistic" or hopelessly "complex." As you will see in the following discussion, both views are partially true.

Biochemical models of emotion date back to the ancient Greeks. Hippocrates proposed that individual differences in emotionality (temperament) were due to the relative proportion of four bodily fluids or humors (blood, black bile, yellow bile, and phlegm). For example, individuals with excessive levels of blood were presumably happy, whereas those with excessive levels of black bile were presumably prone to depression. This simplistic notion that a specific emotional state may be caused by the excess or shortage of a single biochemical has proven extremely durable. Indeed, if you substitute the term *neurotransmitter* for *humor*, you will grasp the essence of a surprisingly large percentage of twen-tieth-century biochemical models of emotion.

The view that biochemical models are so complex that they are incompre-hensible to the average person is due to the relatively recent birth and exponen-tial growth of psychopharmacology (the study of psychological effects of drugs). Since the dawn of recorded history, humans have known that naturally occur-ring chemicals such as caffeine, marijuana, and mescaline have "mood-altering" effects. Most cultures also independently discovered how to manufacture mood-altering chemicals such as alcohol and opium. Yet, prior to the 1950s, little information was available on *how* drugs effected the brain.

Over the past 30 years, the clinical use and public abuse of drugs has produced an explosion of information on chemically induced "altered states" of consciousness. Buried in this huge mass of information are three general findings of interest to emotion researchers. First, specific drugs may at least temporarily abolish abnormal emotional states such as psychiatric levels of depression. Second, specific drugs may temporarily induce abnormal emotional states that mimic specific psychiatric disorders. Third, the psychoactive effects of a given drug may vary with both prior exposure to the drug and with the current dosage of the drug. Some drugs lose their effectiveness with repeated exposure (tolerance), and larger and larger amounts of the drug must be taken to produce an effect. Moreover, tolerance to a given drug may reduce the effectiveness of similar drugs (cross-tolerance). Other drugs increase in effectiveness with repeated exposure (reverse tolerance). Thus, the immediate (acute) effects of a drug may differ from its long-term (chronic) effects.

These three clinical findings strongly suggest that psychoactive drugs may directly alter emotional states by altering the amounts of individual neurotransmitters in the central nervous system. Accordingly, researchers then attempted to isolate *which* specific tracts in the nervous system are influenced by a given drug. Common research techniques with human subjects include autopsies of deceased subjects' brains and urinary and cerebrospinal fluid assays of neurotransmitter metabolites in living subjects. All three of these research techniques provide only rather crude, indirect estimates of neurotransmitter activity.

To provide more direct evidence for the effects of drugs on specific neural tracts, psychopharmacologists have tested drugs on nonhuman species and employed a variety of experimental techniques such as interjecting radioactive isotopes with a given drug to identify which areas of the brain are most effected. Not surprisingly, researchers have found that a number of different drugs may facilitate or interfere with either the presynaptic synthesis, storage, release, reabsorption, or deactivation of a specific neurotransmitter or the postsynaptic binding of a given neurotransmitter. Because the specific mechanisms by which a given drug alters neuronal activity are beyond the scope of this book, we will restrict our discussion to the general effects (facilitation or inhibition) of drugs on neurotransmitters. For a detailed discussion of how specific drugs alter neurotransmission, see Seiden and Dyskstra (1977).

Based on the findings of these early clinical and laboratory studies, researchers naively generated a host of competing "humorlike" models of the human emotions. Because these biochemical models were tightly linked to empirical observations, there has been a high "turnover" rate as older models have been revised or discarded as newer findings have been published. As our knowledge of the biochemistry of the CNS has grown, researchers have proposed increasingly sophisticated models of emotion that attempt to integrate the biochemical effects of diet, drugs, exercise, genetic variation, hormones, and the sleep–wake cycles.

To avoid confusing the reader, no attempt will be made to review all of the various biochemical models of emotion. Rather, we will discuss examples of biochemical models of three classes of emotional states: anxiety-fear, elation, and depression.

12.1. ANXIETY–FEAR

As we have discussed throughout the previous chapters, anxiety is not a unitary phenomenon. Rather, the experience of anxiety is characterized by either threat-related mental images and thoughts (cognitive anxiety), physiological arousal such as sweating (somatic anxiety), or as a complex mixture of cognitive and somatic symptoms.

Such individual differences in the experience of anxiety are quite pronounced in samples of psychiatric patients. Conversion disorder patients report high levels of somatic anxiety but deny experiencing cognitive anxiety. High levels of anxiety are commonly reported by both depressed and psychotic patients. Moreover, even psychiatric patients whose primary symptom is excessive anxiety are subdivided into five disorders: generalized anxiety, obsession-compulsion, panic, phobias, and posttraumatic stress.

Given the diversity of anxiety reactions, it would appear extremely unlikely that all forms of anxieties can be traced to an imbalance of a single neurotransmitter. Not surprisingly, drug studies suggest that different types of anxieties may be linked to different neurotransmitters.

During the 1950s, drugs in the chemical family *phenothiazine* such as Thorazine were tested on mental patients. Because these drugs were quite effective in calming agitated psychotic patients, they were mislabeled *major tranquilizers.* However, these drugs are relatively ineffective in reducing anxiety in either anxiety patients or normal individuals (Davis & Coles, 1975). The "tranquilizing" effects of these drugs appears due to their ability to reduce psychotic symptoms (delusions, hallucinations, etc.) *without* necessarily altering the patients' moods (anxiety, depression, etc.). Because phenothiazines selectively block receptor sites for the neurotransmitter dopamine (Synder, 1976), it would appear that dopaminergic tracts are involved in psychoses but play little or no role in anxiety.

Drugs in the chemical family *propanediol* such as Miltown were also tested on psychiatric patients during the 1950s. These so-called "minor tranquilizers" were effective in reducing anxiety in some but not all patients and were soon replaced with more potent antianxiety drugs in the chemical family *bezodiazepine* (Librium, Valium). Bezodiazepines have been found to be highly effective in the treatment of either anticipatory or generalized anxiety. However, these drugs have also been shown to be ineffective in the treatment of agoraphobia (fear of open spaces), obsessive-compulsive disorder, and panic disorder (Mavissakalian, 1982; Klein, 1984). Thus, it would appear that there are at least two distinct biochemical types of anxiety disorders.

12.1.1. Generalized Anxiety

Researchers have identified how benzodiazepines effect the brain. Specifically, benzodiazepines potentiate (increase) the inhibitory effects of the neurotransmitter GABA on norepinephrine and serotonin tracts but appear to have little direct effect on neurons that release acetylcholine, dopamine, histamine, or peptide neurotransmitters (Krassner, 1983). Conversely, researchers have found that chemicals such as Beta-caroline that inhibit GABA neurons produce increases in anxiety and block the antianxiety effects of bezodiazephines (Marx, 1985). Thus generalized anxiety reactions appear to be linked to the CNS levels of GABA, norepinephrine, and serotonin. However, given that the brain contains a large number of tracts that use these neurotransmitters, isolating which specific parts of the CNS mediate anxiety has proven to be a difficult task.

Gray (1978) proposed that two limbic structures, the hippocampus and the septal area, may play a key role in anxiety. Specifically, surgical destruction of either area mimics the effects of bezodiazepines, whereas electrical stimulation of these limbic areas elicits anxiety-like behavior in rats. He argued that the hippocampus and septal area perform the adaptive function of temporarily blocking ineffective behavior by acting as a "behavioral inhibition system" on norepinephrine and serotonin tracts.

As discussed previously in Chapter 2, studies of the human limbic system would appear to at least partially support Gray's model. Specifically, electrical stimulation of either the hippocampus or septal area can elicit self-reports of anxiety and fear.

12.1.2. Panic Disorders

Before we review the literature on panic disorders, it is important that the reader be familiar with the metabolite, *lactate*. During anaerobic metabolism, the striate muscles convert glucose into lactic acid, a toxic metabolite. Lactic acid is either oxidized into carbon dioxide and water or excreted into the bloodstream as lactate, an ion. The liver normally absorbs lactate from the bloodstream and resynthesizes it into glucose. Because lactate is produced during anaerobic metabolism, blood lactate levels normally rise during moderate to heavy exercise.

Cohen and White (1950) observed that, during exercise, *some* anxiety disorder patients show marked increases in lactate levels relative to healthy controls. This finding was replicated by other researchers who noted that sudden lactate increases in *some* anxiety patients also led to increased reports in symptoms (see Pitts, 1969).

Based on these findings, Pitts and McClure (1967) hypothesized that panic attacks in anxiety patients may be triggered by sudden increases in blood lactate levels. To test their hypothesis, they infusion-injected 14 anxiety patients and 10 control subjects with three different solutions on different testing days. One injection was sodium lactate that in solution separates into sodium and lactate. A second solution was a neutral injection of sodium lactate and calcium. Because lactate and calcium bind chemically, this injection was equivalent to an injection of sodium alone. The third solution was also neutral (glucose in sodium chloride). Injections of either neutral solution had no effect on either anxious or control subjects. However, injections of sodium lactate almost immediately triggered panic attacks in 13 of the 14 anxiety patients and 2 of the 10 "normal" controls.

The physiological effects of lactate are counterintuitive. Specifically, calcium plays an *excitatory* role in both muscle contraction and the adrenal release of catecholamines. Thus, lactate–calcium binding should *inhibit* rather than stimulate peripheral SNS arousal. Pitts (1969) speculated that high blood levels of lactate may trigger panic attacks in susceptible individuals by binding calcium in the CNS. Because calcium stimulates the presynaptic release of neurotransmitters in the CNS, Pitts assumed that the SNS arousal (increased systolic BP, tachycardia, etc.) produced by lactate injections was due to inhibition of unspecified inhibitory tracts in the CNS.

Shortly after the lactate theory was published, other researchers raised serious questions about its empirical validity. For example, Grosz and Farmer (1969) reported that only a subset of anxiety disorder patients showed elevated blood levels of lactate. Ackerman and Sachar (1974) found that normal individuals who reacted to sodium lactate injections with panic attacks did not react with panic attacks after vigorous exercise.

Despite these negative results, researchers remained enchanted with the ability of sodium lactate to trigger panic attacks in some individuals. Scientists have focused on three major issues: (a) who is susceptible to lactate-induced panic attacks; (b) the physiological mechanisms that mediated lactate-induced panic; and (c) whether drugs can block spontaneous and/or lactate-induced panic attacks.

Lactate testing of psychiatric populations produced the surprising discovery that lactate-sensitive individuals fell almost exclusively into two diagnostic categories: panic disorders and agoraphobia. Depending on the sample tested, between 65% and 100% of panic disorder and agoraphobic patients show panic attacks in response to lactate. Surprisingly, the percentage of lactate-sensitive individuals in other anxiety disorders (generalized, obsessive-compulsive, posttraumatic stress, simple and social phobias) appears to be *lower* than in the general population. Thus panic attacks and agoraphobia appear to be qualitatively different from other forms of anxiety disorders.

Researchers now suspect that panic attacks and agoraphobia are simply different phases of the same disorder. Presumably, the panic attack patients develop phobic reactions to the situation cues that are contiguous with the occurrence of spontaneous panic attacks. For example, if an individual experiences a spontaneous panic attack while driving a car, he or she may develop a fear of riding in cars. These simple phobias quickly multiply until the individual literally becomes afraid of almost everything, including the panic attacks themselves. Thus agoraphobia may represent the end state of panic disorders. Epidemiological studies suggest that both lactate sensitivity and panic attacks have a strong genetic predisposition. Researchers have noted a relatively high concordance rate between panic disorder patients and biological relatives who have been diagnosed with major depression or an anxiety disorder (Rifkin & Siris, 1985).

Despite 35 years of research, no physiological mechanism has been identified to account for why lactate elicits panic attacks in some individuals. Contrary to Pitts's (1969) predictions, researchers have consistently failed to find any consistent difference in blood levels of calcium ions during lactate injections between reactive and nonreactive individuals (Fyer *et al.*, 1984). Three alternative biological mechanisms for lactate-induced panic attacks have been proposed.

First, lactate may trigger hyperventilation that, in turn, may cause shifts in blood pH. Although many of the physiological symptoms of hyperventilation and panic attacks are similar, hyperventilation *per se* does not appear to be the biological cause of panic attacks (Haslam, 1974; Gorman *et al.*, 1984; Van den Hout and Griez, 1984). Moreover, Liebowitz and his associates have also failed to find any difference in blood pH in reactive and nonreactive individuals (Liebowitz *et al.*, 1985).

A second commonly proposed biological mechanism for lactate-induced panic attacks is that susceptible individuals have hyperreactive epinephrine or norepinephrine tracts. However, Liebowitz *et al.* (1985) failed to find differences in blood levels of epinephrine between susceptible and nonsusceptible individuals.

A third explanation of lactate-induced panic attacks is that lactate may indirectly effect the CNS by altering liver or body metabolism. However, there is again little evidence to support this hypothesis. For example, insulin levels are normal during lactate-induced panic attacks (Gorman, Liebowitz, Stein, Fyer, & Klein, 1984).

At this point in time, no specific "cause" of lactate-induced panic has been identified. To further confuse matters, chemicals *other* than sodium lactate have also been found to trigger panic attacks. For example, Raskin (1984) reported a case of dexamethasone-induced panic attacks and agoraphobia. Similarly, Gawin and Markoff (1981) reported a case of a depressed patient whose panic attacks were triggered by discontinuation of an antidepressant drug (amitriptyline). Charney, Heninger, and Jatlow (1985) found that caffeine could trigger panic attacks in panic disorder patients. Cohen, Barlow, and Blanchard (1985) found that *relaxation* could paradoxically induce panic attacks in some patients.

To further complicate the situation, researchers have found that drugs that "shouldn't work" may block panic attacks. For example, the "antidepressant" drug, imipramine, is ineffective in reducing generalized anxiety but has been found to be extremely effective in treating both panic and agoraphobic patients. Other "antidepressant" drugs such as phenelzine and MAO inhibitors have also been found to have an "antipanic" effect (see Klein, 1984). We will discuss the biochemistry of these antidepressant drugs in detail later in this chapter.

Recently, the triazolobenzodiazepine drug, alprazolam, was introduced into clinical practice. Because alprazolam is chemically related to the benzodiazepines, psychopharmacologists correctly predicted that alprazolam would be effective in the treatment of anticipatory and generalized anxieties. Surprisingly, researchers discovered that alprazolam also appears to have potent antipanic properties (Charney & Heninger, 1985).

To recapitulate, drug research suggests that generalized anxiety and panic are controlled by different biochemical mechanisms. At this point in time, we have a relatively crude map of the neural tracts involved in generalized anxiety. However, no plausible biochemical model of panic disorders is currently available. We can neither explain why panic disorders occur nor explain why drugs like alprazolam are effective. The effectiveness of "antidepressant" drugs would appear to suggest that panic attacks and depression may be mediated by at least some of the same neurotransmitters. We will return to this issue later in this chapter.

12.2. ELATION

The term *elation* is commonly used to denote four distinct psychological states. First, elation is often used to describe the abnormal state of euphoria characteristic of the manic phases of bipolar disorders. Second, elation is commonly used to denote feelings of extreme joy associated with attainment of a personally meaningful goal. Third, elation is often used to describe euphoriclike religious experiences. Fourth, elation is also used to denote drug-induced states of euphoria.

Although each of these "altered states" of consciousness is triggered by different stimuli, self-reports during all four types of elation are remarkably similar. Specifically, descriptions of the "emotional highs" associated with mania, goal attainment, religious ecstasy, and drug ingestion are often indistinguishable.

One plausible explanation for these findings is that the observed similarities in self-reports are merely a semantic artifact. That is, subjects may have difficulty verbally describing their feelings and thus, may inadvertently select similar metaphors to describe subjectively different states. For example, religious experiences are often described as "orgasmic," whereas orgasms are often described in religious terms.

An alternative explanation is that at least some, if not all, forms of elation might be produced by the activation of the same CNS tracts. As we will discuss in the following section, psychopharmacologists have made a series of discoveries that appear to provide strong empirical support for this hypothesis.

Traditionally, researchers were puzzled by the ease at which plant alkaloids pass through the blood–brain barrier and are absorbed by the CNS. Specifically, both hallucinogenic plant alkaloids (ergot, D-lysergic acid diethylamide, psilocin, and psilocybin) and opiate plant alkaloids (heroin, morphine, and opium) readily cross the blood–brain barrier. Researchers suspected that the ability of plant alkaloids to "fool" the blood–brain barrier was due to their molecular structures mimicking neurotransmitters and/or their precursors. For example, serotonin and the hallucinogenic drugs LSD, psilocin, and psilocybin, all contain an indene (or indole) ring in their molecular structure. The hallucinogenic drug mescaline is similar in molecular structure to epinephrine and norepinephrine (Barron, Jarvick, & Burnell, 1964).

The major criticism of the molecular mimicry model of alkaloid passage through the blood–brain barrier was that there was (then) no known neurotransmitter molecularly similar to opiate alkaloids. Based on the assumption that the mimicry model was correct, Hughes (1975; Hughes *et al.*, 1975) performed a series of opiate assays of guinea pig tissue in an attempt to isolate the "missing" neurotransmitter. They discovered, not one, but two distinct opiatelike peptide (amino acid string) neurotransmitters, leu-5-enkephalin and met-5-enkephalin. Later researchers discovered three additional opiatelike neuropeptides (alpha-, beta-, and gamma-endorphins) in the CNS as well as a number of distinct neuropeptides in the peripheral nervous system (Guillemin, 1978). To further confuse matters, researchers discovered that neuropeptides are also found within the chemical structure of some larger organic molecules. For example, beta-lipotropin, a pituitary hormone involved in fat metabolism, contains both beta-endorphin and met-5-enkephalin within its molecular structure. Researchers currently disagree over whether neuropeptides are the precursors or metabolites of such larger molecules (Edelson, 1981).

Although a number of researchers have speculated that endorphins and enkephalins may be either precursors or metabolites of each other, Bloom and his associates found that independent tracts of beta-endorphin and enkephalin neurons occur in the rat brain (Bloom, Battenburg, Rossier, Ling, & Guillemin, 1978). Beta-endorphin cells are clustered primarily in the hypothalamus and pituitary, whereas enkephalin neurons are found throughout the spinal cord and brain. Enkephalin neurons are highly concentrated in the amygdala, basal ganglia, medial forebrain bundle, and periventricular system.

Synder (1977) noted that the anatomical arrangement of neuropeptide tracts was ideally suited to block pain signals from reaching the cortex. Consistent with this hypothesis, clinical studies have found that injecting pain patients with an opiate receptor blocker, naloxone, increased pain (Lasagna, 1965; Levine, Gordon, Jones, & Field, 1978). Conversely, stimulation of these tracts reduces pain. Hosobuchi, Rossier, Bloom, and Gullemin (1979) found that electrical stimulation of the periaqueductal gray matter in the pons produced both pain relief and an increase in beta-endorphins in the cerebrospinal fluid of three pain patients. Similarly, Akil, Richardson, Hughes, and Barchas (1978) found that electrical stimulation of sites in the periventricular system produced both pain relief and an increase in enkephalins in eight brain patients' cerebrospinal fluid. Not surprisingly, naloxone blocked the analgesic effects of electrical brain stimulation.

Although naloxone increases pain in patients, laboratory studies have rather consistently failed to find naloxone-induced increase in pain in normal subjects. Schull, Kaplan, and O'Brian (1981) noted that experimentally induced and pathological pain may differ both in their intensity and in their emotional significance. Experimentally induced pain (cold pressor, ischemic pain, etc.) may be intense but is rarely anxiety producing because the subjects are aware that the pain will terminate shortly. Conversely, pathological pain is often highly anxiety producing because it reminds the patients that they are ill or injured. Schull and his associates hypothesized that state anxiety may mediate both the analgesic effects of morphine and opiate neuropeptides and the pain-increasing effects of naloxone. To test this hypothesis, 8 female and 6 male volunteers were given cold pressor and ischemic pain tolerance tests on each of 2 consecutive testing days. All subjects were tested alone in an isolation chamber to increase the aversiveness of the testing situation. Half of the subjects received a naloxone injection on the first day of testing and a saline injection on the second day of testing. The remaining subjects received the injections in reverse order. A total of 10 of the 14 subjects displayed marked reduction in ischemic pain tolerance on the naloxone day of testing. Moreover, subjects who received naloxone on the first day of testing reported much higher levels of anxiety at the beginning of the second testing session. The authors speculate that opiate neuropeptides may reduce pain by acting as an antianxiety drug and that naloxone may increase the emotional quality of pain rather than its sensory quality.

Schull's findings are consistent with earlier reports that morphine may have antianxiety properties (Davis, 1979) and that antianxiety drugs may increase pain tolerance (Chapman & Feather, 1973). About the same time as Schull's report, researchers found that exercise was associated both with increases in positive moods and in blood levels of neuropeptides (Carr et al., 1981; Colt, Wardlaw, and Franz, 1981). For example, Carr et al. (1981) found that chronic exercise produced a marked increase in blood levels of both beta-endorphins and beta-lipotropin in nonathletes. Researchers realized that the opiate neuropeptide may be the biochemical link between exercise-induced mood changes and exercise-induced increases in pain tolerance.

Callen (1983) argued that an exercise-induced release of opiate neuropeptides may account for both the antianxiety and anitdepressant effects of exercise and exercise-induced euphoric states such as "runners highs." Presumably, exercising up to the point of pain produces a low-level release of opiate peptides that result in the general elevation in mood without producing a euphoriclike state. Thus, light to moderate exercise may function as a tranquilizer rather than a euphoric (DeVries, 1981). Exercising *beyond* the point of pain, however, may trigger a marked release of opiate neuropeptides that produce a state of opiate intoxication. Callen noted that about two-thirds of 424 runners surveyed reported experiencing "highs" about 44% of the times that they ran.

The inconsistency of such runners highs may be best understood if habitual exercise is viewed as a form of opiate addiction. Suppose we are "out of shape." Even relatively minor physical exercise may become painful. Because neuropeptide release is pain-dependent, an individual who is in a poor state of physical conditioning may experience an elevation in mood at relatively low levels of physical exertion. If individuals exercise chronically, both their physical conditioning improves and their pain threshold increases. Consequently, the individual must exert more and more effort to reach a state of self-induced pain. Moreover, the CNS develops a tolerance for opiate drugs and therefore the individual requires higher and higher dosages of opiates to "get high." Together, these three factors mean that habitual runners must run greater and greater distances to produce a high. For example, the respondents in the Callan study that reported "highs" were running an average of 37.6 kilometers (23.3 miles) per week when they first noted a distinct euphoric state.

Although Glasser (1976) has labeled habitual running a *positive addiction*, it should be emphasized that exercise addiction may be no different than any other form of opiate addiction. Laboratory research suggests that at least two neuropeptides, beta-endorphin (Wei & Loh, 1976) and leu-5-enkephalin (Stein & Belluzi, 1978) are highly addicting. Thus it would appear reasonable to predict that termination of daily exercise may elicit symptoms of opiate withdrawal. Consistent with this prediction, habitual runners frequently report feeling anxious, depressed, and hostile on days that they are prevented from running

(Callen, 1983). Like other opiate addicts, habitual runners may compulsively seek their daily "fix" merely to avoid unpleasant symptoms of withdrawal.

It should be noted that the endorphin addiction model of exercise minimizes the effects of other biochemical changes associated with physical exercise such as increases in lactic acid. Berger and Mackenzie (1980) observed that the *same* female runner reported at least 30 different emotional states while running, ranging from ecstasy to fear.

Stein and Belluzzi (1978) have hypothesized that opiate peptides may also play an important role in regulating everyday emotional states and motivational behaviors. They noted that rewards can be crudely divided into classes: incentives and satisfiers. Incentives produce increases in physiological arousal, whereas satisfiers produce decreases in arousal. For example, drugs such as cocaine act primarily as incentives and increase physiological arousal. Conversely, drugs like morphine reduce physiological arousal and thus act primarily as satisfiers. In everyday life, this distinction may appear rather trivial because the *same* stimuli often act sequentially as incentives and satisfiers. The sensory qualities of food (sight, smell, taste, etc.) initially act as an incentive, and the subsequent sensory feedback from consuming food normally functions as a satisfier.

Stein and Belluzzi argued that neuropeptides may regulate the shift from incentive motivation to satisfaction and thus prevent pleasurable stimuli from becoming aversive. As discussed previously in Chapter 2, both pain and pleasure are conditional due to interactions between the medial forebrain bundle (MFB) and the periventricular system (PS). For example, even highly pleasurable stimuli become aversive in high dosages. Most humans report that continued mechanical stimulation of their genitals immediately after orgasm is unpleasant if not painful. Stein and Belluzzi postulate that, by decreasing physiological arousal, neuropeptide release during orgasm and other rewards normally terminates pleasurable behavior before it becomes painful. In a series of experiments, they demonstrated that (a) either naloxone or norepinephrine inhibitors suppress rats' self-stimulation of the MFB and (b) injections of enkephalins block food-seeking behaviors in hungry rats. Thus, it would appear that either a deficit or an excess of enkepahlin may disrupt the functioning of the MFB.

The literature on pain- and pleasure-induced releases of opiate neuropeptides is also highly consistent with Solomon and Corbit's (1974; Solomon, 1980) opponent-process model of emotion and motivation discussed previously in Chapter 4. Solomon and Corbit argued that the acute effects of opiate drugs (euphoria) decrease with repeated exposure, whereas the rebound effects (abstinence-agony) become more pronounced. Gradually, the individual's motivation shifts from seeking euphoria (State A) to avoiding withdrawal (State B). If we substitute *neuropeptide* for *drug*, their model predicts that novice runners engage in running to "feel good," whereas veteran runners may run to avoid "feeling bad."

Solomon and Corbit also hypothesized that other nondrug satisfiers (food, sex, etc.) elicit similar negative rebounds. For example, consuming your favorite food every meal would quickly elicit negative emotional reactions, for example, "Oh no! Not steak *again!*" Such postsatiation negative rebounds may produce four distinct patterns of incentive motives. First, the individual may attempt to restore the original level of pleasure by increasing the *quantity* of the reward. Thus the individual may compulsively eat, engage in sexual behaviors, and so forth but still derive little pleasure from the behaviors. Second, the individual may attempt to restore the original level of pleasure by altering the *quality* of the reward. The individual may develop a craving for gourmet cooking, sexual novelty, and the like that may temporarily restore some amount of pleasure. Third, the individual may attempt to restore the original level of pleasure by substituting "novel" satisfiers, for example, new foods, new sex partners. Fourth, the individual may find the rebound effects so aversive that they avoid the precipitating behavior. For example, the decline in the frequency of sexual behavior during middle age may be a reaction to satiation rebound rather than due to hormonal changes.

In summary, neuropeptides appear to provide the biochemical link between emotional states such as elation and motives. However, the effect of neuropeptides on other neurotransmitters is poorly understood. Researchers have found that neuropeptides may facilitate and/or inhibit neural tracts of at least three neurotransmitters (dopamine, norepinephrine, and serotonin) that are suspected of mediating emotional states. Moreover, researchers are also uncertain about the interaction of neuropeptides and hormones. What role (if any) neuropeptides may play in normal emotional states or psychiatric disorders is currently unknown.

12.3. DEPRESSION

As discussed throughout previous chapters, the term *depression* is loosely used to denote a variety of psychological states ranging from "blue" moods to suicidal levels of despair. Moreover, depression may be triggered by a real or imaginary psychological "loss" or may occur spontaneously. Given that depression is also associated with a variety of neurohormonal disorders (see Chapter 3), researchers have long suspected that at least some, if not all, forms of depression were linked to biochemical changes in the brain.

Schildkraut (1965; Schildkraut & Kety, 1967; Schildkraut & Freyhan, 1972) noted that drugs such as reserpine that decrease CNS levels of norepinephrine act as mood depressors and in some cases may actually produce suicidal states of depression. Conversely, drugs that increase CNS levels of norepinephrine act as mood elevators and in some cases may produce maniclike states of extreme elation. Based on these clinical observations, Schildkraut hypothesized that emotional states of depression and of mania were both mediated by the level of norepinephrine in the CNS. Presumably, an individual experiences severe depression when norepinephrine levels are extremely low, whereas if norepinephrine levels are abnormally high, the individual experiences manic states. Thus, changes in the biochemical balance of the nervous system may produce the psychiatric disorders of unipolar depression and of bipolar (manic) depression. This deceptively simple humorlike model has stimulated much research.

A number of empirical findings are consistent with Schildkraut's nor-epinephrine theory of depression and mania. First, as shown in Table 12-1, drugs that are commonly used to treat psychiatric disorders that involve hyper-arousal (anxiety, bipolar depression, and functional psychoses) generally do inhibit norepinephrine tracts. Second, drugs that are effective in treating uni-polar depression generally facilitate norephinephrine transmission. Third, ad-ministrations of drugs that facilitate norepinephrine transmission such as amphetamines or l-dopa may trigger maniclike episodes. Fourth, norepin-ephrine levels estimated from urinary MHPG do tend to co-vary with states of hyperarousal (anxiety, mania) and with states of hypoarousal (depression). For example, studies of unipolar depressed patients have found that MHPG levels often are lower during episodes of depression than during nondepressed peri-

Table 12-1. Acute Pharmacological Effects of Drugs Commonly Used to Treat Psychiatric Disorders

Psychiatric disorder	Generic drug	Trade name	Neurotransmitter(s) affected
Anxiety	Chlordiazepoxide	Librium	Dopamine▼ Norepinephrine▼ Serotonin▼
	Diazepam	Valium	Dopamine▼ Norepinephrine▼ Serotonin▼
Panic attacks	Alprasolam	Xanax	Unknown[a]
	Imipramine	Tofranil	Dopamine▲ Norephinephrine▲ Serotonin▲
Depression (unipolar)	MAO inhibitors	Iproniaziad[b]	Dopamine▲ Norephinephrine▲ Serotonin▲
	Amitriptyline	Elavil	Serotonin▲
	Desipramine	Norpramin	Norepinephrine▲
	Imipramine	Tofranil	Dopamine▲ Norepinephrine▲ Serotonin▲
Depression (bipolar)	Lithium salts	Esalith	Norepinephrine▼ Serotonin▲
Functional psychoses	Halaperidol	Haldol	Dopamine▼
	Chlopromazine	Thorazine	Dopamine▼ Norepinephrine▼ Serotonin▼

Note. ▲ indicates that transmission is facilitated. ▼ indicates that transmission is inhibited.
[a]*Physicians' Desk Reference* (39th ED.). Oradell, Medicial Economics Co., 1985.
[b]Due to toxic long term-effects of Iproniaziad treatment, this drug has been replaced in clinical practice by other MOA inhibitors such as Isocarboxazid and Nialamide. These newer drugs also effect dopamine, norepinephrine, and serotonin neurotransmission.

ods. In bipolar depression patients, decreased MHPG excretion accompanies periods of depression, and increased MHPG excretion accompanies manic episodes. In some patients, the shifts in MHPG levels were observed *prior* to changes in the patients' emotional states (Maas, 1975a). Moreover, compared with normal controls, depressed patients excrete lower levels of MHPG (Maas, Fawcett, & Dekirmenjiam, 1972; Schildkraut, 1974).

Given the rather impressive empirical support for the norepinephrine model of emotion, it may come as a surprise to the reader that Schildkraut (1973) dismissed his own model as too simplistic. One of the most common errors in human reasoning is called the *confirmation trap*. In order to objectively evaluate the empirical validity of a theory, one must look at both the positive and negative evidence and not just the positive evidence. After a careful review of available literature, Schildkraut correctly concluded that changes in the norepinephrine tracts alone could not account for depression and mania. To reinforce the importance of reviewing negative evidence, let us now briefly review the findings that do not support Schildkraut's model.

First, drugs that reduce norepinephrine levels are not universally effective in treating bipolar depression. For example, lithium, the drug of choice in treating bipolar depression patients, is effective with only about 70% of patients.

Second, drugs that may be successful in the treatment of unipolar depression do not all increase CNS levels of norepinephrine. For example, amitriptyline increases serontonergic transmission and has almost no effect on catecholamine (dopamine or norepinephrine) tracts.

Third, many drugs that increase norepinephrine levels are ineffective in treating unipolar depressed patients. For example, cocaine is a rather potent stimulant of catecholamine transmission. Yet, cocaine has almost no effect on chronic depressed patients' symptoms. Similarly, l-dopa increases the biosynthesis of both norepinephrine and dopamine but is only an effective treatment for a subset of depressed patients (Goodwin, Murphy, Brodie, and Bunney, 1970).

Fourth, although the majority of depressed patients excrete low quantities of urinary MHPG, about 30% of depressed patients actually secrete normal or elevated levels of MHPG (Beckmann & Goodwin, 1975; Maas, 1975b). Suspiciously, almost an identical percentage of depressed patients show abnormally low levels of the serotonin metabolite, 5-HIAA, in their cerebrospinal fluid (Coppen, 1972; Asberg, Thoren, Traskman, Bertilsson, & Tingberg, 1976). Thus it would appear that there are at least two major subtypes of depression: a "norepinephrine depression" characterized by low levels of MHPG and a "serotonin depression" characterized by low levels of 5-HIAA.

Consistent with this hypothesis, a number of researchers have reported that patients with low MHPG levels respond well to drugs that increase norepinephrine levels (desipramine or imipramine) but not to drugs that increase seratonin levels (amitriptyline). Conversely, depressed patients with normal or elevated MHPG levels respond well to amitriptyline but not desipramine or imipramine (Fawcett, Maas, & Dekirmenjian, 1972; Beckmann & Goodwin, 1975; Hollister, Davis, & Berger, 1980).

Although not all researchers have found a relationship between urinary MHPG levels and patients' responses to drug treatments, the overall pattern of clinical findings tends to strongly support the predictive validity of MHPG levels (Whybrow, Akiskal, & McKinney, 1984). Accordingly, researchers proposed a series of new models of depression. For example, a "double depression" or catecholamine–indoleamine deficiency model was proposed by Schildkraut (1973) and later refined by Mass (1975b). Basically, this model postulates that psychiatric levels of depression are produced by low levels of *either* norepinephrine or serotonin in the CNS. Thus depressive disorders can be seen as analogous to neurohormonal disorders discussed previously in Chapter 3.

Prange and his associates proposed a "permissive" or "balance" model of depression (Prange, Wilson, Lynn, Alltop, & Stikeleather, 1974). They postulated that low levels of serotonin do not cause but rather merely permit depression or mania to develop. Specifically, they hypothesized that emotional states may be mediated by the relative rather than the absolute levels of catecholamines and serotonin in the brain. Presumably, if catecholamine levels drop to the level of serotonin, the individual experiences depression, whereas if catecholamine levels rise extremely high relative to serotonin levels, the individual experiences manic states. It should be noted that this model correctly predicts the therapeutic benefit of lithium in the treatment of bipolar depression.

Although both the double and permissive models can account for the clinical effectiveness of specific drugs, both models also share two major theoretical weaknesses. First, they fail to specify *why* an individual would suddenly develop a specific neurotransmitter deficiency or imbalance. This curious lack of a causal mechanism is partially due to the fact that these models were constructed by reasoning backward from the clinical findings.

Second, these models were based on the effects of *acute* administration of drugs. However, many drugs have no effect on psychiatric patients' emotional states unless they are administered *chronically*. For example, lithium must be administered on a daily basis for at least 5 days and often as long as 2 weeks before any detectable change occurs in the emotional states of bipolar depressive patients. Similarly, MAO inhibitors and tricyclic antidepressants (amitriptyline, desipramine, imipramine, and nortriptyline) must be administered chronically for between 2 to 4 weeks before any therapeutic benefit is observed in unipolar depressive patients. This time lag between initial administration of the drug and change in patients' subjective states raises the obvious question of whether the acute and chronic effects of these drugs are identical.

The distinction between acute and chronic effects of drugs is actually quite a complex issue. Some specific drugs appear to produce identical acute and chronic effects on neural transmission. For example, ethyl alcohol produces a significant elevation of MHPG levels in the cerebrospinal fluid of both alcoholics and normal controls (Borg, Kvande, & Sevall, 1981). Other drugs, however, have *opposite* effects when administered on an acute and on a chronic basis.

Beckmann and Goodwin (1980) assessed the chronic effects of antidepressant drugs by measuring the change in urinary catecholamine metabolites during the course of drug treatment. As predicted by the second generation models, the acute effects of antidepressants was an increase in catecholamine metabolites. However, the chronic effect of antidepressants was a net *decrease* in catecholamine metabolites. Consistent with this finding, other researchers have reported that the chronic effects of antidepressants and many other psychotrophic drugs used in the treatment of mental illness may be exactly opposite of their acute effects (Whybrow *et al.*, 1984). One plausible interpretation of these findings is that the double-depression and permissive models are basically correct but have simply "reversed" the excesses and deficiencies in neurotransmitters that presumably produce specific forms of emotional disorders.

An alternative explanation of the neurophysiological effects of psychotrophic drugs is that the drugs trigger a complex series of neuronal adaptations and that these chronic neuronal changes, rather than the drugs themselves, account for the therapeutic benefit of the drug treatments. Consistent with this hypothesis, comparison of antidepressant drugs and electroconvulsive shock therapy (ECT) have found that ECT is as effective as drug therapies and that ECT produces a faster remission in symptoms (Kilicpera, Albert, and Strain, 1979). Although the effects of ECT on the brain are currently unknown, Masserano, Takimoto, and Weiner (1981) reported that giving rats repeated ECT promotes an acute increase in tyrosine hydroxylase, an enzyme that increases dopamine and norepinephrine levels. Thus it is plausible that *any* therapy (diet, exercise, psychotherapy, etc.) that can trigger an acute change in CNS neurotransmitter levels may also trigger a series of compensatory neuronal changes that may produce a new balance between the levels of different neurotransmitters and symptom remission.

Studies of the effects of termination of drug treatments are also consistent with the view that a change in the balance of neurotransmitters rather than the absolute levels of neurotransmitters may account for the therapeutic benefits of drug treatments. A number of researchers have reported that at least a sizable minority of psychiatric patients show no relapse in their symptoms if they are secretly given placebos or if their drug treatments are terminated completely. Moreover, there have been some reports that placebo treatments alone may "cure" depression. For example, Sato, Turnbull, Davidson, and Madakasira (1984) compared the effects of a placebo and the antidepressant drug, bupropion, in a double-blind experiment. Surprisingly, 32 of 53 depressed inpatients responded to the placebo and reported both a marked reduction in psychological symptoms such as feelings of apathy and guilt and a reduction in somatic symptoms. The 21 placebo nonresponders reported "improvement" in only some psychological symptoms. The individual patient's response to the placebo appeared to be mediated by both the patient's sex and psychiatric disorder. The majority of the placebo responders were female patients who had been diagnosed as depressive neurotics, whereas the majority of nonresponders were male and had been diagnosed as bipolar depressives.

The partial validity of the double-depression and permissive models led researchers to postulate a series of more sophisticated models. These "third generation" models attempted to incorporate two dynamic features, a causal mechanism and a description of the interaction between the catecholamines and other neurotransmitters in the brain.

In terms of complexity, these third generation models represent a quantum leap from the earlier models. For example, depressed patients often display either increased or decreased levels of aggressive, eating, and sexual behaviors.

Antelman and Caggiula (1977, 1980) postulated that such mood-related behavioral changes are mediated by the interactions between the dopaminergic neurons and the neurons that employ acetylcholine, GABA, glutamate, norepinephrine, and serotonin as neurotransmitters that are anatomically arranged into a complex system of excitatory and inhibitory circuits. Unlike earlier models, their theory does not treat neurotransmitters as if they occur in a vacuum but rather recognizes that the level of a given neurotransmitter may be modified by the activity of other neurons using different neurotransmitters. Thus dopaminergic neurons are considered only the final common pathway for the mood-related changes in motivational behaviors.

The major flaw in Antelman and Caggiula's model is that the authors failed to specify *how* neurotransmitter imbalances might occur in a natural setting. Other theorists have proposed that at least four different biological mechanisms may predispose or actually trigger emotion-related imbalances in neurotransmitters: genetic vulnerability, diet, hormones, and circadian rhythms.

First, researchers have frequently reported concordance between a given individual's psychiatric diagnosis and psychiatric disorders in biological (but not adoptive) relatives. For example, individuals with anxious or depressed biological relatives are a high-risk group for affective disorders (Farber, 1982; Wybrow *et al.*, 1984). It should be noted that the issue of genetic predisposition is extremely complex. Obviously, the increased risk of psychiatric disorders among biological relatives may be due to the increased level of psychosocial stress produced by interacting with emotionally disturbed relatives.

Second, diet appears to play an important role in maintaining neurotransmitter levels. Many chemicals that are essential precursors or "blocking blocks" for the biosynthesis of neurotransmitters cannot be manufactured by the body but must be derived directly from the diet. Foods such as eggs, fish, green leafy vegetables, liver, soybeans, and wheat germ are all rich in choline, a precursor of acetylcholine. High protein foods contain two precursors of catecholamines (tyrosine and phenylalanine) and often contain tryptophan, a precursor to serotonin. Moreover, neurotransmitter precursors may be found in any number of dietary sources. For example, ice cream is rich in tryptophan. For a more detailed discussion of the role of diet in neurotransmitter biosynthesis, see Kolata (1976, 1979).

Given that diet supplies the essential precursors for neurotransmitters, it would appear reasonable to predict that diet alone may alter moods. Consistent with this hypothesis, Wurtman and Growdon (1980) found that different groups of psychiatric patients appear to react differently to high-choline diets. Specifically, increasing dietary choline produced an increase in the symptoms of depressed patients but a decrease in the symptoms of manic patients. Similarly, placing psychiatric patients on high carbohydrate diets appears to reduce insomnia and increase the effectiveness of antidepressant drugs in some depressed patients. Gibson and Gelenberg (1983) reported that tyrosine treatments produced symptom remission in four out of six unipolar depressed patients without any of the adverse side effects produced by antidepressant drugs. These findings clearly suggest that diet alone may alter psychiatric patients' emotional states by altering the relative balance of CNS neurotransmitters (Gonzalez, 1984).

Although the therapeutic value of diet in the treatment of psychiatric disorders is, in itself, a fascinating issue, it also raises the larger theoretical question of whether diet may alter emotional states in healthy individuals. Christensen, Krietsch, White, and Stagner (1985) demonstrated that diet may interact with genetic or acquired susceptibility in influencing moods. Three females and one male were placed on a high-protein and low-carbohydrate diet for a 2-week period. Although all four subjects reported mood and personality changes as a function of diet, the specific psychological changes were idiosyncratic. That is, each subject reacted differently to the same diet.

A third biological cause of CNS neurotransmitter imbalances are hormones. As discussed previously in Chapter 3, Grant and Pryse-Davies (1968), Carroll and Steiner (1978), and other theorists have postulated that the sex hormones (androgen, estrogen, progesterone, and prolactin) may indirectly induce states of anxiety, depression, and hostility by altering CNS levels of specific neurotransmitters. Conversely, other theorists have argued that the levels of sex hormones are themselves influenced by the effects of stress hormones (cortisol, thyroxine) on CNS neurotransmitters (McEwen, 1980). For example, corticosteroid responses are clearly elevated, and sex hormone responses are clearly reduced in both anxious and depressed psychiatric patients (Sachar, 1980). Moreover, there have been numerous clinical reports of steroid treatment-induced depression or psychosis. Lewis and Smith (1983) estimated that severe psychiatric reactions may occur in about 5% of patients treated with steroids. Thus the current balance of CNS neurotransmitters may be a product of the complex interaction between the sex hormone control system, the stress hormone control system, and the previous balance of neurotransmitters.

A fourth biological cause of neurotransmitter imbalances is that stress may disrupt the body's "biological clocks" and thus interfere with the temporal regulation of the hormonal and nervous systems. Physiologists have noted that many biological processes oscillate with one of the four major physical cycles on our planet: the tides, day and night, the phases of the moon, and the seasons. The relative importance of each of these biological rhythms varies from species to species. In humans, daily (circadian) rhythms appear to dominate both endocrine gland and neurotransmitter activity. Specifically, many biological processes continue on roughly a 24-hour cycle even if the individual is deprived of information of the external day–night cycle. In adult women, the monthly (circalunar) shifts in sex hormone levels are superimposed upon these circadian rhythms.

In humans, the sleep–wake cycle also plays an important role in mediating circadian rhythms. A sudden shift in the sleep–wake cycle by at least 4 or 5 hours (e.g., jet lag) desynchronizes physiological processes for 2 or 3 days until the CNS adapts to the new sleep–wake cycle. Curiously, complete adaptation does not occur with reversal of the sleep–wake cycle. For example, workers on rotating shifts show deformed (partially shifted) rather than completely inverted circadian rhythms. For a more detailed discussion of human circadian rhythms, see Aschoff (1980).

The observed linkage between human circadian rhythms and the sleep–wake cycle led Hartmann (1973) to propose that sleep helped restore both the body's global biochemical balance and the CNS balance between neurotransmitters. He postulated that nondream or slow wave sleep (SWS) may serve as "rest" to allow the body to recover biochemically from physical exertion. Hartmann also postulated that dream or rapid-eye-movements (REM) sleep may serve as "brain restitution" to allow the CNS to recover from mental exertion by restoring the balance between neurotransmitters. Hartmann noted that both clinical and laboratory findings suggested that CNS catecholamine levels were depleted while awake and restored during REM sleep. Antidepressant drugs that (acutely) increase CNS catecholamine levels decrease REM sleep, whereas drugs that decrease CNS cathecholamine levels increase REM time. Moreover, the proportion of REM time during sleep varies between psychiatric patients and normal controls. Manic patients tend to show lower amounts of REM, whereas depressed patients tend to show increased REM time.

Hartmann's deceptively simple model has had a profound impact on both sleep research and the study of the biochemistry of emotion. Hartmann predicted that physical stressors upset the biochemical balance of the body and thus increase the individuals "need" for SWS. Research on the effects of presleep exercise on the sleep cycle, however, has not consistently found an increase in SWS after physical exertion. Horne (1979, 1981) noted that those studies that found a positive relationship between exercise and SWS time have all employed exercise as a physical stressor (high-intensity exercises) and, conversely, studies that failed to find a relationship between exercise and SWS have employed less stressful exercises.

Hartmann's model also predicts that psychological stress should produce an increased "need" for REM sleep. Cohen (1979a), however, reported that in (presumably) healthy undergraduates, REM "need" was greatest among repressors who habitually denied emotional stress while awake. Moreover, depriving psychiatric patients of REM sleep may actually be therapeutic. For example, Vogel and his associates found that depriving depressed psychiatric patients of REM sleep produces improvements in the patients' moods (Vogel, Traub, Ben-Horin, & Meyers, 1968; Vogel, McAbee, Baker, & Thurmond, 1977). Fahndrich (1983) reported that depressed patients' mood reactions to sleep deprivation may predict their response to tricyclic antidepressants. Patients who show mood improvements with sleep deprivation generally obtain symptom relief with antidepressants that facilitate serotonin transmission such as clomipramine. Conversely, patients who reacted negatively to sleep deprivation responded best to antidepressants such as maprotiline that facilitate norepinephrine transmission.

Although the empirical validity of Hartmann's model is questionable, its heuristic value should not be underestimated. Hartmann's linkage of neurotransmitter levels to the sleep cycle encouraged researchers to reexamine the biochemistry of sleep. Researchers had traditionally assumed that because serotonin levels are normally depleted during sleep, sleep was controlled by serotonergic activity. However, a number of studies suggest that acetylcholine levels in the pons may mediate the oscillation between SWS and REM (Cohen, 1979b). Based on Davis's (1975) model that depression represents acetylcholine dominance of the neurotransmitter balance in the CNS, Cohen (1979b) speculated that REM deprivation may help deplete CNS acetylcholine and thus shift neurotransmitter levels toward a more balanced state.

Clearly, at least three distinct physiological mechanisms (diet, hormones, and sleep) coupled with a genetic predisposition may trigger changes in the balance of CNS neurotransmitters that, in turn, may produce the characteristic symptoms of specific psychiatric disorders. In an ambitious attempt to synthesize the research on potential causal mechanisms and balance theories of emotion, Whybrow, Akiskal, and McKinney (1984) proposed a "fourth generation" biochemical model. Given the sophistication of their model, it is virtually impossible to present more than a brief outline of their theory. They postulated that moods are controlled by at least four major systems: the motor system, neurohormonal system, MFB, and RAS. Like other physiological systems, the homeostasis of the CNS is not static but in a constant state of flux. The dynamic balance between these CNS systems changes with circadian rhythms, the sleep–wake cycle, and other biological clocks. Moreover, these CNS systems are arranged in a mutually inhibitory fashion such that overexcitation of one system stimulates inhibitory tracts that return the entire system to a balanced state.

Whybrow and his associates postulate that a variety of biological and psychosocial factors may disrupt the homeostasis of the CNS and trigger emotional disorders. They argue that the individual's cognitive appraisal of biochemically induced mood shifts may play a central role in whether aversive life events elicit normal emotions or psychiatric levels of emotion. For example, the psychological stress of a significant personal loss such as the death of a parent may trigger physiological changes that the majority of individuals would label as *depression*. If the individual consciously connects the life event and the negative emotional state (i.e., "I am depressed because my father died"), the psychological stress is reduced, and the emotional state gradually passes as the balance in the CNS is restored. However, if the individual focuses his or her attention on his or her inability to cope during the emotional state he or she may inadvertently trigger additional psychological stress that creates a vicious cycle between psychological stress and biochemical imbalances that then would result in a major depressive episode. (Note: from a strict materialist position, Whybrow has committed the cardinal sin of allowing the "ghost into the machine").

One of the powerful features of the Whybrow–Akiskal–McKinney model is that it assumes that *different* biological and psychological factors may elicit the same emotional states. For example, a number of researchers have noted that eating ice cream often results in positive moods. Because ice cream contains the neurotransmitter precursor, tryptophan, the mood-elevation effect of ice cream may be due to increased CNS levels of serotonin. Conversely, ice cream may trigger pleasant childhood memories or occur in the cheerful context of an ice cream parlor (Anonymous, 1986). Alternatively, the taste and physical sensations produced by eating ice cream may directly stimulate the medial forebrain bundles. Thus the pleasure associated with ice cream consumption could, itself, elicit positive moods. According to Whybrow's model, any or all of these factors could elicit positive emotional states in any given individual.

Although Whybrow and his associates' model is an excellent representation of state-of-the-art biochemical theories, it should be stressed that, in psychopharmacology, the state-of-the-art is constantly shifting. New psychotrophic drugs are continuously being introduced into clinical practice. For example, Norman, Maguire, and Burrows (1984) reviewed the development and clinical studies of 11 new antidepressant drugs (amoxapine, bupriopion, ciclazindol, citalopram, deprenyl, femoxetine, mianserin, moclobamide, nomifensine, trazodone, and zimeldine). Moreover, researchers are continuously inventing new assay techniques to identify which types of neurons a given drug chemically binds to and to detect changes in neurotransmitter levels. For example, traditionally researchers had difficulty assaying hormone and neurotransmitters postmortem because these chemicals are quickly destroyed after death. Researchers have discovered that killing animals with microwave radiation effectively "freezes" biochemical activity and allows much more accurate postmortem assays.

Both the development of newer drugs and newer assay techniques has produced a constant stream of empirical findings that often conflict with existing biochemical theories of emotions. For example, researchers have recently discovered that many antidepressant drugs are extremely potent blockers of receptors for the neurotransmitter histamine and are 100 to 1,000 times more powerful than antihistamine drugs (Krassner, 1983). Thus, the antidepressant-induced changes in the levels of catecholamines and serotonin may be produced by inhibition of specific histiminergic tracts or other CNS tracts that contain histamine receptors.

In summary, biochemical models represent a series of fascinating attempts to provide a strict materialist explanation for emotional states. The major strength of these models is that they are closely linked to clinical and laboratory observations and, thus, have a high degree of empirical validity. For example, studies of the effects of benzodiazephines have allowed researchers to isolate the neural tracts involved in generalized anxiety and to document that anxiety and terror (panic) are mediated by different biochemical mechanisms.

The major weaknesses of the current biochemical models is that they have focused only on a few "abnormal" emotional reactions (e.g., psychiatric levels of anxiety, depression, and elation). For example, because there is little or no clinical interest in "antiembarrassment" drugs, we know virtually nothing about the biochemical basis of embarrassment.

SUGGESTED READINGS

Gray, J. A. Anxiety. *Human Nature,* 1978, July, 38–45.
   Lucid theoretical discussion of the biochemistry of the neural tracts involved in generalized anxiety.

Stein, L., & Belluzzi, J. D. Brain endorphins and the sense of well-being: A psychobiological hypothesis. In E. Costa & M. Trabucchi (Eds.), *Advances in biochemical psychopharmacology, Vol. 18. The endorphins.* New York, Raven Press, 1978.
   A theoretical discussion of the role of opiate peptides in everyday emotional-motivational patterns.

Whybrow, P. C., Akiskal, H. S., & McKinney, W. T. *Mood disorders: Towards a new psychobiology.* New York: Plenum Press, 1984.
   An excellent example of contemporary biochemical models of emotion. It also provides a comprehensive review of the literature on the biochemistry of depression.

Physiological Models

Like the biochemical models discussed in Chapter 12, physiological models of emotion are based on the materialist assumption that biological reactions *determine* emotional states. The distinction between biochemical and physiological models is based on the level at which biological events produce emotions. The biochemical models are based on the assumption that causal events occur at a *micro*level, for example, biochemical imbalances in neurotransmitters. Physiological models are based on the assumption that physiological causes occur at a *macro*level of organs and organ systems. It should be noted that these two subclasses of materialist models are complementary rather than mutually exclusive. Obviously, organ activity may directly alter CNS and hormonal activity and vice versa.

As discussed previously in Chapter 10, Darwin (1872) proposed a comprehensive theory of emotional behaviors in both human and nonhuman species. A number of later theorists have attempted to revise Darwin's model to account for both emotional states and behaviors.

13.1. WILLIAM JAMES

Like many other nineteenth-century scientists, William James made significant contributions in a variety of disciplines.

> He began his career, it will be remembered, not as a psychologist, but as a biologist, and it was while he was teaching anatomy in the Harvard Medical School that he made a place in his laboratory for psychological experiments, and thus started almost by accident the first psychological laboratory. The definite shift in his interests toward psychology is marked by his undertaking in 1878 to write *The Principles of Psychology*, a task which occupied him for twelve years. During this time, however, he became interested in philosophy; or rather, philosophy, which had attracted him from his early youth, claimed more and more of his attention. (Heidbreder, 1961, p. 154)

Although James generally favored Darwin's ideas, he felt that Darwin's theory of emotion did not adequately account for emotional states. In 1884,

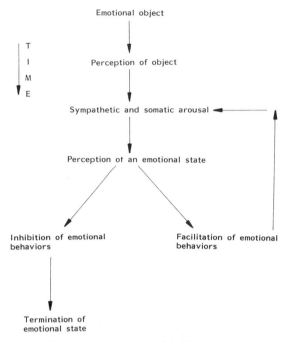

Figure 13-1. James's model of emotion.

James proposed his own physiological model of emotion shown in Figure 13-1. He postulated that emotions are triggered by specific objects or events. The next step in the temporal sequence is the perception of the object or event as emotional. Perception then directly stimulates a distinct pattern of sympathetic and somatic arousal that, in turn, is perceived as a *unique* emotional state. James argued that

> the bodily changes follow directly the perception of the exciting fact, and that our feelings of the same changes as they occur is the emotion. Common-sense says, we lose our fortune, are sorry and weep, we meet a bear, are frightened and run; we are insulted by a rival, are angry and strike. The hypothesis here to be defended says that this order of sequence is incorrect, that the one mental state is not immediately induced by the other, that the bodily manifestations must first be interposed between and that the more rational statement is that we feel sorry because we cry, angry because we strike, afraid because we tremble and not that we cry, strike or tremble because we are sorry, angry or fearful, as the case may be. Without the bodily states following on the perception, the latter would be purely cognitive in form, pale, colorless, destitute of emotional warmth. We might then see the bear and judge it best to run, receive the insult and deem it right to strike but we should not actually feel afraid or angry. (James, 1892, pp. 375–376.)

Despite the relative simplicity of James's theory, three misrepresentations of his model are frequently cited in the emotion literature. The first common misrepresentation of James's model is that because cognitive events *precede* physiological arousal, he hypothesized that cognitive activity *causes* emotional states. Although James conceded that images and memories *could* trigger emotional reactions, he argued that only mental activity that *reproduced* external emotional objects produced emotions. Thus mental events (hallucinations, images, and memories) may produce emotions only when the observer confuses them with sensory input. Moreover, James argued that, although perception may play a role in triggering physiological arousal, in the awareness of arousal and in the termination or maintenance of an emotional state, the emotion *is* the physiological response.

> I now proceed to urge the vital point of my whole theory, which is this: If we fancy some strong emotion, and then try to abstract from our consciousness of it all the feelings of its bodily symptoms, we find we have nothing left behind, no "mind-stuff" out of which the emotion can be constituted, and that a cold and neutral state of intellectual perception is all that remains. (James, 1892, p. 379)

James's insistence that perception during emotional states was a mechanical process created an interesting logical inconsistency in his writings. He described (nonemotional) perception as a dynamic interaction between incoming sensory input, memory, and the ongoing stream of consciousness. Thus James postulated that, in nonemotional situations, both the individual's past experiences and his or her ongoing thought processes influence how current sensory information is interpreted. The sensory message *bear* is obviously perceived differently in the context of a circus performance than in the context of *in my tent*. James clearly recognized that his own dynamic view of perception shifted his model of emotion from the materialist to the interactionist camp, and he intentionally dismissed perception as a "cold" intellectual process to defend his materialist view of emotion.

A second common misrepresentation of James's model in the emotion literature is the notion that *all* emotional states are accompanied by clear patterns of high levels of physiological arousal. James differentiated between "coarser" emotions (anger, fear, love, hate, joy, grief, shame, and pride) that are each presumably associated with distinct patterns of strong physiological arousal and "subtler" emotions that are produced by weaker and more diffuse physiological patterns.

A third major misrepresentation of James theory is the so-called "James–Lange" theory of emotion. Carl Lange (1885) proposed a vasomotor theory of emotion that is extremely similar to James's model. The major distinction between their two models is that Lange emphasized cardiovascular (vasomotor) changes as the primary cause of emotional states. Because the two models were proposed independently at about the same time, many later authors treated the two theories as identical and credited both authors. However, James (1894), himself, rejected Lange's view that cardiovascular changes were the central cause of emotional states and argued that *any* sympathetic or somatic response may trigger emotional states. The reader should note that many of James's examples of physiological causes of emotional states (running, striking, etc.) are clearly somatic responses.

Given that physiological recording instruments were extremely crude at the turn of the century, no direct test of James's model was then possible. Early research on polygraph exams, discussed in Chapter 6, appeared to only partially support James's model. Although lying could be detected in the majority of individuals by examining their physiological responses, a minority of individuals did not show distinct patterns of physiological arousal when lying. However, it was unclear whether the error rate of polygraph exams was due to the primitive recording equipment, incompetent operators, or actual individual differences. Before the technology was available to resolve this issue, Cannon (1927) launched a blistering attack on the "James–Lange" theory that silenced its proponents for about 25 years.

Cannon pointed out five major weaknesses in the "James–Lange" theory. First, cutting the nerves to the internal organs does not eliminate emotional behaviors. Second, global sympathetic arousal, rather than differential patterns of arousal, appears to occur across emotions. Third, the viscera are very poorly represented in the CNS. If individuals normally have only a vague perception of their internal organs, how then could they perceive different patterns of autonomic arousal as distinct emotions? Fourth, emotional states occur rather rapidly, yet, sympathetic nervous system arousal is relatively slow. That is, time is needed to disrupt ongoing physiological activity and produce phasic changes in physiological activity. Fifth, artificial induction of physiological arousal usually does not produce distinct emotional states.

Cannon's critique was generally accepted as demolishing the logical basis of the "James–Lange" theory. However, Mandler (1984) raised the obvious question that, because the "James–Lange" theory never existed, whose model was Cannon attacking, James's or Lange's? Mandler argued that Cannon's criticisms apply to Lange's theory but not to James's model. Specifically, James postulated that *both* somatic and sympathetic arousal were involved in emotional states. Feedback from the somatic nervous system is not lost if the sympathetic nerves are cut (criticism 1); different patterns of somatic activity (frowning, smiling) do occur between emotions (criticism 2); the somatic nervous system is extremely accurately represented in the CNS (criticism 3); somatic nervous system reactions are relatively rapid (criticism 4); and adopting somatic patterns associated with specific emotions may trigger a specific emotion (criticism 5).

As we will discuss later in this chapter, a number of "neo-Jamesian" models of emotion have been proposed that emphasize the role of somatic feedback in emotional states. At this point, it should be noted that the empirical validity of at least three of Cannon's five original criticisms are also debatable. Numerous researchers have found that cutting the sympathetic or vagus nerves may not eliminate all sensory feedback from the viscera (criticism 1). Ax's (1953) and Funkenstein's (1956) studies of cardiovascular responses and Wolf and Wolff's (1947) study of stomach activity suggest that at least two emotions, anger and fear, may be associated with distinct patterns of visceral arousal (criticism 2). Although research has generally supported Cannon's third argument, studies of body perception suggest that *some* individuals may be hyperaware of internal sensations. Cannon's fourth argument (slow SNS response time) has been consistently supported by empirical evidence. However, there are clearly a number of empirical findings that appear to contradict his fifth argument (failure to artificially induce emotions). For example, the physiological symptoms of lactate-induced panic attacks are indistinguishable from spontaneous panic attacks.

The weak empirical support of Cannon's arguments has led a number of theorists to call for reexamination of the validity of James's original model (Goldstein, 1968; Fehr & Stern, 1970). However, it should be emphasized that the bulk of the empirical evidence supports Cannon's (and James's) position that visceral feedback *per se* may play a minor role in *most* emotions. Whether distinct physiological patterns occur during a few "coarser" emotions, as James predicted, is clearly an open question.

Some emotions appear to be closely linked with distinct physiological patterns, whereas other emotions are not. For example, as discussed in Chapter 2, spinal patients often report a decrease in anger and fear after their injuries but little change in their experiences of anxiety and depression. Such findings would appear to support James's original hypothesis. However, other empirical findings appear to flatly contradict James's theory. As discussed in Chapter 9, sexual arousal occurs (a) during masturbation, yet both sexes report experiencing a variety of positive and negative emotions; (b) in some rape victims of both sexes during the assault but the victims report experiencing a wide spectrum of negative emotional states (disgust, fear, humiliation, etc.); and (c) in females with sexual dysfunctions who report a variety of negative emotional reactions and deny sexual arousal. According to James's model, sexual arousal should *always* produce a psychological state of sexual excitement. Clearly, it does not.

Empirical support for other aspects of James's model has also been mixed. As discussed previously in Chapters 4 and 10, research has only partially supported Darwin's and James's position that emotional expression has an anticathartic effect on emotional states.

13.2. JOHN WATSON

At the beginning of the twentieth century, the introspectionist (self-report) movement dominated both American and European psychology. The basic tenet of the introspectionist movement was that psychology should strive to become the science of the *conscious mind*. However, there was little agreement among introspectionists on how consciousness should be studied. Wundt and Titchener argued that researchers should investigate the structure of consciousness, whereas more Darwinian-oriented psychologists such as John Dewey argued that researchers should study the function of consciousness.

The behaviorist movement was originally a reaction against the introspectionists' "obsession" with consciousness. The early behaviorists (Dunlap, Jennings, Loeb, and McDougall) felt that the study of consciousness was unscientific and that, in order for psychology to become a true natural science, it would have to mimic the physical sciences and focus only on observable events, that is, overt and covert behaviors. Hence the label *behaviorists*.

Watson studied with the famous German biologist, Jacques Loeb, who advocated a strict materialist view of animal behavior. Watson argued that the behaviorist position could also account for human thoughts and actions. In 1919, Watson proposed a materialist theory of human emotion that was derived from two major sources: Darwin's theory of emotional behaviors and Pavlov's theory of conditioned reflexes. Based on his own observational studies of human infants (Watson & Morgan, 1917), Watson argued that only fear, love/lust, and rage were inherited and that all other emotions were learned. Thus he adopted two of the major principles of Darwin's theory. One important distinction between Darwin's and Watson's models is that Darwin used the term *emotional expression* to denote that emotional behaviors may reflect human and other animals' emotional states. Watson argued that emotional behaviors *were* the emotions and divided human emotional responses into three distinct components: autonomic responses (visceral habits), movements (manual habits), and verbalizations (laryngeal habits).

Watson also modified Pavlov's model of conditioned reflexes (see Figure 13-2) by proposing that manual, visceral, and verbal responses were being *simultaneously* conditioned. Specifically, a given unconditioned stimulus does not elicit a simple physiological response (e.g., increase in heart rate) but rather elicits a complex pattern of manual, visceral, and verbal responses. Thus, rather than viewing classical conditioning as involving a single physiological response, Watson argued that the entire organism (physiological pattern) is being conditioned. For example, a severe electric shock (US) elicits a complex pattern of striate muscle, smooth muscle, cardiac muscle, and glandular responses that can be collectively labeled *fear* and/or *pain*. If the electric shock is paired repeatedly with a (presumably) neutral stimulus such as a smiling face, the individual will later involuntarily display a complex physiological response to the mere sight of a smiling face. Although Watson used the singular *conditioned emotional response* (CER) to label such acquired responses, it should be emphasized that he intended to denote the *pattern* of physiological responses rather than any single physiological reaction.

Watson hypothesized that acquisition of CERs began shortly after birth. (Note: many later behaviorists argue that conditioning can occur *prior* to birth; see Spelt, 1948). He argued that only three emotions (fear, love/lust, and rage) were unconditioned responses that could be elicited by unconditional stimuli. For example, a newborn may show an unlearned fear reaction to any loud noise. If a neutral stimulus such as darkness was paired with a loud noise (thunder), the infant would be conditioned to fear darkness. Watson argued that because young infants lack language habits, these early CERs are composed of only autonomic and motor components and prelanguage vocalizations, that is, screams. Even though the preschool child gradually learns language between the ages of 6 months and 6 years, the majority of these early words refer only to external objects or events and not to physiological sensations. Thus the CERs acquired by preschool children may have only primitive verbal components and thus may be perceived as "gut" reactions later in life.

Through experience, the preschooler gradually acquires an *idiosyncratic* set of CERs that increase in complexity as more and more motor, visceral, and verbal components are added to each CER. For example, a 6-month-old screams when frightened, whereas a 3-year-old throws his or her hands over the eyes

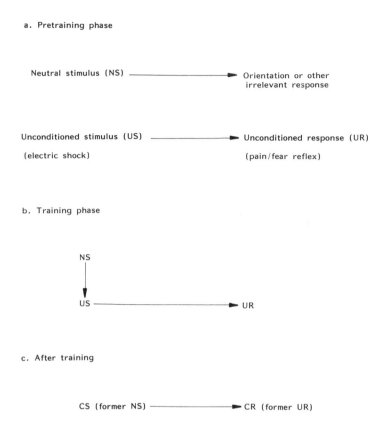

Figure 13-2. Pavlov's theory of conditioned reflexes (classical conditioning). Learning is assumed to occur in three distinct phases. During pretraining and training, the UR is elicited by only the US. Eventually, by pairing the NS and US, the NS becomes capable of eliciting the UR. To indicate that the NS is no longer neutral, it is labeled a *conditioned stimulus* (CS), and to indicate the UR is now responding to a learned stimulus, it is labeled a *conditioned response* (CR).

and shouts, "Mommy, I'm scared!" Depending on the given individual's experiences during childhood, specific CERs may extinguish (become unlearned) or generalize (transfer) to new objects and events. Moreover, because presentation of a given US may disrupt a different ongoing physiological pattern, each child would gradually develop an *idiosyncratic* set of CERs derived from the physiological patterns of fear, love, or rage and ongoing manual and verbal behaviors. Thus, an older child would not only display more complex patterns than a younger child, the older child would display more types of CERs (emotions). Watson also argued that emotional conditioning did not end during childhood but continued throughout the life span. Thus adults acquire "new" emotions, and distinct CERs may be elicited by a variety of abstract symbols such as political slogans. Watson argued that adults' CERs were no more "magical" than children's. Both were presumably acquired through conditioning, and both could be extinguished through learning.

Although Watson's model appears relatively straightforward, it should be emphasized that it is difficult to discriminate between biological development of the nervous system (maturation), conditioning, and cognitive development. Thus findings that appear to support Watson's model also simultaneously support a number of alternative models of emotion such as Freud's psychoanalytic theory (Chapter 14) or Izard's differential emotions theory (Chapter 16). For example, Jones and Jones (1928) tested 51 children's and 90 adult's emotional reactions to a (harmless) 6-foot-long snake. None of the children under age 2 showed the slightest fear of the snake. Distinct fear reactions were observed in the 4-year-old and older children, and the strongest fear reactions were displayed by adults. The authors noted that there are at least three rival interpretations for their findings of age-related changes in the fear of snakes:

> (a) as the result of conditioning, (b) as the result of the ripening of an innate fear of snakes, (c) as the result of a general maturation of behavior, which leads to greater sensitiveness and more discriminatory responses." (p. 142)

Jones and Jones also observed marked individual differences in emotional reactions. Some children and adults absolutely refused to touch the snake. Other children complied with the request with obvious reluctance, whereas some adults who complied showed marked signs of emotional distress such as overt sweating. Although Watson interpreted such individual differences in emotional reactions as due to differences in conditioning history, it is equally plausible to interpret individual differences as evidence for genetic variability in emotional reactivity (see Chapter 16).

Assessment of the validity of Watson's model requires the examination of three related empirical issues: emotional development, the acquisition of specific emotional responses, and the extinction of specific emotional responses.

13.2.1. Emotional Development

Studies of emotional development during infancy have consistently failed to support Watson's view that fear, love, and rage represent the three primary human emotions. Although facial expressions of at least three other emotions (disgust, interest-excitement, and joy) may be present at birth, anger is usually not observed until the infant is at least 2 months old, and distinct fear responses usually are not displayed until 7 months of age (Izard, Huebner, Risser, McGinnes, & Dougherty, 1980; Izard & Malatesta, 1987). Moreover, as we will discuss in Chapter 16, infants do not display distinct attachment behaviors (love/lust?) until 5 or 6 months of age.

Paradoxically, Watson's prediction that emotions gradually differentiate during infancy and childhood has been empirically supported. Longitudinal studies of the same infants have found that infants do gradually acquire both an increased number of emotional responses and more complex emotional responses (Bridges, 1932). Whether such developmental changes represent conditioning, cognitive development, maturation of the nervous system, or a combination of factors has been repeatedly debated. Accordingly, researchers have focused on the acquisition of specific emotional reactions. If Watson's model is valid, then we should be able to demonstrate classical conditioning of specific emotions.

13.2.2. Acquisition of Specific Emotional Reactions

Watson and Rayner (1920) attempted to teach a specific fear to a 11-month-old infant, Albert B. (The unethical nature of this experiment is so obvious, it is difficult to comprehend why Watson actually performed it.) Watson had originally tested Albert with a group of other children at a hospital and selected Albert because he displayed almost no emotional response to any of a series of novel stimuli (burning newspapers, a dog, a monkey, a rabbit, a rat, masks, etc.) but did show fear to loud noises (striking a steel bar with a hammer). Watson and Rayner presented little Albert with a rat and paired the sight of the rat with the loud noise. After a total of only six NS-US pairings, Albert displayed a marked fear of the rat (presented alone) that generalized to other animals (rabbit, dog) and other furry stimuli (a fur coat, a Santa Claus mask with beard). Watson and Rayner tested Albert 2 months later and found that he still displayed the same fears.

Watson and Rayner's study of Albert was (and is) impressive evidence that fears can be acquired through classical conditioning. However, Rachman (1978) has raised six serious objections to Watson's view that fears are classically conditioned in everyday life. First, children and adults often *fail* to acquire fears in life-threatening situations. Second, it is often difficult to classically condition specific fears in human subjects. Third, contrary to Watson's position that any stimulus can become a CS for fear, some stimuli such as lambs are relatively ineffective CSs, whereas other stimuli (snakes) are highly effective CSs. Fourth, the distribution of fears in the general population is nonrandom and is unrelated to the frequency of specific CSs and USs in everyday life. Fifth, phobic patients often cannot identify any specific traumatic event that triggered their fears. Sixth, children and adults may acquire fears through observational learning.

Rachman's criticisms also apply to Watson's explanation of the acquisition of other emotions. For example, infants often fail to form emotional attachments to caretakers who are repeatedly paired with meaningful USs (food, water, warmth, etc.). Yet infants may form strong emotional attachments to caretakers who physically abuse them. Moreover, infants often form emotional attachments to inanimate objects (blankets, stuffed animals, etc.). In strange situations, the presence of such objects may be as anxiety-reducing to the infant as the presence of his or her biological mother (Passman & Weisberg, 1975).

Some emotional reactions clearly can be acquired through classical conditioning. However, such CERs appear to be the exception rather than the norm. Thus cognitive development, observational learning, and/or social reinforcement appear to play a more important role than classical conditioning in acquiring specific emotional reactions.

13.2.3. Extinction (Unlearning) of Specific Emotional Reactions

The myth persists that Watson later cured "poor little Albert" of his fears. However, Albert was taken from the hospital before this new experiment could be performed, and his fate is unknown. The origin of this myth appears to be Watson's later report of the successful treatment of a *different* boy whose fears (rabbits, rats, fur coats, etc.) were virtually identical to Albert's experimentally induced fears (see Keller, 1973).

The first systematic study of using conditioning techniques to eliminate children's fears was reported by Watson's colleague, Mary Clover Jones (1924). Contrary to Watson's predictions, she found that therapeutic techniques that involved presenting either biological or social reinforcements in the presence of the CS were more effective in extinguishing fears than presenting the CS alone.

Later behaviorists argued that the major difficulty in extinguishing fear is that, once the CER is formed, the individual often *voluntarily* avoids the CS and that the avoidance response, itself, is rewarded by fear reduction. Thus, in order to countercondition fear, it may be necessary to first eliminate the avoidance response.

Wolpe (1954, 1958) proposed that the most effective way to eliminate fears was to condition an antagonistic physiological response, relaxation, *prior* to presenting the CS and then to gradually reverse the fear generalization gradient by first presenting a CS that only elicited mild fear reactions. For example, an individual who experiences terror at the sight of a dog may also experience mild distress at even a photograph of a dog. Conditioning the individual to relax to a photograph of a dog helps partially to reduce his or her fear of dogs (desensitization). Wolpe argued that by systematically presenting least feared to most feared stimuli, the individual could learn to overcome his or her avoidance of the feared object and eventually eliminate his or her fears.

Wolpe's *systematic desensitization* technique has proven remarkably successful in the treatment of a wide variety of phobias. For example, Bandura (1967) noted that the cure rate of systematic desensitization for speech phobias approaches 100%. Similarly, after reviewing the clinical literature, Smith and Glass (1977) concluded that, across studies, systematic desensitization averaged an 82% cure rate. They also noted, however, that although systematic desensitization may be the treatment of choice for phobias (approximately 100% cure rate), the therapy is much less effective with neurotic patients (mean cure rate 51%).

Numerous theorists have argued that the success of systematic desensitization depends upon the client's learning cognitive coping skills rather than counterconditioning *per se* (London, 1964; Marcia, Rubin, & Efran, 1969; Bandura, 1974). For example, Rardin (1969) reported a case of a student nurse who was terrified of blood (hemophobia). After completing only part of the systematic desensitization procedure, she discovered that she could cope with other people's injuries by reminding herself, "it's not me."

Behaviorists counter that *only* cognitions that are components of CERs are effective in either eliciting or suppressing emotional responses (Davison & Wilson, 1973). For example, depending upon an individual's prior experiences, the mental image of a lake may elicit boredom, fear, relaxation, or a variety of other reactions. Wolpe (1978) argued that cognitions are conditioned in the same manner as other behaviors.

> All three behavioral modalities—motor, autonomic and cognitive—partici-
> pate in parallel and in sequence. For example, if an attractive woman ac-
> quaintance enters the visual field of a man sitting in a cafe, his first response
> is to perceive her. Then, emotionally aroused, he begins to move toward her,
> while imagining ways of extending the association. It will be argued that
> every bit of this behavior, including the cognitive, has its form determined by
> its antecedents—in contrast to the traditional view that cognitive behavior
> has some degree of autonomy from the causal stream. (p. 440)

Research on extinguishing other emotional reactions (anger, disgust, jeal-ousy, inappropriate sexual excitement, etc.) only partially supports Watson's model. Some emotional reactions can be eliminated through classical condition-ing. However, such cases appear to be the exception rather than the rule. The overall pattern of findings suggests that CERs may account for the acquisition and extinction of only a small subset of emotional responses and thus Watson's model appears to have limited validity.

13.3. NEO-JAMESIAN MODELS

During the 1930s through the 1950s, behaviorist and psychoanalytic models dominated discussions of emotion. During the late 1950s, two concurrent but unrelated trends led to a renewed interest in James's model of emotion. First, the growing influence of the humanistic/existential psychology movement, which emphasizes subjective experience, helped relegitimize the scientific study of consciousness. Second, researchers discovered, or more correctly redis-covered, that specific physiological responses may represent species-specific emotional behaviors. Although a few of these responses involve the autonomic nervous system, the majority of species-specific emotional behaviors in humans involve the somatic (skeletal-muscular) nervous systems. These two trends spawned a series of new (neo) versions of James's model.

A wide variety of theorists, including Ekman (1984), Gellhorn (1964), Izard (1971), Leventhal (1979), and Tomkins (1962) have proposed that skeletal muscle reactions, particularly those of facial muscles, may play a key role in the con-scious experience of emotional states. However, all of these theorists have elabo-rated upon James's basic position and created their own distinct models of emotion. Indeed, classifying the neo-Jamesian models is quite difficult. Some of the theories, such as Tomkins's, are clearly materialistic. Other theories, such as Leventhal's and Izard's, are interactionistic, and some theories, such as Ek-man's, represent a bridge between the strict materialism and interactionism. For the purpose of brevity, we will discuss only two neo-Jamesian models in this chapter: Paul Ekman's and Silvan Tomkin's. We will discuss Leventhal's model in Chapter 15 and Izard's theory in Chapter 16.

13.4. PAUL EKMAN

As shown in Figure 13-3, Ekman's model differs from James's in regard to the role and temporal sequence of autonomic arousal. James postulated that the primitive perception of an emotional event simultaneously triggers both autonomic and somatic responses, which, in turn, produce the perception of an emotional state. Ekman (1984) proposed that the primitive perception of a prototypic emotional situation such as the death of a loved one triggers facial/postural responses, which then simultaneously trigger *both* the autonomic responses and the emotional state. Although the individual is genetically programed to react to specific stimuli as emotional, these innate responses may be modified through learning. The reciprocal relationship between ANS arousal and the perception of emotion merely helps to amplify and maintain ongoing emotional states. The individual's ongoing cognitions may lead to facilitation or inhibition of facial/postural responses due to culturally acquired *display rules* (Ekman & Friesen, 1969a). Ekman argued that each culture prescribes who can display what specific emotion to whom in which social contexts. Such cultural norms produce three distinct types of nonverbal deception responses: (a) attempts to suppress facial/postural responses, (b) referential expressions—attempts to substitute the facial-postural responses of a different emotion and (c) false expressions—displaying facial-postural responses when no emotional state is experienced.

Based on the available literature on nonverbal deception, Ekman concluded that these three types of voluntary motor movements vary in numerous ways from spontaneous emotional expressions and thus normally fail to reproduce the motor patterns associated with spontaneous emotional states. For example, across experiments, only about 10% of subjects can completely suppress both their facial and postural emotional expressions while viewing stressful films. Ekman conceded that in some situations or in some individuals, attempts to

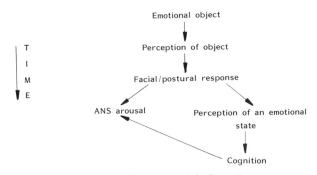

Figure 13-3. Ekman's model of emotion.

suppress facial/postural responses may increase autonomic arousal. However, he argues that the act of attempting to fake an emotion itself may elicit emotional reactions such as anxiety, embarrassment, or guilt.

Although Ekman rather freely used the term *cognition*, it should be emphasized that like James, Ekman argued that the pattern of autonomic and somatic arousal *is* the emotion.

> With three emotion-differentiated systems (e.g. ANS, cognitions and facial/postural expressions) the question is how do they interrelate? We believe that they must be interconnected. Our experiment suggests that changing one (face) changes another (ANS). I presume that usually these three systems operate consistently, and that interrelated variations in each are what produces the color and unique quality of each and every emotional experience.
>
> When are they discrepant? Are they ever discrepant outside the psychologist's laboratory? I suspect that we will have to work hard to make them discrepant. If they are discrepant, is cognition always the master in determining subjective experience? I suspect not. Whether cognition will override the autonomic nervous system patterning in determining a person's impressions as to which emotion is occurring will depend on the strength of the cognitive process, how fixed and strong expectations might be and the strength and nature of ANS activity. There may be individual differences as well.
>
> We are not throwing out, nor denying the importance of cognitive processes in the experience of an emotion. We are only suggesting that cognition is a part of an integrated, differentiated package. The autonomic nervous system activity may be more differentiated and play more of a role in emotional experience than some of the cognitive theorists have presumed. (Ekman, 1984, p. 327)

Because Tomkins's model of emotion has a number of common features with Ekman's model, we will defer discussion of the empirical validity of Ekman's model to avoid redundancy.

13.5. SILVA TOMKINS

Tomkins (1962, 1963) proposed that seven emotional expressions are innate responses that are elicited by the density (rate of neural activity over time) in the CNS (see Figure 13-4). Presumably, both positive and negative emotions are

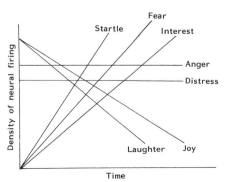

Figure 13-4. Tomkins's model of neural density eliciting specific innate emotions. From "Affect theory" by S. S. Tomkins, 1984. In K. R. Scherer and P. Ekman (Eds.), *Approaches to emotion.* Hillsdale NJ: Lawrence Earlbaum Associates. Copyright 1984 by Lawrence Earlbaum Associates. Reprinted by permission.

elicited by increasing neural density. A sudden steep increase in neural activity elicits a startle–surprise response. A more gradual increase in neural activity triggers a fear–terror response, and a slower increase in neural activity elicits excitement-interest. Prolonged high levels of neural density elicit only negative emotional responses (anger-rage and distress). Two positive emotional behaviors, joy and laughter, are elicited by sudden decreases in neural density. For example, your emotional reaction to a new joke is based on increase in neural density with information processing (interest) followed by a sudden decline in neural firing with the punch line (laughter).

Tomkins argued that two additional emotional expressions—contempt and disgust—are yoked to basic biological drives (hunger, thirst, and oxygen). He originally postulated that contempt and disgust were a unitary *auxiliary motivational* response, but his own research findings convinced him that these two emotions represented two separate responses (Tomkins, 1965). He argued that contempt and disgust are innate defensive reactions to noxious stimuli (smells, tastes) that through learning become associated with nonbiological stimuli. Tomkins postulated that shyness-shame-guilt represent an innate *auxiliary affect* that is elicited by and, in turn, inhibits excitement and enjoyment.

Tomkins proposed that emotional states are influenced by a complex series of feedback loops between facial/postural patterns and neural density. For example, the perception of an emotional stimulus evokes a chain of cognitions that may in turn alter (a) the density of neural firing and thus directly effect the emotional state, (b) ongoing motivational behaviors, and (c) ongoing facial/postural responses.

Tomkins argued that specific cognitive patterns during emotional states are the learned responses to parental postures and ideology during socialization. Presumably, parental styles tend to polarize toward two extremes, a humanistic style and a normative style. The humanistic style is characterized by the belief that positive emotional states are inherently good and therefore should be maximized. Accordingly, humanistic parents' postural and verbal reactions to a child's *positive emotions* tend to amplify the child's feelings. Humanistic parents also use positive emotional displays (hugging, smiling, etc.) to minimize their child's negative emotional states. In contrast, the normative parental style is characterized by the belief that negative emotions are the product of "disobeying the rules" and, therefore, the experience of negative emotions should be maximized rather than minimized. The normative parent tends to amplify the child's negative emotional states, for example, "I told you that you would get hurt, but would you listen?" Tomkins postulates that the child may internalize both the parents' postural responses and ideology. Later in life, children of humanistic parents may be predisposed to smile more frequently, respond with distress rather than anger, and respond with shame rather than contempt (see Tomkins, 1979).

In his most recent revision of his theory, Tomkins (1984) emphasized three major points. First, emotions amplify ongoing motivational patterns by adding hedonic tone. Thus, like the sensation of pain, emotions force the individual to attend to his or her ongoing behaviors. Second, Tomkins argued that voice, visual, and skin feedback may play a co-equal role with somatic muscle feedback in determining a specific emotional state. For example, hearing yourself scream increases your sense of terror, or feeling yourself blush increases your sense of embarrassment. Third, because emotional vocalizations tend to be contagious, all societies proscribe the inhibition of innate vocalizations and thus produce pseudo- or *backed-up* emotional expressions. Tomkins argues that these backed-up emotional displays ultimately produce stress, psychiatric disorders, and psychophysiological disorders.

Although many of the basic features of Ekman's and Tomkins's models are identical, there are also a number of notable differences between their theories. For example, Ekman proposed that humans may be genetically programmed to react emotionally to specific prototypical stimulations. Tomkins disagrees. Ekman classified startle as a reflex, whereas Tomkins classified startle as an emotion. Ekman argued that facial/postural responses evoke specific patterns of ANS activity. Tompkins believed that facial/postural responses may alter the perception of ongoing ANS activity as well.

Research on striate muscle activity during emotional states, discussed previously in Chapters 10 and 11, provides rather strong empirical support for both Ekman's and Tomkins's models. Specifically, (a) posing individuals in emotional faces evokes both specific moods and ANS arousal, (b) specific facial/postural responses are observed during both spontaneous and recalled emotions, and (c) specific facial/postural emotional responses are observed across cultures. Moreover, because Ekman's or Tomkins's theories agree that the emotion *is* the facial response, either model can account for the discrepant emotions commonly observed in the sex research.

One phenomenon that cast some doubt on the empirical validity of both Ekman's and Tomkins's models is emotional lability (EM), that is, involuntary emotional displays in patients with brain dysfunctions. For example, involuntary crying or laughing is commonly observed in amyotrophic lateral sclerosis, anoxia, multiple sclerosis, and stroke patients. Not only do EM patients deny experiencing the corresponding emotional states, but observational studies confirm that they are usually emotionally upset by their own uncontrollable emotional displays and often make concerted, if futile, attempts to inhibit these involuntary behaviors (Rinn, 1984).

Obviously, the occurrence of emotional displays *without* corresponding emotional states would appear to directly contradict both Ekman's and Tomkins's models. In defense of Ekman's model, it can be argued that EM patients recognize that their own involuntary behaviors violate *display rules*, and thus their inappropriate behaviors may act as stimuli for negative emotions such as shame. Similarly, in defense of Tomkins, it can be argued that emotional lability is both a cause and effect of abnormal patterns of neural density.

Another major criticism of Ekman's and Tomkins's models is that because a series of complex cognitive processes (perception, recognition, memory, etc.) *precede* facial expressions and other emotional behaviors, cognitions should be viewed as the cause of emotional states (Lazarus, 1982; Mandler, 1984). According to this position, presentation of an emotional stimulus such as a snake cannot trigger an emotional reaction until *after* the object has been correctly identified. Presumably, the visual image *snake* first elicits a primitive stage of feature analysis during which the brain attempts to identify the primary sensory characteristics of the stimulus (e.g., color, shape, size). The identification of stimulus features, in turn, allows the brain to search its memories for similar objects and to decide if the object is novel or familiar and, if familiar, whether the object is neutral or emotional. Only if the stimulus is identified as emotional is an appropriate emotion (fear, interest, etc.) elicited.

Although this sequence of events (stimulus > feature recognition > object recognition > emotion) might appear to be the *only* logical possibility, Zajonc (1980, 1984a,b, 1985) has raised a number of very serious objections to this theoretical position. He argued that at least some very primitive emotional reactions (good-bad, safe-dangerous, etc.) can and do occur prior to "higher" cognitive processes. For example, an unexpected loud noise in the dead of night may trigger fear *before* we are able to identify the cause of sound.

Zajonc (1980, 1984a,b) summarized a number of different types of empirical findings that are consistent with his view that emotional reactions may precede more sophisticated cognitions. Although preconscious or unconscious recognition of emotional stimuli might account for any or all of these findings (Lazarus, 1982), the overall pattern of findings suggests that very *minimal* cognitive processing may trigger at least some emotions. First, individuals often report primitive preference (like–dislike) reactions to stimuli that are presented too briefly to be consciously recognized. Second, cognitive and emotional reactions are only partially correlated, so that the same individual may have entirely different intellectual and "gut" reactions to a given object. Third, some types of new emotional reactions can be learned with minimal cognitive involvement. For example, taste preferences may develop at such a primitive level that individuals are often not consciously aware of *why* they like or dislike the taste of a new beverage or food. Fourth, emotional development appears to precede rather than follow cognitive development during infancy. Fifth, the limbic system and other brain structures that control emotions are evolutionarily older than many of the brain structures involved in "higher" cognitive processes.

Zajonc (1980) postulated that different types of emotions may be triggered by different patterns of cognitive processes. At the most primitive level, any sudden stimuli such as movement in the visual field, a noise, or an odor may trigger a simple approach/avoidance emotional response *before* either feature or object recognition occurs. Thus, much like a simple spinal reflex, the organism may respond prior to awareness of the specific meaning of the stimulus. Zajonc conceded that more complex emotional reactions such as embarrassment may require much more sophisticated levels of perceptual processing and thus, either feature recognition or object recognition may have to occur prior to some emotions. However, Zajonc (1984a) argued that if we define the occurrence of an emotion as a physiological reaction (autonomic and somatic responses), then the emotion can be conceptualized as independent of the cognitive processes of feature and object recognition.

Although Zajonc's position has been widely criticized by both cognitively oriented and Darwinian-oriented theorists, Ohman (1986) argued that Zajonc's hypothesis may actually complement either the cognitive or Darwinian position.

First, primitive reflexes elicited by crude sensory processes do not in any way imply that cognitive processing of the stimulus stops at the point in time that emotions are generated. Indeed, the experience of an emotion, itself, may elicit both cognitive appraisals and reappraisals of the stimuli. Second, the research on fear suggests that humans and other primates may be genetically programmed to easily acquire fears of either "reptilelike" or "facial" (social) stimuli. Such *biological preparedness* of fears may easily be traced to natural selection. For example, early mammals had to compete with dinosaurs and other reptiles. Given that rapid sensory detection of reptilian predators would give a species a distinct evolutionary advantage, it is not implausible to assume that contemporary mammals have inherited rather primitive sensory "reptile detectors."

A third major criticism of Ekman's and Tomkins's models is that neither theory adequately accounts for cross-cultural variations in emotional displays. Specifically, although both theorists postulated that social cues may elicit different facial patterns in different cultures, neither theorist has offered a plausible explanation of *why* such cultural variation should occur. For example, most cultures interpret being spat upon as an act of contempt. Yet, the African Masai tribe traditionally considered being spat upon a great compliment, particularly if the target was a member of the opposite sex (Thomson, 1887). Although both Ekman and Tomkins predict that any culture might evolve such a bizarre social signal, they are silent on how or why it might do so.

In summary, physiological models attempt to provide simple somatopsychic explanations of human emotions. Presumably, observable physiological events (autonomic responses, somatic responses, and/or brain wave activity) cause specific emotional states. Neo-Jamesian theorists argue that distinct patterns of physiological activities may represent specific emotional states. Conversely, behaviorists argue that emotions are characterized by idiosyncratic patterns of physiological arousal. Thus, neo-Jamesian and behaviorist models fundamentally disagree over the types of physiological patterns that may trigger emotional states.

SUGGESTED READINGS

Ekman, P. Expression and the nature of emotion. In K. R. Scherer & P. Ekman (Eds.), *Approaches to emotion.* Hillsdale, N.J.: Lawrence Erlbaum Associates, 1984.

A concise presentation of Ekman's model of human emotions.

Rachman, S. J. *Fear and courage.* San Francisco: Freeman, 1978.

A critical discussion of the behaviorists' explanation of acquisition and extinction of fears.

Tomkins, S. S. Affect Theory. In K. R. Scherer & P. Ekman (Eds.), *Approaches to emotion.* Hillsdale, N.J.: Lawrence Erlbaum Associates, 1984.

A concise description of Tomkins's current views on human emotions.

Wolpe, J. Cognition and causation in human behavior and its therapy. *American Psychologist,* 1978, *33(5),* 437–446.

A clear presentation of the contemporary behavioristic views of the role of cognitions in human behaviors.

Zonjac, R. B. Feeling and thinking: Preferences need no inferences. *American Psychologist*, 1980, *35(2)*, 151–175.

A stimulating discussion of whether emotional reactions can precede "higher" cognitive processes.

Mentalistic Models

According to mentalistic philosophy, physical existence is merely an illusion, and only mental phenomena exist. Although few Americans accept mentalism in its literal sense, philosophies such as existentialism and phenomenology that incorporate a watered-down "as-if" version of mentalism are popular among college-educated individuals. The basic tenet of as-if mentalism is that, although we may share a common physical environment and common anatomy and physiology, our subjective experiences of the given object or event are idiosyncratic and determined by our own psychological expectations, fantasies, and needs (see Fell, 1977).

As-if mentalistic models are currently quite common in emotional research. For example, as discussed in Chapter 4, visceral feedback plays only a minor role in Schachter and Singer's (1962) theory of emotion. As long as individuals *believe* that they are experiencing physiological arousal, they experience a psychological need to rationally explain *why* they feel aroused. Such cognitive models usually give lip service to the biological substrata of behavior, but the primary cause of emotional states and behaviors is presumably mental. Indeed, some theorists such as Ellis (1974) virtually ignore the fact that humans have bodies and discuss emotions in purely mentalistic terms. In this chapter, we focus on two major theorists: Sigmund Freud and Aaron Beck.

14.1. SIGMUND FREUD

During his lifetime, Freud wrote so copiously that Hogarth Press' *The Standard Edition of the Complete Works of Sigmund Freud* consists of 23 volumes. Freud constantly revised and expanded his theories and he frequently rejected many of his own earlier ideas. For example, Brenner (1955) noted that in his early writings, Freud used the term "ego defense" to denote emotional reactions to ideas or stimuli that were *consciously* perceived as morally offensive. Later, he used ego defense to denote *unconscious* psychological distortions intended to prevent emotionally laden thoughts from entering consciousness. Obviously, such semantic shifts make Freud's writings extremely easy to misinterpret. To further confuse matters, Freud felt no obligation to maintain a fixed metaphysical position and alternately proposed mentalistic, materialistic and interactionist models of the same phenomenon.

Although for the purpose of our discussion we will treat Freud's theories as "as if" mentalistic models, the reader should be aware that any discussion of his theories represents a gross oversimplification of his complex stream of ideas. It should also be emphasized that when discussing Freud the plural case, theories, is appropriate since he published a series of independent theories on the development of human emotions, morals, psychiatric disorders and sex-roles. These theories tend to fall into two major clusters: trauma theories and conflict theories. Since Freud's theories of emotion are integral components of his more global theories, we will briefly examine some of his major models.

14.1.1. Freud's Trauma Models

As discussed previously in Chapter 1, conversion disorders are characterized by physical symptoms such as blindness that have no identifiable physiological basis. Conversion disorders were first recognized by the ancient Greek physician, Hippocrates, who labeled them *hysterias* (disorders of the uterus). Although conversion disorders are relatively rare in the general population, this disorder played a major role in the development of Freud's theories.

During the eighteenth century, the Austrian physician, Friedrich Mesmer, discovered that some hysteric patients could be cured through hypnosis. Mesmer was subsequently rewarded for his discovery by being barred from practicing medicine in both Austria and France. Despite the European medical establishment's official disapproval, many physicians continued experimenting with hypnosis in the treatment of hysteric patients. By the mid-1800s, there were already numerous case reports of successful hypnotic cures of hysteria. These findings suggested that at least some forms of psychiatric disorders were psychogenic rather than biogenic in origin and triggered the (ongoing) debate over the metaphysics of "mental illnesses."

Shortly after Freud completed his medical training, he became an acquaintance of Josef Breuer, a prominent Austrian physician. During their discussions, Breuer confided in Freud that a few years earlier he had secretly cured a female hysteric patient, Anna O., by having her discuss her emotional problems while hypnotized. Although Breuer had already developed a rather sophisticated theory about why his *cathartic method* or "talking cure" worked, he had refused to publish either his findings or his ideas. Freud consulted extensively with Breuer on the treatment of at least two patients and eventually convinced a reluctant Breuer to collaborate on writing a book on hysteria.

In 1893, Breuer and Freud published the first preliminary report of their research, and in 1895, they finally published their now classic work, *Studies on Hysteria*. As Freud's daughter, Anna, noted in her foreword to the English translation of this work, identifying the relative contributions of Breuer and Freud is virtually impossible. Accordingly, we will refer to the Breuer–Freud model in our discussion.

The Breuer–Freud model is based on the assumption that hysterical symptoms are not "purposeless" but are meaningfully related to the individual's history of psychological traumas. For example, a patient with a history of epilepticlike convulsive symptoms was asked while hypnotized what she was conscious of during her attacks. She reported seeing a savage dog. Consultation with family members revealed that her symptoms first began after she had been chased by a large dog. Breuer and Freud proposed that the individual's emotional behaviors *at the time of the trauma* played a key role in the development of hysteric symptoms. If the individual appropriately acted out or even talked about his or her emotional states with others, the emotional release (catharsis) reduced the later psychological impact of the trauma. However, if the individual failed to express his or her trauma-related emotions, these emotions *and* concurrent behaviors become associated with the memory of the trauma.

Breuer and Freud argued that the formation of trauma-related memories is insufficient to trigger hysteric symptoms. They proposed that the occurrence of a variety of strong emotional states (anger, anxiety, disgust, fear, sexual excitement, etc.) coupled with the *inability* to express the specific emotion experienced was necessary for the formation of hysteric symptoms. Given that these individuals were incapable of coping with their emotions during the initial trauma, they are also incapable of coping with the emotionally laden memory of the trauma, and they attempt to block these unpleasant memories from consciousness.

Breuer and Freud fundamentally disagreed over *how* these traumatic memories were kept unconscious. Breuer favored what would now be called *state dependent learning*. Presumably, the trauma elicits an altered (hypnoid) state of consciousness, and memories formed at this time can only be retrieved if the original altered state is restored, as during hypnotic trances. Freud favored a selective forgetting (repression) model of blocking traumatic memories from conscious awareness. The Breuer–Freud model postulated that *either* mechanism could lead to the formation of hysterical symptoms and later produce incomplete recall. Anytime the traumatic memory is triggered, the individual would reexperience the sensorimotor components of the memory *without* consciously recalling the trauma, itself. Thus, the memory of the trauma has been *converted* into a pattern of somatic responses. (Note: the contemporary diagnostic term *conversion reaction* is derived directly from Breuer–Freud theory.)

Theoretical disagreements and personality differences caused Breuer and Freud to abandon their cooperative research. Freud began experimenting with having patients talk about their lives (free association) *without* inducing a hypnotic trance. He discovered that if patients were forced to talk about themselves long enough, they would eventually recall long-forgotten traumata. He labeled his method *psychoanalysis* and devoted the rest of his life to developing both the therapeutic techniques of his "new" therapy and the theoretical basis of psychoanalysis.

14.1.2. Freud's Conflict Models

Freud later incorporated many of the features of the Breuer–Freud model into a number of his conflict (dynamic) models of personality (Freud, 1911, 1920, 1923, 1926, 1939). Specifically, Freud postulated that due to conflicts between the individual's biological instincts and the social demands of his or her specific culture, emotional traumata were inevitable during childhood.

At birth, the individual's behaviors reflect genetically programmed motives. Freud originally proposed two innate classes of instincts—self-preservation and sex (libido). He later argued that aggression and a death wish (thanatos) are also genetically programed drives (see Thompson, 1950). Freud labeled these biological instincts collectively as the *id* and argued that the id supplies the basic psychological "energy" that drives the individual to interact with the environment.

The id is totally irrational and demands immediate gratification (primary-process thinking). Thus newborn infants make a continuous stream of irrational demands on the environment to immediately gratify their every whim. These irrational demands predestine infants to frustration. They soon discover that there are pleasant stimuli (e.g., food) that do not occur whenever wanted and negative stimuli (cold, hunger, etc.) that cannot be "wished" away. This growing sense of (a frustrating) reality gradually becomes a primitive consciousness or *ego* that is dimly aware that its body and the environment are separate entities. The ego presumably is rational and in contact with reality (secondary-process thinking).

The ego slowly evolves during the first few months of life solely to "serve" the id, that is, obtain real gratification for the id's demands. Because the ego is able to differentiate between reality and fantasy, the ego is potentially capable of channeling the id's demands into goal-directed behaviors. Freud, however, emphasized that the ego's ability to inhibit and redirect id impulses varies directly with the infant's cognitive development. As the infant's ego functions (emotions, motor control, memory, perception, and thought processes) develop so does the infant's ability to delay gratification and perform goal-directed behaviors. Thus, a 3-month-old infant can only scream in frustration when it is hungry, a 1-year-old can toddle to the kitchen and point to the refrigerator, and a 2-year-old can chant, "I hungry!" Prior to about 3 years of age, the individual is presumably amoral and totally controlled by the hedonistic demands of the id to seek pleasure and avoid pain.

Freud proposed that emotional development plays an integral role in early personality development. Specifically, the innate emotional reaction of frustration stimulates the formation of the ego and the subsequent development of early emotional attachments. As the infant begins to form mental representations of external objects or events, psychic energy is attached (cathected) to specific mental representations that are associated to drive reduction. These primitive cathexes are essentially conditioned stimuli in that the infant's early emotional attachment to its mother or other primary caretaker is derived from the infant's primitive recognition of its "food source." Obviously, to the young infant who is still incapable of inhibiting its id, the sudden disappearance of the food source represents a severe threat, and the infant's primitive ego is flooded with id impulses whenever its mother is absent. This flood of intense internal stimuli produces a state of *trauma anxiety*. Freud felt that a flood of intense external stimuli could also produce trauma anxiety and hypothesized that post-traumatic stress disorders in both children and adults could be traced to a trauma-related sensory overload of the ego.

As infants' cognitive abilities develop, they eventually begin to *anticipate* mother's absence and other potentially dangerous situations and react with anxiety *before* the traumatic event occurs. This anticipatory or *signal anxiety* serves two important psychological functions. First, signal anxiety stimulates ego development as the child attempts to actually remove or avoid the perceived danger. Thus, unlike a young infant who becomes distressed *after* mother leaves, the older infant may show anticipatory distress when its mother begins to put on a coat. The second important function of signal anxiety is that it triggers the formation of primitive defense mechanisms (anticathexes) to suppress id impulses before they flood into consciousness. For example, if its mother is unavailable, an older infant may *displace* his or her attachment behaviors to other caretakers or pets or inanimate objects such as a stuffed animal.

Freud felt that displacement played the useful function of allowing individuals to partially release their impulses when direct expression is blocked. For example, slamming a door when you feel angry may help reduce the intensity of anger, although it is clearly not as gratifying as striking the individual that elicited the emotion. He also postulated that creativity was a socially acceptable form of displacement. Presumably, the individual's repressed impulses are the source of the creative energy needed to compose a musical score, paint a picture, or write a book. Freud labeled such socially acceptable displacement as *sublimation*.

Freud argued that ego development does not occur in a vacuum but rather in the context of the everyday interactions between the infant and its primary caretaker. He postulated that personality development followed an orderly sequence of inevitable conflicts between the individual's instinctual demands and the cold realities of his or her social environment. During the first year after birth (oral stage), the infant's mouth is the primary locus of both pleasure and frustration. Initially, the infant passively derives pleasure from the environment by sucking and licking milk from the nipple of the breast or bottle.

Freud postulated that *either* over- *or* undergratification of these oral behaviors produced arrested development (fixation). For example, infants who are fed on demand are being simultaneously taught to be passively dependent and have poor reality testing. In the extreme case, the individual develops into an overtrusting and overdependent adult who expects the world to "mother" him or her. Conversely, infants who are undergratified (e.g., fed on a strict schedule) are being taught that the environment is insensitive to their basic needs and to crave oral stimulation in order to provide a sense of emotional security. Such deprivation-induced oral fixations are later unconsciously acted out as oral habits in adulthood. For example, the pleasure derived from socially acceptable forms of sucking such as cigarette smoking or drinking through a straw and from socially acceptable licking behaviors such as eating an ice cream cone may reflect a relative lack of oral stimulation during early infancy.

The development of teeth provides a new source of oral pleasure during the latter half of the oral stage. The infant can now aggressively explore the environment by biting and chewing. Again, over- or undergratification of these oral sadistic needs presumably results in fixation. In the case of extreme overgratification, the individual develops into a sadistic and exploitive adult. If these oral aggressive needs are undergratified, the individual may later display a variety of aggressive oral habits such gum chewing or biting fingernails or pens.

Between the ages of 1 and 3 years (anal stage), the infant is suddenly confronted with maternal demands to inhibit defecation and urination except in socially approved situations. From the infant's perspective, toilet training represents a no-win conflict. Infants can gain parental approval and avoid parental punishment only by denying the pleasurable instinctual urges to defecate when their rectums are full and to urinate when bladder pressure reaches threshold. Given that delaying defecation and urination is often painful, the mother, in essence, is asking her infant to "suffer to please Mommy." If they comply with the maternal request, they are being punished by both the loss of immediate gratification and the physical discomfort associated with retention. If they refuse to comply, they risk the loss of their primary cathexes.

Freud postulated that maternal toilet training methods have a direct effect on emotional development. The infant's nervous system develops in a head-to-tail (cephalocaudal) direction and is usually too immature to control rectal and urethral sphincter muscles until around 18 months after birth. Obviously, delaying toilet training until the child has physically matured reduces the difficulty of learning bowel and bladder control. Presumably, mothers who delay toilet training foster the development of pride as the child develops mastery over its own excretory functions. Mothers who attempt to toilet-train the child prematurely, however, inadvertently increase the child's feelings of anxiety and frustration.

If the mother physically punishes lack of control, the infant may rebel by deliberately defecating and urinating in inappropriate situations to intentionally displease the parent. Thus the parent may inadvertently encourage the development of anger and hostility. If the parent punishes toilet accidents with verbal threats of rejection, the child may express his or her anger indirectly through passive aggression by refusing to defecate on command. Presumably, either extreme of anal rebellion leads to compulsions, obsessions, and excessive stubbornness later in life. Similarly, overgratification may also have negative effects on the child. Mothers who lavish praise on the child's successful use of the toilet may inadvertently be training the child to associate love with material gifts. Specifically, children may confuse mothers' praise of control for her happiness at receiving a "gift" (feces).

Freud argued that maternal emotional reactions toward excrement, toilet accidents, and the genital region of the body also has a profound impact on the child's emotional development. Humans do not have any innate emotional reactions to excrement, and young infants often display obvious delight while playing with their own feces or urine. However, most adults strongly associate excrement and disgust. Even otherwise permissive parents may display strong negative emotional reactions if they discover their child using feces as modeling clay or urine as paint. Such incidents are extremely traumatic to the primitive ego of the child. To avoid repetition or recall of the trauma, the child usually employs the defense mechanism of *reaction formation*, that is, conscious recital of the opposite of the forbidden impulse. Thus, like the parents, the infant begins to label his or her own natural bioproducts (feces and urine) as "disgusting" or "dirty." Freud hypothesized that two additional emotional states, shame and shyness, could also be traced to parent–child interactions during toilet training. Presumably, shyness is a reaction to parental inspections for toilet accidents, whereas shame is derived from parental disapproval of toilet accidents.

Freud argued that the child's toilet-related emotional reactions reflect the formation of an extremely primitive *superego* (psychological representation of cultural norms). The superego includes cultural prescriptions (thou shalt), or the ego ideal, and cultural proscriptions (thou shalt not), or the conscience. However, Freud felt that the 2-year-old's superego was too weak to inhibit the id. Thus, like an adult psychopath, a 2-year-old may be aware of cultural norms, yet violate them anyway.

Between the ages of 3 to 6 years (phallic stage), children display a primitive interest in sexuality. Children are naturally curious about their own bodies and often discover that manual contact with their genitals produces greater pleasurable sensations than touching other parts of their bodies. The child also is curious about the anatomy of others and may engage in primitive heterosexual or homosexual contacts with other children. Freud argued that due to the anatomical differences between the sexes, boys and girls experience different psychosocial conflicts over sexuality and thus are biologically predestined to form different types of personalities.

The boy's emerging sexuality is initially directed at his primary cathexis, his own mother. Although his mother may tolerate her son's partially acting-out his incestual fantasies in displays of affection, his father may react with overt jealousy and hostility. The boy initially fantasizes about displacing his father but realizes that his father is much bigger and stronger than he is. The boy then develops an intense fear that his father will eliminate his competition by making him into a daughter (castration anxiety). Freud labeled the boy's collection of fears and fantasies the *Oedipus complex* after the Greek myth of Oedipus who accidently killed his father and married his mother.

The development of the Oedipus complex places the boy in an extremely traumatic situation. His primitive ego defenses are incapable of inhibiting his socially unacceptable inpulses. Yet he receives increasingly intense parental disapproval of his attempts to act-out either his incestual impulses toward his mother or his hostile impulses toward his father. Castration anxiety eventually increases to the point that the boy breaks his primary cathexes with his mother and attempts to win his father's approval by imitating him. Freud used the term *identification* rather than *imitation* to denote that the boy does not merely attempt to become "like" dad by copying his father's behaviors; he attempts to *become* dad by internalizing (introjecting) his father's superego. Thus the boy adopts his father's attitudes, beliefs, and values, not out of admiration for his father, but to reduce his own feelings of fear and hostility. Freud felt that both the trauma associated with the Oedipus complex and the increased strength of the superego produces extremely strong repression in males. Presumably, inadequate resolution of the Oedipus complex results in homosexuality or psychopathy later in life. Phallic fixations include the unconscious desire to find a mate that is "just like mom."

Freud postulated that girls experience a different sequence of conflicts during the phallic stage. Presumably, the girl discovers to her shock and disappointment that only males have penes and that she has been "castrated by nature." She experiences feelings of shame at her biological inferiority and contempt for both herself and all other females, including her mother. This *penis envy* leads to incestual attraction toward her father and fantasies of obtaining a penis substitute (baby). Although her mother may react with jealousy to affectional displays toward her father, her mother cannot elicit the intense anxiety that fathers presumably elicit in sons. Thus spared the trauma of castration anxiety, the girl may have little incentive to abandon her attachments to her father and at least consciously reidentify with her mother. Freud named this sequence of feminine personality development the *Electra complex* after the Greek myth of Electra who killed her father to prevent her mother from having him.

Freud (1925) hypothesized that the relative lack of trauma associated with the Electra complex makes females' phallic conflicts more prolonged and difficult to resolve than males'. Two deviant patterns of development are presumably common in females. First, the girl may be so overwhelmed by penis envy that she completely renounces her own sexuality by employing the defense mechanism of reaction formation to reduce her intense feelings of inferiority and self-hatred. Freud argued that such girls grow up to become mentally ill women. Second, the girl may refuse to consciously acknowledge her penis envy and fixate on clitorial masturbation. This "delusion" of equality with males presumably leads to lesbianism in adulthood.

Freud postulated that "normal" female superego development eventually occurs when the girl realizes that her wish to obtain a baby can *only* be fulfilled if she makes herself attractive to males by adopting culturally prescribed norms of femininity. She begrudgingly reidentifies with her mother. This delayed reidentification process presumably produces poor superego development and only partial resolution of her Electra complex. Thus later in life she may consciously wish for a mate that is just like "dear old dad."

Once the mature superego is formed, the male or female child has internalized parental norms and thus can no longer avoid "parental" supervision. Children praise themselves with feelings of pride when their behavior matches their ego ideal and punish themselves with feelings of guilt when they violate the rules of their conscience. The child's ego is now permanently trapped between the irrational demands of the ego ideal (perfection), the conscience (absolute norm obedience), and the id (hedonism). Freud labeled the stress associated with such conflicts *moral anxiety*.

Freud postulated that the ego defense mechanisms (self-deceptions) normally help reduce such everyday conflicts. For example, the individual may *rationalize* or *deny* his or her impulses. The ego defense mechanism of *repression* also helps reduce current psychological stress by blocking memories of past emotional conflicts, socially unacceptable impulses, and traumata from consciousness. These emotionally laden thoughts are neither destroyed nor dormant but rather form unconscious impulses that seek expression in the disguised form of everyday "mistakes" such as slips of the tongue or "accidental" motor movements (Freud, 1904), humor (Freud, 1900), and dreams (1900–1901).

Freud argued that the first 6 years after birth are a critical period for personality development during which the child forms basic personality traits that are almost impossible to modify later in life. Accordingly, the remaining two stages in Freud's model of personality development are rather anticlimatic. During the latency period (age 6 to puberty), Oedipus/Electra conflict-induced repression temporarily frees the child's ego from psychological conflict. This "lull before the storm" serves the important function of allowing the child's ego to develop adequate skills to cope with the inevitable conflicts of puberty and adulthood. At puberty (genital stage), hormonal-induced sexual maturation reactivates the individual's dormant sexual impulses, and the adolescent now must cope with renewed id–superego conflicts.

Freud argued that if the individual's personality had been deformed during socialization, his or her unconscious impulses will emerge as deviant behaviors and psychiatric symptoms. For example, psychopathy is presumably caused by the failure of normal superego development. In the case of psychotic- or neurotic-prone individuals, their unconscious impulses are so emotionally charged that they continually threaten to flood into consciousness. This constant threat to the ego produces the emotional state of "free-floating anxiety" where the individual consciously feels anxious but cannot identify a rational source for anxiety. Free-floating anxiety, in turn, may trigger *neurotic anxiety*, for example, fear of losing one's sanity. The ego defenses of psychotic-prone individuals are so weak that eventually their psychological defenses are overwhelmed and their egos disintegrate.

Neurotic-prone individuals attempt to cope with anxiety by developing exaggerated defense mechanisms. Neurosis usually gradually develops as the individual invests more and more energy into "coping with coping" and less and less energy in resolving his or her conflicts. Although the symptoms of various neuroses differ, Freud argued that all neuroses represent the same *process*, that is, desperate attempts to avoid consciously dealing with unconscious impulses. For example, a male who has a strong unconscious fear of women perceives himself as a "macho man" through reaction formation. Dating females, however, would elicit his unconscious impulses. Hysteric symptoms, such as a facial tic, allow him to consciously deny dating anxiety while simultaneously scaring off prospective partners. Similarly, obsessions (repeating the same thoughts), compulsions (repeating ritualistic actions), phobias (exaggerated fears), and other neurotic symptoms may serve the same function.

Freud's theories have had an immense heuristic value in the study of abnormal psychology, child development, motivation, and personality. His prolific writing popularized his psychoanalytic method and attracted numerous followers. Moreover, Freud's theories stimulated numerous other theorists who disagreed with specific aspects of his models to propose their own theories. For example, Freud's blatant sexism stimulated three generations of feminist theorists to propose alternative explanations for female personality development. Theorists such as Clara Thompson (1942) argued that rather than being biologically determined, *penis envy* may be an artifact of the advantages given male offspring in many cultures. A little girl who has never seen a penis may deeply resent being told that her brother can climb trees, play in mud, and so on and that she cannot. Thus "penis envy" may represent culturally induced *privilege envy*.

Assessing the empirical validity of Freud's theories has proven to be an extremely difficult task. First, Freud's own writings contain numerous logical contradictions that were produced by his evolutionary style of theory construction. To state "Freud hypothesized X" is absolutely meaningless outside of the historical context of the specific prediction. For example, in his earliest theories, Freud hypothesized that anxiety was caused by hormonal imbalances produced by excessive sexual activity. He later postulated that undischarged instincts were transformed into anxiety. Still later, he hypothesized that anxiety was caused by either stimulus overloads or anticipation of danger to the ego. Given that Freud frequently abandoned or reformulated his own hypotheses, it serves little purpose to assess the empirical validity of predictions that Freud himself later refuted. Thus to legitimately test Freud's theories, researchers must wade through Freud's massive works to find his "last" prediction on any given topic.

Second, many of Freud's concepts, such as symbolic expression of unconscious conflicts in dreams, are simply untestable. For example, Freud (1917) interpreted a young woman's dream about striking her head on a low-hanging chandelier as menstruation anxiety. Obviously, it is no more possible to prove that Freud's interpretation was correct or incorrect than it is to prove or disprove alternative explanations such as the patient had a repressed fear of walking into low-hanging chandeliers.

Third, although Freud repeatedly used quantitative dimensions such as strong/weak, he failed to specify how to quantitatively measure his concepts (Hall & Lindzey, 1970). For example, an individual's psychological adjustment or maladjustment is presumably determined by the relative strength of his or her id, ego, and superego. Yet, *how* should we measure strength? The frequency of id impulses? The intensity of id impulses?

Despite the problems inherent in testing Freud's theories, there have been numerous efforts to evaluate the empirical validity of his predictions (Fisher & Greenberg, 1977; Masling, 1983). For example, in a series of studies of maternal child-rearing practices, Sears and his associates found at least some empirical support for Freud's prediction that early childhood experiences during weaning, toilet training, and learning to inhibit overt sexual behaviors did relate to the child's emotional development (Davis, Sears, Miller, & Brodbeck, 1948; Sears & Wise, 1950; Sears, Maccoby, & Levin, 1957; Sears, Rau, & Alpert, 1965). However, they also found that the mother's personality, rather than child-rearing practices *per se*, appears to be the primary causal variable. For example, mothers who were rigid, emotionally cold to their children, and had high levels of sexual anxieties tended to punish the children severely for *any* behavioral infraction and thus might form (or deform) their children's personality in their own image. Sears's findings have been independently replicated by other researchers in our own culture (Beloff, 1957; Hetherington & Brackbill, 1963; Pollack, 1979) and in cross-cultural studies (Whiting & Child, 1953; Whiting, 1963; Levine, 1974). Similarly, as we will discuss in Chapter 16, research on parental absence is also only partially consistent with Freud's predictions that maternal or parental absence has a devastating effect on children under the age of 5. Thus, although the general outline of Freud's theories may have some degree of validity, many of the specific details appear to be incorrect.

Developmental psychologists argue that one of the greatest weaknesses in Freud's theories is that he treated the "family" as a dyadic (mother–child) or triadic (mother–father–child) unit and only vaguely referred to the potential impact of other relatives (grandparents, siblings, etc.), other adults (nannies, teachers, etc.), and peers on the child's psychological development. Research on the role of family structure on emotional development strongly suggests that variables such as birth order, number, spacing, and sex of siblings may exert a direct influence on the emotional development of a given child. For example, Sewall (1930) found that siblings who differed between 18 and 42 months in age were most likely to be jealous of each other and that sibling jealousy tended to decrease as family size increased.

Parent–child interactions also vary with the child's birth order. Parents tend to treat their firstborn as a "test case." They tend to have higher expectations and use more physical punishment with firstborn than later born children (Lasko, 1954). Not surprisingly, firstborns tend to be more anxious in stressful situations (Schachter, 1959), more likely to report fear of failure and guilt, and more likely to enter psychotherapy than later born siblings (Rosenoer & Whyte, 1931; Phillips, 1956). Conversely, later born children are more likely to engage in dangerous activities (Nisbett, 1968) and to display higher levels of aggression than firstborns (Feshbach, 1970). This relative lack of anxiety and increased aggressiveness in later born children may account for why they are more successful fighter pilots in combat situations than firstborns (Torrence, 1954).

Studies of the psychophysiology of emotion also provide only partial support for Freud's theories. Freud argued that emotions were normally conscious experiences but noted that the individual's defense mechanisms can block conscious awareness of emotional reactions. Consistent with this prediction, studies of alexithymics and repressors suggest that at least some individuals display physiological reactions to emotional stimuli but misperceive their arousal as physical illness. Moreover, experiments with normal subjects suggest that at least in some situations, adopting specific ego defense may reduce the psychological stress but increase physiological arousal. Empirical support for Freud's catharsis hypothesis, however, is equivocal. Some studies find that expressing your emotional states decreases the intensity of emotional states, whereas other studies have found the exact opposite pattern results.

Laboratory studies of human perception appear to provide some interesting support for Freud's concept of unconscious processes. Cantril (1957), for example, reported an interesting demonstration of inducing hysterical blindness in one eye. Because of the spacial separation between your eyes, each eye normally receives a slightly different image of the external environment. Your brain normally fuses both images and uses the slight disparity between the two retinal images to create the illusion of three-dimensional space (stereopsis). Both the nineteenth-century stereoscope and the modern children's toy, the stereo viewer, use this principle to trick the visual system into seeing 3-D by presenting slightly different views of the same scene to each eye. Cantril asked the obvious question of what would happen if each eye was presented with a completely *different* image? He employed a stereoscope to present an emotional picture (female nude) to one eye and a neutral picture (Madonna with child) to the other eye. Surprisingly, rather than perceiving a fused version of both pictures, observers initially suppressed one visual image completely. Thus some subjects saw only the Madonna (perceptual defense), whereas other observers saw only the nude (perceptual vigilance). Note that in order for subjects to "see" only one picture, they literally had to temporally "go blind" in the other eye. If the observer stares at the pictures for 30 seconds or more, the supressed image may at least partially emerge into consciousness. For example, observers who initially see the Madonna often report that she starts to "strip." Conversely, observers who initially see the nude often report that she starts to "dress."

Paradoxically, the strongest empirical support for Freud's mentalistic models can be derived from the literature on psychobiology. First, studies of motivational changes during stress suggest that humans and other species may involuntarily increase their motivational behaviors (eating, drinking, sexual behaviors) in response to mild stress but decrease their motivational behaviors in response to moderate or severe stress. Clearly, these findings are consistent with Freud's hedonistic view of humans. Second, the automaton behaviors of emotional lability patients are clearly consistent with Freud's view that emotional behaviors can be controlled independently of conscious thought. Third, studies of split-brain patients suggest that humans can perceive and react appropriately to emotional stimuli without conscious awareness that a stimulus was even presented.

14.2. AARON BECK

As a psychiatrist trained in the Freudian psychoanalytic tradition, Beck frequently employed free association with his patients. He began noting that clients often displayed multiple emotions while discussing their personal problems. For example, patients often report a rapid sequence of emotional states such as feeling anger, then guilt, then sadness. Such sequences of emotions are commonly interpreted as simple cause–effect relationships between emotions. One of Beck's patients, however, spontaneously reported that only some of his feelings were related to his free associations and his other emotions were triggered by an unverbalized stream of self-critical thoughts.

Beck began questioning his other patients, and most reported a similar phenomenon of a parallel stream of self-critical thoughts about what they were saying, how they expected the therapist to react, and emotionally laden visual images. The patients reported that these normally unverbalized co-conscious thoughts had four common characteristics: (a) they were extremely rapid and fleeting; (b) they emerged into consciousness without (and often inspite of) volition: (c) they were often "telegraphic" in sentence style (i.e., "Run! Danger!"); and (d) they could become extremely clear to the person *if* the individual focused his or her attention on them. Because this "other" stream of consciousness occurred involuntarily, Beck labeled these ideas *automatic thoughts.*

Beck then began asking his clients to report *any* ideas or images that immediately preceded their emotional states. Surprisingly, most patients reported two different concurrent sets of thoughts. One set of thoughts sounded suspiciously like rationalization based on their previous verbalizations. For example, a female client who reported embarrassment while discussing her sex life might report, "I was thinking about how much difficulty I have discussing birth control with a partner." The other set of thoughts fell into the automatic category such as "I had this fleeting image that we both sitting here nude" or "I sound like a whore." The relative salience of such automatic thoughts varied with the severity of the individual's psychiatric disorder. Extremely disturbed patients frequently mixed their automatic thoughts into their everyday conversations. Thus it would appear that their automatic thoughts had gained primacy over their everyday thought patterns. As the patients' psychological functioning improved, their automatic thoughts became less and less salient and began to resemble vague fleeting ideas and images. Regardless of their clarity, their automatic thoughts were accepted as "plausible" by the patients.

Based on his clinical findings, Beck (1967, 1970,a,b, 1976) gradually evolved a general theory of emotion based on the assumption that both normal and abnormal emotional reactions were caused by conscious thought processes. In the case of normal emotional reactions, the individual correctly perceives a specific event as emotionally meaningful stimuli, and this perception, followed by highly rational thought processes, elicits a pattern of both physiological arousal and the cognitive appraisal of an emotional state. Thus both the physiological arousal and self-perception of an emotion are *caused* by the individual's preceding cognitions. For example, suppose you are a spectator at a basketball game. Whether or not you experience an emotional state in response to the game depends directly on whether or not the outcome is psychologically meaningful to you. Obviously, if you "don't care" who wins, the situation is, by definition, nonemotional. Suppose you really "want" one team to win. Perception that your team lost produces negative emotional reactions, whereas perception that your team won elicits positive emotional states.

In the case of abnormal emotional reactions, the individual either misperceives the event *or* subsequently distorts the meaning of the event. For example, if your team is losing, you may perceive the referees as biased in favor of the other team. Such misperceptions then may trigger an extremely logical sequence of anger-eliciting ideas. Similarly, you may correctly perceive the situation and yet cognitively distort the meaning of the event (e.g., "these bums couldn't beat a team of geriatric patients"). Such cognitive distortions may also elicit a logical sequence of depression-eliciting ideas such as "how stupid of me to root for a bunch of losers."

Beck hypothesized that the specific meaning of an automatic idea may directly determine which emotional state is produced. For example, thoughts about a significant real or imaginary loss to the individual tend to elicit sadness. Conversely, thoughts about a significant personal gain tend to elicit euphoria. Anxiety is elicited by thoughts about significant personal danger, whereas anger is elicited by thoughts of being a direct target of an assault (physical or verbal aggression) or an indirect target of assault (norm violations by others that violate the observer's beliefs and values). Thus, in the same situation, four different individuals may experience four different emotional reactions.

Beck postulated that both normal and psychiatric populations engage in similar types of cognitive distortions. The key distinctions between "us and them" are merely the relative frequency in which such distortions occur, the relative amount of distortion that occurs, and whether the cognitive distortions occur during self-evaluation. For example, Beck, Rush, Shaw, and Emery (1979) found that the following six different types of cognitive distortions occur commonly in the thought patterns of *both* normal individuals and depressed psychiatric patients: (a) *arbitrary inference*—conclusions based on no evidence or even in the presence of contradictory evidence; (b) *selective abstraction*—focusing only on specific details and ignoring the context; (c) *overgeneralization*—deriving a general conclusion from a single incident; (d) *magnification-minimization*—over- or underevaluating the significance of events; (e) *personalization*— relating external events to oneself in the absence of any objective connection; and (f) *absolutistic, dichotomous thinking*—classifying experiences into only extreme categories such as "good" or "evil."

Presumably, normal individuals' logical errors are rather randomly distributed throughout their everyday thoughts and, therefore, even normal individuals may episodically experience a variety of abnormal emotional states. Such irrational reactions are usually misattributed to environmental causes (e.g., "I'm angry because I'm caught in rush hour traffic") rather than attributed to our own faulty logic. If the event has specific personal significance to the individual, he or she may overreact in a fashion similar to psychiatric patients. For example, if being caught in a traffic jam means that you are going to miss your flight at the airport, you may become enraged at the other drivers or depressed over missing your flight. Beck argues that such irrational reactions are not unconscious in origin but rather inevitable products of our own conscious cognitive distortions.

Given the observed similarities between psychiatric patients and normal individuals, why do some individuals develop psychiatric disorders? In a series of studies, Beck (1961, 1963, 1970; Loeb, Beck, & Diggory, 1971) found that patients with the same psychiatric diagnosis tended to share similar types of *idiosyncratic* habitual thought patterns. Beck argued that these idiosyncratic thought patterns function as personal emotional land mines that trigger specific types of automatic thoughts that, in turn, trigger specific "abnormal" emotional states. For example, Beck *et al.*, (1979) cited the example of a female patient who became severely depressed after she was divorced. Both her depression and automatic thoughts could be traced back to a very specific irrational belief that "If I'm nice, bad things won't happen to me." This belief was associated with two other contradictory beliefs—"it's my fault when bad things happen" and "life is unfair." Her automatic thoughts were logical (but invalid) conclusions derived from her own faulty belief system. If bad things happened and she perceived herself as not nice, she concluded that she was "responsible" and therefore experienced depression. If bad things happened and she perceived herself as nice, she then concluded that she was the victim of a cosmic injustice and experienced irrational anger.

Although Beck (1976) hypothesized that emotional disorders were caused by the patients' cognitive distortions, he made two interesting exceptions, psychophysiological disorders and somatoform disorders. He proposed that psychophysiological symptoms could be traced to the *interaction* of cognitive distortions and genetically determined patterns of physiological activity. For example, an individual who primarily showed cardiovascular reactions to stress would display heart rate and BP increases in a wide variety of stressful situations. Although the individual's cognitions determine whether a given event is psychologically stressful or nonstressful, stress-induced physiological arousal, itself, may become a source of psychological stress. The individual may misinterpret his or her own cardiovascular arousal as symptoms of a heart attack or stroke, triggering additional psychological stress. This vicious cycle of cognitive distortion > emotion > physiological arousal > cognitive distortion > emotion eventually leads to physical disease. Beck extended his interactionist submodel to include somatoform disorders and argued that somatoform disorders were produced by misperceptions of physiological activity (somatic imaging). Curiously, Beck was unwilling to attribute more than a minor role to physiological arousal in other emotional disorders and insisted that the individual's cognitions were the cause of both his or her normal and abnormal emotional reactions.

Beck gradually evolved a series of therapeutic techniques collectively called *cognitive therapy* to help patients to detect and correct their own cognitive distortions. Although discussion of the specific techniques employed in cognitive therapy is beyond the scope of this book, it is important that the reader be aware that one of the key components in cognitive therapy is convincing the patient that only *some* of his or her emotional experiences are legitimate and the remainder of his or her emotional states are caused by his or her own distorted thinking. For example, with anxious patients, the therapist initially tries to convince the patient that some of his or her anxieties are actually realistic reactions to potential harm that can be objectively verified. The therapist may point out to a client who is involved in a custody dispute that his or her fear of losing his or her children is quite rational because the threat is real. The therapist then contrasts these "normal" anxieties with the patient's abnormal anxieties and challenges the patient to justify them, for example, "What evidence do you have that you can contract AIDS by brushing your teeth?" Thus the therapist attempts to teach the patient to discriminate between his or her realistic and unrealistic emotional reactions.

Reviews of the clinical literature suggest that cognitive therapy may be an effective treatment for at least a subset of emotional disorders (Beck, 1976; Beck & Shaw, 1977; Shaw & Beck, 1977; Beck *et al.*, 1979). For example, Rush and his associates found that cognitive therapy was more effective in treating unipolar depressives than antidepressant medication (Rush, Beck, Kovacs, & Hollon, 1977). A 1-year follow-up of these patients revealed that patients who had received cognitive therapy still reported lower depression than clients who had completed drug therapy (Kovacs, Rush, Beck, & Hollon, 1981). In a more recent review, Wright and Beck (1983) found that cognitive therapy was at least as effective and an often more effective treatment for depression than antidepressant medications in all studies that compared the efficacy of the two treatments.

The results of laboratory studies of human reasoning also provide strong empirical support for Beck's position that cognitive distortions are commonly found in normal adults (Bem, 1970). However, the results of experimental studies of depression have provided only equivocal support for Beck's model. Krantz and Hammen (1979), for example, found a positive correlation between cognitive distortions and the intensity of depression in college students. Moreover, students who initially reported high levels of both cognitive distortions and depression reported the highest levels of depression 8 weeks later. However, Lewinsohn and his associates tested a large community sample and found that depression-related cognitions did not *precede* depressive episodes but rather occurred concurrently with depression (Lewinsohn, Steinmetz, Larson, & Franklin, 1981). Paradoxically, they also found that depression-related cognitions were negatively correlated with recovery from depression at a 1-year follow-up. Davis and Unruh (1981) found that patients who reported relatively recent onset of depression (mean 5.3 months) reported negative self-evaluations but failed to report irrational negative beliefs characteristic of long-term depression patients (mean onset 74.6 months).

Lewinsohn and his associates compared the agreement between self-rating and staff rating of social skills of 79 depressed psychiatric patients, 59 nondepressed psychiatric patients, and 73 normal controls. Surprisingly, the self-ratings of the depressed patients were closest to that of the staff. Both the nondepressed psychiatric patients and normal controls rated themselves significantly more positively than other people did. The authors noted that

> nondepressed people may thus be characterized by a halo or glow that involves illusory self-enhancement in which one sees oneself more positively than others see one. Clearly, if social reality is defined by the extent of agreement with objective observers, the depressed at the initial assessment were the most realistic in their self-perceptions whereas the controls were engaged in self-enhancing distortions. (Lewinsohn, Miscel, Chaplin, & Barton, 1980, p. 211)

After psychotherapy, the previously depressed patients began to display the distorted self-enhancement characteristic of the control subjects.

Although Lewinsohn and other theorists argue that the overall pattern of empirical findings in the depression literature clearly contradicts Beck's model, such a conclusion may be unwarranted. Beck, himself, argued that the conscious *salience* of an individual's automatic thoughts varied with the individual's emotional state and that only severely disturbed subjects spontaneously reported their automatic thoughts. Given that such negative self-statements are normally not reported during psychoanalysis sessions, it is unlikely that subjects will report them in self-ratings or questionnaires. Thus the halo effect observed by Lewinsohn may reflect the low salience of automatic thoughts in both normal subjects and in psychiatric disorders that are nonemotional in nature.

In summary, mentalistic models assume that our cognitions (thoughts, memories, visual images, etc.) directly *cause* the experience of specific emotional states. Freud and Beck disagree over the *types* of cognitive processes that evoke emotions. Freud stressed the role of unconscious processes in human emotions, whereas Beck emphasized the importance of conscious thought.

SUGGESTED READINGS

Beck, A. T. *Cognitive therapy and emotional disorders*. New York: International Universities Press, 1976.

A good introduction to Beck's model of emotion.

Breuer, J., & Freud, S. *Studies in hysteria*. 1895. Translated by J. Strachey & A. Freud. *The standard edition of the complete works of Sigmund Freud, Vol. II (1893–1895)*. London, Hogarth, 1955.

This classic work provides a number of fascinating insights into Freud's later theories.

Freud, S. *The psychopathology of everyday life*. 1904. Translated by A. A. Brill. *The basic writings of Sigmund Freud*. New York: Modern Library, 1938.

A provocative theoretical discussion of the role of unconscious processes in human emotions and motives.

Interactionist Models I
Physiological Models

The major tenet of all the interactionist models of emotion is that the mind and body are fundamentally inseparable. Given the clarity of this tenet, it might appear simple to classify theories as interactionist or noninteractionist. However, in practice, the distinction between interactionist models and as-if interactionist models is often unclear. For example, Whybrow, Akiskal, and McKinney's biochemical model discussed in Chapter 12 incorporates the view that psychological stressors may cause biochemical imbalances that, in turn, lead to alterations in emotional states. Accordingly, even though they postulate that biochemical states are the immediate cause of emotional disorders, their model may legitimately be classified as an interactionist model.

In sharp contrast, Freud's "interactionist" models discussed in Chapter 14 lack any form of conceptual bridge between mind and body. Specifically, *how* is the id related to neurological and other physiological activity? *How* are emotionally laden ideas converted into physical symptoms? And so on. Freud repeatedly ignored such issues while simultaneously giving lip service to the interactionist view.

To avoid the difficult task of differentiating between interactionist models and as-if interactionist models, the following discussion will focus only on two theorists, Howard Leventhal and Gary Schwartz, who explicitly articulate *how* mind and body interact. Interactionists models that emphasize the role of genetic factors in emotions will be discussed in Chapter 16.

15.1. HOWARD LEVENTHAL

Leventhal's *perceptual-motor* theory of emotion shares a number of common features with the Darwinian-oriented models discussed in Chapter 13. However, two important characteristics distinguish Leventhal's model from most of the Darwinian models. First, Leventhal espoused the interactionist view of a reciprocal relationship between physiological and cognitive processes. Second, unlike most Darwinian theorists, Leventhal emphasized the importance of motor commands (feedforward) in producing emotional states.

Perhaps the best way to explain the concept of *feedforward* is to ask the reader to perform a very simple demonstration. First, keep your head stationary and look upward. Although your visual image changes, the visual world appears to remain stationary. Next, place a finger against your bottom eyelid and gently press your eyeball upward. Notice that the world appears to move. In both instances, your brain receives input that (a) the retinal image has changed and (b) the six muscles attached to your eyeball have changed tension. Why does the world remain stationary when you actively move your eyes but appear to move when your eyeball is passively displaced?

One plausible explanation for this phenomenon is that active and passive movements produce different patterns of neural activities. Although active and passive movements may produce identical kinesthetic feedback from the eye muscles, only active movement is preceded by a motor command (efferent or feedforward signal). Presumably, a hypothetical comparator in the visual system compares the motor command to the subsequent amount of change in the retinal image. If I command my eyes to move 5 degrees to the right and the retinal image changes appropriately, the comparator signals no environmental movement. When the eyeball is displaced passively, the resulting change in the retinal image is not accompanied by a motor command and the comparator, detecting a mismatch, signals environmental movement. Now suppose you visually track a moving object with your eyes. Although the motor feedforward is given, the visual image remains stable. Again, detecting a mismatch, the comparator signals environmental movement. Such relatively simple feedforward–feedback comparator systems can account for a variety of perceptual phenomena, including why the world appears to move if your eye muscles are paralyzed, how we adapt to prism-induced distortions of the visual field, and why it is impossible to tickle oneself (see Schiffman, 1982).

Leventhal (1979, 1980, 1984a,b) hypothesized that such feedforward–feedback systems play an important role in integrating physiological and cognitive activities during emotional reactions. He postulated that adaptive behaviors are simultaneously mediated by two parallel sets of perceptual-motor control systems: a "cold" or nonemotional volition system and a "hot" or emotional system. Each system presumably operates in three distinct stages of processing: (a) a stimulus representation stage, (b) a planning-execution stage, and (c) an appraisal stage.

Suppose you are walking down the street and see a large puddle in your path. If the stimulus is represented as a puddle of water, the nonemotional processing system then generates a motor plan to avoid the puddle based on prior experiences with wet shoes and socks. Obviously, a young child may generate the alternative plan to jump in the puddle. Once the appropriate motor commands are given, the nonemotional system checks for feedback on the success or failure of the coping effort, for example, "Are my feet wet?".

Now suppose that the stimulus is represented as a puddle of blood. Such an emotional representation would cause the emotional control system to simultaneously trigger a facial reaction and the subjective experiences of disgust, fear, or surprise. At the planning–execution stage, the emotional system generates and executes motor plans to alter both the external stimulus situation (problem-based coping) and the subjective emotional experience (emotion-based coping). The emotional system then checks for feedback at the success or failure of the coping efforts. Given that the volitional and emotional systems compete for control of the *same* muscles, the relative dominance of either system determines whether emotions are displayed overtly.

Leventhal (1984b) argued that it is absurd to differentiate between cognition and emotion because both the nonemotional and emotional systems are simultaneously processing the *same* external and internal stimuli and rapidly cycling through all three stages of information processing. Presumably, the "cold" volitional system and the "hot" emotional system simultaneously evaluate external and internal stimuli at an unconscious level. Both systems then generate a set of motor plans or scripts that are simultaneously relayed to the facial muscles and to a feedforward–feedback comparator. If the composite signal of emotional feedforward and facial feedback matches the volitional system's feedforward, the experience is labeled *nonemotional*. However, if the emotional feedforward-facial feedback mismatches the feedforward from the volitional system, then it is experienced as a specific emotion. Unlike the Darwinian models discussed in Chapter 13, Leventhal does *not* postulate that facial feedback is the emotion. Rather, he hypothesized that the match or mismatch of CNS feedforward signals determines whether an emotion is experienced.

To account for both innate and learned components of emotions, Leventhal postulated that the emotional processing system is organized in a heirarchical fashion. The most primitive mode of representing, coping with and appraising emotional stimuli, is an expressive-motor code. Presumably, the newborn is genetically programmed to display both autonomic and facial responses to specific types of stimuli such as loud noises. Such primitive reflexes are later displaced by more adaptive motor behaviors as the organism acquires more sophisticated cognitive abilities.

Schemata (perceptual-motor codes) are developmentally and hierarchically the next level of processing. These codes are specific memories that incorporate representations of a variety of sensory modalities (sights, sounds, smells, kinesthetic feedback, somatic feedback, and autonomic feedback). Because these schemata are *composite* memories of the situational cues that elicited specific emotion and specific motor programs, they are essentially mental representations of emotional experiences.

As the child matures intellectually, he or she gradually acquires two conceptual coding systems for representing-coping-appraising emotional stimuli: language and performance. Specifically, language provides children with an abstract mode for representing and communicating their emotions. Leventhal (1980) argued that verbal codes represent only an incomplete abstract conceptualization of the emotion and are *not* a representation of the emotion itself. Thus, the verbal system may be relatively ineffective in either eliciting or inhibiting emotional reactions *unless* the verbal system triggers a facility or inhibitory schematic representation. For example, verbally thinking about being attacked by a pack of savage dogs may not elicit an emotion unless you generate a vivid image or trigger a personal (episodic) memory of the event.

The child also gradually acquires a set of performance codes for voluntarily decoding and mimicking other people's emotional responses. Children acquire this nonverbal conceptual system by observing the emotional displays of others and by actively participating in their own spontaneous emotional displays, for example, consciously trying to laugh harder.

Leventhal hypothesizes that the performance system plays a key role in overriding situationally elicited emotional reactions. Presumably, the performance system uses verbal and facial cues to *anticipate* expressive-motor and schemata-induced facial reactions and to generate conflicting motor commands to the facial muscles. Although such voluntary "false" faces may not eliminate the emotional experience entirely, they may reduce the *intensity* of the emotional experience by providing nonemotional facial feedback that helps reduce the mismatch produced by the emotional feedforward from the expressive-schematic processing systems.

Leventhal postulated that each of the three levels of processing emotional stimuli is differentially sensitive to specific types of environmental stimuli. The conceptual level responds primarily to verbal stimuli but will also react to other facial expressions. The schematic level responds primarily to facial cues but also may react to either verbal messages or specific stimulus properties such as tone of voice. The expressive level responds primarily to specific stimulus properties but may also be triggered by facial stimuli.

The "cold" volitional processing system presumably interacts directly only with the conceptual (language-performance) level of the emotional processing system. If the individual consciously defines the situation as emotional, he or she automatically triggers the appropriate conceptual associations that, in turn, elicit the appropriate schematic and expressive motor memories in a top-to-bottom fashion. Conversely, consciously focusing attention on the specific stimulus characteristics may reduce emotional reactions indirectly by allowing the individual to nonemotionally anticipate the stimulus and thus generate voluntary facial responses to override involuntary facial patterns produced by the emotional system. Such attempts at voluntarily masking emotional displays may also inadvertently increase the intensity of emotional states by increasing the discrepancy between feedforward signals.

Paradoxically, voluntarily making the appropriate emotional face may serve to reduce the *intensity* of the emotion by reducing the mismatch between volitional and emotional feedforward. For example, in a series of experiments on humor, Leventhal found that instructing subjects to focus their attention on canned laughter tends to reduce the subjects' emotional reactions to cartoons. Similarly, Leventhal has also demonstrated that focusing patients' attention on the stimulus properties of a painful stimulus such as an injection may reduce the severity of pain produced by the stimulus.

Leventhal (1980, 1984a) argued that his model is consistent with the findings of both facial feedback and the findings of studies employing Schachter and Singer's arousal and Vallin's false feedback techniques. However, in an attempt to refute Ekman's and Tomkins's models of emotion, Leventhal (1984a) cited clinical neurological findings that also cast considerable doubt upon the validity of his own model.

As discussed previously in Chapters 10 and 13, voluntary and involuntary emotional displays are controlled by different neural tracts. Specifically, disorders of the pyramidal motor tracts lead to the loss of voluntary facial expression but have little effect on spontaneous emotional displays. Although these patients still experience emotions, their emotional states often mismatch their facial expressions. Thus a patient may smile but report feeling embarrassment. A minority of these patients display emotional lability (involuntary crying, laughing, etc.) but report no or contradictory emotional experiences (Rinn, 1984).

Disorders of the extrapyramidal tract eliminate spontaneous emotional expressions (*mimitic facial paralysis*) without altering voluntary facial expressions. The loss of emotional facial displays, however, may not eliminate the patients' emotional reactions. For example, about one-third of Parkinson's disease patients report depression despite mimitic facial paralysis (Rinn, 1984). Similarly, *Huntington's chorea* is caused by the progressive destruction of the GABA tracts within the extrapyramidal system. Both involuntary motor movements and depression are characteristic of the disease.

Such clinical findings would appear to clearly refute facial feedback models of emotional states. However, whether such clinical findings support Leventhal's feedforward model is debatable. In Leventhal's defense, it can be argued that the loss of voluntary control of facial muscles may increase the salience of involuntary facial responses. The patients' awareness of their involuntary facial displays may act to simultaneously reduce the intensity of facially induced emotional experiences while triggering competing schemata (i.e., embarrassment).

Alternatively, the feedforward tracts to the comparator may be undamaged in many motor disorders. The conflicting facial patterns and emotional states reported by neurological patients may reflect feedforward mismatches that are not apparent in the patient's facial displays because either the volitional or emotional feedforward signals are blocked *beyond* the comparator. For example, *myasthenia gravis* is a progressive disease of the neuromuscular junction that leaves the CNS undamaged. These patients report normal emotional states (anger, anxiety, etc.) but often display abnormal emotional displays such as the "myasthetic vertical snarl" (teeth baring) when smiling (Jefferson & Marshall, 1981). Although this clinical observation neatly fits a postcomparator interpretation, it reveals one of the major weaknesses in Leventhal's model—namely a lack of specificity in the neurological location of his hypothetical feedforward comparator.

Another major weakness in Leventhal's model is that he only vaguely acknowledges that biological states such as fatigue or illness may directly alter both volitional and emotional processing. However, studies of both child development and altered states of consciousness in adults (drugs, sleep deprivation, stress, etc.) indicate that biological states may directly alter both volitional and emotional cognitive processes. For example, Pikunas (1969) noted that by late infancy, toddlers' emotional states are directly yoked to both their internal biological states (hunger, fatigue, etc.) and environmental situations. Infants are

most likely to display *negative* emotional behaviors when they are in a deprived
state and *positive* emotional behaviors in a satiated state.

Research on memory in adults suggests that mood may exert complex effects on recall. In some instances, a given mood may facilitate recall of similarly
emotionally toned memories. Thus an angry mood may make it easier to recall
anger-related memories. A sad mood may make it easier to recall sad memories
(see Teasdale & Fogarty, 1979; Bower, 1981). In other instances, mood may
interfere with recall (Ellis, Thomas, McFarland, & Lane, 1985). Although Leventhal's model could potentially accommodate such complex affect-biological
state-cognitive interactions, the current form of his model poorly accounts for
such phenomena.

A third weakness in Leventhal's model is that he does not adequately take
into account individual differences in habitual coping strategies. Both clinical
and laboratory studies have documented marked individual differences in cognitive coping strategies before, during, and after stressful events. Some individuals attempt to cope with stress by adopting an information-seeking strategy
(monitors), whereas other individuals attempt to reduce stress by distracting
themselves (blunters). Given that subjects enter an experiment with their own
personal coping strategies, it is reasonable to expect that their habitual styles of
coping may interact with the demand characteristics of the experiment. For
example, focusing an individual's attention on the stimulus properties of a
stressor may decrease the stress of monitors but increase the stress of blunters.

Miller and Mangan (1983) examined the role of coping style and the amount
of information given in subjects' reactions to a real-life stressor, a gynecological
examination for cervical cancer. They measured 40 female subjects' physiological
reactions (pulse rate, vaginal muscle contractions, and overt movements such as
hand clenching) and psychological reactions. Based on their self-reports, half of
the subjects were classified as monitors and the remaining half as blunters. Ten
subjects in each group were randomly selected to receive detailed information
about the examination procedures and the physical sensations they might experience (high information treatment). The remaining subjects were only informed
which specific tests (colposcopy, pap smear, etc.) they would be given (low
information treatment). Miller and Managan found that each patient's reactions
to the examination was a product of both her habitual coping style and the
amount of prior information she had received. Blunters who received minimal
information reported less emotional distress and displayed lower physiological
arousal than those who were given large amounts of information. Conversely,
monitors reported increased emotional distress when given only minimal information. Although such findings are consistent with Leventhal's model, he has
failed to address how such habitual coping styles could be incorporated into his
theory.

A fourth major weakness in Leventhal's model is that he has failed to
directly address how normal emotional reactions may be transformed into abnormal emotional reactions. Leventhal speculated that abnormal emotional
states such as phobias might be traced to distorted schematic and conceptual
representations of events. However, he has failed to offer any explicit hypoth-

eses as to *why* one individual would be prone to acquire realistic schemata and another individual would be prone to acquire distorted schemata.

15.2. GARY SCHWARTZ

As the reader has already probably guessed, each theorist's educational and professional experiences tend to color his or her view of emotions. Clinically oriented theorists such as Freud tend to emphasize how normal emotions are transformed into abnormal emotions. Laboratory-oriented theorists such as Leventhal tend to focus primarily on explaining how normal emotional states are elicited and/or suppressed. Not surprisingly, researchers such as Gary Schwartz who are actively involved in both clinical and laboratory studies often attempt to synthesize clinical and laboratory findings.

As one of the early pioneers in the use of biofeedback to treat psychophysiological disorders, Schwartz was impressed by the marked individual differences he observed. In a series of papers, Schwartz (1973, 1975, 1977, 1978; Davidson & Schwartz, 1976) has attempted to provide a general theoretical framework to account for observed individual differences in (a) psychophysiological reactions during emotional states, (b) the development of psychophysiological disorders, and (c) learning to consciously control physiological reactions. Specifically, if we are all basically "built" in a similar fashion, why do we show such diverse physiological and psychological reactions to environmental and psychological stressors?

Schwartz noted that numerous researchers have found that specific *patterns* of cognitive activity (images, verbal thoughts, etc.) tend to elicit very distinct *patterns* of physiological activity. For example, speaking (not singing) the lyrics to a song produces brain activation primarily in the left cerebral hemisphere, whereas humming the tune to a song produces activation in the right hemisphere. Not surprisingly, singing the song leads to activation of both hemispheres (Schwartz, Davidson, Maer, & Bromfeld, 1974).

Schwartz observed that such asymmetrical hemispheric patterns also occur when subjects are asked to answer different types of emotionally loaded questions. For example, asking subjects to report their emotional responses to visual images (e.g., "What emotion do you feel if you imagine your mother's face?") elicited right-hemisphere activation. Asking subjects to describe the difference between the meaning of words used to define emotional states (i.e., "What is the difference between joy and love?") led to activation of both hemispheres. Although such findings would appear to strongly support cognitive models of emotion, Schwartz (1975) disagreed and argued that thoughts may act both as stimuli for emotional reactions and as responses to specific patterns of physiological activity. For example, fear-related thoughts may trigger heart rate acceleration and vice versa.

Pure cognitive or somatic anxiety would appear to contradict this interactionist position. As discussed in previous chapters, some individuals experience anxiety states in the absence of autonomic arousal (cognitive anxiety), whereas other individuals experience somatic symptoms without accompanying anxious cognitions (somatic anxiety). However, Schwartz (1975; Davidson & Schwartz, 1976) argued that only an interactionist model can account for such marked individual differences during the same emotional state. Specifically, he postulated that different coping strategies may elicit at least four distinct patterns of cognitive-physiological activity.

First, an individual may habitually react to perceived threats with verbal (left) cerebral hemisphere activity. Such an individual may experience high cognitive anxiety (e.g., anxiety-laden thoughts) but little physiological arousal. Consistent with this hypothesis, Bell and Schwartz (1973) found that instructing subjects to think arousing thoughts had little effect on heart rate.

A second individual may habitually react to perceived threats with nonverbal (right) cerebral hemisphere activity. Such an individual may experience low cognitive anxiety but experience patterns of somatic activation. The feedback from the peripheral physiological arousal may then be verbally labeled as either *free-floating* anxiety ("I feel upset but I don't know why") or somatic arousal ("I must be getting the flu").

A third individual may habitually adopt a dual verbal-nonverbal cognitive mode for coping with perceived stress. Such individuals would display a strong concordance between physiological arousal and their subjective states and experience mixed (high cognitive and high somatic) anxiety states.

A fourth individual may habitually deny the existence of the threat. Because he or she does not perceive the situation as emotional, neither cortical nor peripheral physiological arousal is elicited (low cognitive and low somatic anxiety).

In each case, the individual's subjective experience of anxiety (or lack thereof) can be directly traced to a unique *pattern* of cognitive and physiological activities. Schwartz (1975) argued that each discrete emotion (anger, sadness, etc.) should not be conceptualized as a unique unitary state but rather should be viewed as an *emergent property* of the complex interaction between cognitions and discrete patterns of physiological activity. For example, emotional imagery may induce facial displays and vice versa. The conscious experience of the emotion is neither the mental image nor the sensory feedback from facial expression but rather the unique product of the ongoing cognitive and physiological activities.

According to the Davidson–Schwartz (1976) model, each emotion consists of an idiosyncratic pattern of cognitive and physiological activities. For example, your subjective experience of anger may be quite different than mine. However, due to the similarities in neurological and neurohormonal controls and the biological constraints of physiological systems, different people may acquire the *same* cognitive-physiological pattern for a given emotional state. For example, Cameron (1944) found that anxiety patients tended to display one of three patterns of physiological responses: skeletal muscle tension, cardiovascular symptoms, or gastrointestinal symptoms. Thus similar physiological responses were observed within each cluster of patients, but *different* patterns of responses were observed across the entire sample.

Similar clusters of individuals with common symptoms have been observed with samples of college students. Pennebaker (1982) asked 177 college undergraduates to rate how they were feeling "right now" on a physical symptom–emotion checklist. Each of the six emotions included on the rating scale (angry, guilty, happy, jealous, tense, sad) were each associated with a unique pattern of physical symptoms. To examine individual differences in emotional experiences, four female and five male subjects were each asked to complete the symptom–emotion checklist an average of 12 times per day on 5 consecutive days. At least three or more of the nine subjects reported the *same* pattern of physical symptoms for each of the six emotions. For example, happiness was negatively correlated with tense muscles and upset stomach and positively correlated with light-headedness.

The literature on test anxiety would also appear to at least partially support the Davidson–Schwartz model of emotion. Liebert and Morris (1967) proposed that worry (cognitive anxiety) inhibits test performance, whereas emotionality (somatic anxiety) is unrelated to performance. Consistent with these predictions, researchers have generally found that worry is negatively correlated with academic performance, whereas emotionality is unrelated to high-school and college students' grades (see Deffenbacher, 1980; Holroyd & Appel, 1980). However, Borkovec, Robinson, Pruzinsky, and Depree (1983) found that worry is not identical to cognitive anxiety. Although worriers did report higher levels of anxiety and obsessional (uncontrollable intruding) thoughts than nonworriers, worriers also reported higher levels of both depression and hostility than nonworriers. Moreover, worriers reported moderate awareness of somatic symptoms such as muscle tension or an upset stomach.

In contrast with other theories of emotion, Davidson–Schwartz's model is an extremely vague conceptual outline. However, Schwartz has made a concerted effort to fill in the specific details of his model empirically rather than theoretically. For example, as discussed previously in Chapter 10, Schwartz and his associates have conducted a series of experiments on the relationship between emotional imagery, facial responses, and autonomic arousal and have repeatedly documented that imagining situations associated with specific emotions elicits distinct patterns of facial responses. Consistent with the findings of nonverbal communication research, they have also found marked sex differences in facial displays (Schwartz, Brown, & Ahern, 1980). In one study, they also found distinct autonomic patterns that accompanied specific imagery-elicited facial responses (Schwartz, Weinberger, & Singer, 1981). This finding was later replicated by Ekman, Levenson, and Friesen (1983).

The second major theoretical issue that Schwartz (1973, 1977, 1978, 1979) has addressed is the relationship between emotional states and psychological disorders. He proposed that psychophysiological disorders can be traced to a variety of factors that may produce a disruption of the neurological-neurohormonal system feedback loops that normally maintain homeostasis, that is, physiological activity within prescribed limits. Homeostatic regulation of physiological activity normally occurs in four stages: (a) environmental demand, (b) CNS information processing, (c) peripheral organ responses and (d) negative feedback.

The external physical environment places a series of never-ending demands on the organism. These environmental demands are literally *categorical imper-atives* (i.e., unconditional demands). For example, in an extremely hot or cold environment, the organism must adjust its body metabolism and heat loss to match the environmental conditions or die. Humans and other animals may also behaviorally adjust to environmental demands by seeking shade in a hot en-vironment or seeking shelter in a cold environment. Although some readers have difficulty accepting Skinner's notion of environmental control, our physical environment does exert immediate control over our physiology and many of our behaviors. That is, we put on a raincoat *because* it is raining.

The external social environment also places a series of never-ending uncon-ditional demands on the organism. For example, social animals such as chim-panzees or wolves usually have recognizable dominance hierarchies. A low-status animal is placed in the frustrating position of having to defer his or her own gratification at the demands of higher status animals or engaging in often futile fights to change his or her position in the dominance hierarchy. Converse-ly, high-status animals are faced with the threat of losing their dominant posi-tion. Although human cultures also display a variety of dominance heirarchies (age, sex, social class, etc.), cultural norms also exert a series of categorical imperatives on the individuals. In cultures where physical aggression is consid-ered normal, the individual is socially pressured into aggressive displays. Con-versely, in cultures where aggression is labeled *abnormal*, the individual is so-cially pressured into inhibiting aggressive displays.

During the second stage of homeostasis, the CNS compares the environ-mental demands with the current state of the internal environment and devises a specific plan to hold the activity of all physiological systems within tolerable levels. For example, in the hot external environments, the individual can main-tain a constant internal temperature by either diverting hot internal blood to the skin or activating one's sweat glands. These two simple biological responses, however, require rather complex adjustments of both the cardiovascular system and the urinary system to compensate for the sudden diversion of blood from the internal organs and the sudden loss of body fluids through sweating.

The third stage of homeostasis represents the actual physiological response of the peripheral organs. As previously discussed in Chapters 4 through 10, a local organ response such as contraction or relaxation of a muscle is only a single component in a complex pattern of highly coordinated physiological activity that involves multiple physiological systems. For example, change in respiration rate is accompanied by changes in both heart rate and blood pressure. As each physiological system is pushed above or below its baseline state, it sends senso-ry signals back to the brain to terminate the change and allow the system to return to baseline. This negative feedback constitutes the fourth stage of homeostasis.

Schwartz postulated that homeostatic *disregulation* rather than regulation may occur at any one of these four stages of homeostatic control and produce psychophysiological disorders. For example, wearing a suit and tie in a hot environment places an extreme demand on the body's thermoregulatory sys-tem, and the peripheral organs send strong negative feedback that core tem-perature is rising. However, if the individual also receives the demand from the social environment to remain properly attired, the stress may become unavoidable and the individual may feel forced to ignore the danger signals from his or her own body. If this situation is prolonged or repeated, the body makes a series of pathological adjustments to the stressor. These adjustments may be changes in (a) the baseline (tonic) activity such as elevated BP that persists when the stressor is removed, or (b) phasic overreactions to the stressor such as vascular headaches, or (c) a combination of tonic and phasic responses such as Raynaud's disease.

Schwartz argued that disregulation by the internal homeostatic mechanisms may cause pychophysiological disorders to develop even if environmental demands are relatively benign. Due to genetically determined hyperreactivity, the CNS may generate inappropriate signals to the internal organs even when no stressor is present. Similarly, due to prior experiences, an individual may misinterpret external stimuli as stressors and generate inappropriate signals to the internal organs. For example, due to either emotionality or prior experiences, a given student may respond to a test situation "as if" his or her life were being threatened. Moreover, due to previous damage or genetic factors, a given organ may either respond inappropriately to CNS signals or send inappropriate feedback signals to the brain. If such internal disregulation is repeated, the individual will eventually develop a specific psychophysiological disorder. Moreover, because organs are organized into interlocking physiological systems, a given patient's psychophysiological disorder may have multiple causes.

Schwartz postulated that the specific *physiological patterns* associated with an individual's emotional states may at least partially account for why he or she may be prone to develop specific psychophysiological disorders. For example, anger may be associated with increased BP, increased acid release in the stomach, and a variety of other physiological responses. Suppose Person A habitually displays a BP response during anger, whereas Person B habitually displays a stomach acid response. Although Person A may be predisposed to essential hypertension and Person B may be predisposed to develop peptic ulcers, neither individual is *predetermined* to develop a psychophysiological disorder *unless* disregulation is triggered at one or more of the four stages of homeostasis.

Suppose both individuals live in benign physical and social environments, realistically cope with external and internal demands, and have healthy peripheral organs. In such an ideal situation, neither individual would develop a psychophysiological disorder. However, Person A would experience anger as pulsing arteries, whereas Person B would experience anger as an upset stomach. Now suppose the environmental demands repetitively elicit anger in Person A but not in Person B. Person A would eventually develop high blood pressure, whereas Person B never develops an ulcer. Conversely, if Person B repetitively thinks angry thoughts whereas Person A does not, only Person B would develop a psychophysiological disorder. Schwartz argues that such a probabilistic approach is needed to account for the wide individual differences observed within psychophysiological populations. Consistent with Schwartz's hypothesis, research on psychophysiological patients has repeatedly failed to identify any single cause for any given disorder, although clusters of causal factors have repeatedly been documented.

The third major theoretical issue that Schwartz has addressed is how individuals learn to consciously *control* physiological patterns. Schwartz argued that our ability to understand how *self-regulation* occurs is limited by our understanding of the complex interactions between conscious thought and our physiological systems that are normally coordinated subcortically. For example, although humans do not normally consciously regulate breathing, they display a high degree of control over respiration during singing and talking. Asking someone to describe *how* they breathe while singing usually evokes a nonsensical answer even from individuals who have had formal training in singing. Similarly, asking someone to describe *how* he or she walks elicits only vague replies. The fact that such behaviors are controlled subcortically, however, does not imply that they are not yoked to conscious thought. Although I may be only dimly aware of how I sing or walk, my conscious decision to sing or not to sing or walk or not to walk elicits the appropriate subcortical programs.

Schwartz (1977, 1978, 1979) postulated that self-control involves consciously recognizing which specific cognitive patterns are associated with unwanted or pathological arousal and learning to substitute more adaptive modes of dealing with stressors. Although many biofeedback therapists argue that patients are being conditioned by feedback to learn direct conscious control over physiological functioning, Schwartz disagreed. He conceptualized biofeedback as providing a form of an external negative feedback loop that allows the patient to discover which cognitive-physiological patterns aggravate or diminish their symptoms.

A given patient may learn to consciously recognize the situations or thoughts that maintain disregulation and learn to eliminate his or her symptoms by changing or avoiding the eliciting situations or cognitions. For example, an individual patient may learn to lower his or her blood pressure by changing his or her life-style or maladaptive cognitions. Once the stressors have been eliminated, homeostasis will at least partially return to the cardiovascular system. Obviously, the amount of damage to the arterial walls previously produced by high blood pressure may limit the amount of recovery possible. Schwartz argued that, although such patients clearly have learned effective self-control strategies through biofeedback, they may not have acquired any direct conscious control over the specific physiological response. That is, they cannot voluntarily "think" their arterial walls into relaxing. Similarly, a given patient may use the information provided by biofeedback to discover which specific voluntary responses are yoked with his or her symptoms. For example, patients may learn to voluntarily lower their heart rate through respiration or through muscle relaxation. Again, patients may acquire an effective strategy for eliminating their symptoms without learning any direct conscious control of the physiological response, for example, they cannot "think" their heart into slowing.

Like the Davidson–Schwartz model of emotion, Schwartz's disregulation and self-regulation models are general conceptual frameworks rather than detailed models. Again, it should be noted that Schwartz has made a concerted effort to fill in the specific details of his model empirically rather than theoretically. However, his approach greatly reduces the heuristic value of his models. For example, given that he postulated that the same disorder can be traced to multiple causes, it is virtually impossible to disprove his hypothesis. Suppose one ulcer patient has a large number of biological relatives who also have ulcers, whereas a second ulcer patient has no biological relatives with ulcers. Although such observations clearly refute the hypothesis that ulceration is a genetically determined disorder, they paradoxically support Schwartz's view of multiple causality.

Clearly, Schwartz's models are excellent *post hoc* explanatory devices that account for a variety of conflicting empirical findings. However, it is extremely difficult to base *a priori* predictions on his models. For example, the age of onset of different psychophysiological disorders varies. Some disorders such as asthma may appear during childhood, whereas other disorders such as essential hypertension may not occur until middle age. Although such findings suggest that the disregulation of specific physiological systems may be age-related, it is impossible to predict, based on Schwartz's models, *which* physiological systems may be most vulnerable to disregulation at a given age.

In summary, Leventhal's and Schwartz's models illustrate different aspects of the interactionist view of emotions. Both theorists emphasize the role of cognitive coping strategies in eliciting (or preventing) discrete emotional states. However, both theorists agree that cognitive and physiological activities are inseparable. The major theoretical advantage of this interactionist approach is that it allows us to avoid the "chicken-versus-egg" argument that dominates materialist-mentalist discussion of emotions. The major theoretical weakness of the interactionist approach is that unless we specifically define *how* mind and body interact, interactionism degenerates into a sterile tautology.

SUGGESTED READINGS

Leventhal, H. A perceptual-motor theory of emotion. In K. R. Scherer & P. Ekman (Eds.), *Approaches to emotion.* Hillsdale, N.J.: Lawrence Erlbaum Associates, 1984.

A good introduction to Leventhal's theory of emotion.

Schwartz, G. E. Biofeedback, self-regulation and the patterning of physiological processes. *American Scientist,* 1975, *63,* 314–324.

A fascinating discussion of the psychophysiology of individual differences in emotions.

Schwartz, G. E. The brain as a health care system. In G. C. Stone, F. Cohen, & N. E. Adler (Eds.), *Health psychology—A handbook: Theories, applications and challenges of a psychological approach to the health care system.* San Francisco: Jossey-Bass, 1979.

An informative presentation of Schwartz's disregulation model of psychophysiological disorders.

Interactionist Models II
Personality/Temperament Models

A common weakness of most models of emotion is that they either ignore genetic variability completely, or worse, they evoke genetics as a tautological explanation. For example, as discussed in Chapter 12, there is a high concordance rate between panic disorders and anxiety and/or depression in biological relatives. Such correlations tell us only that a genetic predisposition *may* exist and *not* that genetic vulnerability does exist. To interpret these findings as "panic disorder patients are genetically vulnerable to panic attacks" is, pure and simply, tautological. It is equally plausible (and tautological) to infer that anxiety and depression may be produced by the intense psychosocial stress of coping with a relative who experiences spontaneous panic attacks. "Wasn't that your uncle Fred who freaked out in the middle of church last week?" A correlation implies only that a relationship exists, but it does not tell us *why* the relationship exists.

16.1. BEHAVIORAL GENETICS

Before we discuss the role of genetics in emotion, a quick review of basic genetics may be helpful. *DNA* (deoxyribonucleic acid) is the basic unit of genetic coding. Complex strings of DNA form structural units called *genes* that are the basic units of genetic codes. Complex strings of genes, in turn, form larger structural units called *chromosomes*. With the exception of reproductive cells (ovum and sperm), all cells in the human body contain 46 chromosomes arranged in 23 pairs. On 22 of these pairs, genes are arranged so that the gene for a given trait is found on corresponding segments of either chromosome pair. Genes on the twenty-third pair, or sex chromosomes, are arranged slightly differently. The "female" chromosome (X) is larger and therefore carries more genetic information than the "male" chromosome (Y). Thus individuals with two female chromosomes (XX) have more genes than individuals with one male and one female chromosome (XY). In nonreproductive cells, the chromosomes duplicate themselves prior to cellular division (mitosis). Thus the two "new" cells have identical chromosomes.

Reproductive cells undergo a different process of cellular reproduction called *meiosis*. Prior to cellular division, genes are randomly exchanged between pairs of chromosomes (crossing-over) through random breakage of the segments of the chromosomes as the pairs separate. Cellular division occurs twice and produces four (instead of two) new cells. These mature reproductive cells contain a random assortment of approximately 50% of the original gene pool arranged on 23 single chromosomes. This process of meiosis produces genetic diversity without mutation, because the same individual produces a large combination of different genes in his or her reproductive cells. At conception, the 23 chromosomes of the ovum fuse with the 23 chromosomes of the sperm and produce a new cell with a unique set of 46 chromosomes. Mitotic cellular division then begins and produces a genetically distinct organism.

An individual's genetic inheritance is called his or her *genotype*, whereas their observable characteristics, such as hair color, are called their *phenotype*. A child has approximately 50%· of his or her genotype in common with either parent and any full siblings. Fraternal (dizygotic) twins develop from two different ovum and thus have only about 50% of the genotype in common. Because identical (monozygotic) twins develop from the same ovum, they have 100% of their genotype in common. Step-siblings (one common parent) have approximately 25% of their genotype in common. With the exception of identical twins, there is obviously much genetic variability within the same family.

Whether a given genotypical trait is expressed (appears) in a given individual's phenotype is determined by a complex interaction of factors. First, some genes are *dominant*, whereas other genes are *recessive*. Dominant traits such as brown eyes normally appear in the phenotype when either the individual inherits two dominant genes (homozygous dominant) or only one dominant gene (heterozygous). A recessive trait such as blue eyes usually appears in the phenotype only when the individual inherits the same recessive gene from each parent (homozygous recessive). However, geneticists have discovered that some individuals *simultaneously* display both dominant and recessive traits (codominance). For example, some "blue-eyed" individuals have small flecks of brown pigment in their eyes. Such individuals are actually heterozygous and thus capable of producing either blue- or brown-eyed offspring.

Second, some phenotypical traits (height, skin color, voice pitch) are characterized by *intermediate expression of heterozygosity*. That is, the heterozygous phenotype is a compromise between the dominant and recessive phenotype. Thus the offspring of one extremely tall and one extremely short parent tend to be of average height.

Third, some genetic traits are dormant unless activated by environmental exposure. For example, allergeries are triggered by environmental exposure to toxins. Although a given individual may be genetically vulnerable to show severe allergic reactions to bee stings, this characteristic would never appear in his or her phenotype *unless* he or she is stung by a bee.

The field of behavioral genetics dates back to human beings' prehistorical attempts at selective breeding of animals. Herders discovered that selective breeding for homogeneous physical characteristics such as wool color also inadvertently produced homogeneous behavioral characteristics such as aggressiveness. Moreover, selective breeding for a specific behavioral characteristic may also inadvertently produce other undesired behavioral traits. For example, thoroughbred horses are selectively bred for speed (a behavioral trait) but are also more emotional than other breeds of horses. Researchers have documented that a variety of emotional-motivational behavioral traits such as aggression, emotionality, and sex drive can be produced through selective breeding in nonhuman species (McClearn, 1970).

Anastasi (1958) noted that the study of human behavioral genetics has undergone three historical periods. Early researchers asked *which* behavioral traits were environmentally determined and which were genetically determined. This approach was eventually abandoned as researchers realized that environmental and genetic factors may interact to produce a given phenotype. For example, an individual's genotypical height may be 6 feet tall, but because of poor diet, he or she may grow to an adult height of only 5 feet tall. Next, reseachers began asking *how much* of a given trait was environmentally or genetically determined. Eventually, researchers realized that asking the question "How much?" is futile, unless we first answer the more fundamental question of *how* do environmental and genetic factors interact? Geneticists currently offer three conflicting explanations for how environmental and genetic factors interact during development: predetermined development, probablistic development, and plasticity.

The predetermined development model is based on the assumption that the genotype contains a fixed blueprint of the adult organism and a set of biological clocks that determine the invariant sequence in which development (maturation) occurs. Presumably, the environment only plays the passive role of providing adequate support for phenotypical development. For example, the onset of some genetic diseases such as Huntington's chorea (a degenerative disease of the nervous system) does not occur until middle age. If an individual with Huntington's chorea genotype lives *long* enough, he or she will inevitably develop the disease. However, if the individual dies prior to middle age, the Huntington's genotype would never have appeared in his or her phenotype, although it may appear in the phenotypes of his or her offspring.

The probabilistic development model is based on the assumption that the genotype contains a series of alternative blueprints and biological clocks that determine *critical periods* during which an alternative blueprint may be implemented. According to this view, environmental factors may play an active role in determining which genotype blueprint is expressed in the phenotype but only during critical periods. For example, as discussed in Chapter 3, phenotypical sex is determined by the levels of androgens in the embryo's bloodstream around the sixth week after conception. If androgen levels are high at this point in time, individuals begin to develop a male phenotype regardless of their genotype. Thus, a genetic female (XX) can be born with a fully developed penis. Conversely, if androgen levels are low, a female phenotype develops, regardless of genotype. Thus a genetic male (XY) may be born with a vagina. Intermediate levels of androgen produce the development of partially male and partially female genitals. Before or after this critical period, androgen levels have relatively little impact on the development of primary sexual characteristics. Thus the development of sexual phenotype is clearly 100% genetic and yet is not 100% genetically determined.

The plasticity model of development is based on the assumption that environmental factors actively interact with genetic factors and, thus, the *degree* to which a genotype is expressed in the phenotype may be environmentally determined. For example, an individual may be genetically predisposed to become a world-class athlete, chess player, or musician. However, even with optimal biological environmental support (e.g., diet), none of these characteristics may ever appear in the individual's phenotype. Moreover, few behavioral traits vary in an either/or fashion. Individuals are not aggressive or nonagressive. Humans differ in both the types of aggressions (physical, verbal, etc.) and the *degree* of aggressive behaviors they display. However, such behavioral traits should not be viewed as "learned" because humans display marked individual differences in their ability to acquire a given trait. Even in cultures that reward extreme aggression, individuals differ in their degree of aggressiveness. According to the plasticity model, an individual's genotype determines the *reaction range* of potential phenotypes he or she could develop, whereas the environment actively determines the actual phenotype (Gottesman, 1963a).

Lehrman (1970) noted that each of these alternative models of development may be valid for different species or for different behaviors in the same species. However, these competing models have created much semantic confusion in the behavioral genetics literature. For example, the term *innate* is used by predetermined theorists to indicate a trait that develops independently of environmental experiences. To probabilistic theorists, the term *innate* implies that the environment may influence the phenotype during specific critical periods of development. To plasticity theorists, the term *innate* implies a range of behaviors that may develop in different environments at specific points during the life span. Such semantic distinctions are nontrivial, and, as we focus our discussion on specific genetic models of emotion, the reader should be aware that each of these models incorporates a specific model of the role of genetics and experience in human development.

Predetermined theorists used the term *temperament* to denote an inherited pattern of emotionality that is independent of environmental influences. In everyday language, the term "temperament" is used to denote specific trait emotions (hothead, scaredy-cat, etc.). Researchers, however, often use the term temperament to represent nonspecific characteristics such as physiological reactivity that may predispose an individual to a variety of emotional reactions.

Buss and Plomin (1975) argued that in order for a given human characteristic to be labeled a component of temperament, it must meet all of the following five criteria: (a) be inheritable; (b) be stable during childhood; (c) be present in adult humans; (d) be present in nonhuman species; and (e) be evolutionarily adaptive. It should be noted that the last two criteria are "strawmen" or bogus arguments. *Any* behavioral trait can be observed across species *if* one is willing to ignore species differences. For example, ant colonies fight organized wars. To argue that both humans and ants share a warlike temperament stretches the sociobiological argument beyond credibility. Similarly, *any* human behavior, however bizarre, can be labeled *adaptive*. Many species display the tonic immobility reflex (i.e., "play dead") if caught by a predator. This behavior is highly adaptive because many predators drop their prey when it no longer struggles. Thus, "playing dead" may give the prey a second chance to escape. Although there is an obvious parallel between tonic immobility and catatonic states in humans, arguing that catatonic states are adaptive is purely speculative.

A considerable body of evidence has accumulated that suggests that at least three human characteristics (general activity level, physiological reactivity, and sociability) may meet all five of Buss and Plomin's criteria for temperament. For example, observations of human newborns have consistently found marked individual differences on these three characteristics within the first week after birth (Shirley, 1931; Gesell, 1937; Bridger & Birns, 1968). Moreover, marked ethnic differences in infants' behaviors have been observed. Specifically, Caucasian infants tend to be more sensitive and irritable than infants of Oriental descent (Chinese, Japanese, Navaho, Polynesian), and Japanese infants were more sensitive and irritable than other Oriental ethnic groups (Freedman, 1979).

Studies of the concordance rates of activity level, physiological reactivity, and sociability in biologically related individuals have also consistently supported the view that these characteristics may be innate. Compared with fraternal twins, identical twins tend to be much more similar in activity level (Scarr, 1966; Willerman, 1973), physiological reactivity (Jost & Sontag, 1944; Lader & Wing, 1966), and sociability (Shields, 1962; Freedman & Keller, 1963; Gottesman, 1963b; Scarr, 1969; Eaves, 1973; Eaves & Eysenck, 1974). Longitudinal studies of the same individuals suggest that individual differences in activity (Neilon, 1948; Tuddenham, 1959), physiological reactivity (Wenger & Cullen, 1972), and sociability (Kagen & Moss, 1962; Schaefer & Bayley, 1963) remain relatively stable throughout the life span.

Clearly, phenotypical differences in temperament may reflect genetic variability. However, researchers disagree over how environmental and genetic factors influence emotional development. We will briefly review four different views of temperament: Hans Eysenck, John Bowlby; Alexander Thomas, and Carroll Izard.

16.2. HANS EYSENCK

Hans Eysenck (1967, 1970) proposed that activity, physiological reactivity, and sociability form the biological substrate of two major personality dimensions: introversion-extraversion and neuroticism (emotional stability-instability). He postulated that introverts have higher tonic levels of physiological arousal than extraverts. According to this view, general activity and sociability are different manifestations of the same genetically determined trait—tonic level of physiological arousal (see Figure 16-1). Presumably, extraverts are chronically underaroused and attempt to raise their own levels of arousal by increasing their general levels of activity and through social stimulation. Conversely, introverts

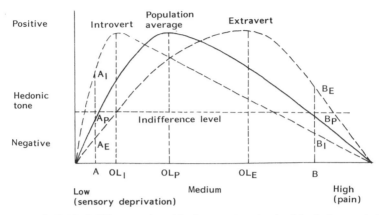

Figure 16-1. Individual differences in subjective reactions to physiological arousal. OL = optimal level; OL$_I$ = optimal level introvert; OL$_P$ = optimal level population; OL$_E$ = optimal level extravert. From "Personality and Drug Effects," H.J. Eysenck (Ed.), (p. 8) by H.J. Eysenck, 1963, in *Experiments with Drugs*, Oxford: Pergamon Press. Copyright 1963 by Pergamon Press. Reprinted by permission.

are presumably chronically overaroused and attempt to lower their arousal level by reducing their general activity level and through social withdrawal. Thus introverts may be genetically predisposed to be "stimulus avoiders," whereas extraverts are predisposed to be "stimulus seekers."

Eysenck also postulated that physiological reactivity predisposes the individual to become emotionally stable or unstable. Presumably, neurotics are hyperreactive to environmental stimuli and may actively avoid external stimuli in order to avoid producing unpleasant levels of phasic physiological activities. Conversely, emotionally stable individuals may be hyporeactive to external stimuli and thus be genetically programmed "stimulus seekers." Because tonic and phasic physiological activities are only partially yoked, two individuals with the same tonic level of physiological arousal may react quite differently to environmental stimuli. Presumably, neurotic introverts should be extreme "stimulus avoiders," whereas stable introverts should show only moderate degrees of avoidance. Conversely, stable extraverts should be extreme "stimulus seekers" and show approach behaviors to a variety of dangerous activities (e.g., skydiving) in order to raise their own physiological arousal to an enjoyable level. Although Eysenck postulates that the environment can modify the individual's specific approach or avoidance responses, he argued that the environment cannot modify an individual's basic temperament. Thus his model clearly incorporates the predetermined model of development.

Eysenck's model has been extensively tested by a large number of researchers. In general, the results of the majority of field and laboratory studies have supported Eysenck's theory (see Morris, 1979). For example, Geen (1984) found that extraverts performed better than introverts on a paired-associate learning task at high levels of background noise but performed worse than introverts at low-noise levels. Extraverts also showed lower physiological arousal than introverts at all levels of noise except extremely high or low levels of stimulation. Thus, as predicted by Eysenck's model, extraverts and introverts appeared to differ in their optimal level of arousal.

Although the empirical support for Eysenck's model appears rather impressive, it should be emphasized that a number of other studies have failed to support his theory. For example, Revelle and his associates found that measures of impulsivity predicted both the effects of circadian rhythms and of caffeine on intellectual performance, whereas measures of introversion-extraversion did not (Humphreys, Revelle, Simon, & Gilliland, 1980; Revelle, Humphreys, Simon, & Gilliland, 1980). Moreover, it should be noted that temperaments and other personality traits are not either/or characteristics but continua or dimensions. Few people are either extreme introverts or extraverts. The majority of the population are ambiverts who display a mixture of introverted and extraverted characteristics. Similarly, only a minority of the population are either extremely stable or neurotic. Most people are semineurotic and display a mixture of stable and neurotic characteristics. Inspection of the introversion–extraversion literature reveals that the Eysenck's model appears to be poor at predicting the behaviors of the "average" person, that is, semineurotic ambiverts.

16.3. JOHN BOWLBY

The probabilistic view of the development of emotions is best illustrated by John Bowlby's (1957, 1958, 1969, 1973) theory of the development of human emotional attachments. Bowlby was a psychiatrist who had been trained in the Freudian psychoanalytic tradition. In the late 1940s he was selected by the World Health Organization of the United Nations to supervise a study of the psychological effects on children of being separated from their parents. After an extensive review of the available literature and numerous clinical observations of institutionalized children, Bowlby (1951, 1953) concluded that prolonged (6 months or more) separation from parents had devastating psychological effects on children under the age of five. These children later had a much higher incidence rate of psychiatric disorders, particularly psychopathy, than children who were not separated from their parents. For example, in one study he compared the family histories of 44 emotionally disturbed children (controls) and 44 juvenile delinquents. Only 2 of the control children but 17 of the juvenile delinquents had a history of early parental separation. Moreover, 14 juvenile delinquents and none of the controls were classified as psychopaths, and 12 of the 14 psychopaths had histories of prolonged parental separation under the age of 5.

Based on his own clinical observations, Bowlby became convinced that neither the Freudian model nor Watson's conditioning model could adequately account for the effects of parental separation on emotional development. Bowlby (1957, 1958) proposed that humans are genetically programmed to form close emotional bonds with a single caretaker (usually female) during infancy. Like emotional attachments in nonhuman species, human infants' early emotional attachments serve the evolutionarily adaptive function of allowing the infant to maintain physical proximity with a source of food, warmth, and protection. He argued that although human attachment behaviors were genetically programmed to appear during maturation, the behaviors themselves were modifiable during critical periods.

In his later writings, Bowlby (1969, 1973) argued that the infant was also genetically programmed to combine attachment behaviors into hierarchical organizations of goal-directed plans at about 1 year of age. For example, a 2-year old child may attempt to gain a parent's attention by verbal signals ("Mommy," "Daddy"). If these behaviors fail, the child may then tug upon the parent's clothes. If tugging also fails, the child might resort to screaming or crying. Although different children may employ different sequences of goal-directed behaviors, a hierarchical sequence does occur.

Bowlby proposed that attachment undergoes three critical periods during early childhood. During the preattachment period (birth to 6 momths), the child indiscriminately displays attachment behaviors (clinging, crying, reaching, visual following, etc.). These responses are initially made to both animate and inanimate objects, and gradually the child directs the responses at *any* caretaker.

During the attachment period (sixth month to one year), the infant *selectively* displays attachment behaviors toward his or her primary caretaker. Bowlby argued that the selectivity of the infant's responses indicates that the infant has formed a strong emotional bond or attachment. Once this caretaker bond has formed, the infant may react with distress to the threat of separation from the caretaker. For example, the child may display mild distress at the presence of strangers (stranger anxiety) and severe distress when suddenly separated from the primary caretaker (separation anxiety).

During the postattachment period (first to fourth year) the child may display at least temporary distress at involuntary separation from his or her primary caretaker. However, the child often voluntarily detaches himself or herself to explore the environment or play with toys. As the child grows older, these voluntary detachments become gradually longer and longer, and by the end of the third year the child may readily accept substitutes (teachers, playmates, etc.) and display little or no distress at the departure of the primary caretaker. However, during periods of physical stress (illness) or psychological stress, older children (and many adults) may seek emotional support from their original caretaker. Bowlby believed that this early infant–caretaker bond allows the child to develop both a sense of independence and the ability to form close emotional attachments later in life.

What happens if during one of these three critical periods, the child is separated from the primary caretaker for prolonged periods? Bowlby argued that children under the age of 4 may permanently lose their ability to form normal attachments and, thus, may be predisposed to develop psychiatric disorders later in life. Studies of hospitalized children suggest that separation initially produces a period of extreme distress followed by a period of depression. After a period of months, the child may show disinterest when reunited with the primary caretaker. Bowlby hypothesized that these children are now prone to develop anxiety, depression, or psychopathy later in life.

Studies of preschool children have found only partial support for Bowlby's model. For example, consistent with his predictions, an infant's age at the time of separation from the parents appears to play a critical role in his or her later adjustment. Children under the age of 4 months at the time of separation do not develop the behavioral disorders characteristic of parental separation in 4- to 9-month-old infants (Yarrow & Goodwin, 1973). Numerous researchers have also documented that most children begin to display behavioral manifestation of attachment to a single caretaker (selective social smiling, separation anxiety, stranger anxiety) at about 5 or 6 months of age.

Other studies suggest that Bowlby may have underestimated the roles of dispositions and situations in infants' emotional responses. For example, infants who have had little contact with strangers are more likely to display stranger anxiety (Schaffer, 1966). Moreover, infants may display either positive or negative emotional reactions toward strangers, depending upon the strangers' age, sex, and behaviors (Brooks & Lewis, 1976).

Researchers have also questioned the role of physical separation of parent and child in later maladjustment. Prugh and Harlow (1962) found that children who remain at home with psychiatrically disturbed parents often develop more severe psychological problems than children who are separated from their parents and placed in institutions. Thus separation between children and parents may be *psychological* rather than physical. Consistent with this hypothesis, Rutter (1972) found that the psychological impact of temporary child–parent separations varies with the status of the family prior to separation. Children from relatively happy households suffer little permanent harm from brief separations. However, children from families in crises may experience more harm from brief separation than from prolonged separation.

Perhaps the most damaging evidence to Bowlby's probabilistic model is reports of the negative effects of parental separation on children *older* than 4 years. Baggett (1967) found that the effects of father absence on children under the age of 8 years varied with both the sex of the child and the cause of absence. For sons, divorce and/or desertion produced more behavioral problems than death of the father. In daughters, father absence for any cause produced an increase in behavioral problems.

Hetherington (1972) found that separations produced by divorce and by death had different long-term effects on older children. Adolescent women whose fathers were absent due to death tended to show excessive sexual anxiety and avoidance of males. Conversely, adolescent women whose fathers were absent due to divorce tended to become highly promiscuous and sexually assertive. Hetherington noted that the daughters' behaviors were almost a mirror image of their mothers' attitudes toward their ex-spouse. Widows tended to express positive attitudes toward their ex-spouse, and their daughters avoided men. Conversely, the divorcées tended to express negative attitudes, and their daughters actively approached males. A control group of adolescent women from intact families fell between these two extremes.

Cross-cultural research has also produced mixed empirical support for Bowlby's model. Across cultures, most children do form primary attachment bonds between the ages of 6 months and a year; they display separation anxiety and the like (Schaffer & Emerson, 1964; Ainsworth, 1967). However, studies of children reared with multiple caretakers have reported equivocal findings. Some studies have found that such individuals later have difficulty forming emotional attachments in adulthood (see Munroe & Munroe, 1975), whereas researchers have found that children raised with multiple caretakers display normal patterns of emotional development (Bettelheim, 1969; Leiderman & Leiderman, 1974).

16.4. ALEXANDER THOMAS

The plasticity model of development is based on the assumption that the environment and genotype continuously interact in a number of complex ways. For example, an adult treats an irritable infant differently than a quiet infant. Although both the infant's and adult's temperament may have a strong genetic predisposition, the interactions between the infant and adult may radically modify both biology and behaviors. For example, infants that are born prematurely often have abnormal social interactions during infancy. Relative to full-term infants, premature infants' cries are more physiological arousing and more aversive to adults. Premature infants are also more difficult to pacify than full-term infants. Not surprisingly, adults tend to hold premature infants further away from their bodies, touch and talk to the infant less, and are less likely to hold them face-to-face (Goldberg, 1979). Thus, regardless of the infant's genetic temperament, the physical immaturity associated with prematurity tends to disrupt infant–parent interactions. A number of theorists, including Hebb (1953), Lehrman (1953), and Schneirla (1956), have argued that such environmental interactions may directly modify the biology of the developing infant within the range proscribed by its phenotype.

One the most commonly cited plasticity models of human emotional development was proposed by Thomas and his associates after a series of longitudinal studies of children from birth through childhood (Thomas, Chess, Birch, & Hertizig, 1960; Thomas, Chess, Birch, Hertizig, & Korn, 1963; Thomas, Chess, & Birch, 1968, 1970; Thomas & Chess, 1977). They identified nine distinct behavioral characteristics (such as adaptability to environmental changes) that appear to define a distinct behavioral profile or temperament within the first few weeks of life. Children's temperaments tended to fall into four distinct clusters: "easy," "slow to warm up," "difficult," and "other." In one study, about 65% of middle-class infants fell into the first three categories (Thomas *et al.*, 1968). Easy infants (40%) were characterized by extremely regular biological rhythms (hunger, sleep, etc.), positive approach to novel stimuli, very adaptable to environmental change, and generally displayed positive moods. Slow-to-warm-up infants (15%) were characterized by low-to-moderate activity levels, initial withdrawal from novel stimuli, moderate behavioral reactions, slow adaptation to environmental change, and displayed slightly negative moods. Difficult infants (10%) present a challenge to any parent. They are characterized by highly irregular biological rhythms, withdrawal from novel stimuli, slow adaptability, intense behavioral reactions, and negative moods.

Consistent with a predetermined view of development, these temperament profiles tended to stay relatively stable throughout childhood. Thus difficult infants often grew up to become difficult 10-year-olds. Thomas, however, rejected the predetermined view that these temperaments are "fixed" and argued that, within limits, environmental factors can modify a child's basic temperament. For example, approximately 70% of the difficult infants later developed behavioral disorders by 17 years of age. However, 30% of the difficult infants did *not* develop later problems. Moreover, about 18% of the easy infants also later developed behavioral disorders. Although temperament predisposes the infant to specific styles of parent–child interactions, parents clearly can and do modify their children's emotional reactions by modifying their child-rearing practices to match the specific child's temperament.

Thomas argued that the range of environmental modifications of temperament are limited by the individual's genotype and that under stress, many children "regress" back to their earlier temperament. For example, a 10-year-old girl named Grace was apparently quite well adjusted until she was transferred to a new school. To the surprise of her parents, Grace suddenly became acutely anxious and fearful. When her longitudinal observational file was examined, Thomas noted that Grace had previously shown strong withdrawal reactions to novel stimuli from infancy through the second grade (Thomas *et al.*, 1968).

The results of other longitudinal studies of infants generally support Thomas's view that within the limits prescribed by genotype, temperament may be relatively stable from birth into adulthood (see Schaffer & Emerson, 1964; Stone, Smith, & Murphy, 1973). However, it should also be emphasized that in Thomas's and in other studies, a sizable minority of children show clear changes in temperament during development.

16.5. CARROLL IZARD

Izard's (1971, 1977) differential emotion theory is difficult to classify. Some aspects of his model are identical to the Darwinian-oriented models discussed previously in Chapter 13. For example, both Izard and Ekman postulate that feedback from emotional facial responses simultaneously triggers autonomic responses and conscious emotional states. Izard and Ekman also agree that an infant's genetically programmed emotional facial expressions are later modified by culturally prescibed display rules. Similarly, Izard and Tomkins agree that, although drives (e.g., pain) and emotions (e.g., sadness) are distinct psychological states, emotions may function as drives and vice versa.

Although Izard's theory might appear to be "another materialistic feedback model," he postulated that cognitions and emotions may interact in a reciprocal fashion. Thus Izard's model shares many of the features of the interactionistic models discussed in Chapter 15.

Izard (1977) argued that 10 primary emotions are found across cultures: anger-rage, contempt-scorn, disgust-revulsion, distress-anguish, fear-terror, guilt, interest-excitement, joy, shame-shyness, and surprise-startle. To clarify the distinctions between drives, reflexes, and motives, he has substituted the term *sadness-dejection* for *distress-anguish* and *surprise-astonishment* for *surprise-startle* in his more recent papers. Each of these fundamental emotions is assumed to have three genetically determined components: a conscious feeling, a facial/postural expression, and neural substrate. Thus, a fundamental feeling such as anger, the facial postural expression of anger, the concordance between the feeling and the expression of anger, the neural circuits producing the physiological pattern of anger, and the amount of stimulation needed to elicit anger (biological threshold) are all presumably genetically determined.

Given the multiple interpretation of the term *innate*, it might appear reasonable to ask whether Izard's view of emotions is predetermined, probabilistic, or plastic. In the case of Izard's theory, a more relevant question is, *"which* components of emotion are predetermined, probabilistic, or plastic?"* Specifically, he postulated that both the feelings and the neural substrate of the primary emotions are invariant (predetermined) across the life span. Emotional expression, the concordance between feelings and expression, and biological thresholds, however, may change radically during development and, thus, are presumably plastic.

Izard proposed that emotional development consists of a complex interaction between the maturation of neural excitatory and inhibitory mechanisms, social experiences, and cognitive development. For example, specific emotions may appear at different times during infancy due to maturation alone. However, once infants display a specific emotion expression such as anger, their caretakers can then respond, positively or negatively, to their emotional states. Through socialization, the infant gradually learns to inhibit some of his or her emotional expressions and, thus, learns to at least partially dissociate facial expressions and feelings. Although such dissociations become highly overlearned responses, the individual may regress during intense emotional states and display prototypical facial expressions at any point during the life span.

The dissociation of feelings and expressions raises the thorny issue of how can the effect (feelings) occur in the absence of cause (facial response)? Izard postulates that three different mechanisms may trigger feelings when facial expressions are suppressed: (a) brief or anticipatory motor responses, (b) motor feedforward commands, and (c) the memory of facial feedback associated with specific emotional states. As discussed in Chapter 15, a feedforward explanation may account for the mismatch between facial expressions and emotional states observed in emotional lability patients.

Izard proposed that learning associations between primary emotions are the second major trend in emotional development. Specifically, the 10 fundamental emotions can be combined in pairs to form 45 dyadic mixed or blended emotions, in triads to form 120 triadic emotions, and so on. Emotions such as anxiety, depression, and love presumably represent a complex combination of primary emotions. Moreover, the composition of such "mixed" emotions may vary with development. For example, 10- and 11-year-old children report that when they experienced depression, feelings of anger are most salient, followed by feelings of sadness (Blumberg & Izard, 1985, 1986). However, adults report that feelings of sadness are primary during depression, and feelings of anger, guilt, and shame tend to be secondary (Izard, 1972). Thus children's and adults' subjective experiences of depression do not appear to be identical.

A third major trend in emotional development is learning associations between emotions and motives. Each fundamental emotion may be paired with specific drives to produce unique emotional-motivational states such as sexual excitement or sexual guilt. Similarly, "mixed" emotions can be combined with drives to produce complex emotional-motivational reactions.

Learning associations between emotions and cognitions is a fourth major trend in emotional development. Emotion–cognition associations may serve a variety of functions. First, cognitions may act as coping mechanisms that allow the individual to terminate his or her emotional responses. Thus the emotion–cognition association may function as a negative feedback loop. Second, cognitions may act as a positive feedback loop and amplify the ongoing emotional state. For example, fear may trigger specific fear-associated cognitions that, in turn, amplify fear into terror. Third, cognitions may trigger related emotional states. Depending on the individual's prior experiences, fear-related cognitions may trigger shame rather than terror. Fourth, emotion-cognitive structures may represent unique subjective states such as admiration or bewilderment. Fifth, emotion-induced cognitions may trigger complex memory clusters (attitudes, beliefs, values, etc.).

Although genotype may limit the impact of socialization experiences, Izard postulated that learning plays a key role in emotional development. Frequent repetition of a situation that elicits a given emotion may predispose the individual to experience a specific set of emotions, emotion-related drives, and emotion-related cognitions. Thus experience may play a critical role in the development of (a) emotional traits such as depression, (b) motivational traits such as erotophilia, and (c) global personality traits such as extroversion (Hyson & Izard, 1985).

Izard (1977) argued that due to the complex network of associations between emotions, between emotions and cognitions, and between emotions and drives, emotions play a key role in motivating and organizing adults' personality processes and social behaviors. Thus emotions should be viewed as dynamic components of personality rather than as reflexivelike responses.

In general, Izard's model is consistent with the results of both cross-cultural and developmental studies of emotional expression (see Izard, 1980; Izard & Malatesta, 1987). Moreover, his model can account for many of the apparently contradictory findings of laboratory and clinical studies of striate muscle activity during emotions. However, it should be noted that two major empirical findings are difficult to reconcile with Izard's model.

First, repressors display exaggerated facial and autonomic responses to emotional events, yet deny experiencing negative feelings. Similarly, conversion reaction patients display anxiety-related physical symptoms (blindness, deafness, paralysis, etc.) but deny experiencing anxiety. In both cases, physiological feedback is present, but the emotional experience is absent. Although Izard (1977) conceded that such dissociations between physiological responses and feelings do occur, he failed to specify how or why such extreme dissociations develop.

Second, as discussed in the preceding chapters, the expression or suppression of a given emotion may produce a baffling array of psychophysiological disorders in different individuals. For example, repetitive anger may lead to high blood pressure in one individual, to migraine headaches in a second individual, to ulcers in a third. Although Izard's conceptual framework could be expanded to account for such individual differences, the current version of his theory offers only a vague explanation of the development of psychophysiological disorders.

In summary, the temperament models provide a unique perspective on the psychobiology of emotions. Unlike most models of emotion, the temperament models assume that individual differences in emotionality are the norm rather than the exception. Moreover, the temperament models emphasize that genetic variability in physiological reactions may be to some degree modified by experiences during socialization and vice versa.

SUGGESTED READINGS

Izard, C. *The psychology of emotions.* New York: Plenum Press, in press.

   Represents the most current version of Izard's model of emotion.

Morris, L. W. *Extraversion and introversion: An interactional perspective.* New York: Halsted Press, 1979.

   A comprehensive review of the empirical validity of Eysenck's model of personality.

Thomas, A., Chess, S., & Birch, H. G. The origin of personality. *Scientific American,* 1970, 223(2), 102–109.

   A highly readable report on the stability of temperament during childhood and adolescence.

17

Beyond Tautologies

Authors differ widely on the type of content that they view appropriate in a final chapter of a book on a scientific topic. Some authors simply stop abruptly after the last topic and leave the task of thrashing out what it all means to the reader. I personally find this approach disappointing. After investing time and energy into reading a book, I expect the author to at least speculate on the future of the field.

Some authors use their final chapters to synthesize material presented in previous chapters. Although such summaries may appear objective, they inevitably reflect the authors' metaphysical and theoretical biases. By definition, scientific truths are probabilistic and not absolute. Hence the decision about whether any single observation is empirically true or an artifact is inherently a subjective judgment and not a pure deduction. Moreover, any single empirical finding may have multiple plausible explanations. Thus when we attempt to summarize a large number of research findings, deciding "what's important" is a highly subjective process.

Other authors use their final chapters to promote their own theoretical views on emotion. This approach is also inherently biased. Textbooks often present a highly distorted picture of the process of constructing scientific theories. Presumably, scientists coldly and objectively review the available information on a given phenomenon and derive specific data-based conclusions through inductive logic. These conclusions are then organized into a working model of the phenomenon from which testable hypotheses can be derived through deductive logic. The new information generated through hypothesis testing is then used to modify the existing theory. Although this idealized description of theory construction accurately mirrors the deductive-inductive thought processes involved, many theorists confess that their own models were constructed in a much less formal and logical manner.

Deductive logic is based on the assumption that *all* the relevant information is currently available. However, scientists frequently have only very partial information available on any given phenomenon and are forced to make numerous assumptions in an attempt to fill in the gaps in our current knowledge. Thus scientists deductions and inductions are often closer to educated guesses than logical deductions or inferences.

Suppose you are browsing at a flea market and notice a shoebox marked "500-piece jigsaw puzzle." Out of curiousity, you purchase the box. When you arrive home and spread out its contents, you discover that you have only 378 puzzle pieces. You have no guarantee that all of the pieces are from the same puzzle or that the original puzzle did not have 1,000 pieces. All you are certain of is that some unknown number of pieces are missing. Moreover, you have no idea of what the finished puzzle should look like. How do you proceed?

The simplest solution is to conclude that because the puzzle is incomplete, it is also irrelevant. Unfortunately, this approach has been adopted by a number of contemporary psychologists. A surprisingly large number of theories of human development, learning, memory, motivation, neuropsychology, perception, personality, problem solving, or social psychology treat humans as emotionless robots whose behaviors can be explained with elaborate flow charts of "cold" cognitive processes. Can we explain human behaviors without including "hot" cognitive processes? Perhaps. But are we willing to accept the psychopath as the prototypical human?

Alternatively, you may decide to accept the intellectual challenge of assembling the pieces of the puzzle that you do have. One potentially fruitful strategy for completing the puzzle of human emotions is to first look for a single cluster of pieces that had been left assembled by a previous owner and then try to find additional pieces that match. This is the essence of the theory-extension approach. For example, James and numerous other theorists have attempted to "fix" Darwin's model of emotion.

The major advantage of the theory-extension approach is that existing theories provide useful conceptual frameworks for organizing at least some small section of the empirical literature. For example, Fonagy and Calloway (1986) found that both anxiety- and depression-inducing tasks lead to increased spontaneous swallowing rates in normal females and males. Although their findings are interesting, without some form of theoretical framework to explain *why* swallowing rates should increase with emotional arousal, these findings are as trival as a single piece of a jigsaw puzzle.

The major disadvantage of the theory-extension approach is that we may end up with a coherent picture of only a small fragment of the puzzle. That is, we may derive a clear explanation of humor, yet be unable to relate humor to other emotions.

A second potentially fruitful strategy for assembling the puzzle of emotions would be to locate multiple clusters of pieces and then try to fit these clusters together into larger units. This is essentially a griffin approach to theory construction. A griffin is a mythical animal built from parts of different animals. Traditionally, a griffin was depicted as having the head and wings of an eagle and the body of a lion. However, how much eagle and how much lion is needed to be a griffin is debatable. Moreover, if we are willing to go beyond the stereotype of a griffin, our mythical creature can have the head of a bull, the wings of an eagle, the body of a lion, the legs of a horse, or any other components that we choose. The griffin approach of theory construction is to borrow parts from different theories and attempt to fuse the parts into a new model. As discussed in Chapters 13 and 15, Ekman's, Leventhal's, and Tomkins's models all represent griffins composed primarily of parts of James's and Darwin's theories.

The major advantage of the griffin approach is that *if* we can detach empirically valid components from specific models, our new hybrid theory may have greater empirical validity than any of the original models. The major disadvantage of the griffin approach is that we may accidently construct a nonviable beast that collapses under the weight of its own logical contradictions. For example, Darwin emphasized the role of learning in human emotional behaviors, whereas James minimized the role of learning in emotional states. Any viable fusion of Darwin's and James's theories requires recognizing this logical contradiction and explicitly excising it.

A third potentially fruitful strategy is to lay out all the assembled and loose puzzle pieces and try to guess the content of the completed picture. Is it an icecream truck? A mountain lake? Such a Gestalt (wholistic) approach is also common in emotion research. Based on the available data, numerous theorists have attempted to construct comprehensive models of human emotions. For example, as discussed previously in Chapter 12, Wybrow and his associates have attempted to integrate the empirical findings on the roles of biochemistry, genetics, neurology, and psychosocial stress in depression.

The major advantage of the wholistic approach is that it provides us with a large conceptual framework in which to organize data and to generate new hypotheses. The major disadvantage of wholistic models is that they often unintentionally blur the distinction between empirical observation and inference. For example, the empirical observation that "70% of chronically depressed patients respond to drug A" may imply that "70% of chronically depressed patients have a deficit or excess in neurotransmitter X." However, any number of other plausible explanations may also account for the effects of drug A. Until a change in neurotransmitter-X levels are documented, it is a hypothesis and not a fact.

A fourth potentially fruitful approach is to systematically sort the available pieces on the basis of their stimulus characteristics (color, shape, etc.) and then use this information as a guide for assembling the puzzle. For example, a single straight edge usually indicates that a piece is a component of the puzzle's border. Assembling all of the available border pieces may, in turn, provide clues about how to organize the remaining pieces, that is, the blue pieces appear to belong in the lower left corner. This empirical approach is informally referred to as *bootstrapping* after the phrase *pull yourself up by your bootstraps* (i.e., improving your economic position through your own efforts). In more formal terms, bootstrapping is referred to as the hypothetico-deductive method of theory construction. As discussed in Chapter 15, Schwartz's models are excellent examples of the bootstrap approach. Obviously, the theory-extension, griffin, and wholistic approaches all also involve bootstrapping to at least some degree.

The greatest strength of the bootstrap approach is that the empirical findings dictate the characteristics of our current theory. Thus, by definition, our theory is empirically valid. Paradoxically, this is also the greatest weakness of the bootstrap approach. By limiting our model to the "known" facts, we inevitably limit the types of predictions we can derive from our model. That is, what we know limits what we can learn. Moreover, because our bootstrap theory is gradually evolving to accommodate new research findings, we risk creating a chameleonlike theory that is virtually impossible to refute.

Fundamental disagreement among researchers over the best strategy for assembling the puzzle of emotions has led to the mass proliferation of theories of emotions. Readers who were overwhelmed by the sheer number of theories presented throughout this book may be shocked to discover that they have been exposed to only a small sample of contemporary theories. Without exaggeration, I can name over a hundred theories of human emotions. Such theoretical plurality is a welcome relief from the monolithic dominance of behaviorist and psychoanalytic models during the 1920s through the 1950s. Different theoretical perspectives encourage intellectual debate and force us to examine different data bases.

Unfortunately, theoretical plurality has also reduced emotion research to an intellectual Tower of Babel. Different researchers often use the same terms (anger, stress, etc.) to denote entirely different physiological or psychological processes. Conversely, researchers may use different terms (augmenter, monitor, sensitizer, etc.) to refer to similar phenomena. Such semantic disagreements have often led to bitter theoretical debates about relatively trival issues, for example, "should startle be classified as an emotion or a reflex?"

Given the current theory-dominated state of the field, there is probably little to be gained by adding one more theory of emotion. Accordingly, I have decided to spare the reader my own personal model of emotions and, instead, offer a general summary of the available empirical data. The reader is forewarned that this summary is by no means objective but rather reflects my own metaphysical and theoretical views.

17.1. THE PUZZLE OF EMOTIONS

Regardless of which strategy we employ to assemble the puzzle of emotions, the first task is to identify what pieces we already have and what pieces are missing. Numerous pieces of the puzzle of emotion are scattered throughout the anthropological, medical, psychiatric, and psychological literatures. These findings tend to fall into three pairs of categories: biological variability-response stereotypy; cultural variability-commonality, and psychological dispositions-situations.

17.1.1. Biological Variability

Most contemporary theories of emotion share the simplistic and erroneous assumption that because all humans are similar anatomically, they are similar physiologically. However, regardless of the organ system studied, biological variability is the rule rather than the exception. Both tonic and phasic physiological activities vary as a function of age, race, or sex. Moreover, within any group, large differences in both anatomy and physiology have been observed (Williams, 1967).

As discussed in Chapters 3 and 12, biological variability is commonly observed at a biochemical level. For example, premenopausal women tend to have much lower adrenal stress hormone responses than their male peers. The stress hormone responses of postmenopausal women, however, are indistinguishable from their male peers. Within any given age and sex, there are also marked individual differences in stress hormone responses. Such complex patterns of between- and within-group differences are also commonly observed in sex hormones and in neurotransmitter metabolites.

There are a number of plausible rival interpretations of the observed variability in biochemistry. First, biochemical variability may represent genetic variability. Second, biochemical variability may be due to a variety of transient biological factors (diet, drug use, health, menstrual cycle, sleep–wake cycle, etc.). Third, biochemical variability may be due to environmental history. For example, Selye's research suggests that prior exposure to stressors may permanently alter an individual's hormonal stress responses. Fourth, biochemical variability may reflect individual differences in cognitive coping strategies.

Biological variability has also been documented with individual organs and organ systems. As discussed in Chapters 4 through 11, between- and within-group differences in tonic and phasic physiological activities are usually observed during emotional states. For example, Type A individuals display much larger increases in heart rate than Type B individuals in competitive situations. Again, there are multiple plausible interpretations of such findings.

As discussed in Chapter 16, between- and within-group differences have been found in global physiological arousal. Specifically, individuals differ in the amount of stimulation needed to trigger an emotion and in their degree of global physiological arousal during emotional states. Because such individual differences in emotionality have been observed in newborns and appear to be relatively stable during childhood, researchers have traditionally assumed that individual differences in temperament are due to genetic variability. However, a newborn is not "new" in any sense of the term. During pregnancy, the maternal and fetal bloodstreams interact via the placenta. Many chemicals ingested by the mother (diet, drugs, etc.) and biochemicals produced by the mother's behaviors (emotional stress, exercise, etc.) may pass directly to the fetus. Given that injecting pregnant rats with male sex hormones directly alters the "sex" of their offsprings' brains, it appears reasonable to suspect that other prenatal factors may alter the offsprings' temperaments.

Regardless of its cause or causes, the existence of biological variability has a number of important implications for theories of emotion. First, we must abandon the simplistic assumption that because all people are similar biologically, all people should display similar physiological reactions during emotional states. Obviously, our premise is empirically false, that is, all people are not "built the same." Hence, according to the law of initial values, it is much more reasonable to predict marked individual differences in physiological reactions during emotional states.

Second, biological variability may produce consistent but idiosyncratic patterns of physiological activity in the same individual during emotional states. Suppose an individual is genetically predisposed to secrete large amounts of adrenal hormones (cortisol, epinephrine, and norepinephrine) in response to stressors. Acute elevations in epinephrine and norepinephrine would produce marked increases in cardiovascular arousal. Elevations in cortisol and feedback from the cardiovascular system, however, would signal CNS control systems to restore homeostasis by inhibiting global sympathetic arousal. During emotional states, this individual would display clear cardiovascular arousal but relatively little change in other physiological systems (EDA, respiration, etc.). Such individual stereotypy has been repeatedly documented in samples of healthy subjects, medical patients, and psychiatric patients.

Third, biological variability may predispose individuals to develop different psychiatric disorders. For example, as discussed in Chapter 12, about 20% of healthy individuals experience panic attacks in response to sodium lactate injections. These susceptible individuals may be predisposed to later develop agoraphobia and/or panic disorders. Similarly, individuals differ in their susceptibility to psychophysiological disorders. Type A individuals have a higher incidence rate of heart disease than Type B individuals.

17.1.2. Biological Response Stereotypy

Despite biological variability, some emotional states are accompanied by stereotyped patterns of physiological activity. For example, both clinical and laboratory studies have consistently found that a small number of emotions (anger, fear, happiness, and sadness) may be differentiated by patterns of autonomic activity (BP, EDA, heart rate, stomach activity, etc.). Similarly, research on human facial reactions during emotional states suggest that at least six emotional states (anger, disgust, fear, happiness, sadness, and surprise) may be characterized by distinct facial muscle patterns.

At least three additional emotions—guilt, humor and embarrassment—may also be accompanied by stereotypical patterns of physiological activity. As discussed in Chapter 6, guilt is associated with breath holding (respiration blocks), whereas humor is associated with respiration irregularities (chuckling, laughing, etc.). Because respiration is at least partially yoked with other physiological systems (EDA, cardiovascular activity, etc.), both guilt and humor may produce distinct patterns of physiological arousal in the majority of individuals. Similarly, embarrassment is accompanied by vasodilation of the face and/or upper chest and by spasmodic bladder contractions (i.e., spurting urination) in at least a large minority of individuals.

The joint occurrence of biological variability and response stereotypy may appear illogical. However, individual stereotypy and response stereotypy are *not* mutually exclusive. Individual stereotypy is not truely idiosyncratic because clusters of individuals display the same patterns of physiological arousal during a given emotional state. Moreover, individual differences are often quantitative rather than qualitative. Specifically, individuals often differ in the intensity of stereotyped responses rather than in their overall patterns of physiological activity. For example, individuals differ in their predisposition to humor and in the intensity of their emotional displays. Two individuals, who rate the same joke as equally funny, may display marked differences in the respiration patterns. One individual may chuckle softly, whereas the second individual may laugh until he or she cries. However, both individuals are displaying the *same* stereotypical response, that is, respiration irregularities.

17.1.3. Cultural Variability

The anthropological literature is laced with hundreds of anecdotal references to cultural differences in emotional displays and in self-reports of emotional states. Thus individuals from different cultures presumably act and feel differently during emotional states. Yet, paradoxically, the cross-cultural literature on emotions is extremely sparse (Izard, 1980). That is, we have relatively few direct comparisons of the emotional reactions of individuals from different cultures. This curious state of affairs can be traced to three primary causes.

First, anthropological research usually involves a Western observer studying an isolated non-Western community. Given that the observer and the observed have radically different cultural backgrounds, it is not surprising that anthropological reports tend to focus on cultural differences and minimize cultural similarities. Behaviors that are common to both the observer's and subjects' cultures such as smiling when being introduced to a stranger are often unintentionally ignored. Conversely, behaviors that are novel to Westerners (e.g., smiling in anger) are often reported.

Second, many cultures define emotions as private events that should be concealed from even family members. The presence of a stranger (the anthropologist) may merely increase the salience of such display rules. Thus otherwise highly emotional individuals may appear inscrutable to the observer. For example, Eibl-Eibesfeldt (1970) noted that anthropological films of non-Western individuals have rarely recorded spontaneous emotional reactions. As soon as the individuals realized they were being photographed, they (a) shifted to a blank facial expression ("poker face"), (b) acted embarrassed, or (c) exaggerated ("hammed") their facial expressions and gestures. As discussed in Chapter 10, all three of these acting styles are also commonly employed by Western subjects when they are instructed to attempt to conceal their emotional states.

Third, prior to the 1950s, anthropologists did not consider emotions *per se* to be an important research topic (Levy, 1984). Traditionally, anthropologists defined culture as an abstract set of customs, rituals, and values. Thus theoretical emphasis was placed on the abstract characteristics of the group rather than on the everyday behaviors of the individuals within the group. Accordingly, cultural differences in emotional displays were often cited merely as examples of cultural differences in social norms.

Obviously, older anthropological reports of cultural variability in emotions should be interpreted with caution. Since the 1950s, anthropologists have attempted to systematically study the influence of culture on emotions and have employed a number of sophisticated research techniques (hidden cameras, linguistic analysis, observational checklists, etc.) to provide less biased cross-cultural comparisons. However, the reader should be aware that emotions are extremely difficult to study in a cross-cultural context and, thus, even well-designed experiments may be biased. For example, Pancheri (1975) compared samples of normal and psychiatrically depressed Italians and Swiss. Each group was administered a standardized test of psychological adjustment (the MMPI) in their native languages. No differences were observed between the two samples of normal individuals, and both groups of psychiatric patients had the same abnormal profile of scores on the MMPI. However, the Italian psychiatric patients' scores were much higher than their Swiss peers. Thus some individuals diagnosed as mentally ill in Switzerland would apparently be labeled normal in Italy and vice versa.

Despite methodological limitations, anthropological studies have documented a wide variety of cross-cultural differences in human emotional behaviors. For example, the meaning attributed to specific gestures varies from culture to culture. A clenched fist with either an upraised thumb, an upraised middle finger, or upraised middle and index finger (reverse peace or victory sign), each represent a vulgar reference to sexual intercourse in Sardinia, America, and England, respectively (Morris, 1977). Such deliberate nonverbal messages are highly culturally specific and are referred to as *emblems* (Ekman, 1980).

As discussed previously in Chapter 10, a small set of spontaneous facial expressions, postures, and vocalizations can be observed in all cultures. However, social norms concerning whether such spontaneous emotional behaviors should be concealed or displayed vary radically from culture to culture. For example, Chinese women were traditionally encouraged to conceal displays of sadness and happiness but to exaggerate displays of grief (Klineberg, 1938).

Cultures also differ in the complexity of their verbal labels for emotional states. Levy (1984) reported that Tahitians use a number of different words to discriminate between various types of anger but have only vague verbal labels for guilt and sadness. Other anthropological studies have found that verbal labels for specific emotional states (disgust, depression, etc.) may be completely absent in some cultures (Plutchick, 1980). According to Whorf's (1956) *linguistic relativity hypothesis*, individuals from such cultures may be incapable of experiencing these emotional states. That is, an individual who grows up not knowing the meaning of fear may literally be incapable of experiencing fear as an distinct emotional state.

Research on Western samples of alexithymics would appear to at least partially support Whorf's hypothesis. Alexithymics' verbal labels for emotions are inappropriate, limited, or nonexistent, and they habitually mislabel their emotional arousal as illness (Neill & Sandifer, 1982). Such mislabeling of emotions has also been reported in other cultures. For example, Tahitians display alexithymiclike reactions in situations such as death of a loved one that would elicit sadness in individuals from Western cultures (Levy, 1984).

Research on psychopaths and repressors, however, would appear to refute Whorf's hypothesis. Psychopaths claim that they do not experience any emotional states, and repressors selectively deny negative emotional states. Although both psychopaths and repressors may have the same emotional vocabulary as other members of their culture, their emotional labels are disassociated from their physiological reactions and overt behaviors. Thus psychopaths may report experiencing guilt but show no physiological responses and later repeat the same antisocial behaviors (Hare, 1985). Conversely, a repressor may deny experiencing guilt but display the stereotypical pattern of physiological arousal associated with guilt (Davidson, 1983b).

Cross-cultural research on the perception of external objects would also appear to refute Whorf's hypothesis. Heider and other researchers have demonstrated that cross-cultural language differences exert little influence on the perception of colors (Berlin & Kay, 1969; Heider, 1972; Heider & Oliver, 1972; Rosch, 1973). Specifically, even members of cultures whose languages have only two words for colors (light and dark) can correctly identify the same hues (blues, greens, reds, yellows, etc.) as individuals from Western cultures.

Unfortunately, the role of linguistic differences in the perception of emotional states has not been extensively studied cross-culturally. Ekman and Friesen (1971) found that New Guinea tribesmen could accurately match emotional facial expressions with stories that represented anger, disgust, happiness, and sadness but had difficulty discriminating the facial expressions of fear and surprise. The authors noted that individuals in this culture frequently label fear-inducing events as *surprising*. Whether these tribesmen experience fear and surprise as one emotion or as two distinct emotional states is difficult to determine.

Culturally prescibed verbal labels for emotions reflect social norms concerning what *feelings* are socially appropriate in a given situation (Hochschild, 1979 1983). Specifically, in our cultures, individuals are not expected to merely *act* happy at weddings; they are expected to *feel* happy. Both display and feeling rules are not idiosyncratic social norms but rather expressions of global attitudes about the individual's role in the culture. For example, cultures that stereotype males as brave explicitly threaten social disapproval for violating the social norms. That is, a male's emotional display or self-report of fear is not merely defined as inappropriate; it is also labeled *unmasculine*. Thus, even if a male consciously experiences fear, he may deliberately attempt to deceive others to avoid social censure.

Culturally acquired attitudes may also alter the individual's conscious experience of specific emotional states. In our culture, many women report highly ambivalent attitudes toward sexual excitement. Although they may privately enjoy sexual excitement, they may also feel that too much enjoyment threatens their femininity. Accordingly, ego defense mechanisms may block sexual excitement from consciousness, and the individual may either deny sexual arousal or misperceive her physiological arousal as a socially acceptable emotion, for example, disgust. Alternatively, the individual may have learned to associate disgust and sexual arousal through social conditioning. Thus, self-reports of experiencing disgust to sexual stimuli could represent accurate perceptions rather than misperceptions of one's emotional state.

Barring the invention of some new "mind-reading" technology, it is impossible to discriminate between deceit, denial, misperception, and social learning. As discussed previously in Chapter 6, polygraph exams have, at best, an average accuracy rate of only 80% to 90%. Hence, we can never be absolutely certain whether a given individual is consciously being deceitful or honest. Moreover, even if we can document that the individual is displaying a physiological pattern associated with fear or sexual arousal in other people, we have no guarantee that the individual is consciously experiencing a similar emotional state.

Cultural differences in display rules, feeling rules, and verbal labels all represent cultural variability in beliefs about emotions. Izard (1971) found that individuals from 10 different cultures tended to respond differently to simple questions such as "which emotion do you understand best or least?" Such findings suggest that cultures may vary on the relative importance placed on specific emotions. For example, the belief systems of some cultures may emphasize guilt (self-disapproval), whereas the belief systems of other cultures may emphasize shame (social disapproval).

17.1.4. Cultural Commonality

Anthropological reports of cultural variability in emotions tend to obscure our common humanity. All humans belong to the same species. Anatomically, physiologically, and psychologically, we have more in common with each other than with other animals. Both biological variability and response stereotypy have been observed in all cultures tested.

Regardless of culture, humans display biological variability. Within every culture, individuals differ in their emotional displays and self-reports of emotional states. Even in cultures that encourage aggression, some individuals are nonaggressive relative to their peers. Conversely, cultures that strongly disapprove of aggression still produce some highly aggressive individuals (Whiting & Child, 1953).

Across cultures, humans display response stereotypy during emotional states. For example, despite cultural differences in emblems and display rules, individuals from different parts of the planet spontaneously display and can correctly identify at least six specific facial expressions associated with distinct emotional states (Ekman, 1973; Izard, 1980). Obviously, it is debatable whether such universal facial expressions are (a) the cause of specific emotional states, (b) biological markers (occur in parallel with emotional states), or (c) triggered by specific emotional states. Nevertheless, six common facial expressions have been observed in a variety of Western and non-Western cultures. Whether other facial expressions or physiological responses are also found universally across cultures is currently an open question.

Numerous authors have argued that anthropological reports of cultural variability in emotions may also mask psychological universals as well as biological universals. Regardless of nationality, humans share a number of common experiences throughout the life span. Freud noted that we are all weaned, toilet-trained, and forced to deal with cultural norms on sexuality and death. Moreover, cross-cultural studies suggest that cognitive, emotional, language, personality, and social development in children occur at about the same rates in all cultures. Given these psychosocial commonalities, why do adults from different cultures appear to differ so radically in their emotional responses?

Edgerton (1971) postulated that cultural differences in emotional behaviors and beliefs may be traced to occupation rather than culture *per se*. Specifically, display rules, feeling rules, and beliefs about emotions vary with social status (socioeconomic class, sex, etc.) within any given culture. For example, our cultural belief that emotional displays are, at best, childish is reflected in our folk myths that poor people of both sexes and women in all socioeconomic classes are more emotional than the rest of the population. Although such beliefs reflect prevailing social stereotypes and prejudices, they may also reflect social realities. For example, individuals whose survival depends upon herding and/or stealing livestock from other tribes should value occupationally adaptive characteristics such as bravery, independence, sexual infidelity, tolerance of pain, and social prestige ("face"). Conversely, due to different occupational demands, farmers should encourage more communally oriented beliefs such as amiability, industriousness, manipulative and verbal skills, and sexual fidelity.

To test his hypothesis, Edgerton selected four East African tribes (Hehe, Kamba, Pokot, and Sebei) whose members included both farmers and herders. At least 30 adult female and 30 adult male representatives of each occupation were tested in each tribe. Each subject was given a structured interview and a battery of projective tests designed to elicit information about the subject's beliefs. For example, subjects were asked questions like "What is the worst thing that can happen to a man (woman)?" Edgerton found that across tribes, herders shared a common belief system that stressed affection, brutality, depression, direct aggression, guilt-shame, and hostility toward the opposite sex. In contrast, the farmers in all four tribes reported a common belief system that emphasized anxiety, fear, hatred, and jealousy of wealth.

Such occupationally related variability in beliefs about emotions can also be observed in our own culture. Hochschild (1979, 1983) argued that many occupations demand that the individual display specific bogus emotions. For example, an employer may demand superficial or surface acting by requiring all his or her salesclerks to mindlessly chant, "Have a nice day." Some occupations, however, demand that the individual's bogus emotional display appear convincing to others (deep acting). For example, stewardesses are instructed to act elated and to suppress all displays of fear in order to convince passengers that nothing can possibly go wrong with the flight. Conversely, bill collectors are encouraged to fake anger/hostility and suppress empathy with the debtor.

Hochschild argued that occupational demands for emotional acting varied with socioeconomic class and sex. In manufacturing industries, middle-class occupations (factory manager) require much deep acting, whereas blue-collar jobs (factory worker) do not. Service occupations such as salesclerk tend to require at least surface acting. However, service occupations stereotyped as feminine are more likely to demand deep acting than occupations stereotyped as masculine. Approximately 81% of female service occupations (e.g., hairdresser, stewardess) but only 38% of male service occupations (baggage porters, barbers, etc.) demand that the individual exert some degree of emotional labor by portraying specific emotions for the benefit of the employer.

Both Edgerton's and Hochschild's findings raise the interesting question of to what degree are cultural beliefs about emotions yoked to the current socioeconomic structure of a given culture. For example, as late as the 1960s, the Miyanmin tribe in Papua New Guinea were politely described as Stone Age by anthropologists and impolitely described as fierce cannibals by members of neighboring tribes. Traditionally, the Miyanmin's existence depended on slash-and-burn agriculture and on hunting small game and an occasional neighbor. When the soil and game around a village were depleted, the Miyanmin simply moved their village. In less than one generation, the Miyanmin shifted from subsistence farmers to commercial vegetable farmers who use a local airstrip to ship their produce. The Miyanmin have also adopted Western dress, education, medicine, religion, and technology. Have they also adopted Western beliefs about emotions? Apparently, yes. One anthropologist who had studied the Miyanmin during the 1960s was shocked to discover that by 1980 the Miyanmin and their traditional enemies were not only abstaining from killing each other but members of each tribe were sending their children to the same school.

17.1.5. Psychological Dispositions

As discussed in Chapter 16, humans consistently differ in both the amount of stimulation needed to elicit an emotion and the intensity of their emotional reactions. Humans also differ in the variety of distinct emotions that they experience. For example, at least some adults fail to consciously experience specific emotional states. These "unfeeling" adults tend to fall into three distinct clusters: alexithymics, psychopaths, and repressors. At the opposite extreme, some individuals report experiencing distinct emotional states with abnormally high frequency and/or intensity. That is, a specific individual may be predisposed to anger, anxiety, depression, elation, fear, guilt, or any number of distinct emotions. Depending upon the culture, extremes of such emotional traits are labeled as childish, criminal, divine, normal, or mental illness.

Although researchers agree that individual differences in the disposition to experience specific emotions do exist, they disagree over the role emotional dispositions play in everyday life. First, theorists disagree over the developmental relationship between emotional traits and other personality characteristics. Izard (1971, 1977), for example, postulated that individual differences in emotionality may predispose the individual to develop specific personality traits. Other theorists, however, argue that an individual's personality may shape his or her emotional reactions (Sommers, 1981, Sommers & Scioli, 1986). Still other theorists argue that cultural norms may alter both personality and emotionality (Levy, 1984).

Second, theorists disagree over the *concurrent validity* of dispositional measures, for example, how accurately does our self-report or behavioral measure of the trait predict *current* behaviors. Although this issue would appear rather straightforward, it represents both a methodological and theoretical bog (see Epstein, 1979). The key question is *which* dispositions predict *which* individuals' behaviors in *which* situations.

In the typical experiment, a self-selected group of subjects are asked to complete a self-report measure of a specific trait such as social anxiety and then placed in a situation designed to elicit the appropriate emotional state. Individuals who report a high disposition to social anxiety would logically be more likely to experience social anxiety and display physiological arousal in a group situation. However, across experiments, the correlations between self-reports of dispositions and current behaviors, physiological responses, or self-reports of emotional states average only about +.3. Thus, our dispositional measures appear to predict the reactions of less than 10% of the population.

Are dispositional measures poor predictors of actual behaviors? Not necessarily. Our self-selected sample may be unrepresentative of the population. However, even when we control sampling error, large individual differences are observed. Some individuals' behaviors are highly predictable, whereas others are highly unpredictable. As discussed in Chapter 16, individuals who report extremely high or low dispositions tend to behave in a highly predictable fashion, whereas the average individual does not. Thus the concurrent validity of our dispositional measure varies with *whose* behaviors we are trying to predict.

The apparent unpredictablity of the average person is at least partially an artifact of the unreliability of our dispositional and behavioral measures. Suppose our trait is normally distributed in the population and we wish to compare each fourth (quartile) of our sample. As shown in Figure 17-1, the majority of the population would score similarly on our dispositional measure. That is, the *average* individual would report neither high nor low social anxiety. Thus, the differences in self-report scores between the second quartile (25th to 50th percentile) and third quartile (50th to 75th percentile) are minimal. Moreover, because our self-report measures do not have perfect reliability, we would expect fluctuations in an individual's scores with repeated testing (standard error of the measurement). Thus some individuals who score in the second quartile on one occasion may score in the third quartile on another occasion and vice versa. Not surprisingly, comparisons of members of the second and third quartiles usually fail to find behavioral differences between the two groups.

Now suppose we compare only the first quartile (0 to 25th percentile) and the fourth quartile (75th to 100 percentile). Each of these groups is composed of a heterogeneous collection of individuals who report moderate to extremely low (or high) dispositions. Even with statistical fluctuations over repeated testing (standard error of the measurement, regression to the mean, etc.), members of

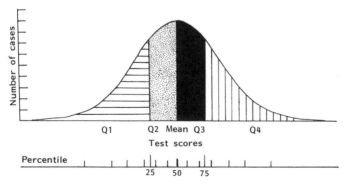

Figure 17-1. Graph of a normal frequency distribution.

these two extreme groups are unlikely to exchange positions. Not surprisingly, comparisons of members of the first and fourth quartiles usually find marked behavioral differences between the two groups.

Simultaneous comparisons of members of all four quartiles often find only small behavioral differences between groups. However, it is unclear whether such findings indicate that dispositions are only weakly related to specific behaviors or whether they reflect the error of variance inherent in our dispositional and behavioral measures.

One potentially fruitful approach for minimizing the error variance in our measures is to repeatedly test the same individuals. According to psychometric theory, chance fluctuations in a given individual's scores should cancel each other over time and, thus, the individual's average score would serve as an unbiased estimate of his or her "true" score (see Nunnally, 1978). Using this approach, Epstein (1979) found correlations of +.8 to +.9 between self-reports of dispositions and measures of emotional states, physical symptoms, physiological arousal, and social behaviors over a 2-week period. Thus it would appear that dispositional measures may account for the average behaviors of between 64% and 80% of the population. Epstein's findings are remarkably similar to those of long-term longitudinal studies of temperament. Specifically, about 65% of the population displays relatively stable temperaments from birth through adulthood.

Clearly, dispositions predict the emotional reactions of some of the people most of the time and most of the people at least some of the time. Depending upon our theoretical biases, one can legitimately argue that our glass is either half empty or half full. Proponents of the dispositional approach argue that the poor to moderate concurrent validity of our dispositional measures is due to flaws in our measuring instruments. For example, despite the repeated documentation of biological variability, many anxiety questionnaires fail to differentiate between cardiovasular, gastrointestinal, and striate reactions. A given individual may experience high levels of anxiety whether or not he or she experiences cold hands and feet. Conversely, subjective awareness of peripheral vasoconstriction may occur during a variety of emotional states. Presumably, the construction of more sophisticated measures of dispositions would improve the accuracy of our predictions.

Critics of the dispositional approach argue that the apparent validity of traits is an artifact of the stability of our psychosocial environments. If you live in a neighborhood with a high crime rate, you may habitually experience fear when walking alone at night. However, your fear reaction may be purely situational. If you move to a low-crime neighborhood, your fear reaction may persist (a disposition) or extinguish.

17.1.6. Psychological Situations

In everyday life, both emotional behaviors and states are complexly related to (a) cultural norms, (b) dispositions, and (c) situational factors. Mischel (1976) argued that most psychological theories grossly underestimate the complexity of both situational and dispositional causes of behaviors. For example, your emotional *state* while sitting in a dentist's office waiting room may be determined primarily by dispositions (emotional traits, past experiences with dentists, etc.). However, your emotional *behaviors* may be determined primarily by situational factors. If other people are present, your emotional behaviors are usually controlled by cultural norms about public displays of emotions. Although you may experience a variety of emotional states (anger, anxiety, boredom, etc.), you will probably display little emotion. If you are alone in the waiting room, your emotional behaviors may more closely match your emotional state. In this instance, a single situational factor (presence or absence of others) may determine the relative *salience* of dispositional and cultural factors.

In other instances, situational factors may override dispositional and cultural factors and elicit similar emotional states and behaviors in most individuals. If you discover a friend's severed head lying on the sidewalk, you will probably experience intense emotional states (disgust, surprise, terror) and display stereotypical emotional behaviors (vomiting, screaming, etc.).

In still other situations, your personal dispositions and internalized cultural norms may play a much more salient role in determining your emotional reactions. For example, if you are alone in the privacy of your own bedroom, how do you feel when you are nude? Some individuals feel quite natural whereas other individuals feel naked (vulnerable) and/or embarrassed (Lowen, 1968). Such individual differences in emotional states in any given situation are commonly observed in emotion research. A trivial event may trigger depression in one individual, elation in another, humor in a third, and so on.

The tasks of identifying the relative importance of dispositions and of situations in eliciting emotions is complicated by the discovery that many dispositions may be highly situationally specific. For example, Turner, Beidel, and Larkin (1986), compared the physiological and psychological reactions of highly socially anxious college students and psychiatric patients and a control group of nonanxious students during three different social situations. Each subject was asked to (a) role-play with a same-sex confederate, (b) role-play with an opposite-sex confederate, and (c) give a brief speech. Across tasks, members of both socially anxious groups reported more frequent negative cognitions and less frequent positive cognitions than control subjects. However, physiological arousal only crudely paralleled self-reports of negative cognitions. Compared with the controls, subjects in both socially anxious groups displayed elevated heart rates and systolic BP during the opposite-sex and speech conditions, but during the same-sex interaction the physiological reactions of members of all three groups were indistinguishable.

17.2 TOWARD A SYNTHESIS

Biological variability-response stereotypy, cultural variability-commonality, and psychological dispositions-situations represent the three largest chunks of pieces of the puzzle of emotions. However, there are numerous smaller clusters of empirical findings that do not appear to neatly fit into any of these three categories. For example, some individuals consistently report that they simultaneously experience unique combinations of emotional states such as fear-surprise. Do such mixed or blended emotions represent biological variability, cultural variability. or psychological dispositions?

Now reflect a moment on *why* you would classify mixed emotions as an example of biological variability or cultural variability or psychological dispositions. Is there some specific set of empirical findings that influenced your decision, or did your decision match your own metaphysical and theoretical biases? Unfortunately, tautological (circular) reasoning is one of the most common errors in human thought processes. The human mind can distort and bend reality to fit its preexisting beliefs with remarkable precision. Our conclusions become proof of our premises, and our premises then become proof for our conclusions.

What type of evidence would support a biological variability interpretation of mixed emotions? For the sake of argument, let us assume that humans are genetically programmed to display a distinct pattern of facial, postural, and autonomic responses during fear and a different pattern of physiological activity during surprise. Would observing the combination of these two patterns prove that mixed emotions exist? No, such reasoning is tautological. How do I know that mixed emotions occur? Because mixed patterns of physiological arousal occur. Why do mixed patterns of physiological arousal occur? Because the individual is experiencing a mixed emotion. Our conclusion and premise are hopelessly intertwined.

An equally plausible biological explanation of mixed emotions is that humans are genetically programmed to react to external events with a rapid sequence of distinct emotions. Mixed emotions may merely represent a transition stage between two distinct emotions. Thus self-reports of fear-surprise may indicate that the individual was initially surprised and then frightened or initially frightened and then surprised. Observing mixed patterns of physiological arousal would support either a mixed or sequential emotion hypothesis. The obvious empirical test of these two rival hypotheses would be to record individuals' physiological responses before, during, and after they report experiencing a mixed emotion.

Suppose we conduct our hypothetical experiment. Empirical support for either a mixed or sequential emotional pattern would allow us to refute one of our hypotheses and yet would not "prove" genetic determinism. Either physiological pattern might be the product of cultural display rules or individual dispositions, that is, when frightened act surprised. In order to provide a non-tautological explanation of emotions, we must examine the validity of all plausible alternative hypotheses.

Based on the available evidence, can we assemble a coherent picture of human emotions? Frankly, no. So many pieces of our puzzle are missing that we can produce only a vague outline of human emotional behaviors and states. Only four emotions (anger, anxiety, depression, and fear) have been extensively studied. Other emotions (disgust, excitement, embarrassment, guilt, happiness, humor, sadness, shame, and surprise) have received much less empirical attention. Moreover, the literature on contempt, jealousy, loneliness, love, and pride is sparse and fragmented. Yet despite our limited data bases, we have accumulated enough pieces of our puzzle to determine what our completed picture will *not* look like.

First, our completed puzzle will *not* be strictly materialistic. Biochemical factors (diet, drugs, fatigue, hormones, motives, etc.) can influence our emotional states, but alone they are often insufficient to elicit emotional reactions. For example, alcohol consumption alters our thresholds for anger, humor, or sexual excitement. However, our expectations, rather than alcohol consumption *per se*, often determine our emotional reactions. Similarly, physiological arousal plays a major role in both the initiation and maintenance of our emotional reactions. Blushing is both a cause and an effect of embarrassment. Yet, physiological arousal, alone, is often insufficient to elicit an emotion.

Second, our completed puzzle will *not* be strictly mentalistic. Our conscious mental activity plays an important role in shaping our emotions. However, emotions and the conscious self may also be completely dissociated. The right hemispheres of split-brain patients are capable of eliciting emotional responses independently of the (conscious) left hemisphere. Similarly, alexithymics and repressors may display the physiological patterns associated with emotions in others, yet deny consciously experiencing emotions. Moreover, a strict mentalist position ignores the powerful role that biological factors can play in human emotions. For example, hormone disorders do not merely *mimic* spontaneous emotional states, they can *produce* them. Steroid-induced depression is not an as-if emotion, nor is steroid-induced suicide an as-if behavior.

Third, our completed picture will *not* be parallel dualistic. Only a small set of psychiatric patients display a complete dissociation of mind and body. Although catatonic states are fascinating phenomena, they are unrepresentative of normal conscious experience. Very few of us "leave our bodies" with any regularity. In everyday life, our conscious experience of our emotions is at least partially yoked to our physiology.

Materialistic, mentalistic, and dualistic positions all have extreme difficulty accounting for psychophysiological disorders. For example, how can we account for pseudocyesis (false pregnancy)? The key issue is not how does the neurohormonal system mimic pregnancy, it is, *why* is pseudocyesis triggered by the psychological desire to have a baby?

The emerging picture of human emotions is clearly interactionistic. Yet we must avoid the simplistic conclusion that "mind and body are inseparable." The relative contribution of our biological states and our cognitions in determining our emotions varies with cultural, dispositional, and situational factors. In some instances, our biology dominates our cognitions. We may experience terror after a sodium lactate injection, despite being consciously aware that the situation is harmless. In other instances, our cognitions dominate our biology. We often can think ourselves in and out of anger, depression, or other emotional states. To further complicate matters, our biological states and psychological states may covary or display marked dissociation.

Given the complexity of mind–body interactions, we should be leery of simple explanations such as "repressed anger causes ulcers." As discussed throughout this book, researchers have repeatedly tested such simple explanations and found them inadequate. If we wish to comprehend the full richness and variety of human emotions, we must develop a greater appreciation of biological, psychological, and cultural variability.

SUGGESTED READINGS

The following books contain excellent summaries of the theoretical positions of a wide variety of emotion researchers:

Candland, D. K., Fell, J. P., Keen, E., Lesher, A. I., Tarpey, R. M., & Plutchik, R. (Eds.), *Emotion.* Monterey, Calif.: Brooks/Cole, 1977.

Izard, C. (Ed.). *Emotions in personality and psychopathology.* New York: Plenum Press, 1979.

Rorty, A. O. *Explaining emotions.* Berkeley: University of California Press, 1980.

Scherer, K. R., & Ekman, P. (Eds.), *Approaches to emotions.* Hillsdale, NJ.: Lawrence Erlbaum Associates, 1984.

References

Abe, K., & Masui, T. Age-sex trends of phobic and anxiety symptoms in adolescents. *British Journal of Psychiatry*, 1981, *138*, 297–302.

Abel, G. G., Murphy, W. D., Becker, J. V., & Bitar, A. Women's vaginal responses during REM sleep. *Journal of Sex and Marriage Therapy*, 1979, *5(1)*, 5.

Abell, T. L., Tucker, R., & Malagelada, J. R. External and internal electrogastrogram in humans. *Psychophysiology*, 1983, *20*, 427. Abstract.

Abrams, D. B., & Wilson, G. T. Alcohol, sexual arousal and self-control. *Journal of Personality and Social Psychology*, 1983, *45*, 188–198.

Abramson, P. R., & Mosher, D. L. Development of a measure of negative attitudes toward masturbation. *Journal of Consulting and Clinical Psychology*, 1975, *43*, 485–490.

Abramson, P. R., & Pearsall, E. H. Pectoral changes during the sexual response cycle: A thermographic analysis. *Archives of Sexual Behavior*, 1983, *12*, 357–368.

Ackerman, S. H., & Sachar, E. J. The lactate theory of anxiety: A review and reevaluation. *Psychosomatic Medicine*, 1974, *36*, 69–81.

Agra, W. S., Leitenberg, H., Barlow, D. H., Curtis, N. A., Edwards, J., & Wright, D. Relaxation in systematic desensitization. *Archives of General Psychiatry*, 1971, *25*, 511–514.

Ainsworth, M. D. *Infancy in Uganda: Infant care and the growth of love.* Baltimore: Johns Hopkins Press, 1967.

Akil, H., Richardson, D. E., Hughes, J., & Barchas, J. D. Enkephalin-like material elevated in ventricular cerebrospinal fluid of pain patients after analgesic focal stimulation. *Science*, 1978, *201*, 463–465.

Alexander, A. B., & Smith, D. D. Clinical applications of EMG biofeedback. In R. Gatchel & K. Price (Eds.), *Clinical applications of biofeedback: Appraisal and status.* New York: Pergamon Press, 1979.

Alexander, F. The influence of psychologic factors upon gastrointestinal disturbances: A symposium. *Psychoanalytic Quarterly*, 1934, *3*, 501–539.

Alexander, F. *Psychosomatic medicine: Its principles and applications.* New York: Norton, 1950.

Alexander, F., French, T. M., & Pollock, G. H. *Psychosomatic specificity.* Chicago: University of Chicago Press, 1968.

Alexander, M. F. *The resurrection of the body.* New York: Delta, 1969.

Al-Issa, I. *The psychopathology of women.* Englewood Cliffs, N.J.: Prentice-Hall, 1980.

Allen, R. A., & Mills, G. K. The effects of unilateral plethysmographic feedback of temporal artery activity during migraine head pain. *Journal of Psychosomatic Research*, 1982, *26*, 133–140.

Almy, T. P., Hinkle, L. E., Berle, B., & Kern, F. Alterations in colonic function under stress: III. Experimental production of sigmoid spasm in patients with spastic constipation. *Gastroenterology*, 1949, *12*, 437–449.

345

Amkraut, A., & Solomon, G. F. From the symbolic stimulus to the pathophysiologic response: Immune mechanisms. *International Journal of Psychiatry in Medicine*, 1974, 5, 541–563.

Anand, B. K., & Brobeck, J. R. Localization of a feeding center in the hypothalamus of the rat. *Proceedings for the Society of Experimental Biological Medicine*, 1951, 77, 323–324.

Anand, B. K., & Dua, S. Feeding responses induced by electrical stimulation of the hypothalamus in cats. *Indian Journal of Medical Research*, 1955, 43, 113–122.

Anastasi, A. Heredity, environment, and the question "how?" *Psychological Review*, 1958, 65, 197–208.

Anders, T. F. What we know about sleep disorders in children. *Medical Times*, 1976, 4, 75–80.

Andersch, B., & Hahn, L. Progesterone treatment of premenstrual tension—A double blind study. *Journal of Psychosomatic Research*, 1985, 29, 489–493.

Anderson, C. D., & Franks, R. D. Migraine and tension headache: Is there a physiological difference? *Headache*, 1981, 21, 63–71.

Anderson, J. L. Women's sports and fitness programs at the U.S. Military Academy. *Physican and Sportsmedicine*, 1979, 7, 72–80.

Andrew, J., & Nathan, P. W. The cerebral control of mituration. *Proceedings of the Royal Society of Medicine*, 1965, 58, 553–555.

Anonymous. Ice cream analysis. *United Cerebral Palsy Contents*, 1986, 2, 20.

Antelman, S. M., & Caggiula, A. R. Norepinephrine-dopamine interactions and behavior. *Science*, 1977, 195, 646–653.

Antelman, S. M., & Caggiula, A. R. Stress-induced behavior: Chemotherapy without drugs. In J. M. Davidson & R. J. Davidson (Eds.), *The psychobiology of consciousness*. New York: Plenum Press, 1980.

Appel, M. A., Saab, P. A., & Holroyd, K. A. Cardiovascular disorders. In M. Hersen & A. S. Bellack (Eds.), *Handbook of clinical behavior therapy with adults*. New York: Plenum Press, 1985.

Appenzeller, O. Vasomotor function in migraine. *Headache*, 1969, 9, 147–155.

Arena, J. G., Blanchard, E. B., & Andrasik, F. The role of affect in the etiology of chronic headache. *Journal of Psychosomatic Research*, 1984, 28, 79–86.

Aronfreed, J. M., Messick, S. A., & Diggory, J. C. Re-examining emotionality and perceptual defense. *Journal of Personality*, 1953, 21, 517–528.

Asberg, M., Thoren, P. Traskman, L., Bertilsson, L., & Tingberg, V. Serotonin depression—A biochemical subgroup within the affective disorders? *Science*, 1976, 191, 478–480.

Aschoff, J. The circadian system in man. In D. T. Krieger & J. C. Hughes (Eds.), *Neuroendocrinology*. Sunderland: Sinauer, 1980.

Asendorpf, J. B., & Scherer, K. R. The discrepant repressor: Differentiation between low anxiety, high anxiety, and repression of anxiety by autonomic-facial-verbal patterns of behavior. *Journal of Personality and Social Psychology*, 1983, 45, 1334–1346.

Aslan, S., Nelson, L., Carruthers, M., & Lader, M. Stress and age effects on catecholamines in normal subjects. *Journal of Psychosomatic Research*, 1981, 25, 33–41.

Astrand, I., & Astrand, P. Aerobic work performance: A review. In F. J. Folinsbee (Ed.), *Environmental stress*. New York: Academic Press, 1978.

Astrand, P. O., & Rodahl, K. *Textbook of work physiology*. New York: McGraw-Hill, 1970.

Athanasiou, R., Shaver P., & Yavris, C. Sex. *Psychology Today*, 1970, 4, 37–52.

Averill, J. R. Autonomic response patterns during sadness and mirth. *Psychophysiology*, 1969, 5, 399–414.

Ax, A. F. The physiological differentiation between fear and anger in humans. *Psychosomatic Medicine*, 1953, 15, 433–442.

Backstrom, T., Sanders, S., Leask, R., Davidson, D., Warner, P., & Bancroft, J. Mood, sexuality, hormones and the menstrual cycle II. Hormone levels and their relationship to the premenstrual syndrome. *Psychosomatic Medicine*, 1983, 45, 503–507.

Baggett, A. T. The effect of early loss of father upon the personality of boys and girls in late adolescents. *Dissertation Abstracts*, 1967, 28 (1-b), 356–357.

Bakal, D. A. *Psychology and medicine: Psychobiological dimensions of health and illness.* New York: Springer, 1979.

Baker, W. M., Sandman, C. A., & Pepinsky, H. B. Affectivity of task, rehearsal time, and physiological response. *Journal of Abnormal Psychology,* 1975, *84,* 539–544.

Balshan-Goldstein, I. Role of muscle tension in personality theory. *Psychological Bulletin,* 1964, *61(6),* 413–425.

Balshan-Goldstein, I. The relationship of muscle tension and autonomic activity to psychiatric disorders. *Psychosomatic Medicine,* 1965, *27,* 39–52.

Balshan-Goldstein, I., Grinker, R. R., Heath, H. A., Oken, D., & Shipman, W. G. Study in psychophysiology of muscle tension: I. Response specificity. *Archives of General Psychiatry,* 1964, *11,* 322–330.

Bancroft, J., & Bell, C. Simultaneous recording of penile diameter and penile arterial pulse during laboratory-based erotic stimulation in normal subjects. *Journal of Psychosomatic Research,* 1985, *29,* 303–313.

Bancroft, J., Sanders, D., Davidson, D., & Warner, P. Mood, sexuality, hormones and the menstrual cycle: III. Sexuality and the role of androgens. *Psychosomatic Medicine,* 1983, *45,* 509–516.

Bandura, A. Behavioral psychotherapy. *Scientific American,* 1967, *216(3),* 78–86.

Bandura, A. Behavior theory and models of man. *American Psychologist,* 1974, *29,* 859–869.

Bandura, A., Taylor, C. B., Williams, S. L., Mefford, I. N., & Barchas, J. D. Catecholamine secretion as a function of perceived coping self-efficacy. *Journal of Consulting and Clinical Psychology,* 1985, *53,* 406–414.

Banks, M. H., & Beresford, S. A. The influence of menstrual cycle phase upon symptom recording using data from health diaries. *Journal of Psychosomatic Research,* 1979, *23,* 307–313.

Bar, L. H., & Kuypers, B. R. Behavior therapy in dermatological practice. *British Journal of Dermotology,* 1973, *88,* 591–598.

Bard, P. A diencephalic mechanism for the expression of rage, with special reference to the sympathetic nervous system. *American Journal of Physiology,* 1928, *84,* 490–515.

Bard, P. On emotional expression after decortication, with some remarks to certain theoretical views. Parts 1 and 2. *Psychological Review,* 1934, *41,* 309–329, 424–449.

Bard, P., & Mountcastle, V. B. Some forebrain mechanisms involved in the expression of rage, with special reference to suppression of angry behavior. In J. F. Fulton (Ed.), *The frontal lobes.* Baltimore: Williams & Witkins, 1948.

Barland, G. H., & Raskins, D. C. An experimental study of field techniques in "lie detection." *Psychophysiology,* 1972, *9,* 275. Abstract.

Barland, G. H., & Raskins, D. C. Psychopathy and detection of deception in criminal suspects. *Psychophysiology,* 1975, *12,* 224. Abstract. (a)

Barland, G. H., & Raskins, D. C. An evaluation of field techniques in the detection of deception. *Psychophysiology,* 1975, *12,* 321–330. (b)

Barlow, W. Anxiety and muscle-tension pain. *The British Journal of Clinical Practice,* 1959, *13,* 339–350.

Barlow, W. *The Alexander technique.* New York: Knopf, 1973.

Barron, F., Jarvick, M. E., & Burnell, S. The hallucinogenic drugs. *Scientific American,* 1964, *210(4),* 29–37.

Basmajiam, J. V., & Blumenstein, R. *Electrode placement in EMG biofeedback.* Baltimore: Williams & Wilkins, 1980.

Beaumont, W. *Experiments and observations on the gastric juice and the physiology of digestion.* Plattsburgh, N.Y.: F. P. Allen, 1833.

Beck, A. T. A systematic investigation of depression. *Comprehensive Psychiatry,* 1961, *2,* 163–170.

Beck, A. T. Thinking and depression. *Archives of General Psychiatry,* 1963, *9,* 324–333.

Beck, A. T. *Depression: Clinical, experimental and theoretical aspects.* New York: Harper & Row, 1967.

Beck, A. T. Role of fantasies in psychotherapy and psychopathology. *Journal of Nervous and Mental Disease,* 1970, *150,* 3–17. (a)

Beck, A. T. The core problem in depression: The cognitive triad. In J. Masserman (Ed.), *Depression: Theories and therapies.* New York: Grune & Stratton, 1970. (b)

Beck, A. T. *Cognitive therapy and emotional disorders.* New York: International Universities Press, 1976.

Beck, A. T., & Shaw, B. F. Cognitive approaches to depression. In A. Ellis & R. Grieger (Eds.), *Handbook of rational-emotive theory and practice.* New York: Springer, 1977.

Beck, A. T., Rush, A. J., Shaw, B. F., & Emery, G. *Cognitive therapy of depression.* New York: Guilford, 1979.

Beck, E., Thompson, J. G., & Adams, M. *The effects of paced respiration and self-vocalizations on heart rate activity during emotional arousal.* Paper presented at the 27th annual meeting of the Southeastern Psychological Association, Atlanta, March 27, 1981.

Beck, J. G., Sakheim, D. K., & Barlow, D. H. Operating characteristics of the vaginal photoplethysmograph: Some implications for its use. *Archives of Sexual Behavior,* 1983, *12,* 43–58.

Beckmann, H., & Goodwin, F. K. Antidepressant response to tricyclic and urinary MHPG in unipolar patients: Clinical response to imipramine or amitriptyline. *Archives of General Psychiatry,* 1975, *32,* 17–21.

Beckmann, H., & Goodwin, F. K. Urinary MHPG in subgroups of depressed patients and normal controls. *Neuropsychobiology,* 1980, *6,* 91–100.

Belar, C. D., & Cohen, J. L. The use of EMG feedback and progressive relaxation in the treatment of a woman with chronic back pain. *Biofeedback and Self Regulation,* 1979, *4,* 345–353.

Bell, B., Christie, M. J., & Venables, P. H. Psychophysiology of the menstrual cycle. In P. H. Venables & M. J. Christie (Eds.), *Research in psychophysiology.* New York: Wiley, 1975.

Bell, I., & Schwartz, G. E. Cognitive and somatic mechanisms in the voluntary control of human heart rate. In D. Shipiro, T. X. Barber, L.V. DiCara, J. Kamiya, N. E. Miller, & J. Stoyva (Eds.), *Biofeedback and self-control. 1972.* Chicago: Aldine, 1973.

Beloff, H. The structure and origin of the anal character. *Genetic Psychology Monographs,* 1957, *55,* 141–172.

Bem, D. J. *Beliefs, attitudes and human affairs.* Belmont, Calif.: Brooks/Cole, 1970.

Benedek-Jaszmann, L. J., & Hearn-Sturtevant, M. D. Premenstrual tension and functional infertility. *Lancet,* 1976, *1,* 1095–1098.

Benjamin, L. S. Statistical treatment of the law of initial values in autonomic research: A review and recommendation. *Psychosomatic Medicine,* 1963, *25,* 556–566.

Bennett, D. H., & Holmes, D. S. Influence of denial (situational redefinition) and projection on anxiety associated with threat to self-esteem. *Journal of Personality and Social Psychology,* 1975, *32,* 915–921.

Ben-Tovin, D. I., Marilov, V., & Crisp, A. H. Personality and mental state within anorexia nervosa. *Journal of Psychosomatic Research,* 1979, *23,* 321–325.

Berger, B., & Mackenzie, M. M. A case study of a woman jogger: A psychodynamic analysis. In W. F. Straub (Ed.), *Sport psychology: An analysis of athletic behavior.* Ithaca: Mouvement Pub., 1980.

Berlin, B., & Kay, P. *Basic color terms: Their universality and evolution.* Berkeley: University of California Press, 1969.

Bermant, G., & Davidson, J. M. *Biological bases of sexual behavior.* New York: Harper & Row, 1974.

Bernstein, A. S. Race and examiner as significant influences on basal skin impedance. *Journal of Personality and Social Psychology,* 1965, *1,* 346–349.

Bernstein, A. S. Phasic electrodermal orienting response in chronic schizophrenics: II. Response to auditory signals of varying intensity. *Journal of Abnormal Psychology,* 1970, *75,* 146–156.

Bernstein, A. S., Schneider, S. J., Juni, S., Pope, A. T., & Starkey, P. W. The effect of stimulus significance on the electrodermal response in chronic schizophrenia. *Journal of Abnormal Psychology,* 1980, *89,* 93–97.

Bernstein, A. S., Firth, C. D., Gruzelier, J. H., Patterson, T., Straube, E., Venables, P. H.,

& Zahn, T. P. An analysis of the skin conductance responses of American, British and German schizophrenics. *Biological Psychology*, 1982, *14*, 155–211.

Bernstein, D. A., & Borkovec, T. D. *Progressive relaxation training.* Champaign, Ill.: Research Press, 1973.

Best, C. H., & Taylor, N. B. *The living body: A text in human physiology* (4th ed.). New York: Holt, Rinehart & Winston, 1966.

Bettelheim, B. *The children of the dream.* New York: Free Press, 1969.

Biron, P., Mongeau, J., & Bertrand, D. Familial aggregation of blood pressure in adopted and natural children. In O. Paul (Ed.), *Epidemiology and control of hypertension.* New York: Stratton, 1975.

Birtchnell, J., & Floyd, S. Further menstrual characteristics of suicide attemptors. *Journal of Psychosomatic Research*, 1975, *19*, 81–85.

Bishop, M. P., Elder, S. J., & Heath, R. G. Intracranial self-stimulation in man. *Science*, 1963, *140*, 394–395.

Bixler, E. O., Kales, A., & Soldatos, C. S. Sleep disorders encountered in medical practice: A national survey of physicians. *Behavioral Medicine*, 1979, November, 13–21.

Blanchard, E. B. Biofeedback and the modification of cardiovascular dysfunctions. In R. J. Gatchel & K. P. Price (Eds.), *Clinical applications of biofeedback: Appraisal and status.* New York: Pergamon Press, 1979.

Block, M. A. *Alcoholism: Its facets and phases.* New York: John Day, 1965.

Bloom, F., Battenberg, E., Rossier, J., Ling, N., & Gullemin, R. Neurons containing beta-endorphin in rat brain exist separately from those containing enkephalin: Immunocytochemical study. *Proceedings of National Academy of Science, USA.* 1978, *75*, 1591–1595.

Bloom, G., Von Euler, U. S., and Frankenhaeuser, M. Catecholamine excretion and personality in paratroop trainees. *Acta Psychologica Scandinavica*, 1963, *58*, 77–89.

Bloom, L. J., & Trautt, G. M. Finger pulse volume as a measure of anxiety: Further evaluation. *Psychophysiology*, 1977, *14*, 541–544.

Blumberg, S. H., & Izard, C. E. Affective and cognitive characteristics of depression in 10- and 11-year old children. *Journal of Personality and Social Psychology*, 1985, *49*, 194–202.

Blumberg, S. H., & Izard, C. E. Discriminating patterns of emotions in 10- and 11-year old children's anxiety and depression. *Journal of Personality and Social Psychology*, 1986, *51*, 852–857.

Blumenthal, J. A., Lane, J. D., Williams, R. B., McKee, D. C., Haney, T., & White, A. Effects of task incentive on cardiovascular response in Type A and Type B individuals. *Psychophysiology*, 1983, *20*, 63–69.

Boeringa, J. A. Blushing: A modified behavioral intervention using paradoxical intention. *Psychotherapy: Theory, Research and Practice*, 1983, *20*, 441–444.

Bolzinger, A., & Ebtinger, R. Value of hypnosis in psychosomatic conditions in children: A case of hyperhidrosis. *Revue de Neuropsychiatre Infantile et d'Hygiene de l' Enfance*, 1971, *19*, 573–579.

Borg, S., Kvande, H., & Sedvall, G. Central norepinephrine metabolism during alcohol intoxication in addicts and healthy volunteers. *Science*, 1981, *213*, 1135–1137.

Borgeat, F., Chagon, G., & Legault, Y. Comparison of the salivary changes associated with a relaxing and with a stressful procedure. *Psychophysiology*, 1984, *21*, 690–698.

Borkovec, T. D., Robinson, E., Pruzinsky, T., & DePree, J. A. Preliminary explorations of worry: Some characteristics and processes. *Behavior Research and Therapy*, 1983, *21*, 9–16.

Bors, E., & Comarr, A. E. *Neurological Urology: Physiology of mituration, its neurological disorders and sequalae.* Baltimore: University Park Press, 1971.

Boucsein, W., Baltissen, R., & Euler, M. Dependence of skin conductance reactions and skin resistance reactions upon previous level. *Psychophysiology*, 1984, *21*, 212–218.

Boudewyns, P. A. A comparison of the effects of stress vs. relaxation instructions on the finger temperature response. *Behavior Therapy*, 1976, *7*, 54–67.

Boulenger, J. P., Uhde, T. W., Wolff, E. A., & Post, R. M. Increased sensitivity to caffeine in patients with panic disorders. *Archives of General Psychiatry*, 1984, *41*, 1067–1071.

Bourne, P. G. *Men, stress and Vietnam.* Boston: Little, Brown and Co., 1970.

Bower, G. H. Mood and memory. *American Psychologist,* 1981, *36(2),* 129–148.

Bowlby, J. *Maternal care and mental health.* Geneva: World Health Organization, 1951.

Bowlby, J. *Child care and the growth of love.* London: Penguin, 1953.

Bowlby, J. An ethological approach to research in child development. *British Journal of Medical Psychology,* 1957, *30,* 230–240.

Bowlby, J. The nature of the child's tie to his mother. *International Journal of Psychoanalysis,* 1958, *39,* 350–373.

Bowlby, J. *Attachment and Loss. Vol. 1: Attachment.* New York: Basic Books, 1969.

Bowlby, J. *Attachment and Loss. Vol. 2: Separation, anxiety and anger.* London: Hogarth, 1973.

Brady, J. V. Ulcers in "executive" monkeys. *Scientific American,* 1958, *199,* 95–100.

Brady, J. V., Porter, R. W., Conrad, D. G., & Mason, J. W. Avoidance behavior and the development of gastrointestinal ulcers. *Journal of Experimental Analysis of Behavior,* 1958, *1,* 69–72.

Brenner, C. *An elementary textbook of psychoanalysis.* New York: International Universities Press, 1955.

Breuer, J., & Freud, S. *Studies in hysteria.* 1895. Trans. by J. Strachey & A. Freud, *The standard edition of the complete works of Sigmund Freud. Vol. II.* London: Hogarth, 1955.

Briddell, D. W., Rimm, D. C., Caddy, G. R., Krawitz, G., Sholis, D., & Wunderlin, J. Effects of alcohol and cognitive set on sexual arousal to deviant stimuli. *Journal of Abnormal Psychology,* 1978, *87,* 418–430.

Briddell, D. W., & Wilson, G. T. The effects of alcohol and expectancy set on male sexual arousal. *Journal of Abnormal Psychology,* 1976, *85,* 225–230.

Bridger, W. H., & Birns, B. Experience and temperament in human neonates. In G. Newton & S. Levine (Eds.), *Early experience and behavior.* Springfield, Ill.: Thomas, 1968.

Bridges, K. M. Emotional development during infancy. *Child Development,* 1932, *3,* 324–341.

Brierley, H. The treatment of hysterical spasmodic torticollis by behavior therapy. *Behavior Research and Therapy,* 1967, *5,* 139–142.

Brobeck, J. R. Mechanism for the development of obesity in animals with hypothalamic lesions. *Physiological Review,* 1946, *26,* 541–559.

Brodtborg, E., Sulg, I., & Gimse, R. The hyperventilation syndrome. *Acta Neurologica Scandinavica,* 1984, *98,* 395–396.

Broer, M. R. *Efficiency of human movement.* Philadelphia: Saunders, 1966.

Brooke, R. I., & Stenn, P. G. Myofascial pain dysfunction syndrome—How effective is biofeedback assisted relaxation training? In J. J. Bonica, U. Lindblom, & A. Iggo (Eds.), *Advances in pain research and therapy.* New York: Raven, 1983.

Brooks, J., & Lewis, M. Infants' responses to strangers: Midget, adult and child. *Child Development,* 1976, *47,* 323–332.

Broughton, R. J. Sleep disorders: Disorders of arousal? *Science,* 1968, *159,* 1070–1078.

Brown, B. B. *Stress and the art of biofeedback.* New York: Harper & Row, 1977.

Brown, E., & Barglow, P. Pseudocyesis: A paradigm for psychophysiological interactions. *Archives of General Psychiatry,* 1971, *24,* 221–229.

Bruch, H. *Eating disorders.* New York: Basic Books, 1973.

Bruch, H. *The golden cage. The enigma of anorexia nervosa.* Cambridge: Harvard University Press, 1978.

Brudny, J., Korein, J., Grynbaum, B. B., Friedmann, L. W. Weinstein, S., Sachs-Frankel, G., & Belandres, P. V. EMB feedback therapy: Review of treatment of 114 patients. *Archives of Physical Medicine and Rehabilitation,* 1976, *57,* 55–61.

Buck, R. W., Savin, V. J., Miller, R. E., & Caul, W. F. Communication of affect through facial expressions in humans. *Journal of Personality and Social Psychology,* 1972, *23,* 362–371.

Buck, R., Miller, R. E., & Caul, W. F. Sex, personality and physiological variables in the communication of affect via facial expressions. *Journal of Personality and Social Psychology,* 1974, *30,* 587–596.

Burgess, E. Elimination of vomiting behavior. *Behavior Research and Therapy*, 1969, 7, 173–176.

Burgess, A. W., & Holstrom, L. L. Rape trauma syndrome. *American Journal of Psychiatry*, 1974, 131, 981–986.

Burglo, K. L., Whitehead, W. E., & Engel, B. T. Behavioral treatment of stress urinary incontinence in elderly women. *Biofeedback and Self-Regulation*, 1983, 8, 323.

Burnam, M. A., Pennebaker, J. W., & Glass, D. C. Time consciousness, achievement striving and Type A coronary-prone behavior pattern. *Journal of Abnormal Psychology*, 1975, 84, 76–79.

Burns, B. H. Breathlessness in depression. *British Journal of Psychiatry*, 1971, 119, 39–45.

Buss, A. H., & Plomin, R. A., *A temperament theory of personality development*. New York: Wiley-Interscience, 1975.

Buss, A. H., Iscoe, I., & Buss, E. H. The development of embarrassment. *Jornal of Psychology*, 1979, 103, 227–230.

Byrne, D., Fisher, J. D., Lamberth, J., & Mitchell, H. E. Evaluations of erotica: Facts or feelings. *Journal of Personality and Social Psychology*, 1974, 29, 111–116.

Byrne, D., Jazwinski, C., Deninno, J. A., & Fisher, W. A. Negative sexual attitudes and contraception. In D. Byrne & L. Byrne (Eds.), *Explaining human sexuality*. New York: Thomas Y. Crowell, 1977.

Cajal, S. R. *Degeneration and regeneration of the nervous system*. New York: Hafner, 1968.

Calhoun, K. S., Atkeson, B. M., & Resnick, P. A. A longitudinal examination of the fear reactions in victims of rape. *Journal of Counseling Psychology*, 1982, 29, 655–661.

Callen, K. E. Mental and emotional aspects of long-distance running. *Psychosomatics*, 1983, 24(2), 133–151.

Cameron, D. E. Observations of patterns of anxiety. *American Journal of Psychiatry*, 1944, 101, 36–41.

Cameron, D. E. Some relationships between excitement, depression and anxiety. *American Journal of Psychiatry*, 1945, 102, 385–394.

Campbell, D., Sanderson, R. E., & Laverty, S. G. Characteristics of conditioned responses in human objects during extinction trials following a single traumatic conditioning trial. *Journal of Abnormal and Social Psychology*, 1964, 68, 627–639.

Cannon, W. B. The James-Lange theory of emotion: A critical examination and alternative theory. *American Journal of Psychology*, 1927, 39, 106–124.

Cannon, W. B. Bodily changes in pain, hunger, fear, and rage. New York: Appleton-Century Co., 1934.

Cantor, J. R., Zillmann, D., & Bryant, J. Enhancement of experienced sexual arousal in response to erotic stimuli through misattribution of unrelated residual excitation. *Journal of Personality and Social Psychology*, 1975, 32, 69–75.

Cantril, H. Perception of interpersonal relations. *American Journal of Psychiatry*, 1957, 114(2), 119–126.

Cappo, B. M., & Holmes, D. S. The utility of prolonged respiratory exhalation for reducing physiological and psychological arousal in non-threatening situations. *Journal of Psychosomatic Research*, 1984, 28, 265–273.

Carpenter, J. A., & Armenti, N. P. Some effects of ethanol on human sexual and agressive behavior. In B. Kissins & H. Begleiter (Eds.), *The biology of alcoholism* (Vol. 2). New York: Plenum Press, 1971.

Carr, D. B., Bullen, B. A., Skrinar, G. S., Arnold, M. A., Rosenblatt, M., Beitins, I. Z., Martin, J. B., & McArthur, J. W. Physical conditioning facilitates the exercise-induced secretion of beta-endorphin and beta-lipotropin in women. *The New England Journal of Medicine*, 1981, 305(10), 560–563.

Carroll, B. J., & Steiner, M. The psychobiology of menstrual dysphoria: The role of prolactin. *Psychoneuroendocrinology*, 1978, 3, 171–180.

Carroll, B. J., Curtis, G. C., & Mendels, J. Neuroendocrine regulation in depression: II. Discrimination of depressed from nondepressed patients. *Archives of General Psychiatry*, 1976, 33, 1051–1057.

Carroll, B. J., Feinberg, M., Greden, J. F., Tarika, J., Albala, A. A., Haskett, R. F., James,

B. M., Kronpol, Z., Lohr, N., Steiner, M. Vigne, J. P., & Young, E. A specific laboratory test for the diagnosis of melancholia: Standardization, validation and clinical utility. *Archives of General Psychiatry*, 1981, *38*, 15–22.

Carroll, B. J., Martin, F. I., & Davies, B. M. Resistance to suppression by dexamethasone of plasma 11-OHCS levels in severe depressive illness. *British Medical Journal*, 1983, *3*, 285.

Carroll, D., Marzillier, J. S., & Merian, S. Psychophysiological changes accompanying different types of arousing and relaxing imagery. *Psychophysiology*, 1982, *19*, 75–82.

Casas, J. M., Beemsterboer, P., & Clark, G. T. A comparison of stress-reduction behavioral counseling and contingent nocturnal EMG biofeedback for treatment of bruxism. *Behavior Research and Therapy*, 1982, *20*, 9–15.

Casler, L. Nudist camps. *Medical Aspects of Human Sexuality*, 1971, May, 92–98.

Castelnuovo-Tedesco, P. Emotional antecedents of perforation of ulcers of the stomach and duodenum. *Psychosomatic Medicine*, 1962, *24*, 398.

Castelnuovo-Tedesco, P., & Krout, B. M. Psychosomatic aspects of chronic pelvic pain. *Psychiatry and Medicine*, 1970, *1*, 109–126.

Cellucci, A. J., & Lawerence, P. S. Individual differences in self-reported sleep variable correlations among nightmare sufferers. *Journal of Clinical Psychology*, 1978, *34*, 721–725.

Chambless, D. L., & DeMarco, D. Pubococcygens, Kegel exercises and female coital orgasm: Reply to Jayne. *Journal of Consulting and Clinical Psychology*, 1985, *53*, 271–272.

Chapman, C. R., & Feather, W. Effects of diazepam on human pain tolerance and pain sensitivity. *Psychosomatic Medicine*, 1973, *35*, 330–339.

Charney, D., & Heninger, G. R. Noradrenergic function and the mechanism of action of antianxiety treatment: I. The effects of long-term alprazolam treatment. *American Journal of Psychiatry*, 1985, *42(5)*, 458–467.

Charney, D. S., Heninger, G. R., & Jatlow, P. I. Increased anxiogenic effects of caffeine in panic disorders. *Archives of General Psychiatry*, 1985, *42*, 233–243.

Chaudhary, N. A., & Truelove, S. C. The irritable colon syndrome. A study of the clinical features, predisposing causes and prognosis in 130 cases. *Quarterly Journal of Medicine*, 1962, *31*, 307–322.

Christensen, L., Krietsch, K., White, B., & Stagner, B. Impact of a dietary change on emotional distress. *Journal of Abnormal Psychology*, 1985, *94*, 565–579.

Clancy, J , Noyes, R., Hoenk, P. R., & Slymen, D. J. Secondary depression in anxiety neurosis. *Journal of Nervous and Mental Disease*, 1978, *166*, 846–850.

Clark, L. What gives women sexual pleasure. *Sexology*, 1970, January, 46–49.

Clark, M. S., Milberg, S., & Erber, R. Effect of arousal on judgments of others' emotions. *Journal of Personality and Social Psychology*, 1984, *46*, 551–560.

Clarke, A. W. Hormones, behavior and the menstrual cycle. *Journal of Psychosomatic Research*, 1985, *29*, 225–233.

Clarke, A., & Ruble, D. Young adolescents' beliefs concerning menstruation. *Child Development*, 1978, *49*, 321–324.

Clarke, P. S. Effects of emotion and cough on airways obstruction in asthma. *Medical Journal of Australia*, 1970, *1*, 535–537.

Clausen, J. Respiratory movements in normal, neurotic and psychotic subjects. *Acta Psychiatrica et Neurologica Scandinanvica*, 1951, Supplementum, 68.

Cleeland, C. S. Behavioral tactics in the modification of spasmodic torticollus. *Neurology*, 1973, *23*, 1241–1247.

Cobb, S., Schull, W. J., Harburg, E., & Kasl, S. V. The intrafamilial transmission of rheumatoid arthritis: I-VII. *Journal of Chronic Diseases*, 1969, *22*, 193–295.

Coe, F. L. Polyuria and nocturia. In K. J. Isselbacher, R. D. Adams, E. Braunwald, R. G. Petersdorf, & J. D. Wilson (Eds.), *Harrison's principles of internal medicine* (9th ed.). New York: McGraw-Hill, 1980.

Cohen, A. S., Barlow, D. H., & Blanchard, E. B. Psychophysiology of relaxation-associated panic attacks. *Journal of Abnormal Psychology*, 1985, *94*, 96–101.

Cohen, A. S., Rosen, R. C., & Goldstein, L. EEG hemispheric asymmetry during sexual arousal: Psychological patterns in responsive, unresponsive and dysfunctional men. *Journal of Abnormal Psychology*, 1985, *94*, 580–590.

Cohen. D. B. Dysphoric affect and REM sleep. *Journal of Abnormal Psychology*, 1979, *88*, 73–77. (a)

Cohen, D. B. *Sleep and dreaming: Origins, nature and functions.* New York: Pergamon, 1979. (b)

Cohen, H. D., Rosen, R. C., & Goldstein, L. Electroencephalograhpic laterality changes during human sexual orgasm. *Archives of Sexual Behavior*, 1976, *5*, 189–199.

Cohen, M. E., & White, P. D. Life situations, emotions and neurocirculatory asthenia (anxiety neurosis, neurasthenia, effort syndrome). In *Proceedings of the Association for Research in Nervous and Mental Diseases, Vol. XXIX: Life stress and bodily disease.* Baltimore: Williams & Witkins, 1950.

Cohen, S. I., Silverman, A. J., & Magnussen, F. New psychological correlates in women with peptic ulcer. *American Journal of Psychiatry*, 1956, *112*, 1025–1026.

Coldsmith, D. "Symbolic" amenorrhea—Emotional factors in secondary amenorrhea. *Medical Aspects of Human Sexuality*, 1979, September, 102–112.

Colt, E. W., Wardlaw, S. C., & Franz, A. G. The effects of running on plasma beta-endorphin. *Life Science*, 1981, *28*, 1637–1640.

Connor, W. H. Effects of brief relaxation training on autonomic response to anxiety-evoking stimuli. *Psychophysiology*, 1974, *11*, 591–599.

Cook, J. R. Repression-sensitization and approach-avoidance as predictors of response to a laboratory stressor. *Journal of Personality and Social Psychology*, 1985, *49*, 759–773.

Cook, T. C., & Cashman, P. M. Stress and ectopic beats in ships pilots. *Journal of Psychosomatic Research*, 1982, *26*, 559–569.

Cooke, G. Evaluation of the efficacy of the components of reciprocal inhibition psychotherapy. *Journal of Abnormal Psychology*, 1968, *73*, 464–467.

Cooper, A. J. A clinical study of "coital anxiety" in male potency disorders. *Journal of Psychosomatic Research*, 1969, *13*, 143–147. (a)

Cooper, A. J. Some personality factors in frigidity. *Journal of Psychosomatic Research*, 1969, *13*, 149–155. (b)

Coppen, A. Indoleamines and affective disorders. *Journal of Psychiatric Research*, 1972, *9*, 163–171.

Cowan, W. M. The development of the brain. *Scientific American*, 1979, *241(3)*, 113–133.

Craig, K. D. Physiological arousal as a function of imagined, vicarious and direct stress experiences. *Journal of Abnormal Psychology*, 1968, *73*, 513–520.

Craig, T. K., & Brown, G. W. Goal frustration and life events in the aetiology of painful gastrointestinal disorder. *Journal of Psychosomatic Research*, 1984, *28*, 411–421.

Cram, J. R., & Steger, J. C. EMG scanning in the diagnosis of chronic pain. *Biofeedback and Self-Regulation*, 1983, *8*, 229–241.

Crawford, D. G., Friesen, D. D., & Tomlinson-Keasey, C. Effects of cognitively induced anxiety on hand temperature. *Biofeedback and Self-Regulation*, 1977, *2*, 139–146.

Crisp, A. H., Plamer, R. L., & Kalucy, R. S. How common is anorexia nervosa: A prevalence study. *British Journal of Psychiatry*, 1976, *128*, 549–554.

Crooks, R., & Baur, K. *Our sexuality* (2nd ed.). Menlo Park, Calif.: Benjamin-Cummings, 1983.

Curt, B. A., Jacobsen, S., & Marcus, E. M. *An introduction to the neurosciences.* Philadelphia: Saunders, 1972.

Cutrow, R. J., Parks, A., Lucas, N., & Thomas, K. The objective use of multiple physiological indices in detection of deception. *Psychophysiology*, 1972, *9*, 578–588.

Dahlem, D. W., & Kinsman, R. A. Panic-fear in asthma: A divergence between subjective report and behavioral patterns. *Perceptual and Motor Skills*, 1978, *46*, 95–98.

Dalton, K. *Once a month.* Claremont: Hunter House, 1979.

Darwin, C. R. *The expression of the emotions in man and animals.* New York: Appleton and Company, 1896. (Originally published in London by Murray in 1872).

Davenport, C., Xrull, J., Kuhn, C., & Harrison, S. Cyclical vomiting. *Journal of the American Academy of Child Psychiatry*, 1972, *11*, 66–87.

Davidson, J. M. The psychobiology of sexual experience. In J. M. Davidson & R. J. Davidson (Eds.), *The psychobiology of consciousness*. New York: Plenum Press, 1980.

Davidson, R. J. Specificity and patterning in biobehavioral systems: Implications for behavior change. *American Psychologist*, 1978, *33*, 430–436.

Davidson, R. J. Affect, cognition and hemispheric specialization. In C. E. Izard, J. Kagan, & R. Zajonc (Eds.), *Emotion, cognition and behavior*. New York: Cambridge University Press, 1983. (a)

Davidson, R. J. Affect, repression and cerebral asymmetry. In C. Van Dyke & L. Temoshok (Eds.), *Emotions in health and illness: Foundations of clinical practice*. New York: Academic Press, 1983. (b)

Davidson, R. J. Hemispheric asymmetry and emotion. In K. R. Scherer & P. Ekman (Eds.), *Approaches to emotion*. Hillsdale, N.J.: Erlbaum, 1984.

Davidson, R. J., & Schwartz, G. E. The psychobiology of relaxation and related states: A multi-process theory. In D. I. Mostofsky (Ed.), *Behavior control and modification of physiological activity*. Englewood Cliffs, N.J.: Prentice-Hall, 1976.

Davis, A. J. Sexual assaults in the Philadelphia prison system and sheriff's vans. In C. Gordon & G. Johnson (Eds.) *Readings in human sexuality: Contemporary perspectives*. New York: Harper & Row, 1980.

Davis, D. T., & Wilson, A. T. Observations on the life history of chronic peptic ulcer. *Lancet*, 1973, *1*, 1354–1360.

Davis, H. V., Sears, R. R., Miller, H. C., & Brodbeck, A. J. Effects of cup, bottle and breast-feeding on oral activities of newborn infants. *Pediatrics*, 1948, *2*, 549–558.

Davis, H., & Unruh, W. R. The development of self-schema in adult depression. *Journal of Abnormal Psychology*, 1981, *90*, 125–133.

Davis, J. M. Critique of single amine theories: Evidence of a cholenergic influence in the major mental illnesses. In D. X. Freedman (Ed.), *Biology of the major psychoses: A comparative analysis*. Research Publications of the Association for Research in Nervous and Mental Disease, Vol. 54. New York: Raven Press, 1975.

Davis, J. M., & Coles, J. O. Antipsychotic drugs. In A. M. Freedman, H. I. Kaplan, & B. J. Sadock (Eds.), *Comprehensive textbook of psychiatry II* (Vol. 2). Baltimore: Williams & Wilkins, 1975.

Davis, M. Morphine and naloxone: Effects on conditioned fear as measured with potentiated startle paradigm. *European Journal of Pharmacology*, 1979, *54*, 341–347.

Davison, G. C., & Wilson, G. T. Processes of fear-reduction in systematic desensitization: Cognitive and social reinforcement factors in humans. *Behavior Therapy*, 1973, *4*, 1–21.

Deffenbacher, J. L. Worry and emotionality in test anxiety. In I. G. Sarason (Ed.), *Test anxiety: Theory, research and applications*. Hillsdale, N.J.: Erlbaum, 1980.

Degen, K. Sexual dysfunction in women using major tranquilizers. *Psychosomatics*, 1982, *23*, 959–961.

DeLeo, D., & Magni, G. Sexual side effects of antidepressant drugs. *Psychosomatics*, 1983, *24*, 1076–1082.

Delgado, J. M. *Physical control of the mind: Toward a psychocivilized society*. New York: Harper Colophon Books, 1971.

DeLong, M. R. Motor functions of the basal ganglia: Single-cell activity during movement. In F. O. Schmitt & F. G. Wordens (Eds.), *The neurosciences*. New York: Cambridge University Press, 1974.

DePaulo, B. M., & Rosenthal, R. Telling lies. *Journal of Personality and Social Psychology*, 1979, *37*, 1713–1722.

Deregowski, J. B. Pictorial perception and culture. *Scientific American*, 1972, *227(5)*, 80–88.

DeVries, H. A. Tranquilizer effect of exercise: A critical review. *Physician and Sports Medicine*, 1981, *9(11)*, 47–55.

Diagnostic and Statistical Manual (DSM) of Mental Disorders (3rd ed.). Washington, D.C.: American Psychiatric Association, 1980.

Diamond, M., & Karlen, A. *Sexual decisions*. Boston: Little, Brown, 1980.

Dittman, A. T., Parloff, M. B., & Boomer, D. S. Facial and bodily expression: A study of receptivity of emotional cues. *Psychiatry*, 1965, *28*, 239–244.

Dixon, N. F. The effect of subliminal stimulation upon autonomic and verbal behavior. *Journal of Abnormal and Social Psychology*, 1958, *57*, 29–36.

Doering, C. H., Brodie, H. K., Kraemer, H., Becker, H., & Hamburg, D. A. Plasma testosterone levels and psychologic measures in men over a two-month period. In R. Freidman, R. M. Richart, & R. L. Wiele (Eds.), *Sex differences in behavior*. Huntingon, N.Y.: Krieger, 1978.

Doleys, D. M. Weiler, D., & Pegram, V. Special disorders of childhood: Enuresis, encopresis and sleep disorders. In J. R. Lachenmeyer & M. S. Gibb (Eds.), *Psychopathology in childhood*. New York: Gardner Press, 1982.

Donat, D. C., & McCullough, J. P. Psychophysiological discriminants of depression at rest and in response to stress. *Journal of Clinical Psychology*, 1983, *39*, 315–320.

Dorpat, T. L., & Holmes, T. H. Mechanisms of skeletal muscle pain and fatigue. *Archives of Neurology and Psychiatry*, 1955, *74*, 628–640.

Dosuzkov, T. Idrosophobia: A form of pregenital conversion. *Psychoanalytic Quarterly*, 1975, *44*, 253–265.

Downey, J. A., Miller, J. M., & Darling, R. C. Thermoregulatory responses to deep and superficial cooling in spinal man. *Journal of Applied Physiology*, 1969, *27*, 209–212.

Doyle, J. A. *The male experience*. Dubuque: Wm. C. Brown, 1983.

Drew, F. L., & Stifel, E. N. Secondary amenorrhea among young women entering religious life. *Obstetric Gynecology*, 1968, *32*, 47–51.

Drillien, C. M. A study of normal and abnormal menstrual function in the A.T.S. *Journal of Obstetrics and Gynaecology*, 1946, *53*, 228–241.

Drummond, P. D. Extracranial and cardiovascular reactivity in migrainous subjects. *Journal of Psychosomatic Research*, 1982, *26*, 317–331.

Drummond, P. D. Cardiovascular reactivity in mild hypertension. *Journal of Psychosomatic Research*, 1983, *27*, 291–297.

Duddle, M. An increase of anorexia nervosa in a university population. *British Journal of Psychiatry*, 1973, *123*, 711–712.

Dudley, D. L., Martin, C. J., & Holmes, T. H. Dyspnea: Psychologic and physiologic observations. *Journal of Psychosomatic Research*, 1968, *11*, 325–339.

Duller, P., & Gentry, W. D. Use of biofeedback in treating chronic hyperhidrosis: A preliminary report. *British Journal of Dermatology*, 1980, *103*, 143–146.

Dutton, D., & Aron, A. Some evidence for heightened sexual attraction under conditions of high anxiety. *Journal of Personality and Social Psychology*, 1974, *30*, 510–517.

Eastman Kodak. *Medical infrared photography*. Rochester: Eastman Kodak Co., 1973.

Eaves, L. J. The structure of genotypic and environmental covariations for personality measurement: An analysis of PEN. *British Journal of Social and Clinical Psychology*, 1973, *12*, 275–282.

Eaves, L. J., & Eysenck, H. J. Genetics and the development of social attitudes. *Nature*, 1974, *249*, 288–289.

Eccles, J. C. *The understanding of the brain*. New York: McGraw-Hill, 1973.

Edelberg, R. Mechanisms of electrodermal adaptations for locomotion, manipulation, or defense. In E. Stellar & J. M. Sprague (Eds.), *Progress in physiological psychology* (Vol. 5). New York: Academic Press, 1973.

Edelson, E. The neuropeptide explosion. *Mosaic*, 1981, May/June, 15–18.

Edgerton, R. B. *The individual in cultural adaptation: A study of four East African peoples*. Berkeley: University of California Press, 1971.

Ehrenkranz, J. R. A gland for all seasons. *Natural History*, 1983, June, 18–23.

Eibl-Eibesfeldt, I. *Ethology: The biology of behavior*. New York: Holt, Rinehart & Winston, 1970.

Eibl-Eibesfeldt, I. Similarities and differences between cultures in expressive movements. In R. A. Hinde (Ed.), *Nonverbal communication*. Cambridge: Cambridge University Press, 1972.

Ekman, P. *Darwin and facial expression: A century of research in review*. New York: Academic Press, 1973.

Ekman, P. Biological and cultural contribution to body and facial movements in the expression of emotions. In A. O. Rorty (Ed.). *Explaining emotions*. Berkeley: University of California Press, 1980.

Ekman, P. Expression and the nature of emotion. In K. R. Scherer & Paul Ekman (Eds.), *Approaches to emotions*. Hillsdale, N.J.: Lawrence Erlbaum Associates, 1984.

Ekman, P. *Telling lies*. New York: Norton, 1985.

Ekman, P., & Friesen, W. V. The repertoire of nonverbal behavior: Categories, origins, usage, and coding. *Semiotica*, 1969, *1*, 49–98. (a)

Ekman, P., & Friesen, W. V. Nonverbal leakage and clues to deception. *Psychiatry*, 1969, *72*, 118–137. (b)

Ekman, P., & Friesen, W. V. Constants across cultures in the face and emotion. *Journal of Personality and Social Psychology*, 1971, *17*, 124–129.

Ekman, P., & Friesen, W. V. Detecting deception from the body or face. *Journal of Personality and Social Psychology*, 1974, *29*, 288–298.

Ekman, P., Levenson, R. W., & Friesen, W. V. Autonomic nervous system activity distinguished among emotions. *Science*, 1983, *221*, 1208–1210.

Ekman, P., Sorenson, E. R., & Friesen, W. V. Pan-cultural elements in facial displays of emotion. *Science*, 1969, *164*, 86–88.

Eller, J. J. Skin disorders and the psyche. *Cutis*, 1974, *13*, 395–416.

Ellis, A. *Humanistic psychotherapy: The rational-emotive approach*. New York: McGraw-Hill, 1974.

Ellis, E. M., Atkeson, B. M., & Calhoun, K. S. An assessment of long-term reactions to rape. *Journal of Abnormal Psychology*, 1981, *90*, 263–266.

Ellis, E. M., Atkeson, B. M., & Calhoun, K. S. An examination of differences between multiple- and single-incident victims of sexual assault. *Journal of Abnormal Psychology*, 1982, *91*, 221–224.

Ellis, H. *Studies in the psychology of sex* (Vol. 3; Part 2). New York: Random House, 1900.

Ellis, H. C., Thomas, R. L., McFarland, A. D., & Lane, J. W. Emotional mood states and retrieval in episodic memory. *Journal of Experimental Psychology: Learning, Memory and Cognition*, 1985, *11*, 363–370.

Ellson, D. G., Davis, R. C., Saltzman, I. J., & Burke, C. J. *A report on detection of deception*. Tech. Rep No. N6onr-18011. Bloomington: Indiana University, 1952.

Elmadjian, F. Excretion and metabolism of epinephrine. *Pharmacological Review*, 1959, *11*, 409–415.

Elmadjian, F., Hope, J. M., & Lamson, E. T. Excretion of epinephrine and norepinephrine in various emotional states. *Journal of Clinical Endocrinology and Metabolism*, 1957, *17*, 608–620.

Elmadjian, F., Hope, J. M., & Lamson, E. T. Excretion of epinephrine and norepinephrine under stress. *Recent Progress in Hormone Research*, 1958, *14*, 513–521.

Engel, B. T., & Chism, R. A. Effects of increases and decreases in breathing rate on heart rate and finger pulse volume. *Pyschophysiology*, 1967, *4*, 83–89.

Engels, W. D. Dermatologic disorders. *Psychosomatics*, 1982, *23*, 1209–1219.

Epstein, S. The stability of behavior: I. On predicting most of the people much of the time. *Journal of Personality and Social Psychology*, 1979, *37*, 1097–1126.

Evarts, E. V. Activity on thalamic and cortical neurons in relation to learned movements in the monkey. *International Journal of Neurology*, 1971, *8*, 321–326.

Evarts, E. V. Brain mechanisms in movement. *Scientific American*, 1973, *229(1)*, 96–103.

Evarts, E. V. Brain mechanisms of movement. *Scientific American*, 1979, *241(3)*, 164–179.

Eysenck, H. J. The appreciation of humor: An experimental and theoretical study. *British Journal of Psychology*, 1942, *32*, 295–309.

Eysenck, H. J. *The biological basis of personality*. Springfield, Ill.: Thomas, 1967.

Eysenck, H. J. *The structure of human personality*. London: Methuen, 1970.

Fahndrich, E. Effects of sleep deprivation as a predictor of treatment response to antidepressant medication. *Acta Psychiatrica Scandinavica*, 1983, *68(5)*, 341–344.

Falkner, W. B. Severe esophageal spasm: An evaluation of suggestion therapy as determined by means of the esophageoscope. *Psychosomatic Medicine*, 1940, *2*, 139–140.

Falls, H. B., Baylor, A. M., & Dishman, R. K. *Essentials of fitness*. Philadelphia: Saunders, 1980.

Farber, S. L. Genetic diversity and differing reactions to stress. In L. Goldberger & S. Bresnitz (Eds.), *Handbook of stress*. New York: Free Press, 1982.

Fava, G. A., Fava, M., Kellner, R., Serafini, E., & Mastrogiacomo, I. Depression, hostility and anxiety in hyperprolactinemic amenorrhea. *Psychotherapy and Psychosomatics*, 1981, *36*, 122–128.

Fava, M., Fava, G. A., Kellner, R., Serafini, E., & Mastrogiacomo, I. Psychological correlates of hyperprolactinemia in males. *Psychotherapy and Psychosomatics*, 1982, *37*, 214–217.

Fawcett, J., Maas, J. W., & Dekirmenjian, H. Depression and MHPG secretion. Response to dextroamphetamine and tricyclic antidepressants. *Archives of General Psychiatry*, 1972, *26*, 246–251.

Featherstone, H. J., & Beitman, B. D. Marital migraine: A refractory daily headache. *Psychosomatics*, 1984, *25*, 30–38.

Fehr, F. S., & Stern, J. A. Peripheral physiological variables and emotion: The James-Lange theory revisited. *Psychological Bulletin*, 1970, 74(6), 411–424.

Feinmann, C. Psychogenic facial pain: Presentation and treatment. *Journal of Psychosomatic Research*, 1983, *27*, 403–410.

Feldman, M., & Fordtran, J. Vomiting. In M. S. Sleisenger & J. S. Fordtran (Eds.), *Gastrointestinal disease: Pathophysiology, diagnosis, management* (2nd ed.). Philadelphia: Saunders, 1978.

Feleky, A. The influence of emotions on respiration. *Journal of Experimental Psychology*, 1916, *1*, 218–241.

Fell, J. P. The phenomenological approach to emotion. In D. K. Candland, J. P. Fell, E. Keen, A. I. Leshner, R. M. Tarpey, & R. Plutchik (Eds.), *Emotion*. Monterey, Calif.: Brooks/Cole, 1977.

Fenz, W. D., & Epstein, S. Gradients of physiological arousal in parachutists as a function of an approaching jump. *Psychosomatic Medicine*, 1967, *29*, 33–51.

Feshbach, S. Aggression. In P. H. Mussen (Ed.), *Carmichael's manual of child psychology* (Vol. 2). New York: Wiley, 1970.

Fielding, J. F. The irritable bowel syndrome: The clinical spectrum. *Clinics in Gastorenterology*, 1977, *6*, 607–622.

Fisch, H. U., Frey, S., & Hirsbrunner, H. P. Analyzing nonverbal behavior in depression. *Journal of Abnormal Psychology*, 1983, *92*, 307–318.

Fisher, C., Gross, J., & Zuch, J. Cycle of penile erections synchronous with dreaming (REM) sleep: Preliminary report. *Archives of General Psychiatry*, 1965, *12*, 29–45.

Fisher, S., & Greenberg, R. P. *The scientific credibility of Freud's theories and therapy*. New York: Basic Books, 1977.

Fishkin, L. P., & King, L. C. Psychiatric aspects of menstrual dysfunction. In R. L. Gallon (Ed.), *The psychosomatic approach to illness*. New York: Elsevier Biomedical, 1982.

Fitts, P. M. Perceptual-motor skill learning. In A. W. Melton (Ed.), *Categories of human learning*. New York: Academic Press, 1964.

Flor, H., Turk, D. C., & Birbaumer, N. Assessment of stress-related psychophysiological reactions in chronic back pain patients. *Journal of Consulting and Counseling Psychology*, 1985, *53*, 354–364.

Flynn, J. P. The neural basis of aggression in cats. In D. C. Glass (Ed.), *Neurophysiology and emotion*. New York: Rockefeller University Press, 1967.

Flynn, J. P., Vanegas, H., Foote, W., & Edwards, S. Neural mechanisms involved in a cat's attack on a rat. In R. E. Whalen, R. F. Thompson, M. Verreano, & N. M. Weinberger (Eds.), *The neural control of behavior*. New York: Academic Press, 1970.

Folkins, C. H. Temporal factors and cognitive mediators of stress reaction. *Journal of Personality and Social Psychology*, 1970, *14*, 173–184.

Foltz, E. L., & Miller, F. E. Experimental psychosomatic disease states in monkeys: I. Peptic "ulcer-executive" monkeys. *Journal of Surgical Research*, 1964, *4*, 445–453.

Fonagy, P., & Calloway, S. P. The effects of emotional arousal on spontaneous swallowing rates. *Journal of Psychosomatic Research*, 1986, *30*, 183–188.

Ford, C. S., & Beach, F. A. *Patterns of sexual behavior*. New York: Harper, 1951.

Ford, C. V. *The somatizing disorders: Illness as a way of life*. New York: Elsevier Biomedical, 1983.

Forsman, L. Note on estimating catecholamines in urine sampled after 75-min. periods of mental work and inactivity. *Journal of Psychosomatic Research*, 1981, *25*, 223–225.

Forsman, L., & Lindblad, L. E. Effect of mental stress on baroreceptor-mediated changes in blood pressure and heart rate and on plasma cathecholamine and subjective responses in healthy men and women. *Psychosomatic Medicine*, 1983, *45*, 435–445.

Frankenhaeuser, M. Framework for psychoneuroendocrine studies. In *Nebraska Symposium on Motivation*. Lincoln: University of Nebraska Press, 1978.

Frankenhaeuser, M., & Jarpe, G. Psychophysiological reactions to mixtures of adrenaline and noradrenaline. *Scandinavian Journal of Psychology*, 1962, *3*, 21–29.

Frankenhaeuser, M., & Rissler, A. Effects of catecholamine release and efficiency of performance. *Psychopharmacologia*, 1970, *17*, 378–390.

Frankenhauser, M., Jarpe, G., & Matell, G. Effects of intravenous infusions of adrenaline and noradrenaline on certain psychological and physiological functions. *Acta Physiologica Scandinavica*, 1961, *51*, 175–186.

Frankenhaeuser, M., Rauste-von Wright, M., Collins, A., von Wright, J., Sedvall, G., & Swahn, C. G. Sex difference in psychoneuroendocrine reactions to examination stress. *Psychosomatic Medicine*, 1978, *40*, 334–343.

Freedman, D. G. Ethnic differences in babies. *Human Nature*, 1979, January, 36–43.

Freedman, D. G., & Keller, B. Inheritance of behavior in infants. *Science*, 1963, *140*, 196–198.

Freedman, R. R., & Ianni, P. Effects of general and thematically relevant stressors in Raynaud's disease. *Journal of Psychosomatic Research*, 1985, *29*, 275–280.

Freedman, R. R., Ianni, P., & Wenig, P. Behavioral treatment of Raynaud's disease: Long-term follow-up. *Journal of Consulting and Clinical Psychology*, 1985, 53, 136.

Freud, S. Formulations regarding two principles in mental functioning. 1911. Translated by M. N. Searl. *Collected Papers* (Vol. 4). London: Hogarth Press, 1925.

Freud, S. The ego and the id. 1923. Translated by J. Riviere. *The standard edition of the complete works of Sigmund Freud* (Vol. XIX). London: Hogarth Press, 1961.

Freud, S. *The problem of anxiety*. 1926. Translated by H. Bunker. New York: Norton, 1936.

Freud, S. *The psychopathology of everday life*. 1904. Translated by A. A. Brill. *The basic writings of Sigmund Freud*. New York: Modern Library, 1938.

Freud, S. *A general introduction to psychoanalysis*. 1917. Translated by J. Riviere. Garden City: Garden City Pub. Co., 1943.

Freud, S. *Beyond the pleasure principle*. 1920. Translated by J. Strachey. New York: Liveright Pub., 1950.

Freud, S. The interpretation of dreams, 1900–1901. Translated by J. Strachey & A. Freud. *The standard edition of the complete works of Sigmund Freud* (Vols. IV, V). London: Hogarth, 1953.

Freud, S. Jokes and their relationship to the unconscious. 1900. Translated by J. Strachey & A Freud. *The standard edition of the complete works of Sigmund Freud* (Vol. VIII). London: Hogarth, 1960.

Freud, S. Some psychical consequences of the anatomical distinctions between the sexes. 1925. Translated by J. Strachey & A. Freud. *The standard edition of the complete works of Sigmund Freud*. (Vol. XIX). London: Hogarth, 1961.

Freud, S. *An outline of psychoanalysis*. 1939. Translated by J. Strachey. New York: Norton, 1970.

Friedlund, A. J., Schwartz, G. E., & Fowler, S. C. Pattern recognition of self-reported emotional state from multiple-site facial EMG activity during affective imagery. *Psychophysiology*, 1984, *21*, 622–637.

Friedman, M., & Rosenman, R. *Type A behavior and your heart*. New York: Knopf, 1974.

Frisch, R. E., & McAuthur, J. W. Menstrual cycles: Fatness as a determinant of minimum weight for height necessary for their maintenance or onset. *Science*, 1974, *185*, 949–951.

Fritz, G. K. Childhood asthma. *Psychosomatics*, 1983, *24*, 959–967.

Frohman, L. A. Neurotransmitters as regulators of endocrine function. In D. T. Krieger & J. C. Hughes (Eds.), *Neuroendocrinology*. Sunderland, Mass.: Sinauer, 1980.

Funkenstein, D. H. Norepinephrine-like and epinephrine-like substances in relation to human behavior. *Journal of Nervous and Mental Disease*, 1956, *124*, 58–67.

Fyer, A. J., Gorman, J. M., Liebowitz, M. R., Levitt, M., Danielson, E., Martinez, J., & Klein, D. F. Sodium lactate infusion panic attacks and ionized calcium. *Biological Psychiatry*, 1984, *19(10)*, 1437–1448.

Gaelick, L., Bodenhausen, G. V., & Wyer, R. S. Emotional communication in close relationships. *Journal of Personality and Social Psychology*, 1985, *49*, 1246–1265.

Gage, D. F., & Safer, M. A. Hemisphere differences in the mood state-dependent effect for recognition of emotional faces. *Journal of Experimental Psychology: Learning, Memory and Cognition*, 1985. *11*, 752–763.

Gagnon, J., & Simon, W. *Sexual conduct*. Chicago: Aldine, 1973.

Galbraith, G. G., & Mosher, D. L. Associative sexual responses in relation to sexual arousal, guilt and external approval contingencies. *Journal of Personality and Social Psychology*, 1968, *10*, 142–147.

Galin, D. Implications for psychiatry of left and right cerebral specialization. *Archives of General Psychiatry*, 1974, *31*, 572–583.

Gallois, C., & Callan, V. J. Decoding emotional messages: Influence of ethnicity, sex, message type and channel. *Journal of Personality and Social Psychology*, 1986, *51*, 755–762.

Gambaro, S., & Rabin, A. I. Diastolic blood pressure responses following direct and displaced aggression after anger arousal in high- and low-guilt subjects. *Journal of Personality and Social Psychology*, 1969, *12*, 87–94.

Gardner, L. I. Deprivation dwarfism. *Scientific American*, 1972, *227(7)*, 76–82.

Garfinkel, P. E., & Gardner, D. M. *Anorexia nervosa. A multidimensional perspective*. New York: Brunner-Mazel, 1982.

Gatchel, R. J. Biofeedback and the treatment of fear and anxiety. In R. J. Gatchel & K. P. Price (Eds.), *Clinical applications of biofeedback: Appraisal and status*. New York: Pergamon Press, 1979.

Gawin, F. H., & Markoff, R. A. Panic anxiety after abrupt discontinuation of amitriptyline. *American Journal of Psychiatry*, 1981, *138(1)*, 117–118.

Gazzaniga, M. S. The split brain in man. *Scientific American*, 1967, *217(2)*, 24–29.

Gazzaniga, M. S. *The bisected brain*. New York: Appleton-Century-Crofts, 1970.

Gazzaniga, M. S. One brain—two minds? In I. Janis (Ed.), *Current trends in psychology*. Los Altos, Calif.: Kaufmann, 1977.

Gazzaniga, M. S., & LeDoux, J. E. *The integrated mind*. New York: Plenum Press, 1978.

Geen, R. G. The meaning of observed violence: Real vs. fictional violence and consequent effects on aggression and emotional arousal. *Journal of Research in Personality*, 1975, *9*, 270–281.

Geen, R. G. Preferred stimulation levels in introverts and extroverts: Effects of arousal on performance. *Journal of Personality and Social Psychology*, 1984, *46*, 1303–1312.

Geen, R. G., & Stonner, D. The meaning of observed violence: Effects on arousal and aggressive behavior. *Journal of Research in Personality*, 1974, *8*, 55–63.

Geer, J. H. Fear and autonomic arousal. *Journal of Abnormal and Social Psychology*, 1966, *71*, 253–255.

Gellhorn, E. Motion and emotion: The role of proprioception in the physiology and pathology of emotions. *Psychological Review*, 1964, *71*, 457–472.

Gentry, W. D. Sex differences in the effects of frustration and attack on emotion and vascular process. *Psychological Reports*, 1970, *27*, 383–390.

Gerrard, M. Sex guilt in abortion patients. *Journal of Consulting and Clinical Psychology*, 1977, *45*, 708.

Gerrard, M. Sex, sex guilt and contraceptive use. *Journal of Personality and Social Psychology*, 1982, *42*, 153–158.

Gesell, A. Early evidence of individuality in the human infant. *Scientific Monthly*, 1937, *45*, 217–225.

Gessel, A. H. Electromyographic biofeedback and tricyclic antidepressants in myofascial pain-dysfunction syndrome: Psychological predictors of outcome. *Journal of the American Dental Association*, 1975, *91*, 1048–1052.

Gessel, A. H., & Alderman, M. N. Management of myofascial pain dysfunction syndrome of the temporomandibular joints by tension control training. *Psychosomatics*, 1971, *12*, 302–309.

Ghose, K., & Coppen, A. Bromocriptine and premenstrual syndrome: A controlled study. *British Medical Journal*, 1977, *11*, 147–148.

Gibson, C. J., & Gelenberg, A. Tyrosine for the treatment of depression. *Advances in Biological Psychiatry*, 1983, *10*, 148–159.

Giles, H., & Oxford, G. S. Towards a multidimensional theory of laughter causation and its social implications. *Bulletin of the British Psychological Society*, 1970, *23*, 97–105.

Gill, W., & Coe, F. L. Dysuria, incontinence and enuresis. In K. J. Isselbacker, R. D. Adams, E. Braunwald, R. G. Petersdorf, & J. D. Wilson (Eds.), *Harrison's principles of internal medicine* (9th ed.). New York: McGraw-Hill, 1980.

Glass, D. C. Stress, behavior patterns, and coronary disease. *American Scientist*, 1977, *65*, 177–187.

Glasser, W. *Positive addiction*. Hagerstown: Harper & Row, 1976.

Goddard, G. V. Functions of the amygdala. *Psychological Bulletin*, 1964, *62*, 89–109.

Goldberg, S. Premature birth: Consequences for the parent-infant relationship. *American Scientist*, 1979, *67*, 214–220.

Goldfried, M. R. Systematic desensitization as training in self-control. *Journal of Consulting and Clinical Psychology*, 1971, *37*, 228–234.

Goldfried, M. R., & Trier, C. Effectiveness of relaxation as an active coping skill. *Journal of Abnormal Psychology*, 1974, *83*, 348–355.

Goldstein, D., Fink, D., & Mettee, D. R. Cognition of arousal and actual arousal as determinants of emotion. *Journal of Personality and Social Psychology*, 1972, *21*, 41–51.

Goldstein, M. L. Physiological theories of emotion; A critical review from the standpoint of behavior theory. *Psychological Bulletin*, 1968, *69(6)*, 78–90.

Golenhofen, K. Zur Topographie der Muskelaktiviat bei Kaltebebalstung des Menschen. *Arch. Phy. Ther. (Lpz)*, 1963, *15*, 435–438. Cited in H. Hensel, *Thermoreception and thermal regulation*. New York: Academic Press, 1981.

Gonzalez, E. R. Drug treatment and nutrient therapy: The distinction blurs. *New York State Journal of Medicine*, 1984, *84(9)*, 467–472.

Gooden, B. A., Feinstein, R., & Skutt, H. R. Heart rate responses of scuba divers via ultrasonic telemetry. *Undersea Biomedical Reseach*, 1975, *10*, 11–19.

Goodman, P., Greene, C. S., & Laskin, D. M. Response of patients with myofascial pain dysfunction syndrome to mock equilibration. *Journal of American Dental Association*, 1976, *92*, 755–758.

Goodwin, F. K., Murphy, D. L., Brodie, H. K., & Bunney, W. E. L-dopa, catecholamines and behavior: A clinical and biochemical study in depressed patients. *Biological Psychiatry*, 1970, *2*, 314–366.

Gordon, B. The superior colliculus of the brain. *Scientific American*, 1972, *227(6)*, 72–82.

Gorman, J. M., Askanazi, J., Liebowitz, M. R., Fyer, A. J., Stein, J., Kinney, J. M., & Klein, D. F. Response to hyperventilation in a group of patients with panic disorder. *American Journal of Psychiatry*, 1984, *141(7)*, 857–861.

Gorman, J. M., Liebowitz, M. R., Stein, J., Fyer, A. J., & Klein, D. F. Insulin levels during lactate infusion. *American Journal of Psychiatry*, 1984, *141(12)*, 1621–1622.

Gotestam, K. G., Melin, L., & Olsson, B. Treatment of erythrophobia by cooling and temperature feedback. *Scandinavian Journal of Behavior Therapy*, 1976, *5*, 153–159.

Gottesman, I. I. Developmental genetics and ontogenetic psychology. *Minnesota Symposia on Child Psychology* (Vol. 8). Minneapolis: University of Minnesota Press, 1963. (a)

Gottesman, I. I. Heriability of personality: A demonstration. *Psychological Monographs*, 1963, *77* (Whole No. 572.). (b)

Gottlieb, H., Strite, L. C., Koller, R., Madorsky, A., Hochersmith, V., Kleeman, M., & Wagner, J. Comprehensive rehabilitation of patients having chronic low back pain. *Archives of Physical Medicine and Rehabilitation*, 1977, *58*, 101–108.

Gottschalk, L. A. Self-induced visual imagery, affect arousal and autonomic correlates. *Psychosomatics*, 1974, *15*, 166–169.

Gottschalk, L. A., Kaplan, S. M., Gleser, G. C., & Winget, C. M. Variations in the magnitude of emotions: A method applied to anxiety and hostility during phases of the menstrual cycle. *Psychosomatic Medicine*, 1962, *24*, 300–311.

Gould, L. N. Auditory hallucinations and subvocal speech. *Journal of Nervous and Mental Disease*, 1949, *109*, 418–427.

Goy, R. W., Phoenix, C. H., & Young, W. C. A critical period for suppressing the behavioral receptivity in adult female rats by early treatment with androgen. *Anatomical Record*, 1962, *142*, 307.

Graber, B., & Kline-Graber, G. Female orgasm: Role of the pubococcygeus muscle. *Journal of Clinical Psychiatry*, 1979, *40*, 348–351.

Graham, D. T. Cutaneous vascular reactions in Raynaud's disease and in states of hostility, anxiety and depression. *Psychosomatic Medicine*, 1955, *17*, 200–207.

Graham, D. T., Stern, J. A., & Winokur, C. Experimental investigation of the specificity of attitude hypothesis in psychosomatic disease. *Psychosomatic Medicine*, 1958, *20*, 446–457.

Graham, J. R., & Wolff, H. G. Mechanism of migraine headache and action of ergotamime tartrate. *Archives of Neurological Psychiatry*, 1938, *39*, 737–763.

Grant, C., & Pryse-Davies, J. Effects of oral contraceptives on depressive mood changes and endometrial monoamine oxidase and phosphates. *British Medical Journal*, 1968, *1*, 777–780.

Gray, J. A. Anxiety. *Human Nature*, 1978, July, 38–45.

Green, E. E., Green, A. M., & Norris, P. A. Self-regulation for control of hypertension. *Primary Cardiology*, 1980, *6*, 126–137.

Griggs, R. C., & Stunkard, A. J. The interpretation of gastric motility: Sensitivity and bias in the perception of gastric motility. *Archives of General Psychiatry*, 1964, *2*, 83–89.

Grings, W. W., & Dawson, M. E. *Emotion and bodily responses*. New York: Academic Press, 1978.

Groen, J. J., Hansen, B., Herrmann, H., Schafer, H., Schmidt, T. H., Selbmann, K. H., Uexkull, T. V., & Weckmann, P. Effects of experimental emotional stress and physical exercise on the circulation in hypertensive and control subjects. *Journal of Psychosomatic Research*, 1982, *26*, 141–154.

Grollman, S. *The human body*. New York: Macmillian, 1964.

Gross, R. J., Doerr, H., & Caldirola, D. Borderline syndrome and incest in chronic pelvic pain patients. *International Journal of Psychiatry and Medicine*, 1980, *10*, 79–96.

Grossberg, J. M., & Wilson, H. K. Physiological changes accompanying visualization of fearful and neutral situations. *Journal of Personality and Social Psychology*, 1968, *10*, 124–133.

Grossman, P., & DeSwart, J. C. Diagnosis of hyperventilation syndrome on the basis of reported complaints. *Journal of Psychosomatic Research*, 1984, *28*, 97–104.

Grossman, P., DeSwart, J. C., & Defares, P. B. A controlled study of a breathing therapy for treatment of hyperventilation syndrome. *Journal of Psychosomatic Medicine*, 1985, *29*, 49–58.

Grossman, S. P. Eating or drinking elicited by adrenergic or cholinergic stimulation of hypothalamus. *Science*, 1960, *132*, 301–302.

Grossman, S. P. Behavioral effects of direct chemical stimulation of central nervous system structures. *International Journal of Neuropharmacology*, 1964, *3*, 45–58.

Grosz, H. J., & Farmer, B. B. Blood lactate in the development of anxiety neurosis: A critical examination of Pitts and McClure's hypothesis and experimental study. *Archives of General Psychiatry*, 1969, *21*, 611–619.

Groth, A. N., & Burgess, W. Male rape: Offenders and victims. *American Journal of Psychiatry*, 1980, *137*, 806–810.

Gruzelier, J. H., & Venables, P. H. Skin conductance orienting activity in a heterogeneous sample of schizophrenics. *Journal of Nervous and Mental Disease*, 1972, *155*, 277–287.

Gruzelier, J. H., & Venables, P. H. Skin conductance response to tones with or without attentional significance in schizophrenic and nonschizophrenic psychiatric patients. *Neuropsychologia*, 1973, *11*, 221–230.

Guillemin, R. Peptides in the brain: The new endocrinology of the neuron. *Science*, 1978, *202*, 390–401.

Hafner, R. J., Stanron, S. L., & Guy, L. A psychiatric study of women with urgency incontinence. *British Journal of Urology*, 1977, *49*, 211.

Hager, J. C., & Ekman, P. The inner and outer meanings of facial expressions. In J. T. Cacioppo & R. E. Petty (Eds.), *Social psychophysiology: A source book*. New York: Guilford Press, 1983.

Hall, C. S., & Lindzey, G. *Theories of personality* (2nd ed.). New York: Wiley, 1970.

Hall, R. C. Psychiatric effects of thyroid hormone disturbance. *Psychosomatics*, 1983, *24*, 7–18.

Halmi, K. A. Anorexia and bulimia. *Psychosomatics*, 1983, *24*, 111–129.

Halmi, K. A., Falk, J. R., & Schwartz, E. Binge-eating and vomiting: A survey of a college population. *Psychological Medicine*, 1981, *11*, 697–706.

Hannon, J. P. Comparative altitude adaptability of young men and women. In L. J. Folinsbee, J. A. Wagner, J. F. Borgia, B. L. Drinkwater, J. A. Gliner, & J. F. Bedi (Eds.), *Environmental stress: Individual human adaptations*. New York: Academic Press, 1978.

Hare, R. D. Cardiovascular components of orienting and defensive responses. *Psychophysiology*, 1972, *9*, 606–614(a).

Hare, R. D. Psychopathy and physiological responses to adrenalin. *Journal of Abnormal Psychology*, 1972, *79*, 138–147(b).

Hare, R. D. Orienting and defensive reactions to visual stimuli. *Psychophysiology*, 1973, *10*, 453–464.

Hare, R. D. Psychophysiological studies of psychopathy. In D. C. Fowles (Ed.), *Clinical applications of psychophysiology*. New York: Columbia University Press, 1975.

Hare, R. D. Comparison of procedures for the assessment of psychopathy. *Journal of Consulting and Clinical Psychology*, 1985, *53*, 7–16.

Hare, R. D., & Blevings, G. Defensive responses to phobic stimuli. *Biological Psychology*, 1975, *3*, 1–13.

Hare, R. D., & Craigen, D. Psychopathy and physiological activity in a mixed-motive game situation. *Psychophysiology*, 1974, *11*, 197–206.

Hare, R. D., & Quinn, M. Psychopathy and autonomic conditioning. *Journal of Abnormal Psychology*, 1971, *77*, 223–239.

Hare, R., Wood, K., Britain, S., & Shadman, J. Autonomic responses to affective visual stimulation. *Psychophysiology*, 1971, *7*, 408–417.

Hare, R. D., Frazelle, J., & Cox, D. N. Psychopathy and psychological responses to threat of an aversive stimulus. *Psychophysiology*, 1978, *15*, 165–172.

Harris, J. C. *Uncle Remus and his friends*. Boston: Houghton Mifflin, 1914.

Harris, V. A., & Katkin, E. S. Primary and secondary emotional behavior: An analysis of the role of autonomic feedback on affect, arousal and attribution. *Psychological Bulletin*, 1975, *82*, 904–916.

Harris, V. A., Katkin, E. S., Lick, J. R., & Habberfield, T. Paced respiration as a technique for modification of autonomic response to stress. *Psychophysiology*, 1976, *13*, 386–391.

Hart, L. S., & Weiss, T. Current psychosomatic approaches to the treatment of cardiovascular disease. In R. L. Gallon (Ed.), *The psychosomatic approach to illness*. New York: Elsevier Biomedical, 1982.

Hartman, W. E., Fithian, M., & Johnson, D. *Nudist society: An authoritative, complete study of nudism in America*. New York: Crown, 1970.

Hartmann, E. I. *The functions of sleep*. New Haven: Yale University Press, 1973.

Haslam, M. T. The relationship between the effect of lactate infusion on anxiety states and their amelioration by carbon dioxide inhalation. *British Journal of Psychiatry*, 1974, *125*, 88–99.

Hassett, J. *A primer of psychophysiology*. San Francisco: Freeman, 1978.

Hastrup, J. L., & Light, K. C. Sex differences in cardiovascular stress responses: Modulation as a function of menstrual cycle phases. *Journal of Psychosomatic Research*, 1984, *28*, 475–483.

Hatfield, E., Specher, S., & Traupmann, J. Men's and women's reactions to sexually explicit films: A serendipitous finding. *Archives of Sexual Behavior*, 1978, *7*, 503–592.

Hawkins, E. R., Monroe, J. D., Sandifer, M. G., & Vernon, C. R. Psychological and physiological responses to continuous epinephrine infusion. *Psychiatric Research Report American Psychiatric Association*, 1960, *12*, 40–52.

Haynes, S. N., Follingstad, D. R., & McGowan, W. T. Insomnia: Sleep patterns and anxiety level. *Journal of Psychosomatic Research*, 1974, *18*, 69–74.

Haynes, S. N., Adams, A., & Franzen, M. The effects of presleep stress on sleep-onset insomnia. *Journal of Abnormal Psychology*, 1981, *90*, 601–606.

Haynes, S. N., Gannon, L. R., Cuevas, J., Heiser, P., Hamilton, J., & Katranides, M. The psychophysiological assessment of muscle-contraction headache subjects during headache and nonheadache conditions. *Psychophysiology*, 1983, *20*, 393–399.

Heath, R. G. Pleasure responses of human subjects to direct stimulation of the brain: Physiologic and psychodynamic considerations. In R. G. Heath (Ed.), *The role of pleasure in behavior.* New York: Hoeber, 1964.

Hebb, D. O. Heredity and environment in animal behaviour. *British Journal of Animal Behavior*, 1953, *1*, 43–47.

Heidbreder, E. *Seven psychologies.* New York: Appleton-Century-Crofts, 1961.

Heider, E. R. Universals in color naming and memory. *Journal of Experimental Psychology*, 1972, *93*, 10–20.

Heider, E. R., & Oliver, D. The structure of color space in naming and memory in two languages. *Cognitive Psychology*, 1972, *3*, 337–354.

Heiman, J. R. A psychophysiological exploration of sexual arousal patterns in females and males. *Psychophysiology*, 1977, *14*, 266–274.

Heiman, J. R., & Rowland, D. L. Affective and physiological sexual response patterns: The effects of instructions on sexually functional and dysfunctional men. *Journal of Psychosomatic Research*, 1983, *27*, 105–116.

Heisel, J. S. Life changes as etiological factors in juvenile rheumatoid arthritis. *Journal of Psychosomatic Research*, 1972, *17*, 411–420.

Held, R. Plasticity of sensory-motor systems. *Scientific American*, 1965, *213(5)*, 84–94.

Henane, R. Acclimatization to heat in man: Giant or windmill—A critical reappraisal. In Z. Szelenyi & M. Szekely (Eds.), *Advances in Physiological Sciences* (Vol. 32). Elsmford:, N.Y.: Pergamon Press, 1981.

Hensel, H. *Thermoreception and thermal regulation.* New York: Academic Press, 1981.

Herman, C. P., & Polivy, J. Anxiety, restraint, and eating behavior. *Journal of Abnormal Psychology*, 1975, *84*, 666–672.

Herrmann, F., Prose, P. H., & Sulzberger, M. B. Studies of sweating. IV. A new quantitative method of assaying sweat-delivery to circumscribed areas of the skin surface. *Journal of Investigative Dermatology*, 1951, *17*, 241–249.

Herzog, D. B. Bulimia: The secretive syndrome. *Psychosomatics*, 1982, *23*, 481–487.

Hetherington, E. M. Effects of father absence on personality development in adolescent daughters. *Developmental Psychology*, 1972, *7*, 313–326.

Hetherington, E. M., & Brackbill, Y. Etiology and covariation of obstinacy, orderliness and parsimony in young children. *Child Development*, 1963, *34*, 919–943.

Hewes, G. W. The anthropology of posture. *Scientific American*, 1957, *196(2)*, 123–132.

Hochschild, A. R. Emotional work, feeling rules and social structure. *American Journal of Sociology*, 1979, *85*, 551–575.

Hochschild, A. R. *The managed heart: Commercialization of human feeling.* Berkeley: University of California Press, 1983.

Hodges, W. E., & Spielberger, C. D. The effects of threat of shock on heart rate for subjects who differ in manifest anxiety and fear of shock. *Psychophysiology*, 1966, *2*, 287–294.

Hohmann, G. W. Some effects of spinal cord lesions on experiencing emotional feelings. *Psychophysiology*, 1966, *3*, 143–156.

Hokanson, J. E. Vascular and psychogalvanic effects of experimentally aroused anger. *Journal of Personality*, 1961, *29*, 30–39.

Hokanson, J. E. Psychophysiological evaluation of the catharsis hypothesis. In E. I. Megargee & J. E. Hokanson (Eds.), *The dynamics of aggression*. New York: Harper & Row, 1970.

Hokanson, J. E., & Burgess, M. The effect of three types of aggression on vascular processes. *Journal of Abnormal and Social Psychology*, 1962, *64*, 446–449. (a)

Hokanson, J. E., & Burgess, M. The effect of status, type of frustration, and aggression on vascular processes. *Journal of Abnormal and Social Psychology*, 1962, *65*, 232–237. (b)

Hokanson, J. E., & Edelman, R. Effects of three types of social process on vascular processes. *Journal of Personality and Social Psychology*, 1966, *3*, 442–447.

Hokanson, J. E., & Shetler, S. The effect of overt aggression on physiological arousal level. *Journal of Abnormal and Social Psychology*, 1961, *63*, 446–448.

Hokanson, J. E., Burgess, M., & Cohen, M. F. Effects of displaced aggression on systolic blood pressure. *Journal of Abnormal and Social Psychology*, 1963, *67*, 214–218.

Hokanson, J. E., Willers, K. R., & Koropsak, E. Modification of autonomic responses during aggressive interchange. *Journal of Personality*, 1968, *36*, 386–404.

Hollender, M. H., Luborsky, L., & Harvey, R. B. Correlates of the desire to be held in women. *Journal of Psychosomatic Research*, 1970, *14*, 387–390.

Hollister, L. E., Davis, K. L., & Berger, P. A. Subtypes of depression based on excretion of MHPG and response to nortriptyline. *Archives of General Psychiatry*, 1980, *37*, 1107–1110.

Holman, C. W., & Muschenheim, C. *Bronchopulmonary diseases and related disorders* (Vol. 2). New York: Harper & Row, 1972.

Holmes, D. S., & Burish, T. G. Effectiveness of biofeedback for treating migraine and tension headaches: A review of the evidence. *Journal of Psychosomatic Research*, 1983, *27*, 515–532.

Holmes, D. S., McCaul, K. D., & Solomon, S. Control of respiration as a means of controlling responses to threat. *Journal of Personality and Social Psychology*, 1978, *36*, 198–204.

Holmes, D. S., Solomon, S., & Rump, B. S. Cardiac and subjective responses to cognitive challenge and to controlled physical exercise by male and female coronary prone (Type A) and non-coronary prone persons. *Journal of Psychosomatic Research*, 1982, *26*, 309–316.

Holmes, D. S., McGilley, B. M., & Houston, B. K. Task-related arousal of Type A and Type B persons: Level of challenge and response specificity. *Journal of Personality and Social Psychology*, 1984, *46*, 1322–1327.

Holmes, T. H., & Wolff, H. G. Life situations, emotions and backache. *Psychosomatic Medicine*, 1952, *14*, 18–33.

Holroyd, K. A., & Appel, M. A. Test anxiety and physiological responding. In I. G. Sarason (Ed.), *Test anxiety: Theory, research and applications*. Hillsdale, N.J.: Erlbaum, 1980.

Holyroyd, K. A., & Gorkin, L. Young adults at risk for hypertension: Effects of family history and anger management in determining responses to interpersonal conflict. *Journal of Psychosomatic Research*, 1983, *27*, 131–138.

Holzle, E. On conjoint spectral gastrography or what surface gastrograms show. *Psychophysiology*, 1983, *20*, 428. Abstract.

Holzle, E. Pathogenesis and clinical features of hyperhidrosis. *Hautarzt (West Germany)*, 1983, *34*, 596–604.

Hoon, P. W., Wincze, J. P., & Hoon, E. F. A test of reciprocal inhibition: Are anxiety and sexual arousal in women mutually inhibitory? *Journal of Abnormal Psychology*, 1977, *86*, 65–74.

Horne, J. A. The effects of exercise on sleep: A critical review. *Biological Psychology*, 1981, *12*, 241–290.

Horne, J. A. Restitution and human sleep: A critical review. *Physiological Psychology*, 1979, *7*, 115–125.

Horrobin, Mtabaji, D. F., Mtabaji, J. P., Karmali, R. A., Manku, M. S., & Nassar, B. A. Prolactin and mental illness. *Postgraduate Medical Journal*, 1976, *52*(Suppl. 3), 79–85.

Hosobuchi, Y., Rossier, J., Bloom, F. E., & Guillemin, R. Stimulation of human preiaqueductal gray for pain relief increases immunoreactive beta-endorphin in venticular fluid. *Science*, 1979, *203*, 279–281.

Hubel, D. H. The brain. *Scientific American,* 1979, *241(3),* 44–53.

Hughes, J. Isolation of an endogenous compound from the brain with pharmacological properties similar to morphine. *Brain Research,* 1975, *88,* 295–308.

Hughes, J., Smith, T. W., Kosterlitz, H. W., Fothergill, L. A., Morgan, B. A., & Morris, H. R. Identification of two related pentapeptides from the brain with potent opiate agonist activity. *Nature,* 1975, *258,* 577–579.

Humphreys, M. S., Revelle, W., Simon, L., & Gilliland, K. Individual differences in diurnal rhythms and multiple activation states: A reply to M. W. Eysenck and Folkard. *Journal of Experimental Psychology: General,* 1980, *109,* 42–48.

Hunt, M. *Sexual behavior in the 1970's.* Chicago: Playboy Press, 1974.

Hutch, J. A., & Elliot, H. W. Electromyographic studies of the paraurethral muscles prior to and during voiding. *Journal of Urology,* 1968, *99,* 759–765.

Hyde, J. S. *Understanding human sexuality.* New York: McGraw-Hill, 1982.

Hyde, J. S., & Rosenberg, B. G. *Half of the human experience: The psychology of women.* Lexington: Heath, 1976.

Hyson, M. C., & Izard, C. E. Continuities and changes in emotional expression during brief separation at 13 and 18 months. *Developmental Psychology,* 1985, *21,* 1165–1170.

Iacono, W. G. Bilateral electrodermal habituation-dishabituation and resting EEG in remitted schizophrenics. *The Journal of Nervous and Mental Disease,* 1982, *170,* 91–101.

Iacono, W. G., Lykken, D. T., Peloquin, L. J., Lumry, A. E., Valentine, R. H., & Tuason, V. B. Electrodermal activity in euythymic unipolar and bipolar affective disorders: A possible marker for depression. *Archives of General Psychiatry,* 1983, *40,* 557–565.

Iacono, W. G., Lykken, D. T., Haroian, K. P., Peloquin, L. J., Valentine, R. H., & Tuason, V. B. Electrodermal activity in euthymic patients with affective disorders: One-year retest stability and the effects of stimulus intensity and significance. *Journal of Abnormal Psychology,* 1984, *93,* 304–311.

Ira, G. H., Whalen, R. E., & Bogdonoff, M. D. Heart rate changes during daily "stressful" tasks. *Journal of Psychosomatic Research,* 1963, *7,* 147–150.

Ivey, M. E., & Bardwick, J. M. Patterns of affective fluctuations and the menstrual cycle. *Psychosomatic Medicine,* 1968, *30,* 336–345.

Izard, C. E. *The face of emotion.* New York: Appleton-Century-Crofts, 1971.

Izard, C. E. *Patterns of emotions: A new analysis of anxiety and depression.* New York: Academic Press, 1972.

Izard, C. E. *Human emotion.* New York: Plenum Press, 1977.

Izard, C. E. Cross-cultural perspectives on emotion and emotion communication. In H. C. Triandis & W. Lonner (Eds.), *Handbook of cross-cultural psychology. Basic processes* (Vol. 3). Boston: Allyn & Bacon, 1980.

Izard, C. E., Huebner, R. R., Risser, D., McGinnes, G. C., & Dougherty, L. M. The young infant's ability to produce discrete emotion expressions. *Developmental Psychology,* 1980, *16,* 132–140.

Izard, C. E., & Malatesta, C. Z. A developmental theory of emotions. In J. Osofsky (Ed.), *The handbook of infant development.* New York: Wiley-Interscience, 1987.

Jacobs, A., & Felton, G. S. Visual feedback of myoelectric output to facilitate muscle relaxation in normal persons and patients with neck injuries. *Archives of Physical Medicine and Rehabilitation,* 1969, *50,* 34–39.

Jacobs, A., & Kilpatrick, G. S. The Patterson-Kelly syndrome. *British Medical Journal,* 1964, *2,* 79–82.

Jacobs, W. J., & Nadel, L. Stress-induced recovery of fears and phobias. *Psychological Review,* 1985, *92,* 512–531.

Jacobson, E. *Progressive relaxation* (2nd ed.). Chicago: University of Chicago Press, 1938.

James, W. What is an emotion? *Mind,* 1884, *9,* 188–205.

James, W. *Psychology: Briefer course.* New York: Holt, 1892.

James, W. The physiological basis of emotion. *Psychological Review,* 1894, *1,* 516–529.

Jayne, C. E. Effects of pubococcygeal exercise on female sexuality: Comment on Chambless *et al. Journal of Consulting and Clinical Psychology,* 1985, *53,* 269–270.

Jeffcoate, T. N. Functional disturbances of the female bladder and urethra. *Journal of the Royal College of Surgery, Edinburgh,* 1961, *7,* 28–47.

Jefferson, J. W., & Marshall, J. R. *Neuropsychiatric features of medical disorders.* New York: Plenum Press, 1981.

Jenkins, C. D. Psychologic and social precursors of coronary disease. *New England Journal of Medicine,* 1971, *284,* 244–255.

Johnson, J. H., & Sarason, I. G. Life stress, depression and anxiety: Internal-external control as a moderator variable. *Journal of Psychosomatic Research,* 1978, *22,* 205–208.

Jones, H. E. The study of patterns of emotional expression. In M. L. Reymert (Ed.), *Feeling and emotions.* New York, McGraw-Hill, 1950.

Jones, H. E., & Jones, M. C. Maturation and emotion: Fear of snakes. *Childhood Education,* 1928, *5,* 136–143.

Jones, H. W., & Jones, S. J. *Novak's textbook of gynecology* (10th ed.). Baltimore: Williams & Wilkins, 1981.

Jones, J. P. *Body awareness in action.* New York: Schocken, 1976.

Jones, M. C. The elimination of children's fears. *Journal of Experimental Psychology,* 1924, *7,* 382–390.

Jost, H., & Sontag, L. The genetic factor in autonomic nervous system function. *Psychosomatic Medicine,* 1944, *6,* 308–310.

Jouvet, M. Neurophysiology of the states of sleep. In G. C. Quarton, T. Melnechuk, and F. O. Schmitt (Eds.), *The neurosciences.* New York: Rockefeller University Press, 1967.

Kagan, J., & Moss, H. A. *Birth to maturity.* New York: Wiley, 1962.

Kahn, R. L. Stress: From 9 to 5. *Psychology Today,* 1969, *3(4),* 34–38.

Kanner, L. *Child Psychiatry* (4th ed.). Springfield, Ill.: Thomas, 1972.

Kantner, J. E., & Ascough, J. C. Physiological and self-report correlates of focusing and induced affect. *Psychotherapy: Theory, Research and Practice,* 1974, *11,* 250–253.

Karacan, I. Nocturnal penile tumescence as a biologic marker in assessing erectile dysfunction. *Psychosomatics,* 1982, *23,* 349–360.

Karasek, R., Baker, D., Marxer, F., Ahlbom, A., & Theorell, T. Job decision latitude, job demands and cardiovascular disease: A prospective study of Swedish men. *American Journal of Public Health,* 1981, *71,* 694–705.

Katkin, E. S. The relationship between a measure of transitory anxiety and spontaneous autonomic activity. *Journal of Abnormal Psychology,* 1966, *71,* 142–146.

Kaufman, A., Divasto, P., Jackson, R., Voorhees, D., & Christy, J. Male rape victims: Noninstitutional assault. *American Journal of Psychiatry,* 1980, *137,* 221–223.

Kegel, A. H. The physiologic treatment of poor tone and function of the genital muscles and of urinary stress incontinence. *Western Journal of Surgery, Obstetrics and Gynecology,* 1949, *57,* 527–535.

Kegel, A. H. Sexual functions of the pubococcygeus muscle. *Western Journal of Surgery, Obstetrics and Gynecology,* 1952, *60,* 521–524.

Keller, F. S. *The definition of psychology* (2nd ed.). Englewood Cliffs, N.J.: Prentice-Hall, 1973.

Kelly, A. and Stinus, L. Neuroanatomical and neurochemical substrates of affective behavior. In N. A. Fox and R. J. Davidson (Eds.), *The psychobiology of affective development.* Hillsdale, N.J.: Lawrence Erlbaum Associates, 1984.

Kelly, D. H. Measurement of anxiety by forearm blood flow. *British Journal of Psychiatry,* 1966, *112,* 789–798.

Kelly, D. H. Emotion and physiological changes in the arm. *Journal of Psychosomatic Research,* 1971, *15,* 445–450.

Kelly, D. H., & Walter, C. J. A clinical and physiological relationship between anxiety and depression. *British Journal of Psychiatry,* 1969, *115,* 401–406.

Kelly, D. H., Brown, C. C., & Shaffer, J. W. A comparison of physiological and psychological measurements on anxious patients and normal controls. *Psychophysiology,* 1970. *6,* 429–441.

Kendrick, D. T., Stringfield, D. O., Wagenhals, W. L., Dahl, R. H., & Ransdell, H. J. Sex differences, androgyny and approach responses to erotica: A new variation on the old volunteer problem. *Journal of Personality and Social Psychology,* 1980, *38,* 517–524.

Kennedy, B. J. Effects of massive doses of sex hormones on libido. *Medical Aspects of Human Sexuality,* 1973, *7,* 67–78.

Kilicpera, C., Albert, W., & Strian, F. Effects of somatic treatments on mood in endogenous depression. *Acta Psychiatrica Scandinavica*, 1979, *60*, 129–136.

Kilpatrick, D. G. Differential responsiveness of two electrodermal indices to psychological stress and performance of a complex cognitive task. *Psychophysiology*, 1972, *9*, 218–226.

Kinsey, A. C., Pomeroy, W. B., & Martin, C. E. *Sexual behavior in the human male*. Philadelphia: Saunders, 1948.

Kinsey, A., Pomeroy, W., Martin, C., & Gebhard, P. *Sexual behavior in the human female*. Philadelphia: Saunders, 1953.

Kirk-Smith, M., Booth, D. A., Carroll, D., & Davies, P. Human social attitudes affected by androstenol. *Research Communications in Psychology, Psychiatry and Behavior*, 1978, *3*, 379–384.

Kleck, R. E., Vaughan, R. C., Cartwright-Smith, J., Vaughan, K. B., Colby, C. Z., & Lanzetta, J. T. Effects of being observed on expressive, subjective and physiological responses to painful stimuli. *Journal of Personality and Social Psychology*, 1976, *34*, 1211–1218.

Kleiger, J. H., & Dirks, J. F. Psychomaintenance aspects of alexithymia: Relationship to medical outcome variables in a chronic respiratory illness population. *Psychotherapy and Psychosomatics*, 1980, *34*, 25–33.

Klein, D. F. Psychopharmacologic treatment of panic disorders. *Psychosomatics*, 1984, *25*(10, Suppl.), 32–35.

Kleinmuntz, B., & Szucko, J. A field study of the fallibility of polygraphic lie detection. *Nature*, 1984, *308*, 449–450.

Klimo, Z., Durindova, Z., Simko, S., & Durinda, M. Contribution to the therapy of primary polydipsia. *Ceskoslovenska Psychiatrie*, 1975, *71*, 151–154.

Klineberg, O. Culture and emotion. *Journal of Abnormal and Social Psychology*, 1938, *33*, 517–519.

Klorman, R. Habituation of fear: Effects of intensity and stimulus order. *Psychophysiology*, 1974, *11*, 15–26.

Klorman, R., Wiesenfeld, A. R., & Austin, M. L. Autonomic responses to affective visual stimuli. *Psychophysiology*, 1975, *12*, 553–560.

Kluver, H., & Bucy, P. "Psychic blindness" and other symptoms following bilateral temporal lobectomy in rhesus monkeys. *American Journal of Physiology*, 1937, *119*, 352–353.

Kluver, H., & Bucy, P. Preliminary analysis of the functions of the temporal lobes in monkeys. *Archives of Neurology and Psychiatry*, 1939, *42*, 979–1000.

Knapp, P. H. Some riddles of riddance: Relationships between eliminative processes and emotion. *Archives of General Psychiatry*, 1967, *16*, 586–602.

Knapp, P. H. Psychotherapeutic management of broncial asthma. In E. D. Wittkower & H. Warnes (Eds.), *Psychosomatic medicine: Its clinical implications*. New York: Harper & Row, 1977.

Knapp, T. W. Treating migraine by training in temporal artery vasoconstriction and/or cognitive behavioral coping: A one-year follow-up. *Journal of Psychosomatic Research*, 1982, *26*, 551–557.

Koch, K. L., & Stern, R. M. Relationship of the electrogastrogram to gastric motor activity in humans. *Psychophysiology*, 1983, *20*, 427. Abstract.

Koeske, R. K., & Koeske, G. F. An attributional approach to moods and the menstrual cycle. *Journal of Personality and Social Psychology*, 1975, *31*, 473–478.

Kohler, I. Experiments with goggles. *Scientific American*, 1962, *206 (5)*, 62–72.

Kohler, I. The formation and transformation of the perceptual world. *Psychological Issues*, 1964, *3* (Whole No. 4).

Kolata, G. B. Brain biochemistry: Effects of diet. *Science*, 1976, *192*, 41–42.

Kolata, G. B. Mental disorders: A new approach to treatment? *Science*, 1979, *203*, 36–38.

Kolodny, R. C., Masters, W. H., & Johnson, V. E. *Textbook of sexual medicine*. Boston: Little, Brown, 1979.

Kopin, I. J. Catecholamines, adrenal hormones and stress. In D. T. Krieger & J. C. Hughes (Eds.), *Neuroendrocrinology*. Sunderland: Sinaur, 1980.

Kopp, S. Short term evaluation of counseling and occlusal adjustment in manibular dysfunction patients. *Journal of Oral Rehabilitation*, 1979, *6*, 101–109.

Korff, J., & Geer, J. H. The relationship between sexual arousal experience and genital response. *Psychophysiology*, 1983, *20*, 121–127.

Kovacs, M., Rush, A. J., Beck, A. T., & Hollon, S. D. Depressed outpatients treated with cognitive therapy or pharmacotherapy: A one year follow-up. *Archives of General Psychiatry*, 1981, *38*, 33–39.

Kovats, F., Kiss, P., Naszlady, A., & Nemeskeri, I. Morphology of breathing movements of the trunk: A dynamic double-view photographic technic. In I. Hutas & L. A. Debreerzeni (Eds.), *Advances in physiological sciences. Vol. 10: Respiration.* New York: Pergamon, 1981.

Krantz, S., & Hammen, C. Assessment of cognitive bias in depression. *Journal of Abnormal Psychology*, 1979, *88*, 611–619.

Krassner, M. B. Brain chemistry. *Chemical and Engineering News*, 1983, *29*, August, 22–23.

Kreuz, L. E., & Rose, R. M. Assessment of aggressive behavior and plasma testosterone in a young criminal population. *Psychosomatic Medicine*, 1972, *34*, 321–332.

Kronecker, H., & Metzer, S. J. Der Schluckmechanismus, seine Erregung seine Hemmung. *Archiv fur Anatomie and Physiologie, Physiologische Abteilung*, 1883, *7*, 328–362 (Suppl. Festgage).

Krupp, M. A., & Chatton, M. J. *Current medical diagnosis and treatment.* Los Altos: Lange Medical Pub., 1975.

Lacey, J. I. Individual differences in somatic response patterns. *Journal of Comparative Physiological Psychology*, 1950, *43*, 338–350.

Lacey, J. I. Psychophysiological approaches to the evaluation of psychotherapeutic processes and outcome. In E. A. Rubenstein & M. B. Parloff (Eds.), *Research in psychotherapy.* Washington, D.C.: American Psychological Association, 1959.

Lacey, J. I. Somatic response patterning and stress. Some revisions of activation theory. In M. H. Apley & R. Turmbull's (Eds.), *Psychological stress.* New York: Appleton-Century-Crofts, 1967.

Lacey, J. I., & Lacey, B. C. Verification and extension of the principle of autonomic response stereotypy. *American Journal of Psychology*, 1958, *71*, 50–73.

Lacey, J. I., & VanLehn, R. Differential emphasis in somatic response to stress. *Psychosomatic Medicine*, 1952, *14*, 73–81.

Lacey, J. I., Bateman, D. E., & VanLehn, R. Autonomic response specificity. *Psychosomatic Medicine*, 1953, *15*, 8–21.

Ladas, A. K., Whipple, B., & Perry, J. D. *The G spot: And other recent discoveries about human sexuality.* New York: Holt, Rinehart & Winston, 1982.

Lader, M. The psychophysiology of anxious and depressed patients. In D. C. Fowles (Ed.), *Clinical applications of psychophysiology.* New York: Columbia University Press, 1975.

Lader, M., & Mathews, A. Physiological changes during spontaneous panic attacks. *Journal of Psychosomatic Research*, 1970, *14*, 377–382.

Lader, M., & Wing, L. Habituation of the psychogalvanic reflex in patients with anxiety states and in normal subjects. *Journal of Neurology, Neurosurgery and Psychiatry*, 1964, *27*, 210–218.

Lader, M., & Wing, L. Physiological measures, sedative drugs and morbid anxiety. *Maudsley Monographs 14.* London: Oxford University Press, 1966.

Laird, J. D. Self-attribution of emotion: The effects of expressive behavior on the quality of emotional experience. *Journal of Personality and Social Psychology*, 1974, *29*, 475–486.

Lamontagne, Y. Single-case study: Treatment of erythrophobia by paradoxical intention. *Journal of Nervous and Mental Disease*, 1978, *166*, 304–306.

Lance, J. W. *Mechanism and management of headache* (3rd ed.). Boston: Butterworths, 1978.

Lang, A. R., Searles, J. Lauerman, R., Adesso, V. Expectancies, alcohol and sex guilt as determinants of interest in and reaction to sexual stimuli. *Journal of Abnormal Psychology*, 1980, *89*, 644–653.

Lang, P. J. Behavior therapy with a case of nervous anorexia. In L. P. Ullman & L. Krasner (Eds.), *Case studies in behavior modification.* New York: Holt, Rinehart & Winston, 1965.

Lang, P. J., & Melamed, B. G. Case report: Avoidance conditioning therapy of an infant with chronic ruminative vomiting. *Journal of Abnormal Psychology*, 1969, *74*, 1–8.

Lang, P. J., Kozak, M. J. Miller, G. A., Levin, D. N., & McLean, A. Emotional imagery: Conceptual structure and pattern of somato-visual response. *Psychophysiology*, 1980, *17*, 179–192.

Lang, P. J., Levin, D. N., Miller, G. A., & Kozak, M. J. Fear behavior, fear imagery, and the psychophysiology of emotion: The problem of affective response integration. *Journal of Abnormal Psychology*, 1983, *92*, 276–306.

Lang, P. J., Melemed, B., & Hart, J. E. A psychophysical analysis of fear modification using an automated desensitization procedure. *Journal of Abnormal Psychology*, 1970, *76*, 220–234.

Lange, C. G. *Om Sindsbevaegelser. et psyko. fysiolog. studie.* Copenhagen: Keonar, 1885.

Lansky, D., & Wilson, G. T. Alcohol, expectations and sexual arousal: An information processing analysis. *Journal of Abnormal Psychology*, 1981, *90*, 35–45.

Lanzetta, J. T., & Kleck, R. E. Encoding and decoding of nonverbal affect in humans. *Journal of Personality and Social Psychology*, 1970, *16*, 12–19.

Lanzetta, J. T., Cartwright-Smith, J., & Kleck, R. E. Effects of nonverbal dissimulation on emotional experience and autonomic arousal. *Journal of Personality and Social Psychology*, 1976, *33*, 354–370.

Lapides, J., Ajemian, E. P., Stewart, B. H., Breakey, B. A., & Lichtwardt, J. R. Further observations on the kinetics of the urethrovesical sphincter. *Journal of Urology*, 1960, *84*, 86–94.

Lapides, J. Sweet, R. B., & Lewis, L. W. Role of striated muscle in urination. *Journal of Urology*, 1957, *77*, 247–250.

Lasagna, L. Naloxone hyperalgesia in post operative patients. *Proceedings of the Royal Society of Medicine*, 1965, *58*, 978–983.

Laskin, D. M. Aetiology of the pain dysfunction syndrome. *Journal of the American Dental Association*, 1969, *79*, 147–153.

Lasko, J. K. Parent behavior towards first and second born children. *Genetic Psychology Monographs*, 1954, *49*, 96–137.

Latimer, P. R. Colonic psychophysiology: Implications for functional bowel disorders. In R. Holzl & W. E. Whitehead (Eds.), *Psychophysiology of the gastrointestinal tract.* New York: Plenum Press, 1983. (a)

Latimer, P. R. Irritable bowel syndrome. *Psychosomatics*, 1983, *24*, 205–218. (b)

Latimer, P. R., Sarna, S., Campbell, D., Latimer, M., & Daniel, E. E. Colonic motor and myoelectrical activity: A comparative study of normal subjects, psychoneurotic patients and patients with the irritable bowel syndrome. *Gastroenterology*, 1981, *80*, 893–901.

Lazarus, R. S. Cognitive and personality factors underlying threat and coping. In M. H. Appley & R. Turmbull (Eds.), *Psychological stress.* New York: Appleton-Century-Crofts, 1967.

Lazarus, R. S. Thoughts on the relations between emotion and cognition. *American Psychologist*, 1982, *37(9)*, 1019–1024.

Lazarus, R. S., & Alfert, E. Short-circuiting of threat by experimentally altering cognitive appraisal. *Journal of Abnormal and Social Psychology*, 1964, *69*, 195–205.

Learmonth, G. J., Ackerly, W., & Kaplan, M. Relationships between palmar skin potential during stress and personality variables. *Psychosomatic Medicine*, 1959, *21*, 150–157.

Leary, M. R., & Dobbins, S. E. Social anxiety, sexual behavior and contraceptive use. *Journal of Personality and Social Psychology*, 1983, *45*, 1347–1354.

Leavitt, F. The value of the MMPI conversion 'V' in the assessment of psychogenic pain. *Journal of Psychosomatic Research*, 1985, *29*, 125–131. (a)

Leavitt, F. Pain and deception: Use of verbal pain measurement as a diagnostic aid in differentiating between clinical and simulated low back pain. *Journal of Psychosomatic Research*, 1985, *29*, 495–505. (b)

Leavitt, F., Garron, D. C., & Bieliauski, L. A. Stressing life events and the experience of low back pain. *Journal of Psychosomatic Research*, 1979, *23*, 49–55.

Lehrman, D. S. A critique of Konrad Lorenz's theory of instinctive behavior. *Quarterly Review of Biology*, 1953, *28*, 337–363.

Lehrman, D. S. Semantic and conceptual issues in the nature-nurture problem. In L.

Aronson, E. Lobach, D. Lehrman, & J. Rosenblatt (Eds.), *Development and evolution of behavior*. San Francisco: Freeman, 1970.

Leiderman, P. H., & Leiderman, G. F. Affective and cognitive consequences of polymatric infant care in the East African highlands. In A. Pick (Ed.), *Minnesota Symposium on Child Development* (Vol. 8). Minneapolis: University of Minnesota Press, 1974.

Lenhart, R. E. Lowered skin conductance in a subsyndromal high-risk depressive sample: Response amplitudes versus tonic levels. *Journal of Abnormal Psychology*, 1985, *94*, 649–652.

Leon, G. R. *Case histories of deviant behavior* (3rd ed.). Boston: Allyn & Bacon, 1984.

Leon, G. R., & Chamberlain, K. Emotional arousal, eating patterns, and body image as differential factors associated with varying success in maintaining a weight loss. *Journal of Comparative and Clinical Psychology*, 1973, *40*, 474–480.

Lerer, B. Hyperhidrosis: A review of its psychological aspects. *Psychosomatics*, 1977, *18*, 28–31.

Lerer, B., Jacobowitz, J., & Wahba, A. Personality features of essential hyperhidrosis. *International Journal of Psychiatry in Medicine*, 1980, *10*, 59–67.

Levenson, R. W. Effects of thematically relevant and general stressors on specificity of responding in asthmatic and nonasthmatic subjects. *Psychosomatic Medicine*, 1979, *41*, 28–38.

Leventhal, H. A perceptual-motor processing model of emotion. In P. Pliner, K. R. Blankstein, & I. M. Spigel (Eds.), *Perception of emotion in self and others* (Vol. 5). New York: Plenum Press, 1979.

Leventhal, H. Toward a comprehensive theory of emotion. In L. Berkowitz (Ed.), *Advances in experimental social psychology* (Vol. 13). New York: Academic Press, 1980.

Leventhal, H. A perceptual-motor theory of emotion. In L. Berkowitz (Ed.), *Advances in experimental social psychology* (Vol. 17). New York: Academic Press, 1984. (a)

Leventhal, H. A perceptual-motor theory of emotion. In K. R. Scherer & P. Ekman (Eds.), *Approaches to emotion*. Hillsdale, N.J.: Lawrence Erlbaum Associates, 1984. (b)

Levi, L. Stress and distress in reponse to psychosocial stimuli. *Acta Medica Scandinavia* (Suppl. 528), 1972, *191*, 55–73.

Levi, L. The urinary output of adrenaline and noradrenaline during pleasant and unpleasant emotional states. *Psychosomatic Medicine*, 1965, *27*, 80–85.

Levy, R. I. The emotions in comparative perspective. In K. R. Scherer & P. Ekman (Eds.), *Approaches to emotion*. Hillsdale, N.J.: Lawrence Erlbaum Associates, 1984.

Levine, J. D., Gordon, N. C., Jones, R. T., & Fields, H. L. The narcotic antagonist naloxone enhances clinical pain. *Nature*, 1978, *272*, 826–827.

Levine, R. A. Parental goals: A cross-cultural view. *Teacher College Record*. New York: Columbia University Press, 1974.

Lewinsohn, P. M., Miscel, W., Chaplin, W., & Barton, R. Social competence and depression: The role of illusory self-perceptions. *Journal of Abnormal Psychology*, 1980, *89*, 203–212.

Lewinsohn, P. M., Steinmetz, J. L., Larson, D. W., & Franklin, J. Depression-related cognitions; Antecedent or consequence? *Journal of Abnormal Psychology*, 1981, *90*, 213–219.

Lewis, D. A., & Smith, R. E. Steroid-induced psychiatric syndromes: A report of 14 cases and a review of the literature. *Journal of Affective Disorders*, 1983, *5*, 319–332.

Lewis, T. *Vascular disorders of the limbs*. London: Macmillan, 1949.

Lewitt, P. A., Newman, R. P., Greenberg, H. S., Rocher, L. L., Calne, D. B., & Ehrenkranz, J. R. Episodic hyperhidrosis, hypothermia and agenesis of the corpus callosum. *Neurology*, 1983, *33*, 1122–1129.

Lichstein, K. L., & Rosenthal, T. D. Insomniacs' perception of cognitive versus somatic determinants of sleep disturbance. *Journal of Abnormal Psychology*, 1980, *89*, 105–107.

Liebert, R. M., & Morris, L. W. Cognitive and emotional components of test anxiety: A distinction and some initial data. *Psychological Reports*, 1967, *20*, 975–978.

Liebowitz, M. R., Gorman, J. M., Fyer, A. J., Levitt, M., Dillon, D., Levy, G., Appleby, I. L. Lactate provocation of panic attacks: II. Biochemical and physiological findings. *Archives of General Psychiatry*, 1985, *42(7)*, 709–719.

Lindemann, C. *Birth control and unmarried young women*. New York: Springer-Verlag, 1974.

LiPiccolo, J., Heiman, J. R., Hogan, D. R., & Roberts, C. W. Effectiveness of single therapists versus cotherapy teams in sex therapy. *Journal of Consulting and Clinical Psychology*, 1985, *53*, 287–294.

Little, B. C., & Zahn, T. P. Changes in mood and autonomic functioning during the menstrual cycle. *Psychophysiology*, 1974, *11*, 579–590.

Lobitz, W. C., & LoPiccolo, J. New methods in the behavioral treatment of sexual dysfunction. *Journal of Behavior Therapy and Experimental Psychiatry*, 1972, *3*, 265–271.

Loeb, A., Beck, A. T., & Diggory, J. Differential effects of success and failure on depressed and nondepressed patients. *Journal of Nervous and Mental Disease*, 1971, *152*, 106–114.

Lomont, J. F., & Edwards, J. E. The role of relaxation in systematic desensitization. *Behavior Research and Therapy*, 1967, *5*, 11–25.

London, P. *Modes and morals of psychotherapy*. New York: Holt, 1964.

Lowen, A. *The betrayal of the body*. New York: Macmillan, 1967.

Lowen, A. In defense of modesty. *Journal of Sex Research*, 1968, *4*, 51–56.

Lowen, A. *Depression and the body*. New York: Penguin, 1973.

Lowen, A. The body in personality theory: Wilhelm Reich and Alexander Lowen. In A. Burton (Ed.), *Operational theories of personality*. New York: Brunner/Mazel, 1974.

Lowen, A. *Bioenergetics*. New York: Penguin Books, 1976.

Luce, G. G. *Body Time*. New York: Pantheon, 1971.

Ludel, J. *Introduction to sensory processes*. San Francisco: Freeman, 1978.

Ludwig, A. A. Rheumatoid arthritis. In E. D. Wittkower & R. A. Cleghorn (Eds.), *Recent developments in psychosomatic medicine*. London: Pittman, 1954.

Ludwig, A. A. Rheumatoid arthritis. In A. W. Freedman & H. T. Kaplan (Eds.), *Comprehensive textbook of psychiatry*. Baltimore: Williams & Wilkins, 1967.

Lum, L. C. Hyperventilation syndrome: The tip of the iceberg. *Journal of Psychosomatic Research*, 1975, *19*, 375–383.

Lundberg, U., Ekman, G., & Frankenhaeuser, M. Anticipation of electric shock: A psychophysical study. *Acta Psychologica*, 1971, *35*, 309–315.

Luthe, W., & Blumberger, S. R. Autogenic therapy. In E. D. Wittkower & H. Warnes (Eds.), *Psychosomatic medicine: Its clinical applications*. New York: Harper & Row, 1977.

Lykken, D. T. The GSR in the detection of guilt. *Journal of Applied Psychology*, 1959, *43*, 385–388.

Lykken, D. T. Psychology and the lie detection industry. *American Psychologist*, 1974, *29*, 725–739.

Lykken, D. T. The detection of deception. *Psychological Bulletin*, 1979, *86*, 47–53.

Lynch, J. J., Long, J. M., Thomas, S. A., Malinow, K. L., & Katcher, A. H. The effects of talking on the blood pressure of hypertensive and normotensive individuals. *Psychosomatic Medicine*, 1981, *43*, 25–33.

Maas, J. W. Biogenic amines and depression: Biochemical and pharmacological separation of two types of depression. *Archives of General Psychiatry*, 1975, *32*, 1357–1361. (a)

Maas, J. W. Catecholamines and depression. In A. J. Friedhoff (Ed.), *Catecholamines and Behavior*. New York: Plenum Press, 1975. (b)

Maas, J. W., Fawcett, J. A., & Dekirmenjiam, H. Catecholamine metabolism, depressive illness and drug response. *Archives of General Psychiatry*, 1972, *26*, 252–262.

Madison, A. S. *Psychophysiological response of female nursing home residents to backmassage: An investigation of the effect of one type of touch*, unpublished doctoral dissertation. Ann Arbor: University Microfilms International, 1973.

Makin, H. J., & Adams, R. D. Pain in the back and neck. In K. J. Isselbacher, R. D. Adams, E. Braunwald, R. G. Petersdorf, & J. D. Wilson (Eds.), *Harrison's principles of internal medicine*, (9th ed.). New York: McGraw-Hill, 1980.

Malinak, L. R. Operative management of pelvic pain. *Clinical Obstetrics and Gynecology*, 1980, *23(1)*, 191–200.

Malmo, R. B. Physiologic study of symptom mechanisms in psychiatric patients under stress. *Psychosomatic Medicine*, 1949, *11*, 25–29.

Malmo, R. B., Shagass, C., & Davis, F. H. Symptom specificity and bodily reactions during psychiatric interview. *Psychosomatic Medicine*, 1950, *12*, 362–376.

Mandler, G. *Mind and body: Psychology of emotion and stress.* New York: Norton, 1984.

Manuck, S. B., Giordani, B., McQuaid, K. J., & Garrity, S. J. Behaviorally-induced cardiovascular reactivity among sons of reported hypertensive and normotensive parents. *Journal of Psychosomatic Research,* 1981, *25,* 261–269.

Maranon, G. Contribution a l'etude de l'action emotive de l'adrenaline. *Revue Francaise d'Edocrinologie,* 1924, *2,* 301–325.

Marcia, J. E., Rubin, B. M., & Efran, J. S. Systematic desensitization: Expectancy change or counterconditioning? *Journal of Abnormal Psychology,* 1969, *74,* 382–387.

Mark, V. H., & Ervin, F. R. *Violence and the brain.* New York: Harper & Row, 1970.

Marshall, G. D., & Zimbardo, P. G. Affective consequences of inadequately explained physiological arousal. *Journal of Personality and Social Psychology,* 1979, *37,* 970–988.

Martin, B. Expression and inhibition of sex motive arousal in college males. *Journal of Abnormal and Social Psychology,* 1964, *68,* 307–312.

Martin, I., & Venables, P. H. *Techniques in psychophysiology.* New York: Wiley, 1980.

Martin, M. J. Tension headache: A psychiatric study. *Headache,* 1966, *6,* 47–54.

Martin, M. J. Muscle-contraction (tension) headache. *Psychosomatics,* 1983, *24,* 319–324.

Martin, P. R., & Mathews, A. M. Tension headaches: Psychophysiological investigation and treatment. *Journal of Psychosomatic Research,* 1978, *22,* 389–399.

Marx, J. L. "Anxiety peptide" found in brain. *Science,* 1985, *227,* 934.

Maslach, C. Negative emotional biasing of unexplained arousal. *Journal of Personality and Social Psychology,* 1979, *37,* 953–969.

Masling, J. (Ed.). *Empirical studies of psychoanalytic theories* (Vol. 1). Hillsdale, N.J.: Lawrence Erlbaum Associates, 1983.

Masserano, J. M., Takimoto, G. S., & Weiner, N. Electroconvulsive shock increases tyrosine hydroxylase activity in the brain and adrenal gland of the rat. *Science,* 1981, *214,* 662–664.

Masso, A., & Pellacani, P. Sur les fonctions de la vessie. *Archives Italian Biology,* 1882, *1,* 97–128, 291–324.

Masters, W. H., & Johnson, V. E. *Human sexual response.* Boston: Little, Brown and Company, 1966.

Masters, W. H., & Johnson, V. E. *Human sexual inadequancy.* Boston: Little, Brown, 1970.

Masters, W. H., Johnson, V. E., & Kolodny, R. C. *Human Sexuality* (Boston: Little, Brown, 1982.

Mathew, R. J., Ho, B. T., & Taylor, D. L. Catecholamines and dopamine-beta-hydroxylase in anxiety. *Journal of Psychosomatic Research,* 1981, *25,* 499–504.

Mathis, J. L. A sophisticated version of voodoo death. *Psychosomatic Medicine,* 1964, *26,* 104–107.

Mavissakalian, M. Pharmacological treatment of anxiety disorders. *Journal of Clinical Psychiatry,* 1982, *43(12),* 487–491.

May, R. R. Mood shifts and the menstrual cycle. *Journal of Psychosomatic Research,* 1976, *20,* 125–130.

McArthur, L. Z., Solomon, M. R., & Jaffe, R. H. Weight differences in emotional responsiveness to proprioceptive and pictorial stimuli. *Journal of Personality and Social Psychology,* 1980, *39,* 308–319.

McBride, G., King, M. G., & James, J. W. Social proximity effects on galvanic skin responses in adult humans. *The Journal of Psychology,* 1965, *61,* 153–157.

McCahill, T. W., Meyer, L. C., & Fischman, A. M. *The aftermath of rape.* Lexington, MA: Lexington Books, 1979.

McCaul, K. D., Solomon, S., & Holmes, D. S. Effects of paced respiration and expectations on physiological and psychological responses to threat. *Journal of Personality and Social Psychology,* 1979, *37,* 564–571.

McClearn, G. E. Genetic influence on behavior and development. In P. H. Mussen (Ed.), *Carmichael's manual of child psychology* (3rd ed.). New York: Wiley, 1970.

McClelland, D. C. Inhibited power motive and high blood pressure in men. *Journal of Abnormal Psychology,* 1979, *88,* 182–190.

McClintock, C. C., & Hunt, R. G. Nonverbal indicators of affect and deception in an interview setting. *Journal of Applied Social Psychology,* 1975, *5,* 54–67.

McCook, R. D., Randall, W. C., Hassler, C. R. Mihaldzic, N., & Wurster, R. D. The role of cutaneous thermal receptors in sudomotor control. In J. D. Hardy, A. P. Gagge, & J. A. Stolwijk (Eds.), *Physiological and behavioral temperature regulation*. Springfield, Ill.: Thomas, 1970.

McCormick, W. O. Amenorrhea and other menstrual symptoms in student nurses. *Journal of Psychosomatic Research*, 1975, *19*, 131–137.

McCreary, C. Empirically derived MMPI profile clusters and characteristics of low back pain patients. *Journal of Consulting and Clinical Psychology*, 1985, *53*, 558–560.

McEwen, B. S. The brain as a target organ of endocrine hormones. In D. T. Krieger & J. C. Hughes (Eds.), *Neuroendocrinology*. Sunderland, Mass.: Sinauer, 1980.

McGee, P. E. *Humor: Its origin and development*. San Francisco: Freeman, 1979.

McGlone, J. Sex differences in functional brain asymmetry. *Cortex*, 1978, *14*, 122–128.

McGuigan, F. J. *Cognitive psychophysiology: Principles of covert behavior*. Englewood Cliffs, N.J.: Prentice-Hall, 1978.

McKechnie, A. A., Wilson, F., Watson, N., & Scott, D. Anxiety states: A preliminary report on the value of connective tissue massage. *Journal of Psychosomatic Research*, 1983, *27*, 125–129.

McKenna, R. J. Some effects of anxiety level and food cues on the eating behavior of obese and normal subjects. *Journal of Personality and Social Psychology*, 1972, *22*, 311–319.

Meares, R. Features which distinguish groups of spasmodic torticollis. *Journal of Psychosomatic Research*, 1971, *15*, 1–11.

Meares, R., & Lader, M. Electromyographic studies in patients with spasmodic torticollis. *Journal of Psychosomatic Research*, 1971, *15*, 13–18.

Meeks, L. B., & Heit, P. *Human sexuality*. Philadelphia: Saunders, 1982.

Merton, P. A. How we control the contractions of our muscles. *Scientific American*, 1972, *226*(5), 30–37.

Metheny, E. *Body dynamics*. New York: McGraw-Hill, 1952.

Michael, R., Bonsall, R. W., & Warner, P. Human vaginal secretions: Volatile fatty acid content. *Science*, 1974, *186*, 1217–1219.

Middlemist, R. D., Knowles, E. S., & Matter, C. F. Personal space invasions in the lavatory: Suggestive evidence for arousal. *Journal of Personality and Social Psychology*, 1976, *33*, 541–546.

Mikkelsen, E. J. Caffeine and schizophrenia. *Journal of Clinical Psychology*, 1978, *39*, 732–736.

Miller, N. E. Motivational effects of brain stimulation and drugs. *Federation Procedings, Federation of American Societies for Experimental Biology*, 1960, *19*, 846–853.

Miller, N. E. Learning and performance motivated by direct stimulation of the brain. In D. E. Sheer (Ed.), *Electrical stimulation of the brain*. Austin: University of Texas Press, 1961.

Miller, S. M., & Mangan, C. E. Interacting effects of information and coping style in adapting to gynecologic stress: Should the doctor tell all? *Journal of Personality and Social Psychology*, 1983, *45*, 223–236.

Miller, R. E. Experimental approaches to the physiological and behavioral concomitants of affective communication in rhesus monkeys. In S. A. Altmann (Ed.), *Social communication among primates*. Chicago: University of Chicago Press, 1967.

Mischel, W. *Introduction to personality* (2nd ed.). New York: Holt, Rinehart & Winston, 1976.

Mittelmann, B., & Wolff, H. G. Affective states and skin temperature: Experimental study of subjects with "cold hands" and Raynaud's syndrome. *Psychosomatic Medicine*, 1939, *1*, 271–292.

Mittelmann, B., & Wolff, H G. Emotions and skin temperature: Observations during psychotherapeutic (psychoanalytic) interviews. *Psychosomatic Research*, 1943, *5*, 211–231.

Miyabo, S., Asato, T., & Mizushima, N. Psychological correlates of stress-induced cortisol and growth hormone release in neurotic patients. *Psychosomatic Medicine*, 1979, *41*, 515–523.

Moldofsky, H. Occupational cramp. *Journal of Psychosomatic Research*, 1971, *15*, 439–444.

Money, J., & Ehrhardt, A. A. *Man and woman, boy and girl*. Baltimore: John Hopkins, 1972.

Money, J., & Tucker, P. *Sexual signatures*. Boston: Little, Brown & Co., 1975.

Moniz, E. *Tentatives operatoires dans le traitement de certaines psychoses*. Paris: Masson, 1936.

Moos, R. H., & Leiderman, D. B. Toward a menstrual cycle symptom typology. *Journal of Psychosomatic Research*, 1978, 22, 31–40.

Moos, R. H., Kopell, B. S., Melges, F. T.. Yalom, I. D., Lunde, D. T., Clayton, R. B., & Hamburg, D. A. Fluctuations in symptoms and moods during the menstrual cycle. *Journal of Psychosomatic Research*, 1969, 13, 37–44.

Moreault, D., & Follingstad, D. R. Sexual fantasies of females as a function of sex guilt and experimental response cues. *Journal of Consulting and Clinical Psychology*, 1978, 46, 1385–1393.

Morgan, H. G. Functional vomiting. *Journal of Psychosomatic Research*, 1985, 29, 341–352.

Morokoff, P. J. Effects of sex guilt, repression, sexual 'arousability,' and sexual experiences on female sexual arousal during erotica and fantasy. *Journal of Personality and Social Psychology*, 1985, 49, 177–187.

Morris, D. *Manwatching*. New York: H. N. Abrams, 1977.

Morris, L. W. *Extraversion and introversion: An interactional perspective*. New York: Halsted Press, 1979.

Morse, D. R., Schacterle, G. R., Esposito, J. V. Furst, M. L., & Bose, K. Stress, relaxation and saliva: A follow-up study involving endodontic patients. *Journal of Human Stress*, 1981, 7, 19–26.

Morse, D. R., Schacterle, G. R., Furst, M. L., & Bose, K. Stress relaxation and saliva: A pilot study involving endodontic patients. *Oral Surgery, Oral Medicine, Oral Pathology*, 1981, 52, 308–312.

Morse, D. R., Schacterle, G. R., Furst, M. L., Brokenshire, J., Butterworth, M., & Cacchio, J. Examination induced stress in meditators and nonmeditators as measured by salivary protein changes. *Stress*, 1981, 2, 20–23.

Morse, D. R., Schacterle, G. R., Furst, M. L., Goldberg, J., Greenspan, B., Swiecinski, D., & Susek, J. The effects of stress and meditation on salivary protein and bacteria: A review and pilot study. *Journal of Human Stress*, 1982, 8, 31–39.

Moruzzi, G., & Magoun, H. Brainstem reticular formation and activation of EEG. *Electroencephalography and Clinical Neurophysiology*, 1949, 1, 455–473.

Mosher, D. L. *The development and validation of a sentence completion measure of guilt*, unpublished doctoral dissertation. Columbus: Ohio State University, 1961.

Mosher, D. L. Interaction of fear and guilt in inhibiting unacceptable behavior. *Journal of Consulting Psychology*, 1965, 29, 161–167.

Mosher, D. L. The development and multitrait-multimethod matrix analysis of three measures of three aspects of guilt. *Journal of Consulting Psychology*, 1966, 30, 25–29.

Mosher, D. L. Sexual callousness towards women. In the *Technical Report of the Commission on Obscenity and Pornography. Vol. 8: Erotica and social behavior*. Washington, D.C.: U.S. Government Printing Office, 1971.

Mosher, D. L. The meaning and measurement of guilt. In C. E. Izard (Ed.), *Emotions in personality and psychopathology*. New York: Plenum Press, 1979.

Mosher, D. L., & Cross, H. J. Sex guilt and premarital sexual experiences of college students. *Journal of Consulting Psychology*, 1971, 36, 22–32.

Moss, R. A., Garrett, J., & Chiodo, J. F. Temporomanibular joint dysfunction and myofascial pain dysfunction syndromes: Parameters, etiology and treatment. *Psychological Bulletin*, 1982, 92, 331–346.

Moulton, R. Psychiatric consideration in maxillo-facial pain. *Journal of the American Dental Association*, 1955, 51, 408–414.

Mullen, B., & Suls, J. The effectiveness of attention and rejection as coping styles: A meta-analysis of temporal differences. *Journal of Psychosomatic Research*, 1982, 26, 43–49.

Munroe, R., & Munroe, R. *Cross-cultural human development*. Monterey, Calif.: Brooks/Cole, 1975.

Munsterberg, H. *On the witness stand*. New York: Doubleday, 1908.

Murray, H. A. Studies of stressful interpersonal disputations. *American Psychologist*, 1963, 18, 28–36.

Murray, J. L. "False pregnancy." *Medical Aspects of Human Sexuality*, 1979, March, 133–134.

Myers, M. B., Templer, D. I., & Brown, R. Reply to Wieder on rape victims: Vulnerability does not imply responsibility. *Journal of Consulting and Clinical Psychology*, 1985, *53*, 431.

Nadelson, C. C., Norman, M. T. Zackson, H., & Gornick, J. A follow-up study of rape victims. *American Journal of Psychiatry*, 1982, *139*, 1266–1270.

Nadelson, C. C., Norman, M. T., & Ellis, E. A. Psychosomatic aspects of obstetrics and gynecology. *Psychosomatics*, 1983, *24*, 871–884.

Naditch, M. P., Gargan, M. A., & Michael, L. B. Denial, anxiety, locus of control and the discrepancy between aspirations and achievements as components of depression. *Journal of Abnormal Psychology*, 1975, *84*, 1–9.

Natelson, B. The "executive monkey" revisited. In F. P. Brooks & P. W. Evans (Eds.), *Nerves and the gut*. Philadelphia: Slack, 1977.

Naquet, R. Effects of stimulation of the rhinencephalon in the waking cat. *Electroencephalography and Clinical Neurophysiology*, 1954, *6*, 711–712.

Neill, J. R., & Sandifer, M. G. The clinical approach to alexithymia: A review. *Psychosomatics*, 1982, *23(12)*, 1223–1231.

Neilon, P. Shirley's babies after fifteen years: A personality study. *Journal of Genetic Psychology*, 1948, *73*, 175–186.

Nestoros, J. N., Demers-Desrosiers, L. A., & Dalicandro, L. A. Levels of anxiety and depression in spinal cord-injured patients. *Psychosomatics*, 1982, *23*, 823–830.

Ney, R. L., Shimizu, N., Nicholson, W. E., Island, D. P., & Liddle, G. W. Correlation of plasma ACTH concentration with adrenocorticol response in normal human subjects, surgical patients and patients with Cushing's disease. *Journal of Clinical Investigation*, 1963, *42*, 1669–1677.

Niki, H. Prefrontal unit activity during delayed alternation in the monkey. I. Relation to direction of reponse. *Brain Research*, 1974, *68*, 185–196.

Niki, H., & Watanabe, M. Prefrontal unit activity and delayed response: Relation to cue location vs. direction of response. *Brain Research*, 1976, *105*, 79–88.

Nisbett, R. E. Birth order and participation in dangerous sports. *Journal of Personality and Social Psychology*, 1968, *8*, 351–353.

Norman, T. R., Maguire, K. P., & Burrows, G. D. New antidepressants: Clinical studies. *Advances in Human Psychopharmacology*, 1984, *3*, 3–27.

Norris, J., & Feldman-Summers, S. Factors related to the psychological impact of rape on the victim. *Journal of Abnormal Psychology*, 1981, *90*, 562–567.

Norris, R. V., & Lloyd, C. W. Psychosexual effects of hormone therapy. *Medical Aspects of Human Sexuality*, 1971, *5*, 129–146.

Nunnally, J. C. *Psychometric theory* (2nd ed.) New York: McGraw-Hill, 1978.

Obrist, P. A. The cardiovascular-behavioral interaction—As it appears today. *Psychophysiology*, 1976, *13*, 95–107.

Obrist, P. A., Howard, J. L., Lawler, J. E., Galosy, R. A., Meyers, K. A., & Gaeblein, C. J. The cardiac somatic interaction. In P. A. Obrist, A. H. Black, J. Brener, & L. V. Dicara (Eds.), *Cardiovascular psychophysiology*. Chicago: Aldine, 1974.

Obrist, P. A., Webb, R. A., Sutterer, J. R., & Howard, J. L. The cardiac-somatic relationship: Some reformulations. *Psychophysiology*, 1970, *6*, 569–587.

Oda, N. Developmental and behavioral characteristics in 3-year old twins. *Journal of Osaka City Medical Center*, 1983, *32*, 359–375. Abstract.

Ohman, A. Electrodermal activity and vulnerability to schizophrenia: A review. *Biological Psychology*, 1981, *12*, 87–145.

Ohman, A. Face the beast and fear the face: Animal social fears as prototypes for evolutionary analyses of emotion. *Psychophysiology*, 1986, *23*, 123–145.

Oken, D. The psychophysiology and psychoendrocinology of stress and emotion. In M. H. Appley & R. Turmbull (Eds.), *Psychological stress*. New York: Appleton-Century-Crofts, 1967.

Olds, J. Adaptive functions of paleocortical and related structures. In H. F. Harlow and C. N. Woolsey (Eds.), *Biological and biochemical bases of behavior*. Madison: University of Wisconsin Press, 1958. (a)

Olds, J. Self-stimulation of the brain. *Science*, 1958, *127*, 315–324. (b)

Olds, J., & Milner, P. Positive reinforcement produced by electrical stimulation of the septal and other regions of the rat brain. *Journal of Comparative and Physiological Psychology*, 1954, *47*, 419–427.

O'Leary, V. E. *Toward understanding women*. Monterey, Calif.: Brooks/Coles, 1977.

O'Moore, A. M., O'Moore, R. R., Harrison, R. F., Murphy, G., & Carruthers, M. E. Psychosomatic aspects in idiopathic infertility: Effects of treatment with autogenic training. *Journal of Psychosomatic Research*, 1983, *27*, 145–151.

Ornstein, R. E. *The psychology of consciousness*. New York: Harcourt Brace Jovanovich, 1977.

Orr, W. C. Studies of esophageal function during waking and sleep. In R. Holzl & W. E. Whitehead (Eds.), *Psychophysiology of the gastrointestinal tract*. New York: Plenum Press, 1983.

Ortega, D. F., & Pipal, J. E. Challenge seeking and Type A coronary prone behavior pattern. *Journal of Personality and Social Psychology*, 1984, *46*, 1328–1334.

Paige, K. E. Effects of oral contraceptives on affective fluctuations associated with the menstrual cycle. *Psychosomatic Medicine*, 1971, *33*, 515–537.

Paige, K. E. Sexual pollution: Reproductive sex taboos in American society. *Journal of Social Issues*, 1977, *33*, 144–165.

Palazzoli, M. S. *Self-Starvation*. New York: Berkeley Press, 1978.

Pancheri, P. Measurement of emotion: Transcultural aspects. In L. Levi (Ed.), *Emotions— Their parameters and measurement*. New York: Raven Press, 1975.

Pankranz, L. A review of the Munchausen syndrome. *Clinical Psychology Review*, 1981, *1*, 65–78.

Papez. J. W. A proposed mechanism of emotion. *Archives of Neurology and Psychiatry*, 1937, *38*, 725–743.

Parlee, M. The premenstrual syndrome. *Psychological Bulletin*, 1973, *80*, 454–465.

Passman, R. H., & Weisberg, P. Mothers and blankets as agents for promoting play and exploration by young children in a novel environment: The effects of social and nonsocial attachment objects. *Developmental Psychology*, 1975, *11*, 170–177.

Patel, C. H. Biofeedback-aided relaxation and meditation in the management of hypertension. *Biofeedback and Self-Regulation*, 1977, *2*, 1–41.

Patkai, P. Catecholamine excretion in pleasant and unpleasant situations. *Acta Psychologica*, 1971, *35*, 352–363.

Patkai, P. Johannson, G., & Post, B. Mood, alertness and sympatheticadrenal medullary activity during the menstrual cycle. *Psychosomatic Medicine*, 1974, *36*, 503–512.

Paul, G. L. Physiological effects of relaxation training and hypnotic suggestion. *Journal of Abnormal Psychology*, 1969, *74*, 425–437.

Pazulinec, R., & Sajwaj, T. Psychogenic treatment approaches to psychogenic vomiting and rumination. In R. Holtzl & W. E. Whitehead (Eds.), *Psychophysiology of the gastrointestinal tract*. New York: Plenum Press, 1983.

Pearce, S., & Beard, R. W. Chronic pelvic pain. In A. Broome & L. Wallace (Eds.), *Psychology and gynaecological problems*. London: Tavistock Publications, 1984.

Penfield, W. Mechanisms of voluntary movement. *Brain*, 1954, *77*, 1–17.

Penfield, W. Functional localization in temporal and deep sylvian areas. *Academy for Research in Nervous and Mental Disease*, 1958, *36*, 210–226.

Penfield, W. *The mystery of the mind*. Princeton: Princeton University Press, 1975.

Penfield, W., & Jasper, H. *Epilepsy and the functional anatomy of the human brain*. Boston: Little and Brown, 1954.

Penfield, W., & Rasmussen, T. *The cerebral cortex of man*. New York: Macmillian, 1950.

Pennebaker, J. W. *The psychology of physical symptoms*. New York: Springer-Verlag, 1982.

Perry, J. D., & Whipple, B. Pelvic muscle strength of female ejaculators: Evidence in support of a new theory of orgasm. *Journal of Sex Research*, 1981, *17*, 22–39.

Persky, H. Reproductive hormones, moods and the menstrual cycle. In R. C. Freidman, R. M. Richard, & R. L. Van de Wiele (Eds.), *Sex differences in behavior*. Huntington, N.Y.: Krieger, 1978.

Persky, H., Hamburg, D. A., Basowitz, H., Grinker, R. R., Sabshin, S., Korchin, S. J., Hertz, M., Board, F. A., & Heath, H. A. Relationship of emotional responses and changes in plasma hydrocortisone level after stressful interview. *Archives of Neurology and Psychiatry*, 1958, *79*, 434–447.

Petersen, P. Psychiatric disorders and primary hyperparathyroidism. *Journal of Clinical Endocrinology,* 1968, *28,* 1491–1495.

Pfeffer, J. M. The aetiology of the hyperventilation syndrome: A review of the literature. *Psychotherapy and Psychosomatics,* 1978, *30,* 47–55.

Pfeiffer, C. A. Sexual differences of the hypophyses and their determination by the gonads. *American Journal of Anatomy,* 1936, *58,* 195–226.

Pflanz, M. Sex differences in abdominal illness. *Social Science and Medicine,* 1978, *12B,* 171–176.

Philips, C. Headaches in general practice. *Headache,* 1977, *16,* 322–329.

Phillips, E. L. Cultural vs. interpsychic factors in childhood. *Journal of Clinical Psychiatry,* 1956, *12,* 400–401.

Physicians' desk reference (39th ed.). Oradell, N.J.: Medical Economics Co., 1985.

Pickering, T. G. Blood pressure during activities, sleep and exercise: Comparison of normotensive and hypertensive subjects. *Journal of the American Medical Association,* 1982, *247,* 992–996.

Pikunas, J. *Human development: A science of growth.* New York: McGraw-Hill, 1969.

Pine, C. J. Anxiety and eating behavior in obese and nonobese American Indians and white Americans. *Journal of Personality and Social Psychology,* 1985, *49,* 774–780.

Pitts, F. N. The biochemistry of anxiety. *Scientific American,* 1969, *220(2),* 69–75.

Pitts, F. N., & McClure, J. N. Lactate metabolism in anxiety neurosis. *The New England Journal of Medicine,* 1967, *277(25),* 1329–1336.

Plutchik, R. The role of muscular tension in maladjustment. *Journal of General Psychology,* 1954, *50,* 45–62.

Plutchik, R. The psychophysiology of skin temperature: A critical review. *Journal of General Psychology,* 1956, *55,* 249–268.

Plutchick, R. A language for the emotions. *Psychology Today,* 1980, February, 68–78.

Plutchik, R., & Ax, A. F. A critique of determinants of emotional state by Schacter and Singer(1962). *Psychophysiology,* 1967, *4,* 79–82.

Polivy, J., & Herman, C. P. Clinical depression and weight change: A complex relationship. *Journal of Abnormal Psychology,* 1976, *85,* 338–340.

Pollack, J. M. Obsessive-compulsive personality: A review. *Psychological Bulletin,* 1979, *86,* 225–241.

Porter, R. W., Brady, J. V., Conrad, D., Mason, J. W., Galambos, R., & Rioch, D. Some experimental observations of gastrointestinal lesions in behaviorally conditioned monkeys. *Psychosomatic Medicine,* 1958, *20,* 379–394.

Poteliakhoff, A. Adrenocortical activity and some clinical findings in acute and chronic fatigue. *Journal of Psychosomatic Research,* 1981, *25,* 91–95.

Prange, A. J., Wilson, I. C., Lynn, C. W., Alltop, L. B., & Stikeleather, R. A. L-triptophan in mania: Contribution to the permissive hypothesis of affective disorders. *Archives of General Psychiatry,* 1974, *30,* 56–62.

Price, K. P., & Clark, L. K. Classical conditioning of digital pulse volume in migraineurs and normal controls. *Headache,* 1979, *19,* 328–332.

Price, K. P., & Tursky, B. Vascular reactivity in migraineurs and nonmigraineurs: A comparison of responses to self-control procedures. *Headache,* 1976, *16,* 210–217.

Prugh, D. G., & Harlow, R. G. "Masked deprivation" in infants and young children. *Deprivation of maternal care: A reassessment of its effects.* Public Affairs Papers, No. 14. Geneva: World Health Organization, 1962.

Purchell, K. Distinctions between subgroups of asthmatic children: Children's perception of the events associated with asthma. *Pediatrics,* 1963, *61,* 486–494.

Purchell, K., & Weiss, J. H. Asthma. In C. G. Costello (Ed.), *Symptoms of psychopathology.* New York: Wiley, 1970.

Rachman, S. Studies in desensitization. I: The separate effects of relaxation and desensitization. *Behavior Research and Therapy,* 1965, *3,* 245–251.

Rachman, S. The role of muscular relaxation in desensitization therapy. *Behavior Research and Therapy,* 1968, *6,* 159–166.

Rachman, S. J. *Fear and courage.* San Francisco: Freeman, 1978.

Rada, R. T., Laws, D. R., & Kellner, R. Plasma testosterone levels in the rapists. *Psychosomatic Medicine,* 1976, *38,* 257–268.

Rader, G. E., Bekker, L. D., Brown, L., & Richardt, C. Psychological correlates of un-wanted pregnancy. *Journal of Abnormal Psychology,* 1978, *87,* 373–376.

Raine, A., & Venables, P. H. Electrodermal nonresponding, antisocial behavior and schiz-oid tendencies in adolescents. *Psychophysiology,* 1984, *21,* 424–433.

Rardin, M. W. Treatment of a phobia by partial self-desensitization: A case study. *Journal of Consulting and Clinical Psychology,* 1969, *33,* 125–126.

Raskin, D. E. Steroid-induced panic disorder. *American Journal of Psychiatry,* 1984, *141(12),* 1647.

Raskin, N. H. Migraine. *Psychosomatics,* 1982, *23,* 897–907.

Rauste-von Wright, M., & von Wright, J. A longitudinal study of psychosomatic symp-toms in healthy 11–18-year-old girls and boys. *Journal of Psychosomatic Research,* 1981, *25,* 525–534.

Rees, L. Physical and emotional factors in bronchial asthma. *Journal of Psychosomatic Re-search,* 1956, *1,* 98–114.

Reich, W. *Character analysis* (3rd ed.). New York: Farrar, Straus and Giroux, 1961.

Reid, J. E., & Inbau, F. E. *Truth and deception: The polygraph ("lie detection") technique* (2nd ed.). Baltimore: Williams & Wilkins, 1977.

Revelle, W., Humphreys, M. S., Simon, L., & Gilliland, K. The interactive effects of personality, time of day and caffeine: A test of the arousal model. *Journal of Experimen-tal Psychology: General,* 1980, *109,* 1–31.

Richmond, J. B., Eddy, E., & Green, M. Rumination: A psychosomatic syndrome of infancy. *Pediatrics,* 1958, *22,* 49–55.

Richter, R., & Dahme, B. Bronchial asthma in adults: There is little evidence for the effectiveness of behavior therapy and relaxation. *Journal of Psychosomatic Research,* 1982, *26,* 533–540.

Ridley, C. K. *Inhibitory aspects of sex guilt, social censure and need for approval.* Unpublished doctoral dissertation, University of Manitoba, 1976.

Rifkin, A., & Siris, S. G. Panic disorder response to sodium lactate and treatment with antidepressants. *Progress in Neuropsychopharmacology and Biological Psychiatry,* 1985, *9(1),* 33–38.

Rimm, D. C., & Litvak, S. B. Self-verbalization and emotional arousal. *Journal of Abnormal Psychology,* 1969, *74,* 181–187.

Rinn, W. E. The neuropsychology of facial expression: A review of the neurological and psychological mechanisms for producing facial expressions. *Psychological Bulletin,* 1984, *95(1),* 52–77.

Riskind, J. H. They stoop to conquer: Guiding and self-regulatory functions of physical posture after success and failure. *Journal of Personality and Social Psychology,* 1984, *47(3),* 479–493.

Roberts, W. W. Both rewarding and punishing effects of stimulation of the posterior hypothalamus of cats with same electrode and same intensity. *Journal of Comparative and Physiological Psychology,* 1958, *51,* 400–407.

Rock, I. and Harris, C. S. Vision and touch. *Scientific American,* 1967, *216*(5), 96–104.

Rodin, J. Elman, D., & Schachter, S. Emotionality and obesity. In S. Schachter & J. Rodin (Eds.), *Obese humans and rats.* Washington, D.C.: Erlbaum/Halsted, 1974.

Roessler, R., Bruch, H., Thum, L., & Collins, F. Physiologic correlates of affect during psychotherapy. *American Journal of Psychotherapy,* 1975, *29(1),* 26–36.

Rogel, M. J. A critical evaluation of the possibility of higher primate reproductive and sexual pheromones. *Psychological Bulletin,* 1978, *85,* 810–830.

Roman, J., Older, H., & Jones, W. L. Flight research program: VI. Medical monitoring of Navy carrier pilots in combat. *Aerospace Medicine,* 1967, *38,* 133–139.

Rook, K. S., & Hammen, C. L. A cognitive perspective on the experience of sexual arousal. *Journal of Social Issues,* 1977, *33,* 7–29.

Rosch, E. On the internal structure of perceptual and semantic categories. In T. E. Moore (Ed.), *Cognitive development and the acquistion of language.* New York: Academic Press, 1973.

Roscoe, A. H. Heart rate changes in test pilots. In R. I. Kitney & O. Rompelman (Eds.), *The study of heart rate variability.* New York: Oxford University Press, 1980.

Rose, R. M., & Sachan, E. Psychoendocrinology. In R. H. Williams (Ed.), *Textbook of endocrinology* (6th ed.). Philadelphia: Saunders, 1981.

Rosenbaum, A. H., Wells, L. A., Schatzberg, A. F., Jiang, N., Jost, F. A., Maruta, T., & Cross, P. D. Urinary free cortisol levels in anxiety. *Psychosomatics*, 1983, *24(9)*, 835–837.

Rosenman, R. H., & Chesney, M. A. Stress, Type A behavior and coronary disease. In L. Goldberger & S. Breznitz (Eds.), *Handbook of stress*. New York: Free Press, 1982.

Rosenoer, C., & Whyte, A. H. The ordinal position of problem children. *American Journal of Orthopsychiatry*, 1931, *1*, 430–434.

Ross, W. D. Musculoskeletal disorders. In E. R. Wittkower & H. Warnes (Eds.), *Psychosomatic medicine: Its clinical applications*. New York: Harper & Row, 1977.

Roth, W. T., Tinklenberg, J. R., Doyle, C. M., Horvath, T. B., & Kopell, B. S. Mood states and 24-hour cardiac monitoring. *Journal of Psychosomatic Research*, 1976, *20*, 179–186.

Rouse, P. Premenstrual tension: A study using the Moos menstrual questionnaire. *Journal of Psychosomatic Research*, 1978, *22*, 215–222.

Rubens, R. L. and Lapidus, L. B. Schizophrenic patterns of arousal and stimulus barrier fuctioning. *Journal of Abnormal Psychology*, 1978, *87*, 199–211.

Rubin, J. Nagler, R., Spiro, H. M., & Pilot, M. L. Measuring effects of emotions on esophageal motility. *Psychosomatic Medicine*, 1962, *24*, 170–176.

Ruble, D. N., & Brooks-Gunn, J. Menstrual symptoms: A social cognition analysis. *Journal of Behavioral Medicine*, 1979, *2*, 171–194.

Ruch, T. C. The urinary bladder. In T. C. Ruch & H. D. Patton (Eds.), *Physiology and biophysics* (9th ed.). Philadelphia: Saunders, 1966.

Ruderman, A. J. Dysphoric mood and overeating: A test of restraint theory's disinhibition hypothesis. *Journal of Abnormal Psychology*, 1985, *94*, 78–85.

Ruderman, A. J., Belzer, L. J., & Halperin, A. Restraint, anticipated consumption and overeating. *Journal of Abnormal Psychology*, 1985, *94*, 547–555.

Rugh, C. D., & Solberg, W. K. The identification of stressful stimuli in natural environments using a portable biofeedback unit. *Proceedings of the Biofeedback Research Society*, 1974, *p. 54*. Abstract.

Rugh, J., Perlis, D., & Disraeli, R. (Eds.). *Biofeedback in dentistry*. Phoenix: Semantodontics, 1977.

Rugh, J. D., & Johnson, R. W. Temporal analysis of nocturnal bruxism during EMG feedback. *Journal of Periodontology*, 1981, *52(5)*, 263–265.

Rusalova, M. N., Izard, C. E., & Simonov, P. V. Comparative analysis of mimical and autonomic components of man's emotional state. *Aviation, Space and Environmental Medicine*, 1975, September, 1132–1134.

Rush, A. J., Beck, A. T., Kovacs, M., & Hollon, S. D. Comparative efficacy of cognitive therapy and imipramine in the treatment of depressed outpatients. *Cognitive Therapy and Research*, 1977, *1*, 17–37.

Russek, H. I., & Russek, L. G. Is emotional stress an etiological factor in coronary heart disease? *Psychosomatics*, 1976, *17*, 63–67.

Russell, G. F. Psychological and nutritional factors in disturbances of menstrual function and ovulation. *Postgraduate Medical Journal*, 1972, *48*, 10–13.

Russell, P. L., & Brandsma, J. M. A theoretical and empirical integration of the rational-emotive and classical conditioning theories. *Journal of Consulting and Clinical Psychology*, 1974, *42*, 389–397.

Rutter, M. *Maternal deprivation: Reassessed*. Baltimore: Penguin, 1972.

Ryan, W. G. *Endocrine disorders: A pathophysiological approach*. Chicago: Year Book Medical Publishers, 1975.

Sachar, E. J. Hormonal changes in stress and mental illness. In D. T. Krieger & J. C. Hughes (Eds.), *Neuroendocrinology*. Sunderland: Sinauer, 1980.

Sackeim, H. A., Gur, R. C., & Saucy, M. C. Emotions are expressed more intensely on the left side of the face. *Science*, 1978, *202*, 434–435.

Sajwaj, T., Libet, J., & Agras, S. Lemon-juice therapy: The control of life-threathening rumination in a six month old infant. *Journal of Applied Behavioral Analysis*, 1974, *7*, 557–563.

Salter, A. *Conditioned reflex therapy*. New York: Creative Age Press, 1950.

Sanders, D., Warner, P., Backstrom, T., & Bancroft, J. Mood, sexuality, hormones and the menstrual cycle. I: Changes in mood and physical state: Description of subjects and method. *Psychosomatic Medicine*, 1983, *45*, 487–501.

Sarrel, P. M., & Masters, W. H. Sexual molestation of men by women. *Archives of Sexual Behavior*, 1982, *11*, 117–131.

Sassin, J. F. Sleep-related hormones. In R. R. Drucker-Colin & J. L. McGaugh (Eds.), *Neurobiology of Sleep and Memory*. New York: Academic Press, 1977.

Sato, T. L., Turnbull, C. D., Davidson, J. R., & Madakasira, S. Depressive illness and placebo response. *International Journal of Psychiatry in Medicine*, 1984, *14*, 171–179.

Scarr, S. Genetic factors in activity motivation. *Child Development*, 1966, *37*, 663–673.

Scarr, S. Social introversion-extraversion as a heritable response. *Child Development*, 1969, *40*, 823–832.

Schachter, S. *The psychology of affiliation*. Stanford: Stanford University Press, 1959.

Schachter, S. Cognitive effects on bodily functioning: Studies of obesity and eating. In D. C. Glass (Ed.), *Neurophysiology and emotion*. New York: Rockefeller University Press, 1967.

Schachter, S. Obesity and eating. *Science*, 1968, *161*, 751–756.

Schachter, S. Some extraordinary facts about obese humans and rats. *American Psychologist*, 1971, *26*, 129–144.

Schachter, S., & Latene, B. Crime, cognition and the autonomic nervous system. In M. R. Jones (Ed.), *Nebraska Symposium on Motivation*. Lincoln: University of Nebraska Press, 1964.

Schachter, S., & Singer, J. E. Cognitive, social and physiological determinants of emotional states. *Psychological Review*, 1962, *69*, 379–399.

Schachter, S., & Singer, J. E. Comments on the Maslach and Marshall-Zimbardo experiments. *Journal of Personality and Social Psychology*, 1979, *37*, 989–995.

Schachter, S., Goldman, R., & Gordon, A. Effects of fear, food deprivation and obesity on eating. *Journal of Personality and Social Psychology*, 1968, *10*, 91–97.

Schaefer, W. S., & Bayley, N. Maternal behavior, child behavior and their intercorrelations from infancy through adolescence. *Monographs of the Society for Research in Child Development*, 1963, *28*(Serial No. 87), 1–127.

Schaffer, D. The association between enuresis and emotional disorders: A review of the literature. In I. Kolvin, R. C. MacKeith, & S. R. Meadow (Eds.), *Bladder control and enuresis*. Philadelphia: Saunders, 1973.

Schaffer, H. R. The onset of fear of strangers and the incongruity hypothesis. *Journal of Child Psychology and Psychiatry*, 1966, *7*, 95–106.

Schaffer, H. R., & Emerson, P. The development of social attachments in infancy. *Monographs of the Society for Research in Child Development*, 1964, *29(3)*, No. 94.

Schally, A. V. Aspects of hypothalamic regulation of the pituitary gland. *Science*, 1978, *202*, 18–28.

Schiffman, H. R. *Sensation and perception: An integrated approach* (2nd ed.). New York: Wiley, 1982.

Schildkraut, J. J. The catecholamine hypothesis of affective disorders: A review of supporting evidence. *American Journal of Psychiatry*, 1965, *122*, 509–522.

Schildkraut, J. J. Norepinephrine metabolites as biochemical criteria for classifying depressive disorders and predicting response to treatment: Preliminary findings. *American Journal of Psychiatry*, 1973, *130*, 695–698.

Schildkraut, J. J. Biogenic amines and affective disorders. *Annual Review of Medicine*, 1974, *25*, 333–348.

Schildkraut, J. J., & Freyhan, F. A. Neuropharmacological studies of mood disorder. In J. Zubin (Ed.), *Disorders of mood*. New York: Grune & Stratton, 1972.

Schildkraut, J. J., & Kety, S. S. Biogenic amines and emotion. *Science*, 1967, *156*, 21–30.

Schneck, J. M. Blushing and unconscious hostility. *Diseases of the Nervous System*, 1967, *28*, 679.

Schneirla, T. C. The interrelationships of the "innate" and "acquired" in instinctual behavior. In P. Grasse (Ed.), *L' Instinct dans le comportement des animaux et de l'homme.* Paris: Masson, 1956.

Schreiber, F. *Sybil.* New York: Warner, 1974.

Schreiner-Engel, P., Schiavi, R. C., Smith, H., & White, D. Sexual arousability and the menstrual cycle. *Psychosomatic Medicine,* 1981, *43,* 199–214.

Schull, J., Kaplan, H., & O'Brian, C. P. Naloxone can alter experimental pain and mood in humans. *Physiological Psychology,* 1981, *9(3),* 245–250.

Schuster, M. M. The irritable bowel syndrome: Applications of psychophysiological methods to treatment. In R. Holzl & W. E. Whitehead (Eds.), *Psychophysiology of the gastrointestinal tract.* New York: Plenum Press, 1983.

Schwab, J. J., Fennell, E. B., & Warheit, G. J. The epidemiology of psychosomatic disorders. *Psychosomatics,* 1974, *15,* 88–93.

Schwartz, G. E. Biofeedback as therapy: Some theoretical and practical issues. *American Psychologist,* 1973, *28(8),* 666–673.

Schwartz, G. E. Biofeedback, self-regulation and the patterning of physiological processes. *American Scientist,* 1975, *63,* 314–324.

Schwartz, G. E. Psychosomatic disorders and biofeedback: A psychobiological model of disregulation. In J. D. Maser & M. E. Seligman (Eds.), *Psychopathology: Experimental models.* San Francisco: Freeman, 1977.

Schwartz, G. E. Psychobiological foundations of psychotherapy and behavior change. In S. L. Garfield & A. E. Burgin (Eds.), *Handbook of psychotherapy and behavior change: An empirical analysis* (2nd ed.). New York: Wiley, 1978.

Schwartz, G. E. The brain as a health care system. In G. C. Stone, F. Cohen, & N. E. Adler (Eds.), *Health psychology—A handbook: Theories, applications and challenges of a psychological approach to the health care system.* San Francisco: Jossey-Bass, 1979.

Schwartz, G. E., & Logue, A. *Facial thermography in the assessment of emotion.* Unpublished manuscript, 1977. Cited in J. Hassett *A Primer of Psychophysiology.* San Francisco: Freeman, 1978.

Schwartz, G. E., & Shipiro, D. Biofeedback and hypertension: Current findings and theoretical concerns. *Seminars in Psychiatry,* 1973, *5(4),* 493–503.

Schwartz, G. E., Davidson, R., Maer, F., & Bromfeld, E. Patterns of hemispheric dominance during musical, emotional, verbal and spatial tasks. *Psychophysiology,* 1974, *11,* 227.

Schwartz, G. E., Fair, P. L., Greenberg, P. S., Friedman, M. J., & Klerman, G. L. Facial electromyography in the assessment of emotion. *Psychophysiology,* 1974, *11,* 237. Abstract.

Schwartz, G. E., Fair, P. L., Greenberg, P. S., Mandel, M. R., & Klerman, G. L. Facial expression and depression: An electromyographic study. *Psychosomatic Medicine,* 1974, *36,* 458. (Abstract).

Schwartz, G. E., Fair, P. L., Salt, P., Mandel, M. R., & Klerman, G. L. Facial muscle patterning to affective imagery in depressed and nondepressed subjects. *Science,* 1976, *192,* 489–491. (a)

Schwartz, G. E., Fair, P. L., Salt, P., Mandel, M. R., & Klerman, G. L. Facial expression and imagery in depression: An electromyographic study. *Psychosomatic Medicine,* 1976, *38,* 337–347. (b)

Schwartz, G. E., Brown, S. L., & Ahern, G. L. Facial muscle patterning and subjective experiences during affective imagery: Sex differeces. *Psychophysiology,* 1980, *17,* 75–82.

Schwartz, G. E., Weinberger, D. A., & Singer, J. A. Cardiovascular differentiation of happiness, sadness, anger and fear following imagery and exercise. *Psychosomatic Medicine,* 1981, *43,* 343–364.

Schwartz, M. F., & Bauman, J. E. *Hyperprolactinemia and sexual dysfunction in men.* Paper presented at the seventh annual meeting of the Society for Sex Therapy and Research, New York, March 1981.

Scott, D. S., & Gregg, J. M. Myofacial pain of the temporomandibular joint: A review of the behavioral-relaxation therapies. *Pain,* 1980, *8,* 207–215.

Sears, R. R., & Wise, G. W. Relation of cup-feeding in infancy to thumbsucking and oral drive. *American Journal of Orthopsychiatry,* 1950, *20,* 123–138.

Sears, R. R., Maccoby, E. E., & Levin, H. *Patterns of child rearing*. New York: Harper & Row, 1957.

Sears, R. R., Rau, L., & Alpert, R. *Identification and child rearing*. Standford: Standford University Press, 1965.

Seer, P. Psychological control of essential hypertension: Review of the literature and methodological critique. *Psychological Bulletin*, 1979, *86*, 1015–1043.

Seiden, L. S., & Dykstra, L. A. *Psychopharmacology: A Biochemical and Behavioral Approach*. New York: Van Nostrand Reinhold, 1977.

Selye, H. *The stress of life*. New York: McGraw-Hill, 1956.

Sewall, M. S. Two studies of sibling rivalry: I. Some causes of jealousy in young children. *Smith College Studies of Social Work*, 1930, *1*, 6–22.

Shanan, J., Brezezinski, H. Sulman, F., & Sharon, M. Active coping behavior, anxiety and cortical steroid excretion in the prediction of transient amenorrhea. *Behavior Science*, 1965, *10*, 461–465.

Shagass, C., & Malmo, R. B. Psychodynamic themes and localized muscular tension during psychotherapy. *Psychosomatic Medicine*, 1954, *16*, 295–314.

Shapiro, A. H. Behavior of Kibbutz and urban children receiving an injection. *Psychophysiology*, 1975, *12*, 79–80.

Shaw, B. F., & Beck, A. T. The treatment of depression with cognitive therapy. In A. Ellis & R. Griegers (Eds.), *Handbook of rational emotive theory and practice*. New York: Springer, 1977.

Sheehy, T. W. Gastroenterology and the elderly. In S. R. Gambert (Ed.), *Contemporary geriatric medicine* (Vol. 1). New York: Plenum Press, 1983.

Sherman, A. R., & Plummer, I. L. Training in relaxation as a behavioral self-management skill: An exploratory investigation. *Behavior Therapy*, 1973, *4*, 543–550.

Shields, J. *Monozygotic twins brought up together and apart*. London: Oxford University Press, 1962.

Shipman, W. G., Oken, D., Balshan-Goldstein, I., Grinker, R. R., & Heath, H. A. Study in psychophysiology of muscle tension: II. Personality factors. *Archives of General Psychiatry*, 1964, *11*, 330–345.

Shirley, M. M. *The first two years: A study of twenty-five babies*. Minneapolis: University of Minnesota Press, 1931.

Shochet, B. R., Lisansky, E. T., Schubart, A. F., Fiocco, V., Kurland, S., & Page, M. A. A medical-psychiatric study of patients with rheumatoid arthritis. *Psychosomatics*, 1969, *10*, 271.

Siegel, A., & Chabora, J. Effects of electrical stimulation on the cingulate gyrus upon attack behavior elicited from the hypothalamus in the cat. *Brain Research*, 1971, *32*, 169–177.

Siegel, A., & Skog, D. Effects of electrical stimulation of the septum upon attack behavior elicited from the hypothalamus in the cat. *Brain Research*, 1970, *23*, 371–380.

Siegel, J. M., Mattews, K. A., & Leitch, C. J. Blood pressure variability and the Type A behavior pattern in adolescence. *Journal of Psychosomatic Research*, 1983, *27*, 265–272.

Silver, B. V., & Blanchard, E. B. Biofeedback and relaxation training in the treatment of psychophysiological disorders: Or are the machines really necessary? *Journal of Behavioral Medicine*, 1978, *1*, 217–239.

Silverman, A. J., Cohen, C. I., & Zuidema, C. Psychophysiological investigations in cardiovascular stress. *American Journal of Psychiatry*, 1957, *113*, 691–693.

Silverman, A. J., Cohen, C. I., Shmavonian, B. M., & Kirschner, N. Catecholamines in psychophysiologic studies. *Recent Advances in Biological Psychiatry*, 1961, *3*, 104–117.

Sim, M. *Guide to psychiatry*. Baltimore: Williams & Wilkins, 1963.

Singh, B. S. Ventilatory Response to CO_2: II Studies in neurotic psychiatric patients and practitioners of transcendental meditation. *Psychosomatic Medicine*, 1984, *46*, 347–362.

Sintchak, G., & Geer, J. H. A vaginal plethysmograph system. *Psychophysiology*, 1975, *12*, 113–115.

Slade, P. Premenstrual emotional changes in normal women: Fact or fiction? *Journal of Psychosomatic Research*, 1984, *28*, 1–7.

Slater, E., & Glithero, E. A followup of patients diagnosed as suffering from hysteria. *Journal of Psychosomatic Research*, 1965, *9*, 9–13.

Slochower, J. Emotional labeling and overeating in obese and normal weight individuals. *Psychosomatic Medicine*, 1976, *38*, 131–139.

Smith, B. The neurological lesion in achalasia of the cardia. *Gut*, 1970, *11*, 388–391.

Smith, B. M. The polygraph. *Scientific American*, 1967, *216*, 25–31.

Smith, D. R. Discussion of Bors-Turner. *Transactions of the Western Section American Urological Association*, 1959, *27*, 148–149.

Smith, M. L., & Glass, G. V. Meta-analysis of psychotherapy outcome studies. *American Psychologist*, 1977, *32(9)*, 752–760.

Smith, S. M., Brown, H. O., Toman, J. E., & Goodman, L. S. The lack of cerberal effects of d-turbocurarine. *Anesthesiology*, 1947, *8*, 1–14.

Smith, T. W., Houston, B. K., & Zurawski, R. M. Finger pulse volume as a measure of anxiety in response to evaluative threat. *Psychophysiology*, 1984, *21*, 260–264.

Smith, T. W., Snyder, C. R., & Handelsman, M. M. On the self-serving function of an academic wooden leg: Test anxiety as a self-handicapping strategy. *Journal of Personality and Social Psychology*, 1982, *42*, 314–321.

Solomon, R. L. The opponent-process theory of motivation: The costs of pleasure and the benefits of pain. *American Psychologist*, 1980, *35(8)*, 691–712.

Solomon, R. L., & Corbit, J. D. An opponent-process theory of motivation: Temporal dynamics of affect. *Psychological Review*, 1974, *81*, 119–145.

Sommers, S. Emotionality reconsidered: The role of cognition in emotional responsiveness. *Journal of Personality and Social Psychology*, 1981, *41*, 553–561.

Sommers, S., & Scioli, A. Emotional range and value orientation: Toward a cognitive view of emotionality. *Journal of Personality and Social Psychology*, 1986, *51*, 417–422.

Sovak, M., Kunzel, M., Sternbach, R. A., & Dalessio, D. J. Is volitional manipulation of hemodynamics a valid rationale for biofeedback therapy of migraine? *Headache*, 1978, *18*, 197–202.

Spelt, D. K. The conditioning of the human fetus in utero. *Journal of Experimental Psychology*, 1948, *38*, 338–346.

Sperry, R. W. Hemisphere deconnection and unity in conscious awareness. *American Psychologist*, 1968, *23*, 723–733.

Sprague, K. *The athlete's body*. Los Angeles: J. P. Tarcher, 1981.

Spiesman, J. C., Lazarus, R. S., Mordkoff, A., & Davison, L. Experimental reduction of stress based on ego-defense theory. *Journal of Abnormal and Social Psychology*, 1964, *68*, 367–380.

Spitzer, R. L., Skodol, A. E., Gibbon, M., & Williams, J. B. *DSM-III Casebook*. Washington, D.C.: American Psychiatric Association, 1981.

Springer, S. P., & Deutsch, G. *Left brain, right brain*. San Francisco: Freeman, 1981.

Srole, L., Langner, T. S., Michael, S. T., Opler, M. K., & Rennie, T. A. *The Midtown Manhatten Study: Mental health in the metropolis* (Vol. 1). New York: McGraw-Hill, 1962.

Sroufe, L. A. Effects of depth and rate of breathing on heart rate and heart rate variability. *Psychophysiology*, 1971, *8*, 648–655.

Stacher, G., Schmierer, G., & Landgraft, M. Tertiary esophageal contractions evoked by acoustical stimuli. *Gastroenterology*, 1979, *77*, 49–54.

Stacher, G., Steinringer, H., Blau, A., & Landgraft, M. Acoustically evoked esophageal contractions and defense reactions. *Psychophysiology*, 1979, *16*, 234–241.

Stanton, S. L. Psychosomatic aspects of female urinary incontinence. *Journal of Psychosomatic Research*, 1981, *25*, 417–419.

Starker, S., & Hasenfeld, R. Daydream styles and sleep disturbances. *The Journal of Nervous and Mental Disease*, 1976, *163*, 391–400.

Starkman, M. N., Marshall, J. C. LaFerla, J., & Kelch, R. P. Pseudocyesis: Psychologic and neuroendocrine interrelationships. *Psychosomatic Medicine*, 1985, *47*, 46–57.

Stamler, J., Stamler, R., Riedlinger, W. F., Algers, G., & Roberts, R. H. Hypertension screening of 1 million Americans. *Journal of the American Medical Association*, 1976, *235*, 2299–2306.

Stein, L., & Belluzzi, J. D. Brain endorphins and the sense of well-being: A psychobiological hypothesis. In E. Costa & M. Trabucchi (Eds.), *Advances in biochemical psychopharmacology, Vol. 18.: The endorphins*. New York: Raven Press, 1978.

Steiner, M. The treatment of severe premenstrual dysphoria with bromocriptine. *Journal of Psychosomatic Obstetrics and Gynaecology*, 1983, *2(4)*, 223–227.

Steinhardt, M. J. Modes of therapy in emotional aspects of respiratory dysfunction. *Psychosomatics*, 1970, *11(3)*, 169–172.

Stern, D. B. Handedness with the lateral distribution of conversion reactions. *Journal of Nervous and Mental Disease*. 1977, *164*, 122–128.

Stern, R. M., & Anschel, C. Deep inspiration as stimuli for responses of the autonomic nervous system. *Psychophysiology*, 1968, *5*, 132–141.

Stern, R. M., & Lewis, N. L. Ability of actors to control their GSRS and express emotions. *Psychophysiology*, 1968, *4*, 294–299.

Stern, R. M., Ray, W. J., & Davis, C. M. *Psychophysiological recording*. New York: Oxford University Press, 1980.

Sternback, R. A. The effects of instructional sets on autonomic responsivity. *Psychophysiology*, 1964, *1*, 67–72.

Stevens, C. F. The neuron. *Scientific American*, 1979, *241(3)*, 54–66.

Stevenson, I., & Ripley, H. S. Variations in respiration and in respiratory symptoms during changes in emotion. *Psychosomatic Medicine*, 1952, *14*, 476–490.

Stoller, R. J. Sexual deviations. In F. A. Beach (Ed.), *Human sexuality in four perspectives*. Baltimore: Johns Hopkins University Press, 1977.

Stone, L. J., Smith, H. T., & Murphy, L. B. *The competent infant*. New York: Basic Books, 1973.

Stoyva, J. Self-regulation and the stress-related disorders: A perspective on biofeedback. In D. I. Mostofsky (Ed.), *Behavior control and modification of physiological activity*. Englewood Cliffs, N.J.: Prentice-Hall, 1976.

Straub, L. R., Ripley, H. S., & Wolf, S. Disturbance of bladder function associated with emotional states. *Journal American Medical Association*, 1949, *141*, 1139–1143.

Straub, L. R., Ripley, H. S., & Wolf, S. Disturbance of bladder function associated with emotional states. *Research publications of Association of Nervous and Mental Diseases*, 1950, *29*, 1019–1029.

Stretch, R. H., Vail, J. D., & Maloney, J. P. Post-traumatic stress disorder among army nurse corps Vietnam veterans. *Journal of Consulting and Clinical Psychology*, 1985, *53*, 704–708.

Striegel, R. H. *Hunger perception: Comparison of normally weighted, obese and anorexic persons*. Paper presented at the 27th annual meeting of the Southeastern Psychological Association, March 1981.

Stunkard, A. J. Obesity and the denial of hunger. *Psychosomatic Medicine*, 1959, *21*, 281–289.

Stunkard, A. J., & Koch, C. The interpretation of gastric motility: Apparent bias in the reports of hunger by obese persons. *Archives of General Psychiatry*, 1964, *2*, 74–82.

Suinn, R., & Richardson, F. Anxiety management training: A nonspecific behavior therapy program for anxiety control. *Behavior Therapy*, 1971, *4*, 498–511.

Sullivan, M. J., & Brender, W. Facial electromyography: A measure of affective processes during sexual arousal. *Psychophysiology*, 1986, *23*, 182–188.

Surwitt, R. S., Williams, R. B., & Shapiro, D. *Behavioral approaches to cardiovascular disease*. New York: Academic Press, 1982.

Sveback, S. Respiratory patterns as predictors of laughter. *Psychophysiology*, 1975, *12*, 62–65.

Svensson, J. C., & Theorell, T. Cardiovascular effects of anxiety induced by interviewing young hypertensive male subjects. *Journal of Psychosomatic Research*, 1982, *26*, 359–370.

Synder, M. Self-monitoring of expressive behavior. *Journal of Personality and Social Psychology*, 1974, *30*, 526–537.

Synder, S.H. The dopamine hypothesis of schizophrenia. *American Journal of Psychiatry*, 1976, *133*, 197–202.

Synder, S. H. Opiate receptors and internal opiates. *Scientific American*, 1977, *236(3)*, 44–56.

Szucko, J. J., & Kleinmuntz, B. Statistical versus clinical lie detection. *American Psychologist*, 1981, *36*, 488–496.

Tal, A., & Miklich, D. R. Emotionally induced decreases in pulmonary flow rates in asthmatic children. *Psychosomatic Medicine*, 1976, *38*, 190–199.

Tarler-Benlolo, L. The role of relaxation in biofeedback training: A critical review of the literature. *Psychological Bulletin*, 1978, *85*, 727–755.

Taskahashi, K., Takahashi, Y., Takahashi, S., & Honda, Y. Growth hormone and cortisol secretion during noctural sleep in narcoleptics and in dogs. In N. Hadotani (Ed.), *Psychoendocrinology*. Basel: Karger, 1974.

Taylor, C. B., & Fortmann, S. P. Essential hypertension. *Psychosomatics*, 1983, *24*, 433–448.

Teasdale, J. D., & Fogarty, S. J. Differential effects of induced mood on retrieval of pleasant and unpleasant events from episodic memory. *Journal of Abnormal Psychology*, 1979, *88*, 248–257.

Teitelbaum, P., & Stellar, E. Recovery from the failure to eat, produced by hypothalamic lesions. *Science*, 1954, *120*, 894–895.

Thach, W. T. Discharge of cerebellar neurons related to two postures and movements. I. Nuclear cell output. *Journal of Neurophysiology*, 1970, *33*, 527–536. (a)

Thach, W. T. Discharge of cerebellar neurons related to two postures and movements. II. Purkinje cell output and input. *Journal of Neurophysiology*, 1970, *33*, 537–547. (b)

Thach, W. T. Correlation of neural discharge pattern and force of muscular activity, joint position, and direction of intended next movement in motor cortex and cerebellum. *Journal of Neurophysiology*, 1978, *41*, 654–676.

Thackray, R. I. The stress of boredom and monotony: A consideration of the evidence. *Psychosomatic Medicine*, 1981, *43*, 165–176.

Thomas, A., & Chess, S. *Temperament and development*. New York: Brunner/Mazel, 1977.

Thomas, A., Chess, S., Birch, H., & Hertizig, M. E. A longitudinal study of primary reaction patterns in children. *Comprehensive Psychiatry*, 1960, *1*, 103–112.

Thomas, A., Chess, S., Birch, H. G., Hertizig, M. E., & Korn, S. *Behavioral individuality in early childhood*. New York: New York University Press, 1963.

Thomas, A., Chess, S., & Birch, H. G. *Temperament and behavioral disorders in children*. New York: New York University Press, 1968.

Thomas, A., Chess, S., & Birch, H. G. The origin of personality. *Scientific American*, 1970, *223*(2), 102–109.

Thomas, C. B., & Greenstreet, R. L. Psychological characteristics in youth as predictors of five disease states: Suicide, mental illness, hypertension, coronary heart disease and tumors. *Johns Hopkins Medical Journal*, 1973, *132*, 16–43.

Thomas, L. J., Tiber, N., & Schireson, S. The effects of anxiety and frustration on muscular tension related to the temporomandibular joint syndrome. *Dental Research*, 1973, *36*, 763–768.

Thompson, C. *Psychoanalysis: Evolution and development*. New York: Hermitage, 1950.

Thompson, C. Cultural pressures in the psychology of women. 1942. In M. R. Green (Ed.), *Interpersonal psychoanalysis: The selected papers of Clara Thompson*. New York: Basic Books, 1964.

Thompson, D. S. (Ed.). *Everywomen's health: The complete guide to body and mind*. Garden City: Doubleday, 1980.

Thompson, J. G., Griebstein, M. G., & Kuhlenschmidt, S. L. Effects of EMG biofeedback and relaxation training in the prevention of academic underachievement. *Journal of Counseling Psychology*, 1980, *27*(2), 97–106.

Thomson, J. *Through Masai land*. London: Low, Marston, Searle and Rivington, 1887.

Tillman, F. A., Berofsky, B., & O'Conner, J. *Introductory philosophy*. New York, Harper & Row, 1967.

Tinbergen, N. Ethology and stress disease. *Science*, 1974, *185*, 20–27.

Tolis, G. Prolactin: physiology and pathology. In D. T. Kreiger & J. C. Hughes (Eds.), *Neuroendocrinology*. Sunderland: Sinaur, 1980.

Tomkins, S. S. *Affect, imagery, consciousness. Vol. 1. The positive affects*. New York: Springer, 1962.

Tomkins, S. S. *Affect, imagery, consciousness, Vol. 2. The negative affects*. New York: Springer, 1963.

Tomkins, S. S. Script theory: Differential magnification of affects. In H. E. Howe & R. A.

Dienstbier (Eds.), *Nebraska Symposium on Motivation, 1978* (Vol. 26). Lincoln: University of Nebraska Press, 1979.

Tomkins, S. S. Affect theory. In K. R. Scherer & P. Ekman (Eds.), *Approaches to Emotion.* Hillsdale, N.J.: Lawrence Erlbaum Associates, 1984.

Toone, B. K., & Lader, M. H. Salivary secretion in the affective disorders and schizophrenia. *Acta Psychiatrica Scandinavica,* 1979, *59,* 529–535.

Torrence, E. B. *A psychological study of American jet aces.* Paper presented at the meeting of the Western Psychological Association, Long Beach, California, 1954.

Traue, H. C., Gottwald, A., Henderson, P. R., & Bakal, D. A. Nonverbal expressiveness and EMG activity in tension headache sufferers and controls. *Journal of Psychosomatic Research,* 1985, *29,* 375–381.

Truax, S. R. *Determinants of emotion attribution: Cognitive effects of relative ambiguity and subjective salience.* Paper presented at the 52nd annual meeting of the Midwestern Psychological Association, May 3, 1980.

Tuddenham, R. D. The constancy of personality ratings over two decades. *Genetic Psychology Monographs,* 1959, *60,* 3–29.

Turner, S. M., Beidel, D. C., & Larkin, K. T. Situational determinants of social anxiety in clinic and nonclinic samples: Physiological and cognitive correlates. *Journal of Consulting and Clinical Psychology,* 1986, *54,* 523–527.

Udry, J. R., & Morris, N. M. Distribution of coitus in the menstrual cycle. *Nature,* 1968, *220,* 593–596.

Udry, J. R., & Morris, N. M. Effects of contraceptive pills on the distribution of sexual activity in the menstrual cycle. *Nature,* 1970, *227,* 502–503.

Vaernes, R., Ursin, H., Darragh, A., & Lambe, R. Endocrine response patterns and psychological correlates. *Journal of Psychosomatic Research,* 1982, *26,* 123–131.

Valenstein, E. S. *Brain control: A critical examination of brain stimulation and psychosurgery.* New York: Wiley, 1973.

Valenstein, E. S., & Valenstein, T. Interaction of positive and negative reinforcing neural systems. *Science,* 1964, *145,* 1456–1458.

Valins, S. Cognitive effects of false heart-rate feedback. *Journal of Personality and Social Psychology,* 1966, *4,* 400–408.

Valins, S. The perception and labeling of bodily changes as determinants of emotional behavior. In P. Black (Ed.), *Physiological correlates of emotion.* New York: Academic Press, 1970.

Valone, K., Goldstein, M. J., & Norton, J. P. Parental expressed emotion and psychophysiological reactivity in an adolescent sample at risk for schizophrenia spectrum disorders. *Journal of Abnormal Psychology,* 1984, *93,* 448–457.

Van den Hout, M. A., & Griez, E. Panic symptoms after inhalation of carbon dioxide. *British Journal of Psychiatry,* 1984, *144,* 503–507.

Van Egeren, L. F., Abelson, J. L., & Sniderman, L. D. Interpersonal and electrocardiographic responses of Type A's and Type B's in competitive socioeconomic games. *Journal of Psychosomatic Research,* 1983, *27,* 53–59.

Van Pelt, S. J. Hypnotherapy: Not merely a treatment, more a way of life. *Journal of the American Institute of Hypnosis,* 1975, *16,* 44–45.

Victor, R., Weipert, D., & Shapiro, D. Voluntary control of systolic blood pressure during postural change. *Psychophysiology,* 1984, *21,* 673–682.

Vierling, J. C., & Rock, J. Variation in olfactory sensitivity to exaltolide during the menstrual cycle. *Journal of Applied Physiology,* 1967, *22,* 311–315.

Vogel, G. W., Traub, A. C., Ben-Horin, P., & Meyers, G. M. REM deprivation II: The effects on depressed patients. *Archives of General Psychiatry,* 1968, *18,* 301–311.

Vogel, G. W., McAbee, R., Baker, K., & Thurmond, A. Endogenous depression improvement and REM pressure. *Archives of General Psychiatry,* 1977, *34,* 96–97.

Voors, A. W., Berenson, G. S., Dalfere, E. R., Webber, L. S., & Schuler, S. E. Racial differences in blood pressure control. *Science,* 1979, *204,* 1091–1094.

Wabrek, A. J. Effects of metroclopramine on ejaculatory threshold in a group of premature ejaculators. *Neurology and Urodynamics,* 1984, *3,* 155–161.

Wadden, T. A. Relaxation therapy for essential hypertension: Specific or nonspecific effects? *Journal of Psychosomatic Research*, 1984, *28*, 53–61.

Waldron, I. Why do women live longer then men? *Human Stress*, 1976, *2*, 2–30.

Wallbott, H. G., & Scherer, K. R. Cues and channels in emotion recognition. *Journal of Personality and Social Psychology*, 1986, *51*, 690–699.

Ward, M. M., Mefford, I. N., Parker, S. D., Chesney, M. A., Taylor, C. B., Keegan, D. L., & Barchas J. D. Epinephrine and norepinephrine responses in continuously collected human plasma to a series of stressors. *Psychosomatic Medicine*, 1983, *45*, 471–486.

Waters, W. F., & McDonald, D. G. Autonomic responses to auditory, visual and imagined stimuli in a systematic desensitization context. *Behavior Research and Therapy*, 1973, *11*, 577–585.

Waters, W. F., McDonald, D. G., & Koresko, R. L. Psychophysiological responses during analogue systematic desensitization and non-relaxation control procedures. *Behavior Research and Therapy*, 1972, *10*, 381–393.

Watson, J. B. *Psychology from the standpoint of a behaviorist*. Philadelphia, Lippincott, 1919.

Watson, J. B., & Morgan, J. J. Emotional reactions and psychological experimentaion. *American Journal of Psychology*, 1917, *28*, 163–174.

Watson, J. B., & Rayner, R. Conditioned emotional reactions. *Journal of Experimental Psychology*, 1920, *3*, 1–14.

Weaver, J. B., Masland, J. L., Kharazmi, S., & Zillmann, D. Effects of alcoholic intoxication on the appreciation of different types of humor. *Journal of Personality and Social Psychology*, 1985, *49*, 781–787.

Webb, J., Millian, D., & Stoplz, C. Gynecological survey of American female athletes competing at the Montreal Olympic games. *Journal of Sports Medicine and Physical Fitness*, 1979, *19*, 405–412.

Weerts, T. C., & Roberts, R. The physiological effects of imagining anger-provoking and fear-provoking scenes. *Psychophysiology*, 1976, *13*, 174. Abstract.

Wei, E., & Loh, H. H. Physical dependence on opiate-like peptides. *Science*, 1976, *193*, 1262–1263.

Weideger, P. *Menstruation and menopause: The physiology, the psychology, the myth and the reality*. New York: Knopf, 1976.

Weinberg, M. S. Sexual modesty, social meanings and the nudist camp. *Social Problems*, 1965, *12*, 311–318.

Weinberg, M. S. Embarrassment: Its variable and invariable aspects. *Social Forces*, 1968, *46(3)*, 382–388.

Weinberger, D. A., Schwartz, G. E., & Davidson, R. J. Low-anxious, high-anxious and repressive coping styles: Psychometric patterns and behavioral and physiological responses to stress. *Journal of Abnormal Psychology*, 1979, *88*, 369–380.

Weiner, H. *Psychobiology and human disease*. New York: Elsevier, 1977.

Weiner, H., Thaler, M., Reiser, M. F., & Mirsky, I. A. Etiology of duodenal ulcer: I. Relation of specific psychological characteristics to rate of gastric secretion (serum pepsinogen). *Psychosomatic Medicine*, 1957, *19*, 1–10.

Weiss, J. M. Effects of coping responses on stress. *Journal of Comparative and Physiological Psychology*, 1968, *65*, 251–260.

Weiss, J. M. Somatic effects of predictable and unpredictable shock. *Psychosomatic Medicine*, 1970, *32*, 397–408.

Weiss, J. M. Effects of coping behavior in different warning signal conditions on stress pathology in rats. *Journal of Comparative and Physiological Psychology*, 1971, *77*, 1–13. (a)

Weiss, J. M. Effects of coping behaviors with and without a feedback signal on stress pathology in rats. *Journal of Comparative and Physiological Psychology*, 1971, *77*, 22–30. (b)

Weiss, J. M. Effects of punishing the coping response (conflict) on stress pathology in rats. *Journal of Comparative and Physiological Psychology*, 1971, *77*, 14–21. (c)

Weiss, T. Medical uses of biofeedback. In M. T. Orne (Ed.), *Biofeedback: Task Force Report No. 19*. Washington, D.C.: American Psychiatric Association, 1980.

Weiss, T. N. Urethral manipulation: An unusual paraphilia. *Journal of Sex and Marital Therapy*, 1982, *8*, 222–227.

Weitzman, E. D. Biological rhythms and hormonal secretion patterns. In D. T. Krieger & J. C. Hughes (Eds.), *Neuroendocrinology*. Sunderland: Sinauer, 1980.

Wells, K. F. *Kinesiology: The scientific basis of human motion* (5th ed.). Philadelphia: Saunders, 1971.

Welsh, D. K. Hypnotic control of blushing: A case study. *American Journal of Clinical Hypnosis*, 1978, *20*, 213–216.

Wenderlein, J. M. Urinary bladder function in women psychometric aspects. *Geburtshilfe Frauenheilkd*, 1980, *40*, 246–252.

Wenger, M. A., & Cullen, T. D. Studies of autonomic balance in children and adults. In N. S. Greenfield & R. A. Sternbach (Eds.), *Handbook of psychophysiology*. New York: Holt, 1972.

Werbach, M. R., & Sandweiss, J. B. Peripheral temperatures of migraineurs undergoing relaxation training. *Headache*, 1978, *18*, 211–214.

White, C. A. The effects of viewing films of different arousal content on the eating behaviors of obese and normal weight subjects. *Dissertation Abstracts International*, 1973, *34(5-B)*, 2324.

Whitehead, W. E. *The use of biofeedback in the treatment of gastrointestinal disorders*. Denver: Biofeedback Society of America, 1978.

Whitehead, W. E., & Schuster, M. M. The treatment of functional gastrointestinal disorders. In R. L. Gallon (Ed.), *The psychosomatic approach to illness*. New York: Elsevier Biomedical, 1982.

Whitehead, W. E., Blackwell, B., DeSilva, H. & Robinson, A. Anxiety and anger in hypertension. *Journal of Psychosomatic Research*, 1977, *21*, 382–389.

Whitehead, W. E., Engels, B. T., & Schuster, M. M. Irritable bowel syndrome: Physiological and psychological differences between diarrhea-predominant and constipation-predominant patients. *Digestive Diseases and Sciences*, 1980, *25*, 404–413.

Whitehead. W. E., Winget, C., Fedoravicius, A. S., Wooley, S., & Blackwell, B. Learned illness behavior in patients with irritable bowel syndrome and peptic ulcer. *Digestive Diseases and Sciences*, 1982, *27(3)*, 202–208.

Whiting, A. W., & Child, I. L. *Child training and personality*. New Haven: Yale University Press, 1953.

Whiting, B. B. (Ed.). *Six cultures: Studies of child rearing*. New York: Wiley, 1963.

Whitlock, F. A. The aetiology of hysteria. *Acta Psychiatrica Scandinavia*, 1967, *43*, 144–162.

Whorf, B. L. Science and linguistics. In J. B. Carrol (Ed.), *Language, thought and reality: Selected writings of Benjamin Lee Whorf*, Cambridge: M.I.T. Press, 1956.

Whybrow, P. C., Akiskal, H. S., & McKinney, W. T. *Mood disorders: Toward a new psychobiology*. New York: Plenum Press, 1984.

Wieder, G. B. Coping ability of rape victims: Comment on Myers, Templer and Brown. *Journal of Consulting and Clinical Psychology*, 1985, *53*, 429–430.

Wilkinson, R. T., El-Beheri, S., & Gieseking, C. C. Performance and arousal as a function of incentive, information load and task novelty. *Psychophysiology*, 1972, *9*, 589–599.

Willerman, L. Activity level and hyperactivity in twins. *Child Development*, 1973, *44*, 288–293.

Williams, R. J. *You are extraordinary*. New York: Random House, 1967.

Williamson, D. A., Kelley, M. L., Davis, C. J., Ruggiero, L., & Blouin, D. C. Psychopathology of eating disorders: A controlled comparison of bulimic, obese and normal subjects. *Journal of Consulting and Clinical Psychology*, 1985, *53*, 161–166.

Wilson, G. T. Alcohol and human sexual behavior. *Behavioral Research and Therapy*, 1977, *15*, 239–252.

Wilson, G. T., & Lawson, D. M. Expectancies, alcohol and sexual arousal in male social drinkers. *Journal of Abnormal Psychology*, 1976, *85*, 587–594. (a)

Wilson, G. T. & Lawson, D. M. Effects of alcohol on sexual arousal in women. *Journal of Abnormal Psychology*, 1976, *85*, 489–497. (b)

Wilson, G. T., & Lawson, D. M. Expectancies, alcohol and sexual arousal in women. *Journal of Abnormal Psychology*, 1978, *87*, 358–367.

Wincze, J. P., Hoon, E. F., & Hoon, P. W. Physiological responsivity of normal and sexually dysfunctional women during erotic stimulus exposure. *Journal of Psychosomatic Research*, 1976, *20*, 445–451.

Winer, D. Anger and dissociation: A case study of multiple personality. *Journal of Abnormal Psychology*, 1978, *87*, 368–372.

Wise, T. N. Sexual dysfunction in the medically ill. *Psychosomatics*, 1983, *24*, 787–805.

Wishner, J. Neurosis and tension: An exploratory study of the relationship of physiological and Rorschach measures. *Journal of Abnormal and Social Psychology*, 1953, *48*, 253–260.

Witkin-Lanoil, G. *The female stress syndrome*. New York: Newmarket Press, 1984.

Wolf, S., & Almy, T. P. Experimental observation on cardiospasm in man. *Gastroenterology*, 1949, *13*, 401–421.

Wolf, S., & Wolff, H. G. *Human gastric function: An experimental study of a man and his stomach*. New York: Oxford University Press, 1947.

Wolpe, J. Reciprocal inhibition as the main basis of psychotherapeutic effects. *Archives of Neurology and Psychiatry*, 1954, *72*, 205–226.

Wolpe, J. *Psychotherapy by reciprocal inhibition*. Stanford: Stanford University Press, 1958.

Wolpe, J. Cognition and causation in human behavior and its therapy. *American Psychologist*, 1978, *33(5)*, 437–446.

Wood, C. G., & Hokanson, J. E. Effects of induced muscular tension on performance and the inverted U function. *Journal of Personality and Social Psychology*. 1965, *1*, 506–509.

Woodworth, R. S., & Schlosberg, H. *Experimental psychology* (2nd ed.). New York: Holt, Rinehart & Winston, 1952.

Worsely, A., & Chang, A. Oral contraceptives and emotional states. *Journal of Psychosomatic Research*, 1978, *22*, 13–16.

Wright, B. Demystifying Reichian therapy. *Issues in Radical Therapy*, 1982, *10*, 32–39.

Wright, J. H., & Beck, A. T. Cognitive therapy of depression: Theory and practice. *Hospital and Community Psychiatry*, 1983, *34*, 1119–1127.

Wurtman, R. J., & Growdon, J. H. Dietary enhancement of CNS neurotransmitters. In D. T. Krieger & J. C. Hughes (Eds.), *Neuroendocrinology*. Sunderland: Sinauer, 1980.

Yarrow, L. J., & Goodwin, M. S. The immediate impact of separation: Reactions of infants to a change in mother figures. In L. J. Stone, H. T. Smither, & L. B. Murphy (Eds.), *The competent infant*. New York: Basic Books, 1973.

Yates, A. J. Tics. In C. G. Costello (Ed.), *Symptoms of psychopathology*. New York: Wiley, 1970.

Yemm, R. Masseter muscle activity in stress. *Archives of Oral Biology*, 1969, *14*, 1437–1439. (a)

Yemm, R. Variations in the electrical activity of the human masseter muscle occurring in association with emotional stress. *Archives of Oral Biology*, 1969, *14*, 873–878. (b)

Yerkes, R. M., & Dodson, J. D. The relation of strength of stimulus to rapidity of habit formation. *Journal of Comparative and Neurological Psychology*, 1908, *18*, 459–482.

Young, S. J. Psychiatric considerations in irritable bowel syndrome. *Practical Gastroenterology*, 1979, *3(4)*, 29–34.

Young, S. J., Alpers, D. H., Norland, C. C., & Woodruff, R. A. Psychiatric illness and the irritable bowel syndrome: Practical implications for the primary physician. *Gastroenterology*, 1976, *70*, 162–166.

Zahn, T. P., Rosenthal, D., & Lawlor, W. G. Electrodermal and heart rate orienting reactions in chronic schizophrenia. *Journal of Psychiatric Research*, 1968, *6*, 117–134.

Zajonc, R. B. Feeling and thinking: Preferences need no inferences. *American Psychologist*, 1980, *35(2)*, 151–175.

Zajonc, R. B. The interaction of affect and cognition. In K. R. Scherer & P. Ekman (Eds.), *Approaches to emotion. Hillsdale, N.J.: Lawrence Erlbaum Associates, 1984. (a)*

Zajonc, R. B. The primacy of affect. In K. R. Scherer & P. Ekman (Eds.), Approaches to emotion. Hillsdale, N.J. Lawrence Erlbaum Associates, 1984. (b)

Zajonc, R. B. Emotion and facial efference: A theory reclaimed. *Science*, 1985, *228*, 15–21.

Ziegler, D. K., Hassanein, R. S., & Couch, J. R. Characteristics of life headache histories in a nonclinical population. *Neurology*, 1977, *27*, 265–269.

Ziegler, D. K., Rhodes, R. J., & Hassanein, R. S. Association of psychological measurements of anxiety and depression with headache history in a non-clinical population. In A. P. Friedman & M. Critchley (Eds.), *Research and Clinical Studies in Headache* (Vol. 6). Basel: Karger, 1978.

Zillmann, D. The role of excitation in aggressive behavior. *Proceedings of the Seventeenth International Congress of Applied Psychology*, 1971. Brussels: Editest, 1972.

Zillmann, D., Johnson, R. C., & Day, K. D. Attribution of apparent arousal and proficiency of recovery from sympathetic activation affecting excitation transfer to aggressive behavior. *Journal of Experimental Social Psychology*, 1974, *10*, 503–515.

Zillmann, D., Katcher, A. H., & Milavsky, B. Excitation transfer from physical exercise to subsequent aggressive behavior. *Journal of Experimental Social Psychology*, 1972, *8*, 247–259.

Zimbardo, P. G. *Shyness*. Reading: Addison-Wesley, 1977.

Zimbardo, P. G., Pilkonis. P. A., & Norwood, R. M. *The silent prison of shyness*. (ONR tech. Rep Z-17.) Standford: Standford University, 1974.

Zimny, G. H., & Miller, F. L. Orienting and adaptive cardiovascular responses to heat and cold. *Psychophysiology*, 1966, *3*. 81–92.

Zola, P., Meyerson, A. T., Reznikoff, M., Thornton, J. C., & Concool, B. M. Menstrual symptomatology and psychiatric admission. *Journal of Psychosomatic Research*, 1979, *23*, 241–245.

Zuckerman, M. Physiological measures of sexual arousal in the human. *Psychological Bulletin*, 1971, *75*, 347–356.

Zuckerman, M., Hall, J. A., DeFrank, R. S., & Rosenthal, R. Encoding and decoding spontaneous and posed facial expressions. *Journal of Personality and Social Psychology*, 1976, *34*, 966–977.

Author Index

Subject Index